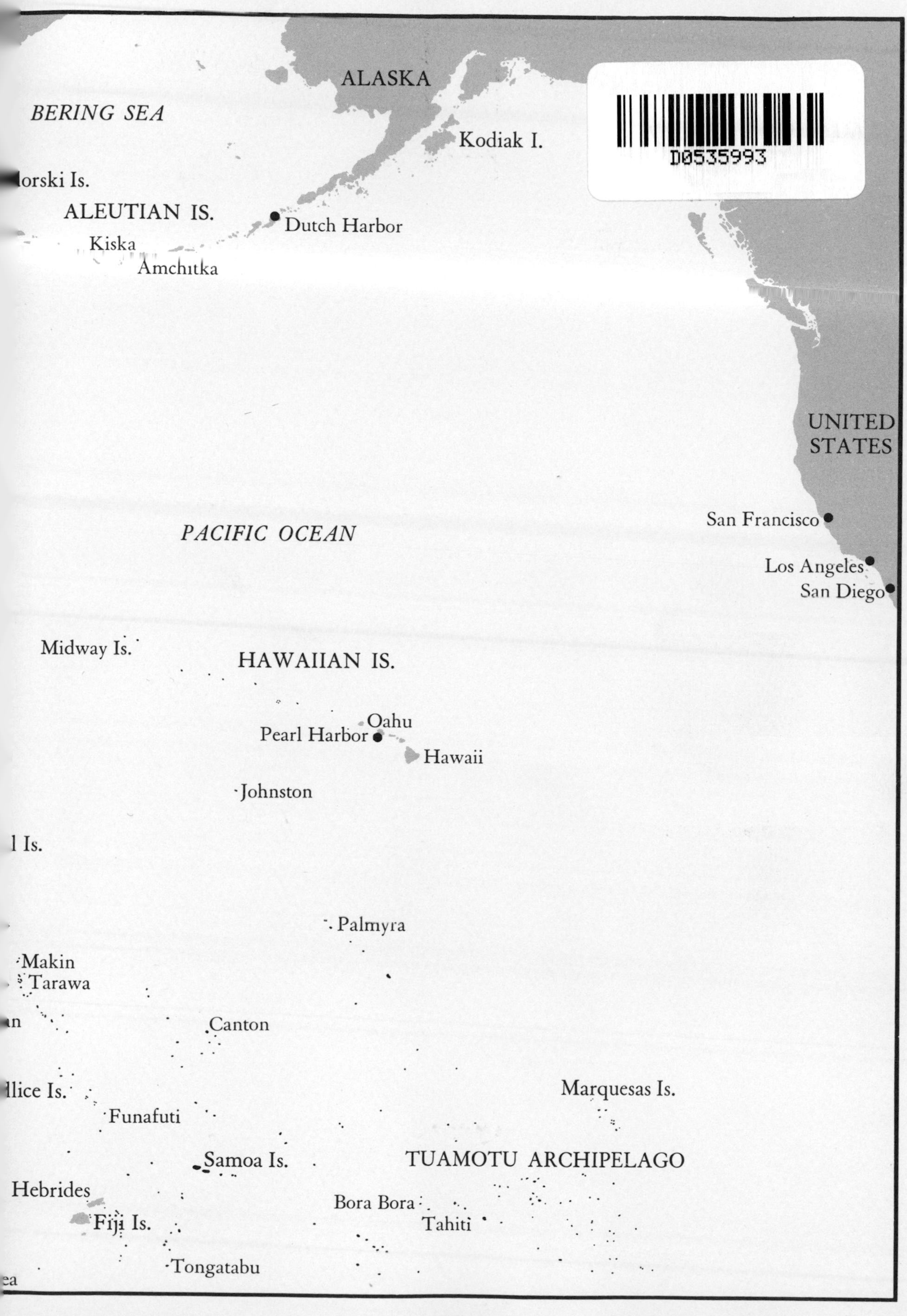

ALASKA

BERING SEA

Kodiak I.

orski Is.

ALEUTIAN IS.

Dutch Harbor

Kiska

Amchitka

UNITED STATES

PACIFIC OCEAN

San Francisco

Los Angeles

San Diego

Midway Is.

HAWAIIAN IS.

Oahu

Pearl Harbor

Hawaii

Johnston

l Is.

Palmyra

Makin

Tarawa

an

Canton

llice Is.

Marquesas Is.

Funafuti

Samoa Is.

TUAMOTU ARCHIPELAGO

Hebrides

Bora Bora

Fiji Is.

Tahiti

Tongatabu

ea

BULL HALSEY

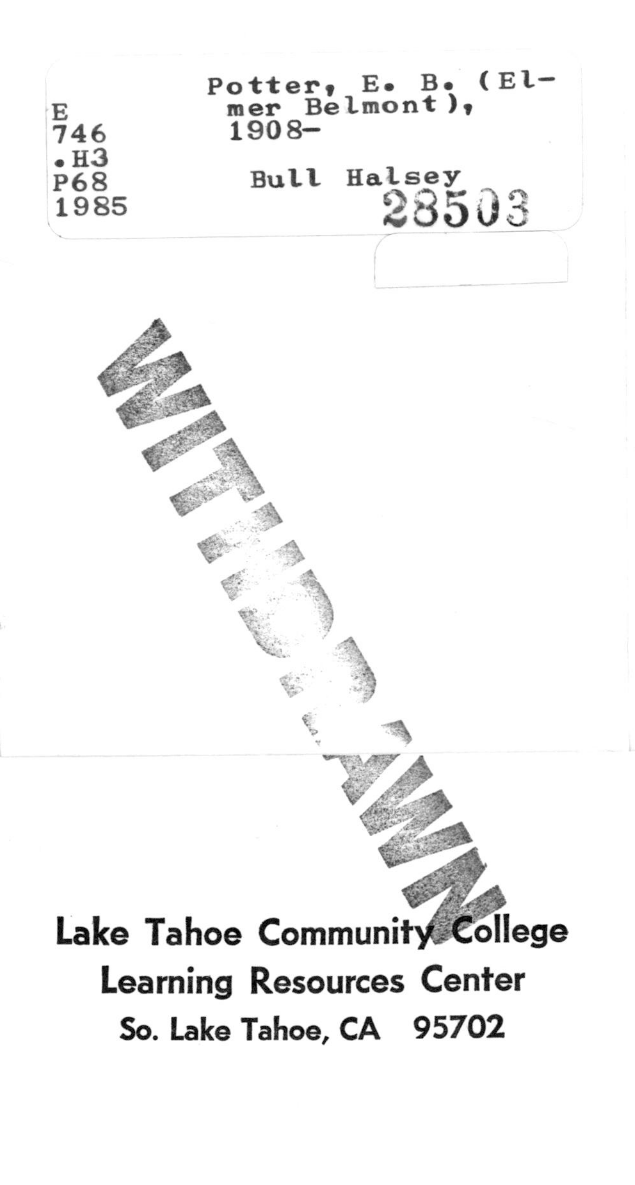

E. B. POTTER

BULL HALSEY

NAVAL INSTITUTE PRESS
ANNAPOLIS, MARYLAND

Library of Congress Cataloging-in-Publication Data

Potter, E. B. (Elmer Belmont), 1908–
  Bull Halsey, a biography.
  Bibliography: p.
  Includes index.
  1. Halsey, William Frederick, 1882–1959. 2. Admirals—United States—Biography. 3. United States. Navy—Biography. 4. World War, 1939–1945—Naval operations, American. I. Title.
E746.H3P68 1985 940.54'26'0924 [B] 85-15419
ISBN 0-87021-146-3

Printed in the United States of America

To Grace

CONTENTS

MAPS

PREFACE

WHEN THE NAVAL INSTITUTE PRESS asked me to write a biography of Admiral Halsey, I was reluctant to do so. During the Second World War I had become aware of his reputation as a no-holds-barred fighter, applauded by the public and revered by men who served under him, but I myself had reservations about him.

I first saw Halsey at the end of August 1942, when he spoke at the U.S. Naval Academy, where I was on the faculty as a naval reserve officer. After a hot day in various offices in Washington, he arrived in wrinkled khakis to speak before an audience of white-uniformed midshipmen and other officers. He gave a tough-guy impression, called the Japanese "yellow-bellied sons of bitches," and in a rambling, unprepared speech described his early 1942 raid on the Marshall Islands, leaving us with only the vaguest impression of how it had been carried out. To his credit, however, he was not boastful; he praised everybody but himself.

The nickname Bull, which the press bestowed on Halsey, presented, to my mind at least, an image of witless bellicosity. The salty comments attributed to him did little to erase this impression. It was reinforced by his January 1943 prediction, carried in all the newspapers, that the war with Japan would conclude with an Allied victory before the end of the year.

In 1944, while I was on duty at Pearl Harbor, Halsey arrived to take command of the fleet. I was favorably impressed when on his departure he sent letters of thanks to all the agencies that had helped him and his staff prepare for the fleet command.

At war's end, back at the Naval Academy, I was one of a committee appointed to accept from Halsey two trophies for the museum: a captured Japanese flag and a saddle presented to him in response to his expressed desire to ride the emperor's white horse. The admiral invited us to spit on the flag and told with obvious relish the story of the Japanese battleship commander who was humiliated when the Americans ordered him to haul down his own colors.

Out of uniform and on the Academy's civilian faculty, I launched a career of teaching and writing naval history. This beginning coincided with the publication of criticisms charging Halsey with ineptitude in the handling of his fleet in the Battle for Leyte Gulf. Some officers who had served in ships under him expressed the opinion that he was not sufficiently skilled to command a fleet. Though I tried to be objective, my own writing tended to support that view.

My impression of Halsey began to change when I was associated with Admiral Nimitz in the writing of the Naval Academy textbook *Sea Power*. The former commander in chief of the Pacific Fleet, whose opinions I greatly respected, had high regard for Halsey's character and ability. Later, working on a biography of Nimitz, I was obliged to make a closer study of Halsey's operations and personality. What I found raised him considerably in my estimation. When *Nimitz* was published, some of Halsey's friends expressed satisfaction with the portrait I had drawn of him in the book.

Debating whether to write a Halsey biography, I mentioned the project at a small gathering that included Mrs. Joseph Taussig. The wife, daughter, and mother of Naval Academy graduates, she was accustomed to sizing up naval officers. Moreover, her father was Robert B. Carney, former chief of naval operations, who during the Second World War had been Halsey's chief of staff and remained his friend and confidant. Of Halsey Mrs. Taussig said, "He was a dear man."

I went to Richmond, Virginia, to call on Joseph Bryan, who was associated with Halsey during the war and subsequently collaborated with him on *Admiral Halsey's Story*. Bryan, I found, regarded the admiral with respect and affection. I next proceeded to Raleigh, North Carolina, and visited William Ashford, Halsey's aide from 1937 to 1943. I found Ashford intensely admiring of and fiercely loyal to his old commanding officer. The same attitude prevailed among other Halsey associates: Douglass Moulton, Harold Stassen, Robert Carney, and above all William Frederick Halsey III, who regarded the admiral with reverence not all sons show their fathers.

Despite these golden opinions, I began writing this book with lingering reservations about Halsey's character and abilities. My critical attitude reveals itself in several passages in the first part of the book. I have decided to retain them, hoping the reader will sense and participate in my gradual conversion to a Halsey admirer.

I had hitherto regarded the Battle of Midway as the turning point in America's war with Japan. In a sense it was, but it did not force the Japanese to shift to the defensive. After Midway they landed and commenced building an airfield on Guadalcanal and in the next few months challenged the Americans in two more carrier actions, the battles of the Eastern Solomons and Santa Cruz Islands. In October 1942, five months after Midway, the Japanese were still on the offensive but only on Guadalcanal, where they and the Americans were deadlocked, with operations turning increasingly in favor of the former. At this time of crisis Halsey arrived in the South Pacific, relieved a defeatist

U.S. command, and in thirty extraordinary days completely reversed the course of the conflict, throwing the Japanese on the defensive, from which they never recovered. This was the real turning point of the Pacific war.

In the light of this achievement, I have reexamined Halsey's later controversial operations and statements and drawn conclusions that I trust the reader will find convincing. As I complete the writing of this book, I see in Admiral Halsey a man not without shortcomings but with qualities of leadership, courage, judgment, good will, and compassion that utterly outweigh his faults. I now fully concur with Admiral Nimitz's appraisal of Halsey written toward the end of the Guadalcanal campaign: "He is professionally competent and militarily aggressive without being reckless or foolhardy. He has that rare combination of intellectual capacity and military audacity, and can calculate to a cat's whisker the risk involved in operations when successful accomplishments will bring great results. He possesses superb leadership qualities which have earned him a tremendous following of his men."

BULL HALSEY

CHAPTER 1

PEARL HARBOR AND WAKE

THE OFFICERS WHO ATTENDED the 27 November 1941 conference at Pacific Fleet headquarters, Pearl Harbor, would later vividly recall the proceedings. Vice Admiral William F. Halsey, commanding the Pacific Fleet carriers, would write that he remembered the discussions with special clarity.

The U.S. government had cut off the flow of American oil on which Japan depended for its conquests on the Asian mainland. As its price for reviving the flow, the United States demanded that the Japanese get out of China—a price Japan would not pay. A favorable outcome of negotiations, Washington warned, was doubtful.[1]

Denied American oil, Japan could be expected to make a grab for the nearest alternate source, the Dutch East Indies, now orphaned by the German conquest of the Netherlands. To clear the flanks for such a southward drive, the Japanese would probably make surprise attacks on Guam, the Philippines, and the peninsular approaches to Singapore, as they had on Chinese forces in 1894 and on Russian forces ten years later.

The conference had been called by Admiral Husband E. Kimmel, commander in chief of the Pacific Fleet (CinCPac). Halsey was there by special invitation. Kimmel, setting great store by his common sense and seagoing savvy, tried to have him present at all major conferences. Kimmel and Halsey had been friends since their days at the Naval Academy in Annapolis, where they were classmates. As it turned out, 27 November was the last day they would be in contact until after the Japanese had raided Pearl Harbor, bringing the United States into the war.

They were both gifted leaders, administrators, and shiphandlers, who by hard work and devotion to duty had risen to the top of their profession, but their styles contrasted sharply. Kimmel's honesty, fairness, and obvious ability had won him the respect of his officers and men; but self-contained, imperious, every inch the stern commander, he was a difficult man to know. Halsey was no less honest, fair, and able, but he wore the mantle of leadership more lightly. Gregarious and approachable, he won his subordinates' affection as well as their respect.

Halsey's fighting-cock stance, barrel chest, and beetle brows embodied the popular conception of an old sea dog. He could scowl fiercely and make strong men wince under the lash of his invective, but the wrinkles around his eyes were not from scowling. He was a genial, likable man, known to his intimates as Bill and affectionately referred to by his subordinates as Admiral Bill.

The main business before the meeting was deciding what planes to send to Wake and Midway. Guam, because of nearby Japanese bases in the Marianas, was written off as untenable in the event of war with Japan. The outlying atolls of Wake and Midway, though vulnerable, were considered defensible. To each of these Kimmel had sent as many additional guns and marine reinforcements as he could spare, and on both of them civilian construction teams were completing airstrips.

The War and Navy departments had authorized sending fifty P-40s, the army's newest fighter planes. Major General F. L. Martin, commander of the army air forces in Hawaii, proposed that they retain the P-40s and instead send out older planes they could better afford to lose. Lieutenant General Walter C. Short, commanding general of the Hawaiian Department, contended that the outposts, likely to be attacked first by the Japanese, should have the best planes, not the poorest. Short's chief of staff, Lieutenant Colonel James A. Mollison, disagreed with his boss, pointing out that their primary mission was to defend Oahu. Shipping out their best army planes, he said, would compromise their ability to do so.

"Why are you so worried about this?" Kimmel wanted to know. "Do you think we are in danger of attack?"

"The Japanese have such a capability," Mollison replied.

"Capability, yes, but possibility?" Kimmel turned to his war plans officer, Captain Charles H. McMorris. "What do you think about the prospects of a Japanese air attack?"

"None, absolutely none," replied McMorris. It was clear to him that the War and Navy departments were of the same opinion; else they would never have authorized stripping Hawaii of half its best army fighters. In fact, almost no one in the U.S. high command believed the Japanese would risk sending a carrier force across 3,500 miles of open sea to within striking range of America's most powerful Pacific base.[2]

Halsey, who had been listening in silence, now had a question for General Martin. "Is it not a fact," he said, "that the army pursuit flyers are forbidden to venture more than fifteen miles from the shoreline?"

"That is true," replied Martin.

"Then," said Halsey, "they are no good for this purpose."[3]

That obvious fact apparently had occurred to no one else. Pilots tied to the shoreline and untrained in overwater navigation would be virtually useless for island defense. Moreover, the planes would have to be delivered to the islands by carrier, and no one knew whether army fighters were capable of taking off from a flight deck. So it had to be naval planes. Kimmel decided to send the best fighters he had, Grumman F4F Wildcats. Those intended for Wake, the island farthest out, would leave first, on board the carrier *Enterprise*—"the Big E." The delivering would have to be done by Halsey, whose additional duty was commanding Task Force 2, the *Enterprise* force. Departure was scheduled for the following morning.

The commander in chief cautioned those present to maintain the strictest silence about the project. Under no circumstances should any Japanese agents in Hawaii be given reason to suspect that the Americans were arming Wake and Midway with planes. He then adjourned the meeting and asked Halsey to return after lunch.

That afternoon, with Halsey at his side, Kimmel sent for two officers who needed to know about the forthcoming operation, Commander Miles Browning, Halsey's chief of staff, and Major Paul Putnam, commander of Marine Fighter Squadron 211, selected to go to Wake. For security reasons Putnam was directed to tell his pilots that they were merely going out in the *Enterprise* for three days of maneuvers.

Later in the day Kimmel was handed a startling message from the Navy Department. It began, "This despatch is to be considered a war warning. Negotiations with Japan looking toward stabilization of conditions in the Pacific have ceased and an aggressive move by Japan is expected within the next few days." All signs, the message continued, pointed to an amphibious expedition against the Philippines, against the approaches to Singapore, or directly against the oil-rich East Indies island of Borneo. Kimmel was ordered to execute an appropriate defense deployment before carrying out the tasks assigned in the navy's basic war plan.

Halsey read the message with foreboding. His destination, Wake, was closer to Japan than to Pearl Harbor. He was more than half convinced that he would be in a fight before he got back—a chilling thought, he later testified. But from what is known of Halsey it is safe to say that he was also not a little exhilarated at the possibility of soon exercising command in a battle at sea.

"Do you want to take the battleships with you?" Kimmel asked him.

"Hell, no! If I have to run, I don't want anything to interfere with my running."[4]

Kimmel understood. None of the old battlewagons could make twenty knots, while the rest of the ships in the force could all do better than thirty. But to make it appear as if the force were departing on a routine practice maneuver, they decided that Halsey should take the battleships out and then detach them at sea, out of sight of land. The rest of the force would proceed nearly 2,000 miles westward, into waters about which Japan had earlier shown special sensitivity. They had to face the fact that here any overt act might easily precipitate war.

It was nearly 1800. Halsey rose to leave. "How far do you want me to go?" he asked.

"Goddammit," replied Kimmel, "use your common sense!"

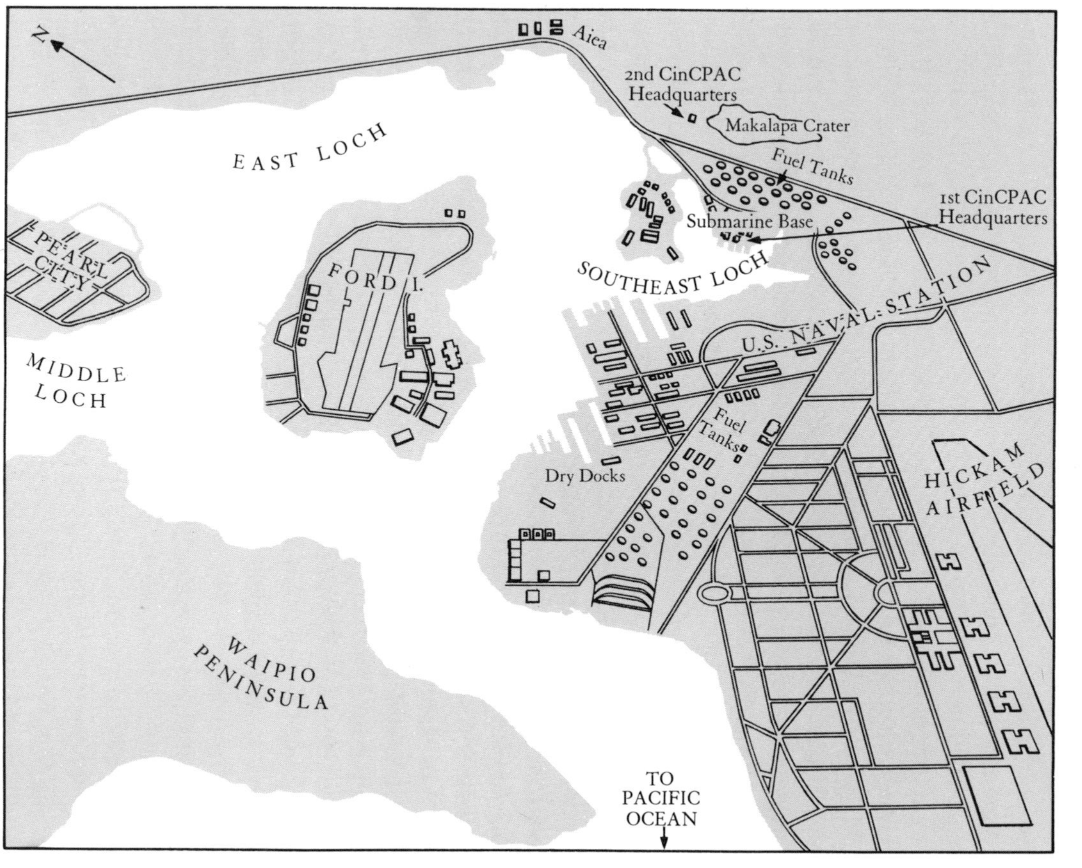

Pearl Harbor, 1942

Halsey grinned. He knew that his old friend wasn't trying to pass the buck. Kimmel was simply giving Halsey, the man at the scene of action, complete authority to handle the situation according to his own best judgment and assurance that he would be backed to the hilt. Said Halsey later, "I consider that as fine an order as a subordinate ever received."[5]

Halsey had already issued orders for Task Force 2 to be readied for departure the following morning, a Friday. The timing was bound to cause a stir, because it was Admiral Kimmel's settled policy to keep the fleet in port through Sunday and permit the men weekend liberty. But with war imminent, Halsey dared not lose a single day getting those planes to Wake. Using a cover story, he got on the telephone and invited friends, including members of his staff, to an impromptu dinner party at Waikiki's Halekulani Hotel, where he and his wife, Fan, had quarters. During the meal Halsey feigned an air of nonchalance, but his little scheme backfired. He had made the mistake of confiding to Fan that he might be in combat within the next few days, and she remained in a state of such obvious agitation all evening that the guests left convinced something out of the ordinary was afoot.[6]

When Halsey's Task Force 2 sortied the next morning, the *Enterprise,* contrary to normal procedure when leaving port, was carrying planes—two army P-40s. At the request of the army air forces, they had been hoisted on board at dockside. Army planes were not constructed to land on carriers, but the air force wanted to find out if they could take off from a flight deck, a capability that might prove useful.[7]

After clearing the channel, Halsey formed the *Enterprise,* three heavy cruisers, and nine destroyers into Task Force 8, directing his second senior in command to take charge of the three battleships and remaining cruisers and destroyers and proceed with them to the drill area for normal maneuvers. As a feint, Task Force 8 temporarily stood to eastward.

From his easterly course Halsey presently turned into the wind to let the P-40s take off, which they did without incident. When Task Force 8 was clearly beyond the observation of these planes and the battleship group, it wheeled to starboard and shaped course a little south of west for Wake.

In mid-morning the distant roar of many planes could be heard from astern the *Enterprise,* and presently they came into view, approaching the carrier in neat wedge-shaped formations. Halsey, anxious to get his task force well under way before slowing down to turn again into the wind, let the planes circle for more than an hour. At last, a little before noon, the appropriate flag hoist was raised, and at the execute all ships wheeled together until the wind blew directly down the carrier's deck. Then on signal the planes approached and began to land—eighteen TBD Devastator torpedo bombers, thirty-six SBD Dauntless dive-bombers, and thirty F4F Wildcats. Eighteen Wildcats belonged to the Big E's Fighting Six, twelve to Putnam's Marine Fighter

Squadron 211, assigned to Wake. Several of the pilots of Putnam's squadron would never get home again; the others would return only after four years in Japan's barbarous prisoner-of-war camps. Having been led to believe that they were going out for a routine weekend exercise, the marines had brought little more than a razor, a toothbrush, and an extra pair of skivvies (shorts).[8]

The airmen were surprised to be ordered immediately to their squadron ready rooms. Awaiting them was a far greater surprise. When they were seated, each was handed a mimeographed sheet. It read:

U.S.S. ENTERPRISE

At Sea
November 28, 1941

BATTLE ORDER NUMBER ONE

1. The ENTERPRISE is now operating under war conditions.
2. At any time, day or night, we must be ready for instant action.
3. Hostile submarines may be encountered.
4. The importance of every officer and man being specially alert and vigilant while on watch at his battle station must be fully realized by all hands.
5. The failure of one man to carry out his assigned task promptly, particularly the lookouts, those manning the batteries, and all those on watch on deck, might result in great loss of life and even loss of the ship.
6. The Captain is confident all hands will prove equal to any emergency that may develop.
7. It is part of the tradition of our Navy that, when put to the test, all hands keep cool, keep their heads, and FIGHT.
8. Steady nerves and stout hearts are needed now.

G. D. MURRAY,
Captain, U.S. Navy
Commanding

Approved: November 28, 1941.
W. F. HALSEY,
Vice Admiral, U.S. Navy,
Commander Aircraft, Battle Force[9]

The astonished buzz of voices that followed the reading of this order was silenced by briefing officers, who announced to the airmen that the task force was bound for Wake, where the marine fighters would be landed.

Commander William H. Buracker, Halsey's operations officer, the mimeographed battle order in hand, bounded up to the flag bridge. "Admiral," he said, breathing hard, "did you authorize this thing?"

"Yes."

"Do you realize that this means war?"

"Yes."

"Goddammit, Admiral, you can't start a private war of your own! Who's going to take the responsibility?"

"I'll take it," replied Halsey. "If anything gets in my way, we'll shoot first and argue afterwards."

Halsey had made sure before leaving Pearl that no U.S. or Allied shipping was in the waters he had to cross. His orders were to get the marine fighters and their pilots to Wake in secret, and he was prepared to shoot down any plane and sink any submarine that attempted to snoop his force, preferably before the snooper could get off a radio report. In view of the previous day's war warning, he believed that any Japanese ships he might encounter could only be en route to launch one of their treacherous prewar raids. In these circumstances, probably his only chance for survival—or even of flashing a warning to Kimmel—was to strike the first blow, and he had no compunction about doing so. But running across any ship would have surprised Halsey. He knew that a huge Japanese attack force had been detected heading south. In common with other U.S. military and naval leaders, he did not believe the Japanese had the power simultaneously to dispatch a second major attack force in another direction.

The truth was that three days earlier a fleet comprising all six of Japan's large carriers, supported by two battleships, three cruisers, and nine destroyers, had departed the Kuril Islands and was now pounding east, heading for an air raid on Pearl Harbor.

After evening mess Halsey had another visitor. Major Putnam arrived on the flag bridge with a question that had been bothering him. "I know I'm on my way to Wake," he said, "but what in hell am I supposed to do when I get there?"

"Putnam," said the admiral benignly, "your instructions are to do what seems appropriate when you get to Wake. You're under my direct and personal orders and will not report for duty to the island commander." He held out his hand. "Have a pleasant cruise."[10]

The reply was Halsey's counterpart to Kimmel's advice to him. Halsey believed firmly in the old leadership rule, Tell your man what to do but not how to do it; if you have to tell him how to do it, you have picked the wrong man for the job. He was sure that Putnam was the right man, and that when the chips were down he would do the right thing.

In compliance with Admiral Halsey's battle order, all hands exerted themselves to get the *Enterprise* and her aircraft combat ready. Inflammables had been removed from the ship several weeks earlier. Now torpedo gangs broke out warheads and attached them. Crews belted and clipped ammunition for guns on the ship and on planes and attached 500-pound bombs under the wings of the dive-bombers.

Halsey imposed strict radio silence. The five-inch guns and antiaircraft batteries were manned continuously. Airmen, carrying out daytime antisubmarine patrols and searching the ocean to a distance of 300 miles morning and evening, were under orders to attack any Japanese or unidentified aircraft that approached the force. Halsey himself remained on the bridge or took catnaps in the nearby emergency cabin.

At dawn on 4 December the *Enterprise* was 174 miles north of Wake. Major Putnam's F4Fs were on her flight deck, ready to take off. All hands who could be spared from duties came topside or paused to watch them depart. The marine aircraft were followed by a navigational escort of several *Enterprise* planes. An officer on board the carrier remarked that the marine aviators were good, but that just a dozen of them was "kind of light to take on the whole Jap air force."

The escorting airmen accompanied the marines to within sight of the low-lying atoll, waved farewell, and turned back under menacing skies. They found Task Force 8 already heading toward Pearl, where it was scheduled to arrive on Saturday, 6 December.

Several hundred miles to the north, the Japanese carrier force was on a parallel course, headed toward the same destination.

The *Enterprise* now ran into stormy seas, and high winds buffeted the carrier and her accompanying vessels for several days. A destroyer cracked a seam. The task force was obliged to slow down. Halsey found it necessary to reschedule arrival time. The Big E would reach Pearl Harbor at noon on Sunday, 7 December.[11]

On Saturday Task Force 8 at last passed out of the stormy area and reached calm seas and clearing skies. That morning at Pacific Fleet headquarters Admiral Kimmel, sitting nonchalantly, his feet on his desk, was being interviewed by newly arrived war correspondent Joseph C. Harsch.

"Is there going to be a war out here?" Harsch asked.

"No," replied Kimmel.

"Would you please explain why you seem so confident that there won't be a war?"

"Yes. Since you have been traveling over recent days, you probably do not know that the Germans have announced that they are going into winter quarters in front of Moscow. That means that Moscow is not going to fall this winter. That means that the Japanese cannot attack us in the Pacific without running the risk of a two-front war. The Japanese are too smart to run that risk."[12]

The Japanese carrier force was now on course southeast, heading for Pearl Harbor, which it was scheduled to raid the following morning. The commander of the force was disappointed to learn from spies in Honolulu, via

Tokyo radio, that there were no carriers in Pearl Harbor for him to attack. The *Lexington* had departed the day before to take planes to Midway.[13]

By dawn on 7 December the Big E, under clear skies, was 150 miles from her destination. On her flight deck, the eighteen scout bombers of Scouting Squadron 6 were preparing to search ahead of the task force and land at Ford Island in the middle of Pearl Harbor. Before the pilots manned their planes, they were surrounded by officers and men requesting them to telephone their wives and notify them of the force's imminent arrival. Like their husbands, the wives had supposed the *Enterprise* was going out only for weekend maneuvers. She had been gone nine days.

Admiral Halsey, still on the flag bridge, watched the planes take off. Now at last he could relax. At that moment he probably had mixed emotions—of relief because his mission was successfully accomplished, of regret that there had been no opportunity for action against an enemy. He went below to flag quarters, shaved, bathed, and put on a fresh uniform. Then he joined his flag secretary, Lieutenant Douglass Moulton, for breakfast. He was having a second cup of coffee when the telephone rang. The flag secretary answered it. "Moulton. . . . *What?* . . . Roger!"

"Admiral," he said, "the staff duty officer says he has a message that there's an air raid on Pearl."

Halsey sprang to his feet. "My God," he shouted, "they're shooting at my own boys! Tell Kimmel!"

Halsey knew that the planes of Scouting 6 would be arriving at about that time. Because he was operating under radio silence, he had necessarily skipped the usual procedure of notifying Pearl Harbor to expect them. Trigger-happy antiaircraft gunners must have failed to recognize them and opened fire.

At least one *Enterprise* plane had indeed been hit by ground fire. Down in the code room the radiomen had heard the voice of Ensign Manuel Gonzales: "Please don't shoot! Don't shoot! This is an American plane." A few seconds later, evidently to his rear sea gunner, he cried out, "We're on fire. Bail out!" Next they received a report from Lieutenant Earl Gallaher, executive officer of Scouting 6, whose voice was calm and controlled: "Pearl Harbor is under attack by enemy planes! May be Jap planes."[14]

At 0758 the *Enterprise* radiomen received a keyed message from the command center at Ford Island to all ships and stations: "Air raid, Pearl Harbor. This is not drill." CinCPac headquarters promptly echoed the warning: "Enemy air raid, Pearl Harbor. This is not a drill." At 0812 Admiral Kimmel announced to the Pacific Fleet, "Hostilities with Japan commenced with air raid on Pearl Harbor." Captain Murray relayed the announcement to all hands by loudspeaker and sent the Big E to general quarters.[15]

At 0921 CinCPac radioed an order to all ships and forces afloat to rendezvous as directed by Commander, Task Force 8, thus giving Admiral Halsey temporary command of every available ship of the Pacific Fleet. While waiting for these to join, Halsey maneuvered off Kaula Rock, some 150 miles west of Pearl.

The Americans were eager to seek out and strike back at the enemy, but they had no idea where to find him and inadequate power to deal with him if they did. Only a dozen fully operational army patrol planes on Oahu had survived the attack. Halsey's scout bombers on Ford Island joined them in the search, but only thirteen of these were left. Besides Gonzales's plane, shot down by "friendly" fire, four others had been destroyed by enemy aircraft.

Based on the strength and direction of the raid, Kimmel estimated that the Japanese force included as many as six carriers and was on a retirement course northwest of Pearl. He ordered Halsey to seek out and attack it. This was quite an assignment for a commander with one carrier and no battleships. At any rate, Halsey could not go steaming off to the northwest until he had assembled his forces, as Kimmel had previously directed, and he could not spare planes for searches. He needed those he had left on board for combat air patrol and offensive action when the enemy was found. Nevertheless, he gave orders to hoist the signal to prepare for battle.[16]

The confusions of the day were compounded by mistaken observations and false reports. Observers afloat and ashore reported enemy troops landing on the north shore, paratroops landing elsewhere. A man excitedly telephoned the army intelligence office to report in all seriousness that "a dog down on Ewa Beach was barking in code to a submarine off shore."

Radio direction finders at last came up with something solid. A radio transmission from a Japanese carrier revealed that it bore 358 degrees, almost due north. But the direction finder indicated both the true direction and its reciprocal, and the choice was a matter of estimation. The operators chose the latter and passed their estimate to CinCPac. Kimmel then notified Halsey that "D/F bearings indicate enemy carrier bearing 178 from Barbers Point," almost due south. It happened that the heavy cruiser *Minneapolis* was just then rounding Barbers Point en route to join Task Force 8. She intercepted Kimmel's message and radioed CinCPac, "No carriers in sight," but the message, garbled in transmission, was interpreted as "Two carriers in sight." Bombers promptly came streaking down from Hickam Field. Luckily the pilots, able to tell a cruiser from a carrier, left the *Minneapolis* alone. Another pilot, operating far to the south, was less perceptive. He mistook the heavy cruiser *Portland* for a Japanese carrier and dropped two bombs. By good fortune his marksmanship was as defective as his powers of observation. Both bombs fell astern of their target.

In midafternoon Rear Admiral Milo Draemel left Pearl Harbor with survivors of the morning raid—four cruisers and a number of destroyers—and headed south to join Halsey. Scout planes reported this force to be Japanese carriers. The report was relayed to Draemel, who began searching for himself. At about the same time, a B-17 from Hickam Field began a bomb run on the *Enterprise* but turned away when guns on the carrier and her escorts opened fire.

Eventually Draemel gave up the search for the supposed carrier force and shaped course for his rendezvous with Task Force 8. On arriving, he gave Halsey his first news of the fate of the Pacific Fleet battleships. In the understatement of the day, Draemel said he feared they were "incapacitated."[17]

The numerous false reports of carriers south of Hawaii gave credence to the opinion expressed by several officers that the enemy attack force had come from and was returning to the Marshall Islands, site of the Japanese bases closest to Pearl Harbor. Radio traffic analysis had recently detected carriers in the Marshalls.

In late afternoon Halsey received a new dispatch reporting a carrier south of his position. Convinced by then the enemy force was retiring in that direction, he made an all-out effort to attack it. First he formed all his ships except the *Enterprise* and her plane-guard destroyers into a scouting line and ordered it to make contact with the enemy and open fire. Then he turned his carrier into the wind and launched all his available torpedo planes, accompanied by six fighters for cover and six dive-bombers equipped with smoke tanks to screen the torpedo attack. Neither the scouting line nor the planes found anything. The latter searched far and wide until sunset, then headed back in growing darkness. There was neither a moon nor stars that night. The Wildcats, leading the way, found the Big E only by means of her phosphorescent wake.[18]

Rather than risk a night landing on the carrier, Halsey ordered the fighters to proceed to Pearl Harbor. Though both the ship and the planes notified the base that the Wildcats were coming, exhausted, raw-nerved gunners on shore shot down two of them as they approached the airfield.

The pilots of the other planes, short of fuel, had no choice but to land on the carrier, though few of them had training or experience in night landings. When the TBDs came down, all hands held their breath. Never before had torpedo-armed aircraft been brought on board a carrier at night. Admiral Halsey and Captain Murray watched from the bridge as the planes landed—without mishap, thanks to the landing signal officer's illuminated green wands.

One Devastator made a hard landing, snapping the metal band holding her torpedo. There were several moments of near panic on board as the deadly "fish" went slithering along the flight deck. If the detonator in its nose had struck the island, the exploding warhead would have blown the structure to smithereens and killed many men. Fortunately the torpedo continued straight toward the bow, and before it reached the wire barrier the deck crew stopped and disarmed it.[19]

While the *Enterprise* and her destroyers maneuvered independently through the night, Halsey reviewed the events of the preceding day. He was disgusted by the false reports and misleading information that had sent him and forces under his command searching hither and yon while the enemy attack force retreated farther and farther beyond their reach. On the other hand, if American aircraft or radio direction finders had pinpointed the attack force, and either the *Enterprise* or *Lexington,* which was then near Midway, had advanced to intercept it, what would have been the outcome? Apparently for the first time, he gave serious thought to that question. Clearly the Japanese would have been overwhelmingly superior.

Halsey had said he would shoot first and argue afterwards. He was also prepared, it would seem, to shoot first and think afterwards. Even after extended reflection, it did not occur to him that it might have been a mistake to expose America's slender carrier forces to ruinous odds. Years later he was to write, "I have the consolation of knowing that, on the opening day of the war, I did everything in my power to find a fight."[20]

A little after daybreak on 8 December the Big E rejoined the combined forces. Halsey detached the cruisers and destroyers that had gone with him to Wake and ordered them to Pearl for refueling. He intended to follow later with the carrier. She had only fifty percent of her fuel, not enough to take her to the United States. Should the Japanese capture Oahu or in another attack destroy the oil storage and pumping facilities on the island, she would be left adrift at sea.[21]

At breakfast time the survivors of Scouting 6 returned from Oahu to their carrier. With them was Lieutenant Commander Bromfield Nichol, assistant operations officer, whom Halsey had sent to Pearl Harbor with the scouting group the preceding morning to give the commander in chief a verbal report on Wake and to make arrangements for berthing and supplies for the task force. From Nichol Halsey got a vivid account of the disaster at the base.

Nichol had occupied the rear seat of the squadron commander's plane. While approaching Oahu, he noticed antiaircraft fire in the distance and wondered why the gunners were breaking precedent by training on Sunday. Equally surprising, over Pearl Harbor he saw many planes in the air. When one of them dived at him, he thought at first some young army smart aleck was trying to scare the navy. Next, however, he noticed bits of metal being struck off one of his own wing tips. His plane was being attacked! As the belligerent aircraft pulled away he caught sight of orange circles under its wings and realized that his assailant was Japanese. He swung about to unlimber a gun, but before he could get it into operation his plane was letting down for a landing.

Nichol lost no time making his way to CinCPac headquarters. He was standing in Admiral Kimmel's office watching the ongoing raid through a window when the *Arizona* exploded in a giant fireball with a blast that rattled every pane in the building. By then all the battleships, traditional backbone of the fleet, were knocked out. Nichol was sure some of them could be repaired, but it would be an extensive and time-consuming task.

Halsey wanted to know how his friend Kimmel had held up in the face of this disaster. Nichol replied that the commander in chief's conduct and bearing were splendid.[22]

Throughout the morning Halsey's forces continued to patrol and send out air searches, but neither ships nor planes found anything to report. Toward noon the *Enterprise,* accompanied by several destroyers, shaped course for Pearl. Commander Browning flew ahead to advise those responsible for loading planes on board the carrier *Saratoga,* which was to proceed from San Diego to Pearl Harbor and come under Halsey's command. Browning also had the important mission of making sure all antiaircraft gunners on Oahu were notified that the Big E's remaining planes would be coming in ahead of their carrier and were not to be fired at.

The sun was setting when, in single file, the *Enterprise* and her escorts entered the narrow mouth of the harbor. On board the carrier every man not otherwise employed stood silently watching. All along the shore near Hickam Field they could see antiaircraft guns manned by obviously exhausted soldiers. One called out derisively, "Where in hell were *you?*" Another shouted, "You'd better get the hell out of here or the Japs will nail you too."[23]

A pall of smoke lay over the main anchorage, and the water was coated with stinking black oil. The column passed close aboard the shattered *Nevada,* which had been beached off Waipio Point when she tried to make a run for the open sea during the attack. In the gathering dusk, as they approached Ford Island, some of the ships' company were half nauseated by the acrid odor of burnt flesh. Observers on board could discern the line of wrecks strung out along Battleship Row—the *California,* little more than her superstructure now showing above water; the *Oklahoma,* capsized, only the bottom of her hull visible; the *West Virginia,* a mere scorched hulk; the *Arizona,* her masts and part of her superstructure projecting above the surface and still burning. More than a thousand of her ship's company had perished.

Observers on board the *Enterprise* could make out the charred skeletons of burnt-out hangars ashore. As the carrier swung west around Ford Island, the men could see the hull of the old *Utah,* bottom up, at the Big E's usual mooring space. Admiral Halsey, his face expressing dismay and deepening anger, had been silently surveying the scene. At last he was heard to growl, "Before we're through with 'em, the Japanese language will be spoken only in hell!"[24] This was vintage Halsey—uttering the quotable quote, proclaiming his abhorrence of the enemy and the fearful retribution he intended to inflict upon him. Such statements, widely repeated, became his trademark and went far toward creating the public character known as Bull Halsey.

The Big E anchored to await refueling by naval oiler. Commander Browning had arranged for Admiral Halsey to be conveyed to a nearby pier by bos'n's chair. From here they went by boat to CinCPac's landing. The total blackout saved them from the machine-gunners, who were firing at all moving objects.

At fleet headquarters Halsey found Admiral Kimmel and staff members busily at work. They were haggard and unshaven. Their Sunday white uniforms, which they had never removed, were wrinkled and dirty, spotted with mud from inspections carried out in the rain. There was a dark splotch on Kimmel's chest. Halsey had been told the story. While Kimmel was standing at his office window the day before, watching in horror as the Japanese planes destroyed his fleet, a spent machine-gun bullet had crashed through the window, struck him, and fallen to the floor. Picking it up, he had murmured, "It would have been merciful had it killed me."[25]

Kimmel and his staff had now overcome the first shock. Despite their untidy appearance and obvious fatigue, their operations were coolly professional. Confused reports of enemy ships and enemy landings were still coming in. Most of these were absurd, but Kimmel preferred not to ignore them. He knew now that the Japanese had attacked Wake, Midway, Guam, and the Philippines, and that they had made a landing on the Malay Peninsula. Only two days earlier he had believed the Japanese incapable of carrying out more than one major military operation simultaneously. Now it was hard to know what to believe.

A new report came in. Japanese gliders and paratroopers were landing at Kaneohe. This was too much for Halsey. He burst out laughing. Kimmel wheeled on him. "What in the hell are you laughing at?"

"I've heard many damn fool reports in my life," Halsey replied, "but without exception that is the damnedest fool one I've *ever* heard. The Japs can't possibly tow gliders here from their nearest base, and certainly they're not going to waste their precious carrier decks on such nonsense."

For perhaps the first time in two days, Kimmel smiled. "You're right," he said.[26]

At about 2400 Halsey returned to the *Enterprise*. The oiler *Neosho* was alongside, linked to the carrier by fuel hoses. Lighters were arriving with munitions, victuals, and other supplies, which working parties were hoisting on board and stowing at record speed. Replenishing the carrier was normally a twelve-hour job, done in daylight at a wharf with the help of shore-based cranes. On this winter night the men, working in almost total darkness, finished the job in eight. Having seen what happened to the trapped battleships, they had no desire to be caught in the harbor at dawn, the target of another enemy air raid. At 0500 the job was completed, and the Big E prepared to sortie.[27]

The *Enterprise* force left Pearl Harbor to hunt down the swarms of enemy submarines believed to be lurking in the area. Halsey couldn't help wondering if his force was now placed at maximum risk. Japanese submariners would have liked nothing better than to sink any U.S. warships the carrier aviators had missed.

When the American force was well out to sea, the Big E took on board her Fighting Squadron 6, flying from Oahu. The flyers had spent an uncomfortable night at Wheeler Field, where hangars and other installations had been burned and nearly fifty combat planes had been totally destroyed. The men had been fed in blacked-out dining areas and assigned beds in vacant private quarters but had found sleep almost impossible because of repeated firing by nervous sentries carrying small arms.

The Pacific to which the *Enterprise* returned after witnessing the horror of Pearl Harbor was no longer the friendly sea of previous cruises. The men had not before experienced war. Now everywhere they felt the invisible presence of the enemy. Green officers and enlisted men imagined snoopers or oncoming bomber squadrons in every low-hanging cloud, submarines beneath every wave. The nerves of the aviators were frayed by the sight in wardroom and ready rooms of the empty seats of their comrades lost over Oahu. All hands were startled out of their sleep by the nightmare screams of new men on board, survivors of the sunken and burned ships at Pearl Harbor who had been distributed among the undamaged vessels.

Admiral Halsey, sensing that his aviators were jittery, came to the Big E's wardroom before lunch on the tenth and bucked them up with a short talk. The words are not recorded, but the effect is summarized by an entry in the Fighting 6 diary: "Those Japs had better look out for that man."

Meanwhile the raw nerves of the task force produced a spate of spurious contact reports. Sonar operators identified whales as submarines, a deck swab lost overboard and floating vertically was likely to be reported as a periscope, a playful porpoise heading at night for the bow of ship while streaming phosphorescent bubbles might be mistaken for a torpedo. False identifications sent the ten thousand men of the task force hurrying night and day to battle stations, caused the destroyers to expend dozens of depth charges, and sent the other ships maneuvering at high speed, which wasted hundreds of barrels of fuel oil. Once, when the destroyer *Benham* was running down a supposed contact, a young officer on the Big E's bridge suddenly shouted, "Look! She's sinking! There she goes!"

Halsey quickly put his glasses on the *Benham*. She was hull down in a trough but rose up on the crest of the next swell. The admiral turned wrathfully upon the young man. "If you ever make another report like that," he shouted, "I'll have you thrown over the side!"

When the lookouts continued to report nonexistent submarines, Halsey, his patience exhausted, signaled the task force: "If all the torpedo wakes reported are factual, Japanese submarines will soon have to return to base for a reload, and we will have nothing to fear. In addition, we are wasting too many depth charges on neutral fish. Take action accordingly."

Only the flyers on their air patrols appear actually to have seen submarines, but even their reports are not beyond question. One plane came back with a particularly vivid description of a sinking it had executed. The crew of the Big E was cheered in the belief that their ship had scored the first kill of the war. Postwar studies, however, show that no Japanese submarine was sunk on that date.

News of world events flowed into the carrier by radio, and the major items were printed in the ship's newspaper for all the crew to read. Guam had fallen and was occupied by the enemy. Japanese planes had bombed the U.S. naval base at Cavite in Manila Bay. Other enemy aircraft had sunk the British battleship *Prince of Wales* and battle cruiser *Repulse* off Malaya. On the tenth came a piece of news that elated all hands: the U.S. marines on Wake had thwarted an attempt by the Japanese to land, sinking two of the enemy destroyers. What the news did not reveal was that only two of the twelve Wildcats the Big E had delivered to the island were still operational.

During the cruise Halsey's destroyers fueled from the cruisers, but damage to one of the destroyers, caused by high winds and seas, compelled Task Force 8 to return to Pearl Harbor on the afternoon of 16 December.[28]

The next day Halsey was shocked to learn that Admiral Kimmel had been relieved of his command. Kimmel was to be replaced by Rear Admiral Chester W. Nimitz, chief of the Bureau of Navigation. In midafternoon Kimmel turned over his command to Vice Admiral William S. Pye, commander of Task Force 1, who would be acting CinCPac pending Admiral Nimitz's arrival from Washington. Facing one another, each read his orders. Then they shook hands, and Kimmel walked out of what had been his office.[29]

In addition to CinCPac, Kimmel had been temporary commander in chief of the U.S. Fleet (CinCUS), but Pye did not assume the latter title. The CinCUS command had been separated from the area fleet commands, and its authority had been enormously expanded. Admiral Ernest J. King, whom President Roosevelt appointed to the post, would in fact exercise operational control of the entire U.S. Navy. To King the short title CinCUS, following the Pearl Harbor attack, sounded like a bad joke. He changed it to CominCh (commander in chief).[30]

On 18 December Admiral Pye sent for Halsey. Pye was implementing a plan conceived and set in motion by Kimmel for the relief of Wake. Kimmel's second but by no means secondary objective was to bring about a battle between U.S. and Japanese naval forces in circumstances favorable to the former. Kimmel had early contemplated using Wake, relatively far from everything else but closer to Japanese than to American bases, as bait. In a memorandum to the Navy Department the preceding April he had written that in the event of war U.S. defense of the island might induce the Japanese to attack it with part of their fleet, thereby giving the Americans an "opportunity to get at naval forces with naval forces."

Now time was crucial. The defenders had thrown back the first attempted landing on Wake, but every day since then bombers from the Marshalls had pounded the island, and Japanese naval forces were sure to return in greater force than before in a second endeavor to seize it.

As part of Kimmel's relief plan, the *Lexington* force under Rear Admiral Wilson Brown had departed Pearl Harbor on 14 December to raid Jaluit in the Marshalls, supposed base of the bombers that were attacking Wake. On the morning of the sixteenth, a force built around the newly arrived *Saratoga* and commanded by Rear Admiral Frank Jack Fletcher had left Pearl and was carrying to Wake supplies, ammunition, and equipment and eighteen F4F Wildcats of Marine Corps Fighter Squadron 221 to reinforce the battered remnant of Major Putnam's Squadron 211. The *Saratoga* force was expected to bring away the wounded and as many civilians as possible. Pye issued Halsey secret orders to proceed with the *Enterprise* force to a position near Midway to cover the Hawaiian Islands or support Brown or Fletcher as needed.

Halsey sailed in the morning of 20 December. He was prohibited from announcing the objective of his sortie, but Captain Murray had a chart of the Pacific pasted on a bulkhead of the *Enterprise*'s flight deck, and each morning the ship's position was recorded on it. The spirit on board changed abruptly. The jitters and discontent that had disheartened the crew while the force was steaming north of Oahu, aimlessly, it seemed, was replaced by a sort of excited elation. The men were receiving daily bulletins of the struggle at Wake. The chart showed that their ship was heading west. The consensus was that they were speeding to the relief of that embattled island and of the marines the Big E had lately delivered there. Only Halsey knew that something had gone wrong with the relief plan. The *Lexington* had abandoned its mission of attacking Jaluit and had been ordered to support the *Saratoga* force.

Bombers from the Marshalls continued to pound Wake, joined on 21 December by carrier planes, evidently from the Pearl Harbor attack force returning to Japan. In the early hours of the twenty-third, Wake flashed a message, "Enemy apparently landing," followed some two hours later by, "The enemy is on the island. The issue is in doubt." At 0630 came a final message reporting that the island was surrounded by enemy ships, then silence. Wake had fallen. Not long afterward, a message from Pearl Harbor canceled the relief operation and recalled the *Lexington* and *Saratoga* forces. The *Enterprise* force was ordered to cover the *Saratoga* force as it delivered to Midway the marine fighter squadron and supplies originally intended for Wake.

Word went around the Big E that when Admiral Halsey learned of the cancellation he swore for half an hour and had to be dissuaded from disregarding orders and advancing to Wake to attack the enemy. Chances are he would have recaptured the island, because the Japanese carriers were by that time far away to the west.

On December 24, while supporting the delivery of marines, planes, and equipment to Midway, the *Enterprise* force crossed the international date line westbound, whereupon Halsey hoisted a Merry Christmas signal. The following day the force recrossed the line, eastbound, and Halsey again signaled Merry Christmas, this time with the "first repeater" pennant. The galley saw to it that the men got two days of turkey and trimmings, but the second Christmas was for them even less merry than the first. The eastward course seemed like a craven retreat. On the twenty-eighth the task force received orders to return to Pearl. It reentered the harbor on the thirty-first.[31]

CHAPTER 2

ORIGINS OF A WARRIOR

In his autobiography Admiral Halsey discreetly states that he never knew why the Wake relief expedition was recalled, but we may be sure he made it his business to find out. On the approaches to Wake Admiral Fletcher had wasted time in unnecessary fueling of his destroyers. Admiral Pye, overestimating enemy strength both in the Marshalls and at Wake, ordered Admiral Brown to cancel his proposed attack on the Marshalls and join Fletcher. Before Brown reached Fletcher or Fletcher reached Wake, the Japanese had seized the island. After some hesitation Admiral Pye recalled the expedition rather than risk presenting Admiral Nimitz on his arrival with news of an additional loss of ships.

In the wake of the first shock produced by Japan's raid on Pearl Harbor came anger and a determination to strike back. But the failure to save Wake, following hard on the loss of Guam, brought gloom and dejection. Bill Halsey was frustrated not only by his country's defeats but by his own failure to get at the enemy. This was not to be the last time. Repeatedly throughout the war he would be diverted just as he was about to come to grips with the Japanese fleet.[1]

Halsey's fighting spirit and love of the sea had ample family precedent. In *Admiral Halsey's Story* he wrote that many of his remote ancestors "were seafarers and adventurers, big, violent men, impatient of the law, and prone to strong drink and strong language." One of them was Captain John Halsey, commissioned a privateer by the governor of Massachusetts during Queen Anne's War (1703–13) and sent to attack French shipping. When the coming of peace left him without legitimate prey, Captain John, like many another privateer, turned buccaneer. Some of his more colorful depredations are described in *The History of the Lives and Bloody Exploits of the Most Noted Pirates.*

The Halsey family, after being grounded for a century, again took to the sea in the person of Captain Eliphalet Halsey, first to sail a Long Island whaler around Cape Horn into the South Pacific. A succession of Halsey whaling masters followed the same course.[2]

A more sedate faction of the family was represented by Charles Henry Halsey, who had two successful careers, first as a lawyer, then as an Episcopal clergyman. He married Eliza Gracie King, daughter of Charles King, president of Columbia College, and granddaughter of Rufus King, U.S. senator, minister to Great Britain, and Federalist candidate for the presidency. Charles Henry and Eliza had six or seven children—the record is not clear on this point. The youngest was William Frederick Halsey, father of the future fleet admiral. Two years after the birth of William, his father was killed. While inspecting a rectory under construction, he had an attack of vertigo and fell out of a window. Eliza settled in Elizabeth, New Jersey, and brought up the children by herself.

George M. Robeson, Charles Henry's former law partner, maintained his connections with the Halsey family and tried to be helpful, particularly in finding jobs for the boys. When William was fourteen or fifteen years old, Robeson, who recently had been appointed secretary of the navy by President Grant, called on the Halseys and repeated his offer of help to the boys. To everybody's surprise William spoke up, saying, "I would like to go to the Naval Academy." He explained that reading the adventure stories of George Alfred Henty had made him want to be a sailor.

In this post–Civil War period few appointments were being made to the service academies from Southern states. Robeson gave William one that had lapsed in Louisiana, and ever since Halsey has been listed in the records as being appointed from that state. Following his graduation from the Naval Academy in 1873, William served for a period in the South Pacific, where his forebears had whaled and where in World War II his son, Admiral Halsey, would make his greatest contribution to the American victory.

In 1880 Halsey, then a lieutenant, married Anne Brewster, a neighbor whom he had known since childhood. Anne was one of fourteen children of James Drew Brewster, a ship broker, and the former Deborah Grant Smith. During the day the Brewster household was usually in turmoil, because Mrs. Brewster had trouble controlling her huge brood. In fact, she could scarcely remember all their names. If she wanted to chastise one of the children, she usually tried calling off three or four names before chancing on the right one. When Father Brewster, a dour man and a harsh disciplinarian, came home in the evening, the turmoil ended, and at the dinner table there was dead silence or subdued conversation. Afterward Mr. Brewster would settle in his favorite chair in the living room to read, with two or three large dictionaries on the table beside him. He apparently paid little attention to the quiet conversation going on elsewhere in the room. But if somebody pronounced a word in an unfamiliar way, he would perk up. A stickler for correct speech, he would begin thumbing through his dictionaries and at length announce pontifically, "I find there are several authorities for the pronunciation of that word, but the majority of the authorities say that it is pronounced so."

Anne Brewster Halsey, a direct descendant of William Brewster, spiritual leader of the Plymouth Colony, shared the fortitude, frugality, and Spartan spirit of her Puritan ancestors. These virtues stood her in good stead at a time when promotions in the navy were rare and a lieutenant was paid two hundred dollars a month. She was beautiful in her youth and always possessed a warm personality, but because she held herself very erect and had strict notions of right and wrong, people who did not know her well were inclined to regard her as austere.

Not long after his marriage Lieutenant Halsey was ordered to sea, his wife, then pregnant, remaining in Elizabeth at her father's home. In this house of turmoil William Frederick Halsey, Jr., the future admiral, was born on 30 October 1882, and here he learned to walk and prattle by day and endured enforced quiet and dictionary pronouncements by night. His mother called the boy William, but nearly everybody else early started calling him Willie.

When Lieutenant Halsey was at last transferred ashore, for duty at the Hydrographic Office in New York, Willie was two and a half years old. Lieutenant Halsey's reaction at seeing his son for the first time was one of shock. Willie was sporting long yellow curls. To Mrs. Halsey's dismay, her husband hustled the boy to the barber shop and had the curls lopped off. He kept them, though, and whenever Willie was naughty his father brought him quickly into line by threatening to paste the curls back on.[3]

The Halseys briefly acquired a home of their own, also in Elizabeth, and here Willie's sister Deborah was born. Like most navy families, however, they were soon on the move. After two years at the Hydrographic Office, Lieutenant Halsey was transferred to the Pacific for duty on board a survey vessel operating along the coasts of Baja California and the Mexican mainland.

In the 1880s the navy, in addition to parsimonious pay, provided no transportation for dependents. Lacking funds adequate to move herself and her children by train from coast to coast, Anne Halsey solved the problem by sailing with them in a freighter to Colón (at that time called Aspinwall), then by rail crossing the Isthmus of Panama, from which the French canal builders had lately been driven by raging yellow fever. At Panama City they took passage on a nondescript vessel, which Willie remembered as a barge, that worked its way with many stops slowly up the coast to Coronado. Here the family spent the winter at the picturesque Hotel del Coronado and Willie went to kindergarten. The following winter they lived near the Mare Island Navy Yard in a somewhat run-down boarding house at Vallejo, where the boy continued his education in public school.

In the summer of 1891 Lieutenant Halsey was ordered to the Naval Academy to serve as an instructor in physics and chemistry. This was welcome news indeed, for father, mother, and children would be together and William and Anne would be near their parents.

The preceding spring Willie, while playing baseball, had been struck in the temple by a bat and suffered a wound that required stitches. Some thirty-six hours before the family's departure for Annapolis, Willie was the victim of another accident. At the navy yard he had been horsing around with some of his bluejacket friends, who had nicknamed him Billy Bighead. One of the sailors picked him up by his coat, the buttons in front gave way, and the boy fell to the ground, striking his head and suffering a concussion. In great alarm, his father was prepared to cancel the family's reservations on a vessel sailing from San Francisco. But Willie was a sturdy little fellow. In a couple of days he was as good as new, and the family returned to the East Coast by the same route Anne and the children had followed coming west.

At the Naval Academy the Halsey family was assigned an apartment on Goldsborough Row, a site later occupied by the Officers' and Faculty club. Willie promptly got into trouble with the city of Annapolis and earned a spanking from his father when he broke the globes of some street lights with a slingshot.

But the tour at the Naval Academy proved one of the happier periods of the boy's life and strengthened the resolve, which he had had as long as he could remember, of following his father's footsteps into the navy via the Academy. Willie avidly kept up with all the athletic events there and was a member of a small boys' football team that called itself the Little Potatoes because, as he later wrote, "we considered ourselves hard to peel." He continued his education in a desultory fashion, attending a private school run by women. After two years his father was detached and ordered out to the Asiatic station. Before departing overseas Lieutenant Halsey was granted a long summer leave, which the family spent at Bay Head, New Jersey. Here Willie passed most of his days and some of his evenings in the water.

Anne intended to join her husband in the Orient as soon as conditions following the Sino-Japanese War of 1894–95 permitted. But Willie spoiled her plans by developing an acute attack of Bright's disease, which he believed was brought on by repeated immersion in the often chilly Atlantic. Anne and the children had gone back to Elizabeth to live and Willie had entered the Pingry School there when the disease struck. The boy was placed under the care of a doctor who put him on a diet consisting of two glasses of milk and a piece of dry, thin toast three times a day. That was what he lived on for six months, from the autumn of 1894 to the spring of the following year. He had never cared for milk. Now he came to detest it. As an adult Halsey drank many things, but not milk.

In the summer of 1895 Willie was well enough for Anne to take him and his sister to Capon Springs, West Virginia, to recuperate. At this delightful resort he so regained his strength that in the fall his mother entered him in Swarthmore Grammar School, near Philadelphia. Here he played on the football team, and here for the first time he spent two successive years at the same school.[4]

Because he was approaching fifteen, the youngest age for a naval cadet, Willie began thinking about an appointment to the Naval Academy. Having no connections in Congress or in the hierarchy of the navy, he did not know how to go about getting one. Deciding it would do no harm to start at the top, he wrote a letter to President McKinley:

Swarthmore Grammar School
Swarthmore, Pa.

Jan. 26, '97

Major William McKinley.
Dear Sir:—
I do not suppose you remember the note some of the boys of school sent you. If you do I wish to say that my note is not of the same character. It may not be as nice to you as theirs was; although I hope sincerely it will be. I want to ask you, if you have not already promised all your appointments to the Naval Academy that you will give me one. My father is a Naval officer, and is at present navigator on the U.S.S. Montgomery. As you know as a general rule Naval officers have not much influence, and the presidents are generally willing to give their appointments to a naval officer's son if he has not promised all of his appointments. I know people do not like to give important positions such as this away without knowing the person they are giving them to. But then you know that a naval officer would not keep his position long if he were not the right kind of a man. I know plenty of respectable people who would testify to my good character. My father was appointed by Secretary Robinson [Robeson] of the Navy, who had been a law partner of my grandfather. I have been with my father on shore and on ship board a great deal, and have always wanted to enter the Navy. My parents encouraged me in this desire and gave me their consent to enter if I could get an appointment. I do not know any congressman, and the appointment from the district where I live which is Elizabeth, N.J. is at present filled. I have lived three years at the Naval Academy where my father was instructor in English. I am at present a border [*sic*] of this school and am in the class that graduates in 1898. I was fourteen last October, the thirtieth. My father is now senior lieutenant about 95 on the list for promotion. It is almost needless to congratulate you on your grand victory which every good American sees is for the best. It has been told you so many times by men it is hardly worth while for us boys to say it.

Yours respectively [*sic*],
W. F. Halsey, Jr.[5]

Willie apparently left no explanation why he addressed the president by his Civil War rank, why he claimed to have lived three years at the Naval Academy instead of two, or why he said that his father had been an instructor of English instead of science. It is possible, of course, that in the somewhat freewheeling academic programs of the 1890s Lieutenant Halsey taught some English classes.

Willie and his mother waited in vain for an answer from the president.

Willie at the Pingry School, 1894 (courtesy of U.S. Naval Academy Museum)

Meanwhile, they wrote letters to anyone who might be of assistance. Willie looked up his father's record to find where he had been appointed from and was surprised to find it was a district in Louisiana. He wrote to the current congressman representing that district and asked for an appointment. After some correspondence the boy was told that if he came and lived in the congressman's district he would be placed on the list. In desperation, Willie was on the point of moving when the congressman died, ending that hope.

When Lieutenant Halsey was transferred back to Annapolis the following summer, he joined the campaign to get Willie an appointment, with equally negative results. There was no Secretary Robeson to help his son. The fact was, like many navy families, Lieutenant Halsey's had moved around too much to establish roots and make useful political connections.

Willie was now old enough to get to know and appreciate his father. He saw the aging lieutenant as a tactful man, thoughtful of others, a deeply religious and regular churchgoer who, when irritated, was not above giving vent to a sailorman's oath. He was a firm disciplinarian, stern when necessary but always just. He took Willie sailing and impressed him with his seamanship, thereby implanting in the boy a determination to acquire similar skills.

Despite his disappointment over failing to get an appointment for his son, Lieutenant Halsey, anticipating better luck the following year, decided to enter Willie in one of the several cram schools that had sprung up in the Annapolis area to prepare appointees and would-be appointees for the stiff Naval Academy entrance examinations. He chose one run by Professor Wilmer, a retired naval officer.

Wilmer was known as Buck; his school, as Buck Wilmer University. He was an able teacher, but he had an explosive temper and, when aroused, an extraordinary range of profane language—both of which made him fair game for roguish students. Early in his first semester Willie and his friends played the old bucket-of-water-over-the-door trick. They made a noise, Buck opened the door, got soaked, and began sounding off with a choice line of anathema while the boys took to the woods. Buck complained to the parents, and Lieutenant Halsey applied the stern but just discipline that Willie had come to respect.

When another campaign to get Willie an appointment to the Naval Academy ended unsuccessfully, the Halseys held a family council. They decided that if he could not enter the navy as a naval cadet, he would follow the example of his closest friend, Karl Osterhaus, and get in through a side door, as a medical officer. Karl, another navy junior whose father was on duty at the Academy, was planning to attend the University of Virginia medical school. The Halseys made the financial sacrifice that enabled their son to go to Charlottesville in the autumn of 1899.

It was all most quixotic. If Lieutenant Halsey had had any knowledge of universities or academics beyond what he had picked up at the Naval Academy, which in those days was scarcely a typical college, he would have known better than to send a seventeen-year-old boy, just out of high school, with an inferior academic record, to study such arcane subjects as anatomy, histology, and medical chemistry. In later times no young man could dream of getting into a medical school without at least two years of college premed studies behind him.

Predictably, young Halsey was soon over his head in studies, but socially he had a wonderful time. Dropping the nickname Willie, too juvenile for a college man, he introduced himself as Bill Halsey and adopted a more sophisticated manner to go with his new name. He made many friends, some for life—notably Wiley Grandy of Norfolk and Joseph St. George ("Pat") Bryan of Richmond. With them and Karl Osterhaus he was inducted into the Delta Psi fraternity, and ever thereafter he proudly wore the Delta Psi emblem on his watch chain.

Bill Halsey lost no time moving from his dormitory, Randall Hall, to St. Anthony Hall, which was occupied entirely by Delta Psi brethren. The pride of the house was an expensive human skeleton, which the brothers passed among themselves to work out problems in anatomy. When Halsey's turn came to have the skeleton, he found another use for it. He seated "Mr. Bones" in a rocking chair next to his bed and then by various means induced the more timorous of his friends from outside to enter the room in his absence—after placing himself where he could hear and savor their astonished exclamations.

Bill himself had a bad scare at "Stiff Hall," where the dissecting room was located. He thought he had overcome an early squeamishness and learned with the other medical students to be casual about working among cadavers. Early one morning, at about four, he rose from bed and went by himself to the dissecting room to prepare for a test. Several cadavers had been brought in since his last visit. Poking around in the darkness, trying to find the light switch, he stumbled over one of them and sprawled over two others. "I never found the switch," he said later, "and I don't think I stopped running for the first mile after I left there."

Bill's habitual tendency to neglect his studies was heightened by infatuation with football. He wasn't good enough to make the varsity, but from time to time the coaches let him play with the second team. In the final practice before an important Georgetown game, he was with the scrubs, at left end. A play came toward him. Bill gave it the old college try, and by some miracle he was chiefly instrumental in stopping it. When the players were untangled, the star Virginia quarterback was found to have a broken leg. Bill's teammates were faced with a question not unknown in warfare: Do we court-martial this guy or give him a Medal of Honor? The student body would gladly have hanged Bill, but the coach let him go to Washington with the team. Many years later Halsey wrote in his autobiography, "Most stories like this end with the despised scrub redeeming himself by the winning touchdown. My story is an exception. I didn't even get into the game."

Bill did not utterly disgrace himself in academics at Virginia, thanks chiefly to Wiley Grandy. Somewhat older than the others, Grandy was a sort of father confessor for the Delta Psi chapter. He took Halsey aside one day and gave him the devil for his negligence. Abashed, Bill buckled down and tried to make amends. It was too late to save everything. He flunked histology and medical chemistry but by dint of really hard work managed to make a passing grade in anatomy and comparative anatomy.

By now, however, he had his eyes fixed on other sites. Congress had passed a bill authorizing five additional presidential appointments to the Naval Academy. Bill and his father were all for writing another letter to the president, but Mrs. Halsey, scorning this demonstrably ineffective approach, took matters into her own hands. She went to see Edgar Grigg, attorney general for New Jersey and a family acquaintance, and asked him to get her an appointment with President McKinley. After pulling some strings Grigg, a powerful political figure, accompanied Anne Halsey to the White House. He explained why young Halsey deserved an appointment to the Academy.

"I have been praying," added Anne softly. "I have been praying very sincerely."

"Madam," said the president benignly, "your prayers have been answered."

From the grisly cadavers and formaldehyde odors of Virginia's dissecting room, Bill sped back to Annapolis and set to cramming as never before, even under the tongue-lashing of Wiley Grandy. By the sweat of his brow he prepared himself and struggled through the cruel entrance examination. On 7 July 1900 William Frederick Halsey, Jr., was sworn in as a naval cadet at the U.S. Naval Academy.[6]

The Naval Academy that Halsey entered was in poor shape architecturally. Most of the red brick buildings, dating back to the post–Civil War superintendency of David Dixon Porter or earlier, were dilapidated, and some were dangerous. The dormitory, completed in 1869 and still called New Quarters, had cracked outside walls, floors with open seams, and so many doors torn loose from their frames that kitchen and laundry fumes permeated the cadets' rooms. The Academy, like the U.S. Navy itself, had been the government's neglected stepchild.

But the Academy and the navy were on the eve of a glorious renaissance. In the recent Spanish-American War the navy had stimulated national pride by destroying two enemy fleets. The victory over Spain had gained the United States a respected position in world affairs and secured it an imperial foothold overseas that required naval protection. In response to the 1898 Board of Visitors report that the Academy's recitation hall had become structurally unsafe, Secretary of the Navy John D. Long asked Congress for one million dollars to begin reconstruction of the whole establishment. He already had a blueprint in hand—an architectural and topographical plan financed by a wealthy graduate, Colonel Robert M. Thompson, developed by Ernest Flagg, eminent New York architect, and endorsed by a board of survey.

When Halsey entered the Naval Academy, the yard had been extended and construction of Dahlgren and Macdonough halls begun. The year he left, those two halls were completed and work on a new dormitory, the future Bancroft Hall, was nearing completion. The student body numbered 238 when he matriculated and more than 600 when he graduated in 1904.[7]

Halsey's academic standing at the Naval Academy was considerably

Bill as a plebe, U.S. Naval Academy, 1900 (courtesy of U.S. Naval Academy Museum)

better than that at the University of Virginia. He passed all his courses, and in a graduating class of sixty-two—from which twenty-two men dropped out through failure or for other reasons—he stood forty-third, or roughly two-thirds of the way from the top. He received more than his share of demerits, but he was a social success and a football star.

Early in his plebe year Bill joined the Hustlers, the junior varsity football team. This relieved him of a good deal of hazing, but he still had his share, being made to endure such inconveniences as double-timing down the corridors, changing directions at sharp right angles, and eating rigidly at attention while sitting on the forward two inches of his chair.

Like his peers, Bill disliked parades, but he took some pleasure in marching at the second inauguration of President McKinley, who had sent him to the Naval Academy. The cadet body left Annapolis on an old, slow train bound for Washington. While the parade was forming, the West Pointers stood opposite the Annapolis cadets. Among the former was third-classman Douglas MacArthur, whom Halsey was to meet for the first time forty-two years later in Brisbane, Australia, under very different circumstances. In the march up Pennsylvania Avenue to the Capitol, the Annapolis men were led by Cadet Lieutenant Commander Ernest J. King, the battalion commander, under whom many of the cadets present would again serve in World War II. During McKinley's inaugural address, their spirits were dampened by a rainstorm that soaked their uniforms and cascaded off their bodies in ripples.

In those days cadets got no leave during the academic year, not even at Christmas, and the second semester was followed directly by a summer cruise, at the end of which they were at last granted a month's absence. Bill's father had been ordered to Manila to command the U.S. governor-general's yacht, and his mother and sister had followed him to the Philippines. Thus, with no particular attachments, Bill spent his leave visiting friends and relatives and finally wound up at the University of Virginia, where his erstwhile classmates were still dismembering cadavers.

It happened that he arrived in the midst of the fraternity rushing season. Various fraternity brothers, taking Bill for a particularly attractive and apparently well-heeled candidate, invited him to parties and introduced him to pretty girls. Halsey, recognizing a good thing, made the most of the situation. Finally Wiley Grandy took him aside again and gave him another piece of stern advice: Bill was to get the hell out of Charlottesville and stop diverting the fraternity workers from bona fide candidates. He agreed on one condition, that Grandy lend him five dollars to buy a railroad ticket back to Annapolis. The well-heeled impression was all front; actually Bill was broke. Grandy was glad to lend him the price of the ticket.

The students who returned to the Naval Academy in the autumn of 1901 rejoiced in a new title, or rather the restoration of an old one. They were no longer to be called naval cadets, a term that sounded as if they might be a subspecies of the West Point cadet corps. By act of Congress they were henceforth to be called midshipmen, a rank long accorded young gentlemen in Britain's Royal Navy and held by students at the U.S. Naval Academy from 1870 to 1882.

In his third-class (sophomore) year at the Naval Academy, Halsey had more than his share of demerits, mostly for such offenses as smoking, being late for formations, and talking in ranks. More serious was an evening of unauthorized leave in town, a practice known at the Academy as frenching, short for taking French leave. He and a midshipman who had accompanied him were discovered absent from quarters at taps. Next morning, right after reveille, they were ordered by voice tube to report to the company office. Here the officer in charge, a lieutenant commander, fixed them with a baleful glare.

"Where were you two last night?" he demanded. But knowing that the offense of frenching would cost the young men fifty demerits and might result in expulsion, he said quickly, "I won't ask that. You reported for quarters after taps."

"Aye, aye, sir," replied Halsey and his fellow culprit, enormously relieved at being branded with a lesser offense.

They were ordered to the commandant's office, where they were penalized with twenty-five demerits and two weeks' incarceration in the USS *Santee,* the Academy's prison ship. Shortly afterward the administration plugged the loophole through which Halsey and his friend had escaped. To those absent from quarters after taps it assigned a fifty-demerit penalty.

Toward the end of Bill Halsey's third-class year his father, now a commander, was ordered back to the Naval Academy to serve as head of the Department of Seamanship. He brought with him Bill's mother and sister, and they settled in quarters on Blake Row. Following his summer cruise of 1902, Bill spent leave with his family at the Naval Academy.

To the dismay of his mother and against the earlier advice of his father, he had come back from sea with a tattoo on his shoulder—a foul anchor in blue with a red USNA on the crown and the chain forming the numbers *04*. Bill and a few friends had dreamed up the idea to betoken their status as real sea dogs. One of them had drawn the design, and they employed the services of a coal passer and off-duty tattoo artist who was in the brig for drunkenness.

That fall Bill was in danger of bilging out. In a grading system in which 4.0 was perfect and 2.5 barely passing, his mark in theoretical mechanics fell to 2.28. Commander Halsey strongly advised his son to drop football and was exasperated when Bill said he'd rather bilge. Luckily for Bill, so many other midshipmen were unsatisfactory in the subject that the department decided to give them a break. The instructors staged a crash review program, explaining problem after problem. When the midshipmen compared notes and found that all the instructors were reviewing the same problems, they figured some of them would appear on a crucial upcoming test and induced the brighter members of the class to work them out. Bill took his copy of the answers and crammed as he had not done since he prepared himself for the Academy entrance exam. When he walked into the classroom to take the test, he had every problem memorized.

Later that day, Bill went to his father's quarters for lunch. The commander met him at the door and asked if the marks for mechanics had been posted.

"Yes, sir."

"How did you come out?"

"Pretty well, sir."

"What did you make on the test?"

"I made 3.98."

The commander stared at his son a full minute. "Sir," he asked finally, "have you been drinking?"

In football that year Bill made the varsity. Just before the opening game, the regular fullback was badly injured and Halsey was thrown in as substitute. He kept the job all that year and the next, his last. The team on which he played, however, was possibly the poorest in the Naval Academy's history. Army beat them 22 to 8 in 1902 and 40 to 5 in 1903, the worst trouncing Navy received from Army in the history of their rivalry. In the latter game, however, Bill had his moment of glory. Early in the second half, as noted in *The Philadelphia Public Ledger,* "Halsey electrified the Navy contingent by making the longest run of the game. Catching the ball from a kick off on his 4 yard mark he sprinted straight up the field, dodging and eluding half a dozen West Point tackles until he reached the 43 yard line, where he was brought to earth."

In those days the Naval Academy had no stadium, not even a grandstand. At home games, chairs were brought to the edge of the playing field for the accommodation of female spectators and older males; everyone else stood. Commander and Mrs. Halsey regularly attended games in which their son participated. At this stage in her life Mrs. Halsey had attained a state of such awesome dignity that she showed little reaction to the various plays. There was one exception. While she was watching a game one Saturday, Bill was tackled by a player on the opposing team, whereupon a woman seated directly in front of her, evidently a friend or relative of the player, shrieked, "Kill him! Kill him!" This was too much for the sedate Mrs. Halsey. She rose to her full height, flourished her parasol, and would have swatted the offending female had she not been restrained.

In the summer of 1903 Bill embarked on his third and last midshipman's cruise. As was customary at that time, the mids spent half their time on a windjammer, half on a steamship. The sailing ship this summer was the *Chesapeake,* a steel square-rigger. Bill, by this time no mean sailor, had worked up to port captain of the maintop, the second most responsible job for a first classman and one that gave him particular satisfaction, because his father was acting captain of the ship. One night, when Bill was mate of the deck, a gale blew them into the Bay of Fundy, obliging all hands to lay aloft and reef topsails. This gave him an opportunity to display to his father his expertise under trying conditions. Later in the summer he served on board the old battleship *Indiana,* then a part of the Atlantic Fleet.

In his first-class (senior) year, shortened to meet the demand for officers in a fast-growing navy, Bill Halsey shone. Powerfully built and ruggedly handsome, he exuded confidence and good will. He was fond of most of his associates and they returned his affection. He was on the varsity football team and served on the class German committee and on the staff of *The Lucky Bag,* the class yearbook. As battalion adjutant, he had a respectable rank that authorized him to wear two stripes. He was elected president of the athletic association and awarded the Thompson Trophy Cup, which went annually to the first-classman who did most during the year to promote athletics at the Academy. Also, for the first time in his Academy career, he managed to maintain above-average grades.

"Everybody's friend," the yearbook called him. "A real old salt. Looks like a figurehead of Neptune." In common with all midshipmen at that time, he had nicknames: "Pudge" and "Willie," one he had never entirely succeeded in shrugging off. Some called him Stud in recognition of his rumored successes with young ladies. "Started out in life to become a doctor," the yearbook continued, "and gained in the process several useful hints."

On graduation day, which had been moved forward to 1 February 1904, Bill was elated, ready to undertake any task the navy might assign him. He had his sights lowered a bit, however, when he went to say good-bye to the Academy's chief master-at-arms. "I wish you all the luck in the world, Mr. Halsey," said the older man, "but you'll never be as good a naval officer as your father."[8]

CHAPTER 3

COUNTERATTACK

WHEN THE *Enterprise* force put into Pearl Harbor on the afternoon of 31 December 1941, Vice Admiral Halsey reported to his new commander in chief, Admiral Chester W. Nimitz. Since his days at the Naval Academy Halsey had known Nimitz, who was in the class of 1905. They had not served together since then, but from time to time their paths had crossed, and they would use the occasion to swap a few funny stories, which each collected.

Nimitz and Halsey, both effective leaders, had contrasting styles and personalities. Each was friendly and accessible, but Nimitz was polished, a gentleman of the old school, whereas Halsey was somewhat rough-hewn. Though both were courteous and considerate, Nimitz was noted for his serene self-control, while Halsey was impetuous, quickly moved by his emotions. Nimitz, widely read in military literature, based his moves on careful reasoning; Halsey tended to operate on hunches backed by innate shrewdness. Nimitz was almost obsessively discreet, whereas Halsey had a tendency to speak first and think afterward—a characteristic one war correspondent called "an affinity between his foot and his mouth." The two also had much in common: dedication to duty, decisiveness, utter fearlessness, and unswerving loyalty to seniors and subordinates—traits that won them lasting respect and affection from all but a few who ever served with them.

Secretary of the Navy Frank Knox was well acquainted with the service records of both Nimitz and Halsey. He had in fact made it his business to get to know and evaluate all the navy's top officers. After the raid on the Pacific Fleet he had flown out to Pearl Harbor for a quick inspection. On his return to Washington he recommended to President Roosevelt new employment for the two officers he considered ablest—Admiral King, to be given operational control of the entire navy, and Rear Admiral Nimitz, to command the Pacific Fleet. Roosevelt, himself a shrewd judge of persons, concurred.

Nimitz, as chief of the Bureau of Navigation (later more suitably called the Bureau of Naval Personnel), lingered in Washington long enough to get his successor at the bureau off to a good start, then traveled across the United States by train to give himself time to think things over. Flying from the West Coast, he arrived at Pearl Harbor on Christmas morning, greeted by the grim sight of wrecked and sunken ships and the somber news that Wake had fallen.

Nimitz decided to have a look around before assuming command. The condition of the ships and the news about Wake depressed his spirits, but, constitutionally optimistic, he began to see the bright side of the situation at Pearl Harbor. For being taken by surprise, Kimmel had been relieved of his command—unjustly, Nimitz believed. But what if he had had timely warning of the enemy's approach? Would he not have gone to sea, joined the ships from Pearl Harbor to the *Enterprise* and *Lexington* groups, and advanced to intercept the attacking force?

The Americans now knew that the Japanese had six large carriers and a considerable speed advantage. Had Kimmel met the enemy at sea, his entire fleet would almost certainly have been sunk—in deep water, beyond hope of salvage, with a loss of at least ten times as many men as were killed at Pearl Harbor. But the Japanese had missed the carriers, and most of the battleships sunk in the shallow water of Pearl Harbor could be salvaged. Three had already been raised and, with temporary repairs, were en route to the West Coast for rehabilitation. In any case, the old, slow battleships would be of little use in the kind of warfare the Pacific Fleet faced in the next year or so; their trained crews would serve in the carrier and amphibious forces that would now carry the burden of the war.

The Japanese had failed to hit the repair shops. They had failed to hit the submarine base, from which the opening attack on Japan was already being launched. They had failed to hit the tank farm with its immense reservoir of four and a half million barrels of fuel oil. Had they destroyed the oil, the Pacific Fleet would have been forced back to the West Coast. In short, the Japanese had scarcely impaired America's military potential, but had instead united a seriously divided nation in stubborn resolution to stay the course to final victory, whatever the cost.

On the morning of 31 December, a few hours before Halsey's arrival at Pearl, Admiral Nimitz in a short ceremony assumed command of the Pacific Fleet. He would have preferred to bring in as his advisers and assistants officers with whom he was accustomed to work, but as a gesture to raise morale he announced that he was retaining Admiral Kimmel's staff organization. It was a shrewd move. These officers felt tainted by the Pearl Harbor defeat and disgraced by the failure to relieve Wake. They expected Nimitz, the new broom, to sweep them away to far-off, inhospitable billets. Instead, he expressed faith in them and asked that they stay in their posts to provide continuity. The announcement went far toward restoring the men's self-respect. Their renewed confidence was contagious, raising spirits throughout the base, spirits that had been cast down by bad news and inaction.[1]

No record was kept of the New Year's Eve meeting between the new CinCPac and the commander of Task Force 8, but their known habits and attitudes suggest what they might have said. Halsey no doubt commented bitterly on the failure to relieve Wake. Nimitz, though in complete agreement, was probably noncommittal. The unhappy outcome had presented him with serious problems, but there was nothing to be gained by issuing postmortem criticisms of the officers who had planned and executed the operation, particularly since he would now be in daily association with them.

Admiral Kimmel was still in Hawaii testifying before the Roberts Commission, which the president appointed to investigate the failure of U.S. defenses at Pearl Harbor. On being relieved, he had promptly vacated CinCPac quarters, a large residence across the highway from the naval station, and moved in with Admiral and Mrs. Pye. Nimitz had asked Pye to remain at Pearl Harbor, at least temporarily, as his adviser. Frank Jack Fletcher would continue to command Pacific Fleet carrier forces.

Nimitz's discretion did not include withholding strategic information from his senior subordinates. He undoubtedly told Halsey that he, Nimitz, had orders from Admiral King to guard the Hawaiian Islands, including Midway, and to protect shipping between Hawaii and the United States and between the United States and Australia as far southwest as Samoa. King had also ordered Nimitz to make plans to raid enemy island bases as a possible means of diverting the Japanese from their advances in southeast Asia, the Philippines, and the Netherlands East Indies.

The chief of naval operations (CNO) was transferring the carrier *Yorktown* to the Pacific and had assigned a marine brigade to strengthen the defenses of Samoa, which appeared threatened by a Japanese advance from the Marshalls into the British-governed Gilbert Islands. Samoa had to be kept out of enemy hands because Japanese based there could intercept vital communications between the United States and Australia.

Admiral Fletcher was flying to San Diego to meet the *Yorktown,* form a task force around her, and escort the marines to Samoa. Nimitz's orders to Halsey were to complete replenishment of the *Enterprise* force as quickly as possible and then go on antisubmarine patrol in the approaches to Oahu, paving the way for a major convoy en route from the United States.

Halsey was startled to learn that in his absence all dependents of Pacific Fleet personnel had been sent back to the States. He was concerned about Fan's frail health, and he was worried because, had she gone by sea as he supposed, it might have been through submarine-infested waters. He was relieved to get word that she had arrived safely at the home of their married daughter in Greenville, a suburb of Wilmington, Delaware. He received further assurance in a letter from his friend, Rear Admiral William L. Calhoun, commander of the Base Force, who had been in charge of the stateside transfer of the dependents. Calhoun said that Mrs. Halsey, along with other wives and children with health problems, had been returned to the States by airplane under the care of a navy nurse.

Halsey replied in part, "Many thanks for your letter of 7 January 1942 and the trouble you went to. It is much appreciated.

"Mrs. Halsey arrived safely and is now being looked out for by my daughter—thank God. As you say, it leaves me free for one job and one job only—to get those yellow bastards."[2]

At the first opportunity, Halsey had called on his old friend Admiral Kimmel and found him both despondent and angry. Until Secretary Knox had come out on his inspection trip to Pearl Harbor, shortly after the raid, it had not occurred to Kimmel that he might be held responsible. Even though he knew after Knox's visit that a case was being made against him, he was shocked when on 17 December orders from the president relieved him from his duties.

Shortly afterward the Roberts Commission—two generals, two admirals, and Supreme Court Associate Justice Owen J. Roberts—arrived in Oahu to hold hearings. On 23 December they called their first major witness, Lieutenant General Walter C. Short, commanding general of the Hawaiian Department, who also had been relieved. Short had made careful preparations and spoke frankly but failed to convince the commission that he had adequately carried out his duties.[3]

Kimmel began his testimony on the twenty-seventh. He soon reached the conclusion earlier reached by Short—that one of the generals and one of the admirals were out to get the two of them. Halsey, sharing Kimmel's anger, offered to appear before the commission and give testimony on his former commander in chief's behalf. Kimmel at once accepted the offer and put in a request for the commission to hear Halsey before 3 January, when he was due to begin his patrol. The commission juggled its schedule and summoned Halsey to appear before it on the morning of the second.

In the course of rescheduling, somebody confused names and titles. When Halsey's turn came the legal adviser, a marine colonel, announced, "Admiral Halsey, damage control officer of the *Arizona,* is here." Six months later certainly no marine—officer or enlisted man—and probably few American civilians would fail to recognize that Admiral Halsey was much more than a damage control officer.

The essence of Halsey's testimony was that Kimmel had kept him "fully informed at all times of everything," and that, like Kimmel, he had concluded the Japanese would not attack Pearl Harbor.

Questions posed by one of the generals brought out the fact that Halsey was in disagreement with the battleship admirals, whose ideas had dominated Navy Department thinking on the eve of the U.S. entry into war.

"Admiral," said the general, "do you consider the carrier primarily an offensive or defensive weapon?"

"An offensive," replied Halsey.

"Would you give the commission a very brief opinion on the strategy of the operations of a carrier force?"

"I think General Forrest's description is the best thing I know, to get to the other fellow with everything you have and as fast as you can and to dump it on him.* You have to scout out and find it, and as soon as you find it, send everything you can at him and hit him with it."

"As a commander of a task force, you would have no hesitancy in using your carrier as an offensive weapon?"

"I would consider myself to be a very poor specimen of a naval officer if I thought in any other direction."

"You do not believe a carrier is designed primarily to protect the heavy units of the fleet?"

"No, sir, decidedly not."[4]

The *Enterprise* force sortied the following day. After a singularly uneventful patrol, it entered Pearl Harbor in the afternoon of the seventh and commenced fueling and provisioning. The convoy from the States had arrived safely.[5]

On 8 January Halsey and his cruiser commander, Rear Admiral Raymond A. Spruance, attended the CinCPac morning conference. The participants discussed the advisability of sending carrier strikes against the Gilberts and Marshalls. A successful blow there would safeguard Samoa, possibly divert the Japanese from their advance in the southwest, and certainly raise morale in the American services and public by answering the questions newspapers were beginning to ask: Where is the navy? What's the navy doing?

Admiral Pye had worked out a plan. He cautiously assumed that the Japanese had learned of the forthcoming reinforcement of Samoa and might try to forestall the marines' landing. He therefore proposed that an additional carrier be sent to support the *Yorktown* force in covering the debarkation. Both carrier groups would then head for the Marshalls and Gilberts to meet and intercept any approaching enemy. If no enemy were encountered, the two U.S. task forces would raid points in those islands while a third attacked the airfields at Wake, partly to prevent planes flying from there in defense of the Marshalls. The fourth carrier force would remain near Hawaii to cover Pearl Harbor.[6]

Admiral Nimitz favored the Pye plan. So did Nimitz's war plans officer, Captain Charles H. McMorris. Halsey thought it excellent and certainly worth putting into effect. Hence he was astonished at the vehemence with which some officers opposed it—or any raiding at all of Japanese bases. Nimitz, at a disadvantage because he was not an aviator and had never

*Nathan Bedford Forrest was a Confederate cavalry general. His simple rule of operation was "Get there first with the most men."

commanded a carrier or carrier force, courteously heard them out. They argued that the success of the Pearl Harbor attack had demonstrated to the Japanese that such raids were feasible. They would thus be on guard against any such raid the Americans might attempt in retaliation. They would be on the qui vive particularly in the Gilberts and Marshalls, site of the Japanese bases closest to Pearl Harbor and hence most likely to tempt the Americans.

Halsey heard these arguments with growing irritation. At last he rose and cleared the air by roundly denouncing such defeatism. The plan was risky, he conceded, but they'd never get the war off the ground without taking a few risks. He not only supported the Pye plan but offered to lead the attack himself. Because he had long experience with carriers and was liked and respected by all, his words carried weight.

Halsey, by backing Nimitz and the raiding plan, won his commander in chief's lasting gratitude. Long afterward, when Halsey came under criticism, Nimitz recalled this interlude. "Bill Halsey came to my support and offered to lead the attack," he said. "I'll not be a party to any enterprise that can hurt the reputation of a man like that."[7]

On 9 January Nimitz sent for Halsey, whose offer was accepted. Halsey would activate the Pye proposal and lead the raid on the islands. Nimitz reminded him of the Orange Plan, which they had studied at the Naval War College.* It specified that if Japan attacked the Philippines the United States would capture points in the Marshall and Caroline islands as part of a drive across the central Pacific. For the time being such large-scale operations were out of the question, mainly because the country lacked ships and trained men for amphibious assaults. However, a sharp blow at the spearhead of the enemy's advance via the Marshalls and Gilberts might prevent his proceeding farther through the Ellices to Samoa.

They discussed the Marshalls. At the end of World War I these and other German islands in the Pacific had been mandated to Japan by the League of Nations, which stipulated that no military installations were to be installed on any of them. The Japanese had promptly sealed them off, admitting no foreigners. It was generally suspected that they had disregarded the stipulation, which they had sworn to observe, and built airfields on and otherwise fortified the islands.

Tackling such positions from the sea would be hazardous, Nimitz pointed out. But, he added, it presented Halsey with a rare opportunity. Nimitz meant, of course, that a successful attack would make a potent contribution to the

*American military and naval planners often used a color code to replace names of nations: United States, blue; Japan, orange; Great Britain, red; Germany, black; Mexico, green; and so on. During World War II Americans often referred to the opposing fleets in the Pacific as the Blue Fleet and the Orange Fleet.

American war effort, but he undoubtedly had in mind another advantage that he knew would appeal to Halsey. The officer who led the first successful counterattack against the Japanese would emerge a national hero.[8]

To the crew of the *Enterprise* it soon became evident that a major operation was forthcoming. The carrier had never before been so heavily refueled, rearmed, and replenished. A pilot of Scouting 6 wrote in his diary, "Loaded for bear." Admiral Halsey himself took a hand in the replenishment. Having learned that the doctors were administering sleeping pills to wakeful pilots exhausted by constant overwater searches, he directed the senior medical officer to take on board a large quantity of bourbon whiskey to dispense instead.[9]

On 10 January Halsey dropped by CinCPac headquarters for final instructions and "to say what I hoped was au revoir." Nimitz walked with him down to the wharf. "All sorts of luck to you, Bill!" he called as Halsey stepped into his barge.

At noon the following day the *Enterprise,* escorted by the heavy cruisers *Chester, Northampton,* and *Salt Lake City,* seven destroyers, and an oiler, put to sea with Admiral Halsey and Captain Murray on the bridge. Officers in the know, afloat and ashore, had cause for apprehension. Left guarding the Hawaiian Islands were only the *Saratoga* and *Lexington* forces, the latter scheduled to attack Wake. Radio intelligence indicated that the same six-carrier Japanese striking force that raided Pearl Harbor had departed Japan on 6 January. Its destination could be Midway, Pearl Harbor, the Gilberts and Marshalls, or Samoa. Before the day was over, Halsey received the shocking news that the *Saratoga* had been hit by a submarine torpedo and was limping heavily damaged back to Pearl.[10]

A jinx seemed to settle on the *Enterprise* force as it headed toward Samoa. One of the destroyers lost a man overboard. A seaman was killed in a turret accident on board the *Salt Lake City.* An *Enterprise* scout plane crashed on deck, killing a machinist's mate. Another plane fell into the sea. Two of the destroyers collided and had to return to Pearl for repairs. A torpedo bomber with three men failed to return to the ship. A search by aircraft located neither plane nor flyers.

Halsey's natural impulse was to deploy his surface ships in a hunt for the missing aviators, a routine action in time of peace. But the immutable deadlines of war permitted no such merciful detours. The task force plowed on toward its destination. But the flyers, lost and low on fuel, made a smooth ditching. For thirty-four days they drifted on a rubber raft under tropical skies with little food or water, at length reaching Pukapuka Island, 750 miles from where they went down.

Despite the jinx, the *Enterprise* force arrived right on schedule, 20 January, at the rendezvous point north of American Samoa. But planes winging out

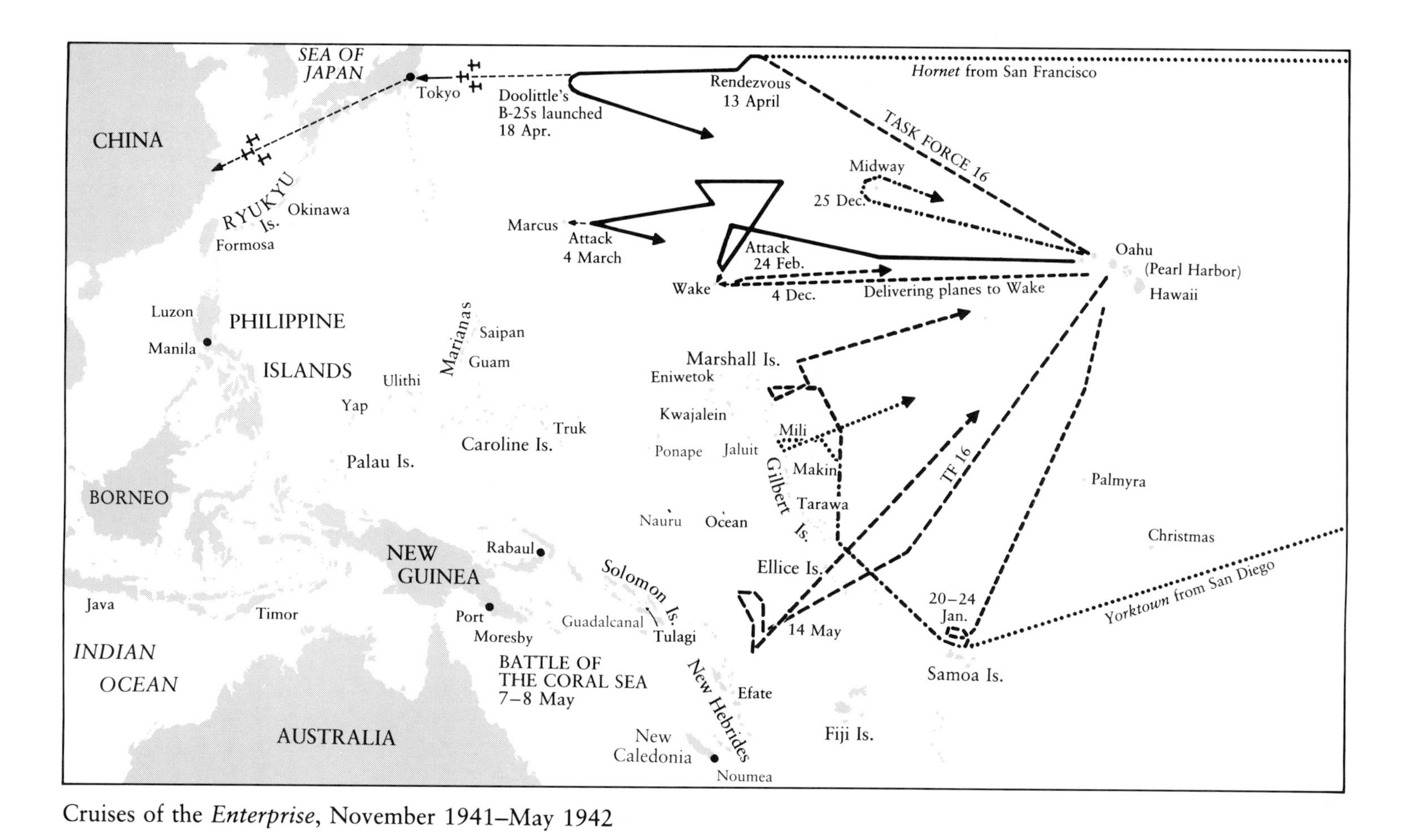

Cruises of the *Enterprise*, November 1941–May 1942

over the harbor of Pago Pago discovered no signs of Fletcher's *Yorktown* force. While awaiting its arrival, Halsey's ships patrolled an east-west line, the Big E's Wildcats maintaining combat patrol overhead and her scout planes fanning out to the northwest in the direction of the enemy. On the twenty-third the *Yorktown* force at last arrived, having been delayed by another of Admiral Fletcher's unscheduled refuelings.

The next day, when the marines and their equipment had all been landed at Pago Pago, the *Enterprise* force moved in closer to the islands, affording the men in the ships a glimpse of green shoreline. The force then shaped course northwest, toward the Marshalls, 1,600 miles away. The *Yorktown* task force, which now came under Halsey's command, fell in behind, following at a distance.

For lack of information about Japanese fortifications in the islands, Admiral Nimitz had given Halsey only the most general orders concerning the forthcoming raid, leaving the details to his discretion. Halsey had turned the planning over to his chief of staff, Miles Browning. On the latter's recommendation, he directed Fletcher to attack Makin in the Gilberts and Jaluit and Mili in the southern Marshalls, reserving for his stronger force the older and presumably more heavily developed bases of Wotje and Maloelap in the northeastern Marshalls.

Until their attack on the islands revealed their presence to the enemy, the task forces were of course to maintain radio silence. But Nimitz could and did keep in touch with them by radio. He informed Halsey and Fletcher that their prospects appeared better than first estimated. Reconnoitering U.S. submarines reported that the Marshalls were not nearly so well developed and fortified as had first been feared and that the greatest concentration of ships and aircraft was at Kwajalein Atoll, evidently the site of Japanese headquarters. More important, the Japanese carriers were not coming their way. They were heading south to support a Japanese landing on New Britain, planned to capture the port of Rabaul.

Browning now urged Halsey to take bolder measures. The admiral should have his cruisers bombard the outer islands of Wotje and Maloelap under the cover of Wildcat fighters while the *Enterprise* penetrated the archipelago and sent bombers against Kwajalein. At any rate, Browning pointed out, unless they kept all air bases in the Marshalls busy defending themselves, the bases would send their planes against the *Enterprise,* which could hardly hope to survive a massed air attack. Halsey was convinced. He adopted the Browning proposal and sent word of the change by carrier plane to Fletcher. "It was one of those plans," said Halsey, "which are called 'brilliant' if they succeed and 'foolhardy' if they fail."

On 28 January, as the task forces neared the target islands, Halsey ordered fueling. The oiler came alongside the *Enterprise* at 2000 and finished fueling at

0130. It was the first time a heavy ship had been fueled at night in the open sea. No lights were showing and the darkness was intense, but the operation was completed without incident.

The force crossed the international date line on 29 January and thus passed into 30 January, east longitude date. Halsey now ordered all ships rigged with gear that would permit vessels damaged in action to be quickly taken in tow.

The following day the force was on course due west, heading directly for the northern Marshalls for a dawn attack on 1 February, still east longitude date. In the afternoon Halsey received the disturbing information that an enemy plane had been picked up and was being tracked by the ship's radar. He hastened to radar plot to have a look, and the radio operators pricked up their ears to catch the pilot's broadcast warning. But the pilot did not break silence. His plane passed within thirty-four miles of the U.S. formation, which apparently was concealed by a light haze.

"That yellow belly is just thinking about his fish and rice," said Halsey. "Let's go and blast them out of the Marshalls." Then, with a playful mischievousness that was a part of his nature, he sent for his Japanese language officer and dictated a message to the enemy commander in the Marshalls: "It is a pleasure to thank you for having your patrol plane not sight my force." He ordered copies printed in Japanese to be dropped the next day along with the bombs.

At 1830 the force, as scheduled, split into three task groups for the final run-in. The *Northampton,* the *Salt Lake City,* and a destroyer, under Rear Admiral Spruance, would bombard Wotje. The *Chester* and two destroyers, commanded by Captain Thomas M. Shock, would bombard Maloelap. Under Halsey's direct command, the *Enterprise,* accompanied by three destroyers, would hit both Wotje and Maloelap but concentrate on Kwajalein.

To reach Kwajalein with her planes the Big E would have to pass within sight of two or three Japanese islands. "To bring a carrier within visual distance of an enemy-held position," said Halsey, "is not considered good practice in the best regulated families and is not recommended." He was aware that in so exposing his carrier he was courting disaster but, weighing the advantages and disadvantages, he had decided to take the chance.[11]

While Spruance's and Shock's groups, diverging to the southwest, were still visible from the *Enterprise,* Halsey was handed a message from CinCPac: "It is essential that the attacks be driven home. Exploit this situation by expanding operations, utilizing both task forces in such repeated air attacks and ship bombardments as developments and logistics make feasible. If practicable, extend offensive action beyond one day."[12]

It would be interesting to know why this mischievous message was sent. We can guess with what emotions Halsey received it. It will be recalled that he declared Admiral Kimmel's order to use common sense the finest any subordinate ever received, and had himself directed Major Putnam to do what seemed appropriate. Now Admiral Nimitz, who had never piloted a plane, commanded a carrier, or fought an engagement, was telling Admiral Halsey, the navy's senior carrier commander, how to fight his battle. Such a message was altogether unlike Nimitz, who in every other recorded instance was extremely reluctant to interfere with the commander at the scene of action. Halsey must have been outraged at this unneeded and unwanted advice, but he was too loyal and disciplined an officer to reveal his feelings.

Through the calm and moonlit evening the *Enterprise* bored steadily westward. Within a few hours Halsey would be locked in combat with an enemy whose fighting potential he had no way of assessing. Mixed emotions of eager anticipation and dread drew his nerves taut. Feeling incapable of presenting the image of calm composure he thought a commanding officer on the eve of his first action should display, he withdrew into his emergency cabin, out of sight.

Halsey lay down and closed his eyes, but sleep eluded him. He turned and twisted. He drank coffee. He smoked cigarettes. He read. Finally, an hour and a half past midnight, he gave up and returned to flag plot. At about 0300 the staff duty officer dashed in from the bridge with a startling report. He had felt sand blowing into his face. Halsey knew that the charts they were navigating with, the only available ones, were based on old and dubious surveys. They might show the islands in wrong positions. That was another risk he had had to take.

The sand was evidence that land was close aboard. Any minute the Big E could come to a violent end, her bow driven into an uncharted beach. Halsey ordered the duty officer to investigate further. The officer hastened out. In a few minutes he came back laughing.

"What the hell are you laughing about?" asked Halsey.

On a sudden inspiration the officer had picked up some sand grains with a wetted finger and tasted them. They tasted sweet. At that moment, on the range-finder platform forward of the bridge, he dimly made out a sailor stirring a cup of coffee.[13]

All hands had now been called, and the crew went to breakfast. The aviators, facing their first attack on enemy territory, ate in silence, keeping their thoughts to themselves. In their ready rooms they received last-minute instructions and quickly studied charts showing the location of their planes on the flight deck, above. Proceeding topside, they found the calm sea glistening under a full moon. In the shadows bluejackets were bellowing numbers to guide the flyers to their aircraft. The pilots climbed into their cockpits, buckled seat belts, and fastened shoulder harnesses.

"Stand by to start engines!" the bull horn blared. The Big E forged ahead to thirty knots, giving the planes a wind for takeoff. "Start engines!" Engines began to roar, and the big props spun. At 0443 the first of thirty-seven dive-bombers sped past the island and rose into the night sky. These were followed by nine torpedo bombers. All headed for Kwajalein, the world's largest atoll. The target for the SBDs was the air base on the atoll's northernmost island, Roi; that for the torpedo bombers was the anchorage off Kwajalein Island, at the southern end of the island-encircled lagoon.

After a two-hour flight the dive-bombers reached the great atoll. Here, baffled by morning mists and poor charts, they circled about, searching for Roi, which they did not identify until 0705. By that time the roar of their engines had alerted the enemy, who had ample time to man his antiaircraft batteries and get his fighters into the air. The U.S. squadron commander, Lieutenant Commander Hallsted Hopping, released the first bomb of the war to land on Japanese soil. He was promptly shot down by a combination of ground and aircraft fire, and three more SBDs were similarly dispatched. The squadron destroyed three enemy fighters, strafed planes parked on the ground, dropped bombs on several structures, and hit an ammunition dump, which exploded with a flash and a thunderclap audible to the flyers.

Radios in the dive-bombers and on board the Big E picked up the voice of Commander Howard Young, the group commander and attack coordinator. Shouting over the roar of battle, he kept repeating, "Targets suitable for heavy bombs at Kwajalein anchorage!" In response, all the dive-bombers in the Roi area that had not expended their 500-pound bombs were promptly detached and headed south. Nine torpedo planes held in reserve on the *Enterprise* also headed for Kwajalein Island. The bombers from Roi found plenty of targets afloat, no fighter opposition, and only erratic antiaircraft fire.

When the reserve torpedo planes reached the anchorage, they could see that the preceding attacks had found targets among the anchored Japanese ships, and they set out eagerly to complete the destruction. Back in the *Enterprise,* Admiral Halsey put on earphones and listened with satisfaction to their exuberant shouts: "Get away from that cruiser, Jack! She's mine!" "Bingo!" "Look at that big bastard burn!"[14]

Immediately after the *Enterprise* had launched her Dauntlesses and her first flight of Devastators for Kwajalein, six of her Wildcats took to the air and remained over the carrier and her escorts to guard against counterattack. At 0610 the Big E's remaining twelve fighters, armed with machine guns and 100-pound bombs, began to take off and head for Maloelap and Wotje, where they would cooperate with the surface bombardments. The moon had now set, and one of the six Wildcats intended for Maloelap became disoriented in the darkness and dived into the water, killing the pilot.

On Taroa, largest island in the Maloelap Atoll, the five remaining F4Fs found a well-developed base with mile-long concrete runways, a navy yard,

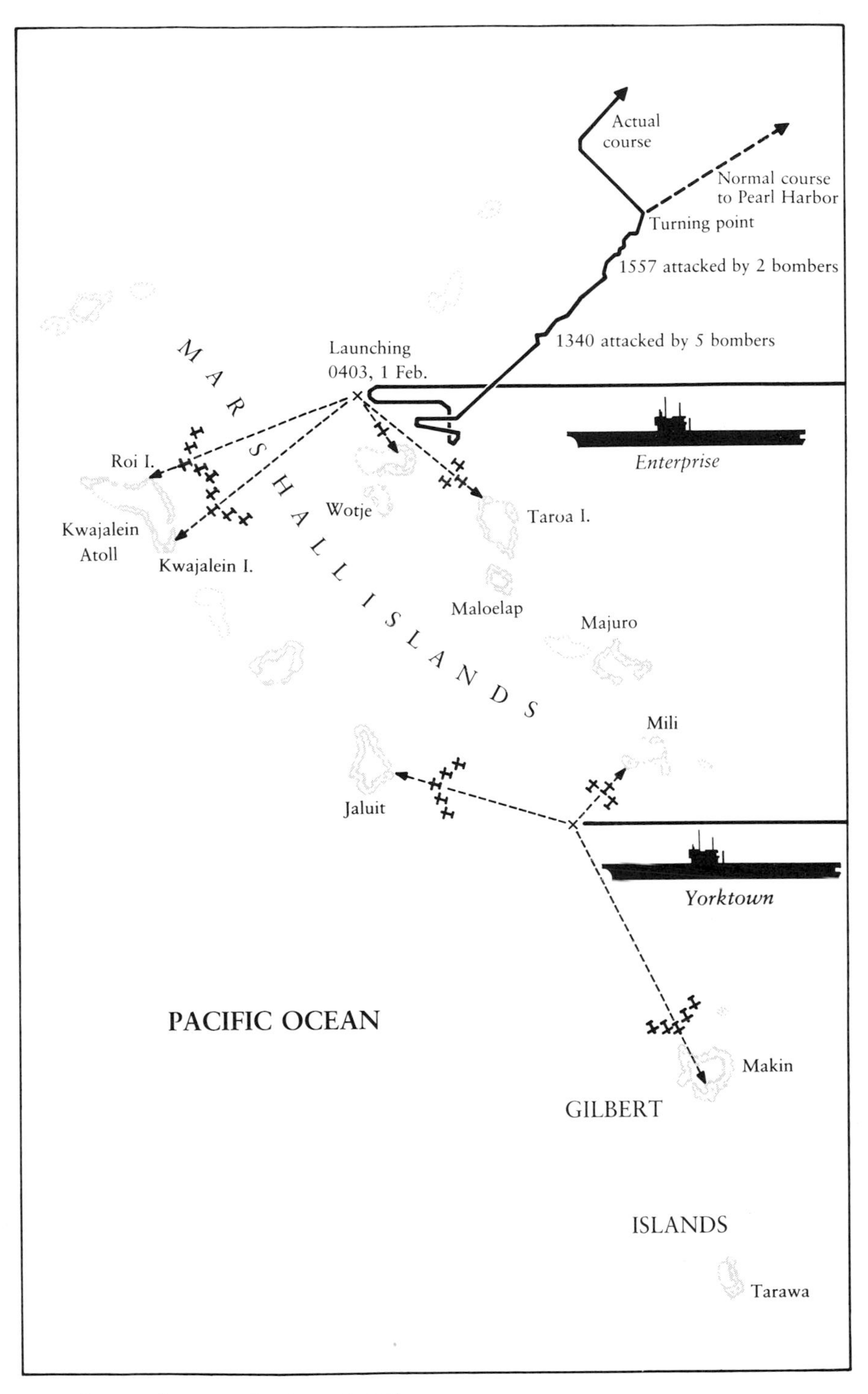

Attacks on the Marshalls and Gilberts

and a radio station. They dropped their light bombs on buildings in the navy yard and strafed bombers parked on the airfield before coming under serious attack by enemy fighters. All five Wildcats made it back to their carrier, but the section leader's plane, following the others at a distance, was riddled with more than thirty bullet holes. As he landed, the last of his fuel drained out through a perforated tank. The ship's supply officer remarked that the plane "looked like the moths had been at it in the attic all summer."

Meanwhile Captain Shock's *Chester* and two destroyers had Taroa under fire. Despite strafing from the air and bombardment from the sea, eight twin-engined bombers succeeded in taking off from the airfield. They concentrated on the cruiser. The *Chester* dodged all their bombs except one, which penetrated her main deck, killing eight men and wounding eleven.[15]

While Shock's bombardment group attacked Taroa, Spruance's headed for Wotje, largest island in the Wotje Atoll. At sunrise, according to plan, six F4Fs from the *Enterprise* swept over the island, bombing and strafing the installations there. At the same time a small gunboat darted out as if to engage the whole Spruance group. "Take it," the admiral ordered his destroyer, which peeled off and in a hail of shells sank the tiny but gallant guardian of the atoll.

Again according to plan, the group formed into column and opened fire on ships inside the lagoon, believed to be merchantmen. Before the cruisers attained any sure hits, a lookout in the *Northampton* reported a periscope. Though Spruance doubted that there were any submarines in the area, he ordered a cease-fire and a radical change of course that disrupted his cruisers' fire-control solution and gave the merchantmen time to dart behind islands.

When the group moved in to begin the bombardment, shells from guns ashore threw up geysers near the cruisers. As one exploded abeam the flag bridge Spruance's chief of staff ducked. Alongside him, the admiral, apparently unperturbed, continued erect and unflinching. Shelling from the cruisers set structures ashore on fire, but presently lookouts reported more periscopes, evidently the tips of gunpowder cases that had been thrown overboard. Disregarding Spruance's signal to ignore such sightings, the rattled cruiser captains repeatedly turned away.

A little before 1000, on schedule, the bombardment group broke off action and headed toward a rendezvous with the *Enterprise* group. Spruance still appeared calm and collected, but his impassive demeanor concealed rage and frustration at the spoiling of his plan and the poor showing of his force.[16]

Throughout the morning Admiral Halsey, wearing a leather windbreaker and an old white sun helmet, remained on the Big E's flag bridge. When his staff suggested that he shift to less conspicuous headgear, he grunted, "Gives 'em something better to shoot at."

All *Enterprise* planes returned from the attack on Kwajalein anchorage. After each flight came on board, the pilots compared observations and the leader reported to Halsey. On the basis of such reports it was concluded that the Big E's bombers and torpedo planes had sunk sixteen Japanese ships at the anchorage, including four auxiliaries, two submarines, a light cruiser, and a small carrier. But the aviators, not experienced in recognizing ship types and assessing damage, had grossly overestimated their achievements. Their actual score at the anchorage was one transport and two smaller vessels sunk and eight other ships damaged.

At Browning's suggestion Halsey had the dive-bombers from Kwajalein refueled, rearmed with 500-pound bombs, and sent to continue the attack on Maloelap and Wotje. After each strike the bombers would return, and during further refueling and rearming their pilots and crews would take a break. Then out they would go again. "These young pilots," said Halsey, "acted as if they were playing football. They'd fight like the devil, then take a short time-out, and get back into the fight again."

In the course of the morning, the Big E launched twenty-one strikes, all the time maneuvering inside a rectangle only five by twenty miles, frequently within sight of Wotje. Halsey was thus exposing his ships to appalling risks. "Surely," wrote naval historian Samuel Eliot Morison, "some kind angel was guarding them from submarines and air bombers."

For one of Halsey's flight leaders, Lieutenant Commander William R. Hollingsworth, enough was enough. At about 1300, after his third strike and following his third report to Halsey, he added, "Admiral, don't you think it's about time we got the hell out of here?"

"My boy," replied Halsey, "I've been thinking the same thing myself." He thereby inaugurated the legendary club "Haul Ass with Halsey."

The hauling didn't get under way quickly enough. Down out of an overcast sky swooped five twin-engined Japanese bombers, which glided steeply toward the *Enterprise*. The whole reassembled task force threw up a fountain of antiaircraft fire, but the gunners were not well versed in leading. When the shells arrived the bombers had swept past. Untouched, they straightened out and dropped their bombs. "Down!" Miles Browning shouted. Halsey was already on the deck.

Captain Murray, conning the ship, had seen the bombs in time and expertly spun the carrier out of their path. They struck the water alongside, raising 200-foot-high geysers that poured onto the flight deck like rain. Bomb fragments riddled the side of the ship, cut a gasoline line, igniting the spilled fuel, and shattered the leg of a seaman manning a machine gun on the port catwalk. The wounded man continued to fire until the action was over but died a couple of hours later.

Meanwhile one of the Japanese bombers, both engines afire, dropped out of formation, circled about, and headed again for the *Enterprise,* apparently intent on making a suicide crash among the planes parked at the forward end of her flight deck. Captain Murray once more took evasive action, but the crippled plane turned with the carrier.

At that moment Halsey, who was again on his feet, was astonished to see a helmeted, jerseyed figure dash across the deck, leap into the rear seat of the sternmost dive-bomber, grab its gun, and open fire at the approaching bomber. Murray threw his helm over. The fire from the dive-bomber must have killed the pilot in the big plane, because this time it failed to turn with the ship. It hit the flight deck and skidded on a diagonal path while gasoline from its ruptured fuel tanks sprayed the island and drenched the navigation bridge. The plane's right wing tip slashed off the tail of the rearmost SBD, not three feet from the impromptu gunner, who continued firing as the fuselage hurtled into the sea and one wheel leapt a couple of hundred feet into the air. The chief gunnery officer had the presence of mind to order a cease-fire before the high-octane gas on the deck and bridge was ignited.[17]

Halsey took a deep breath after that and tottered into the flag plot to steady his nerves with a cup of coffee. While he was drinking it, he happened to look up and notice that the yeoman of the day was grinning at him.

"What are *you* laughing at?" Halsey demanded.

Embarrassed, the young man mumbled, "Nothing, sir."

Turning to Browning, Halsey said, "Who is this man?"

"Why, Admiral,"replied the astonished Browning, "that's Bowman. He's on your staff."

"I don't mean that. What's his rate?"

"Yeoman first class, sir."

Now Halsey was grinning. "That's where you're wrong," he said. "He's a *chief* yeoman. Any man who can grin like that while my knees are cracking together deserves to be promoted."[18]

This was a story Halsey afterward liked to tell in his style of humorous self-depreciation. But a member of his staff said, and the others agreed, "We always had to watch him before an action to keep him from worrying too much. We'd have to send him out of the chart room and see that he got some sleep. But as soon as the shooting started, he was as cool and quiet as you please."

The task force reformed and retired at a steady thirty knots. Halsey learned that the intrepid fellow who had fired at the attacking bomber from the rear seat of the Dauntless was Bruno Gaido, aviation machinist's mate second class. Captain Murray, as a reward for valor, had already promoted him to machinist's mate first class.[19]

At 1555 two more Japanese bombers appeared overhead. Because the Big E's Wildcats couldn't catch them and the antiaircraft gunners on the ships apparently couldn't hit them, Lieutenant Commander Wade McClusky, the fighter squadron skipper, then flying combat air patrol, coached the gunners by radio. The latter succeeded in damaging one of the bombers, but it stayed on course. In the face of the heavy gunfire, however, the enemy planes remained at 14,000 feet, from which altitude their bombs predictably fell wide of their targets.

The Wildcats now were closing in. "Knock off antiaircraft fire," said McClusky. "We'll take 'em."

The fighters chased the enemy bombers into a large cumulus cloud. Halsey, watching, could no longer see any planes, but he heard McClusky on his earphones: "Get out of my way, and let me knock that oriental son of a bitch out of the sky!" A moment later, in sight of the task force, one of the bombers came streaking out of the cloud and crashed into the sea trailing fire and smoke.

During the afternoon the *Enterprise* force was repeatedly snooped, but the Wildcats succeeded in chasing away all would-be attackers. At nightfall the combat air patrol had to be called in. At this early period in the war there were no trained night fighters in the U.S. Navy.

When the moon rose in a cloudless sky, Halsey's worries intensified. In the bright moonlight he could see the thirty-knot wakes of his force stretching back to the horizon. He dared not change course until he had cleared the Marshalls and any outlying shallows and coral heads, a fact he knew the Japanese would be counting on. When at last he was clear he began to breathe more easily.

The direct course to Pearl Harbor was northeast, but Halsey's sharp-eyed flag lieutenant and signal officer, Lieutenant William H. Ashford, made out what appeared to be a line squall to the northwest and suggested they get behind it for concealment. They could ride it out instead of holding the track to Pearl Harbor, which the Japanese would expect them to take. Halsey thankfully accepted the suggestion and gave the necessary orders.[20]

For the next couple of days the task force moved through rain and mist so thick that lookouts at times could not see from ship to ship. Radar tracked enemy planes vainly searching the direct course to Pearl Harbor but, except for a couple of submarine scares, the force was unmolested. In the evening of 2 February Halsey sent a message to all hands: "Well done! You have made history in the Marshalls. I am proud to have the honor to command you. God bless you!"

While the *Enterprise* was manuevering in the Marshalls with all three groups visible to the Japanese, Halsey had temporarily abandoned radio silence to communicate with Fletcher and report to Nimitz. From the former he learned that the *Yorktown* force had been partially defeated by bad weather, but that it was undamaged and would soon be heading back to base.

On the morning of the fifth, as the *Enterprise* force approached Pearl Harbor, Halsey directed all hands on his ships, if their duties permitted, to put on white uniforms and stand at quarters as they entered the channel. Lieutenant Ashford had the Big E's huge battle flag raised, and the other ships of the force, seeing it, hoisted their biggest flags.

As the force passed Hickam Field, where two months before it had been asked derisively, "Where in hell were you?" khaki-clad troops came to the shore cheering. This time they knew where the ships had been. Word had got around. So too at Hospital Point doctors, nurses, corpsmen, orderlies, patients yelled and waved. Inside the big harbor ships blew their sirens and whistles, and crews manned the rails and sounded off with prolonged cheers, which the men of the Big E returned.

As the *Enterprise* came alongside the wharf, Admiral Nimitz, not waiting for the brow to be lowered, went over the side in a bos'n's chair. "Nice going!" he shouted, grabbing Halsey's hand.

Rear Admiral Robert A. Theobald, Commander, Destroyers, Pacific, earlier one of the chief opponents of the proposed carrier raids, came aboard right behind Nimitz and shook his finger in Halsey's face. "Damn you, Bill," he said, "you've got no business getting home from that one! No business at all!"

Bill Halsey grinned while tears of pride stained his weather-beaten cheeks. He and his men had brought back to Pearl Harbor America's first victory of the war.[21]

CHAPTER 4

TARGET: TOKYO

WHEN ADMIRAL FLETCHER'S *Yorktown* force arrived at Pearl Harbor on 6 February, it attracted only moderate attention. The base had apparently exhausted its store of enthusiasm greeting the Big E the preceding day. In truth, the *Yorktown* force had little to celebrate, having been hampered by bad weather in its sector and by Fletcher's unwillingness to risk his ships, all of which returned unscratched.

Admiral Nimitz's public relations officer had arranged a press conference for Halsey and Fletcher that afternoon. The latter, naturally somewhat taciturn, had little to say. Halsey, on the contrary, proved a photographer's and newsman's dream. When discussing the navy's achievements he grinned from ear to ear; at any mention of the Japanese he assumed a ferocious scowl—both faces were equally photogenic. Without boasting about his own achievements or intended achievements, and indeed sometimes amusingly belittling himself, he described what his navy was going to do to the enemy in the salty language that would become his trademark. Here was a likable fellow whom correspondents could with pleasure build up into a national hero. They lost no time at all enshrining him as the nemesis of the Japanese, a half-fictitious character whom they named "Bull Halsey."[1]

Admiral Spruance did not attend the press conference. Perfectionist that he was, he remained secluded in his cabin on board the *Northampton*, depressed over the poor showing of his task group in the Marshalls raid. In any case, he preferred not to be present. Though Spruance had been friends with Halsey for many years and would remain so for life, he deplored his chummy relations with newsmen and his obvious enjoyment of publicity.[2]

Halsey was loud in his praise for all who had participated in the Gilberts-Marshalls raid. On his recommendation, many medals were awarded. He himself received the Navy Distinguished Service Medal for his achievement as overall commander of the operation. Because Halsey insisted that the strategic planning for the Marshalls raid was the work of Miles Browning, Browning also was awarded a Distinguished Service Medal and was promoted to captain. Though Spruance considered his own participation in the raid a failure, Halsey thought otherwise and saw to it that he was awarded a Navy Commendation Medal.[3]

In an impressive ceremony on the *Enterprise*'s flight deck, with all participants wearing whites, Admiral Nimitz pinned on the various medals. When the ceremony was over, Halsey summoned his staff. Pointing to his medal, he said, "This is as much for you as it is for me. You made it possible."

That evening the Big E's crew had assembled on the hangar deck to enjoy the nightly movie when Halsey appeared. Voices were hushed, followed by the scraping of chairs and benches as the men stood. "Carry on," said Halsey, and they all sat back down and resumed their conversations. They fell silent again when they noticed that the admiral was still standing, before the screen, facing them.

After a few seconds of silence Halsey held up the medal he had been awarded that morning. "Men," he said, "this medal belongs to you. I am honored to wear it for you." He paused as if at a loss for words. Then, his voice husky, he added quickly, "I am so damned proud of you I could cry," and sat down. All over Pearl Harbor, lookouts on board ships and night crews in shops and on wharves listened in wonder at the sound of prolonged cheering they could hear coming from the *Enterprise*.[4]

To the disgust of newsmen, the censors held up their stories of the Gilberts-Marshalls raid for fear the Japanese might discover that the task forces had returned to Pearl Harbor and were concentrated there, a target for retaliatory raids. Not until mid-February, when the forces were again at sea, did a full account of the attack appear in the newspapers. The stories were based on the aviators' overblown estimate of their achievements, now officially accepted. The *New York Times* headline read, "U.S. Navy Sank 16 Ships in Marshall Raid, Including Carrier, Cruiser, Destroyer." An aerial photograph of smoking installations on an enemy island was captioned, "The Navy Begins to Even a Score in the Pacific." Other newspapers, less restrained, proclaimed, "Pearl Harbor Avenged!" The nation had its answer to the oft-repeated question, What's the navy doing? Morale rose appreciably in the U.S. armed forces and among the American public. Feature stories played up the character and personality of the leader of the attack. The public was becoming aware of the formidable Bull Halsey and his exploits.[5]

The Gilberts-Marshalls raid had no discernible effect on enemy operations elsewhere. In the Philippines the Japanese continued to push the American and Filipino troops to the tip of Bataan Peninsula and nearby Corregidor Island. Their drives on Rangoon and Singapore and into the Netherlands East Indies showed no signs of losing momentum. Having occupied Rabaul in the Bismarcks, the enemy was obviously developing it into a major air and naval base, from which his bombers would be able to strike at Port Moresby, the Australian base on the south coast of New Guinea.

As the Allied situation in the southwest worsened, Admiral King, now CNO as well as CominCh, called on Nimitz for more diversionary operations in the central Pacific, using all available forces, including the half-dozen battleships then based on the West Coast. Nimitz was convinced, and Halsey and the CinCPac staff concurred, that any blow their modest forces could strike in the central Pacific would be unlikely to affect enemy operations in the southwest. To them, King's directive to use the old battleships for raiding seemed particularly quixotic. The battleships were too slow to keep up with the carriers, and it would be fatal to slow down the carriers to the speed of the battleships. There were not enough cruisers and destroyers in the Pacific Fleet to screen both types operating separately, and carrier forces were more effective than battleship forces because they had both planes and guns for offense and defense.

King seemed to believe the Japanese incapable of launching a powerful attack in the central Pacific while heavily involved elsewhere—a view the Japanese themselves had demolished the preceding December. Nimitz, complying with King's apparent intentions, reluctantly combined the *Enterprise* and *Yorktown* forces and prepared to send them to attack Wake and Eniwetok or Marcus. Such raids, if they did nothing more, would give the men experience and raise American morale, and he hoped they would satisfy King. As for the battleships, he refused to send them out on offensive missions with inadequate screens and have them sunk by enemy submarines or aircraft.

Nimitz was grimly conscious that once the new raids were under way there would be no carrier air power defending Pearl Harbor or central Pacific communications. Feeling he could not resolve such a risky situation by radio, he sent Admiral Pye to Washington to do some fast arguing. As emissary to King, Pye was an inspired choice. He was a highly respected strategist and an experienced commander of large forces. Somewhat cautious by nature, he could be counted on to counsel prudence. Until lately he had been commanding the Pacific Battle Force, so his advice against attempting to use the old battleships would carry weight. By no means least important, he was a Naval Academy classmate of King and one of his few intimate friends.

Halsey would of course command the raids. He always insisted he was not superstitious, but he exploded when his combined force, designated Task Force 13, was scheduled to set sail on Friday, 13 February. He at once dispatched his hot-tempered chief of staff to raise hell at CinCPac headquarters over the outrage.

War Plans Officer McMorris was not the least bit superstitious, but he was tolerant of human frailties. Agreeing with Browning that too many hoodoos were being hung on Halsey's risky expedition, he changed the designation to Task Force 16 and assured Halsey's chief of staff that an overdue oiler would hold up the sortie until the fourteenth.[6]

On the fourteenth, then, Halsey got under way with the *Enterprise* and her screen. Fletcher's *Yorktown* force was to follow the next day. On Sunday the fifteenth there came a conciliatory dispatch from CominCh, apparently reflecting the good offices of Pye. King, it now appeared, would be satisfied with occasional raids on Japanese bases in the central Pacific, and he conceded that a force should be held in reserve to counter possible surprise thrusts by the enemy. Nimitz immediately canceled Fletcher's sailing instructions and ordered him to cruise with the *Yorktown* force, designated Task Force 17, between Pearl Harbor and Samoa. Fletcher's first assignment was to cover the merchantman *President Taylor,* which had run aground in the harbor of Canton Island.

Halsey's Task Force 16, the *Enterprise,* the *Northampton,* the *Salt Lake City,* seven destroyers, and an oiler, continued westward for a raid on Wake. Some of the officers on board expressed the opinion that it was little short of ridiculous to steam 4,000 miles to Wake and back and to employ so much power against so insignificant a target, but this was what CominCh demanded, and it did provide the men with some useful training. It also demonstrated the value of aerial photography in naval operations. A plane from Midway photographed Wake from the air. The photos were rushed to Pearl for developing and interpretation and then delivered to the force at sea by plane drop. The Japanese on Wake unwittingly assisted their attackers by sending out weather reports in a code the Americans had broken.

On the evening of the twenty-third the cruisers and two destroyers, under Spruance, steamed to the west of Wake to carry out a dawn bombardment. It was assumed that the defenders would have difficulty spotting the vessels against the dark western horizon. But the atoll was in a direct line with the rising sun, and the glare on the water blinded the gun-director officers in the ships. The bombardment was supposed to coincide with a strike by dive-bombers from the *Enterprise,* a hundred miles to the north. That didn't work out either. The Big E was caught in such a heavy rain squall that she could not launch on time, and the need for radio silence prevented Halsey from warning Spruance. But the Americans were fortunate: rain concealed the carrier, and the defenders could send against the bombardment vessels only three lumbering seaplanes, whose bombs fell wide. On the atoll some buildings were destroyed and in the lagoon three flying boats were damaged. Two small patrol vessels were sunk by Spruance's destroyers, one of which rescued four survivors. The Americans lost three planes, two destroyed by foul weather and one shot down by ground fire.

While heading for a rendezvous with his bombardment group and the oiler, Halsey received a dispatch from CinCPac: "Desirable to strike Marcus if you think it feasible." This was quite an order. Marcus Island was less than a thousand miles from Tokyo and within easy bombing range of the Japanese base on Iwo Jima. Halsey was ready to take the risk, because a strike so close to home might induce the Japanese at last to divert strength from the southwest. The feasibility of the raid depended on whether continuing tempestuous seas would permit his reassembled force to be fueled in time to have enough oil left after the attack to get back to Pearl.

Halsey barely made it. By 1 March he had succeeded in fueling only his carrier and his two cruisers. With these he began a high-speed dash for Marcus, leaving his destroyers with the oiler. Hours before dawn on the fourth, 125 miles northeast of the island, he launched thirty-two bombers and six fighters and guided them to the target by means of radar. The enemy was taken completely by surprise. His radio station had just begun to sound an alarm when it was silenced by a direct hit. He got no planes into the air, but his antiaircraft fire destroyed one of the American bombers. The attacking planes smashed several buildings and set a fuel tank on fire.

Task Force 16's long cruise back to home base was enlivened only by a couple of dubious submarine contacts. When it arrived at Pearl on 10 March the destroyer with the four Japanese prisoners of war on board secured to a pier and sent for a marine guard to take custody of them. Just as the marines brought the first prisoner topside, a pneumatic riveter opened up on a nearby ship. The three Japanese still below, supposing their comrade had been met with machine-gun fire, began yelling with fear.[7]

During Task Force 16's expedition against Wake and Marcus the Japanese completed their conquest of Malaya with the capture of Singapore and made good their hold on the East Indies with the surrender of Java. Their surface forces had destroyed the Allied surface force in the Battle of the Java Sea. Their carrier force had bombed the Australian port of Darwin and was operating in the Indian Ocean and the Banda Sea. Neither the U.S. carrier raids in the central Pacific nor a raid on 10 March by the *Lexington* and *Yorktown* on enemy bases in New Guinea seemed to have the slightest effect on Japanese operations elsewhere. Of the U.S. raids one officer expressed the opinion, "The Japs didn't mind them any more than a dog minds a flea."

He was mistaken. The raids had caused the Japanese considerable anxiety. Admiral Isoroku Yamamoto, commander in chief of Japan's Combined Fleet, feared the Americans would attempt a carrier raid on Tokyo and thus endanger the sacred emperor, whose safekeeping was traditionally the first duty of the Japanese armed forces. To forestall any such sacrilege and close a gap in Japan's defense perimeter, but mainly to draw out the carrier-centered U.S. Pacific Fleet, Yamamoto proposed the capture of Midway.[8]

Admiral Nimitz received word from Admiral King that he was sending Captain Donald B. Duncan to Pearl to explain a project that had King's backing and support. Nimitz knew only that the project, whatever it was, had to be important for King to be sending an officer all the way from Washington to talk it over.

Duncan arrived in late March. As soon as Nimitz learned that the plan he had come to discuss involved carriers, he sent for Halsey, who reported to CinCPac headquarters accompanied by Browning. Duncan said that early in the war President Roosevelt had called for an air raid on Tokyo as suitable retaliation for Pearl Harbor. Fulfilling this demand presented problems. No Allied air base was within bombing range of Japan. Using carriers and carrier planes would be suicidal, because the latter had a radius of action limited to 300 miles. Japan had land-based planes with ranges far in excess of that.

In January Captain Francis B. Low, Admiral King's operations officer, had put forward an idea. Perhaps inspired by Halsey's early experiment in flying army planes off the flight deck of the *Enterprise,* he suggested sending against the target long-range army bombers that would take off from a carrier operating at a considerable distance from the shore. Low's suggestion—endorsed by King and the commanding general of the army air forces, Henry H. ("Hap") Arnold, and developed by Duncan and army Lieutenant Colonel James H. ("Jimmy") Doolittle—grew into a plan for launching B-25 medium bombers from the new carrier *Hornet.* Led by Doolittle, the B-25s would bomb Tokyo and then, since they could not land on the short carrier deck, continue to friendly airfields in China.

Seventy officer and 130 enlisted volunteers of the army air forces, trained by Doolittle, would service and operate the bombers. Only sixteen of the planes, one deckload, could be carried because the wingspread of the B-25 was too great for the *Hornet*'s elevators. To clear the flight deck for the B-25s, the carrier's own planes would be struck below on the hangar deck. The expedition would thus require the participation of another carrier to provide air cover on the outward voyage. That was part of what Duncan had come to arrange with Nimitz.

The *Yorktown* and *Lexington* were in the South Pacific. Only the Big E was at Pearl Harbor. Before making her available, Nimitz asked Halsey, "Do you think it would work, Bill?"

"They'll need a lot of luck," Halsey replied.

"Are you willing to take them out there?"

"Yes, I am."

"Good!" said Nimitz. "It's all yours."

Captain Duncan, as soon as he had settled a few details with Admiral Halsey, sent a message to General Arnold: "Tell Jimmy to get on his horse."

Arnold relayed the message by telephone to Doolittle. The business thus settled, Doolittle began moving his volunteers and their B-25s to California, whither the *Hornet* also was bound, via the Panama Canal.[9]

It occurred to Halsey that the operation would run more efficiently if he and Browning had a face-to-face conference with Doolittle, whom they had never met. Nimitz agreed and issued them stateside orders. By prior arrangement they met Doolittle and Duncan on 31 March in the bar of San Francisco's Fairmont Hotel, where Halsey and Browning were staying.

The bar was obviously no place to discuss top-secret matters. Nor was it possible to discuss much of anything else there—everybody who came in seemed to be Jimmy's friend and wanted to talk. This sort of situation Halsey ordinarily would have enjoyed, but there was a war on and they had to get cracking. Besides, their being seen together might make people think something unusual was afoot.

So they retreated upstairs to Halsey's room. Here they spent several hours thrashing out the whole project. In the course of their discussion Halsey was impressed with the extraordinary risks Doolittle and his airmen would be facing and how slight was their chance of survival. Doolittle, for his part, came to realize that the navy was also undertaking a perilous mission. The task force, by penetrating almost to the shores of Japan, could lose half the Pacific Fleet's carriers, fourteen other ships, and the lives of several thousand men, including three of the navy's most experienced officers—Halsey, Spruance, and Captain Marc A. Mitscher, commanding officer of the *Hornet,* a pioneer naval aviator.

Halsey and Doolittle decided that the *Enterprise* and *Hornet* groups would meet at sea, and that Bill would try to sneak Jimmy to a point 500 miles from the coast of Japan. They agreed that if the combined force was discovered earlier they would launch Jimmy's bombers anyway, provided they had a chance of reaching either Tokyo or Midway. If they were not within flying range of either, the B-25s would have to be pushed overboard so the *Hornet* could use her own planes to defend the ships.[10]

They shook hands and parted. The next day Doolittle took his bombers from their temporary base at McClellan Field, near Sacramento, to Alameda Naval Air Station, across the bay from San Francisco. The *Hornet* was there, all her planes struck below. Navy handlers drained the B-25s of gas and a dockside crane picked them up and placed them on the carrier's flight deck, where they were lashed down.

The *Hornet* task group, including the light cruisers *Nashville* and *Vincennes,* four destroyers, and the oiler *Cimarron,* sortied in the morning of 2 April in a thick fog that concealed it from the shores and from traffic on the Bay and Golden Gate bridges, under which it had to pass. It had instructions to take a circuitous route to the rendezvous point to keep the *Hornet*'s unusual cargo from being sighted by vessels on the regular sea routes.[11]

Halsey and Browning had expected to be back at Pearl Harbor on 2 April, but strong westerly winds prevented flights to Honolulu. As days passed with no naval or commercial plane able to fly west, Halsey became increasingly restless. It was at this time that he developed an itching rash, the beginning of the dermatitis that was to torment him over the next two months.[12]

On the morning of the sixth he was too ill to rise from his bed, suffering from what he believed was the flu. Browning discovered a navy doctor in the lobby who, "at my insistence," Halsey wrote, "dosed me with dynamite pills." It is perhaps worth noting that Halsey, not the doctor, diagnosed the illness as flu. What the doctor prescribed was liquids and bed rest.

In the evening Halsey, learning that one of the three planes available to him, the Pan American passenger Clipper, would be able to take off that night, rose from his bed of pain and with Browning hastened to the air terminal. On board the Clipper were nine other passengers. Halsey took more pills, climbed into his bunk, and promptly fell asleep. The next morning when the plane lost altitude, he woke up with a severe nosebleed. "This and the dynamite pills," he says, "effectively drove away the flu." One is tempted to speculate that not the pills but Halsey's much-delayed arrival at Pearl Harbor is what drove away whatever had put him in bed. The dermatitis, however, remained.[13]

Halsey now wasted no time. He conferred briefly with Nimitz and at greater length with the CinCPac planning staff. Before the day was over, the staff had prepared and Nimitz had approved CinCPac operation plan no. 20-42, which stated, "This force will conduct a bombing raid against the enemy objective specified in Annex 'C' which is being furnished Commander Task Force Sixteen only." Halsey arranged for two U.S. submarines to maintain patrol stations off Japan and report any enemy forces that might threaten his force. All other American submarines would be routed south of the equator, far away from Halsey's line of advance. He ascertained that any ships or submarines he sighted west of the rendezvous point—latitude 39 north, longitude 180—could be presumed enemy.[14]

At noon the following day, 8 April, Task Force 16 filed out of the harbor—the *Enterprise,* with Halsey on board, the heavy cruisers *Northampton* and *Salt Lake City,* four destroyers, and the oiler *Sabine.* When the *Enterprise* air group landed on board, a couple of hours after the force had left port, the fighter pilots were flying a new breed of Wildcat, the F4F-4. The planes were equipped with cockpit armor and self-sealing fuel tanks and had folding wings, which facilitated stowage and shipboard handling. "Everyone except the pilots loved the folding wings," recorded the Big E's historian. "They made the pilots uneasy. It was like sailing a ship with a removable bottom or driving a car with collapsible wheels."[15]

Because Halsey's delay in San Francisco had postponed his departure from Pearl, CinCPac radioed the *Hornet* to defer her scheduled rendezvous with the *Enterprise* twenty-four hours. The revised schedule brought the two forces together at 0600 on the thirteenth. They merged, forming an enlarged Task Force 16 under Halsey's command.[16]

Among the crew of the Big E, the sight of giant planes on the *Hornet*'s flight deck caused wild speculation. All binoculars and long glasses were trained on them.

"They're B-25s!" one sailor exclaimed.

"You're crazy, sailor," an aviator replied. "A B-25 could never take off with a load—and if it did, it could never land aboard again."

"They won't have to carry a load, you dope, and they won't have to land. They're reinforcing some land base."

"Out here? Which land base?"

"I'll bet we're going through the Aleutians and deliver them to a secret Siberian base."

"Are they using army pilots on carriers? If so, our careers are over. Let's join the marines."[17]

The *Hornet* group had already been told the nature of its mission. Halsey now passed word to the ships from Pearl Harbor—by semaphore to his cruisers and destroyers, directly by squawk box to the Big E: "THIS FORCE IS BOUND FOR TOKYO."

"In all my experience in the navy," said Halsey, "I have never heard such a resounding cheer as came up from the ship's company."[18]

At midnight the admiral ordered time in his force changed to zone minus twelve, and since longitude 180, on which the rendezvous had taken place, coincided in this area with the date line, he ordered the date advanced one day. Thus Halsey's sailors and Doolittle's soldiers went directly from 13 to 15 April.

Halsey became uneasy on the sixteenth when his Japanese language officer handed him a translation of a propaganda broadcast from Radio Tokyo: "Reuters, British news agency, has announced that three American bombers have dropped bombs on Tokyo. This is a most laughable story. They know it is absolutely impossible for enemy bombers to get within five hundred miles of Tokyo. Instead of worrying about such foolish things, the Japanese people are enjoying the fine spring sunshine and the fragrance of cherry blossoms."[19] The Americans never found the source of this false information.

On 17 April, when Task Force 16 was 1,000 miles from Japan, Halsey fueled his larger vessels. Then, as in the Marcus raid, he left his destroyers behind with the oilers and began a high-speed run with his carriers and cruisers. If all worked out according to the optimum plan, he would arrive undetected at a point 500 miles off the Japanese coast in the afternoon of the eighteenth.

Doolittle's plane would then take off, timed to arrive over Tokyo at dusk, and drop incendiary bombs. The rest of the B-25s would be launched at sunset. Four would individually drop their bombs on the cities of Yokohama, Nagoya, Osaka, and Kobe. The remainder would head for Tokyo, where the fires set by Jimmy's bombs would guide them to appropriate targets, which included factories and other buildings of military value. Hospitals, schools, and the imperial palace were to be rigorously avoided.

After passing across Japan in darkness, the bombers at dawn would be over the East China Sea approaching the Chinese coast. With luck they would have enough gas left in their tanks to locate the friendly airfields, well inland, where they were expected to land.

During the afternoon of the seventeenth, as the streamlined task force forged steadily westward, Doolittle called a meeting of the eighty men who would make the flight—three commissioned officers and two enlisted men to each of the sixteen planes—and went over the plan in detail.

"We should have plenty of warning if we're intercepted," he said. "If all goes well, however, I'll take off so as to arrive over Tokyo at dusk. The rest of you will take off two or three hours later and can use my fires as a homing beacon."

"Colonel," said one of the pilots, "what should we do if we lose an engine or something else goes wrong and we have to crash-land in Japan?"

Doolittle replied that it was up to each individual to decide what he would do. As for himself, he didn't intend to be taken prisoner. "If my plane is crippled beyond any possibility of fighting or escape," he said, "I'm going to bail my crew out and then dive it, full throttle, into any target I can find where the crash will do the most damage."

For the last time he gave the men a chance to back out. None did.

At 0300 on the eighteenth, when the task force was 700 miles from land, the Big E's radar detected two ships 21,000 yards off the port bow. Using short-range, high-frequency radio, Halsey ordered the task force to alter course to avoid detection. An hour later, as the strange ships faded from the radar screen, he ordered a resumption of the westerly course.

At first light the *Enterprise* launched a reconnaissance flight of three scout bombers. One returned and dropped a beanbag container with a message reporting another vessel forty-two miles almost dead ahead of the task force. The pilot believed the enemy had seen his plane. It appeared the B-25s would have to be launched very soon, but Halsey ordered another course alteration and pushed on westward. Every mile he could carry the army bombers closer to Japan increased by that much their chance of reaching a friendly Chinese airfield before they ran out of gas.

An hour later two lookouts on the *Hornet* sighted a small patrol craft. Halsey began to suspect, correctly, that he had run into an enemy picket line. A U.S. submarine had earlier seen picket vessels on watch off the Japanese coast but had reported them much nearer the shore than this.

The *Hornet*'s radio operator intercepted a Japanese communication being transmitted from nearby. Obviously the presence of the American carriers was being reported to authorities in Japan. Task Force 16 still continued westward.

Presently Radio Tokyo came on the air. The Big E's Japanese language officer, though a trained cryptanalyst, could not decrypt the coded message. But he had brought with him a list of call signs. Comparing these, he determined that the dispatch was addressed to various military and naval units. One call stood out like a lightning flash. It was the sign of the big Japanese carrier force. If it was taking traffic directly from Tokyo, it was clearly no longer in the Indian Ocean and might even be back in Japanese home waters. Maybe Task Force 16 was running into a trap.

Halsey waited no longer. He had a message flashed to Mitscher on the *Hornet:* "Launch planes. To Col. Doolittle and gallant command. Good luck and God bless you. Halsey."

Doolittle, on the *Hornet*'s bridge, shook hands with Mitscher and dashed below, calling out, "OK, fellas, this is it! Let's go!" The Klaxon shrieked. The loudspeaker barked, "Army pilots, man your planes!"

The prospects for Doolittle and his aviators were not good. The wind, at almost gale force, had whipped up thirty-foot waves. Spray from these and from intermittent rain squalls drenched the exposed decks and deck crews. The army flyers had been counting on surprise. Now they would have to bomb an alerted Tokyo in daylight and then in darkness find their way to and over unfamiliar terrain in China. The *Hornet* was 620 miles from Japan, which meant that to reach friendly airfields the bombers would have to fly 120 miles farther than originally planned.

In preparation for the takeoff the *Hornet* increased speed, and the navy crews topped off gas tanks and loaded ten extra five-gallon gas cans in the rear compartment of each B-25. Doolittle's plane was in front. He was to take off first, with just 467 feet of runway. If he could make it, presumably the rest could.

On signal Doolittle started his engines and gradually gave them full throttle. Crewmen yanked the wheel blocks away, and his plane began to move forward into the teeth of the wind while all hands watched tensely. The *Hornet*'s bow was tilting up on a rising wave. As her stem plowed through its crest, Jimmy's plane seemed to leap into the air with yards to spare. He circled the carrier once and then headed for Tokyo.

Because of the change in launching time, there was no delay before the next takeoff. The second plane took to the air five minutes after Doolittle's. The remaining bombers rolled forward one at a time, and hundreds of onlookers in the ships sweated each into the air. The last left at 0920, exactly an hour after the first. To conserve fuel, the pilots wasted no time getting into formation. Each plane proceeded independently toward its target.

When the last of the bombers had disappeared to the west, Halsey ordered the ships of Task Force 16 to reverse course and at flank speed head east in the now-familiar maneuver known as Haul Ass with Halsey.

Naval headquarters at Tokyo, warned by the patrol boat's report, alerted all available aircraft—90 fighters and 116 bombers—and ordered six heavy cruisers and ten destroyers to sortie at once from Yokosuka Naval Base and attack the American force. Other forces, surface and subsurface, including the carrier force arriving from the Indian Ocean, were ordered to intercept the Americans. All these preparations were undertaken on the assumption that the U.S. carriers would have to approach within 300 miles of the Japanese coast, the operational radius of carrier planes. The raid, it was believed, could not be attempted before the morning of 19 April.

On the morning of the eighteenth, by coincidence, an air-raid drill commenced in Tokyo about the time the last of the B-25s were taking off from the *Hornet.* It ended at noon. Barrage balloons were lowered, and most of the Zero fighter planes returned to their airfields. At 1230 the first of the B-25s arrived over the city. Because the American wing markings of that period somewhat resembled the Japanese orange circle, most citizens of the sprawling capital merely assumed that these were their own planes staging a realistic climax to the morning drill. There was a little ineffective antiaircraft fire, and the few Zeros over Tokyo were unable to overtake the swift American bombers.

The B-25s dropped their bombs and continued unmolested across Japan. One pilot, his fuel supply dangerously low, turned northwest and headed for the nearest neutral airfield, at Vladivostok. Arriving there at dusk, the plane was impounded by the Russians and the crew interned. The rest of the bombers were overtaken by darkness in the long flight across the East China Sea. Not one of these made it to an airfield. One went down off the Chinese coast and two of its crew were drowned. The remaining crews either bailed out of their planes or crash-landed. Doolittle, who bailed out, was among those who landed safely, but one man was killed and others were seriously injured. Most of the Americans who reached China were helped by friendly Chinese to safety inland. Eight who landed in occupied areas, however, were taken prisoner by the Japanese and sentenced to death in a mock trial. Of these, three were executed by rifle fire. The others had their sentences reduced to life imprisonment. One died of malnutrition. The remaining four, after nearly three years of solitary confinement, regained their freedom at the end of the war.

The damage done by the American bombing of Japanese cities was not extensive, but government and military leaders, humiliated by the supposed danger posed to the divine emperor and the indignity done to their sacred soil, reacted with rage. To punish the Chinese for helping the Americans and to destroy airfields that Americans might use in the future, the Japanese army launched a campaign that thrust 200 miles into the interior of eastern China. The Japanese plowed up the landing fields and tortured and killed anyone even remotely suspected of having aided the Doolittle crews. General Claire Chennault, then serving in China, reported, "Entire villages through which the raiders had passed were slaughtered to the last child. . . . A quarter million Chinese soldiers and civilians were killed in the three-month campaign."

The Japanese had no means of retaliating immediately against the Americans, but all opposition to Admiral Yamamoto's project for invading Midway collapsed, and the assault was scheduled for the first week in June.[20]

CHAPTER 5

BATTLES MISSED

AFTER LAUNCHING DOOLITTLE'S B-25s, the *Hornet*, on retirement course, brought some of her own planes to the flight deck and launched them on a search to the southwest to warn of aircraft that might be approaching from Japan. Then, as Task Force 16, eastbound, again neared the warning line of enemy patrol craft, both carriers sent bombers ahead to sink any boats in the area. They found plenty, about fifteen, and also a submarine. They dropped all their bombs and did a great deal of strafing, but it is not certain that they sank anything. As one of the Japanese patrol boats came into view of the task force, men in the ships, putting their glasses on her, could see that she was armor-plated. The *Nashville*, ordered by Halsey to sink the boat, circled her for twenty minutes firing five- and six-inch guns before the craft began to go down. The cruiser then sent a boat to pick up survivors.

Of the five men brought on board one, a seaman second class, told a strange story. On watch early that morning he had seen some planes and roused his skipper to report them. The latter, supposing them to be an air patrol from Japan, stayed in his bunk. A little later the sailor was back with another report. "Sir," he said, "there are two of our beautiful carriers now dead ahead."

The skipper, suddenly wide awake, rushed to the deck and studied the carriers through his binoculars. "They are beautiful," he said sadly, "but they are not ours." He went below, took a pistol out of his seabag, put it to his temple, and fired.[1]

Early that afternoon radios in the speeding task force began picking up Tokyo broadcasts announcing the air raid. None of the speakers seemed to know whose planes had done the raiding or where they had come from. The announcers agreed, somewhat hysterically, that the raiders' bombs and bullets had been aimed exclusively at civilian targets. One, speaking in English, reported the unspeakable outrage to the world in a voice half choked with emotion:

> There has been no damage at all to military objectives, but several schools, hospitals, and shrines have been destroyed. Thirty primary-school children on their way home from morning classes were machine-gunned in the street. This attack on the civilian population, this killing of little helpless children,

> was quickly dealt with. Our patrol planes were already in the air when this armada of Chinese, American, and Russian planes came in from the sea. Our antiaircraft batteries went into action at once. Nine of the enemy bombers were shot down. The others were turned about and forced to fly southward. Others are being pursued by our fighters and they won't escape us.

Halsey and his staff assessed this announcement as mere propaganda. Doolittle's aviators were unlikely to disregard his strict orders to bomb only military targets. The fact that the Japanese had not identified the planes meant that none had in fact been shot down. It meant also that the bombers had come over Tokyo flying high, and they would scarcely have sacrificed the advantage of altitude to machine-gun a bunch of school kids.

When the *Enterprise*'s radar picked up an enemy search plane thirty-five miles away, Halsey considered sending fighters to shoot it down before it could report the position and course of his ships. But as he, Captain Murray, and the radar officer watched intently, the plane closed to thirty-two miles, then turned to course northwest and faded from the scope. Evidently the snooper had seen nothing.

By 1730 the last of the carrier planes had been recovered and, to everyone's relief, darkness soon fell. Through the night each hour put the force twenty miles farther from the vengeful enemy's reach. At dawn on 19 April lookouts on the *Enterprise* discerned the tops of Task Force 16's destroyers on the horizon ahead. These soon joined her, providing added protection against enemy submarines.

That morning Tokyo broadcasts finally identified the attacking planes as American B-25s, information gleaned from the development and analysis of photographs. Japanese and other radio commentators now devoted themselves to speculating whence the raiders had come. The Americans were at some pains not to let them find out. Admiral Halsey had already passed word that under no circumstances were his men to reveal, discuss, or hint at the nature of their mission. All hands complied fully; the origin of the Doolittle raid proved one of the best-kept secrets of the war. President Roosevelt, at a press conference, announced that the bombers had come from the mythical land of Shangri-La. It was a good idea to keep the enemy wondering whether the Americans had built a superplane that could fly from Midway to China or a supercarrier that could handle twin-engine army planes.[2]

At 1400 on the nineteenth officers and enlisted men on the Big E's signal bridge sighted inside the task force screen what appeared to be a periscope. One of their number, Flag Lieutenant Ashford, signaled the location of the object to the task force. A cruiser, without awaiting orders, promptly opened fire. Captain Miles Browning, dozing in his cabin after being up most of the night, awoke with a start, leapt from his bunk, and, in a rage, stormed up to the bridge. He ordered a cease-fire, then turned wrathfully on Ashford, whom he proceeded to chew out, calling into question his competence, his judgment, even his intelligence. He broke off his tirade only when Admiral Halsey appeared on the bridge.

Ashford, convinced he had seen the periscope, told his story to the admiral. He recommended that fueling, scheduled to begin at 1600, be postponed. The task force should continue on course until well after nightfall, then wheel ninety degrees and proceed on the new course for about an hour. Fueling would be carried out under cover of darkness. Browning strongly opposed Ashford's recommendation and resumed his denunciation of the flag lieutenant. Halsey silenced his chief of staff with a glance and directed Ashford to put his proposed plan into effect. Browning paled, stalked off, and went below to sulk.

Such conduct surprised no one. Browning was widely known in the navy as a smart eccentric of whom almost anything might be expected. Historian Samuel Eliot Morison called him "one of the most irascible and unstable officers ever to earn a fourth stripe, but a man with a slide-rule brain." Some observers wondered why Halsey put up with him. The fact was that the admiral leaned heavily on Browning for advice. He had learned how to handle the man and was able to recognize and disregard his chief of staff's occasional screwball ideas.

Fueling was carried out successfully under the revised plan. The next day a sailor brought Ashford a photograph he had taken while standing on the flight deck at the time of the sighting and gunfire. The picture left no doubt that what they had seen was indeed a periscope. Ashford showed it to Admiral Halsey.

"Shortly after I went below and was in my cabin," said Ashford later, "Browning came in. He said that the admiral had directed him to apologize to me for the things he had said. He further said that he had never apologized to anyone in his life and proceeded to talk for about twenty minutes, giving reasons why he should not apologize. Nevertheless, at that point I felt he had said enough, and I said, 'I accept your apology.' That ended the conversation."[3]

At dawn on Saturday, 25 April, Task Force 16 was approaching Pearl Harbor under cloudless skies. A little later the carriers launched their planes, which sped away in formation toward airfields on Oahu. Around 1100 the force filed through the narrow harbor mouth to its anchorage. There was no cheering this time. News of the Tokyo raid led by Jimmy Doolittle, America's most famous ace, had been joyfully received at Pearl Harbor, as elsewhere, but nobody connected it with the carrier force.[4]

Admiral Halsey, standing on the bridge, had lost weight. His expression was grim. His dermatitis now seemed to be spreading over his entire body. He itched continually and was not sleeping well. Oatmeal-water baths prescribed by the ship's doctor gave him only temporary relief. He looked forward to an extended period of rest and recreation ashore—a respite he felt that he and all his men had fully earned. Instead, Task Force 16, including both carriers, was allotted just five days for upkeep, after which it was to hasten to the Coral Sea to hurl back an enemy thrust expected in that area.

Halsey learned that during his absence the strategic picture had changed radically. When Task Force 16 was leaving for its mission against Tokyo, the Japanese carriers were culminating their operations in the Indian Ocean with attacks on British ships and positions in and around Ceylon. They sank two cruisers and the carrier *Hermes* and raided the bases of Colombo and Trincomalee. That same week the Japanese army in the Philippines completed its conquest of Bataan. Alarmed by these surges of enemy power, Washington called on Commander Joseph Rochefort, heading the Pearl Harbor Combat Intelligence Unit, for an opinion concerning Japan's immediate and long-range plans.

Rochefort's Pearl Harbor unit, like the intelligence units at Washington and Melbourne, specialized in predicting the enemy's forthcoming operations by studying his radio communications—analyzing traffic, locating and tracking transmitters, and decoding the messages through cryptanalysis. The units had lost some credence through their failure to warn Admiral Kimmel of the impending attack on Pearl Harbor, but that was an enemy operation they had no means of anticipating. The Japanese had kept all mention of the plan off the air, the attack force had maintained strict radio silence while crossing the Pacific, and for good measure, a few days before the raid the Japanese navy had changed its principal operational code, which the Americans called JN25.

Following the raid, Rochefort placed his unit on a twenty-four-hour war footing. In their secret, vault-like basement under the Fourteenth Naval District administration building, he and his assistants, operating with a minimum of sleep, analyzed the intercepts picked up by their several radio listening stations in the Pacific area. By early spring of 1942 they had rebroken JN25 and were making forecasts on which Admirals King and Nimitz began relying with increasing confidence.

Rochefort, after reviewing his sources of information and consulting with his staff, replied to the query fromWashington with a four-part estimate: (1) The Japanese had concluded operations in the Indian Ocean, and their carrier force was withdrawing to home bases; (2) they had no plans to invade Australia; (3) they would soon launch an operation to seize the eastern end of New Guinea; (4) they would follow this move with a much bigger operation in the Pacific Ocean, an operation involving most of the Combined Fleet.

Admiral Nimitz and his staff tentatively accepted the Rochefort estimate. To control eastern New Guinea, they reasoned, the Japanese would have to seize the Australian base at Port Moresby in the Coral Sea, since bombers from there could reach not only all of eastern New Guinea but also the Japanese base at Rabaul.

As for the coming Pacific Ocean operation, Nimitz and his planners estimated that the Japanese would attack the Aleutians, Pearl Harbor, or Midway. Whatever their ultimate objective, it seemed unlikely that they would bypass Midway, the westernmost fortified U.S. outpost in the central Pacific.

Nimitz began deploying his forces to defend Port Moresby. He ordered Fletcher's *Yorktown* force (Task Force 17), operating in the Coral Sea area, to proceed to Tongatabu for quick replenishment and upkeep and then return to the Coral Sea. Here on 1 May it would be joined by Rear Admiral Aubrey Fitch's *Lexington* force, which had just completed a three-week overhaul at Pearl Harbor, and by a U.S. cruiser and destroyer from Noumea. On 4 May three Australian cruisers based at Sydney would join up, further reinforcing Task Force 17. Halsey's Task Force 16, with the *Enterprise* and *Hornet,* was to depart Pearl Harbor not later than 30 April and race the 3,500 miles to the Coral Sea. If it arrived in time, Halsey would combine his force with Fletcher's and assume overall command.

On 24 April Admiral Nimitz and members of his staff left Pearl Harbor to join Admiral King and his staff in the first of regular CominCh-CinCPac conferences, held this time in San Francisco. Enemy ships were already concentrating at Rabaul and at Truk, an island base 700 miles to the north. Japanese search planes were fanning out on the approaches to Port Moresby, and decrypted enemy dispatches were referring to the forthcoming campaign as Operation MO.[5]

When Nimitz returned to Pearl Harbor on the twenty-eighth, he conferred with Halsey and confirmed decisions made in his absence. He pointed out that, in entering the Coral Sea, the Pacific Fleet forces would be penetrating General Douglas MacArthur's Southwest Pacific Area. Based in Australia and at Port Moresby, MacArthur had some two hundred army planes that could be counted on for a limited amount of reconnaissance, but the pilots were not trained for overwater operations or for ship recognition. If the Japanese were to be stopped at sea, the navy's carrier planes would have to do the stopping.

The Southwest Pacific Area, embracing Australia, the Solomons, the Bismarcks, New Guinea, the Netherlands Indies (except Sumatra), and the Philippines, had been created specifically to give MacArthur something to command. He had been a general since 1918 and had worn four stars in the early 1930s as army chief of staff. When it appeared that the Philippines, where MacArthur was with his troops, would fall to the enemy, public figures, particularly in the U.S. government, demanded that he be transferred and his long experience and demonstrated skills be used to win the war. MacArthur, however, intended to remain with his troops and share their fate. He would not have obeyed an order to abandon them if it were issued by a military officer, because no one in the army or navy matched him in seniority. It took a direct order from the president, as commander in chief, to force him out. At the request of General George C. Marshall, army chief of staff, President Roosevelt ordered MacArthur to report to Australia.

In compliance with the presidential order, MacArthur, with his family and key staff members, made a dramatic night escape from Corregidor on a PT boat. From Mindanao the general flew to Australia, where he announced, "I came through, and I shall return."

Weeks before MacArthur reached Australia, a debate was in progress about what to do with him. One congressman introduced a bill to establish a supreme war command over all the Allied armed forces with MacArthur at its head. Neither President Roosevelt nor Prime Minister Churchill would have accepted any such arrangement, and Roosevelt did not want him in the United States as a possible rival for the presidency. General Marshall hoped MacArthur would command all Allied forces in the Pacific theater, but Admiral King would not stand for that. The navy had been studying and training for twenty years to fight a war with Japan. King would not subject his forces to army command in the area of the navy's particular interest, nor would he let the fleet be controlled by an officer who, in King's opinion, did not understand the uses of sea power. On the other hand, MacArthur could not be expected to accept a command subordinate to Nimitz, who had been a lieutenant commander when the former was a general.

Because the British had conceded command of the Pacific theater to the United States, it was up to the U.S. Joint Chiefs of Staff, Generals Marshall and Arnold and Admiral King, to solve the command problem.* They did so by dividing the Pacific theater into four military operational areas—north, central, south, and southwest. With the president's approval, they appointed MacArthur "Supreme Commander of the Southwest Pacific Area, and of all armed forces which the governments concerned have assigned, or may assign to this area." An exception was the Pacific Fleet; if for strategic considerations it should have to enter MacArthur's Southwest Pacific Area, it would remain under Nimitz's command.

Nimitz would also command all Allied armed forces within the other three areas, which together were designated Pacific Ocean areas. As CinCPac he continued to command U.S. ships and sailors. As Commander in Chief, Pacific Ocean Areas (CinCPOA), he commanded all armed forces—U.S., Canadian, New Zealand, French, and British, army or navy—in or entering his assigned areas.

MacArthur raised no objections to being given command of only one of

*In July 1942 Admiral William D. Leahy, then chief of staff to the president, became ex officio chairman of the Joint Chiefs of Staff.

the four Pacific areas. After all, his Southwest Pacific Area was the chief area of Japanese advance, and hence for the present and foreseeable future it would be the main arena of the Pacific war. To match Nimitz's commander-in-chief title, however, he changed his own title from supreme commander to Commander in Chief, Southwest Pacific.[6]

Thus the Pacific theater of operations was placed under divided command, with each commander in chief responsible directly to the Joint Chiefs of Staff in Washington. The forthcoming defense of Port Moresby would bring segments of the Pacific Fleet into MacArthur's Southwest Pacific Area and be the first test of how effectively the two commands worked together.

On 29 April Admiral Halsey was issued CinCPac operation plan no. 23-42, ordering him to "check further advance by the enemy in the New Guinea–Solomon area by destroying enemy ships, shipping and aircraft." Warm weather had intensified his dermatitis, and he knew that a dash to the south would expose him to more heat and more misery. But, ardent for battle, he concealed his infirmity from Nimitz, lest the latter relieve him for reasons of health.

At about 0800 on the thirtieth Task Force 16 stood out to sea—the *Enterprise* and *Hornet,* three heavy cruisers, seven destroyers, and two oilers. Two more cruisers and a destroyer would leave Pearl as soon as they were readied for sea and race to catch up with the rest of the ships under Halsey's command. After a brief target practice off the island of Maui, Task Force 16 shaped course southwest for the Coral Sea. Each of the carriers received on board, in addition to her own planes, nine F4Fs of Marine Corps Fighter Squadron 212 for delivery to Efate, now garrisoned by a marine defense battalion and two army infantry companies. Seabees were constructing an airfield on the island.[7]

The intelligence units at Pearl Harbor, Washington, and Melbourne had been diligently tracing the movement of Japanese ships with radio traffic analysis and the occasional segments of coded enemy messages they succeeded in breaking. Using in addition to other channels a miniature unit consisting of a Japanese language officer and three radio intercept men on board the *Enterprise,* intelligence officers forwarded all relevant information to Halsey. Thus he knew that three carriers were among the enemy warships recently assembled at Truk. One, the light carrier *Shoho,* had not yet been identified, but the others were known to be the *Shokaku* and *Zuikaku,* big carriers from the force that had raided Pearl Harbor, Darwin, and Ceylon. The intelligence units had now clearly established that Port Moresby was to be the principal Japanese target, but they knew also that the enemy was planning to invade one of the islands in the eastern Solomons, probably Tulagi. What they could not tell Halsey was when, because the Japanese took the precaution of concealing dates and times in a cipher, which was then encoded along with the rest of the

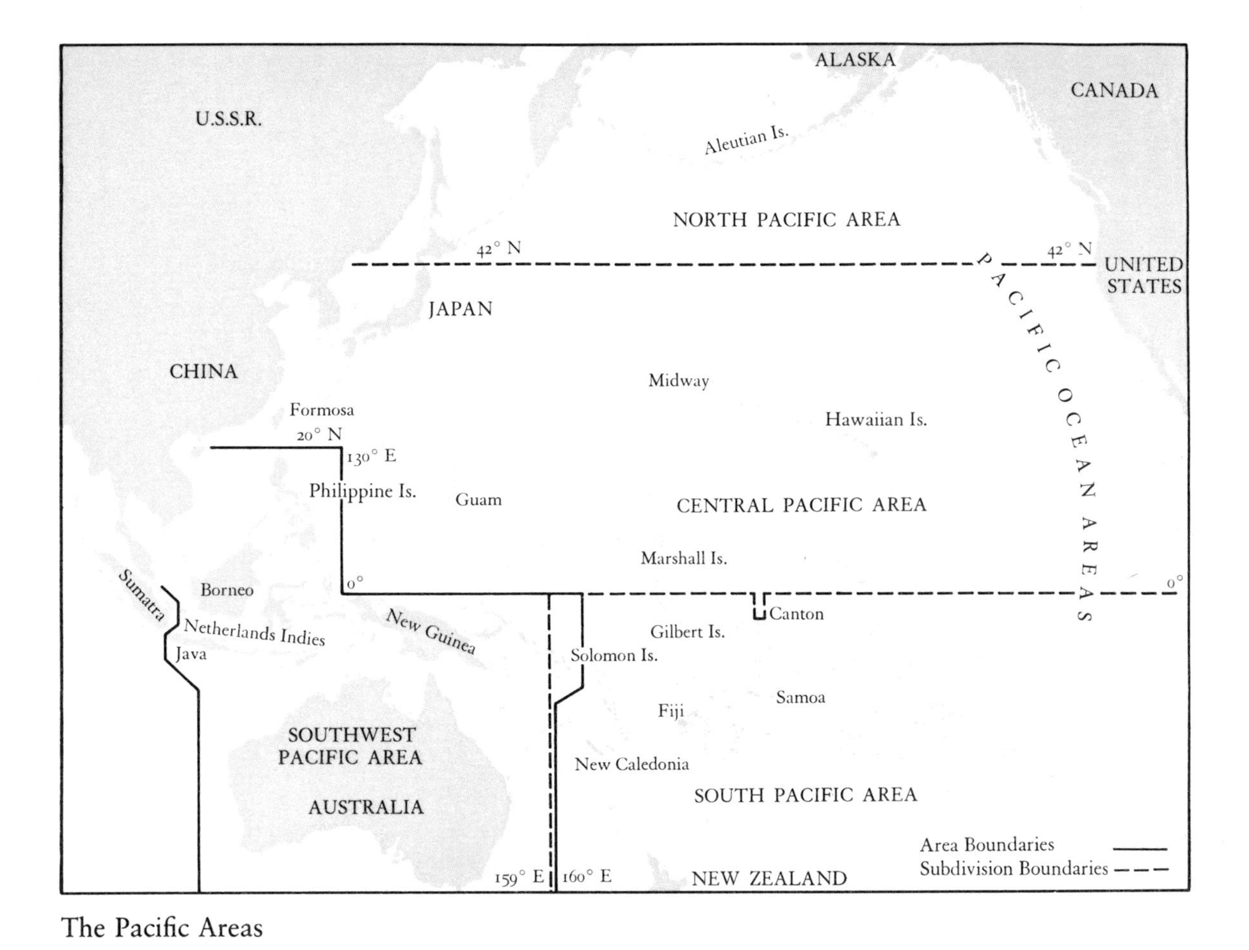

The Pacific Areas

BROKEN VERTICAL LINE IS SOUTH-SOUTHWEST PACIFIC BOUNDARY AS REVISED AUGUST 1, 1942

message. The port director at Truk obligingly came to their assistance. On 30 April, using a simple code that the Americans had long since broken, he announced the departure of four heavy cruisers that with the unidentified carrier comprised a group the Japanese called the MO Covering Force. Since this group had to go only a third as far as Halsey to reach the Coral Sea, it seemed unlikely that Task Force 16 would arrive in time to participate in the defense of Port Moresby.[8]

Halsey appears to have banished that unwelcome probability from his mind. As Task Force 16 approached the equator, he announced that there would be no suspension of drills to observe the Court of Neptune ritual that in peacetime initiated men crossing the line for the first time. "This force," he said, "is preparing for battle expected soon in the Coral Sea."

The *Enterprise*'s radio intercepted a message from MacArthur to Fletcher stating that Southwest Pacific Area planes had sighted Japanese ships debarking troops at Tulagi. Two days later, on 4 May, west longitude date, the Big E overheard Fletcher's report to Nimitz. While the *Lexington* was fueling, Fletcher had dashed north with the *Yorktown* and sent her dive-bombers and torpedo planes in a raid on Tulagi, where the enemy was now establishing a seaplane base. He reported fantastic results, concluding his message with the exclamation, "Some fun!"

From Pearl Harbor Admiral Nimitz jubilantly radioed back, "Congratulations and well done to you and your force. Hope you can exploit your success with augmented force."[9]

Further aerial reconnaissance proved Fletcher's claims grossly exaggerated, reflecting the extreme difficulty aviators had assessing their results in the heat of battle. Only a few minor naval craft had in fact been sunk. But the battle was on, and more action was obviously impending. Halsey and his men hoped it would last long enough for them to arrive on the scene and share some of Fletcher's "fun." A correspondent on board one of the cruisers could see for himself that the task force was spoiling for a fight. "The days pass in target practice and drill and drill and target practice—and simulated battery-firing on a spotting board in the wardroom," he wrote. "There is no doubt in anybody's mind that we are getting whetted up for battle. Morale has been honed to a keen edge."

On 5 May grievous tidings arrived from the Philippines. Lieutenant General Jonathan Wainwright, whom General MacArthur had left in command on Corregidor, had been obliged to surrender his beleaguered, half-starved army, thereby relinquishing the whole Philippine archipelago to the enemy.

Meanwhile, it was obvious that the Japanese and American naval forces in the Coral Sea area were failing to make contact. If this situation lasted a couple of days longer, Halsey would be able to bring his own two carriers into action—an outcome the admiral devoutly wished for. Despite oppressive heat and an itching body, he found himself urging his ships forward as if by act of will.

The battle did not await the arrival of the *Enterprise* and *Hornet.* It resumed on 6 May and reached a climax on the seventh, west longitude dates. The word got around, and such a crowd flocked to the radio shacks for the latest news that the chiefs had to chase men away so the operators could work. The crew did manage to glean information from public broadcasts. American radio reported nine enemy ships sunk, three badly damaged. Australian broadcasts claimed eighteen were sunk. The Japanese announced that they had sunk the *California, Yorktown,* and *Lexington* and put the British battleship *Warspite* out of action. But the British denied any involvement in the battle, and the men of Task Force 16 had recently seen the *California,* heavily damaged in the 7 December raid, undergoing repair in a dry dock at Pearl Harbor.

During the night of 7 May the task force crossed the 180th meridian into 9 May, east longitude date.[10]

From Pearl Harbor Admiral Halsey eventually received a corrected report of the action, which had become known as the Battle of the Coral Sea. It had opened with Fletcher's raid on Tulagi on 4 May, east longitude date. After a two-day lull it resumed on the morning of the seventh, when aircraft from the Japanese striking force, built around the carriers *Shokaku* and *Zuikaku,* attacked the American oiler *Neosho* and her accompanying destroyer *Sims,* which Japanese search planes had identified as a carrier and a cruiser. The aircraft sank the destroyer and left the oiler a drifting derelict.

In the meantime aircraft from Fletcher's Task Force 17 attacked the Japanese invasion force as it was coming down from Rabaul to assault Port Moresby. The American planes sank the light carrier *Shoho,* obliging the rest of the force to turn back.

The climactic action came on the morning of 8 May, when the Japanese and American carrier forces at last located each other and attacked almost simultaneously in about equal strength. American planes put the *Shokaku* out of action with three bombs and shot down most of the *Zuikaku*'s aircraft. Japanese aircraft dropped a series of bombs that just missed the *Yorktown,* and one struck her with a bomb that penetrated three decks. The *Lexington,* hit by two torpedoes, was able to recover her returning planes, but ruptured aircraft fuel lines spilled gasoline into her hold. The deadly vapor eventually exploded, setting off such uncontrollable fires that she had to be abandoned. To keep her out of enemy hands, one of her own destroyers sank her with torpedoes.

Loss of the "Lady Lex" was a severe blow to the navy, in no way offset by the sinking of the small *Shoho.* With the *Saratoga* still under repair at

Bremerton and the *Yorktown* seriously damaged, Nimitz could be reasonably sure of only the *Enterprise* and *Hornet* to counter the air power of the entire Combined Fleet in the forthcoming heavy attack Rochefort had predicted. On the other hand, for the first time a Japanese advance had been repulsed. In that sense the Battle of the Coral Sea was a strategic victory for the Allies. It was bound to impose a degree of caution on the Japanese, who for five months had appeared invincible.

Once again Halsey was deeply disappointed at not having come to grips with the Japanese fleet. But if he felt that in the Coral Sea operation, as in the Wake expedition of the preceding December, mismanagement in higher echelons had deprived him of his sea battle, he was too discreet to record or air his thoughts.

In fact, imminent action between Task Force 16 and a segment of the Japanese fleet remained a possibility. Halsey, informed of enemy intentions by radio bulletins from Pearl Harbor, had learned on 7 May that the Japanese, in an extension of Operation MO, planned to seize the British-controlled islands of Nauru and Ocean, evidently to secure their rich phosphorus resources. Two days later Halsey was told that, as a result of the Coral Sea battle, the Japanese had temporarily shelved their plan to attack Port Moresby but would proceed with their occupations of Nauru and Ocean. It was up to Halsey to repulse and if possible destroy their occupation force.

On 11 May, as Task Force 16 approached the New Hebrides, Halsey sent two aircraft over Efate to see if the airfield there was ready to receive the marine fighter squadron he was transporting. When the planes gave a negative report, he sent them to Noumea with messages to be transmitted from there while he maintained radio silence. One of the messages ordered Rear Admiral Thomas C. Kinkaid to form a task group of two heavy cruisers and three destroyers from Fletcher's retiring Task Force 17 and with these to proceed to a designated rendezvous point, where they would join Halsey's Task Force 16.

Halsey had hoped the *Zuikaku* would operate in support of the enemy occupation force and thus provide his carrier planes with a worthwhile target. He was not happy to learn that the *Zuikaku* was heading for Japan in the wake of the heavily damaged *Shokaku*.

Meanwhile, Halsey refueled and marked time. If he revealed his presence too soon, the occupation force would be able to retreat to the safety of Rabaul. He knew that air searches extended 700 miles south of the Japanese base on Makin in the Gilberts, and that from the new seaplane base they had set up at Tulagi in the Solomons the air searches reached 600 miles eastward. The two search patterns overlapped in an area Task Force 16 would have to cross to reach the Nauru-Ocean area. The overlapping took place, however, only at the outer limits of the searches. The search planes would fan out from Makin and Tulagi early in the morning, reach their outer limits toward noon, make a short dogleg right or left, and head back to base. Thus in the afternoon Task Force 16 could make a dash northward through the ever-widening aperture in enemy air coverage. By noon the next day, when the planes again reached the farthest point of their search, their warning would be too late to enable the occupation force to escape Halsey's torpedo planes and bombers.

Japanese bombers flying southward from the Marshalls could just reach the Nauru-Ocean area, but no farther. Thus Task Force 16, coming up from the south, would be able to send its planes against enemy ships in the vicinity of these islands while its own ships remained safely beyond the operational radius of the bombers from the Marshalls. That Halsey had some such strategy in mind is implied in a message he sent Kinkaid on the afternoon of 14 May. It canceled the original rendezvous order and directed Kinkaid to join Task Force 16 at 0900, 16 May, at a point 500 miles farther north—that is, 500 miles nearer the Nauru-Ocean area.

At about 1800 on the fourteenth, Halsey received from CinCPac a pair of communications that killed any plans he had to force a battle. The first relayed a message from CominCh: "I consider operations of Task Force 16 inadvisable in forward areas beyond own shore-based air cover and within range of enemy shore-based air until necessity requires such operations to oppose major enemy offensive or unless especially favorable results are to be expected."

King understandably opposed unnecessarily risking the only two undamaged U.S. carriers in the Pacific, but his caution enraged Halsey. "This made me mad as hell!" he wrote. Believing his local knowledge better than that available to the authorities in Washington, he considered himself the victim of unwarranted and stupid interference. The only Allied airfields in the area were at Noumea in New Caledonia, 600 miles to the south, and at Nandi in the Fijis, 600 miles to the southeast. To comply with King's advice to remain under "shore-based air cover," Halsey would have to retire to within 200 miles of one of these fields.

King's message was of course not an order but an opinion, which he expected Nimitz to turn into an order for Halsey. Nimitz, who did not concur with King's opinion but knew better than to flout it, merely passed the message on to Halsey—a move that gave it the force of an order without endorsement. At the end of the CominCh dispatch Nimitz stated his belief that King, in his phrase "enemy shore-based air," meant only combat planes, not search planes.

CinCPac's interpretation of "enemy shore-based air," standing by itself, would probably have meant little to Halsey. But Nimitz followed King's dispatch with a private "eyes only" dispatch ordering Halsey to move Task Force 16 the following day to a point where it could be observed by the Japanese search planes—a move that would not oppose King's wishes, as interpreted by Nimitz. As soon as the sighting had occurred, Halsey was to withdraw to avoid an attack on his carriers.

Shortly after reading Nimitz's secret order, Halsey changed course to northwest. Early the next morning search planes launched from the *Enterprise* fanned out northward to a radius of 200 miles but spotted no enemy ships. At 1015, when Task Force 16, under exceptionally clear skies, was 450 miles almost due east of Tulagi, radar on board the Big E revealed an approaching snooper at a distance of seventy miles. When the plane, a Tulagi-based flying boat, had arrived within sixty miles, it sighted the task force and radioed its report, using a simple code that the intelligence unit on board the *Enterprise* easily broke. Halsey now scrambled his fighters to intercept the snooper. By the time the Wildcats gained altitude, several more Japanese planes had approached the force and reported their observations. The F4Fs went after them, but the scouts so adroitly eluded the fighters that Halsey mistakenly supposed that the enemy aircraft were equipped with some sort of airborne radar.

At 1424, when Halsey was satisfied that Japanese headquarters had been amply and accurately apprised of the position, course, and composition of his force, he turned away to heading 090°, due east. Shortly afterward he radioed a new time and place of rendezvous to Admiral Kinkaid, who by this time must have been sorely puzzled by the frequent changes. Kinkaid finally joined Task Force 16 the following morning.[11]

Nimitz's secret order grew out of a difference of opinion concerning the appropriate reaction to forthcoming Japanese strategy. American code breakers and traffic analysts had been predicting another Japanese grab for Port Moresby and an attempted enemy occupation of Kiska and other far-western Aleutian islands. Of the two anticipated operations, King and MacArthur regarded a repeat attack on Port Moresby as the greater peril. Hence they wanted Halsey and his carriers to remain on guard in the South Pacific.

Nimitz himself, recalling Rochefort's prediction that the original Port Moresby attack would be followed by a major operation in the Pacific involving most of the Combined Fleet, suspected Midway of being in greater danger than the Aleutians. Occupation of a couple of desolate unfortified islands at the end of the Aleutian chain did not seem the sort of operation that would require massive support. A map hobbyist, Nimitz spent some time nearly every day studying his charts. It struck him more than ever that if the Japanese were going to unleash a major campaign in the Pacific they were unlikely to spare Midway. On 1 May, with the initial attack on Port Moresby pending, he flew out to Midway with some of his staff to take a look at the atoll's defenses.

While the Coral Sea battle was under way, enemy radio traffic was decrypted that indicated the Japanese were actively preparing for their Pacific Ocean expedition. On 11 May a major segment of the Combined Fleet was ordered to "proceed to the Saipan-Guam area and wait for the forthcoming campaign." Two days later the cryptanalysts at Pearl Harbor learned that this force, "concerned with the occupation of MI," was scheduled to depart the Saipan-Guam area on the twenty-seventh. Another message on the same date designated the place to be occupied with the letters AF, which the Combat Intelligence Unit had already tentatively identified as the designator for Midway.

To nail down the identification, the commandant of the Fourteenth Naval District (under whom the Combat Intelligence Unit then served) sent a message to Midway by underwater cable ordering it to transmit a fake radio dispatch in plain language stating that its water-distillation plant had broken down. The Hawaiian Sea Frontier, in on the stratagem, replied in an equally fake plain-language message that it would send out a bargeload of fresh water immediately. The next day the Combat Intelligence Unit decrypted an intercepted report from Wake Island notifying Tokyo that AF was short of fresh water. Thus it was confirmed that AF was actually Midway.[12]

By 14 May, when Pearl Harbor relayed CominCh's message ordering Halsey to keep out of reach of enemy shore-based air and remain under cover of his own, Nimitz was convinced that the Japanese would direct their next main attack against Midway, along with a secondary attack against the Aleutians. In ordering Halsey to expose Task Force 16 to Japanese search planes and then retire, Nimitz attained several objectives. Halsey's maneuver, without endangering his carriers, caused the Nauru-Ocean occupation force to turn back and induced Japanese headquarters, at least temporarily, to cancel the operation. This backdown by the enemy left King and MacArthur less concerned about keeping the *Enterprise* and *Hornet* in the South Pacific. Meanwhile, the Japanese, having sighted the *Enterprise* and *Hornet* in southern waters and believing they had sunk the *Yorktown* and *Lexington,* would be less cautious when coming against Midway.

On 15 May Nimitz, having been apprised of Wake's report to Tokyo that Midway was short of fresh water, sent the following message to King along with copies to MacArthur and Halsey:

> Present indications [are] that there may well be three separate and possibly simultaneous enemy offensives: one, involving cruisers and carriers, against the Aleutians, possibly Dutch Harbor; second, against Port Moresby, involving present forces that will probably be reinforced; third, against Midway-Oahu line, probably involving initially a major landing attack against Midway, for which it is believed the enemy's main striking force will be employed. The time these offensives will be delivered is not clear, but believe sighting Halsey in South yesterday caused postponement Ocean and Nauru operations and will expedite northern and central operations.

The next day Nimitz notified all task force commanders that the Japanese had indeed canceled their Nauru-Ocean operation.* To Halsey he radioed, "Desire you proceed to the Hawaiian area." In a subsequent message he warned Halsey against attacking enemy positions on the way back, adding, "Consider it important that you not be sighted by the enemy." When Halsey dallied over the assembly of his oilers and supply vessels, Nimitz ordered him sharply, "Expedite return." Admiral Fletcher, then refueling and reprovisioning at Tongatabu, also received orders to head for Hawaii. Admiral Fitch had reported that the *Yorktown* could be repaired at Pearl Harbor but that it would take ninety days. Admiral Nimitz hoped she could be made reasonably battleworthy in far less time than that. Meanwhile, he was being very tactful in his dealings with Washington. He made CominCh the information addressee in his new orders to Halsey, half expecting King to countermand them. In a separate message he assured King that he would "watch situation closely and return Halsey to southward if imminent concentration in that area is indicated."

Nimitz need not have worried. King, kept fully informed of the findings of the cryptanalysts at Pearl Harbor and Melbourne, had at last reached an estimate not very different from CinCPac's. Moreover, like Nimitz, he had concluded that the principal objective of the Japanese in attacking Midway was to draw out the Pacific Fleet for destruction. He warned Nimitz to "employ strong attrition tactics and not, repeat *not,* allow our forces to accept such decisive action as would be likely to incur heavy losses in our carriers and cruisers."[13]

The sharp tone of Nimitz's "expedite" message, with its implication that Task Force 16 should return to base at fuel-consuming speed, plus daily CinCPac radio bulletins describing current and impending enemy ship movements, convinced Halsey that conditions were arising for a major confrontation at sea—a clash on a larger scale and potentially far more decisive than the recent Coral Sea battle. He wanted nothing more than to participate in the forthcoming action but suspected that the condition of his health would sidetrack him. His dermatitis more violent than ever, he was scarcely sleeping at all, and he had lost twenty pounds. The medical officer, unable to give him any relief, said that Halsey would have to go to the hospital. When the admiral protested, the doctor is said to have replied, "Sir, where your health is concerned, I am the one who gives the orders."

On the morning of 26 May Task Force 16 filed into Pearl Harbor, and the *Enterprise* tied up at her usual Ford Island berth. Halsey called for his barge.

*The Japanese finally occupied Nauru and Ocean on 25–26 August 1942, while the U.S. Pacific Fleet was deeply involved in the Guadalcanal campaign, and held them until the end of the war.

Accompanied by Lieutenant Ashford, he made his way to CinCPac headquarters. When he appeared, gaunt and hollow eyed, before Nimitz, the latter was shocked. He ordered Halsey to report to the hospital without delay. First, however, he asked him whom he recommended to command Task Force 16 in the forthcoming operation. Halsey replied at once: Ray Spruance. It was a surprising recommendation, because Spruance was not an aviator, and several officers with aviation experience and greater seniority were available for the command. But Nimitz accepted the suggestion without comment. He had long been acquainted with Spruance and knew his reputation for outstanding performance. Nimitz had in fact requested orders for Spruance to join him as his chief of staff, but that new duty could wait.

Halsey and Nimitz left the office together. Halsey said to Ashford, who had been waiting outside, "Go back to the *Enterprise* and tell Ray Spruance he's to take the task force out, using my staff. Tell him to shift his flag to the *Enterprise*." Ashford darted away.

The admirals walked slowly to the main entrance, where a car had been called to convey Halsey to Hospital Point. On his arrival there, the doctors lost no time putting him to bed. Here the misery of his dermatitis was exceeded by the misery of his deep disappointment. "This was a sad occasion for me," he said, "as it prevented my taking part in the Battle of Midway, where I would have been senior officer present. This was my greatest regret in the whole war."[14]

Spruance, on learning that he was to command Task Force 16, reported to CinCPac headquarters, accompanied by his flag lieutenant, Robert J. Oliver. Before being briefed by Admiral Nimitz, he sent Oliver to collect additional information from CinCPac's intelligence officer, Lieutenant Commander Edwin J. Layton. On the way back to the *Northampton* Oliver repeated to Spruance what he had just learned and on their arrival at the cruiser promptly set about having his admiral's personal gear transferred to the *Enterprise*.[15]

That afternoon Spruance, still with Lieutenant Oliver, went to the hospital to call on his bedridden friend and erstwhile boss. He said he was pleased to take over Halsey's experienced staff, needing their expertise and council, but proposed keeping Oliver and making Ashford available to Halsey. Retaining their personal aides was a sound suggestion to which Halsey readily consented.

After a few minutes of small talk, Spruance excused Oliver and got down to business, explaining the strategic situation to Halsey and seeking his advice. The Japanese planned to occupy Midway and a pair of western Aleutian islands. To pave the way for and support these operations, they would raid the U.S. naval air stations at Midway and at Dutch Harbor in the Aleutians. The Dutch Harbor raid, to take place on 3 June, would be carried out by a two-carrier force. The following day a four-carrier force, coming down from the northwest, would raid Midway.

This disclosure of the Midway operation plan rates as one of the great feats of military intelligence. It was achieved mainly through cryptanalysis, but, contrary to what some books have stated, the Japanese never transmitted their plan by radio. Joseph Rochefort and his colleagues in the Combat Intelligence Unit, working night and day through the month of May 1942, had tackled thousands of radio intercepts but succeeded in decrypting only fragments of occasional messages. These Rochefort would discuss with Commander Layton, usually on the secure telephone line that connected their offices. Both had earlier been sent by the navy for an extended stay in Japan to learn the Japanese language. For many months now they had been studying the Japanese navy. They had learned to perceive significance in a communication, a movement, a combination of units that would mean nothing to persons less initiated. From the snippets of information provided by the cryptanalysts, they gradually pieced together a bare outline of the enemy plan.

Admiral Nimitz was sending a small force north to try to prevent the occupation of the Aleutian islands, but all hands recognized that the key to the whole operation was the four-carrier force coming to raid Midway. The carriers were the ones that had raided Pearl Harbor—minus the *Shokaku* and the *Zuikaku*, the former having been heavily damaged and the latter stripped of planes in the Battle of the Coral Sea. If this force were defeated, the rest of the Japanese fleet would have to retreat or be destroyed.

Task Forces 16 and 17 would deal with the enemy carrier force. Task Force 17, Spruance told Halsey, was not due in till the next day, but the Pearl Harbor repair superintendent, the master shipfitter, and a team of navy yard planners and estimators had already flown out to have a look at the damaged *Yorktown*. They had radioed back that with an all-out effort she might be made barely battleworthy in three days. Workmen were already positioning blocks to receive her in dry dock no. 1.

Thus Nimitz would have three carriers, the *Yorktown*, the *Hornet*, and the *Enterprise*, to meet the Japanese four. He counted on Midway itself to serve as his fourth, if stationary, aircraft carrier. For weeks he had been sending out men and materials to strengthen the two islands of the atoll, Sand and Eastern, and to operate from the airfield on the latter he had managed to scrape together various army, navy, and marine corps planes.

The U.S. plan was to have the two American task forces, under the overall command of Admiral Fletcher, northeast of Midway at dawn on 4 June. Here they would be on the flank of the oncoming enemy carrier force. When search planes sighted and reported the approaching force, torpedo planes and bombers from Midway and from Task Forces 16 and 17 would be launched for an attack. With luck, the American planes would get the jump on the enemy carriers while at least half their planes were away raiding the atoll.[16]

Despite his physical misery, Halsey listened with the most profound interest. He was, as Nimitz later expressed it, "itching to get into the fight."

Itching Halsey certainly was. His entire body covered with a soothing ointment, he lay naked under a single sheet. He was kept awake most of the night, not only by the dermatitis but also by hammering and riveting in the nearby dry dock as successive teams of workmen swarmed over the *Yorktown* in an intense drive to make her ready for battle. On the morning of 28 June, from his hospital window, Halsey watched Task Force 16, with the *Hornet* and the *Enterprise*, the latter wearing Spruance's flag, pass Hospital Point en route to the Pacific. The following morning Task Force 17 filed out, with the *Yorktown* showing no visible signs of her ordeal in the Coral Sea. The two forces were to meet 350 miles northeast of Midway, at a position optimistically designated Point Luck.

Halsey says he followed the Battle of Midway while flat on his back in the hospital, but he doesn't say how. On the day of the main action, 4 June, CinCPac headquarters was the scene of such confusion, uncertainty, and frantic activity that Nimitz had little opportunity to send bulletins to the hospital, and the following day Halsey was en route to the United States.

Whenever and however Halsey learned the facts about Midway, he must have realized that it constituted a major turning point in the war. For the Americans the day began with the dawn takeoff of Catalina search planes from Eastern Island. A few minutes before 0600, one of the planes reported sighting the enemy force, "carriers and battleships bearing 320°, course 135°, speed 25," prompting Nimitz to remark to Layton, "Well, you were only five miles, five degrees, and five minutes off." The American task forces, which had been standing out so that search planes from the enemy carriers could not sight them prematurely, now began to close in. Midway launched as soon as its radar detected enemy planes approaching.

In supplying Midway with additional air power, Nimitz had scraped the bottom of the barrel. Included in the motley collection of aircraft were antique Buffalo fighters and Vindicator dive-bombers, many with pilots untrained in attacks at sea. The squadrons became separated and made five separate attacks on the Japanese carrier force without achieving a single hit with bomb or torpedo. They suffered heavy losses, mainly from the enemy's agile Zero fighters. Next to attack, one at a time, were the three squadrons of torpedo planes from the American carriers, a total of forty-one aircraft. These too failed to achieve a single hit, and thirty-seven of them were shot down.

Meanwhile, the Japanese carriers recovered their planes from the raid on Midway and began to rearm and refuel them. While the carriers were in this state of maximum vulnerability, dive-bombers from the *Enterprise* and *York-*

town found three of them, grouped close together. No amount of planning or rehearsal by the Americans could have set up a situation so deadly for the Japanese. The two squadrons of dive-bombers, coming from different directions and unaware of each other's presence, dove simultaneously and hurled their bombs into the three carriers. All three exploded like firecrackers. Planes from the surviving enemy carrier found and disabled the *Yorktown* with bombs and torpedoes, but before nightfall the American dive-bombers sought out the survivor and set her fatally ablaze.

By midnight, Nimitz knew that forces under his command had won a momentous victory. To them he signaled, "You who participated in the Battle of Midway today have written a glorious page in our history. I am proud to be associated with you. I estimate that another day of all-out effort on your part will complete the defeat of the enemy."

Someone probably saw to it that the good news announced in this widely broadcast message reached the bedridden Halsey. However, it could do nothing to alleviate the misery of his dermatitis, which actually got worse in the hospital. Halsey attributed the deterioration to coral dust blown in from an area half a mile away, where workmen were excavating and blasting for a new dry dock, and the continual polishing of the linoleum hospital floors. The fine coral particles from outside and the finer particles kicked up by the polisher adhered to the ointment covering his body and penetrated to his skin. Disgusted, Halsey asked to be transferred to a stateside hospital. On 5 June he was placed on board the light cruiser *Detroit*, about to depart for San Francisco. Lieutenant Ashford traveled with the admiral to look after his needs.

On the fifth there was a hiatus in the battle. Admiral Fletcher, having transferred from the disabled *Yorktown*, quite properly turned over the command of both forces to Spruance, who pursued the retreating Japanese all day without bringing them within reach of his planes.

The Battle of Midway ended while Halsey was at sea, still flat on his back. On 6 June Spruance came within range of two enemy heavy cruisers that had been slowed down by collision damage. His bombers sank one and so battered the other that she was out of action for a year.

The Japanese got in the last blows after all. On the sixth one of their submarines found the *Yorktown* northeast of Midway under tow. It fired a spread of torpedoes that sank a destroyer alongside and damaged the carrier. She went down on the morning of the seventh. That day the Japanese landed troops on the U.S. islands of Attu and Kiska.[17]

The whole Allied world knew that the Americans had won a major victory. The Japanese had not only been repulsed; through the heavy loss of first-rate aviators, they had been deprived of the means of recovery. Within a few months they would be forced into the retreat that would eventually end in surrender in Tokyo Bay.

The hospital at Pearl Harbor had sent ahead a report on Halsey's condition to Twelfth Naval District headquarters at San Francisco. When the *Detroit* arrived at the Alameda Naval Air Station, the admiral was still in bed. A senior medical officer from the naval district came on board and told Halsey that he had arranged to have him placed in the care of the foremost allergist in the United States, Dr. Warren T. Vaughan of Richmond, Virginia. The medical officer, his assistant, and Ashford then went to the air station and arranged to have seats removed and a bed installed in a twin-engine Douglas transport. The next day the converted plane, with Admiral Halsey and Lieutenant Ashford on board, took off for Richmond.

The plane, after several stops for fuel, landed a little after noon on 14 June at Richmond's Byrd Airport. Dr. Vaughan and his assistant were waiting with an ambulance, which took them to Johnston-Willis Hospital. As soon as the admiral was placed in his room, attendants bathed him with a soothing solution and covered him with a sheet. He still could not bear to wear pajamas. A physical examination showed him in good health "but for a generalized allergic dermatitis." When the doctors told him they would begin making allergy tests to determine the cause, Halsey smiled wanly. "Make your first test a test of Scotch whiskey," he said.[18]

CHAPTER 6

JUNIOR OFFICER

SEVERAL SUCCESSIVE Naval Academy classes, including Bill Halsey's class of 1904, were graduated months ahead of schedule to help meet the pressing need for junior officers in President Theodore Roosevelt's rapidly expanding navy. On graduation they became "appointed" officers, with the rank of passed midshipman. They were eligible to be commissioned ensigns only after serving the navy satisfactorily for two years and passing an examination.

Bill and five of his classmates forfeited their graduation leave in order to secure billets in the battleship *Missouri*, considered choice duty. They graduated on 1 February, joined the ship in Hampton Roads on the seventh, and sailed with her for Guantánamo on the tenth.

Bill began his seagoing career in one *Missouri*, the "Mizzy," and ended his wartime duty in another, the "Mighty Mo." The forty years between them witnessed changes in the dimensions and capabilities of battleships: the Mizzy displaced 12,500 tons and could make 18 knots; the Mighty Mo, 45,000 tons and 32.5 knots. Though each at the time Halsey served on her was the newest battleship in the fleet, both were obsolescent. The Mizzy and her sisters with their mixed-caliber main armament of eight- and twelve-inch guns were soon to be superseded by the all-big-gun dreadnought. The Mighty Mo was the last battleship commissioned in the U.S. Navy. Battleship guns were far outranged by carrier planes.

After normal winter training, including boat, landing, and abandon-ship drills and small-arms practice ashore, the Mizzy left Cuban waters for target practice off Pensacola. Here, on 13 May, Halsey was witness to a catastrophe that left him with nightmarish memories and a strong distaste for the thirteenth of any month.

As the ship moved down the range, Halsey, on the bridge, was watching practice firing by the after twelve-inch turret, on top of which stood an enlisted observer. Suddenly a pillar of flame shot out of the open top hatch to a height of several hundred feet, enveloping the observer, who jumped or was blown to the deck and then, his clothing on fire, leaped over the side and was not seen again. There followed an ear-numbing blast, accompanied by another giant flash. Four ninety-pound powder bags in the turret had caught fire, and sparks from these had ignited more bags in the ammunition-handling room below. Within seconds twenty-six enlisted men and five officers, including some of Halsey's closest friends, had been roasted alive.

Fires threatened to ignite the nine or more tons of powder in the after magazines. The captain turned the ship over to the navigator and hastened aft to superintend the rescues and fire fighting. Half expecting the exploding magazines to blow holes in the ship's hull and leave her sinking, the navigator called for full speed and headed for the beach and shallow water. Halsey, ordered by the navigator to investigate and report, also hurried aft. He found the fire under control, but the hoses had left the handling room and adjacent passageways hip deep in water, in which charred bodies were floating.

That evening the ship put in to Pensacola. Since the doctors were all busy tending the injured, and Halsey had had some medical training, he was given the gruesome job of directing the undertakers who came on board to remove the bodies and prepare them for a mass funeral, to be held the following day.

The *Missouri* turret disaster demonstrated one of the numerous flaws in early American battleship design. Turrets in most European vessels were compartmentalized to prevent sparks falling from the guns into the handling room. In the next three years three more turret explosions, each killing ten men, occurred in American battleships. Only then did the U.S. Navy provide flame-proof scuttles between turrets and handling rooms and between handling rooms and magazines, and an air blast to clear from the powder chamber and gun bore explosive gases that remained after firing.[1]

When the Newport News shipyard had completed repairs on the *Missouri*, she spent the summer of 1904 cruising the Mediterranean. At the end of this and the following summer the Mizzy was at Hampton Roads, where Bill participated with the ship's football team in a series of games culminating both years in a championship match against the team of another battleship—the *Kentucky* in 1904, which won; the *Alabama* in 1905, which lost. After each of the games, Halsey was detached to the Naval Academy for temporary duty as assistant backfield coach under Professor Paul Dashiell of the chemistry department. In an attempt to pull the Navy team out of its losing streak, Dashiell, a notable amateur athlete, had taken over as head coach from the professionals. Army had beaten Navy 22 to 8 in 1902 and 40 to 5 in 1903. In 1905 they tied, and the following year Navy won, 10 to 0.

When Halsey returned to the Mizzy at the end of the 1905 football season, he had reason to feel satisfied with his progress and with his prospects for the future. He had stood practically every type of watch, junior and senior, and served as assistant engineer. He was now appointed division officer and looked forward to a pleasant cruise. In December, however, his anticipations were foiled when orders arrived detaching him from the *Missouri* and sending him to the Norfolk Navy Yard for service in the USS *Don Juan de Austria*. Rated as a cruiser in the Spanish navy, the *Don Juan* had been severely battered by Commodore George Dewey's Asiatic Squadron in the Battle of Manila Bay. Repaired, she had been taken into the U.S. Navy as a gunboat and had seen active service during the Filipino insurgency.

Now the *Don Juan*, after a long period at anchor, was being recommissioned to help enforce President Roosevelt's so-called corollary to the Monroe Doctrine. When prolonged civil strife left the Dominican Republic bankrupt, European creditor nations, notably Germany, suggested that they had a right to collect their debts by force of arms. Not so, said Roosevelt: if any situation in Latin America required intervention, the United States and a force of marines would do the intervening. He took over the Dominican Republic's customs collection and allocated fifty-five percent of the annual receipts to the settlement of its foreign debts.

The function of the *Don Juan* in this operation was simply to back up the customs collectors by showing the flag, a symbol and reminder of U.S. authority. Halsey found the duty stupefyingly monotonous. For six straight months the vessel did not stir from Samana Bay. The only diversions were the weekly mail steamer from the United States and the monthly visit by a collier for refueling.[2]

Two events during his otherwise tedious tour left Bill with happy memories. The first took place while the vessel was still at Norfolk. He was drilling men on deck one afternoon when something soft hit him in the head and knocked off his cap. As the men began to laugh, Halsey, frowning, looked to see what had hit him. Lying on the deck next to his cap was a lady's muff. Standing nearby, beside the executive officer's wife, was the pretty girl who had thrown it. Grinning, Bill turned to his men: "Dismissed!"

The girl had come on board with the exec's wife for tea. Catching sight of Bill, very straight, very serious, she had asked her hostess, "Who is that young officer over there who takes himself so seriously?"

"Midshipman Halsey."

Then she had tossed the muff. When Bill picked it up and approached her, she held out her hand for her property. Bill refused to surrender it until she had made amends by telling him her name. She was Fanny Grandy, of Norfolk. It turned out that Wiley Grandy, Charlie Hunter, and Armistead Dobie, who had been friends of Bill at the University of Virginia, were all first cousins of hers.[3]

Halsey lost no time in calling at the Grandy home. The more he saw of Fanny, the more she attracted him. Blonde, blue-eyed, vivacious, she had a keen mind and a sharp tongue, with which she skewered bores, bigots, and braggarts. To Halsey, who relished good-natured gibes even at his own expense, her merry banter was part of her charm. Her wit, though keen, he noted, was never malicious or vulgar but always held in check by fairness, innate reserve, and evident good breeding. When he sailed for the Caribbean, he had Fanny's image implanted in his memory, and he made good use of the weekly mail steamer to keep in touch with her.

Bill's second pleasant memory from his *Don Juan* days was receiving his first commission in the navy, that of ensign, two years and a day after his graduation from the Naval Academy. Now he was entitled to wear on his sleeve a gold stripe, of which he was inordinately proud. He also received a substantial raise in pay and began to wonder if he was making enough to get married.[4]

Shortly afterward, Halsey gleefully helped take back to Norfolk for renewed decommissioning the wretched ark on which he had been serving. Then, on being detached, he was granted ten days' leave and went to Washington, D.C., where his family was now living. Their place of residence had the special attraction of being near Miss Grandy, who was visiting relatives in Baltimore. Bill took the train over to pay her a call.

What Halsey did not yet realize was that, despite the good word his friends from the University of Virginia put in for him, the Grandy family did not view with unalloyed enthusiasm the attentions of a Yankee officer to one of their Southern girls. Memories had not yet faded of Civil War days, when Union forces were blamed for devastating much of Virginia, including the burning of Richmond, and Norfolk had been occupied by federal troops under the hated General Ben Butler. Many of the Grandy relatives and friends had fought, and some had died, for the Confederacy. The uncle Fanny was now visiting in Baltimore had in fact been chief engineer of the *Merrimack* when she battled the *Monitor* in Hampton Roads almost within sight of the Grandy home.

Bill, oblivious to the Grandy family's prejudice, did what he had been ardently planning during his year of dull duty in the Caribbean: he asked Fanny to marry him. She accepted his proposal but pointed out that she needed time to accustom her parents to the idea of bringing a Northerner into the family.[5]

His brief leave over, Bill proceeded to his next duty with mixed feelings. This was to be on board the battleship *Kansas,* just built and currently at Philadelphia awaiting commissioning. Again Bill would serve in the newest battleship in the navy. She was bigger and more heavily armed than the *Missouri,* displacing 16,000 tons and carrying a main armament of four twelve-inch, eight eight-inch, and twelve seven-inch guns. In the navy it was rumored that she had been hurried to completion in order to participate in a cruise to the West Coast. There was even talk of a possible round-the-world cruise. The prospect excited Bill but would mean a long separation from his fiancée.

After her commissioning, in the spring of 1907, the *Kansas* proceeded to Hampton Roads partly for drill and shakedown but mainly to serve, along with several other battleships, as colorful background to the ongoing Jamestown exposition, held at the site of the future Norfolk Naval Base. To the disgust of officers and men, the vessels were open daily to visitors. That meant almost continuous painting and cleaning to keep them spotless. It also entailed repeated changing of white uniforms, which the humidity quickly wilted. To entertain the sightseers crews staged rowing exhibitions afloat and football games on shore. Bill participated in both.

In late summer the fleet went to sea for parade-ground maneuvers of the type that would be useful for entering and leaving ports and cruising in formation. At the end of October the ships scattered to various yards and bases for repairs, replenishment, and refueling.

Though not yet officially announced, it was now generally understood in the battle fleet that it would soon embark on a world cruise. The plan was President Roosevelt's. He would bill it as an extended training exercise, but his real motive was to enhance national prestige by parading his fine new ships and demonstrating the skill of his sailors. The people he wished most to impress were the Japanese, who in the Battle of Tsushima in 1905 had virtually destroyed the czar's fleet. Though victorious, they were almost bankrupted by the war. They had requested Roosevelt to serve as mediator at the treaty talks. The resulting Treaty of Portsmouth was far from popular with the Japanese, because Russia was not forced to pay them the indemnity they expected to restore their ravaged treasury. Roosevelt denied them the indemnity, arguing that at war's end the Russians still had an army intact on the field.

To escape Japan's depressed postwar economy, thousands of Japanese laborers and their families emigrated to California, where their children, with little knowledge of English, flowed into the public schools, causing disruption. In 1906 the San Francisco school board thought it had found a solution to this vexing problem by setting aside a special school for young immigrants from the Orient.

When news of the action reached Japan, it triggered an outburst of public indignation. The recent victors over the world's most populous white country were outraged over the apparent imputation of racial inferiority. Magnified by yellow journalism in both Japan and the United States, the situation produced a full-blown diplomatic crisis. Roosevelt, with no authority over the internal affairs of the state of California, nevertheless found means to induce the San Franciscans to cancel their plan of segregation. Now to prove to the Japanese that his intervention had been an act of fairness, and not fear of them, he was going to show them the naval power that lay behind American diplomacy.

By 12 December all sixteen first-line battleships of the U.S. Navy had entered Hampton Roads and anchored in neat rows. This was Roosevelt's Great White Fleet. While the rest of the world was painting its warships gray to reduce their visibility, the American ships gleamed snowy white and sported varicolored crests on their prows.

The advent of smokeless powder and improved gunnery enabled the twelve-inch guns on battleships to hit an enemy more than two miles away. Any battle would be decided before their smaller guns came within range. Hence the navy had decided to eliminate secondary batteries in new construction and install more big guns in their place. Converting battleships already built was impractical, but in 1905 American shipyards had laid down the *Michigan* and *South Carolina,* each with an armament of eight twelve-inch guns and no secondary battery. These ships were due for completion in 1909.

Meanwhile Britain's Royal Navy had reached the same conclusion. In October 1905 it laid down its own all-big-gun ship, the famous *Dreadnought.* Rushed to completion in utmost secrecy, she was launched in February 1906, an all-time record in battleship construction. She was completed, commissioned, and revealed to the world in late 1907. With ten twelve-inch guns mounted in five turrets, she had two and a half times the effective firepower of any other battleship afloat, thereby rendering obsolete all the others, including the sixteen assembled in Hampton Roads. Roosevelt was aware of these facts, but he had not yet realized that among knowledgeable navy men everywhere, his vaunted Great White Fleet would increasingly be viewed as a parade of handsome floating antiques.

Few of the men who served in the fleet and almost none of the thousands of civilians who flocked to the Hampton Roads area to see it off were aware of the ships' deficiencies. To entertain the sightseers the ships' teams staged football, baseball, and rowing matches. The festivities reached a climax on the evening of Friday, 13 December, in the grand ballroom of the stately Chamberlin Hotel on Old Point Comfort, overlooking the Roads. Between walls hung with flags and bunting social leaders from Norfolk, Richmond, Washington, and Baltimore mingled with naval officers in blue and gold and with red-uniformed army artillery officers from nearby Fortress Monroe. Not least proud among those present was Bill Halsey, with his fiancée on his arm. The mood, said the *New York Herald* of 15 December 1907, was bittersweet. The waltzers exchanged "many a brave smile," but the following week the women "would be drenching their pillows with tears, and the one prayer would be 'Bring him safely back.'"

On Saturday a fifty-mile gale drowned all festivities. Sunday was the day for good-byes. We may be sure that Bill and Fanny, whom he now called Fan, were together as much as possible. At least a year would pass before they would see each other again.

Early Monday morning, 16 December, crowds began gathering on the shores to see the fleet depart. Rear Admiral Robley D. ("Fighting Bob") Evans, commander in chief of the Atlantic Fleet, was in command. He had announced that his ships were ready for anything, "a feast, a frolic, or a fight." This morning the ships, flags and pennants flying from every line, lay in two rows, forming a passageway along which the presidential yacht *Mayflower* paraded at a stately pace. On her foredeck Roosevelt was standing, holding on to his top hat with one hand and saluting with the other as each ship in succession honored him with twenty-one-guns followed by the national anthem. Soon afterward the *Mayflower* led the way through the capes and stood by as the battleships wheeled right and shaped course for the Caribbean and South America.[6]

On invitation, the fleet paused ten days at Rio de Janeiro, where the men had the liberty of the city, the officers were guests at balls and receptions, and Brazilian dignitaries and social leaders were entertained on board the ships. Bill thought that as a lowly ensign he might be spared most of the ceremonial festivities, but it turned out otherwise. Late one afternoon, in the process of coaling ship, wearing dungarees and black with dust, he was hailed and given half an hour to get cleaned up and in a white dress uniform. He had to attend a ball at a palace in Petropolis, Brazil's summer capital.

At Punta Arenas, Chile, the world's southernmost city, the fleet spent several days taking on coal. Here Bill had the first of his many tours of duty with the shore patrol. He was sent to the red-light district to relieve the patrol officer during the evening meal. He found some bluejackets who had downed a few drinks having a fine time putting on a "smokestack jag," pretending to be very drunk. Since the boat landing was some three miles away, they had convinced themselves that this young officer would never figure how to get them there in their apparently helpless condition. They were mistaken. Halsey had the patrol hire a horse and carriage, drive the culprits to the wharf, and return with the carriage. The culprits had to pay the fare. That ended the smokestacking stunt, at least when Halsey had the duty.

Bill found working with the shore patrol instructive in that it forced him to learn a good deal about handling men. On a few occasions he found it necessary to straighten out officers considerably senior to himself. They had to be informed by Halsey that the enlisted shore patrolmen making the arrests were representatives of the commander in chief. "Two or three knuckles had to be severely rapped," Halsey later said, "until this fact had been driven home."[7]

After passing through the Strait of Magellan, the Great White Fleet moved up the west coast of South America, stopping next at Callao, the port of Lima, capital of Peru. Here a carefully selected shore patrol, including Halsey, was enjoined to be particularly vigilant. What had been acceptable conduct in frontier-like Punta Arenas, where women as well as men chewed tobacco, might be intolerable in the urbane setting of Lima.

"The patrolmen," said Halsey, "were a fine-looking group of American sailormen, and they did their jobs right up to the handle. It must be remembered that there were liberty parties from sixteen battleships, plus some destroyers and small craft and auxiliaries that accompanied the fleet, all turned loose in a strange and foreign city. Their conduct was excellent and I believe far better than the conduct of the same number of college boys turned loose without supervision would have been."

Part of the overall record of good conduct resulted from prompt and decisive action by the shore patrol. Halsey explained, "At the first sign of a man beginning to lose control of himself, it is very much better to place him under supervision and return him to his ship. This not only saves the man in question trouble, but it saves the spectacle of a man in uniform misbehaving in a public place. If handled promptly and with decision, a man will rarely ever get out of hand."

After visits to several southern California ports, the fleet in May 1908 put in to San Francisco, still partly in ruins from the earthquake of two years before. Many of the officers were near exhaustion from the constant round of social engagements, and Fighting Bob, who had begun the cruise with a serious case of gout, had to turn the command over to Rear Admiral Charles S. Sperry and leave the fleet.

Halsey was assigned regular patrol duty on the Barbary Coast, then at the height of its notoriety. Here, from his repeated inspections of whorehouses, he became a familiar figure, known to the girls and their sponsors as Big Bill. Actually, the only time he encountered serious trouble was one night when he was off duty, returning alone to his hotel from a patrol. He heard the muffled shriek of a police whistle coming from a house across the street. When he climbed the porch he heard a tremendous hubbub inside. Knocking and receiving no response, he threw his shoulder against the door and forced it open. Inside he saw a sailor, whom he recognized as a member of the shore patrol, being assailed by several screaming women, inmates of the house, one of whom had in her hand a beer bottle that she was about to bring down on the bluejacket's head. Halsey grabbed the sailor by the collar and, pulling him clear, told him to head for the nearest navy patrol station and send over some patrolmen.

Halsey meanwhile tried to quell the noise. He told the women that he was deputized by the civil authority to make arrests and would exercise that prerogative if they didn't pipe down. When the patrolmen arrived, he ordered them to search the rooms, make no arrests, but put out of the house any sailors or marines they found. That done, he stationed a patrol at the front door with instructions to admit no men in uniform.

A few days later Halsey happened to encounter Captain A. W. Grant, chief of staff to Admiral Sperry. "I have a serious report against you," said Grant severely. "It has been reported that you have been interfering with legitimate business in San Francisco."

When the captain saw that Halsey was dumbstruck, he could no longer suppress his laughter. "A woman signing herself as Navy Bess said she ran one of the most respectable houses that San Francisco had known and that she was a great friend of the navy and for no known reason you had placed a patrol in front of her house and forbidden enlisted men to enter."

Bill laughingly pleaded guilty.[8]

After an exhausting round of parades and entertainments in the San Francisco area, the fleet put to sea, heading for Honolulu and more of the same. From Hawaii the double line of white ships steamed south to visit Auckland, New Zealand, and Sydney and Melbourne, Australia.

In these ports the Americans received a frenzied welcome. The pageantry opened in each city with the officers and men of the fleet and their sixteen bands marching under miles of specially built arches, past buildings draped with Old Glories and Union Jacks. People lining the streets were trampled. Others fell off buildings where they had perched to watch the parades. A grandstand toppled over and a bridge collapsed under the weight of crowds. These mishaps did not discourage girls from darting into the streets to kiss the passing sailors.

The constant round of dinners, dances, and parties the officers were expected to attend scarcely left them time to sleep. Sometimes they had to sit through Admiral Sperry's well-rehearsed speech a dozen times a day. The speeches of local dignitaries were almost as repetitious, stressing the themes of common language, ancestry, traditions, and political institutions. The locals also kept sounding off about the "yellow peril," a subject the Americans were careful to avoid, at least in public.

The fact was that New Zealanders and Australians felt isolated from Europe by the great mass of Asia. They were especially fearful of the Japanese, who, having recently defeated the armies and navies of both China and Russia, had lately been rattling the saber. They felt Britain had let them down by forming and renewing an alliance with Japan and that, in any case, their mother country was militarily on the decline, unable to shield them, half a world away. The United States, on the other hand, had become a Pacific power with the visible means, now in their very ports, of keeping the Japanese contained. Their enthusiasm over the American visit was understandable.

Bill Halsey's youthful vigor enabled him to take the many parties in stride. He was not especially displeased, however, when shore patrol duty spared him the boredom of listening to those speeches.

The problems of the patrol were immensely complicated by drunkenness such as Halsey had not encountered in any ports previously visited by the fleet.

It often began when a friendly civilian offered to buy a visiting sailor a drink, or two, or three. One forenoon in Auckland Bill was startled to see one of his own patrolmen at a bar having a drink with a New Zealander. A strictly enforced order forbade an officer or man on patrol duty to consume any alcoholic beverage. Halsey walked up and tapped his man on the shoulder. When the latter turned and found himself looking into the stern eyes of an officer, he almost dropped his glass. The man was soon returned to his ship under arrest.

On another occasion Halsey, at the head of a small patrol force, found himself threatened by a big sailor crazy with drink and holding a two-by-four. Halsey ordered the man to drop his weapon, at which the fellow snarled, "No son-of-a-bitch here can make me."

That put Bill on the spot. He could have ordered his patrolmen to rush the man, but somebody probably would have been hurt. Instead he began moving toward the fellow, slowly and carefully. "Those next two or three steps," said Halsey, "were the longest miles I ever walked in my life."

As he expected, or at least hoped, the man wavered, then dropped his weapon. Bill had him put under a strong guard for return to his ship.

Referring to this episode, Halsey wrote, "An officer should never attempt personally to put a man under arrest or manhandle him, except in the most extreme cases for self-protection or to prevent injury to some person. To do so lays him open not only to the possibility of bodily injury but the loss of reputation amongst his personnel. I have never had to use personal force in any of my dealings with enlisted personnel, although there have been occasions when I had to make the implied threat to do so."

Patrol duty undoubtedly helped shape Halsey's style of command. Unlike officers who felt that to impose their will they had to assume an imperious mien or maintain an unbridgeable distance between themselves and their subordinates, Halsey was always approachable and at ease, confident that he could handle any situation that might arise.

In addition to drunks, the shore patrol was plagued by the continual need to head off or retrieve deserters. Many bluejackets, impressed by the lavish hospitality of their hosts, decided that New Zealand or Australia was the place to be and took measures to stay behind. Some local families hampered the patrol's efforts by concealing deserters in their homes until the fleet had departed.

The would-be expatriation was not all one way, as Halsey discovered one afternoon at Melbourne when he was officer of the deck. The liberty boat came alongside and men swarmed on board. Noticing a parcel left behind in the boat, Halsey called out to the last man, "Lad, bring that package up with you."

His answer, a breezy "Right you are, sir!" took Halsey aback. That didn't sound like an American. When the man reached the deck Bill questioned him, noted his Aussie accent, and wrung from him the fact that he and an American bluejacket had made a deal to swap clothes and countries. The poor Aussie was stripped of the uniform and sent ashore to the local police in a disreputable old suit in which an earlier straggler had been picked up. His accomplice was never caught.[9]

After coaling at Albany, Western Australia, the fleet proceeded via Lombok and Makassar straits to the Philippines. Halsey tells of an unusual experience during a morning watch: "From the time I took over before four o'clock in the morning till I was relieved at eight, I did not have to touch the engine revolutions [to adjust the ship's speed] and kept in perfect station. It was the only time in my entire naval career when I have been able to go four hours without touching the engine revolutions. This incident will convey to you the efficiency which the fleet had achieved by this time."

The Great White Fleet steamed majestically into Manila Bay on 1 October 1908 and anchored near the place Commodore Dewey had destroyed the Spanish fleet ten years before. There it stayed until the tenth. To the disappointment of the people of Manila and to the rage of its merchants, who counted on parting the sailors from a good share of their pay, nobody from the ships was allowed ashore. Cholera was raging in the city, and Admiral Sperry could not risk having it sweep through his fleet—particularly at this time, for the next port of call was Yokohama, Japan.

It was with mixed feelings that Roosevelt had accepted the invitation for the fleet to visit Japan. He wanted to impress the Japanese with evidence of American power, but he distrusted them. So did Sperry and his senior officers. They spoke of the fate of the battleship *Maine* in Havana harbor.* They spoke also of Japanese sneak attacks on Chinese naval forces in 1894 and on Russian naval forces in 1904, each preceding a declaration of war. Bill Halsey, while not participating in his seniors' discussions, shared their suspicions.

En route to Japan the fleet ran into a typhoon that scattered the ships, wrenched the fore-topmast off one, swept two men overboard, shattered bridge windows, and stripped off wireless antennas. Delayed by the storm, the American fleet entered Tokyo Bay on 18 October, two days overdue. The officers on board were tense, half expecting a trap. They knew that the main Japanese fleet, which included ten battleships and twenty-nine armored cruisers, was at sea "on maneuvers." It could easily return and block Uruga Strait, the narrow entrance to the bay.

But the Japanese, with eyes on Manchuria, where they hoped to make

*The battleship was torn apart by an explosion that killed 260 of her crew. This catastrophe, which the Americans attributed to a mine planted by the Spaniards, was a major cause of the Spanish-American War.

gains without U.S. interference, had prepared a full-scale welcome for the Americans. For reasons of prestige the pageant had to be grander, both afloat and ashore, than anything the Chinese could manage. The Japanese ambassador in Washington had already sought and received assurance that the White Fleet in its entirety would visit Japan but not China.

Both hosts and guests took the utmost care to see that no misconduct marred the visit. The local police in Yokohama and Tokyo issued instructions on how to behave toward the visitors. Japanese citizens were told, for example, to give up their seats in streetcars and trains to foreigners. The visiting officers would be obliged to drink toasts, but they were warned by their superiors that any drunkenness would end in court-martial. The conduct of the enlisted men was regulated by a veritable army of shore patrols. This duty kept Halsey too busy to participate in many of the festivities, but at one reception he heard a children's chorus sing "Hail, Columbia" in English, and he did attend a ball for the American officers on board the famous old battleship *Mikasa.*

The *Mikasa* had been the flagship of Admiral Count Heihachiro Togo, who had commanded the Japanese fleet that was victorious over the Russians in the Battle of Tsushima. Togo himself was host that evening and began festivities with a tour of the ship while he lectured in English on the Tsushima battle. Halsey, knowing the admiral had participated in the sneak attacks against Chinese ships and later Russian ships, both of which the young American considered acts of criminal treachery, was not impressed.*

Available was a plentiful supply of liquor, of which the Americans partook sparingly, fearing court-martial. But the Japanese drank freely, and some became very jolly indeed, insisting upon paying Admiral Sperry the Japanese honor of the "toss." They laid hands on their tall, thin guest and gave him three gentle tosses, crying "Banzai!" each time. Understanding that he had been paid a rare tribute, Sperry managed to gasp, "Thank you."

"Naturally," says Halsey, "we had to return the compliment to Admiral Togo. We were big and he was a shrimp, so instead of tossing him gently, we gave him three real heaves. If we had known what the future held, we wouldn't have caught him after the third one."[10]

The Americans left Japan with varied impressions. Some of the officers and enlisted men believed that the Japanese had given them a heartfelt welcome and that the visit had canceled old hostilities, laying the foundation for genuine friendship between their two nations. Others, including Halsey, believed the motives behind Japanese courtesy were spurious, that with few exceptions the Japanese despised them and were merely obeying strict orders

*For details of the very different impression Admiral Togo made on Passed Midshipman Chester W. Nimitz, see note 10, page 396.

the authorities, for their own devious reasons, had issued. The Japanese had presented to the visitors medals confirming the good will existing between the two governments. The Americans accepted them with varying degrees of enthusiasm. After Pearl Harbor some men sent their medals to Halsey, requesting that he return them to Japan at the earliest opportunity. Just before the April 1942 Tokyo raid Halsey handed them over to Jimmy Doolittle, who dropped them on the city along with his bombs.

Following orders, Sperry detached eight battleships, his third and fourth divisions, to visit China. With the rest of his fleet, including the *Kansas,* he returned to Manila. Here, the cholera epidemic having abated, the crews had shore leave.

In sending to China only half a fleet, the United States insulted China and set off anti-American riots in several Chinese cities, a situation exacerbated by the fact that the Americans chose the small southern port of Amoy to visit. The Chinese government, fearful that its outraged citizens might attack the visitors, had the ships bypass Amoy and anchor off "Pleasure City," which they had built on an uninhabited stretch of shoreline to receive the Americans. The Chinese, by spending more than seven times what any other country had to entertain the Americans—a sum the equivalent of a million 1908 dollars—felt that it was the latter who in the end lost face.[11]

The reassembled Great White Fleet passed through Makassar Strait into the Indian Ocean, where it made one stop, at Colombo, Ceylon, mainly to take on coal. After passing through the Red Sea and the Suez Canal, the fleet split up to visit several points in the Mediterranean simultaneously. It had to do this in order to reach Hampton Roads on 22 February 1909, Washington's birthday, when President Roosevelt was to review the returning fleet and bask in the glory of its achievement before his presidency ended on 4 March.

Sperry's first division, including the *Kansas,* was fortunate to draw Villefranche on the French Riviera, then one of the world's most fashionable resorts. The battleships anchored in a semicircular cove rimmed by a white beach from which rose an amphitheater of steep wooded hills dotted with pink and yellow villas. Sailboats quickly surrounded the ships. Swimmers, taking advantage of the unseasonably warm weather, swam out with greetings and requests to be hoisted on board.

A few wives had followed the fleet since it left San Francisco, joining their husbands in Melbourne and Tokyo. A couple of the ladies even made it to Pleasure City. Learning that the first division was scheduled to visit Villefranche, a crowd joined their husbands there, planning on savoring the fleshpots of the Côte d'Azur. Among them was Halsey's sister Deborah, now married to his shipmate Passed Midshipman Archie Turnbull.

The French went all out to welcome the visitors. In part their hospitality reflected a fear of the Germans, who had defeated them thirty-eight years earlier and were acting belligerent again. The French were happy to take to their bosoms any potential ally who could sail sixteen battleships around the world.

The festivities lasted thirteen days. At that time all Europe was saddened by the recent destruction of Messina, flattened by an earthquake that killed thousands, but the only concession at Villefranche was the informal dress worn at the almost continuous round of parties. At length the older officers reached such a state of exhaustion that they had difficulty being pleasant. The wives, however, kept going strong. At their head was Mrs. Rutherford Stuyvesant, sister of the American ambassador, who arrived from Paris in a black and silver limousine and opened her villa as social headquarters. Here one evening she had Admiral Sperry and former premier Leon Bourgeois to an intimate dinner, whence they repaired to Nice and joined the officers at a ball in the casino. Sperry lost money playing roulette, an outcome that did nothing to cool his smoldering temper.

The young officers, including Bill Halsey, were enjoying the merrymaking. In addition to social functions Bill participated in an exhibition football game, after which the city of Nice awarded his *Kansas* team a prize of six thousand dollars for defeating the *Minnesota* team 6 to 2. Whenever possible the junior officers slipped down to the beach to gawk at the ladies in their daring bathing costumes—no stockings, no sleeves, low-cut necks, and skirts reaching just below the knee.[12]

In early February 1909 the fleet reassembled at Gibraltar and began the voyage across the Atlantic, which was so continuously stormy that sleep was difficult and proper ship maintenance impossible. Even the hardy Halsey had a spell of seasickness after consuming too much cheese. The storm at last abating, the armada dropped anchor off Cape Henry on the evening of 21 February to convert the ships, now grown dingy, into a fleet suitable for presidential inspection on the morrow. In the glare of searchlights sailors on scaffolds slung over the sides applied the last coat of white paint ever to go on an American man-of-war.

On the twenty-second hundreds of small craft afloat and thousands of spectators lining the shores were on hand to greet the fleet, now gleaming once more, as it reentered Hampton Roads. Whistles tooted and foghorns blared. The lame-duck president arrived, again standing at the rail of the *Mayflower,* to acknowledge twenty-one-gun salutes from every ship. Hotel Chamberlin, which had almost gone broke during the fourteen-month absence of the fleet, had been obliged to place cots in the corridors to accommodate the influx of wives and sweethearts who had come to welcome home their men.

"The Round-the-World Cruise," wrote Halsey, "in my opinion—the opinion of a young and inexperienced officer—was a success by every standard." Not all officers agreed with that assessment, but certainly it was a stunning technical achievement. The Great White Fleet had traveled farther on a single cruise than any other fleet in history, and more remarkably it had done so without a serious breakdown, accident, or other mishap. If the appearance of the *Dreadnought* made the American battleships obsolete, it did the same to the battleships of other countries. In that class of warship, every navy, including Britain's, was forced back to square one. If the United States could build and man predreadnoughts that went around the world unscathed, presumably it could do the same and more with dreadnoughts.

Bill Halsey was invited to most of the receptions, presidential balls, Navy League dinners, and other social functions that occupied the next two days, but he dodged as many as possible to spend time with Fan Grandy. He had, he said, "bombarded her with souvenirs and ardent letters from every port on the World Cruise."[13]

CHAPTER 7

DESTROYERMAN

FOLLOWING THE WELCOME-HOME FESTIVITIES in the Hampton Roads area, the Great White Fleet scattered to various navy yards for upkeep, repairs, and repainting. Halsey went with the *Kansas* to Philadelphia. Here workmen proceeded to pry the fancy crest off her prow and paint her gleaming white hull battleship gray, the color of other warships the world around.

Long before the work was completed, Halsey was ordered to Washington to be examined for promotion. It was with some misgivings that he went. The exams would be tough, and on the world cruise he had had little time to prepare for them. With six other ensigns Bill toiled for a week, six to eight hours a day, answering questions and solving problems in marine and electrical engineering, ordnance and gunnery, seamanship and navigation, and communications. Rather to his surprise, he was one of the four candidates who passed. Ordinarily they would have to serve as lieutenants, junior grade, at least two years, but because there were numerous vacancies in the next higher rank, all four were sworn in at once as senior lieutenants.[1]

Halsey's next orders took him to the Charleston Navy Yard and command of the torpedo boat *Du Pont*. Another Spanish-American War relic, she was 165 feet long, displaced 165 tons, and had a crew consisting of Lieutenant Halsey, a passed midshipman, and twenty-three enlisted men. Outmoded by the newly developed destroyers (originally called torpedo-boat destroyers), her type was about to disappear from the navy. But it was Halsey's first command, and he was a proud man when he saw the colors and commissioning pennant hoisted on the little craft.

In mid-summer of 1909 the *Du Pont* proceeded up the coast with a destroyer flotilla, which made a brief call at Norfolk, affording Halsey an opportunity to visit Fan. His double promotion and the considerable raise in pay that came with it gave him reason to urge her to set a date for their wedding. When she hesitated, Bill put forward what he considered a compelling argument: "Do you realize you are being offered the heart and hand of a skipper in the United States fleet? How can you afford to delay?"

To which Miss Grandy is said to have replied, laughing, "Well, now that you make it sound so attractive, I suppose I would be foolish to procrastinate any longer."

But there was to be no rush to the altar. In line with Grandy family tradition, Fan was to have a proper church wedding with all the customary preliminaries and follow-ups. Halsey's duties would not permit him to take sufficient leave for that sort of thing any time soon. So off he went with the flotilla via New York and Long Island Sound to the waters off Provincetown, where the *Du Pont* participated in the first of several exercises with the fleet.[2]

In autumn, when the flotilla headed back south, it paused at Norfolk a little longer. Fan was away, visiting a cousin, Mrs. Edell Jenkins, and the latter's mother, Mrs. Margaret Dobie, at Blue Ridge Summit, Pennsylvania. Halsey obtained a five-day leave of absence and proceeded thither by the first available train.

By this time the Halsey charm, which had won Bill the title "everybody's friend" in the Naval Academy yearbook, had completely won over the Grandy family. At Blue Ridge Summit, however, he met an unexpected obstacle in the person of Mrs. Jenkins's maid, who all but slammed the door in his face when he appeared at the threshold.

In her youth the maid, Mary Harrill, had accompanied her father, a bumboatman, on his trips to sell articles to crews of ships in port or offshore and had acquired a poor opinion of seafarers. After many years serving the Jenkins family, she still retained her bias. She also presumed to exercise a certain degree of dictatorial control. When Mary learned that Fan was planning to marry a naval officer, she was aghast. She hurried to Mrs. Dobie.

"Miss Maggie," she protested, "you ain't gonna let that little gal marry one of them seafaring men, is you?"

When Mrs. Dobie brushed the question aside, Mary was indignant. At first she treated Bill with ill-concealed scorn, but like all the others, she soon fell victim to the Halsey captivation. Before he left she sought him out privately.

"Lieutenant," she said, "I don't like seafaring men, and when you fust came up here I was very angry. Now I is praying for you."[3]

Bill returned to his ship which, with the flotilla, went back to Charleston and then proceeded to Jacksonville, Florida, for a protracted stay. Having foreseen this opportunity, Halsey had applied for and obtained a month's leave, and the Grandy family had begun preparing for the wedding. As Bill was packing his gear to go to Norfolk, Lieutenant Harold ("Betty") Stark, who commanded one of the destroyers, came on board the *Du Pont* and inquired what train he intended to take. When the time came for Bill to leave his ship, he was surprised and gratified to find Stark and a couple other fellow officers waiting in an elegant carriage alongside his ship, prepared to see him off in style.

Bill, deeply touched, climbed unsuspectingly into the vehicle. Then, as the carriage rounded the first corner, he beheld a band lined up and waiting, instruments at the ready. On a sign from Stark, it struck up the wedding march and escorted them through the streets of Jacksonville to the railway station. To spectators drawn to the sound of music the officers nodded pleasantly and pointed to the red-faced Halsey.

Bill arrived in Norfolk in time to participate in the last of the preliminaries. The wedding took place at 2000 on 1 December 1909 in Christ Church. Fan's sister Margaret was maid of honor. Halsey's best man was Dave Bagley, and the ushers were Tommy Hart, Husband Kimmel, and Carl Ohnesorg, all young naval officers.

At the reception, when the time came to cut the cake, Fan was startled to note, by the inscription, that she was using a borrowed sword. A few days before, while Bill was going over his ship's side by Jacob's ladder, his scabbard struck a step and upended, and his sword dropped into the water. The replacement was not yet engraved with Halsey's name.

It had been foreseen that the reception would last beyond the hour when the last train left Norfolk with connections for New York, whither the young couple were bound for their wedding trip. A railwayman cousin of Fan's had solved the problem by obtaining for their use a tug that took them from Norfolk to Old Point Comfort to catch the C&O out of Newport News, with connections at Richmond.[4]

After the honeymoon Bill returned to the *Du Pont,* leaving Fan in Norfolk. In February 1910 he was ordered to Philadelphia to help commission and serve as executive officer of the 750-ton, turbine-driven destroyer *Lamson.* From this date until June 1932 all of Halsey's sea duty, except for one year as executive officer of the *Wyoming,* was in destroyers.

Bill's tour of duty on board the *Lamson* was his shortest. In April 1910 he was detached and ordered to the Norfolk Navy Yard at Portsmouth, Virginia, to take charge of an apprentice seaman training camp. He was assigned the only house on the station, a comfortable dwelling on the Elizabeth River. He and Fan always remembered it with affection as the original home of Lieutenant and Mrs. William F. Halsey, Jr. Here at 0500 on 10 October 1910 their first child, a daughter, was born. They named her Margaret Bradford, for two of Fan's relatives and Bill's Academy roommate, Brad Barnette. By 0800, when the seamen held their morning muster, word of the new arrival had got around and the band led off the parade playing, "I Love My Wife, But Oh, You Kid!"[5]

Such was Bill's happiness in this first tour of shore duty that he was strongly tempted to resign from the navy, pursue a civilian career, and settle down in a permanent home with his wife and child. But in August 1912, when he was ordered to take command of the destroyer *Flusser,* he readily complied. This was the first of a series of such commands in which Halsey became a master in the science of shiphandling and developed leadership skills that enabled him to train crews that were both happy and disciplined. He also came under the approving observation of men who were later in positions to influence his career.

The year after taking command of the *Flusser,* for example, he was ordered to report for duty to the summer residence of Assistant Secretary of the Navy Franklin D. Roosevelt on Campobello Island. The assistant secretary wished to survey naval installations on Frenchman Bay, Maine. "At this time," says Halsey, "Mr. Roosevelt was a splendid-looking, vigorous man, full of vitality."

On the way back to Campobello after the inspection, Roosevelt suggested they take a shortcut through the strait between Campobello and the mainland and offered to serve as pilot. Halsey gave him the conn (steering control) but stood by to take over in case of emergency. He knew that Roosevelt had had extensive experience in small craft and yachts, but that was no guarantee that he could handle a high-powered vessel in narrow waters. Halsey soon realized, however, that there was nothing to worry about. When making a turn, Roosevelt looked aft to check the swing of the stern. By that act he showed he knew his business as a shiphandler. On a turn two-thirds of a destroyer is aft of the pivoting point, so that the stern swings through an arc twice as wide as the bow arc. Thus while the bow is pointing directly down the channel the stern may be in trouble. Roosevelt obviously understood these principles, earning Halsey's respect. This short cruise was the beginning of a friendship between the two that was renewed on later voyages and lasted until Roosevelt's death.[6]

In August 1913 Lieutenant Halsey was given command of the oil-burning destroyer *Jarvis,* which served with the Atlantic Destroyer Flotilla, commanded by Captain William S. Sims, an officer with a remarkable past and a brilliant future. The flotilla's main assignment under Sims was to devise new uses for destroyers, now that torpedo boats, their original prey, were being phased out.

Not long after Halsey took command of the *Jarvis,* he and the other skippers of the flotilla were summoned to Captain Sims's flagship, the light cruiser *Birmingham,* for a conference. Halsey found Sims impressive. As a speaker he was crisp and decisive, with an air of benign authority. Tall, slim, and erect, he had a handsome, aristocratic countenance with a mustache and neatly trimmed Vandyke beard just turning gray. He gave the destroyermen a little pep talk, including a demand for excellence. He said he planned to call frequent conferences of all the commanding officers. With himself serving as moderator rather than dictator, he expected them to engage in full and frank discussions concerning their aims and problems. In the meantime he wanted the skippers to submit to him what they conceived to be the mission of the destroyers.

From these opinions Sims drew up a tentative plan: "The mission of the

Flotilla shall be to determine the manner in which the Flotilla may best assist the Fleet in accomplishing its main objectives, before, during, and after battle." No mention was made of escort duty and submarine hunting, because in the summer of 1914 the deadly role of the submarine as commerce raider was unforeseen.

During late summer and fall the flotilla went through the usual maneuvers with the fleet and engaged in target practice and high-speed torpedo runs off the Virginia Capes. In early January 1914 it headed south and based on Guantánamo Bay, Cuba. Here Sims, in meetings with his carefully selected staff and in conferences with his destroyer captains, worked out on the game board a series of operations that were to serve as a foundation for effective destroyer doctrine. They then took the flotilla to sea to try out the tactical moves they had devised. As Sims had freely predicted, no more than half the maneuvers so carefully worked out on shore proved feasible at sea. And so it was back to the game board.

One maneuver that proved eminently practical was a substitute for the movement by which all ships turned simultaneously to a new course. For a long column such a turn could easily lead to confusion, with ships blanketing each other's fire, especially at night, when the flotilla expected to strike its most deadly blows. Before the development of radar, if the van ship led off in a ripple maneuver in darkness and the remaining ships turned in succession, collisions could be expected. The flotilla's solution was to begin the ripple maneuver with the ship at the rear. The rest of the ships would turn separately after the destroyer immediately astern had begun to turn. This is the famous *Gefechtskehrtwendung*, by which Admiral Scheer in the Battle of Jutland two years later twice extracted his High Seas Fleet from the clutches of Britain's Grand Fleet.

Sims drilled his flotilla like a football team. By constant practice each participant knew precisely what his and his fellows' duties were in any particular maneuver. No long descriptive orders were needed; like a quarterback identifying a particular formation by the number assigned to it, Sims needed to transmit only a few key words to put a complex maneuver into play.

At Guantánamo the captain liked to hold his flotilla conferences in the officers' club. He frequently arrived in tennis clothes carrying several tennis balls. If a speaker waxed verbose or veered from the point at hand, Sims was likely to toss a ball at him. By this time the destroyers' skippers were the best of friends and utterly devoted to their commander in chief. Elting Morison, Sims's biographer, has aptly compared them to Nelson's Band of Brothers.

In maneuvers one night in the waters just east of Cuba, a division of battleships was designated enemy and the destroyer flotilla prepared to attack them. In jet darkness the destroyers worked around to an upwind position and, making smoke, raced past the battleships at a distance where the danger of being hit by gunfire at night was not too great. Then when the smoke had drifted into the battleship gunners' eyes, the destroyers raced back along the edge of the drifting smoke clouds in a simulated torpedo run.

Several commentators have suggested that if the British destroyers in the Battle of Jutland had been trained by Sims, night would have presented the German fleet not with an opportunity to escape but with a real risk of annihilation. Sims's destroyer doctrine never came into actual use, because in World War I the Americans fought no fleet battles, and in World War II the advent of the carrier as capital ship outmoded the Jutland type of battle.

From Guantánamo, the flotilla proceeded to Pensacola. Here, in common with all other U.S. naval forces in the Gulf of Mexico, it was placed on alert. Anarchy reigned in Mexico, where a number of Americans had been killed. President Wilson, calling for the resignation of tyrannical Victoriano Huerta, who had attained the presidency by murdering his predecessor, permitted sales of munitions to Huerta's rivals and stationed warships off the Mexican coasts.

The situation was exacerbated on 9 April, when authorities at Tampico illegally detained an American boat party and then refused to make a suitable apology. On 21 April, as a German merchantman was about to land a cargo of arms at Veracruz for Huerta to use against the United States, Wilson, with congressional consent, ordered his navy to seize the port.

Already the ships at Pensacola had blown a series of blasts on their whistles that summoned on board all personnel ashore. After rapid provisioning and fueling the flotilla put to sea and headed at highest speed for Veracruz. En route it received orders by radio to participate in an amphibious assault, an unusual assignment for destroyers. Lacking the khaki uniforms required for landing forces, all hands were directed to boil their whites in coffee, a time-consuming process, which, Halsey says, made his destroyer smell like a Greasy Spoon.

Communicators in the *Jarvis* intercepted a query from Captain Sims to Lieutenant Commander William Jeffers, Halsey's division commander: "Are Lieutenant Halsey's services available for duty as adjutant of the landing force?" Jeffers promptly replied with a cryptic no. Just as promptly Sims signaled back, "Lieutenant Halsey is detailed as adjutant of the landing force."

Halsey envisioned himself in one of the small landing boats rowing ashore in the face of heavy Mexican fire. No such fate awaited him, however, because long before the flotilla reached Mexico, radio announced that Veracruz was in American hands. It had been seized by marines and bluejackets already in the area, following heavy bombardment from the fleet. The flotilla accordingly was shunted to Tampico, where Americans were waiting to be evacuated.

At Tampico Halsey had the job of carrying out the orders of the battalion commander regarding the organization of boats in the landing force. These stood on guard off the port while the evacuees came out, crowded into a pair of American yachts, one under the charge of a British officer and flying a British ensign, the other under the charge of a German officer and flying the German naval flag. Halsey found it humiliating to sit idly by while neutrals brought American citizens out of an enemy port that was not too well defended, but the flotilla was under strict orders not to provoke further incidents, and the Mexicans were careful not to give it cause to intervene. The evacuees boarded the *Dixie,* the flotilla's only tender, and sailed away for Galveston, leaving the destroyers in broiling heat without a source for fresh provisions or ice.

Its assignment completed, the flotilla proceeded to Veracruz, which was now quiet and, under American occupation, operating almost normally. Bluejackets were running the streetcars as motormen and conductors, and marines were running the police. The streetcar operators charged Mexican passengers the regular fares, which they turned in, but allowed their buddies free rides. By this time relations between the occupiers and citizens had been reestablished, and there were no untoward incidents. As a matter of fact, says Halsey, the Mexicans in general were rather friendly. Of course, the people he encountered may merely have been reacting to the potent Halsey charm.

Bill met some old friends among the occupying marines, and they invited him to lunch. Afterward he accepted their additional invitation to go for a horseback ride, a bad decision since he had had no experience at all with horses. The waggish marines saw to it that their neophyte horseman got a spirited steed. No sooner had Bill climbed on board than his mount spun about and started to gallop, hurdling a trash heap that lay in his way. "The horse started making forty knots," says Halsey, "and there I was in the stern sheets with no steering or engine control. If someone hadn't had mercy on me and overhauled us, he might be running yet."

About this time Wilson, anxious not to plunge the United States into another full-fledged war with Mexico, gratefully accepted the proffered mediation of Argentina, Brazil, and Chile. The Americans withdrew from Veracruz, and Huerta went into voluntary exile.[7]

With war thus averted, the destroyers left Mexican waters and proceeded temporarily to their home port of Norfolk, where the Halseys had taken an apartment. To the dismay of Fan and the delight of Margaret, Bill arrived with a handsome Brazilian parrot by the name of Pedro. They placed his cage at an open window, where the sunlight would gleam on his varicolored feathers. Unfortunately Pedro had only two talents: he could sound off like a boozer laughing or wail like a beaten child. Horrified, Mrs. Halsey imagined her neighbors saying, "That lieutenant has been drunk ever since he got home and repeatedly brutalizes that poor child of his."

Bill was rather amused at the possibility of acquiring such a reputation, but finally Pedro tried even his long-suffering patience. The parrot had acquired another talent, that of unlatching his cage and escaping. One day Bill noticed that Pedro had been unusually quiet. Investigating, he found the bird at large, happily chewing out the crown of his only civilian hat—a serious matter because Halsey always had a difficult time finding big enough headgear to fit his size 7⅞ head. In a flash of temper Bill hurled the parrot across the room. After that Pedro had no use for Halsey and would try to take a nip at him whenever he approached.[8]

When World War I broke out in August 1914, the Atlantic Destroyer Flotilla began neutrality patrols off U.S. ports. One of its assignments, in line with the strict rules of neutrality then in force, was to prevent belligerents from purchasing and carrying away privately owned vessels for military use. Halsey, in the *Jarvis*, operated off Sandy Hook, keeping an eye mainly on the fast yacht *Winchester*, built along the lines of a destroyer. Out past the three-mile limit a British man-of-war paraded back and forth, watching the same vessel.

In the early autumn, after maneuvering some 600 miles on various courses and at various speeds under an overcast that precluded celestial fixes, Halsey had only the vaguest notion where he was. Suddenly the *Jarvis* popped out of a fog bank and he saw the British man-of-war a few hundred yards away. There ensued a tense quarter hour as the two ships looked each other over, half expecting the trigger-happy crew of the other to open fire.

Halsey was relieved to reenter the concealing fog, but presently he sensed another danger, perhaps from the drag of shoaling water or the sudden appearance of large swells at his vessel's stern. Instinctively he ordered, "Full speed astern!" As the ship lost way, he made out a fishing boat close aboard and hailed the fisherman, asking for his position.

The man bellowed back, "If you keep going for half a mile, you'll be right in the middle of the Fire Island Life Saving station!"

In 1915 Halsey was ordered to report to the Naval Academy. This rather pleased him. He had happy memories of his years there both as a midshipman and as a "navy brat." Hoping to improve himself professionally, he requested teaching duty in the Department of Electrical Engineering. To his disgust he was assigned to the Discipline Department. He would have to occupy a room in Bancroft Hall, where the midshipmen lived, and take action against their misconduct. He was sure to have to report midshipmen from navy families, young men whose fathers were friends of his.

The evening after the upperclassmen returned from summer leave, he had a feeling that something of the sort was about to happen. On a routine tour of inspection after supper he walked into a room full of tobacco smoke. Midshipmen were not allowed to smoke in their rooms. "Who's in charge of this room?" he asked.

A fine-looking lad replied, "I am, sir."

"What's your name?"

"Midshipman Macklin."

"Are you a son of General Macklin?"

"Yes, sir."

"My God, I knew it!" cried Halsey. "My first report *would* have to be on the son of an old friend." The elder Macklin, president of the Naval Academy class of 1892, had resigned from the marine corps and eventually became adjutant general of the Maryland National Guard. Halsey knew him well.

After years of experience as a division officer, shore patrol officer, and skipper of his own ship, Halsey figured he would have no trouble controlling midshipmen. He planned to chew out minor offenders without reporting them and to throw the book at major offenders. It didn't work out quite that way. He had forgotten that among midshipmen evading regulations is a game. The person who could break the most rules and not get caught acquired special prestige. Such a devil-may-care fellow was known as a touge. In his plebe year Halsey had particularly admired the skill of Ernest J. King, then the four-striper and near the top of his class academically, who frenched out regularly after supper without ever getting caught. In the year following Bill's graduation Chester Nimitz walked brazenly past the guards at the Academy gate carrying a suitcase full of beer. That night he and his friends, including classmate Royal Ingersoll, the future CinCLant, staged a beer party on the roof of unfinished Bancroft Hall and threw the empty bottles over the side. Had Ingersoll and Nimitz been caught, the Academy would have lost two of its brightest students and the history of the navy in World War II might have been different.

In the class of 1916 there was a genius who rigged a smoke consumer in his shower. It worked; cigarette smoke literally disappeared. Then there was the genius who drove the Discipline Department crazy reversing or short-circuiting the current to bells, buzzers, announcing systems, and elevators in Bancroft Hall. Halsey was glad he had not been around for that. With incidents like these, the lot of a discipline officer was not a happy one.

Somewhat different was the case of the plebe from Louisiana, who each day on rising enjoyed a nonregulation chew of tobacco. At morning inspection Halsey noticed the bulge in his cheek. "Are you chewing tobacco?" he asked.

The boy's Adam's apple rose and fell and the bulge disappeared. "No, sir," he replied truthfully as beads of sweat broke out on his forehead.

Halsey looked at the boy with something like admiration. "Very well," he said. "I thought you were."

The scene was repeated several times thereafter. It seemed to Halsey that the young man was growing pale, and he learned that he wasn't eating regularly. "Marvelous, in a way," Halsey remarked to another officer. "The boy must have been weaned on the stuff."

The young Louisianian finally capitulated. At morning inspection Halsey noticed his bulgeless cheek. "I see you're not," he said.

"No, sir!"

Two events brightened this somewhat unsatisfactory period in Halsey's career. On 8 September 1915 his son, William Frederick Halsey III, was born. The following year Congress passed a bill enlarging the navy. As a result Halsey became eligible for the rank of lieutenant commander, which he attained after a particularly tough examination that left him exhausted. The new rank brought him a raise of about a hundred dollars a month, useful for a growing family. Around this time he was able to move his family out of a rented house in Annapolis and into recently vacated quarters at 39 Upshur Row, on the Academy grounds.

As the war raged in Europe, Bill grew increasingly restless and dissatisfied with shore duty. His hopes soared in April 1917 when the United States declared war. He expected a call to arms at any moment. Nothing of that sort happened, but at least he was relieved of the distasteful job of playing nursemaid to the midshipmen. He was made director of athletics and assigned the additional duty of drilling a class of naval reserve officers who had been ordered to the Naval Academy for a period of intensive instruction.

Weeks passed, then months. Halsey began to fear the war would be over without his participation. Then, unexpectedly, his hopes were fulfilled by William Sims, his old destroyer flotilla commander.

The United States had been brought to the brink of war by Germany's submarines, which, no longer restricted, were sinking American ships and taking American lives. The Navy Department decided to send an officer to England to survey the situation and make recommendations for the employment of the U.S. Navy should America enter the war. Chosen for this mission was Sims, now a rear admiral and president of the Naval War College. By the time he reached England, the United States had joined England and France against the Central Powers.

Sims was shocked to learn that the sinking of its shipping by U-boats had brought Britain to the verge of defeat. The Royal Navy had been patrolling sea routes to combat the U-boat, but that was not working. Studies made by a group of young British officers had convinced Sims that convoys would do the job. The Admiralty opposed convoys on the grounds that they were merely defensive. Sims won over Prime Minister Lloyd George, who put pressure on the Admiralty. Convoys were instituted and sinkings declined dramatically.

Sims informed the Navy Department that what Britain needed most of all were destroyers to escort convoys. In response, the department sent six destroyers, the first of many, to operate out of Queenstown (Cobh), Ireland, on the flank of the western approaches to England. Sims was ordered to take command of all American destroyers operating out of British ports. Subsequently he was commissioned a vice admiral with the title Commander, U.S. Naval Forces Operating in European Waters.

In view of his new responsibilities, Sims drew up a list of names, stars he had trained in his old destroyer flotilla, and sent it to the Bureau of Navigation with a request that as many of the officers as possible be assigned to him. The bureau chose to ignore the list. The U.S. destroyers then in service already had their skippers. The bureau saw no point in replacing them with officers serving in other billets. At any rate, the kind of training Sims had given them, however excellent, scarcely prepared them for the routine of convoy duty.

In November 1917 a friend of Halsey's, happening to be in the Navy Department, saw Sims's list, noted that Bill's name was on it, and told Bill. Halsey promptly swung into action, both at the Naval Academy and through friends in Washington. At the Academy his immediate superior, the commandant of midshipmen, said that if the superintendent agreed and proper relief could be secured, Halsey could go. The superintendent agreed. Bill's friends in Washington got the wheels spinning there, a relief was found, directives were issued, and on 26 December 1917 he was detached from the Naval Academy with orders to proceed to Queenstown.[9]

Halsey was due to sail on the liner *New York* on 7 January. A few days earlier he went to New York, the port of embarkation. Fan accompanied him to sightsee and do some shopping. One morning Bill, in uniform, chose to wait outside a department store while his wife took a swing around inside. Presently a formidable-looking dowager approached Halsey and said to him imperiously, "Call my car!"

Within a brief period eight more persons came up to Halsey and asked how to reach various departments in the store. He was disgusted that American citizens, especially in time of war, knew so little about U.S. uniforms that they could not tell a naval officer from a doorman. To each of the information seekers he gave the same advice, "Go to the top floor, walk to the opposite side of the store, then turn right and go as far as you can. There's your department."

On board the *New York* in the passage to Liverpool were many reserve officers of both services and a few regulars, of whom Halsey was the most senior.

One young army reserve officer unwittingly provided amusement for all hands. He had brought along a Sam Browne belt, which at that time was an innovation. The army did not permit its use in the United States; only the troops in Europe were eligible to wear it. Scarcely had the ship cleared the harbor when the young officer appeared sporting his Sam Browne. Each day he hung an additional piece of equipment on it, so that by the time the liner reached the Irish Sea he resembled a Christmas tree. Unfortunately for him, one of his handy belt gadgets was a flashlight. At about 0400 on the morning the *New York* entered the Irish Sea, the ship's armed guard opened fire on what they took to be a submarine. The noise awakened all hands, some of whom arrived on the weather deck in dressing gowns to have a look. Not the young army reserve officer. Before going outside he put on his uniform, Sam Browne belt, dangling attachments, and all. Because it was a particularly dark night, when he tried to go back inside he could not find the door. Confused, he took the flashlight off his belt and turned it on. An enlisted man of the armed guard, patrolling nearby, was aghast at seeing light being used in submarine waters. He rushed to the spot, knocked the officer down, took the flashlight away from him, and heaved it overboard. When he had brusquely conducted the owner inside, he was shocked to find that the person he had knocked down and taken into custody was a commissioned officer. He apologized and released the man. Then, considerably perturbed, he reported the facts to the officer in charge of the armed guard, who in turn went to Halsey. The latter listened to the story, burst out laughing, and told the officer in charge that he would probably never hear anything more about the incident. He never did.

Lieutenant Commander Halsey arrived at Queenstown on 19 January 1918. Here he reported for duty to Captain Joel R. Poinsett Pringle, USN, Admiral Sims's chief of staff. Because Sims was usually in London, Pringle, who remained in Queenstown, acted as his stand-in. And because the destroyers and their attendant vessels at Queenstown were under the operational orders of Admiral Sir Lewis Bayly, RN, Pringle was appointed chief of staff to him also. Thus he was entered on the British navy list. Only an officer of Pringle's consummate tact and outstanding professional competence could have functioned in this awkward dual role.

Captain Pringle assigned Halsey a month's duty in the destroyer *Duncan* as a "makee-learn" (apprentice). The main task of the destroyers was convoy escort. They would also do some submarine hunting and rescue work. In their capacity as escorts, the destroyers picked up a convoy at a French, English, or Irish port and conducted it to a point 500 miles westward, beyond the usual World War I U-boat patrols. Here they picked up an incoming convoy and conducted it to port. When two or more Queenstown-based vessels operated together, the senior officer present, whether British or American, would assume overall command.

The destroyers normally spent five days at sea and three at Queenstown, and five days after each fifth trip to clean boilers. Admiral Bayly, not unkindly but crusty and demanding, expected all ships and personnel, short of a major catastrophe, to remain in top operational condition with this schedule. When a skipper reported to Bayly for orders, the admiral would address him by his ship's name rather than by his own and follow this immediately by asking him what the condition of his vessel was.

The expected answer was, "Quite all right, sir."

"When will you be ready to go to sea?"

The skipper who knew his way around would reply, "I'm ready now, sir," or at most, "As soon as I can complete with fuel, sir."

One young skipper, not yet initiated into this routine, replied to the first question with a list of needed repairs. Bayly heard him out, then replied with old-world courtesy, "Quite right! Quite right! If you are not prepared to get under way at three o'clock, no doubt you can find a tug to take you in tow, and you can complete repairs on the way to Kinsale Head."

On 7 February Halsey was promoted to the temporary rank of commander. On the nineteenth Captain Pringle gave him a destroyer of his own, the *Benham*. She was a fine ship but inexcusably dirty, the fault of her previous skipper. Halsey called his officers together and read them the riot act. They were good men, well meaning, but they had been badly led. They assembled their divisions, started to work, and in a few days had the *Benham* gleaming to their skipper's entire satisfaction.

It became evident to Halsey that the greatest danger to the destroyers and the ships they were escorting was not submarines but collisions, especially at night and in heavy weather. The *Benham* had several narrow escapes. The U.S. destroyer *Manley,* not so lucky, collided with a British vessel, jarring off the latter's deck several depth charges. These detonated in the water, setting off the *Manley*'s charges, which blew off her stern.

On 23 February, while the *Benham* was at sea escorting a troop convoy, Bill made an entry in a diary he was keeping at that time:

> Can see the *Antigone,* our nearest ship, is crowded with soldiers. Keep them on deck as much as possible while in submarine zone. Suppose other transports are equally crowded. You look at them and pity them having to go in the trenches. Suppose they look at us and wonder why anyone is damn fool enough to roll and jump around in a destroyer. Anyway we are all here for the same purpose, to get the Kaiser, and may that time be soon!

At 0430 on 15 March two lookouts on the *Benham* reported a large wake, which churned through the phosphorescent water toward the destroyer's bow, then apparently stopped. Halsey's impression was that a surprised U-boat had been forced to dive under the *Benham*'s bow. He thought surely he had a Fritz and was about to drop a depth charge when he looked over the side again and saw the wake jumping in all directions. It was a school of fish.

On 9 April Bill laid his first egg. The destroyer *O'Brien* made a submarine signal and picked up speed. Halsey called his ship to general quarters and sped after her. The *O'Brien* dropped a depth charge. Halsey didn't see anything, but he released a depth charge in the same area for good measure. Neither destroyer hit anything, and Halsey seriously doubted that there had been anything to hit.

On 18 May Halsey completed his last trip as commanding officer of the *Benham*. He called the crew to quarters and read his orders. He was assigned to command the *Shaw*, another destroyer. Leaving the *Benham*, Bill noted in his diary, "was quite a wrench, as I [had] grown fond of the crowd on board."

Obviously his fondness for the crew was fully reciprocated. His executive officer on the *Benham*, Lieutenant Julian Wheeler, recalled many years later that

> he was a perfectly marvelous character. He just exuded good nature, good feeling. Apparently he never disliked anyone. . . . Hardly five minutes would go by without his breaking into a smile. . . . He was the best shiphandler I've ever seen. He would put the destroyer alongside of a dock and, honestly, I think you could have put an egg in between the ship and the dock and it wouldn't have broken. It was beautiful. It was a work of art to see him handle the ship. . . . I remember when he was detached from the destroyer . . . , he'd only been in command a few months, why, every man on the ship manned the rails and some of them had tears in their eyes when he left.

Not long after taking his new command, Bill found himself senior officer present of a group consisting of the *Shaw*, another American destroyer, and two British sloops. It was "my first experience in multiple command in the war zone," he said. "I was as proud as a dog with two tails."

The monotony of convoy duty was relieved by the three-day breaks. These were generally lively, thanks in part to the hospitality of the Royal Cork Yacht Club, which the destroyermen called the Royal Uncork Yacht Club. For officers who had trouble getting back to their ships after a merry evening there, they created a special decoration—the "F.I.R.," for "fell in river."

One evening there Halsey and another destroyer skipper began bragging about their prowess hunting U-boats and wound up betting each other five pounds on the first person to bag one. As it turned out, neither skipper ever collected a farthing. In the few months since the Americans and British had adopted the convoy, the latter had been fully rescued from the danger of starvation, and U-boats had become hard to find.

Some were still being sunk, of course, and some were still sinking Allied shipping. Halsey never witnessed either event, but he was involved in a spectacular rescue attempt. On the evening of 1 July he intercepted an SOS from the U.S. troopship *Covington* reporting that she had been torpedoed and giving her position as 150 miles southwest of Brest. In the *Shaw* Halsey headed for her at twenty knots and reported his action by radio to Admiral Bayly. He did not request instructions, and he knew that Bayly did not expect him to do so. The admiral had stated more than once, and Halsey totally agreed, that the man on the spot is so much better informed than the man at headquarters that it would be superfluous for the latter to attempt issuing instructions.

When the *Shaw* found the wounded *Covington* around 0830 the next morning, three tugs had her under tow toward Brest, and two destroyers were standing by. She had delivered her troops to France and begun her homeward voyage in a convoy escorted by seven destroyers. By this period of the war U-boats were generally avoiding convoys, deeming them too hazardous to attack, but in this instance a bold German submariner had slipped in, fired one torpedo at the *Covington,* and departed unscathed.

The torpedoed transport was under easy tow at about five knots, a little down by the stern, listing to port about ten degrees. She had already made it about a third of the way back to port. To Halsey it appeared certain she could be saved, but at 1430 one of the tugs signaled to get the crew off immediately, whereupon the destroyers moved in and began lowering boats. By 1500 all hands were clear of the stricken vessel. Bill watched with dismay as her stern settled and sank, leaving some 200 feet of her bow sticking almost perpendicularly out of the water. Then she went down fast. When her bow disappeared beneath the surface, the water foamed and bubbled furiously under a cloud of black smoke.

It is worth recalling that transports carried more than two million Americans overseas without a single loss on the eastward voyage. On the return trip three empty American transports, including the *Covington,* were sunk by U-boats.

On the afternoon of 8 July the *Shaw* struck a submerged object. Oil appeared on the surface along with a keg marked "S.S. *Reserve,* c/o N.S.O. Aberdeen." Halsey thought his ship had surprised a submarine at periscope depth and rammed it before it could complete its dive. He radioed the facts and his opinion to headquarters, where the latter was received with hilarity. When he got back to port, he found that his fellow submariners had dubbed him "the Duke of Aberdeen," and some miscreant had even dashed off a song about his exploit:

> Last night over by Aberdeen,
> I saw a German submarine.
> The funniest sight I've ever seen
> Was old Bill Halsey's submarine.

On returning to Queenstown on 19 August, Halsey found his detachment orders. He called his crew together to say good-bye and express heartfelt regrets at leaving them. His officers, in a gesture of respect and affection, rowed him ashore. That evening the Uncork Club rocked as all the destroyermen ashore gathered to express their farewells to "old Bill, who sank a submarine from Aberdeen."

Two days later Bill sailed from Liverpool in the British liner *Aquitania.* His old ship, the *Shaw,* escorted her out. As the destroyer parted company with the liner, there rose on the *Shaw*'s signal lines message after message from old shipmates bidding Halsey bon voyage.

While the *Aquitania* plowed out into the Atlantic, Bill experienced a mixture of emotions: melancholy at the rupture of his many friendships formed in and out of Queenstown, cheerfulness at the prospect of an early reunion with his family, and vague dissatisfaction. Through no fault of his own he had entered combat too late, had in effect missed the war. That recurring thought filled him with a sense of frustration second only to the disappointment he was to feel twenty-four years later on missing the Battle of Midway.[10]

CHAPTER 8

AVIATOR

ON HIS RETURN to the United States from Queenstown, Lieutenant Commander Halsey had a brief vacation with his family and then reported to Philadelphia to take command of the new destroyer *Yarnall.* While he was awaiting her commissioning, the war ended, the armistice was signed, and President Wilson announced that he would attend the peace conference in Paris. Halsey, seeing the possibility for a brief, interesting shakedown cruise for his destroyer, requested and obtained an appointment to join the escort of the president's flagship, the *George Washington.*

As the presidential convoy, including the battleship *Pennsylvania,* approached Brest, it was met and conducted into port by a division of battleships flying the flag of Halsey's old commander, Admiral Sims, now commanding all U.S. naval forces in Europe. President Wilson went ashore in France on 13 December 1918. Instead of the early return home Halsey had anticipated, the presidential business in Europe was strung out over six months, during which time the *Yarnall* was assigned chiefly to ferry duty in the English Channel and North Sea.

Among the personnel ferried from the Continent were American mariners who were to man German merchantmen that their own crews had brought to England and surrendered. The ferrying assignment from England that Halsey found most enjoyable was conveying his old friend Assistant Secretary of the Navy Franklin Roosevelt and party from Dover to Ostend.

The most exciting task assigned the *Yarnall* during this period was supporting the first successful transatlantic flight. Three U.S. Navy seaplanes took off from Long Island in an attempt to fly to England via Newfoundland, the Azores, and Portugal. Halsey's destroyer was one of sixty surface vessels stationed along the line of flight for rescue missions. The *Yarnall*'s station was north of Spain, on the last leg.

The pilots undertaking the flight, all friends of Halsey, were Commander John H. Towers, Lieutenant Commander Patrick N. L. Bellinger, whose second in command was Lieutenant Commander Marc A. Mitscher, and Lieutenant Commander Albert C. Read. Bellinger and Towers were forced down on the first leg; the former was picked up by a freighter, and the latter contrived to taxi into the Azores. Read made it all the way. Halsey and his crew watched with pride as his northbound plane passed overhead.

On 29 June 1919, the day following the signing of the Treaty of Versailles, the presidential convoy sailed for the United States. Of an all-too-brief visit with his family at Blue Ridge Summit, Pennsylvania, Bill noted somewhat plaintively, "The children had grown much, but they remembered me."

Returning to New York, Halsey took the *Yarnall* to Hampton Roads, where she joined the new Pacific Fleet, then being formed to counterbalance the growing threat of Japan. Before the fleet sailed for the Panama Canal, Halsey was given additional duty as commander of a division of six destroyers. On arriving in the Pacific, the fleet as a whole visited several U.S. and Canadian west coast ports. The destroyers then established themselves at San Diego, which was to be their permanent base.

During this period a turnabout in the navy's shipbuilding program coupled with rapid demobilization made things rough for American destroyermen. The wartime shift from unneeded battleships to much-needed antisubmarine vessels led to an oversupply of destroyers at war's end. At the same time, officers and men who had joined the navy for the duration were seeking and obtaining discharges. As a result many destroyers had to be placed in reserve, and those that remained in service had barely enough men to keep operating.

Postwar unemployment at length brought in raw recruits to replace the dischargees. Then it was the task of the professional cadres to mold the newcomers into a body of effective destroyermen. Fortunately, superintending this process on the West Coast as Commander, Destroyers, Pacific Fleet, was Rear Admiral Henry A. Wiley, who throughout the lean days permitted no relaxation of discipline, smartness, or efficiency. His drive for excellence raised morale and inspired pride. Halsey says that at the end of Wiley's tour one could spot a Pacific Fleet destroyerman by the cock of his cap and the way he carried himself.

In January 1920 several of the fleet's destroyers, including the *Yarnall,* were ordered to the China station. The Orient-bound ships were commanded by officers commencing tours of sea duty. Since Halsey had been at sea two years, he stayed with the ships based at San Diego, where he commanded successively the destroyers *Chauncey, John F. Burns,* and *Wickes,* all the while maintaining his extra duty as division commander.

In June 1920, on returning from maneuvers, Halsey received from his mother the sad news that his father had died of a heart attack and been buried in Arlington National Cemetery. The elder Halsey had retired in 1907 in the rank of captain. Recalled to active duty during the war, he had been in charge of the equipment desk in the Bureau of Construction and Repair.

Admiral Wiley's successor in command of Pacific Fleet destroyers was Captain William V. Pratt, the future CNO. Pratt, taking over the superb organization his predecessor had shaped, drilled it into a fighting team. Wiley had given the destroyers smartness and self-respect; Pratt taught them teamwork and tactics. The latter had been Sims's chief of staff and right-hand man in the prewar Atlantic Destroyer Flotilla; he now carried on the Sims tradition and brought it to new heights.

Pratt's star squadron, which included Halsey's division, was commanded by Captain Frank Taylor Evans, son of "Fighting Bob." Halsey considered Evans a superlative seaman and shiphandler and said he knew more about marlinespike seamanship than any officer he had ever known. Evans drilled his nineteen destroyers in smoke work and in day and night maneuvers, using novel formations, which, TBS not yet being available, he controlled largely by whistle signals, much faster than flag signals or flashing light.

Of the three six-destroyer divisions in Evans's squadron, Halsey's was the outstanding one. And next to Halsey himself, the top performer of this division was Lieutenant Commander Raymond A. Spruance, skipper of the destroyer *Aaron Ward*. Spruance's biographer, Commander Thomas B. Buell, USN, himself a destroyerman, describes Halsey's commanding officers driving their 1,200-ton greyhounds at flank speed through intricate, audacious maneuvers that left observers awestruck: "Devout destroyermen beamed with approval (and sometimes envy) upon the division of graceful destroyers: bones in their teeth, rooster tails churning astern, pirouetting in unison with signal flags snapping in the breeze, plunging into steep seas and shaking green water from their forecastles—six commanding officers understanding one another perfectly, a brotherhood of proud and confident fighters and seamen."

In the spring of 1921 the squadron that included Halsey's division was ordered to simulate a torpedo attack on four battleships operating out of Long Beach. The squadron commander being ill, Halsey, as senior division commander, took over for this operation, and Ray Spruance took command of Halsey's division. With an independent flagship and three six-destroyer divisions, Halsey now had the biggest command thus far of his career.

He was directed to proceed to a position some 10,000 yards from the battleships and await a radio signal to launch the attack. There were no rules or restrictions; Halsey was free to improvise. In the role of observers, Captain Pratt was on Halsey's bridge and Captain Taylor Evans, now Pratt's chief of staff, was on the battleship flagship. Halsey positioned two of his divisions on parallel columns 1,000 yards apart, with the third division trailing—prepared to divide and reinforce the leading columns or to take an intercepting course should the "enemy" attempt to evade. When Halsey received the signal to attack, he led the way at twenty-five knots on what he hoped was an intercepting course and signaled his squadron to make smoke.

"What do you intend to do?" asked Pratt.

"What's the limit?"

"The sky."

"If the battleships maintain their course and speed," replied Halsey, "I intend to put them between my two columns and fire at them from both sides."

Because Halsey had been allotted only seventy-two torpedoes, he did not arm his flagship. He led one column at a converging angle toward the battle line, then turned away at 3,000 yards from the leading battleship and ducked into the smoke. The rest of the column followed in succession, each destroyer firing as she reached the assigned range. The second destroyer column made a similar attack on the far side of the battle line. The attackers fired thirty-six torpedoes and made twenty-two hits.

Each torpedo carried a dummy warhead with a soft metal nose that was intended to crush on impact, absorbing the blow and preventing damage to both weapon and target ship. It was driven by steam, produced by the combustion of a highly compressed air-water-fuel mixture carried in a so-called air flask. By the time the last destroyers in Halsey's column reached firing point, their distance from the leading battleship had been reduced to about 700 yards. At so short a range the air flasks were far from drained of their explosive mixture.

When a torpedo rammed into the *Texas,* its air flask detonated with a blast that crushed the battleship's steering engine room. The impact blew all her circuit breakers, thereby paralyzing most of the ship's electric gear. Two or more torpedoes exploded among the *Mississippi*'s screws and sent her to the yard for repairs. An explosive hit in the flagship *New Mexico* ruptured her shell plating and flooded her paint locker. Of the four battleships, only the *Idaho* was spared. In a minute and a half Halsey's destroyers had done a million and a half dollars' worth of damage.

Shortly before a similar exercise scheduled for the following day, Halsey and Captain Pratt were summoned to the flagship. Here the admiral gave them a dressing down, telling them in no uncertain terms that there was to be no repeat of yesterday's performance. They were to fire their torpedoes at no range closer than 5,000 yards. Thus restricted, the destroyers achieved only half a dozen hits. The battleships, moreover, were avenged when a torpedo ran wild and exploded under the stern of one of Halsey's ships, which had to be towed to Mare Island Navy Yard for extensive repairs. On returning to port, Halsey was startled to see in a San Diego newspaper a headline that read, "Destroyers Decisively Defeat Battleships."

The tour with the Pacific Fleet destroyers that brought Bill Halsey and Ray Spruance together laid the basis for their lifelong friendship. Spruance admired Halsey for his good fellowship and fighting spirit. Halsey respected Spruance's intellect and integrity. They shared utter devotion to duty and outstanding skill as leaders and shiphandlers. Their methods, however, differed. Spruance was a meticulous planner; Halsey operated at least partly on hunches. Halsey was public; Spruance was private. A key to Spruance's personality was economy. He went straight to the point with no superfluous moves. He gave no unnecessary orders. Many people regarded him as a cold fish, but Halsey knew better. A funny story or ridiculous situation that might cause Bill to roar with laughter would bring a mere twinkle to Ray's eye, but it was a twinkle of appreciation. By nature, Spruance practiced economy even in mirth.

Both Fan Halsey and Margaret Spruance had moved to the West Coast with their children to be near their husbands, whose friendship brought them together as well. In 1921 Halsey's daughter, Margaret, was a schoolgirl, aged eleven; Spruance's daughter, also named Margaret, was an infant. The boys, Billy Halsey and Edward Spruance, both six and just starting school, became great pals, forming another link between the two families.

The Pacific Fleet destroyermen were a hard-working, hard-playing, hard-drinking lot. Their weekend carousals became legendary. Bill and Fan Halsey took the boozy picnics, boisterous beach parties, and evening revels in stride, but for Ray and Margaret Spruance it was a new and rather startling experience. Because Ray's economy extended to his financial and social life, they had never done much entertaining. Though they tried to join in the fun with their friends they could never quite overcome their natural restraint.

At these affairs Ray learned an important fact about himself: he could not hold liquor. Each time he drank he suffered a ghastly hangover. One Sunday morning, after a beach party followed by a late-night fling at a popular Coronado tavern, Ray remained in bed with a numbing headache, exacerbated by the realization that his Panama hat was missing. Margaret, aware how much Ray prized it, set out on a search. The hat had been retrieved from the top of a palm tree, and they were holding it for him at the tavern. The story went around, and Spruance took a ribbing, mainly from Bill. For the rest of his life Ray either avoided liquor altogether or at social gatherings took no more than a sip and, after holding the glass a reasonable length of time, found a way to dispose of its contents.

In June 1921 Halsey attained the permanent rank of commander. In September he was detached from the destroyers and ordered to Washington for duty in the Office of Naval Intelligence. He left his command on a happy note, for on the day of his detachment ships of his division were awarded two of the navy's top accolades. The *Zeilin* had achieved the best record in gunnery of any destroyer in the navy. Halsey's own ship, the *Wickes,* received the battle efficiency pennant for general excellence.[1]

On a passenger vessel the Halsey family traveled from the West Coast to the East via the Panama Canal. Bill visited Fan's family a few days in Norfolk, then proceeded to Washington to assume his new duties.

It was the first time he had served in the Navy Department, also the first time he had commanded an LSD—large steel desk. He appreciated the value of intelligence gathering but had no training in it and hated paper work. In an organization like the Office of Naval Intelligence, dealing in large part with secret information, middle-ranking officers like Halsey—outsiders with almost exclusively seagoing career backgrounds—were likely to be consigned to the periphery, shuffling papers of no particular moment.

Those were the kind of papers Bill shuffled, at first. But he had a way of absorbing information and finding his way around, and within a few months he was handling more important work. When the post of naval attaché to Germany opened, he considered himself qualified for the billet and applied for it. His seniors also thought him qualified and endorsed his application. Halsey got the job.

He had no overwhelming desire to go to Germany, but at least the change would get him away from the papers and the LSD. He attended the Berlitz School for a quick course in German. Then in September 1922 he set sail by passenger liner from New York with Fan, Margaret, and young Bill. Disembarking at Plymouth, Halsey called on his old commander in chief, Admiral Sir Louis Bayly, and then with his family proceeded to London and Paris. In each city he paid a visit to the U.S. naval attaché for a briefing.

An attaché served in a dual capacity. He acted as adviser and aide to the ambassador, in which position he wore aiguillettes on the left shoulder. He also collected and sent to his department information of naval interest, gathered usually not by covert means but by observation and the study of public sources and any documents the host government made available to him.

The Halsey family left Paris after dark in a train that crossed during the night into Germany, where there was a change of railway personnel. The Halseys had dined in the *wagon-restaurant;* they now breakfasted in the same car, which had become the *Speisewagen.* As the waiter approached, Bill prepared to use his German, but the man sounded off with a rush of speech that was certainly faster than anything Bill had heard in the language school.

"What did he say?" asked Fan.

"How the hell do I know?" replied Halsey disgustedly.

At that the waiter burst out laughing and addressed them in American English. He had lived in the United States.

In Berlin, as soon as Halsey had made his family comfortable in a hotel, he

Halsey (*top row, second from left*) as a naval attaché in Germany, 1924 (courtesy of George Behrens)

went to the American embassy and presented his credentials to the ambassador, Alanson Bigelow Houghton of New York. Then he and Fan began hunting for living quarters. This took some doing. Not a thing was to be had in central Berlin. In the suburbs they found an apartment that cost a good deal more than Commander Halsey felt he could afford, but he had no choice. These were the days of Germany's wild postwar inflation. A mark could lose half its value overnight. The previous tenant had in fact given the apartment up because he could no longer afford the cost of transportation to his place of employment. He had taken lodgings for himself in the inner city and sent his family to Egypt, where living was cheaper—and safer, in view of the violence then rocking Germany.

For lack of fuel there was no heat or hot water in the Halsey apartment, but there were plenty of quilts and blankets. When the weather was especially cold the Halseys either stayed with friends who had heat or covered themselves with bedclothes. Somehow, possibly with electricity, the housekeeper who came with the apartment managed to do some cooking.

Commander Halsey had expected to send his children to school, but he dropped that plan when he realized with what intense hostility the Germans regarded nationals of the Allied powers. Their resentment grew out of the harsh terms of the Treaty of Versailles, which included annexation by victorious neighboring nations of territory Germany considered its own and ruinous demands for reparation payments to which most Germans attributed their country's widespread unemployment and runaway inflation. The United States had not fought as a formal ally of any nation, had not ratified the Versailles Treaty, did not threaten Germany in any way, and thus far was the only one of Germany's former antagonists to reestablish diplomatic relations with the defeated nation. The average German, however, unappreciative of these distinctions, lumped Americans with his former European enemies as objects of abomination.

Under the circumstances, Halsey asked Fan to find a governess for Margaret and little Bill. Mrs. Halsey hoped the children would learn to speak German, but the governess would have to have a fair command of English. One thing Fan learned right away was that by unwritten but ironbound tradition no governess in Berlin would take care of more than one child, even in desperate days like these when work was hard to find. After much interviewing, during which she tried to make herself understood in German with the dubious aid of a ten-cent dictionary, Fan found herself the employer of two reasonably acceptable women. That problem was solved only to give way to another one. Bill's governess had a *von* before her name and regarded herself as an aristocrat. She would have nothing to do, would not even sit down to a meal, with Margaret's tutor, whom she considered a commoner.

While Fan was refereeing tiffs between the hired help and running a household in an isolated apartment in a half-starved, semirebellious foreign city, her husband was more often than not out of town attending to his country's business. He visited Friederichshafen, where a small staff of American naval officers was observing the building of a zeppelin, the *Los Angeles*, for the U.S. Navy. He checked in at Koblenz, where U.S. army occupation forces were cooperating with the Joint Allied Commission for the Rhineland, and made the rounds of various plants in whose products his navy was interested, including the Goetz and Zeiss optical works and the Krupp plant at Essen. In his travels and in Berlin he was approached by various persons offering to sell inventions to the United States, often implying that if it did not buy, they would make a deal with the Japanese. Halsey, impressed with an improved range finder thus submitted, recommended it to the U.S. Navy, which tested and adopted it. Accredited also to the legations in the Scandinavian countries, Halsey had occasion to travel to Denmark and Sweden several times.

Because of the unwholesome atmosphere and the poor food in Germany, the Halseys decided to send Margaret to school in Switzerland in the fall of

1923. When she returned to Berlin the following summer, she was fluent in both German and French and could make herself understood in Italian. Bill, too young to leave his parents, remained in Berlin, where, says Halsey, he learned to speak German better than Halsey spoke English. Halsey insisted that he himself never advanced beyond the stage of poor "kitchen" German. One day Fan asked little Bill, "Who speaks better German, Daddy or I?"

Bill, evidently a born diplomat, replied, "Daddy knows more words than you do, but you say them better."[2]

In July 1924 Halsey was relieved as naval attaché and given command of the *Dale*, one of a half dozen American destroyers operating in European waters, mainly to show the flag. He settled his family in Switzerland for the duration of his tour.

In June the following year Halsey was transferred to command of the *Osborne*, then at Gibraltar with three other American destroyers. On 4 July the flagship of Admiral Sir Roger Keyes, commander in chief of the British Mediterranean Fleet, entered the harbor. To the gratification of the Americans present, Admiral Keyes had his ship fully dressed in honor of the U.S. national holiday.

Halsey's official call on the commander in chief was returned by Keyes's chief of staff, Commodore Dudley Pound, who as Britain's First Sea Lord in World War II would represent his navy on the Combined Chiefs of Staff. When Pound's barge, handled by a midshipman (called a "snotty" in the Royal Navy), came alongside the *Osborne*, it accidentally damaged the destroyer's prized teakwood gangplank. Pound promptly had it repaired and that afternoon sent the offending midshipman, a fine upstanding young redhead, over to apologize to Halsey. The latter did what he could to relieve the boy's obvious embarrassment. Afterward, Halsey told Pound plainly that no American naval officer would submit a junior to such humiliation, but when he mentioned the incident to other British officers, the invariable response was, "Splendid of Pound! Excellent training for the snotty!"

Cruising eastward in the *Osborne*, Halsey at Malta beheld his first aircraft carrier, HMS *Hermes*, on which he made an official call. To Bill, accustomed to the clean lines of modern surface warships, the carrier appeared ungainly and off-center, like a ship model built by a singularly ungifted child. Little did he foresee that two decades later he would command task forces of British as well as American carriers and come to appreciate their inherent grace and beauty.

Cruising in the Adriatic Sea, the *Osborne* reached Venice in September. Commander Halsey took leave to visit his family and bring them to Venice, where he established them at Hotel Grünwald on the Grand Canal. The Grünwald was a scant hundred yards from the *Osborne*'s anchorage. Ready to return to his ship in the morning, Halsey would step out on the balcony of his bedroom and hail the officer of the deck, who would send over a boat to pick up his skipper at the hotel's canal porch.

One day Halsey proudly brought young Bill, then ten years old, on board the *Osborne* to eat lunch in the officers' mess. During the course of the meal the boy remarked, "Daddy, this silver is just like ours."

Halsey agreed that the pattern was similar but reminded him that the family silver was engraved with his mother's initials, whereas the silver on the ship bore the initials USN.

"But, Daddy," protested young Bill, "we have some silver with USN on it, too."

It is not recorded that Commander Halsey again brought his son on board for lunch.[3]

In the fall of 1925, learning that Raymond Spruance would soon relieve him of command of the *Osborne*, Halsey called his high-spirited young officers together and warned them not to be deceived by their new skipper's sober manner. He assured them that they would never have a fairer or more capable commanding officer. After being detached, he took his family back to the United States, got them settled in Asheville, North Carolina, and the following January reported as executive officer of the USS *Wyoming*, then at New York.

During the year Halsey served in her, the *Wyoming*'s operations were fairly routine—spring maneuvers in the Caribbean with the battle fleet from the Pacific, followed by the usual practice at Guantánamo; back to the Caribbean in the summer on the midshipmen's cruise; and into the Philadelphia Navy Yard in the fall for conversion of the ship from coal to oil burner. It was during this tour that Halsey met and became friendly with a shipmate, Lieutenant Commander Oliver ("Scrappy") Kessing, an officer with whom he would be closely associated in World War II.

Selected in the spring of 1926 for the rank of captain, Halsey took his examination the following summer. As a consequence of his impending promotion, he was detached from the *Wyoming* in January 1927 and ordered to the Naval Academy as commanding officer of the USS *Reina Mercedes*. The *Reina*, like the *Don Juan de Austria*, was a former cruiser captured from the enemy in the Spanish-American War. Sunk by U.S. army guns in the harbor of Santiago, she was raised and brought to Annapolis for use as a receiving ship. Among her other functions, she served as a residence for the commanding officer, a prison ship for midshipman transgressors, and a barracks for various enlisted instructors and personnel who maintained the Naval Academy's boats.

When Fan Halsey came on board the old hulk and saw where she and her family were expected to live, she was appalled. "This will never do," she said. "I will never live here. It isn't a fit place for human beings."

There was much to be said for Mrs. Halsey's point of view. Except for cutting away partitions, not much had been done to make the living quarters, in the after part of the ship, habitable. The deck, which slanted upward toward the stern, was grimy, and there was everywhere a look of disrepair. On the other hand, the captain's living quarters were certainly commodious, and a stretch of uncovered afterdeck, which served as his porch or patio, provided a splendid view of the Severn River and the distant Chesapeake Bay, both of which on fine days blossomed with white sails. Steam for heating was piped in from the Academy's central heating plant. A cook, a steward, and a stewardsman were on board to look after the family's needs.

Facing the fact that she had no choice and weighing the advantages, which were not to be scorned, Fan relented. She would move in with the children, she said, provided she had a free hand to make the place livable. Halsey gave her the go-ahead.

Fan, superintending her staff and extra help, had the quarters scoured from deck to overhead, made sure that all needed repairs were carried out, and oversaw the conversion of dusty cabins into dainty powder rooms. She ransacked the navy warehouse for furniture to replace the less acceptable pieces already on board and pored over books and magazines for ideas on how to make the portholes look like curtained picture windows. Lastly, she brought in ferns and other plants to soften the nautical look of the living spaces. She thus turned the captain's quarters in the old *Reina* into a showplace where the Halseys were proud to entertain callers.

Among the most frequent were midshipmen. Captain Halsey, delighted when they appeared, undertook to entertain them with his seemingly inexhaustible collection of sea yarns—that is, until Mrs. Halsey pointed out the real reason for their coming. Halsey had been away from his family so much that he had the impression his daughter Margaret was still a little girl, instead of an attractive young lady approaching seventeen.

As for eleven-year-old Bill, Captain Halsey characterized him as "a typical dirty-faced boy with shirttail hanging out." He told the boy that he never wanted him to tell tales about the midshipman prisoners on board the *Reina*. But tattling on the midshipmen was far from Billy's mind. Each day he asked his father if he planned to attend the movie at the Academy that evening. If Halsey said no, Billy let the prisoners know the coast was clear for them to sneak out and see the show.

Halsey always remembered his three-and-a-half years on board the *Reina Mercedes* as one of the pleasantest tours of his career. His not-too-arduous duties—he was in charge of the midshipmen prisoners and of the boats and the men who handled them—left him ample time to enjoy the Academy's social and athletic events with his family and to make an occasional excursion to Washington or Baltimore, each less than an hour away.

In the spring of 1927 the Naval Academy received its first permanent aviation detail. It was based on the *Reina* under Captain Halsey's direct command; operations were controlled by Lieutenant Dewitt C. ("Duke") Ramsey and his executive officer, Lieutenant Clifton A. F. ("Ziggy") Sprague. Halsey, not wanting to take responsibility for something he didn't understand, told Ramsey he expected to be educated.

"Fine!" said Duke. "Let's go flying!"

Thereafter Halsey flew as often as Duke or Ziggy could find time to give him a ride. Like many a neophyte, he became an enthusiast and couldn't get enough of flying. His instructors at length let him take the controls, and eventually he began to consider himself an ace.

News of the lessons traveled. When his tour of duty at the Naval Academy was approaching its end, he received a letter from Rear Admiral James O. Richardson, chief of the Bureau of Navigation, saying that he understood Halsey was interested in aviation. Would he like to take the course at Pensacola? Bill jumped at the opportunity. He passed the general physical, but when it came to the very rigorous test for vision, he failed. This was hard for him to believe. He had always passed the usual eye examinations. But the aviators' test was much stiffer than anything he had encountered. Twice again at intervals of a few days he took the test and flunked.[4]

So it was back to the destroyers. In June 1930 Halsey was detached from the *Reina Mercedes* and ordered to assume command of Destroyer Squadron 14 of the Atlantic Fleet. It was not exactly a letdown. Halsey loved the destroyers and, as it turned out, he could pursue his newer love too. Planes now spotted the destroyers' torpedo runs, and Halsey was able to watch half the torpedo practices from his bridge and half from a plane, thereby running up an impressive record of hours in the air.

In January 1932, in response to the Japanese invasion of Manchuria, most of the U.S. warships remaining in the Atlantic, including Halsey's squadron, were transferred to the Pacific to join the main body of what was now called the U.S. Fleet. At about the same time the division was reduced from six to four ships, so that Halsey's squadron—three divisions and a flagship—shrank from nineteen to thirteen ships. In June, almost before he had got used to handling his diminished unit, Halsey was detached from his command.

Except for one year in the *Wyoming*, his seagoing duty for twenty-two years had been in destroyers. Now he was saying good-bye to them forever. For sheer length of service in the type his was an unmatched record, but the notion had got around that for an officer of Halsey's rank, diversified seagoing experience was indispensable for career advancement. Evidently some angel in the Bureau of Navigation thought otherwise. He was sending Halsey to Newport, as a student officer at the Naval War College, traditionally the gateway to high command.

Bill made arrangements to fly east commercially, a slightly risky venture in the tiny passenger planes of 1932, low-flying hedgehoppers that bounced in up-and-down drafts and made frequent stops for refueling. Fan Halsey, learning of her husband's travel plans, raised strong objections. "I received orders from my wife not to fly east," said Halsey. "We compromised, and I did not fly east."

The usual leisurely journey by sea and the Panama Canal was now out of the question, because daughter Margaret's wedding was impending. So Bill went by train and joined the families of the bride and groom assembling at Annapolis. On the evening of 25 June he proudly marched his daughter up the aisle of the "cathedral of the navy," as the stately Naval Academy chapel is called, and turned her over to her intended—tall, dark Lea Spruance. Margaret had vowed many times that she would marry only a naval officer, but as it turned out the man who won her heart didn't know the starboard from a sideboard. A distant relative of Ray Spruance, he was a rising star in the Du Pont enterprises. He took Margaret to live in Wilmington, Delaware, headquarters of the Du Pont empire.

Young Bill had come to the wedding from boarding school. His parents had sent him there to get him as far away as possible from reminders of the navy. He, like his father before him, had had his heart set on entering the Naval Academy. In every respect except for his eyesight he was qualified, and there was nothing wrong with his eyes that glasses could not correct. But in a superfluous holdover from sailing ship days, when glasses could be a real hindrance in storms at sea, the navy admitted to the line only officers with 20/20 eyesight.*

Trying to improve his vision, young Bill besieged oculists and ate carrots till he was sick of them, but he could never read the charts right. At last he gave up and went, not too unhappily, to Princeton, where he followed his father's Academy curriculum as closely as possible. For athletics, however, he chose boxing instead of football.[5]

In preparation for Captain Halsey's attendance at the War College, the Halseys moved again. Somebody once asked Fan her overall impression of navy life. Without hesitation she replied, "Buying and abandoning garbage cans all over the world." She and Bill rented a house at Jamestown, a small town on Conanicut Island in Narragansett Bay. From here each morning Bill took the boat across to the college, located on Coaster's Island, a stone's throw from the city of Newport.†

*In World War II a number of senior U.S. naval officers wore spectacles regularly while on duty. After the war otherwise suitable young men (and, later, women) with eyesight that had to be corrected by glasses were admitted to the Naval Academy.

†Conanicut was subsequently joined by bridges both to Newport and to the western shore of the bay.

There were two dominant studies that year at the Naval War College. One was a detailed analysis of the 1916 Battle of Jutland, the only engagement between the British and German battleship fleets. The other was the scrutiny of the so-called Orange Plan for relief or recapture of the Philippines, should they be invaded by the Japanese—a possibility considered not unlikely in view of Japan's recent conquest of Manchuria and attack on Shanghai.

The first study, carried out for its tactical lessons, proved largely a waste of time. In World War II there were only two battleship battles, both at night under atypical circumstances, and there was no engagement at all between battle lines. Like the Battle of Lepanto (1571), between galley fleets, and the Battle of Trafalgar (1805), between fleets of sailing ships of the line, Jutland was the culminating clash between obsolescent fleets of ships.

The second study proved immensely valuable. It acquainted future U.S. naval leaders with the geography of what was to be their principal World War II theater of operations. More important, it prepared them for the fantastic logistic efforts required to support the Orange Plan, which the Pacific Fleet actually put into effect in its 1944 drive across the Pacific.

Captain Halsey, aged fifty, was old to be taking the junior course. Chester Nimitz had taken it in 1922, when he was thirty-seven. Ray Spruance had taken it when he was forty, after six months as skipper of the *Osborne.* Now Spruance was again at the Naval War College, this time on the faculty. Captain Ernest J. ("Ernie") King, aged fifty-four, was there that year, but he was taking the senior course, having covered the basic studies years earlier by correspondence. King, it will be recalled, was the four-striper at the Naval Academy when Halsey was there as a plebe. Afterward their paths had crossed when both commanded destroyers in Sims's Atlantic Flotilla.

Admiral Sims was living nearby. Following World War I, he had been reassigned at his own request as president of the Naval War College. On his retirement in 1922, he continued to reside part of the year in Newport, and occasionally, when invited, gave lectures at the college. Both Halsey and King, at different times, paid social calls at the home of their former flotilla commander.

Aged seventy-four, the old warrier, still straight as an arrow, still handsome, had grown garrulous. While his visitors listened politely, he sounded off at length, explaining what was wrong with the navy. In his opinion, the Naval Academy, which he called a cross between a monastery and a trade school, was not preparing its students adequately to meet their problems either as officers or as adults. The selection process then in use, he insisted, was overlooking the best men for promotion. The navy, instead of scrapping its battleships, which Sims called obsolete, was preparing to build more of them as soon as the disarmament treaties lapsed. We may be sure that Halsey, staunch admirer of the old admiral, listened with rapt attention, whether he agreed with him or not.

In early April 1933 the student officers at Newport were shocked to learn that the navy's huge airship *Akron* had crashed in a storm off the New Jersey coast with a loss of seventy-three lives, including that of Rear Admiral William A. Moffett, chief of the Bureau of Aeronautics since its establishment in 1921. Captain King, who had served briefly as assistant chief of the bureau, now left Newport to attend his old chief's funeral—and to lobby for his job. Most naval aviators thought Captain John H. Towers, one of the navy's earliest flyers, should have the post, and certainly Towers himself thought so, but King had seniority, having been at the Naval Academy five years ahead of Towers, and he had just been selected for rear admiral. King got the job, and Towers had to wait his turn. At the end of the Naval War College course, King dropped by Newport to pick up his diploma.

Halsey received his diploma too, but his pride in it was overshadowed at that moment by a greater pleasure. Margaret in September had presented the Halsey and Spruance families with her firstborn, Peter.

The bad news was that Halsey had been ordered to command the naval station at Guantánamo, Cuba. Bill disliked the tropics in general and Guantánamo in particular. As it turned out, his good angel in Washington was still looking after him and the orders to Guantánamo were revoked. He was one of six naval or marine officers selected annually to attend the Army War College in Washington, while six army officers went to Newport.

For Bill Halsey it was another interesting year of study. In Washington the student officers analyzed famous campaigns of military history from the high-command point of view. Among Bill's classmates were Major Omar Bradley and Lieutenant Colonel Jonathan ("Skinny") Wainwright, whose names the public would know well in World War II.

In the spring of 1934, toward the end of his year in Washington, Halsey received a letter from Ernie King at the Bureau of Aeronautics offering him command of the carrier *Saratoga*. He would first have to take the aviation observer's course at Pensacola. This requirement grew out of congressional legislation specifying that commanding officers of naval air stations, seaplane tenders, and carriers had to be qualified aviators. Unfortunately, the experience of most qualified aviators was limited largely to flying. They had neither the training nor the seniority to command ships and stations. To fill these commands, selected senior officers were put through a course in aviation and designated aviation observers. The course was no mere subterfuge to evade the law, as some commentators supposed; it involved several months of intensive training in engines, radio, aerial navigation, gunnery, bombing, torpedoes, takeoffs, landings, and aerial tactics—everything, in fact, except solo flight.

The decision to step from destroyers to aircraft carriers required some thought. The *Saratoga* and her sister, the *Lexington*, were the largest warships in the world. Converted from unfinished battle cruisers by the terms of the 1922 Washington Conference, they displaced 33,000 tons and had a complement of 3,373 men—twenty-two times the tonnage and thirteen times the complement of Halsey's largest destroyers. Bill asked Fan to think over the offer for a couple of days and give him her opinion. She suggested that they seek the advice of Rear Admiral William D. Leahy, chief of the Bureau of Navigation, an officer whose judgment they greatly respected. Leahy, who may have been Halsey's angel in Washington, advised Bill by all means to accept the assignment.

Halsey, with happy recollections of the Newport area, rented another house in Jamestown for Fan and for his son when the latter was home from college. Then he began the long drive to Pensacola. At Tallahassee, his last overnight stop, doubts set in again. Fifty-one years old and a grandfather, he was about to begin competing with men less than half his age. He took a stiff belt of Scotch and didn't touch another drop of liquor for a solid year.[6]

When Captain Halsey arrived at Pensacola on 1 July 1934, Lieutenant Bromfield Nichol, his future assistant operations officer, was assigned as his instructor. Training began at once, half a day on the ground, half a day in the air.

Halsey arrived with, or soon conceived, a fixed intention of changing his designation from student observer to student pilot. As a carrier commander, he wanted to have a better understanding of a pilot's problems and mental processes than he could gain as a mere observer. As a possible passenger in a combat situation, he wanted to be able to take the controls should his pilot be killed or wounded. He made the change, still without being able to pass the pilots' test for eyesight. In his autobiography he discreetly professes ignorance of how he managed this impropriety, or who managed it for him.

Now Halsey was in direct competition with vigorous, keen-eyed young men, aged twenty-two or thereabouts. He was determined to play it straight, neither requesting nor accepting any special consideration. An instructor offered to have his parachute carried out to his plane before every flight. Bill would have none of that. He would carry out his own parachute like everyone else.

Student pilots were expected to make their first solo flight after no fewer than eight and no more than twelve hours of dual instruction. Bill went after twelve and had the thrill of his life during his solo. He was the last man in his class to go, and Pensacola custom decreed that the last soloist be tossed into the harbor, clothes and all. Halsey taxied up the seaplane ramp, where the rest of the class was waiting for him. When the grizzled captain stepped from his plane, the young officers, mostly ensigns, hesitated to lay hands on him. With a grin, Bill challenged them to comply with custom, and into the drink he went.

Halsey dreaded telling Fan about becoming a student pilot, particularly since he had failed to consult her about changing over. Finally he broke the news in a letter. By chance his announcement arrived in Jamestown the morning Margaret was due for a visit. When she got off the ferry from Newport, her mother came charging toward her angrily waving Bill's letter. "What do you think the old fool is doing now?" she demanded. "He's learning to fly! It must be that flying is the only thing left that will make him feel young again. He can't turn somersaults on the ground any more, so he's going to turn them up in the air. Did you ever hear such a thing? It's all your fault! You made him a grandfather!"

In the second phase of their training, the students practiced three-plane formation flying and were taught such elementary stunts as snap rolls, falling leaf, loops, and split-S. These and more complex stunts were no mere showoff antics but means of evading or gaining an advantage over an enemy. One day Halsey overshot the landing strip and had to ground-loop to avoid hitting a fence. The maneuver harmed nothing, but it knocked the growing cockiness out of the pilot.

So as not to advertise his nonregulation status, Halsey avoided wearing his spectacles. He had in mind also that if he became dependent on them for flying, he would be helpless if they became lost or broken. Without glasses he could not read his instruments and hence never knew precisely how fast, how high, or in what direction he was flying. He baffled pilots flying in formation with him as he unintentionally changed speed, altitude, and heading. Once on a cross-country flight it was Halsey's turn to lead the way back to base. Uncertain of his course, he tried an old trick, following the railroad track, or in aviation parlance, "flying the iron compass." Unluckily for Bill, this particular iron compass branched, and he picked the wrong branch. An instructor who regularly flew in the formation to "herd the sheep" when necessary let them follow Halsey's false lead for a while to teach them a lesson. What they learned was not to trust Halsey's sense of direction. At last, before the formation had flown out of the state, the instructor turned around and the pilots headed back to base, where they arrived long overdue. Their absence had caused some anxiety, but then the base was always anxious when Halsey was in the air.

The class next shifted from trainers to service planes, and Halsey soon distinguished himself in this type by flipping one over on its back. He claimed his landing had been fine until the plane's wheels hit a soft spot, whereupon the tail rose in the air and made a 180° arc. From across the field a crash truck and an ambulance, their sirens screaming, arrived only to find Halsey unhurt but very voluble in expressing his annoyance at what had happened. The instructors urged him to take a breather to soothe his nerves, but Halsey refused. Demanding another plane, he took off, put it through some of the more intricate stunts, and came back down as cool as you please.

From time to time a student pilot taxied into a boundary light, a mishap that won him membership in the "Order of the Flying Jackass." In due course Halsey's plane hit a light and went over on its nose. The squadron commander lined up his students and enlisted men, read out a citation, and buckled on Bill's chest the flying jackass emblem, to be worn at all times except when flying or in bed until another student "won" it by hitting a light. That happened in a couple of weeks, but Halsey refused to surrender the Jackass. "No," he said, "I want to keep it. I won't wear it around here any more, but when I take command of the *Sara*, I'm going to put it on the bulkhead of my cabin. If anybody aboard does anything stupid, I'll take a look at the Jackass before I bawl him out, and I'll say, 'Wait a minute, Bill Halsey! You're not so damn good yourself!' "

When Halsey arrived in Pensacola he weighed about two hundred pounds. Once he began taking the course, he lost weight a little too rapidly. It was nerves, no doubt, and the stifling summer heat, but Bill attributed it also to the poor rations being served in the mess hall. When the loss continued, he compromised his intention of living exactly like the other student officers by arranging to take his evening meals with a family in town.

The home cooking appealed to him, but even after autumn put an end to the summer heat, he continued to lose weight. At last Fan decided she had better come south, not only to look after her husband's health but to prevent his doing anything else foolish. When she arrived at Pensacola and caught a glimpse of Bill, she was aghast. He had weighed as much as 230 pounds. Even then, because he had a large frame, he had carried the weight well and not appeared fat. Now, weighing a mere 155 pounds, he was positively gaunt. At the hotel Fan expressed her dismay at Bill's loss of weight. He passed it off lightly, saying his new sylphlike figure rather became him. At that, Fan marched him over to a mirror and grabbed a handful of loose skin hanging from his jaw. "What are these wattles?" she demanded. "You look like a sick turkey buzzard!" What magic Fan invoked is not recorded, but by the time Bill got his wings he was up to 175.

Halsey was satisfied that he could fly a plane safely without wearing his glasses. What convinced him to the contrary was an operation called jumping the rope. The students, as practice for landing on a short field, were required to come in low, barely clear a rope hung with streamers and suspended between poles, and land as close to it as possible. On the approach, Halsey couldn't see the rope and streamers in time to adjust his flight path. Thereafter he wore spectacles until corrective lenses could be fitted into his goggles. As a result his flying improved noticeably. He never became an ace—his flying was started too late in life for that—but he was a competent pilot.

To meet his deadline for taking command of the *Saratoga*, Halsey was obliged either to shorten or condense the final stage of his training. He insisted on the latter, wanting to skip nothing. As a result his daily operations became a three-ring circus. He'd fly a fighter, dash to the beach for a flight in a patrol plane, then hustle back to the fighters. In twenty-eight days he spent more than eighty hours in the air.

At last it was over. The commandant of the Pensacola Naval Air Station pinned on Bill wings that he had honestly earned. He was now Captain William F. Halsey, naval aviator.[7]

CHAPTER 9

CARRIER COMMANDER

After leaving Pensacola, Captain and Mrs. Halsey spent most of his leave visiting their daughter and son-in-law. The Halseys then drove across country to Long Beach, where the captain took command of the *Saratoga*.

With her enormous mass the *Sara* was slower getting under way than the smaller vessels Halsey was used to, and she had to begin losing way at a much greater distance from anchorage or wharf. In other respects he found that, despite her vast size and power, she handled much like the destroyers he had put through their paces for twenty-two years. Once in an emergency situation in Coronado Roads, he employed with her the flying anchorage he had often used with destroyers. While she was making nine knots, he dropped the hook and backed her full. She was dead in the water by the time seventy-five fathoms of chain had been paid out.

Halsey knew little about carrier operations. He found himself in the odd situation of having to learn from his officers and men while as their commanding officer being fully responsible for their actions.

Most fascinating to Halsey was the intricate ballet of the flight deck. First, the aircraft were spotted, with fighters forward—the lightest of the planes, they needed the least length of deck to take off. Once the engines began to roar, drowning out the bull horn, orders had to be passed by flag and gesture. The Fox flag at the dip indicated that flight operations were imminent. The carrier heeled over as the captain headed his ship into the wind. The flag rippled up to the yard, an order to commence launching. Now the flight-deck officer and his assistants, by nodding, headshaking, beckoning, and pointing, maneuvered the planes one at a time to the takeoff spot and sent them hurtling along the deck. As the planes gained momentum, their tails lifted, and next, just short of the bow, their wheels left the deck.

Halsey, watching, sweated each plane into the air. A lack of momentum at takeoff or engine failure would drop the aircraft into the water. The wheels, if still down, could flip it over on its back. The pilot's chances of drowning were multiplied if he was knocked unconscious, if his safety belt or canopy jammed, or if he was run down by his own ship.

A carrier pilot, especially of a fighter plane, required training far in excess of the basic one-year course Halsey had taken. In addition to flying his plane, he had to know how to shoot, bomb, operate a radio, and navigate. His navigation was generally over empty seas with no "iron compasses" or other guides. There was always the danger that engine failure would force him to make a water landing and, during a war, the even greater danger of being shot down by enemy fire. Ship- and land-based seaplanes usually made a determined search for surviving flyers, but some wartime situations forbade such rescue operations.

The pilot, if he survived his mission, had to return, perhaps several hundred miles, to his carrier, which had also moved a considerable distance from the position where he left her and might now be hidden from his view by a low overcast. Radio could help him locate his ship, of course, but in heavy weather radio might fade, and in certain situations it was imperative that both ships and planes maintain radio silence.

When the pilot found his ship, he had the problem of landing over her stern with split-second timing. In even moderately heavy seas, he had to put his plane down, usually in the face of gusty and shifting winds, on a deck that, in addition to moving forward, was rising and falling and swinging right and left as much as thirty feet.

Halsey regarded the courage and skill of his aviators with deepest respect. To give them every possible break, he employed all legitimate measures—and some measures not so legitimate, as when, soon after Pearl Harbor, in defiance of Navy Secretary Josephus Daniels's famous order 99, he requisitioned bourbon to soothe the tense nerves of aviators returning from hazardous flights.

As carrier commander, Halsey had to deal not only with more complex operational and personnel problems but with expanded social responsibilities as well. There was for example the matter of the traditional courtesy call. Navy custom requires all subordinate officers and their wives to call on the commanding officer, who with his wife returns the call. During his destroyer days Halsey found the custom no great burden, but he foresaw that going through this routine with the numerous officers of the *Saratoga* and their wives would present formidable problems. So he resorted to the device necessarily used at large shore stations—a reception for all the families, with all calls thus considered made and returned. He picked what appeared a suitable date and had invitations sent out for an afternoon reception on the huge flight deck of the carrier. As it turned out, this was an unfortunate choice both of time and place.

In 1935 the *Saratoga* and *Lexington* anchored regularly beyond the Long Beach breakwater. The guests would thus arrive by boat and enter the ship via the accommodation ladder, a stairway outside the hull from the waterline to the hangar deck. As fortune would have it, the afternoon of the reception saw heavy swells rolling in from the Pacific. The motion thus imparted to the ship was accentuated on the high flight deck, and the platform of the accommodation ladder began to rise and fall. By the time Captain Halsey realized how ominous the conditions were it was too late to call off the party—the guests were on their way, none so bold as to defy the Old Man's summons.

On arriving alongside the *Saratoga*, even pilots accustomed to heavy-weather carrier landings found their agility and sense of timing sorely taxed when they tried to help the ladies out of the rocking boats and onto the undulating platform. The most effective technique, discovered after a series of mishaps, was to toss a lady onto the platform each time it and the boat reached nearly the same level. The wives then had to mount two more steep, narrow stairways. They arrived on the flight deck in a state of disarray. Here deck chairs were beginning to slide about, hors d'oeuvres were rolling off the tables, and the punch—unspiked, in compliance with Daniels's order 99—was sloshing in the bowls.

In no time at all ladies, some of whose faces had turned pale green, were retreating to sick bay. The rest of the guests, and Halsey himself, waited impatiently until someone could with propriety lead off by saying his farewells and departing. At last a brave couple made the move. The boats were sent for, and the remaining guests followed as swiftly as decorum permitted. All headed for the ladders. At the platform the wives who had been tossed on were now tossed off. Miraculously, except for a few bruises, there were no injuries.

Halsey was aware that his reception had been a fiasco. He regretted causing his guests such discomfort, but at least he had made the gesture: all calls were in effect made and returned. Or were they? Halsey's officers, who had already developed great affection for him, were sorry about the reception and decided to treat it as if it had never happened. One and all they and their wives came to pay courtesy calls on Captain and Mrs. Halsey. The Halseys, for their part, chose to consider the calls already returned.

Halsey soon found something else to fret about. Each time his gig approached the naval landing at Long Beach, there were Japanese ships at the nearby merchant pier, usually taking on scrap iron. The years since he had visited Tokyo with the Great White Fleet had done nothing to lessen his suspicion of the Japanese. He expressed the opinion that in due course they would be hurling the scrap back at the Americans in the form of bombs and shells. On putting out to sea, his ship encountered Japanese tankers heading in for oil. Regarding Japanese fishing boats as potential spy craft, he was irked when, in the midst of U.S. naval maneuvers, they seemed to pop up out of nowhere.

In the winter of 1935–36 the *Saratoga*, flying the flag of Vice Admiral Henry V. Butler, joined the U.S. Fleet to participate in Fleet Problem XVII, to be conducted in the Panama-Pacific area. Admiral Butler was Commander, Aircraft, Battle Force—usually called the carrier command—in which capacity he commanded all the carriers in the U.S. Fleet.

In working out the problem, CinCUS, Admiral Joseph M. Reeves, prepared to take his ships across the equator, an occasion for the shellbacks, who had crossed before, to initiate the pollywogs, who had not. Halsey had been over the line many times, beginning with his cruise in the Great White Fleet, which in circumnavigating the world crossed four times.

Admiral Butler, despite his sixty-one years of age and extensive naval experience, had never once been south of the equator. Halsey and other shellbacks dropped ominous hints within his hearing that it was unthinkable that any pollywog whatever should escape the initiation, which to put it mildly is anything but dignified. Halsey believed they had the admiral worried for a couple of days, but when the time of crossing came, the shellbacks magnanimously excused him from undergoing the prescribed indignities.

Fleet Problem XVIII, carried out the following winter in the vicinity of Hawaii, included war games. As usual, both the *Lexington* and *Saratoga* participated. The latter again wore the flag of Commander, Aircraft, Battle Force, now Vice Admiral Frederick J. Horne, whose chief of staff was Jack Towers, Ernie King's recent rival for the post of chief of aeronautics.

For the mock battles, the battle fleet was divided into two nearly equal parts. The *Saratoga* went with one part, the *Lexington* with the other. In imitation of the Battle of Jutland, the battleships cruised in columns abreast with an antisubmarine screen of destroyers and with cruisers and destroyers searching ahead. The carriers brought up the rear, each attended by a couple of plane-guard destroyers to rescue downed aviators.

When the opposing half fleets made contact the battleships of each, as at Jutland, deployed into single, usually parallel, columns. The *Saratoga* and *Lexington* took station on the disengaged side of their respective battleship lines. For air operations the carriers turned into the wind and moved about freely while remaining within visual range of their battleships. The assigned function of the carriers was fourfold: reconnaissance and shadowing, spotting fleet gunfire in surface actions and shore bombardments, helping to protect the fleet (particularly the carriers themselves) from attacks by enemy submarines and aircraft, and attacking a fleeing enemy force to slow it down so the pursuing surface ships could catch up and take it under fire.

Such exercises were of course highly unrealistic preparation for the sort of naval battles that were to be fought in World War II. A few farsighted officers had been advocating reform. In 1921 Billy Mitchell had demonstrated the vulnerability of ships to air attack. William S. Sims, when president of the Naval War College, had established on the game board that the carrier was preeminently an attack vessel, replacing the battlewagon as capital ship. In

1922 Sims's officer students at the college had invented the highly flexible circular formation and used the board to demonstrate its advantages. The following year, one of the students, Chester Nimitz, introduced the circular formation into the fleet. In 1925 he brought what was then the navy's lone carrier, the *Langley*, into the circular formation. The following year he and his patron, Admiral Samuel S. Robison, who had just been successively Commander in Chief, Battle Fleet, and CinCUS, were both assigned to shore duty. Thereafter the circular formation and the fleet-integrated carrier fell into disuse—either through negligence or because their merits were not recognized.

In the famous Fleet Problem X of January 1929 Admiral Reeves, then Commander, Aircraft, Battle Force, with his flag on the *Saratoga*, detached the carrier from the battle force with only its plane guard and steamed with her through the night toward the Panama Canal, against which he launched a surprise air attack at dawn. Theoretically, according to the umpires, the *Saratoga*'s planes blew up two sets of canal locks and damaged two airfields, demonstrating that a carrier not only could be used offensively but that it could operate successfully against shore targets.

Forrest P. Sherman, in 1931, advocated the carrier-centered circular task-force formation that was later to become standard, but carriers were not assigned permanent screens of cruisers and destroyers until after the Pearl Harbor attack. Then, with the battleships sunk or disabled, the carriers at last took over as the capital ships of the Pacific Fleet.

In 1937 Captain Halsey was little concerned with such tactical matters, if indeed he was aware of them. His business was to operate the *Saratoga*. En route to the scene of battle he took his orders from the commander of his half fleet; during air operations, from Admiral Horne.

Halsey enjoyed the games, in which umpires assessed damages to the ships, which were then expected to act accordingly by, for example, decreasing speed. When they declared a ship "sunk," she was required to haul clear and hoist her out-of-action signal. Such decisions, Halsey found, added realism to the games, but they also led to a great deal of dickering between ships' officers and umpires.

From Hawaii the *Saratoga* proceeded to San Francisco, where in June 1936 Jack Towers relieved Bill Halsey of his command. The latter then went to San Diego and, at North Island Naval Air Station, he was given an offer to return to the East Coast as copilot in a fast two-seater. In a telephone conversation with Fan, then in Wilmington, he mentioned the opportunity and received from her the most peremptory order to forget it. Bill explained that the pilot was an excellent aviator. That made no difference to Fan. He was not to fly across the country, particularly in a two-seater.

Bill couldn't resist the challenge. Deciding not to "compromise" this time, he took his place in the two-seater and headed east. The volume of his radio was too high throughout the flight and he thus arrived in Washington temporarily deafened. When he telephoned Fan to report his arrival, she realized from the slight time lapse since his last call that he had come by air. She thereupon ran up a considerable long-distance bill expressing her strong displeasure. Bill caught her tone but, his hearing still impaired, happily missed her words.[1]

Captain Halsey's next duty was as commandant of the Pensacola Naval Air Station, where he had lately been a student pilot. Here he met old friends and made new ones. The commandant's residence was venerable but well built, with high ceilings that made it comfortable in hot weather. To enjoy the night breezes, he and Fan slept on an upstairs screened porch. At first the roar of planes warming up in early morning at the nearby airfield made Fan nearly jump out of bed, but she soon became accustomed to the sound and slept through the daily pandemonium.

The superintendent of aviation training at Pensacola was Commander Gerald F. Bogan, who in World War II would command a Third Fleet task group under Halsey. In May 1937, recognizing Bogan's abilities, Halsey had him transferred to his own office to be executive officer. Many years later, when Bogan, then a retired vice admiral, was asked how Halsey impressed him at that time, he said that the captain had been "very friendly and cooperative. . . . [A] very fine man. Not a mastermind, by any means, but a very sound, fine person."

In June 1937 Lieutenant William H. Ashford arrived at Pensacola and reported to Commander Bogan. If, as it appears, the lieutenant's services had been requested by Halsey, Ashford was unaware of the fact. Bogan informed him that he would be aide to the commandant. Ashford, who had heard a great deal about Halsey, all of it good, was delighted.

Thus began a long and friendly association. It will be recalled that Bill Ashford was still Halsey's aide and flag lieutenant at the time of the Pearl Harbor attack and subsequently, in the same capacity, accompanied him to the United States when Halsey required special treatment for dermatitis.

The duties of commandant not being particularly burdensome, Captain Halsey decided to retake the student pilot course to catch up on developments in aviation, particularly increased reliance on instruments. At that period the student, in the front cockpit, had a hood placed over him so that, unable to see anything but the instruments, he was obliged to rely on them. An experienced safety pilot sat in the back cockpit, prepared to take over if the student got himself in a jam. Halsey was so fascinated with instrument flying that he kept increasing his time in the air until the instructors protested that they were neglecting their regular students.

One duty Halsey enjoyed at Pensacola was entertaining officers, officials, and other dignitaries who came to observe the aviation school's methods of instruction. At evening meals in the commandant's quarters Fan showed herself ever the witty and gracious hostess, yet it was during this period that she began to experience the spells of depression, alternating with hyperactivity and talkativeness, that would cast a deepening shadow over her and Bill's lives.

Halsey had been selected for rear admiral in December 1936, but he was not promoted until March 1938, when a vacancy occurred in the grade. Much as he enjoyed the post at Pensacola, he now had to move on to a billet more suitable for his new rank. In May, relieved as commandant by his friend Captain Aubrey W. ("Jake") Fitch, Rear Admiral Halsey was ordered to take command of Carrier Division 2, comprising the brand-new sister carriers *Yorktown* and *Enterprise*.[2]

When Halsey arrived at Norfolk to assume his new duty, the *Yorktown* was on her shakedown cruise. The *Enterprise*, back from her own shakedown, was undergoing repair and alterations in the navy yard. Bill was aware of the challenge of preparing his two new carriers and their green air crews to join the veterans *Lexington, Saratoga,* and *Ranger* in the next fleet problem. Wasting no time, he hoisted his flag on the immobilized Big E and moved to the Norfolk Naval Air Station, where the two carrier air groups were forming. Here he actively participated in operations to get the groups in shape.

From time to time, especially when foul weather grounded the planes, Halsey would assemble the pilots in a big drill hall for lectures, discussions, and war games. After studying various fleet formations, the groups unreservedly favored the circular over the line formation for carrier operations. Further studies concerned such matters as how to provide for antisubmarine support when a carrier was involved in launch and recovery and whether to turn the entire force into the wind or let a carrier go off on its own to conduct air operations.

Admiral Halsey had early spotted one of the squadron commanders, Lieutenant Commander Miles Browning, as intelligent and knowledgeable and appointed him his deputy in conducting the discussions. Thomas H. Moorer, a future CNO and chairman of the Joint Chiefs of Staff, then a junior lieutenant, recalls the difference in their styles. Halsey, says Moorer, "had a knack of involving everybody in the discussion." He was genuinely interested and recognized merit in good ideas whether coming from himself or the most junior officers. "Everybody," according to Moorer, "was crazy about Admiral Halsey."

Browning, on the contrary, they found somewhat cold. He tended to lecture rather than hold discussions, often opening on a sarcastic note such as,

"If you are so fortunate as still to be in the navy when we encounter the Japanese. . . ." He knew his business, the pilots agreed, but his aloof and condescending manner prejudiced them against his opinions and advice.

During the summer Halsey's two air groups were invited to participate in a Red Cross celebration in Washington, D.C. They accepted and flew over the city in the formation of a cross, with Halsey at the controls of his plane leading the parade. The cross, said Halsey, "was a rather cumbersome thing to make a 180° turn with, but we succeeded in doing it."

By the end of 1938 both the *Yorktown* and *Enterprise* were shaken down, repaired, appropriately modified, and ready to go. Accompanied by four destroyers, they departed Hampton Roads on the second day of 1939 and headed for the Caribbean to join the battle fleet in spring maneuvers. They touched at St. Thomas, put into Guantánamo for fuel and provisions, then headed for a rendezvous near the Panama Canal.

Whenever weather and other conditions permitted, Halsey exercised his carriers and their air groups. He flew his flag alternately on the *Yorktown* and *Enterprise* to better judge the qualifications and progress of their officers and men, air and surface. There is no record of his opinion of Captain Charles A. Pownall, commanding officer of the *Enterprise*. It is known only that Pownall entered World War II with an unblemished service reputation but failed to measure up in combat as commander of the Pacific Fleet carrier force. On the other hand, there is a record of Halsey's irritation at the indecisiveness of the *Yorktown*'s Captain Ernest D. McWhorter. Gerry Bogan, who at this time was McWhorter's navigation officer, tells a story:

> One day in the Caribbean we were landing planes and we had about four more to put on the deck. There was a very light wind, and we were making perhaps twenty-eight knots. Up ahead of us was one of those little tropical showers with a rainbow through it—nothing serious. Captain McWhorter began to worry about what to do, so I said, "Captain, there'll be a few drops of rain on the planes. It won't bother the pilots at all. Just go ahead with the landing." He got more and more concerned, and finally he said, "I think I'll go down and ask the admiral." So he went down to the flag bridge where Admiral Halsey was.
>
> I thought Halsey would throw him off the ship, so I leaned over the railing of the ladder to see what would happen, and all Halsey said was, "Well, Mac, I don't care. If you're not in a hurry, why don't you just go around [the storm]? It'll only take a few minutes." The decision had been made for him, and McWhorter's face lighted up like a Christmas tree. He got to the first step of the ladder and said, "Admiral, shall I use right or left rudder?" . . . Halsey's aide told me that . . . Halsey was so mad he said, "I'll see that he never gets promoted."

But Halsey didn't have the heart to do anything of the sort. McWhorter made rear admiral and commanded the air group of four carriers during the U.S.

invasion of French Morocco in November 1942. Thereafter he held no command of major consequence.

In the forthcoming maneuvers Halsey would be serving directly under Ernie King, now vice admiral and Commander, Aircraft, Battle Force. As a fellow destroyerman and student at the Naval War College, Halsey had found him pleasant company, but King was ruthlessly ambitious, and in a position of command he was known to be an utter perfectionist—harsh, arrogant, impatient, demanding. Halsey, with a pair of greenhorn carriers, looked forward with some trepidation to operating under him.

In participating in Fleet Problem XIX the preceding year, King had won navy-wide fame by staging successful mock air raids on Pearl Harbor and the Mare Island Navy Yard. Widespread illness on board the *Lexington* kept her out of the first attack, but with the *Saratoga* King approached Pearl Harbor from the northwest under a weather front, achieving complete surprise and incidentally providing a scaled-down preview of the Japanese attack of three and a half years later. He had both carriers for the raid on Mare Island and managed to whisk them safely away in darkness, using the *Pensacola*, lighted up like a passenger vessel, to distract the picket destroyers.

King counted on this stunning success, plus any kudos he could garner in the forthcoming Fleet Problem XX, to trigger a quantum jump in his career. He had his eyes on nothing less than the navy's top professional command, CNO, a post currently held by Admiral William D. Leahy, who was due to retire in May 1939.

For King Fleet Problem XX was crucial, not only because it was taking place just before the post he coveted fell vacant but because both Admiral Leahy and President Roosevelt would be present to observe the windup. Roosevelt, who often referred to the U.S. naval service as "my navy," personally selected officers to fill the top naval billets, sometimes without the advice of the secretary of the navy, the CNO, or the chief of the Bureau of Navigation.

King was aware of obstacles in the way of his goal. One was his reputation for heavy drinking. Another was his lack of experience commanding battleships. The battleship admirals who dominated the navy in 1939 tended to regard naval aviators as specialists, unsuited for the highest commands.

Two days after Halsey's Carrier Division 2 left Norfolk, the U.S. Fleet sailed from West Coast ports for the Canal Zone. The *Saratoga*, in need of an overhaul, had to be left behind. When Carrier Division 1, the *Lexington*, King's flagship, and the much smaller *Ranger*, passed through the canal, King stood on his bridge in considerable pain, his face grim. A few nights before, walking on the darkened deck, he had stumbled on a deck grating and injured his leg. The ship's doctor had ordered him to stay in bed until it was better. King, having heard rumors that he was drinking at sea, dared do nothing of the sort. If he failed to show himself, the rumormongers might pass word that he was drunk in his cabin. As Carrier Division 1 stood off Cristobal to rendezvous with Halsey's division, King was in the foulest of moods.

James S. Russell, an officer in the *Yorktown*, describes the rendezvous from Carrier Division 2's point of view:

> As *Lexington* and *Ranger* came over the horizon, *Lexington* blossomed with an unbelievably large display of signal flags. In *Yorktown* our signalmen were hard put to bend the flags on the many hoists, yet they were intent on speed and smartness. In the intense activity on the signal bridge, one signalman failed to get a snap hook into the ring on the downhaul of a hoist. This hoist of four flags therefore took off and flew horizontally from our yard as if it were a clothesline of dirty linen . . . [A]n opportunity did not arrive for at least a half hour for us to haul down the offending flag hoist which was thus adrift and advertising our ineptness.

At his first inspection of the combined carrier divisions, King humiliated Halsey by detaching three officers of his staff, which he considered too large.

On leaving Cristobal, King formed his two carrier divisions, together with their assigned plane-guard destroyers, into a single formation, making, as he said, "an impressive and unprecedented display."

Whenever Admiral Edward C. Kalbfus, Commander, Battle Force, released the four carriers from his battle line, King would operate them together or in pairs, using screening vessels Kalbfus assigned them. King requested the permanent assignment of a destroyer squadron and a division of heavy cruisers, which he would train to operate exclusively with his carriers. This arrangement became standard practice early in World War II, but in 1939 the traditionally minded line admirals believed the cruisers and the best of the destroyers could not long be spared from scouting and screening for the battleships. Hampered, King nevertheless solved most of the problems carrier forces would face during operations in the coming war.

Halsey was his most apt pupil, but apt or not, he more than once felt the lash of his senior's temper. One morning, for example, an officer on the hangar deck of one of the carriers of Halsey's division made a mistake that delayed launching. King, timing the drill with a stopwatch, promptly cracked down with a signal demanding to know who was responsible. Halsey made the only possible reply: "ComCarDiv 2," that is, himself. King's signal had been absurd; he knew perfectly well that Halsey and Halsey alone was responsible for everything in his division; if one of his people committed a fault, it was up to Halsey to see that that person was penalized or at least reprimanded.

Early in February the U.S. Fleet steamed across the Caribbean Sea and based most of its ships in Guantánamo Bay, sending the overflow to anchor in the Gulf of Gonaives across the Windward Passage in Haiti. From these anchorages it carried out the four-part Fleet Problem XX.

In part one, which consisted of a mock battle, Halsey had a success that King was quick to acknowledge. Despite the latter's habitual scolding, he actually held Halsey in high regard. Kalbfus had tried using King's carriers as bait to lure the enemy cruisers within reach of his battleship guns. The ruse failed. "Finally," said King, "when the time for the end of the problem had nearly arrived, Halsey was permitted to forge ahead with his two new carriers and locate the enemy. Being a good fighter, he succeeded in disposing of the enemy cruisers by air attack alone without the aid of Kalbfus's heavy ships."

From this point on Admiral Halsey was little more than an onlooker. In part two the carriers served merely to reconnoiter for the battle force. In part three Kalbfus put King in command of a raiding force that included the *Lexington* and *Enterprise*. Halsey went along chiefly for the ride. The fourth and last part, witnessed by President Roosevelt in the cruiser *Houston*, consisted of an antiquated Jutland type of action. Of the carriers, only the *Ranger* participated, and she achieved nothing.

Following this unimpressive conclusion, all the participating ships joined the *Houston* in an anchorage off the island of Culebra. Here the flag officers of the fleet, led by the CinCUS, Admiral Claude C. Bloch, called on Commander in Chief Roosevelt to pay their respects. King and Halsey boarded the *Houston* together.

To Halsey, Roosevelt had always been a regal figure. Now, although his legs were shrunken with polio and he was unable to rise without help, Roosevelt appeared even more majestic than in his vigorous youth. He was in high spirits this afternoon. He knew all the admirals and greeted them each by name with a bit of good-natured, personal banter. Among the callers there was considerable fawning. Most of them had stars in their eyes, hoping to fill the forthcoming vacancy as CNO or one of the other top commands at the president's disposal.

For King, with only four more years before mandatory retirement at age sixty-four, it was now or never. Yet when his turn came, he could not bring himself to follow the example of some of the others, who were trying a little too hard to ingratiate themselves with Mr. Roosevelt. Rather stiffly he said that he hoped the president was pleased with recent progress in naval aviation. Yes, Mr. Roosevelt was pleased. They chatted for a few moments, then the president laughed and warned King half teasingly to watch out for the Germans and Japanese.

Halsey, unselfconscious, greeted Roosevelt as an old friend. He was one of the few officers present with no favors to seek. As one of four U.S. naval aviators with flag rank, he had only to wait his turn to fleet up to the billet King now had. There would be time enough then to think about what he next aspired to.

Halsey was aware of King's ambitions, as were most of his fellow flag officers. King was not reticent about his goals. On his fitness reports he had stated that his next duty preference was either CNO or the equally responsible and only slightly less prestigious billet of CinCUS. To his bitter disappointment, he got neither. Harold R. Stark was selected as the next CNO and James O. Richardson as the next CinCUS.

King, reverting from vice to rear admiral, was appointed to the General Board, an honorable but not particularly distinguished retreat, traditionally awarded as the final billet for flag officers who didn't quite make the grade. Apparently King's otherwise brilliant career was at an end. Nobody could have foreseen that in less than three years he would be the only officer in the history of the navy to hold simultaneously both the high posts to which he had aspired.[3]

Following Fleet Problem XX, the U.S. Fleet went north to Hampton Roads, whence after a few days it was expected to proceed to New York to participate in the gala opening of the 1939 World's Fair. On 19 April, however, while Halsey was driving his car in Norfolk, an excited yeoman from his staff waved him down with the news that the New York visit was canceled. The fleet had been ordered to depart early the next morning for the Pacific. The change was so sudden and unexpected that some officers and men failed to get the word and had to rejoin their ships on the West Coast. By the time the fleet had transited the Panama Canal and reached San Diego on 12 May, whatever war scare had dictated its hasty remove had apparently dissipated.

Not long afterward, Vice Admiral Charles A. Blakely relieved King as Commander, Aircraft, Battle Force, and the latter departed for Washington to assume his duties with the General Board. Blakely was one of the navy's four aviators with flag rank. His assumption of the carrier command meant that Halsey's turn was one step nearer. Meanwhile, Bill enjoyed a slight rise in seniority on being detached from Carrier Division 2 and ordered to Carrier Division 1, with his flag in the *Saratoga*.

In the summer of 1939 the U.S. Fleet conducted war games jointly with the army. The battle fleet convoyed a division of invasion troops to a California beach, which was defended by other troops. Halsey commanded the "air force," one carrier and its planes, which harassed the army's shore-based air. Halsey's planes made simulated attacks on the army's airfields, on one occasion penetrating 200 miles inland to blast bombers from the East Coast newly based at Reno. The commanding officer at Reno, certain that carrier planes could not reach so far, had not bothered to post patrols. Some of Halsey's fighter pilots dropped alarm clocks by parachute with notes suggesting it was high time the army woke up.

Fleet exercises for the spring of 1940 were to be in the Hawaiian area. On 1 April, the evening before the fleet was to depart San Pedro for Hawaii,

Admiral Richardson invited his flag officers to dine on board the flagship *Pennsylvania* and meet Charles Edison, the new secretary of the navy, who would go with them. The secretary was accompanied by two naval aides, a civilian friend, and to the surprise of Halsey and the other officers, Ernie King, whom they supposed to be safely on the shelf with the rest of the General Board.

The officers cornered the younger aide, Lieutenant Robert H. Rice, to find out why King was along. Rice wasn't sure. He knew only that the secretary was visiting fleet and shore installations to acquaint himself with the navy. Even King would have been surprised to learn that he was there on the advice of Mr. Roosevelt. The president had telephoned Edison and suggested that since King was available and well informed on all naval matters, the secretary might wish to include him as a tour guide.

While commanding Carrier Division 1, Halsey introduced, over considerable opposition, two time-saving measures modifying communications between ships and aircraft. Initially, each ship and its planes shared a private radio wavelength. A cruiser notified of a contact by its scout plane would readdress and relay the message to the flagship, which would readdress and relay it to the carriers before the carrier commanders could take action. Under the Halsey plan all scout planes shared the same wavelength so that any contact reported would immediately alert the carriers.

Halsey's second reform replaced key transmission with radiophone. Teaching Morse code takes months; learning to use a radiophone takes minutes. The communicators set up a test to substantiate their contention that voice radio can easily be jammed, but ships and planes 150 miles apart still exchanged oral reports with ease.

Halsey's turn to fleet up came at last. On 13 June 1940 he was detached from his command and relieved Admiral Blakely as Commander, Aircraft, Battle Force. He was also assigned duty as Commander, Carrier Division 2, and promoted to the temporary rank of vice admiral. He now commanded all the carriers and carrier air groups in the U.S. Fleet.

Not long after the fleet reached Hawaii, the CNO, Harold Stark, notified Admiral Richardson that it would be based at Pearl Harbor indefinitely. Richardson, in considerable dismay, demanded to know why. "You are there," replied Stark, "because of the deterrent effect which it is thought your presence may have on the Japs going into the East Indies."

To Richardson, such reasoning was arrant nonsense. Pearl Harbor at that time was a comparatively primitive base, lacking adequate repair shops, fuel storage, wharves and docks, and cranes and other loading equipment to service a major fleet. Moreover, most supplies for ships based there would have to be hauled 2,000 miles from the mainland. A fleet kept in readiness at West Coast ports, he believed, was a more credible deterrent than one ill served and exposed in the middle of the ocean. He saw to the construction of facilities and housing at Pearl but continued to complain, twice visiting Washington to urge the Navy Department, the State Department, and the president to bring the fleet back to the United States. Early in 1941 Roosevelt, losing patience, ordered Richardson relieved and replaced him with Halsey's friend and classmate, Rear Admiral Husband E. Kimmel, Commander, Cruisers, Battle Force.

Meanwhile, with the outbreak of war in Europe, the Atlantic Squadron had been redesignated Patrol Force, U.S. Fleet, and given the task of keeping belligerent forces out of American waters. Following the fall of France in June 1940, Congress appropriated four billion dollars to begin building the two-ocean navy that had long been under discussion. In September, when Japan formed an alliance, the Tripartite Pact, with Italy and Germany, the U.S. armed forces concluded that war was inevitable, and the navy assumed that it would indeed be fighting in two oceans. In line with this thinking, the Navy Department reorganized its operational forces. On 1 February 1941, the day Kimmel relieved Richardson, the much-enlarged Atlantic Patrol Force became the U.S. Atlantic Fleet, and the U.S. Fleet became the U.S. Pacific Fleet. Admiral King, now off the shelf for good, was appointed commander in chief of the former (CinCLant); Admiral Kimmel, commander in chief of the latter (CinCPac). Vice Admiral Halsey, commanding the carrier forces of the newly designated Pacific Fleet, retained the title Commander, Aircraft, Battle Force, but was now informally, and more accurately, called Commander, Carriers, Pacific.

Kimmel, in becoming commander in chief with the temporary rank of admiral, jumped up thirty-one numbers. He was surprised, as were most other officers, at his being elevated over so many men until lately his seniors. Halsey was not surprised. A longtime close friend of Kimmel, he considered him superbly competent and attributed his selection to the impression Kimmel must have made on Secetary of the Navy Frank Knox when the latter had visited the fleet the preceding summer.

As his foremost task Admiral Kimmel trained a core of officers and petty officers, surface and air, for the torrent of new construction that would result from the congressional appropriations for a two-ocean navy. While retaining his office on board the flagship *Pennsylvania*, he established headquarters ashore at the Pearl Harbor submarine base to make himself more accessible.

Admiral Richardson, observing that the fleet's regular anchorage at Lahaina Roads, between Maui and Lanai, was exposed to submarine attack, had concentrated the ships inside Pearl Harbor. Admiral Kimmel divided them into three task forces, each comprising battleships, cruisers, destroyers, and one or two carriers, and each commanded by one of his three vice admirals, William S. Pye, Halsey, and Wilson Brown. Despite a critical fuel shortage, Kimmel tried to keep two of the task forces at sea at all times exercising the men and the guns. To maintain morale, however, he normally brought most of the ships into Pearl Harbor for weekends.

One bitter fruit of Kimmel's training plan was that, to form cadres for new construction, trained men were steadily drained away from the Pacific Fleet and replaced by raw recruits. At any given time more than half of Kimmel's officers were newly commissioned reserves, and there were occasions when seventy percent of the men on board some ships had never heard a gun fired.

The pilots who came to the carriers were not newly commissioned—they had had basic training and more at schools like Pensacola—but Halsey realized better than most senior officers that they were not getting sufficient experience on shore before attempting war games with the carriers. John S. ("Jimmy") Thach, destined to be one of the navy's outstanding aces, shared Halsey's concern. When his squadron was ordered on board the *Enterprise* to participate in a big fleet problem, he knew his men were not ready. He fought his way past even the irascible Miles Browning, now chief of staff, to lodge his protest directly with Halsey.

Far from taking offense at the young officer's effrontery, the admiral listened sympathetically while Thach explained that his "kids" hadn't even had an opportunity to fire a gun. "I've got to have a thirty-day period at least where I would like to fly day and night, including weekends."

Halsey asked him when he wanted to begin. "As soon as possible," replied Thach.

"How about this afternoon?"

"Wonderful," said Thach, "but we're going into this fleet problem."

"I'll just let you out of the fleet problem," said the admiral and ordered Thach to fly ashore with his squadron before the *Enterprise* traveled beyond flying range of Oahu.

Halsey was enormously encouraged when the navy began equipping his ships with a mysterious top-secret invention, radar, by means of which his officers would be able to detect enemy ships and planes in darkness or in fog. "If I were to give credit to the instruments and machines that won us the war in the Pacific," he wrote, "I would rank them in this order: submarines first, radar second, planes third, bulldozers fourth."

Halsey noted with grim satisfaction that, in response to the continued aggressions of the Japanese, the United States had embargoed the shipment to Japan of iron and steel, including those shiploads of scrap over which he had fretted at Long Beach. In July 1941, when the Japanese extended their occupation to all of Indochina, the United States, Britain, and the Dutch government-in-exile countered by freezing Japan's assets, thus cutting off its supply of oil from the United States, the Persian Gulf, and the East Indies. Since the country could not continue its conquest of China without oil, the U.S. armed forces were more than ever convinced that Japan would invade the Dutch East Indies, its nearest source, as well as the Philippines and other positions flanking the shipping lane from the East Indies to the home islands. B-17 bombers that would have been priceless in defending Pearl Harbor passed through Hawaii, proceeding via Wake and Guam, to the Philippines. Meanwhile, the Pacific Fleet was putting itself on a war footing, taking measures that included stripping ship, that is, removing all inflammable or splinter-prone gear not required for fighting.

Halsey was gratified in mid-September when his old friend Raymond Spruance, now a rear admiral, arrived at Pearl Harbor to assume command of the four heavy cruisers of Cruiser Division 5 in Halsey's Task Force 2. Ray had brought his wife and daughter with him on board the passenger liner *Lurline*. Fan Halsey had come out the preceding year, and she and Bill had set up housekeeping in the Halekulani Hotel at Waikiki. The Spruances found quarters nearby.

Though it was the army's duty to defend the Hawaiian Islands and also the ships of the Pacific Fleet when they were in Pearl Harbor, Admiral Kimmel maintained close liaison with Lieutenant General Walter C. Short, commanding the Hawaiian Department, and organized a committee to work out plans for supplementing the army's defense of Pearl Harbor. Halsey's representative on the defense committee was Commander Miles Browning.

Halsey cautioned Browning to be on his good behavior at the committee meetings and at all costs to keep his temper in check. Browning managed to maintain his cool and impressed fellow members with his intelligence and quick thinking, but when things were not to his liking, he used his superb command of *Robert's Rules of Order* to tie the conference in knots over questions of procedure.

During the last months of peace in the Pacific, Admiral Kimmel tried to foresee every contingency that might arise with what he regarded as the inevitable and imminent outbreak of war in the area. He conferred frequently, individually or together, with his senior officers, Vice Admirals Pye, Halsey, and Brown, and Rear Admirals William L. Calhoun, Commander, Base Force, and Claude Bloch, now commandant of the Fourteenth Naval District. While their other duties, particularly the periodic seagoing exercises of the vice admirals and their task forces, did not permit all five advisers to assemble often, Kimmel passed on to each of them every piece of military intelligence or other pertinent information that reached him.[4]

By chance, Halsey and his Task Force 2 were in port when Washington authorized the sending of fighter planes to Wake. He was at the 27 November conference convened to decide which fighter planes to send. There he assumed the task of making the delivery. As a result, his ships were absent from, but approaching, Pearl Harbor when the Japanese struck.

CHAPTER 10

COMMANDER, SOUTH PACIFIC

In the summer of 1942 the presence of Admiral Halsey as a patient at Richmond's Johnston-Willis Hospital presented complications. The admiral himself was considerate, his doctors and nurses agreed, but naval district headquarters had warned the hospital administration that his return to the United States was to be kept secret. With visitors coming and going and a large staff circulating at all hours, complying with this injunction posed a problem—particularly in warm weather when the patients' doors were left open. The administrators struggled with the dilemma, but it was the admiral himself who divulged his presence. He had a private telephone placed in his room and did quite a bit of telephoning. Somebody to whom he talked did some talking of his own, and soon Halsey's whereabouts were known.

Among Bill's early visitors at the hospital was St. George Bryan of Richmond. They talked about their days at the University of Virginia together, about their subsequent careers, and about their sons, all now commissioned officers in the naval reserve. Young Bill Halsey was en route to the Pacific theater as a supply officer. The eye troubles that had kept him out of the Naval Academy now barred him from the line. One of St. George's boys was in the Atlantic, the other in the southwest Pacific. Halsey hoped soon to be going back into action and assured his friend that if the opportunity arose, he would try to get in touch with Bryan's sons.

Under the ministrations of the ingenious Dr. Vaughan, Halsey's dermatitis began to subside, and he was relieved to be able to wear pajamas again. At the end of a week he was well enough to leave the hospital. He remained under the doctor's care, however, for six more weeks, during which time he resided at Richmond's Jefferson Hotel. When his gums were found to be ulcerated, a dentist removed several of his teeth, obliging him, as he said, to eat like a rabbit. During his period of convalescence, Halsey took several trips to Delaware to visit Thornby, the home of Margaret and Lea Spruance at Greenville, near Wilmington. Fan had been living there with her daughter and son-in-law since her return from Honolulu.

On 5 August, fully cured of dermatitis and ulcerated gums, Bill left Richmond for good. After stowing his gear at Thornby, he headed for Washington to find out what the navy was planning for him. In that hectic period the Navy Department was working at full capacity through the weekends and around the clock. U.S. marines had just invaded Guadalcanal, the battle against the German U-boat was raging in the Atlantic, and planning was in progress for an early Anglo-American invasion of North Africa. Despite the hubbub, Halsey received his orders: he was to take leave for the rest of the month and then report back for duty. The next three weeks Halsey spent largely at Thornby, enjoying his family, receiving friends, and playing with his grandchildren—two boys and two girls.

In Washington on the last day of August, Admiral Halsey joined Captain Miles Browning, who had flown in from Pearl Harbor, and William Ashford, now a lieutenant commander. Ashford had not spent an idle summer. At an apartment in Virginia Beach near some friends, he remained on the alert to run errands for Admiral Halsey, being directed by telephone, from the admiral's hospital room, from the hotel, and finally from Thornby. Between his missions he had met, courted, and married a young lady on vacation from the staff of *Harper's Bazaar*, and at Virginia Beach's Cavalier Hotel they had had a honeymoon, interrupted only a few times by Halsey.

At the end of their day together in Washington, Halsey, Browning, and Ashford went by government car to Annapolis, where the admiral had agreed to speak at the Naval Academy. In somewhat wrinkled khakis, the three of them walked into the auditorium of Mahan Hall, which was filled with midshipmen and other officers in starched, high-necked whites. Halsey, after being presented to the audience, introduced Browning and Ashford as shipmates and then proceeded with his speech. "Missing the Battle of Midway," he said, "has been the greatest disappointment of my life, but I am going back to the Pacific where I intend personally to have a crack at those yellow-bellied sons of bitches and their carriers."

This announcement brought applause and cheers. When these had died down, Halsey told the story of the raid on the Marshalls while Browning, on the stage with him, illustrated with a pointer on a large map, which had been set up in advance at Halsey's request.[1]

The next day Halsey, with his chief of staff and flag lieutenant, headed by air for the West Coast. Here he proceeded to inspect aviation facilities. On 7 September he dropped in on Admiral Nimitz at the St. Francis Hotel in San Francisco. Nimitz had flown from Pearl with members of his staff for another of his periodic meetings with Admiral King. He took Halsey along to the Federal Building for the opening conference. Here Bill was enthusiastically received with much handshaking and backslapping. In the course of the next three days he sat in on a number of the conferences, less to participate than to listen and bring himself abreast of the changing situation in the Pacific theater.

He was already aware of the new American base on Efate Island in the New Hebrides and, as we have seen, had attempted to deliver a squadron of marine corps fighter planes there. Before entering the hospital, he learned that Admiral King had activated Admiral Nimitz's South Pacific Area under the direct command of Vice Admiral Robert L. Ghormley, who proposed early construction of an additional base on Espíritu Santo Island, between Efate and the Solomons. The dual purpose of these moves, Halsey had been informed, was to block Japan's evident plan to advance from Rabaul via the Solomons and New Hebrides in order to cut U.S. communications with Australia, and to support an eventual advance by U.S. forces via the Solomons to recapture Rabaul.

Directly after Halsey left the hospital, the whole world learned through the media and other sources that U.S. marines had landed on the Solomon islands of Guadalcanal and Tulagi. Newspapers and news magazines told the public, including Halsey, that Japanese cruisers had attacked the Allied amphibious force at these islands and been thrown back, that the first echelon of Japanese reinforcements to land on Guadalcanal had been wiped out by the marines, and that the approach of a second echelon had brought about a battle at sea in which the enemy fleet had been repulsed, its light carrier possibly lost, several other ships heavily damaged, and many of its planes shot down.

It appeared that the long-awaited Allied offensive was well under way with no setbacks and with all services and commands operating in harmony. To Halsey this must have been great news. At the conferences and in private conversations, however, he now learned facts that the newspapers had not reported, and these cast a new light on the whole campaign.

For one thing, planning the invasion of the Solomons had begun not with the services in harmony but rather with a veritable donnybrook over who was to command. General MacArthur, backed by General Marshall, had insisted that any such Allied operation must be under him, because all the Solomon Islands were within his Southwest Pacific Area. Admiral King had contended that Admiral Nimitz, operating through Admiral Ghormley, his deputy in the South Pacific Area, should do the commanding, because the landing force and all the supporting ships would be drawn from Nimitz's Pacific Fleet and Pacific Ocean areas. The deadlock was finally broken by shifting the boundary between areas so that Guadalcanal and Tulagi were brought just within the South Pacific Area. Ghormley would thus be in overall command, with MacArthur providing air searches from Port Moresby.

Both MacArthur and Ghormley urged postponement of the invasion, scheduled for early August, until what they considered adequate forces could be built up. Delay was out of the question, however, when code breaking revealed that the Japanese were building an airfield on Guadalcanal. Obviously whoever first had aircraft operating from the island would be difficult to dislodge.

Though in general command, Ghormley, busy shifting his headquarters from Auckland, New Zealand, to Noumea, New Caledonia, had in fact little to do with the planning, rehearsal, or execution of the invasion. The expeditionary force was commanded by Frank Jack Fletcher, now a vice admiral. The semi-independent amphibious force was commanded by Rear Admiral Richmond Kelly Turner, who on the morning of 7 August put ashore Major

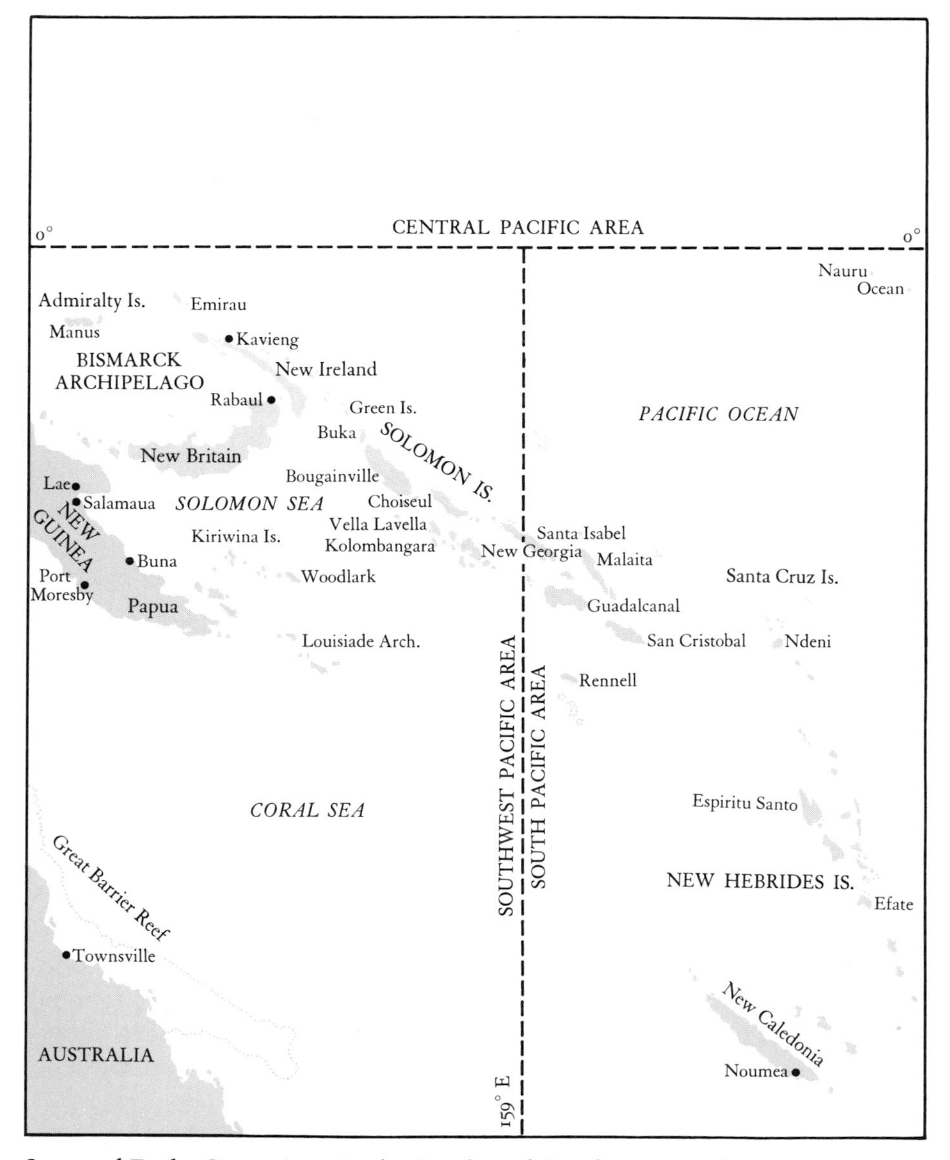

Scene of Early Operations in the South and Southwest Pacific Areas

General A. Archer Vandegrift's reinforced First Marine Division—ten thousand marines on Guadalcanal, three thousand on the much smaller Tulagi and adjacent islets.

The Americans on Tulagi engaged in a series of sharp fire fights to seize the Japanese seaplane base from its defenders, but those on Guadalcanal, encountering mostly construction workers who fled into the jungle, occupied the unfinished airfield on the second day. To fend off Japanese bombers flying down from Rabaul, Fletcher maintained south of Guadalcanal—temporarily, as it turned out—three carrier groups, built around the *Enterprise*, the *Wasp*, recently brought from the Atlantic, and the *Saratoga*, now repaired from her torpedoing of the preceding January.

The Japanese cruisers mentioned by the newspapers as having attacked and been turned back by the Allied amphibious force had in fact struck by surprise, at night, in a raid that took a thousand Allied lives, sank four desperately needed heavy cruisers—three American and one Australian—and damaged three other ships. It was the severest defeat ever suffered by the U.S. Navy at sea.

Had the U.S. carriers still been off Guadalcanal at the time of the battle, their bombers could have overtaken the enemy cruisers at dawn and sunk some, possibly all. But Fletcher had retreated far to the southeast. Having lost two carriers in previous actions, he had no desire to remain in disputed waters while enemy forces closed in on him.

With the carriers gone, Turner had no choice but to withdraw his amphibious force with only about half its supplies unloaded. The sixteen thousand marines left behind, subsisting on canned rations eked out by captured rice, completed the airstrip and named it Henderson Field after a marine major killed in the Battle of Midway.

Admiral Ghormley considered the possibility of sending fast vessels to retrieve the stranded marines. He dropped the evacuation plan, however, when on 20 August an American escort carrier approached Guadalcanal and flew twelve dive-bombers and nineteen fighters in to Henderson Field. The Japanese, if they intended to retake and retain Guadalcanal, would now have to capture the field and operate their own planes from it. Evidently underestimating the size of the American garrison, they made their first attempt with only nine hundred troops, put ashore at night. The marines quickly disposed of these new arrivals.

With his three-carrier force Fletcher now began patrolling the approaches to Guadalcanal. He was taken by surprise when patrol planes reported the approach of a second Japanese reinforcement echelon escorted by a carrier fleet. Fletcher had sent his *Wasp* group south for refueling, thus reducing his strength by a third. Nevertheless, as the newspapers correctly reported, in the ensuing battle the Americans were victorious. The papers failed to mention, however, that the *Enterprise* suffered severe bomb damage.

A few days later, the *Saratoga* for the second time in 1942 was put out of action by a submarine torpedo. Both the *Enterprise* and *Saratoga* had to retire to Pearl Harbor for repairs, leaving in the South Pacific only two U.S. carriers, the *Wasp* and the *Hornet*, the latter newly arrived from Pearl Harbor.

The United States had named the action in which the four cruisers were lost the Battle of Savo Island and the encounter in which the *Enterprise* was damaged, the Battle of the Eastern Solomons. The navy quite properly did not release news of the Allied losses. Publication in newspapers would give the information away to the Japanese. It was important to keep the enemy guessing.

Despite setbacks, the Japanese still intended to recapture Henderson Field. Each night Rabaul sent destroyers or small transports speeding down the Slot, a passage through the central Solomons, to land troops on Guadalcanal—an operation the U.S. marines began calling the Tokyo Express.

The Japanese were also intent on capturing Port Moresby. Having failed to take it by sea, they proposed now to take it by land. Troops put ashore on the north coast of New Guinea bird tail were advancing over the mountain range toward the Australian base.

At the San Francisco conference King, Nimitz, and their staffs spent some time analyzing the Battle of Savo Island. They criticized the state of American intelligence and alertness and the curious night deployment. Their discussion turned into a review of the whole South Pacific campaign. Admiral King was beginning to wonder about Admiral Ghormley's command control. He had heard rumors about defeatism and indecisiveness at South Pacific headquarters. Was Ghormley in good health, able to stand up physically to the strain? Nimitz said he would check the results of Ghormley's last physical examination and let King know what he found.

Because Admiral Fletcher was slightly wounded when the *Saratoga*, then his flagship, was torpedoed at the end of August, he had been granted stateside leave. It was high time. He was exhausted, having been almost continuously at sea since the outbreak of the Pacific war and having lately commanded in three major battles. Since April three carriers under his command had been torpedoed, and two of them, the *Lexington* and *Yorktown*, had gone down. With such a record, it was generally agreed that he must be extraordinarily unlucky or extraordinarily inept. Fletcher had been ordered to report for temporary duty in Washington following his leave, presumably in order for a skeptical King to look him over.[2]

At the close of the conference Halsey, having been fairly well informed concerning the military situation in the Pacific, flew with Nimitz and staff members to Pearl Harbor. Here he was given temporary duty as Commander, Air Force, Pacific Fleet, and installed in an office in the recently completed CinCPac headquarters building. A concrete, bomb-proof structure, with two stories above ground and one below, it was situated on high ground across the highway from the Pearl Harbor Naval Shipyard.

In a sense Halsey's new post was a descendant of his older one, Commander, Aircraft, Battle Force, but it was now a land-bound command administering aviation personnel, equipment, and ships. He was to occupy the billet only between the departure of Rear Admiral Aubrey W. Fitch, being transferred to the South Pacific to command land-based air under Ghormley, and the arrival from Washington of Fitch's replacement, Vice Admiral John H. Towers, just completing a tour as chief of the Bureau of Aeronautics.

The *Enterprise* was in dry dock at Pearl having her battle damage repaired. With the rest of Task Force 16 she had arrived on 10 September wearing the flag of Rear Admiral Thomas C. Kinkaid. Kinkaid, former commander of Cruiser Division 6, had relieved Spruance of temporary command of Task Force 16 following the Battle of Midway, when the latter became Nimitz's chief of staff.

When repairs to the *Enterprise* were completed, Halsey was to join her again and resume his command of Task Force 16. As commander of a single task force, he would normally revert back to rear admiral, but nobody so much as suggested that the raider of the mandate islands and Tokyo should suffer any diminution of rank, particularly since in future carrier battles, even when other carrier forces were operating with Task Force 16, he, as senior officer present, would have the overall command. Apparently, from the looks of things in the South Pacific, Halsey would soon have his chance to fight a battle at sea.

At noon on 21 September the torpedo-damaged *Saratoga* entered Pearl Harbor. The following day, after she had been placed in dry dock, all hands lined up on the flight deck and Admiral Nimitz arrived to present decorations. Probably few officers or men on board recognized the officer accompanying him. It was Bill Halsey. Nimitz had decided the time had come to reveal Halsey's return to duty and considered no place more appropriate than the flight deck of the ship that had been his first carrier command and later his flagship. There had been a tremendous shift of personnel since then. The intervening years must have dimmed even the memories of the few holdovers. Newspapers and magazines had thus far only sparsely displayed Halsey's picture. But his name and reputation as first American victor over the Japanese had resounded throughout the navy and around the world. In every sailorman's book he was down as the fighting admiral who had first smacked the enemy. Nimitz, stepping up to the microphone, beckoned Halsey forward and announced, "Boys, I've got a surprise for you. Bill Halsey's back!" The ship's company, supposed to be at attention, abandoned decorum in a resounding cheer, while Halsey's eyes filled.

That afternoon, at a party Nimitz and Halsey were attending at the Walter

Dillinghams' in Honolulu, the latter was astonished and delighted to be suddenly confronted by his son. Nimitz, having been informed that Ensign Halsey was on Ford Island awaiting assignment, contrived to have him released from duty and invited to the Dillinghams' to surprise his father.

A couple of days later Admiral Nimitz invited both Halsey and his son to dinner and to spend the night at his quarters. During the meal Nimitz turned to young Bill and told him the story of his dad's enthusiastic reception on board the *Saratoga*. After dinner, the Filipino messboy set up a miniature pistol range out in back of the quarters, and Nimitz and the two Halseys took turns firing rubber darts at a target. Young Halsey always believed that the commander in chief, strongly impressed by his father's *Saratoga* reception, had him over for the evening to size him up and decide how best to make use of his abilities. The objective of the target practice might have been to see how steady the admiral's hands were, how fully he had recovered from the case of nerves that had brought on the dermatitis. Possibly Nimitz was making up his mind about the son too. At any rate, a few days later Ensign Halsey was ordered to the *Saratoga* as aviation supply officer.[3]

Admiral Halsey regularly attended the CinCPac morning strategy conferences. These commenced each day at 0900 in Nimitz's office or in a nearby conference room, depending on how many officers were present. Commander Ed Layton opened the proceedings with an intelligence briefing. This usually began with a report on the situation in the South Pacific, where conditions varied from favorable to decidedly unfavorable.

The Tokyo Express had lately been employing more vessels in its nightly runs down the Slot, pouring reinforcements onto Guadalcanal. By mid-September Japanese troop strength had been increased to about six thousand. Again the enemy tried to capture Henderson Field. The Combined Fleet came down from the island base of Truk to fly planes in to the airfield when their infantry had succeeded. But the Japanese were still underestimating the strength of the American garrison, which now amounted to roughly eleven thousand. In the Battle of the Bloody Ridge, 12–14 September, the Americans repelled the attackers with fearful slaughter, and the Combined Fleet returned to Truk.

Nine hundred miles west of Guadalcanal, in eastern New Guinea, Japanese troops, after surging through a pass in the Owen Stanley Range and down the southern slope, had repulsed MacArthur's Australians and come almost within sight of Port Moresby. Then, just as the fall of the base appeared imminent, the Japanese unaccountably retired over the mountains. One theory was that, having at last correctly estimated American strength in the Solomons, they were going on the defensive in New Guinea to concentrate their forces for the recapture of Guadalcanal. This theory seemed to be confirmed when the reinforcement operations of the Tokyo Express were suddenly redoubled.

To offset the enemy buildup Ghormley rushed an additional regiment of marines to Guadalcanal. The men arrived safely, but while the convoy was still at sea, enemy submarines penetrated the circle of escorting vessels and within fifteen minutes torpedoed the carrier *Wasp*, the new, 27-knot battleship *North Carolina*, and a destroyer. The destroyer sank. The carrier, fatally ablaze, was scuttled. The battleship was put out of action with a long underwater slash in her hull. Loss of the *Wasp* left the *Hornet* America's sole operational carrier in the Pacific.

Other bad news from the south concerned the ever-worrisome command situation. Officers and journalists reaching Pearl Harbor after visits to Noumea and Brisbane reported defeatism at both headquarters. Neither Ghormley nor MacArthur believed the Americans could hold Guadalcanal much longer. This view surprised and annoyed Nimitz. He pointed out that the Japanese were already massing their full available strength against Guadalcanal and were losing men, ships, and above all, aircraft far faster than they could replace them. Allied strength, real and potential, was only just beginning to be brought to bear on this point of contact. If the marines could hold out a little longer, Nimitz insisted, the tide was bound to turn.[4]

Concluding that he had better take a personal look at conditions in the South Pacific, Nimitz at the end of September flew to Noumea with members of his staff. On arrival, they found Ghormley haggard with fatigue and anxiety. He and his staff officers were bogged down in detail, stymied by indecision, and infected with the pessimism that had seeped across the Coral Sea to Brisbane. Here in tropical waters the officers and men of the South Pacific command were all living and working in the headquarters vessel, the *Argonne*, an old repair ship with no air-conditioning. Ghormley had scarcely left the vessel since he arrived at Noumea just before the invasion of Guadalcanal. Nimitz wondered why he had not taken more comfortable and commodious headquarters ashore. It appeared that the local French authorities had offered nothing of the sort, and Ghormley had not insisted.

The funk of defeatism, Nimitz discovered, was confined to the rearward headquarters. In visits to Espíritu Santo and Guadalcanal he found that the nearer he got to the combat zone the greater was the confidence. He was relieved to note in General Vandegrift and his senior officers a quiet determination to hold Guadalcanal and a strong conviction that they could do so.

On returning to Noumea, Nimitz again conferred with Ghormley, urging better employment of the naval forces and manpower at his command. Why, he asked, were the South Pacific warships not being used to derail the Tokyo Express? Why were the garrisons of the southern islands not being rolled up to reinforce Guadalcanal and eventually relieve the war-weary First Marine Division? Denuding the southern islands, including New Caledonia, he pointed out, was not too great a risk, because, while the Japanese were fighting to recapture Guadalcanal and maintain a foothold in New Guinea, they would scarcely have sufficient forces available to stage amphibious assaults elsewhere. On his return to Pearl Harbor, Nimitz set an example by stripping the central Pacific of planes for the defense of Guadalcanal and alerting the army's Twenty-fifth Division, then on Oahu, to prepare to move south.[5]

In response to Nimitz's prodding, Ghormley dispatched to Guadalcanal a strongly escorted convoy carrying a regiment of soldiers from his New Caledonia garrison. At the same time a cruiser-destroyer force under Rear Admiral Norman Scott advanced to derail a Tokyo Express that aviators had reported coming down the Slot. This particular express, it turned out, was not composed of transports bringing reinforcements but of cruisers and destroyers en route to bombard Henderson Field. On the night of 11–12 October Scott's force and this express tangled northwest of Guadalcanal in the Battle of Cape Esperance, in which the Americans sank a cruiser and a destroyer and lost a destroyer. Ghormley's reinforcements reached Guadalcanal on 13 October, and the convoy that brought them there retired safely.[6]

Nimitz decided to send his chief of staff, Ray Spruance, and Rear Admiral William L. Calhoun, his service force commander, to the South Pacific to confer with commanders, inspect bases, and study problems and needs. Halsey suggested that he, too, had better go along to acquaint himself with the area and the officers with whom he would serve. Nimitz agreed and issued the necessary orders.

Halsey planned to take with him his chief of staff, Miles Browning, and his intelligence officer, Major Julian Brown, but not his flag lieutenant, Bill Ashford. He ordered the latter, now a lieutenant commander, to report for duty as Admiral Kinkaid's tactical officer. Ashford, Halsey believed, had been a flag lieutenant long enough to further his career. Thus Ashford and the rest of Halsey's old staff remained with Task Force 16, of which Kinkaid retained temporary command. As soon as repairs to the *Enterprise* were completed, Kinkaid would take the force to the South Pacific and turn it over to Halsey at some designated port.

On the morning of 14 October Halsey, Spruance, Calhoun, Browning, and Brown departed Honolulu in a Coronado seaplane and flew 800 miles to Johnston Island, where they spent the afternoon inspecting facilities. On the fifteenth they flew on to Canton Island for another overnight stop.[7]

At Pearl Harbor that evening Admiral Nimitz reached a decision, over which he had been agonizing for several days, about what to do with Admiral Ghormley. Ghormley was an intelligent and dedicated officer as well as an old and cherished friend. Nimitz dreaded subjecting him to the humiliation of being relieved and wondered if a change of command at this juncture would really help matters.

He called a special meeting, mainly of staff members who had accompanied him to the South Pacific. He wanted to hear their impressions of the command situation there. Was Admiral Ghormley tough enough to meet the approaching challenge? More important, did he have the personality to inspire his subordinates to heroic measures beyond their known capabilities? Each officer present expressed the opinion that Ghormley lacked the required traits and that the atmosphere at his command headquarters was intolerable.

"All right," said Nimitz. "I'm going to poll you." He pointed to each officer in turn and put the question to him: "Is it time to relieve Admiral Ghormley?" Every one of them replied yes.

They discussed possible replacements. Admiral Turner came to mind, a grizzled and vociferous warrior, a leader, no doubt, but of the driving sort, a characteristic that had earned him the nickname Terrible Turner. Also he was repeatedly in dispute with General Vandegrift and other marine officers concerning strategy for defending Guadalcanal. Apparently to resolve such differences the South Pacific needed a commander senior to them all and one just as stubborn as Turner. Halsey filled the bill. He had the required rank and firmness and was moreover a popular leader, but he was especially needed as a carrier force commander. Besides, he had had little experience as an administrator and was believed not to be at his best behind a desk.

Without announcing any decision, Nimitz thanked those present and closed the meeting. He had made up his mind what to do but chose to sleep on the matter before acting. The next morning by radio he requested permission from Admiral King to have Halsey relieve Ghormley and received a prompt affirmative. Nimitz then composed a dispatch to Ghormley:

> After carefully weighing all factors, have decided that talents and previous experience of Halsey can best be applied to the situation by having him take over duties of ComSoPac [Commander, South Pacific] as soon as practicable after his arrival Noumea 18th your date. I greatly appreciate your loyal and devoted efforts toward the accomplishment of a most difficult task. I shall order you to report to Halsey for the time being, as I believe he will need your thorough knowledge of situation and your loyal help. CominCh has approved this change. Orders will follow shortly.

Nimitz then prepared the necessary dispatch orders to be given to Halsey on his arrival at Noumea.

Halsey had intended to visit Guadalcanal before going on to Noumea, but when the Coronado reached Canton Island he was handed a dispatch from Ghormley advising him to cancel his proposed call at Guadalcanal because of the tactical situation there. Halsey replied that he would visit the island as planned unless otherwise directed, and sent copies of both messages to CinCPac. He was awakened at 0200 the next morning and handed CinCPac's reply. He was to proceed directly via Fiji to Noumea.

The Coronado touched down in Noumea Harbor at 1515 on the eighteenth, not far from the *Argonne*. Hardly had the seaplane's four propellers ceased turning when a whaleboat came alongside. As Halsey stepped into the craft, Ghormley's flag lieutenant saluted and handed him a sealed envelope. Because he would be on board the *Argonne* in a few minutes, Halsey realized that a message so delivered must have the highest priority. He opened the envelope at once, then tore open an inner envelope marked Secret. Inside was another dispatch from CinCPac: "Immediately upon your arrival at Noumea, you will relieve Vice Admiral Robert L. Ghormley of the duties of Commander South Pacific and South Pacific Force."

Halsey, incredulous, read the message again. "Jesus Christ and General Jackson!" he exploded. "This is the hottest potato they ever handed me!"

Halsey says that his reaction was one of astonishment, apprehension, and regret—astonishment because he had had no inkling of the appointment; apprehension because he would have to handle personnel—from the U.S. army and from New Zealand—with whom he had had no experience in a situation he did not understand under circumstances that Ghormley and MacArthur had pronounced hopeless; and regret at having to relieve a Naval Academy football teammate and friend of forty years' standing. No doubt there was also some regret at the prospect of again being sidetracked on the eve of a possible major carrier battle, of being stuck behind another LSD when he would infinitely have preferred to be standing again on the flag bridge of the Big E.[8]

Spruance and Calhoun were taken to Kelly Turner's flagship, the transport *McCawley*, where they were expected. Halsey, Brown, and Browning went to the *Argonne*. Ghormley met Halsey as he stepped on board. Both men were cordial and friendly but ill at ease.

"This is a tough job they've given you, Bill," Ghormley said.

"I damn well know it," replied Halsey.

Ghormley led Halsey to his cabin and briefed him on the situation and the major problems facing him. He then had the ship's company called to quarters, and both men read their orders in accordance with navy custom.

One of Halsey's first official acts as Commander, South Pacific, was to release a radio message to all of the area's commanding generals and naval task force commanders and to the commander in chief of the southwest Pacific, MacArthur: "Vice Admiral William F. Halsey has this date relieved Vice Admiral Robert L. Ghormley as Commander South Pacific Force and South Pacific Area."

The news traveled rapidly. In the south and southwest Pacific areas only a few men knew Halsey personally, but apparently everybody knew his name and reputation, and in general the appointment was received with jubilation. An air combat intelligence officer on Guadalcanal recalled the effect: "I'll never forget it! One minute we were too limp with malaria to crawl out of our foxholes; the next we were running around whooping like kids."

Though Nimitz had ordered Ghormley to remain at Noumea as long as necessary to indoctrinate his successor, Halsey released him after a couple of days. Perhaps he preferred to make a clean break without guidance from a pessimist who had fallen short. More likely, he recalled the painful experience of his friend Kimmel, who had been obliged to remain at Pearl Harbor, the scene of his humiliation, until the Roberts Commission had completed its sittings.

One decision Halsey had to make promptly was whether to implement plans to build an airfield on Ndeni, one of the Santa Cruz Islands. At the time Henderson was America's sole advanced airfield. Enemy bombers had demonstrated that they could put it out of commission, at least temporarily, and an hour's heavy rain could turn it into a quagmire. The nearest supporting airfield was on Espíritu Santo, 600 miles from Guadalcanal. The field on Ndeni would be 200 miles closer.

U.S. army engineers had landed on Ndeni to make the necessary surveys, and troops were en route from Tongatabu to occupy the island. Vandegrift, however, bitterly opposed sending them to Ndeni, insisting that he needed every available soldier and marine to help him hold Guadalcanal. Turner and Ghormley had maintained that Ndeni was vital as a backup for Henderson, also for reconnaissance and for protecting supplies on their way to Guadalcanal. Ghormley had believed, moreover, that he had no choice but to carry out the Santa Cruz occupation, since it was part of the original instruction issued by the Joint Chiefs and endorsed by CominCh and CinCPOA.

Halsey, faced with this and other knotty problems, regretted that Nimitz had not let him stop, even briefly, at Guadalcanal. He could not visualize the situation. Ghormley and his senior staff members were of little help. They had been too bogged down in paperwork and details to visit the front. Halsey, with unfamiliar problems to solve and an unfamiliar staff, could not for the time being leave his headquarters. So he radioed General Vandegrift, asking him to fly down to Noumea as soon as the conditions on Guadalcanal permitted.

Vandegrift arrived on 23 October, accompanied by Lieutenant General Thomas Holcomb, commandant of the marine corps, who had been visiting Guadalcanal. After dinner Halsey settled down with his visitors for a conference. Among those present at the meeting were Major General Millard F. Harmon, South Pacific army commander, who also had recently visited Guadalcanal; Major General Alexander M. Patch, commander of the ground forces in New Caledonia; and Rear Admiral Kelly Turner, in his capacity as Commander, Amphibious Force, South Pacific.

Halsey opened the proceedings by calling on Vandegrift to describe conditions on Guadalcanal. The general reviewed the campaign to date and then outlined the current situation. Air attacks by day and bombardments from enemy battleships and cruisers at night had destroyed most of his planes. The redoubled exertions of the Tokyo Express had poured troops onto Guadalcanal until there were now about as many of them on the island as there were Americans—some twenty-two thousand. Moreover, most of the Japanese troops were fresh, whereas the majority of the Americans were battle weary and weakened by malaria, restricted diet, and sleeplessness from night bombardments. He absolutely must, he said, have air and ground reinforcements without delay. Generals Harmon and Holcomb strongly supported his statement.

Halsey was drumming on the desk with his fingers. He looked at Vandegrift and asked, "Can you hold?"

"Yes, I can hold," replied the general, "but I have to have more active support than I've been getting."

Kelly Turner insisted that the navy was already giving all possible support with what it had. It was losing transports and cargo ships much faster than they could be replaced because there were not enough warships available to protect them. When Turner had finished his grim recital, Halsey turned again to the commander of the First Marine Division. "You go on back there, Vandegrift," he said. "I promise you everything I've got."

The meeting, among other results, enabled Halsey to make up his mind about Santa Cruz. The following morning, without so much as a by-your-leave, he radioed orders to the convoy from Tongatabu to change course and deliver its troops to Guadalcanal instead of Ndeni, thereby in effect canceling the Santa Cruz operation. Such high-handed disregard of the Joint Chiefs' plan brought Halsey some criticism, but nobody countermanded his order, and the Ndeni field was never missed.

The Santa Cruz question was by no means the only one about which Turner and Vandegrift disagreed. To the latter's intense annoyance, Turner had repeatedly intervened in marine corps strategy for defending Henderson Field. When General Holcomb visited Guadalcanal, Vandegrift requested the commandant's help in getting the admiral off his back. Holcomb was glad to comply. He drew up a dispatch for Admiral King suggesting that the landing force commander be on the same level as the naval task force commander and have unrestricted authority over operations ashore. Taking the dispatch with him to Noumea, Holcomb persuaded Halsey to sign it and send it up the chain of command. En route back to the States, Holcomb paused at Pearl Harbor to pay his respects to Nimitz, who showed him the dispatch, newly arrived from Halsey, and asked him if he concurred with the suggestion. When Holcomb stated emphatically that he did, Nimitz endorsed the dispatch and sent it on to King. It was in Washington when the commandant arrived there. King showed it to him and asked his opinion. Holcomb assured King that he considered it a much-needed reform. King passed the plan on to the Joint Chiefs, who adopted it for future operations in the Pacific.[9]

When General Vandegrift returned to Guadalcanal from Noumea, Japanese soldiers had launched a massive new drive to capture the airstrip. Admiral Fitch's land-based planes were searching the waters north of the Solomons for a large enemy carrier fleet known through traffic analysis to have departed Truk. Presumably it was now steaming about, wasting fuel while awaiting an opportunity to send in aircraft to operate from the captured field.

Task Force 16, with the repaired *Enterprise* and strengthened by the recent addition of the new battleship *South Dakota,* had left Pearl Harbor on 16 October, two days after Halsey had departed by air. In early afternoon on the twenty-fourth, on schedule, Task Force 16 joined Task Force 17, the *Hornet* force, east of Espíritu Santo and began to refuel.

By radio Halsey ordered Kinkaid to take command of the two forces, which, when combined under a single commander, became Task Force 61. He also told Kinkaid to detach certain staff members—Commanders Bromfield Nichol and Leonard Dow, Lieutenant Commanders Douglass Moulton and William Ashford, and several designated enlisted men, all from the Big E. These transferred to the oiler, which took them to Espíritu Santo, where a plane was waiting to convey them to Noumea.

Kinkaid was sorry to lose good men, but it must not be supposed that Halsey had callously stripped him of his staff. On board the *Enterprise* there were in fact three staffs, which overlapped. There was the staff of the carrier's skipper, Captain O. B. Hardison, replacing George Murray, now a rear admiral commanding Task Force 17. Then there was the staff under Kinkaid, Commander, Task Force 16, made up largely of officers and men he had brought with him from his previous command. Lastly there was the staff of Commander, Task Force 61, the combined *Enterprise-Hornet* command that Halsey had just turned over to Kinkaid. It was from this group, actually the admiral's old staff—which had served him in the raids on the mandates and on Japan, and Spruance in the Battle of Midway—that Halsey had drawn men to serve him at Noumea.

The four officers from the *Enterprise,* arriving on board the *Argonne* at about 2000, were conducted at once to Halsey's cabin. The admiral was sitting alone at his desk reading dispatches. He looked up and growled, "It's a goddamn mess." The situation on Guadalcanal, he said, was touch and go. If the Japanese took Henderson Field, it was up to Tom Kinkaid, facing a fleet twice as strong as his own, to see to it that the enemy never made use of it. He rang for a steward and told him to get some food for the new arrivals. The admiral remarked as they prepared to leave his cabin, "Look around and see what's to be done, and do it."

The officers from the *Enterprise* soon perceived why Halsey had felt he simply must have fresh and dependable help. "Admiral Ghormley's staff members aboard the *Argonne,*" said Ashford, "were so exhausted from lack of sleep, overwork, and the strain being placed on their shoulders that they were in a kind of daze. I felt they had just about reached the limit of human endurance."[10]

When the *Enterprise* and *Hornet* forces had completed fueling, Halsey daringly ordered Kinkaid to advance with them to the area north of the Santa Cruz Islands. Here they would be on the left flank of any enemy force approaching Guadalcanal from the northwest, the direction of Truk. Halsey was undoubtedly trying to reproduce the conditions of the Battle of Midway, which he had studied minutely. In that battle the American carrier commanders had achieved victory by learning the enemy's location before he learned theirs. This knowledge enabled the Americans to get the jump on the enemy while his planes, armed and fueled, were on deck.

Now, as in the days before the Midway battle, the Americans knew that the Japanese fleet was at sea, and its destination was obvious. At noon on 25 October one of Jake Fitch's Catalinas out of Espíritu Santo reported a segment of the enemy fleet with two carriers on a southeast course, about 360 miles from the assigned position of the American carrier forces, which were maintaining radio silence. The resemblance to the preliminaries of the Battle of Midway was striking.

Espíritu-based Catalinas reported the location of the enemy fleet in the early morning of the twenty-sixth at 0011 and again at 0310. The second report placed it within attack range of the American carriers. There was no evidence that the Japanese had discovered the location or even the presence of the American forces. Here apparently was an opportunity for the latter to launch an attack force in darkness for a dawn strike, thus beating the enemy to the punch. Halsey refrained from offering tactical advice to the man at the scene of action. Instead, hoping to spur Kinkaid into prompt action, he flashed the general message: "Attack—repeat—attack!"

Radio intercepts reaching Halsey in the next few hours presented a confusing picture, but it soon became evident that this battle was to be no repeat, after all, of the American triumph at Midway. When all the reports were in and intercepted enemy transmissions analyzed, it was found that the Americans were put at an initial disadvantage by a communications failure. The Catalina making the 0310 contact report sent it not to the carriers but by special frequency to Espíritu Santo, which through some mixup delayed two hours in relaying it. When the report reached the *Enterprise,* it was light and Kinkaid had already launched a sixteen-plane search to find out what the 0310 report could have told him.

The American search planes not only found the main enemy force; they also bombed the light carrier *Zuiho,* setting her afire and blasting a fifty-foot hole in her flight deck. By this time Japanese search planes had found the Hornet, and the carriers *Zuiho, Zuikaku*, and *Shokaku* had launched a strike

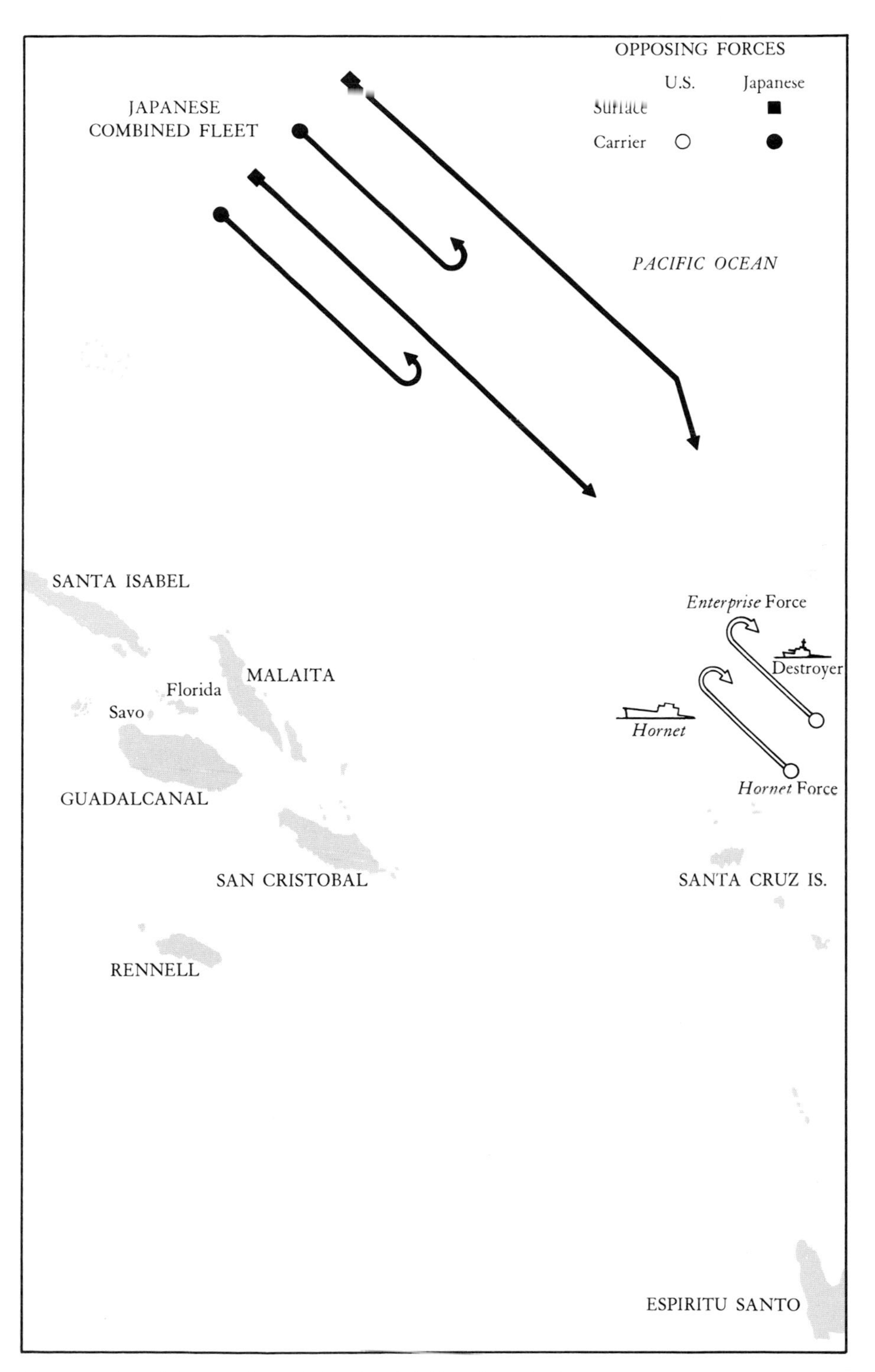

The Battle of Santa Cruz Islands, 26 October 1942

against her. Twenty minutes later the Americans launched a strike against the Japanese fleet. Thus the Japanese got the jump on the *Hornet,* which was obliged to accept battle over her own deck before her fighters attained altitude. She was put out of action by five bombs and two torpedoes.

In a second Japanese air attack, the *Enterprise* was heavily damaged by three bomb hits, and a torpedo plane crashed into a destroyer, setting her ablaze. A third attack damaged the *South Dakota* and the antiaircraft cruiser *San Juan*. The *Enterprise* force, after scuttling a destroyer that had been hit by a submarine-fired torpedo, retired to the southeast. Meanwhile, American carrier planes had obtained two bomb hits on the heavy cruiser *Chikuma* and heavily damaged the carrier *Shokaku.**

The *Hornet,* without fighter cover, became the target of several shattering afternoon air attacks and at length had to be abandoned. Halsey received word at Noumea and flashed the order: "Sink *Hornet* with torpedoes." She was not to fall into enemy hands. Two U.S. destroyers left behind to dispatch the carrier fired sixteen torpedoes and more than four hundred rounds of shell at her without producing any effect other than starting new fires. Approaching enemy surface forces then chased away the destroyers. The Japanese, unable to take the carrier in tow, sent her down with four of their outsize Long Lance torpedoes.

Though tactically the Americans fared worse in the sea battle, which became known as the Battle of the Santa Cruz Islands, they found solace in their estimate that the Japanese had lost nearly twice as many planes as they. Part of the reason, the Americans decided, was that they had learned a great deal about fighter techniques and had vastly improved the accuracy of their antiaircraft fire; they also concluded that the Japanese had already expended their best-trained and most experienced carrier aviators and were not able to train replacements fast enough.

It was the American soldiers and marines on Guadalcanal who foiled the enemy's plans. They held firm while the Japanese attack on land rose to a crescendo and finally died out on the twenty-sixth. Henderson Field remained in American hands, and enemy casualties were roughly ten times those of the Americans. But it had been a close call. Nobody doubted that the Japanese would make another grab for the airfield.

The continuing deadlock at Guadalcanal coincided with an outpouring of Allied military power all around the world. The Russians, having been supplied by Allied shipping via Murmansk and the Persian Gulf, were more than holding their own at Stalingrad. Three Allied expeditionary forces were at sea en route to invade northwest Africa. The Battle of the Atlantic was at its

*The Japanese carrier *Junyo* also participated in the battle but apparently was never sighted by the Americans.

height—in October nearly 600,000 tons of Allied shipping was sunk, a figure that was to be topped in November. Remaining Allied shipping was being stretched to the limit to transport supplies via the Cape of Good Hope and the Suez Canal to the British army in Egypt. There General Bernard Montgomery had been poised for the decisive Battle of El Alamein, which began 23 October. Forces were being assembled in the United Kingdom for a cross-Channel attack on Hitler's Festung Europa. General Arnold was concentrating air power in England for the strategic bombing of Germany.

Under the circumstances the harassed Joint Chiefs of Staff, with the exception of Admiral King, were inclined to overlook the portents of disaster in the South Pacific. Despite the sacrificial efforts of the soldiers and marines guarding Henderson Field and the dedicated energies of Admiral Halsey and the whole South Pacific command, Guadalcanal might have fallen had President Roosevelt not intervened. On 24 October he sent to the Joint Chiefs a memorandum indicating his desire "to make sure that every possible weapon gets in that area to hold Guadalcanal, and that having held it in this crisis, that munitions and planes and crews are on the way to take advantage of our success."

As a result, on the eve of the invasion of North Africa additional artillery and aircraft reached the beleaguered island, and Halsey was able to lay hands on six thousand more soldiers and marines for early transport thither. This reinforcement came none too soon, for it was becoming increasingly clear that the Japanese were determined to make good in November the victory they had missed in October. Nearly every night their destroyers steamed down through the Slot bringing men and weapons for a renewed attack on Henderson Field.[11]

CHAPTER 11

THE CRISIS

THE JAPANESE, having been rebuffed from Henderson Field in October, were obviously getting ready for an all-out effort to take it in November. On the night of the second the Tokyo Express landed fifteen hundred troops near Koli Point, east of the American position. Between the second and the tenth sixty-five destroyer loads and two cruiser loads of troops joined the main Japanese force west of the Americans. These reinforcements constituted only part of the vast preparations Japan was making. Information from traffic analysis, coastwatchers, and aerial observation revealed Japanese ships assembling in large numbers at Truk and Rabaul and in the Shortland Islands of the upper Solomons.

With trouble looming, Halsey dared not send the damaged ships of Task Forces 16 and 17 to distant Pearl Harbor for repairs. He had them brought to Noumea, where they were patched up sufficiently to be seaworthy if not entirely battleworthy. Though the Anglo-American invasion of North Africa, scheduled for 8 November, had first priority, Roosevelt's intervention on behalf of the Guadalcanal campaign soon had cruisers, destroyers, submarines, aircraft, and men heading for the South Pacific. The arrival of fresh troops from New Zealand and the United States emboldened Halsey to strip the remainder of his island garrisons and rush six thousand soldiers and marines, escorted by Turner's surface forces, to Guadalcanal.[1]

Concluding that he needed to have a brief look at the combat area, Halsey headed for Guadalcanal in a B-17 army bomber, accompanied by his war plans officer, Brigadier General Dewitt Peck of the marine corps, and his new flag lieutenant, Lieutenant William D. Kitchell. Their plane landed at Henderson Field at noon on 8 November. Vandegrift greeted them with pleasure. Halsey's visit, he said afterward, was "like a wonderful breath of fresh air." With only an afternoon to spare, Halsey wanted to see as much as he could. So he, Vandegrift, and the two South Pacific staff officers piled into a jeep and toured the defense perimeter and installations.

From time to time Halsey had the driver stop so he could talk with the men, mostly marines who had been on the island since early August. They were now gaunt from repeated bouts with malaria, and their young faces were prematurely lined from the strain of virtually continuous combat. Meeting and talking with the admiral obviously raised their spirits. The old Halsey magic was at work. What in his youth had been called charm had evolved with age and eminence into powerful charisma.

Shortage of time permitted only a few such stops. Most of the men who saw Halsey ride past had not the slightest notion who he was. He wore no decorations, and the three small stars on his khaki collar and garrison cap were scarcely discernible at a distance. Peck and Kitchell urged him to do something—stand up or at least wave—to attract the men's attention as they passed. Halsey would have none of that. "It smells of exhibitionism," he said. "The hell with it."

Halsey's presence became known to the few newsmen on the island, and they were waiting for him when he returned to the command post. As always, he was glad to see them and give them as much as he could of the information they wanted without compromising security. When they asked him to sum up his strategy for winning the war, he replied, "Kill Japs, kill Japs, and keep on killing Japs." One correspondent asked the admiral how long he thought the Japanese could hold out. Halsey snapped, "How long do you think they can take it?"

Dinner that evening was, for Guadalcanal, a rare delight. Halsey had heard of the poor food on the island, but the meal served him on this occasion featured excellent steaks and fresh apple pie. Anticipating the admiral's visit, Vandegrift had had an aide commandeer the best food the supply vessels in Guadalcanal had. Halsey, who rarely failed to praise a worthy accomplishment, decided he had to congratulate somebody. "By golly," he said, "I have to see the cook who can make a pie like that under these conditions."

Vandegrift said it wasn't necessary, but Halsey insisted he had to compliment the man who made that pie. At a gesture from the general, an aide left the room and eventually returned with Sergeant "Butch" Morgan, the general's cook. In khaki pants and skivvy shirt and sporting a bushy red mustache, Morgan bore a striking resemblance to the famous World War I cartoon character Old Bill. He stood stiffly at attention while Halsey poured on the praise. Cooking like that, said the admiral, was a real contribution to victory. A man could serve his country with a skillet as well as with a gun. As Halsey continued, Butch's face flushed with embarrassment and he began nervously fingering his skivvy shirt. Finally he blurted, "Aw, horseshit, Admiral. 'Twarn't nothin'."

All the diners, including Halsey, burst out laughing, and Morgan fled from the room.

The admiral and his two staff members spent the night in Vandegrift's shack. Not long after they had turned in, an enemy ship entered Ironbottom Sound, so called because of the many ships sunk there, and commenced lobbing shells in their general direction. On shore Japanese and American artillery began exchanging insults. Halsey found sleep impossible. In his usual self-depreciating manner, he attributed his wakefulness not to noise but to fear. It is worth noting, however, that only he himself ever accused Bull Halsey of cowardice.

Early the next morning the admiral decorated some officers and men, and then with Vandegrift and his two staff members proceeded to the airfield. Before boarding his plane, he turned to the general, his eyes twinkling. "Vandegrift," he said, "don't you do a thing to that cook."

On his return to New Caledonia, Halsey stopped at Efate, where he visited the base hospital. He paused at the bedside of a young naval officer whose head was swathed in bandages. "What happened, son?" he asked.

"I don't know, Admiral," the bandaged officer replied. "Last thing I remember, I was talking to you at the 'Canal last night."

Halsey was pleased at evidence that at least the navy's South Pacific medical department was operating efficiently. Here was a man, a dozen hours after being wounded, safe in a hospital 700 miles behind the lines.

News of Halsey's hospital visit spread throughout the area. The South Pacific now had a commander, it was said, who really cared.[2]

When Halsey arrived on board the *Argonne* the afternoon of the tenth, he hardly expected to be greeted by cheerful tidings, but what his chief of staff, Miles Browning, had to tell him was little short of appalling. In August, September, and October, enemy attacks had come near the end of the month. Halsey, expecting the Japanese to repeat that pattern, had been counting on at least a week more to get his defenses in order. But code breaking now revealed that the Japanese planned to launch their November assault before mid-month. Aircraft would bomb the American position on Guadalcanal on the eleventh, ships would bombard Henderson Field during the night of the twelfth, carriers would strike on the thirteenth, and at the end of that day a large contingent of Japanese troops would land on the island.

Halsey's six thousand reinforcements, together with food, ammunition, and supplies, were en route to Guadalcanal in two convoys. One was supported by a cruiser-destroyer force under Rear Admiral Norman Scott. The other was escorted by a similar force under Rear Admiral Daniel J. Callaghan. It was imperative that the transports carrying the men and supplies be unloaded and clear of the area before the evening of the twelfth, so Scott's and Callaghan's cruisers and destroyers would be free to deal with the enemy bombardment vessels scheduled to arrive that night off Guadalcanal.

At Noumea were the *Enterprise*, the battleships *South Dakota* and *Washington*, one heavy and one light cruiser, and eight destroyers. Halsey ordered Kinkaid to take these to sea the minute the *Enterprise* and *South Dakota*, still under repair, were able to sail.

When the ships, designated Task Force 16, left early on the eleventh, the

South Dakota's forward turret was incapable of firing. The *Enterprise,* in worse condition, still had eighty-five repairmen on board. Seventy of her officers' staterooms had been destroyed, and the refugees were crammed into the undamaged quarters together with the original tenants. In the area blasted by one of the Santa Cruz bombs, watertight integrity was nonexistent. The workmen reported the damaged forward elevator repaired, but Captain Hardison refused to let it be tested lest it jam in the down position, in which event the *Enterprise* would have a huge hole in her flight deck and be useless as a carrier. There were two after elevators, but with the forward one inoperable, no planes could be taken below until all had landed, thus greatly slowing flight operations.

With only one flight deck at his command and that one impaired, Halsey had no intention of exposing the *Enterprise* to unnecessary risk. She was to take station in the Coral Sea southwest of Guadalcanal. So that her presence would not be revealed, her planes were ordered to stage through Henderson Field and operate with aircraft based there.

Though the reinforcement operation was being carried out under the overall command of Kelly Turner, Halsey kept close track of it by radio. Scott's convoy, with marines and their supplies in three transports, arrived at the Guadalcanal anchorage at 0530 on 11 November and began to unload, the men going ashore first. After sunrise enemy dive-bombers attacked. Most were shot down before making any direct hits, but one of the transports had her hull so riddled by near-misses that she had to retire with half her cargo still on board. That night, while the remaining two transports continued unloading, high-flying aircraft from Rabaul arrived on schedule to drop bombs around Henderson Field.

At dawn on the twelfth the second convoy arrived with soldiers and their equipment in four transports, one of them Turner's flagship, the *McCawley.* While these transports were putting the men ashore, patrol planes reported an enemy surface force, including two battleships, 335 miles to the north, headed for Ironbottom Sound. This was undoubtedly the bombardment force scheduled to arrive in the sound during the night and blast Henderson into a wasteland. The transports' captains and crews worked hard to get their ships completely unloaded and well out to sea by nightfall. They would have succeeded had not a report of approaching enemy planes obliged them to leave the anchorage for maneuvering room. Most of the planes were shot down by the ships' antiaircraft fire or fighters from the airfield before they could ram home their attack. One Japanese pilot, however, managed to crash his burning plane into the cruiser *San Francisco,* knocking out a gun director and a fire control radar and wounding or killing fifty men.[3]

Despite the delay, the later arrivals among the transports were ninety percent empty when, according to plan, they left Guadalcanal at dusk. In compliance with the written orders, Scott and Callaghan escorted them out of Ironbottom Sound and then returned with the heavy cruisers *San Francisco* and *Portland,* the light cruisers *Atlanta, Helena,* and *Juneau,* and eight destroyers. Callaghan, as senior officer present, was commanding in the *San Francisco,* and Scott, his second-in-command, was in the *Atlanta.* Their mission was to protect Henderson Field from the approaching enemy bombardment force.

Though Callaghan was conforming to orders approved, and possibly originated, by Halsey, the latter must have been sorely tempted to countermand them upon realizing he was sending cruisers and destroyers against battleships. Such a mission would surely cost good ships and good men without much chance of preventing the bombardment. He put aside any temptation to countermand, however. Archie Vandegrift needed more support, and Halsey had promised to give him everything he had. That promise the navy was now making good.

At around 0130 on Friday, 13 November, the men on Guadalcanal were aroused by the thunder of distant guns. Staring out into the moonless night, they could see flashes of gunfire and an occasional searchlight beam. "For nearly an hour," says Vandegrift, "we watched naval guns belch orange death with such rapid vehemence that the island seemed to shake beneath us." There ensued only silence and blackness.

Guadalcanal informed Noumea, where Halsey had been walking the decks of the *Argonne* chewing his nails, that there had been a very hot battle indeed. No results were known except one: *Henderson Field had not been bombarded.*

Hours passed with no further word. For Halsey the tension was mounting. He continued to pace the decks, restudied reports and charts, conferred with staff members. "I must have drunk a gallon of coffee and smoked two packs of cigarettes," he said. He tried to read a magazine, but the words blurred before his eyes.

Morning had grayed the skies and the sun had risen before the first official word reached Halsey. It was an intercepted message from the *Portland,* which was requesting a tow. She reported that her steering room was flooded and her rudder jammed from a torpedo hit. Half an hour later a cry came from the *Atlanta:* "Help needed!" At about 0900 the *Helena,* designating herself senior ship, reported that she was retiring toward Espíritu Santo in company with the *San Francisco,* the *Juneau,* and three destroyers. "All ships are damaged," the *Helena*'s message concluded, "so request maximum air coverage." Where were the *Portland,* the *Atlanta,* and the other five destroyers? The fact that the *Helena* designated herself senior ship in the presence of the flagship *San Francisco* implied that Dan Callaghan was dead or severely wounded.

Later, recalling this somber morning, Halsey wrote,

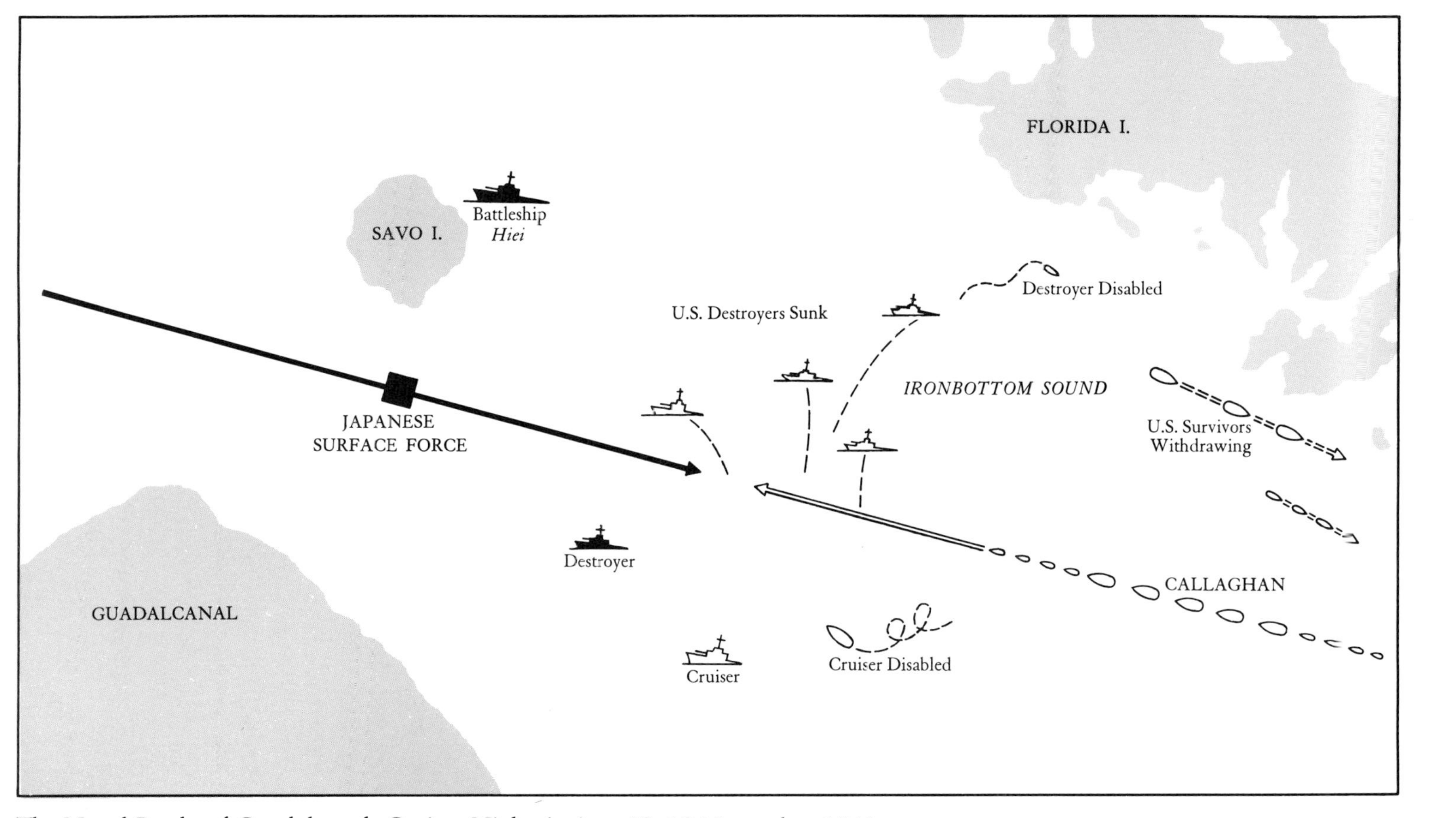

The Naval Battle of Guadalcanal, Cruiser Night Action, 12–13 November 1942

> Bad news always comes first. There was no report of the enemy's losses. This is the hardest thing an area commander in the rear has to face. Your feeling is one of complete helplessness. You know you have put your men into a fight, and you hope you have done everything possible to make that fight successful, but you are always searching your mind for something you may have left undone. It is a great mental agony. You not only have your individual responsibility to your country and to the cause of the Allied Powers, but you have the responsibility of many lives on your shoulders, plus the material damage that may be inflicted on your forces.

In the afternoon, reports from Guadalcanal began to complete the picture. Dawn had revealed a Japanese battleship disabled off Savo Island with five destroyers trying to take her in tow. Bombers and torpedo planes from Henderson Field chased away the enemy destroyers and set the battleship ablaze. Small craft from Guadalcanal had picked up hundreds of Japanese and American survivors, many burned or wounded, from Ironbottom Sound.

The rest of the story came out gradually over the course of the next few days. When Callaghan's cruisers and destroyers were reentering the sound from the east, the Japanese bombardment force was entering it from the west. In darkness, as they sped toward each other on a collision course, radar failed to give adequate warning. Ships intermingled, resulting in a half-hour melee that for confusion and fury is scarcely paralleled in naval history. Both formations broke and the engagement became a series of individual ship duels with each of the opposing forces at one time or another firing on its own vessels.

One of the Japanese battleships, later identified as the flagship *Hiei,* riddled by more than fifty shells, was left helpless off Savo, where, as has been noted, she was set afire and completely wrecked after daylight by aircraft from Henderson Field. In addition, two Japanese destroyers were sunk. In the American force, Admirals Callaghan and Scott and most of their staff members were killed. The cruiser *Atlanta,* gutted by flames and shelled by friend and foe, had to be sunk. Four American destroyers were lost. The cruiser *Portland* and a destroyer were unnavigable. All the remaining American vessels except one destroyer suffered damage. The cruiser *Juneau,* retiring from battle with a weakened keel, was torpedoed by a submarine and went down, carrying nearly seven hundred of her crew.

Loss of life in both forces was tremendous. Though the figures have never been published, it is known that far more Americans were killed than Japanese. Halsey, saddened by the loss of men under his command, was particularly affected by the death of the two admirals. Norm Scott had been one of his closest friends. Dan Callaghan had been Ghormley's chief of staff when Halsey took over command of the South Pacific. To install Captain Browning as chief of staff, Halsey had given Callaghan the sea command.

Such a change of duty would ordinarily be interpreted as a step upward, permitting the officer transferred an opportunity to exercise the chief skills for which he had been trained. But instead it brought Callaghan's career to an untimely end.

In calculating the risks to be taken next, Halsey, as area commander, had to consider losses not abstractly but in relation to what the enemy might be expected to do. Repulsed, the Japanese, a most determined foe, could be expected to try again. Halsey had to weigh how much of the force at his disposal he could afford to lose in stopping him. "That," he said, "is what a commander is for. On his judgment at this moment depends the end of the campaign. We were on the defensive at this moment. If I have any principle of warfare burned within my brain, it is that the best defense is a strong offense. Lord Nelson expressed this very well: 'No captain can do very wrong if he places his ship alongside that of an enemy.'"[4]

In the early hours of 13 November Halsey, in the Nelsonian spirit, had placed Callaghan's ships alongside the enemy in Ironbottom Sound and lost them as an effective fighting force. But the sacrifice had saved Henderson Field from bombardment, and eleven enemy transports bringing 13,500 troops to Guadalcanal had turned back to the Shortlands. However, the Japanese retreat was only temporary—a one-day postponement in the schedule of operations. A coastwatcher reported cruisers leaving the Shortlands, presumably on a mission to bombard the Guadalcanal airfield. Now was the time for Halsey to play his other card—Tom Kinkaid's Task Force 16, built around the *Enterprise*.

Halsey, assuming that the *Enterprise* had reached her assigned operating area southwest of Guadalcanal, radioed Kinkaid instructions to detach his battleships, the *South Dakota* and *Washington*, together with a screen of four destroyers, and send them speeding ahead under the command of Rear Admiral Willis A. Lee, Jr., to protect Henderson Field from the Japanese cruisers. But in fact the task force was far short of its assigned position. It could proceed northward no faster than the *Enterprise*, which had to turn back into the prevailing south wind each time she launched or landed planes for scouting or antisubmarine patrol. Kinkaid, so as not to break radio silence, sent a destroyer fifty miles eastward to report to South Pacific headquarters that Lee could not possibly reach Ironbottom Sound before 0800 the following day.[5]

Under the circumstances, Halsey was not surprised after midnight on the fourteenth to receive a report from Vandegrift that Henderson Field was being heavily shelled. The bombardment, by two heavy cruisers, abruptly ended thirty-five minutes later. Halsey and his staff at Noumea wondered about the sudden end. Later they attributed it to a pair of torpedo boats that had darted out from Tulagi and made three runs on the Japanese cruisers, firing torpedoes. A report arriving from Guadalcanal after dawn brought the welcome news that the bombardment had caused less destruction than had been anticipated. Only three planes had been damaged beyond repair. Seventeen others were battered but reparable. Henderson Field was still operational. The results were mild compared with what the battleships might have achieved the night before had they not been repulsed.

Sunrise on 14 November revealed to American search planes the Japanese bombardment cruisers together with a covering force of destroyers and other cruisers on a westerly retirement course south of the central Solomons. On an opposite course, heading from the Shortland Islands via the Slot toward Guadalcanal, were eleven large transports escorted by as many destroyers. These were the transports that had turned back the preceding day, now making a fresh start. Intelligence estimated the total number of enemy troops in the Guadalcanal-bound convoy at between ten and fifteen thousand.

Political and military leaders in Washington viewed the situation with alarm. Having assumed that Scott's and Callaghan's sacrifice had secured Guadalcanal from enemy bombardment and reinforcement, they were shocked to learn that the enemy had succeeded after all in shelling Henderson Field and, several hours later, that Japanese transports were heading for Guadalcanal, apparently unopposed. After the war Secretary Forrestal recalled, "[T]he tension I felt at that time was matched only by the tension that pervaded Washington the night before the landing in Normandy." The normally optimistic Roosevelt wondered if it were necessary, or even possible, to get the Americans off Guadalcanal.[6]

Top U.S. commands in the South Pacific viewed the situation differently. To them the deployment of the enemy forces represented an unparalleled opportunity. Bombers took off promptly from Henderson Field and the *Enterprise* and attacked the enemy cruisers, sinking one and damaging three others. In response to a radioed command from Halsey that their objective was the transports, they began working over the convoy, a gratifying operation which the B-17s from Espíritu Santo joined in the afternoon.

The irrationality of Japanese planning was now becoming manifest. The convoy was the heart of the whole November offensive. The attempted bombardment of Henderson Field by battleships early on the thirteenth, the successful bombardment of the field by cruisers twenty-four hours later, the Japanese carrier fleet hovering to the north as in the previous offensives—all were aimed at assuring the safe arrival at Guadalcanal of the transports with their troops and supplies. Yet the transports themselves had come down the Slot shielded by a mere handful of destroyers and a meager cover of fighter planes operating out of the upper Solomons and at extreme range from the distant Japanese carriers.

The slaughter of the lumbering transports went on all afternoon. They came under repeated attack by the high-flying B-17s, the steep-diving Dauntlesses, and torpedo bombers skimming the surface to hurl their lethal weapons. Smoke screens laid by the darting Japanese destroyers mingled with the smoke of burning transports as one after another the latter went down or blazed beyond control. By nightfall seven of the troop-carrying ships were sunk or sinking, and the surface was dotted with the heads of men who had been blown overboard or had abandoned ship to escape the flames. When the report of the day's work reached Halsey, he showed the dispatch to his staff, exclaiming, "We've got the bastards licked!"[7]

Archie Vandegrift knew that the battle was not over. Henderson-based search planes had reported a big enemy combatant force coming down from the north, presumably to give the airfield the devastating bombardment it had thus far escaped. Vandegrift knew also that Lee was coming from the south in the *Washington* with the *South Dakota* and four destroyers. These two forces were certain to clash during the night.

Out in Ironbottom Sound torpedo boats were scouting with a view to attacking, or at least discouraging, any enemy force that might arrive. A little before 2300 a plain-English radio communication was brought to Vandegrift's attention: "Refer your big boss about Ching Lee. Chinese, catchee? Call off your boys!" Vandegrift recognized at once that the speaker was Admiral Lee, identifying himself by unconventional means. The admiral was a friend of long standing, who went by his Naval Academy nickname, which the midshipmen had taken from a Chinese laundry named Lee. Vandegrift ordered the torpedo boats to steer clear.

A little later the men on Guadalcanal witnessed the flashes of another night battle, which ended abruptly in half an hour. Neither they nor Admiral Halsey, who was maintaining radio contact with Guadalcanal, had any means of knowing the result. One thing, however, they did know: as on Friday the thirteenth, *Henderson Field had not been bombarded.*

Not until after the war did anybody understand fully what had happened. Admiral Lee, attempting to ambush the enemy force, was himself ambushed. Japanese gunfire sank all four American destroyers and badly damaged the superstructure of the *South Dakota,* which was obliged to retire. The admiral was thus left in his unscathed battleship *Washington* to face the whole Japanese force. With the advantage of radar fire control, at which he was expert, Lee took on the largest target, which happened to be the enemy flagship, the battleship *Kirishima.* In seven minutes he achieved some fifty hits with his five- and sixteen-inch guns, leaving the *Kirishima* helplessly turning in circles. The Japanese admiral abandoned ship, ordered his flagship and a disabled Japanese destroyer scuttled, and with his remaining force left the area.[8]

At dawn the American soldiers and marines on Guadalcanal could see in the west the four surviving Japanese transports, which had arrived, beached,

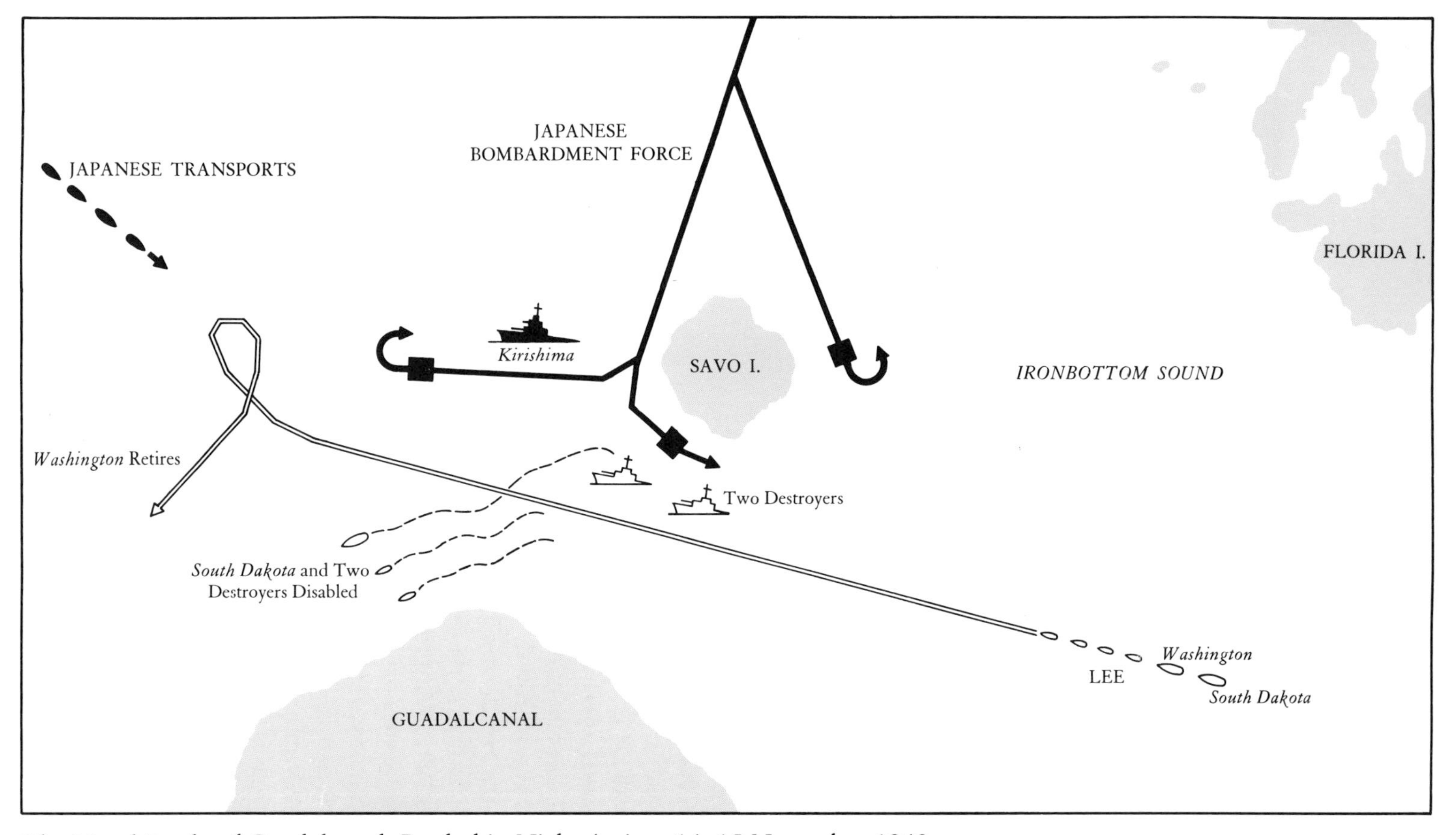

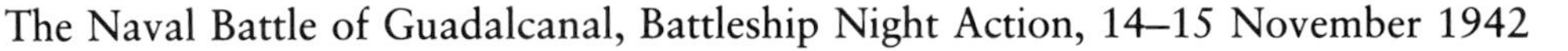

The Naval Battle of Guadalcanal, Battleship Night Action, 14–15 November 1942

and discharged their troops during the night. There had not been enough time to unload their supplies. Long-range U.S. artillery and bombers from Henderson Field and the *Enterprise* worked all four ships over until they were ablaze. The Japanese garrison on Guadalcanal now had additional men to feed and provide for without additional victuals or equipment.

Archie Vandegrift, bone weary as he had been for the last three terrible months, viewed the scene with satisfaction. To him it was obvious that the Japanese, and not the Americans, had reached the end of the line. He had remarked to Nimitz during his September visit to Guadalcanal, "Out here too many commanders have been far too leery about risking their ships." Halsey had put ships and men on the line and suffered heavy casualties in both, but the risks had paid off.

From Halsey came a message addressed to South Pacific ships and commanding generals: "To the superb officers and men on land, on sea, in the air, and under the sea who have performed such magnificent deeds for our country in the past few days: You have written your names in golden letters on the pages of history and won the undying gratitude of your countrymen. No honor for you would be too great. Magnificently done! God bless each and every one of you. To the glorious dead: Hail heroes! Rest with God."[9]

He typically disclaimed the praise that came his way. "President Roosevelt, Secretary Knox, Admiral King, Admiral Nimitz, and others sent me messages of congratulations," he wrote. "I had no illusions about who deserved them, so I passed them on to the men who had done the fighting."

Together the night surface action of 12–13 November, the air attacks on Japanese naval forces on the fourteenth, and the night surface action of 14–15 November are called the Battle of Guadalcanal. The importance of this protracted struggle in the history of the Pacific war can scarcely be exaggerated. For the first time in the war the Battle of the Coral Sea threw back a Japanese advance. The Battle of Midway cost the enemy losses that helped equalize the strength of the opposing naval forces. It was the Battle of Guadalcanal, however, that marked the actual Allied shift in the Pacific theater from defense to offense. The Japanese made no further attempt to reinforce Guadalcanal; they merely held on there while they strengthened their defenses in the central Solomons. In eastern New Guinea General MacArthur also was shifting to the offensive. He was enabled to do so because the Japanese had emphasized Guadalcanal at the expense of everything else.

From the start the Battle of Guadalcanal was touch and go. With better sources of intelligence and better planning, the Japanese might have readily routed U.S. ships and aircraft. In that event the American marines and soldiers on Guadalcanal and Tulagi would have been utterly isolated, with no prospect of reinforcement or resupply. Guadalcanal would have been another Bataan; Archie Vandegrift, another Skinny Wainwright. The Americans on the island would have suffered misfortunes comparable to those their countrymen had suffered in the Philippines, perhaps including another death march. With Guadalcanal as a secure base, its American defenders at sea and in the air defeated, the Japanese might have carried out their original purpose—to advance southeastward via the New Hebrides and sever U.S. supply lines to New Zealand and Australia.[10]

Despite his disclaimer, Halsey received his full share of the credit. Newspapers everywhere declared him the victor. Everybody heard about the conquests of Bull Halsey. The mayor of Elizabeth, New Jersey, Halsey's native city, proclaimed 20 November Halsey Day and ordered schools closed early, church bells rung, and public buildings decorated. Columnist H. J. Phillips celebrated the occasion with a ballad, which included this stanza:

> The foe bore down from Bougainville,
> Our lesser force to pin.
> He met with Halsey and Callaghan
> And soon bore back again.

The 30 November 1942 issue of *Time* magazine carried Bill's picture on the cover with the caption "Halsey of the South Pacific: When an attacker is attacked . . ." The story inside, "Battle of the Pacific: Hit Hard, Hit Fast, Hit Often," opened with an appraisal of Halsey written personally by Admiral Nimitz:

> Halsey's conduct of his present command leaves nothing to be desired. He is professionally competent and militarily aggressive without being reckless or foolhardy. He has that rare combination of intellectual capacity and military audacity, and can calculate to a cat's whisker the risk involved in operations when successful accomplishments will bring great returns. He possesses superb leadership qualities which have earned him a tremendous following of his men. His only enemies are Japs.

A reporter described Halsey in the *Argonne* at Noumea as he read reports on the battle that had evoked Nimitz's tribute: "The face which looked down on those reports was itself like a battlefield. Everything about it was big, broad, strong. The weather had been on it, and personal suffering behind it. The huge mouth looked like command, and above it, the nose was pugnacious. The eyes were aggressive. They and their screen of brow above the weariness below were as impressive and busy-looking as a couple of task forces."[11]

Like Nimitz, Halsey held daily 0900 conferences, which the senior officers of all services attended. As they assembled for the conference of 19 November, one of them congratulated Halsey.

"What for?"

Captain Browning swearing Halsey in as a four-star admiral, 27 November 1942

"You have just been nominated for a full admiral."

The news had been announced in a radio broadcast that Halsey had missed. Subsequently he read Nimitz's comment to the press: "For his successful turning back of the Jap attempt to take Guadalcanal in mid-November he has been nominated by the President for the rank of Admiral, which reward he richly deserves."

Congress approved the nomination on 26 November. Halsey thus became the sixth four-star admiral in the U.S. Navy, joining the lofty company of King; Nimitz; William D. Leahy, chief of staff to the president; Harold R. Stark, Commander, Naval Forces, Europe; and Royal E. Ingersoll, CinCLant.

"Naturally, I was very proud and happy," said Halsey, "but with the full realization that, although it was an individual award, it was intended for acceptance by me as a recognition of the splendid work that the South Pacific force had been continuing to do, and I was promoted as the representative of that force."

While navy four-star pins of regulation size were being cut for Halsey, Rear Admiral William L. Calhoun obtained four larger two-star pins from a marine major general, had them welded in pairs, and insisted that Halsey put the makeshifts on at once. He refused to do anything of the sort until he had received official notification of his promotion and had passed the required physical examination. After Miles Browning had sworn him in, he exchanged the three-star pins on his khaki collar for four-star. He handed his old pins to Calhoun and said, "Send one of these to Mrs. Scott and the other to Mrs. Callaghan. Tell them it was their husbands' bravery that got me my new ones."[12]

CHAPTER 12

GUADALCANAL RECAPTURED

ADMIRAL HALSEY recognized at once that for the South Pacific command to operate efficiently he had to have an adequate staff of officers and a decent place to house them. To him it was clear that many of Ghormley's difficulties had arisen from the fact that he had tried to handle a big job with too little help and too little space.

Ghormley was by no means alone in being shorthanded. Many senior officers took pride in getting by, and seeing that their subordinates got by, with minimum staffs. We have seen how on the eve of Fleet Problem XX Admiral King had humiliated Halsey by removing some of the latter's staff officers. Since then, however, King, as CominCh, had learned from experience that there were distinct limits to thrift in manpower. On assuming the navy's top operational command, he had had his flag secretary, Commander George Dyer, arrange for office space. Studying previous major commands and staff sizes, Dyer had concluded that King would need space for a staff of four hundred. King hit the overhead. He had run the Atlantic Fleet with a staff of fourteen, he said, and he was damned if he was going to have a staff of more than fifty as commander in chief. In due course, Dyer was rotated to sea duty, was wounded, and recuperated at the naval hospital at Bethesda. When he was up and about, King invited him to pay a call at CominCh headquarters. After Dyer arrived, the admiral showed him a report he had just received from his current flag secretary. It said that King's staff then numbered 416.[1]

Unlike many of his contemporaries, Halsey was determined to have the staff he needed to run his command efficiently. He intended to delegate as much authority as possible, refusing to oversee details others could handle. He would conserve his energies for conferences, decisions, inspections, and ceremonial functions that only Commander, South Pacific, could carry out. Retaining key members of Ghormley's staff, he added to them Miles Browning and Julian Brown, who had come south with him, and Bromfield Nichol, Leonard Dow, Doug Moulton, and Bill Ashford from the *Enterprise.* From Nimitz he borrowed Rear Admiral William L. Calhoun, CinCPac service force commander, to unsnarl the South Pacific command's logistic tangle, and Captain John R. Redman, CinCPac communication officer, to straighten out South Pacific's communications. Exercising the authority of his four stars, he kept prodding the Bureau of Personnel for more good men until he had twenty-five competent officers devoting full-time attention to operations alone.

Long before he reached that happy number, Halsey had to find living and working space for his officers and men. Ghormley's headquarters, the old repair ship *Argonne,* overcrowded and without air conditioning, was hopelessly inadequate. Summer, fast approaching in these latitudes south of the equator, would turn her compartments into unbearable sweatboxes. Ghormley had wanted to move ashore but the local authorities had told him they had no housing to offer. Halsey was determined to find housing.

New Caledonia, French territory, reflected the divisions among Frenchmen in Europe and elsewhere. The Germans were occupying northern and western France. From the city of Vichy the rest of the country was governed under German sufferance by a provisional government of French politicians who believed they could best serve their countrymen by cooperating with the victorious Nazis. In London General de Gaulle had placed himself at the head of the Free French movement, which did not recognize the French defeat and continued the struggle against the Axis. Most of the French islands in the Pacific had declared for de Gaulle, but many of the French on New Caledonia were pro-Vichy. Others resented the presence of the Americans, fearing corruption of their cherished French customs. Local elements managed to report all Allied ship and troop movements to the Japanese.

Halsey appointed Julian Brown his emissary to get suitable housing ashore. Aware of the tense situation and also of the Frenchman's respect for decorations, he had Colonel Brown, who had served with French forces, array himself in his dress uniform. This included all his ribbons, a fourragère on his shoulder, and the Croix de Guerre—the last two attesting to his gallantry in the French service. Thus adorned, Brown presented himself at the government building and was promptly escorted into the presence of His Excellency Monsieur Montchamps, governor of New Caledonia. After an exchange of politenesses, Colonel Brown stated his mission—the Americans' need for quarters ashore in Noumea.

The governor pondered a moment. "What do we get in return?"

Brown replied coldly, "We will continue to protect you as we have always done."

His Excellency frowned. He said he would see what he could do, and the audience was at an end.

When nothing happened, Colonel Brown returned to the government building. The governor was in no position to deny him an audience, but all he offered were more empty promises. Repeatedly Brown returned. At the end of a month, when he had been offered nothing definite, he burst out, "We've got a war on our hands, and we can't continue to devote valuable time to these petty concerns. I venture to remind Your Excellency that if we Americans had not arrived here, the Japanese would have."

His Excellency shrugged and turned away, and Colonel Brown stormed out of the building.

By this time Admiral Halsey had ceased to resent Governor Montchamps, having learned that he was little more than a figurehead. The actual sovereignty of New Caledonia was being exercised in absentia by Rear Admiral Georges Thierry d'Argenlieu, high commissioner for the Free French in the Pacific. While d'Argenlieu's duties took him elsewhere, his authority was administered in New Caledonia by his chief of staff, who alone had been entrusted with the French code, the sole means of classified official communication between New Caledonia and the high commissioner or the Free French government in London. The situation was complicated by the fact that d'Argenlieu had developed a strong suspicion of American intentions. In the early days of the Pacific war, when Australians were building airfields on New Caledonia to protect their supply line with the United States, d'Argenlieu had notified the United States that, unless he could be assured of adequate and early protection, he would stop all work on the airfields lest they induce the advancing Japanese to attack the island.

In fact, fifteen thousand troops had been earmarked under Brigadier General Alexander M. Patch for New Caledonia, and these were soon under way, but the United States did not inform d'Argenlieu of this development, because all the messages sent to his headquarters in the past seemed inevitably to have reached the Japanese. When Patch arrived with his troops at Noumea in May 1942, he found that d'Argenlieu had been arrested by the French natives in retaliation for his high-handed maintenance of French sovereignty. Though General Patch obtained his release, d'Argenlieu blamed the Americans for the indignity he had suffered.[2]

Halsey made a survey of vacant real estate in Noumea. With cool disregard for French pretensions, he took over for office space nothing less than the headquarters of the absent high commissioner himself. As his official residence he and his staff appropriated the Japanese consulate, the consul having been interned in Australia at the outbreak of war. One of the few brick houses in Noumea, the consulate crowned a hilltop where the breezes were cool and the view superb. With deep satisfaction Halsey attended the morning ceremony when marine guards raised the American flag over the erstwhile Japanese property. Inside he found the chairs and tables too low for his comfort and the decorations too Japanese for his taste, but he accepted these drawbacks as the inevitable hardships of warfare. His Filipino mess attendants were puzzled but gratified when the admiral reacted to their breaking a piece of the consul's china by saying, "The hell with it. It's Japanese." For additional office space, the Americans took over a run-down French house, which they named Havoc Hall, and set up two Quonset huts, christened Wicky-Wacky Lodge.

As Commander, South Pacific, Admiral Halsey commanded everything in the huge South Pacific Area—troops, ships, planes, and supplies of America's and New Zealand's army, navy, and marine corps. He reported only to CinCPac, and through him to CominCh. Since the planned advance up the Solomons to Rabaul would involve amphibious operations, with the army, navy, and marine corps in close coordination, interservice friction had to be avoided. There had to be, in effect, a unification of the services. Halsey found General Harmon, commanding his army ground and air forces, and General Vandegrift, his marine corps commander, in complete agreement with him on this point.

To make sure that unity penetrated the ranks, Halsey called a meeting of his subordinate commanders. "Gentlemen," he said, "we are the South Pacific Fighting Force. I don't want anybody even to be thinking in terms of Army, Navy, or Marines. Every man must understand this, and every man *will* understand it, if I have to take off his uniform and issue coveralls with 'South Pacific Fighting Force' printed on the seat of his pants."

To contribute to uniformity, Halsey ordered the navy men and marines in his area to leave off their neckties. They were uncomfortable in the hot latitudes, but his real reason was that the army was not required to wear them. He figured that the more the men looked alike the easier it would be for them to forget their differences. For the benefit of new arrivals he had a sign placed over his office door:

> Complete with black tie
> You do look terrific,
> But take it off here:
> This is the South Pacific![3]

Meanwhile, the Americans had been closely scrutinizing the Guadalcanal campaign for its lessons. One fact stood out clearly. The early failure to make any serious attempt to sidetrack the night-running Tokyo Express, which in September, October, and early November had poured 30,000 enemy troops onto the island, had emboldened the Japanese to dispatch 13,500 additional troops there in an ill-protected convoy by daylight.

The near destruction of this convoy, together with evidence that the South Pacific was now in the hands of an area commander prepared to risk men, ships, and planes to make good his occupation of the island, had obviously impressed the Japanese. They knew and the Americans knew that but for the U.S. Navy's sacrifice of ships and men Japanese battleships would have so blasted Henderson Field that aircraft could not have used it, and the convoy would have reached Guadalcanal with relative impunity.

The Japanese made no further attempt to reinforce their Guadalcanal garrison. To keep their troops on the island alive, they contrived a streamlined Tokyo Express of fast night-running destroyers that dropped floating drums of food and medical supplies offshore and then darted back up the Slot before daylight.

An examination of surface actions, beginning with the Battle of Savo Island, in which the Allies lost four heavy cruisers, underscored the fact that the Americans had a great deal to learn about night-fighting surface tactics and the use of radar, of which they had a monopoly. A reevaluation of the October Battle of Cape Esperance revealed that the Americans had achieved less of a victory than they originally supposed. Through sheer luck they had "capped the enemy's T," but they had reversed course by column movement, thereby masking part of their own fire and providing the enemy with a stationary point of aim.

In subsequent night actions the Americans had adopted the same formation they had used in the Cape Esperance battle—single file, with destroyers leading and sometimes also following, in which positions they proved unable to employ their torpedoes. Tactical maneuvers, if any, were carried out only by the Japanese.

Despite the urgent needs of the Atlantic and North African campaigns, the navy had quickly replaced the ship and personnel losses suffered in the Battle of Guadalcanal. Halsey assigned a force of newly arrived cruisers and destroyers to Tom Kinkaid with orders to derail the new Express. The latter, with long experience in such types, was determined to meet the Japanese on better than even terms.

Kinkaid had no intention of employing a blind approach or a single, unbroken column. In night engagements he planned to employ floatplanes for early warning, using parachute flares when needed. His destroyers were to speed ahead to make a surprise torpedo attack and then turn away. His cruisers, holding off at 12,000 yards, out of visual range of the enemy, were to open fire the moment the torpedoes hit.

The plan was sound, but Kinkaid never had an opportunity to use it. He was whisked away to recapture the Aleutian islands occupied by the Japanese in the Battle of Midway. The change was unfortunate for the South Pacific command and disastrous for the professional reputation of newly arrived Rear Admiral Carleton Wright, on whom fell the task of executing the Kinkaid plan. On 30 November, two days after Wright's arrival in the South Pacific, Halsey ordered him to take his cruiser-destroyer force into Ironbottom Sound to intercept an approaching Tokyo Express. The resulting contact brought on the Battle of Tassafaronga, so named for a Guadalcanal coastal point, north of which the battle was fought.

As Wright's force of five cruisers and six destroyers approached from the

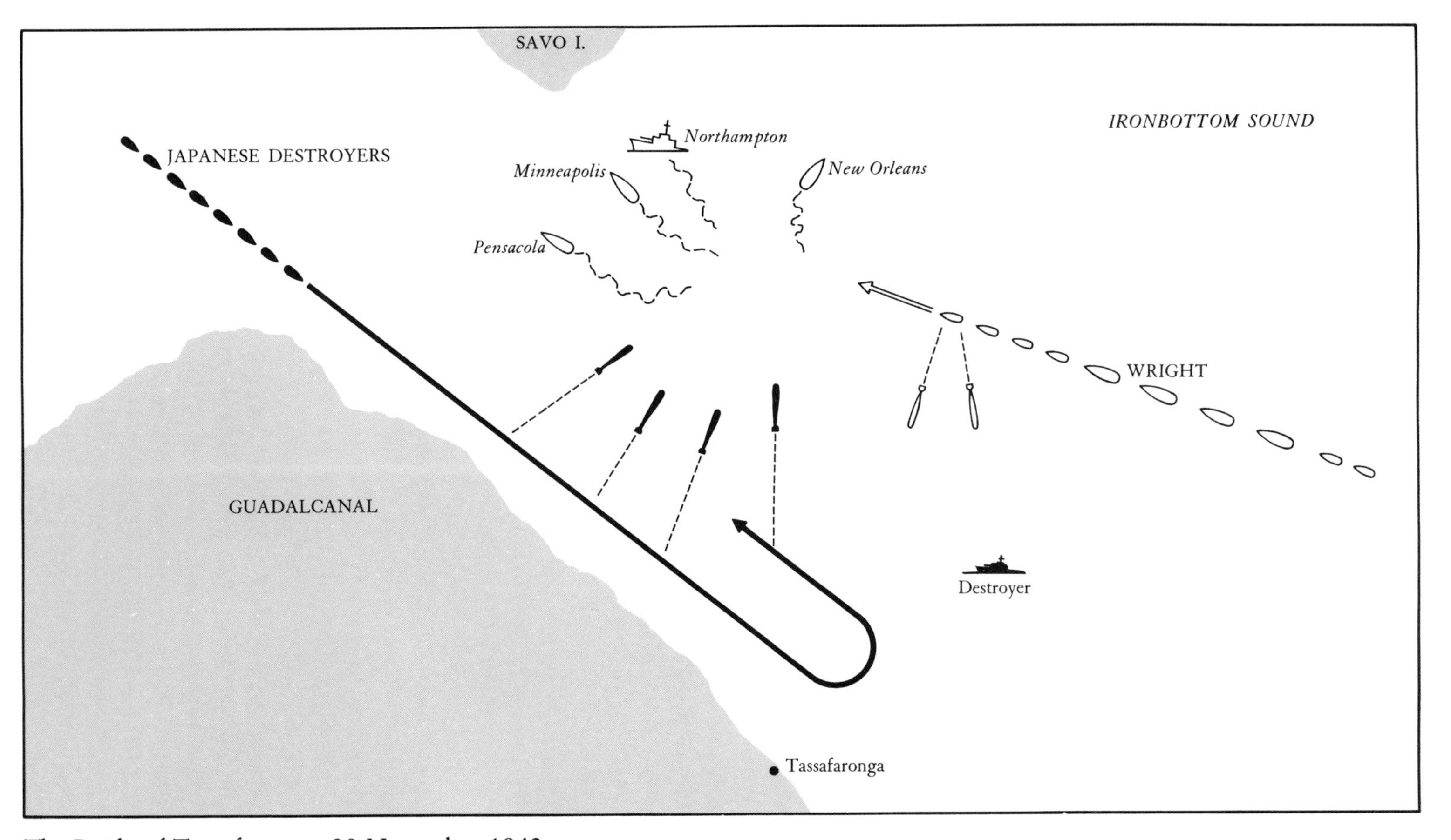

The Battle of Tassafaronga, 30 November 1942

east in total darkness, an express of eight destroyers entered the sound from the west, but of this Wright was unaware. The floatplanes that were to give him warning had been unable to rise from the water because of a dead calm. Wright's flagship at last made radar contact with the Japanese destroyers speeding southward on an opposite course, but because they hugged the Guadalcanal shoreline, Wright could get no clear radar data and hesitated to release his van destroyers. His cruisers, however, opened fire on one of the enemy destroyers, somewhat nearer than the rest, and sent her down in flames.

The other Japanese destroyers had now reversed course and were running along the shore parallel to the American course. Because the Americans were not provided with flashless powder, their successive gun flashes had enabled the enemy to determine the cruisers' range, bearing, course, and speed. The Japanese released a score of torpedoes toward a point where the American cruisers would be when the weapons reached the end of their runs. They were well aimed and ran true, and Wright's cruisers maintained course and speed, so the torpedoes inevitably found their targets. All the cruisers except the *Honolulu* took one or more hits. The *Minneapolis* and *New Orleans* had their bows ripped away. The *Pensacola,* her after engine room flooded and three of her turrets knocked out, was quickly wreathed in oil fires. Worst hit was the *Northampton;* as water poured into the gashes in her side and blazing oil drenched her decks, the crew abandoned ship and she heeled over and sank. By that time the seven surviving Japanese destroyers were far up the Slot. This brief battle, which besides vitally needed cruisers cost the Americans four hundred lives, provided a sort of textbook, later well studied, on how not to combat the powerful and accurate Japanese torpedo.[4]

The three damaged cruisers that remained afloat made their way to Tulagi, where they hid in coves, concealing themselves from the enemy by means of nets and foliage. Here their crews, with the help of technicians and machinists from a tender and three fleet tugs, used coconut logs to get their ships into barely seaworthy condition. The *Pensacola* reached Pearl Harbor on one propeller. The *Minneapolis* made it to Espíritu Santo for further patching up before proceeding to Pearl and eventually to Mare Island.

On 12 December the *New Orleans,* her engineering plant intact but with a coconut-log false face, set out for Sydney, Australia, shepherded by two destroyers. What followed proved to be a nightmare voyage. Even in smooth water the *New Orleans* could make no better than six or seven knots, but whenever the wind blew she had to turn around and back so as not to break her wooden bulkhead—in which awkward posture she could make no more than three knots. The battered cruiser and her escorts, maintaining radio silence and taking an unfrequented route, at length intercepted radio messages inquiring about them. Were they lost? Still under silence, the little group could not reply as it was tempted to do.

They arrived at Sydney on Christmas Eve, 1942. None of the voyagers hailed the arrival with greater delight than members of the crew of the escorting destroyer *Lansdowne*. Much involved in the Guadalcanal campaign, they had not had a single overnight liberty in seven months. A little before 1500 on 24 December, their commanding officer, Lieutenant Commander William R. Smedberg III, got on the loudspeaker. "Men," he announced, "your entire stay at Sydney is to be devoted to liberty and relaxation!" The exhausted crew mustered enough strength to sound off with cheer after cheer.

As Smedberg left the microphone, a signalman handed him a dispatch from a station on the headland. From Admiral Halsey, it read, "*Lansdowne* fuel and depart immediately. Conduct troopship *Mount Vernon* to Noumea."

In disgust, Smedberg turned to his executive officer, Lieutenant Frank Foley. "Frank," he said, "what does 'immediately' mean to you?"

With a twinkle in his eye, Foley replied, "Captain, to me 'immediately' means seven o'clock tomorrow morning."

Smedberg nodded. "Frank, " he said, "that's exactly what it means to me. I'll take the ship alongside the fuel tender and get her fueled. You go down and divide the officers and crew into two parts. Just as soon as you get ready, you can let one half of the ship go on liberty. Try to pick the light drinkers for the first half. They have to be back at ten o'clock tonight. Then, as they get back, the man who's been assigned as each man's relief can go ashore, and he has to be back at 6:30 in the morning. We will sail at seven."

Having made these arrangements, Smedberg went ashore himself and spent the night partying. "I danced with all the beautiful Australian girls," he said, "and had a wonderful time with my two groups of officers, the first group and the second group." Exhilarated from a night of dancing and drinking, Smedberg arrived back at his ship at a quarter to seven and was gratified to learn that every man of his ship's company had reported back by 0630. Said he to the officer of the deck, "Are you ready to get under way?"

"Yes, Sir, all is prepared for getting under way."

"Tell the executive officer to take the ship to sea at seven o'clock. I'm going to turn in."

Apparently the exec had spent his liberty carousing not wisely but too thoroughly. His friends had had to lug him back to the ship. "We've been unable to rouse him," said the officer of the deck.

Declaring that he would have a try at it, Smedberg went to Foley's cabin. He shook the exec, pulled his hair, rolled him out of his bunk onto the deck. The man couldn't be awakened. So Smedberg, after a night on the town, perforce spent the following day on the bridge.

On arriving at Noumea, Smedberg made his official report and then asked to see the admiral. Ushered into Halsey's office, he laid his cards on the table. "Admiral," he said, "you almost had a mutiny on your hands recently."

"Is that right?" said Halsey. "What happened?"

"Sir," replied Smedberg, "the crew of the USS *Lansdowne* almost mutinied, and the mutiny was almost led by her captain." He then proceeded to tell Halsey what had happened. "We almost mutinied," he repeated.

"By God, I would have!" Halsey exploded. "Captain," he said, "I wouldn't have obeyed that order. If you ever get an order like that, send a dispatch and say why you can't do it."

"Well, Sir," replied Smedberg, "you've got four stars on, and I'm a lieutenant commander. I can't do that."

Halsey measured his words. "If you ever get in a fix like that again," he said, "the needs of your crew come first."

Recalling that period, Smedberg said of Halsey, "He had the ability to make each one of us feel that we were part of his team and that he knew exactly what we were doing all the time. Every now and then he'd send a message to an individual ship, 'That was a great job you did' at such and such a time. He would . . . come on board ship now and again, . . . say hello to you, and you got the feeling that you knew him and he knew you. He developed a great esprit."[5]

After the Battle of Tassafaronga, the Americans found new ways to deal with the supply-bearing Tokyo Express, which attempted night runs to Guadalcanal at four-day intervals. At twilight on 3 December fighters from Henderson Field discovered ten enemy destroyers, covered by Japanese fighters, coming down the Slot. The Americans attacked, damaging one destroyer, shooting down three enemy planes, and losing two of their own. At dawn other American planes found hundreds of supply-filled drums off Tassafaronga. Evidently the Japanese garrison was too exhausted and weakened to haul many ashore during the night. The American planes sank the floating drums with machine-gun bullets.

On 7 December the Tokyo Express, attacked by American aircraft before dark and by PT boats later, turned back without delivering any supplies. The 11 December express passed unscathed through the usual sunset air attack and dropped several hundred drums off Cape Esperance. As the destroyers were withdrawing, however, the American PT boats discovered them, sank one of the destroyers, and chased the others away.

In December the bone-weary U.S. First Marine Division, after four months of combatting the enemy, malaria, and foul weather seven days a week, began leaving the green hell of Guadalcanal for well-earned rest and recreation in Australia. They left behind the 147th Infantry, two regiments of the Second Marine Division, and two regiments of the army's Americal

Division (so called because it was the first American division to reach New Caledonia). On 9 December General Patch relieved General Vandegrift as ground force commander on Guadalcanal.

In exchange for the First Marine Division, which now came under Commander, Southwest Pacific, General MacArthur diverted to Commander, South Pacific, the army's Twenty-fifth Infantry Division, then en route from Pearl Harbor to Sydney. The transports bringing the division put in to Noumea, and the commander, Major General J. Lawton Collins, reported to Halsey. He was delighted to see Joe Collins, whom he had known since the latter was a colonel. Joe, said Halsey, was "a small man, quick on his feet, and even quicker in his brain." Joe was also full of vinegar. He called his command "the finest regular division in the Army."

"Give me three weeks to unload my transports and combat-load them," he assured Halsey, "and I'll be ready to go anywhere."

Bill Halsey burst out laughing. Joe wanted to know why. Halsey explained, "Your division is leaving for Guadalcanal tomorrow!"

The Twenty-fifth Division, in three transports escorted by five destroyers, arrived at Guadalcanal on 29 December. Without docks, and with insufficient lighterage and few trucks, they unloaded in less than two days 7,737 officers and men, 180 vehicles, and 7,110 tons of cargo.[6]

Americans on Guadalcanal now numbered nearly fifty thousand. No Japanese reinforcements had reached the island since the four surviving but battered ships of the ill-fated eleven-transport convoy had arrived on the night of 14–15 November, bringing the enemy garrison strength up to about thirty-five thousand. American aircraft and PT boats had seen to it that few supplies had reached Guadalcanal from Japanese sources. The Americans assumed, correctly as it turned out, that the garrison was being decimated by disease and starvation.

In late November Halsey was notified that the Japanese, partly concealed by a coconut grove, were building a new airfield at Munda in the southwest end of New Georgia Island in the central Solomons, only 175 miles from Henderson Field. From the point of view of the Japanese, this was an operation they should have undertaken long ago to provide adequate fighter-plane support for their bombers attacking Guadalcanal and their ships transiting the Slot.

Though aircraft from Guadalcanal struck repeatedly at the new airfield and the ships supplying it, the Japanese kept on doggedly repairing damages and continuing construction. Halsey would have given a great deal to know if the new field was intended to support a renewed campaign to recapture Guadalcanal or if the Japanese were merely holding on tenuously to the island to keep the Americans busy while they prepared a new advance position in the central Solomons.

Bill Halsey was not the sort to so immerse himself in strategic problems that he overlooked social requirements. He had to operate at least partly under French authority. Very well. In the period following World War I he had learned to cooperate with the French. He could do it again. Bill began with Governor Montchamps, with whom Julian Brown had crossed swords. As early as 20 December he could write to Nimitz: "Our personal relations are fine. The Governor is a nice old boy, a good and tried soldier—albeit a bit futile. Two members of my staff and I are dining with him tonight."

Ever since Halsey had taken over as Commander, South Pacific, the New Zealand government had been urging him to pay a visit. Toward the end of December, with no major actions imminent, he accepted the invitation. New Zealand was entirely within his South Pacific Area. American personnel with American equipment had established depots there. In due course he would have to deal with New Zealand officials, and New Zealand soldiers, sailors, and ships would be serving under him.

With Julian Brown and Bill Kitchell he took off from Noumea in his Coronado at 0730 on 2 January and reached Auckland at 1630 that afternoon. Halsey was gratified to be met at the wharf by Peter Fraser, the prime minister, who accompanied him to his hotel. Fraser was worried. New Zealanders, fearful of a Japanese breakthrough followed by an attack on their country, wanted Fraser to bring home the New Zealand divisions serving in North Africa. Prime Minister Churchill and President Roosevelt insisted that they stay. General Montgomery, after pursuing Rommel's Afrika Korps across the Libyan desert, needed every man under his command in order to break into Tunisia. Fraser had no desire to jeopardize the situation in Africa, but he was afraid he would have to surrender to war cabinet demands unless he was backed by strong reassurances from Halsey.

"What do you want me to say," asked the admiral, "and when and where?"

Fraser had it all arranged. Editors and reporters were waiting at the hotel to interview him. Asked by the newsmen what he expected Japan's next move would be, he replied, "Japan's next move will be to retreat. A start has been made to make them retreat. They will not be able to stop going back."

Word had preceded Halsey that he was predicting a complete Allied victory in 1943. The New Zealand journalists wanted to know if he still stood by that prediction. "That is right," Halsey replied. "We have 363 days left to fulfill my prediction and we are going to do it."

Was he satisfied, the newsmen asked, with the progress of operations against the Japanese? "We have their measure in the air, on and under the water, and on the land," Halsey said. "When we first started out against them I held that one of our men was equal to three Japanese. I have now increased this to twenty. They are not supermen, although they try to make us believe they are."

How about Japanese naval tactics? Were they hard to meet? "Like everything else about them, they are tricky, but not too hard to fathom," Halsey replied. "There is nothing to be worried about in their tactics. Any normal naval officer can lick them."

Asked if the forces in the combat zone under his command were now optimistic about the future, Halsey replied that they had been confident from the beginning and they continued to be confident.

Fraser was delighted. Halsey had given his people just the kind of pep talk the prime minister thought they needed. The next day the admiral toured military installations in Auckland, including U.S. military hospitals crowded with American wounded from Guadalcanal.

He made an outstanding impression on the New Zealanders, evidenced by a 7 January 1943 editorial in *The New Zealand Herald:*

> Few people can live up to their reputations. Admiral Halsey is one of them. The bold actions fought in the Gilberts, the Marshalls, and the Solomons had made of him a legend for enterprise and hard hitting. His recent visit to Auckland showed all who were privileged to meet him the embodiment of the legend. For all his unassuming manner and quiet speech, none could fail to identify in him the leader, the man of action, the fighter. . . .

After a tour of Wellington hospitals and installations, Halsey returned to Noumea on 6 January. January promised to be a full month. A U.S. surface force had just carried out a night bombardment of the Munda airfield, and another was scheduled. The Tokyo Express supply system was again running nighttime operations, and measures were being devised to thwart it. General Patch was planning an all-out westward drive, to be launched on the tenth. Secretary of the Navy Knox and Admiral Nimitz were coming from Pearl Harbor for an inspection tour and a conference. Rear Admiral John Sidney McCain, chief of the Bureau of Aeronautics, was en route from Washington to assess the South Pacific's need for aircraft and naval airmen.[7]

"Slew" McCain was coming to visit a post he had left less than six months earlier when, in a game of naval musical chairs, Jake Fitch, erstwhile Commander, Aircraft, Pacific, had come from Pearl Harbor to relieve him as Commander, Aircraft, South Pacific. McCain had gone to Washington to relieve Jack Towers as chief of the Bureau of Aeronautics, and Towers had gone to Pearl Harbor to relieve Halsey as Commander, Aircraft, Pacific, Halsey having recently relieved Fitch in that post.

There were few wiser or more competent officers in the navy than Slew McCain, but whenever his name came up, somebody had a ridiculous story to tell about him—and many of the stories were true. Possibly his reputation for comical adventures had something to do with his appearance. With bony frame, hooked nose, and sunken cheeks, he looked at least ten years older than his age. Junior officers and enlisted men often referred to him as Popeye the

Admirals Nimitz and Halsey conferring on board the *Curtiss* at Espíritu Santo, 20 January 1943

Sailor Man, whom he superficially resembled. Apparently unable to get false teeth that fitted, his speech was interspersed with whistles.

Admiral Nimitz, too, was acquiring an undesirable reputation—as a man who had hard luck with airplanes. He had been in a crash while heading stateside after the Battle of Midway and in another at the beginning of his current tour of bases with Secretary Knox. Fortunately he was not seriously injured in either accident.

On 20 January McCain, Nimitz, Knox, and Halsey met for a conference at Espíritu Santo on board Jake Fitch's headquarters flagship, the tender *Curtiss*.

Bill Halsey had arrived with some grievances, the result of his continued fight to get and retain the officers he believed he needed for his South Pacific staff. He tore first into a startled Slew McCain, whom he encountered on the *Curtiss* quarterdeck. His dispute with McCain was in a sense a continuation of the feud that had begun when Nimitz was chief of the Bureau of Navigation (later the Bureau of Naval Personnel) and Jack Towers chief of the Bureau of Aeronautics. Tradition allocated responsibility for the training and assignment of naval personnel to the navigation-personnel bureau, but Towers, as chief of the new Bureau of Aeronautics, insisted that training and assignment of naval aviators were his prerogative.

The feud had continued under Nimitz's and Tower's successors, Randall Jacobs and Slew McCain, and Bill Halsey had joined the fight. His current beef was over an order recently received by a junior member of Halsey's staff, Lieutenant Commander Paul Stroop, transferring him back to his previous billet in the Bureau of Aeronautics. Neither Halsey nor Stroop liked the order. The admiral intended to oppose it and had brought Stroop along to Espíritu as exhibit A. Halsey protested so vehemently that the racket attracted news cameramen, who began photographing the scene. Bill took the situation in stride, but McCain was reduced to whistling through his teeth. When he finally regained use of his voice, he promptly rescinded the objectionable order.

Halsey next turned his attention to Admiral Nimitz, though whether in the latter's capacity as former chief of the Bureau of Personnel or as sponsor of the present chief, Admiral Jacobs, was not clear. Halsey told the ex-bureau chief a bitter story. Shortly after he had relieved Ghormley as Commander, South Pacific, the commander of the naval base at Tulagi had become ill, and Halsey had to find a relief for him without delay. He thought at once of Commander Oliver Owen ("Scrappy") Kessing, able officer and old friend, and requested the Bureau of Personnel to order him to the South Pacific in the temporary rank of captain. The bureau replied, "Regret his services unavailable," to which Halsey, who knew better, replied hotly, "Make his services available." After a further exchange of snappish radio messages, the bureau capitulated in part. It notified Halsey that Kessing was on his way, but said nothing about the promotion.

Halsey told Nimitz that he was fed up with the bureau's obstructionism and swore that, if the requested promotion had not come through by the time he got back to Noumea, he would send a message to Kessing and an information copy to the bureau: "You will assume rank, uniform, and title of captain, U.S. Navy."

Nimitz threw up his hands. "No! For God's sake, don't do it!" he exclaimed. "You'll foul up everything!"

"You wait and see," replied Halsey.

If Nimitz took action, he left no record of it. The fact remains, however, that confirmation of Scrappy's promotion arrived in time to prevent a showdown between Halsey and the bureau.

After an evening conference, all hands turned in on board the *Curtiss*. Hardly had they done so when enemy bombs started falling. The attack did not last long and it produced only a few craters on the beach, but since this was Espíritu's first air raid in several weeks, there was speculation about the enemy having information of the high-ranking assemblage there.

The next day Halsey, McCain, Nimitz, and Knox flew to Guadalcanal. The island was still far from being a resort, but Halsey and Nimitz noted at once that the installations and the condition of the men had improved enormously since their last visit. Henderson Field had become a respectable, all-weather airstrip, supplemented by a fighter strip not far away. Malaria was still very much of a problem, but the men little resembled the weary wraiths of earlier days. Most of these, including all of the pioneer First Marine Divison, had been relieved by fresh, vigorous men, ready and eager to destroy what remained of the enemy garrison. Though Guadalcanal was still being bombed from time to time, the Americans had won substantial command of the air over and the sea around Guadalcanal.

It so happened that the enemy chose to bomb that night, a vicious attack lasting from 2030 until daybreak. Now almost everybody was convinced that the Japanese were after big game—and knew exactly where to find it.

At the first *bang!* Halsey, Knox, and McCain abandoned their comfortable hut on the double and dived into the nearest trench. There is some question concerning what sort of trench Slew McCain jumped into. According to one story that circulated through the South Pacific, it had been the ditch under a latrine. Workmen had shifted the latrine housing to a fresh spot but had not yet covered the old ditch with dirt. Halsey and other witnesses do not mention McCain's poor choice of foxhole—either because the story wasn't true or because they wished to spare their friend embarrassment.

One fact, however, is clear: Chester Nimitz remained in bed in his hut. He had missed his sleep the night before, he said, and needed to catch up. Anyway, he was afraid of mosquitoes. Halsey, Knox, and McCain spent the night outdoors, half naked, in miserable conditions—and McCain apparently in extraordinarily miserable conditions. As it turned out, Nimitz, who slept under a sheet, behind screens, was the only member of the party to catch malaria.

The next day the travelers took off for Noumea, and the Guadalcanal communication officer prepared to file the routine departure dispatch. "Do me a favor, will you?" said his shaken assistant. "Send it in Japanese. I want 'em to know for sure that the high-priced help has left here!"[8]

On the afternoon of 23 January the high-priced help was assembled at a conference table in Halsey's Noumea headquarters. Present also were De Witt Peck, now a marine brigadier general, and a little later, General Harmon.

Admiral Nimitz, his malaria still latent, opened the meeting at 1520. "The object of this meeting," he announced, "is to review the situation in the South Pacific and to exchange views. No decision will be reached. Indeed, we may not agree on all points. First, as to Guadalcanal. What is ComSoPac's view as to progress, approximate date Japs will be eliminated? Shall we need more troops? What number should be left as a garrison on completion of the operation?"

Halsey, who had had a good deal to say on the trip to Guadalcanal, now let his subordinates do most of the talking. General Peck estimated that the Japanese would be eliminated from the island not later than 1 April. Nimitz expressed surprise that it should take so long. Peck replied that his estimate was based on the possibility that the Japanese might use delaying tactics. In any event, he said, there were enough U.S. troops on Guadalcanal. He then turned to future plans. During Halsey's absence, the South Pacific staff hatched a scheme to occupy the Russell Islands, thirty miles northwest of Guadalcanal, chiefly as a PT-boat base and staging point for landing craft.

"It seems reasonable to me," Halsey said.

The discussion turned to the forthcoming drive up the Solomons. A primary task would be taking out the new Japanese airfield at Munda Point.

"When do you think you can move against Munda?" Nimitz asked.

"April first," said Peck, provided a division of amphibious troops was available and ready at that time.

These apparently would be available, but what about aircraft? McCain promised more naval planes and offered to pressure the army into providing more aircraft.

Nimitz wanted to know when the new airstrip on Guadalcanal, then under construction, would be finished.

"It should be ready for heavy bombers by the end of February," replied Halsey, "but in emergency it could be used by the middle of February."

Once South Pacific forces began their advance up the Solomons, how did they plan to use Guadalcanal? Nimitz wanted to know. As a supporting base, he was told.

"It is my idea," said Nimitz, "that no permanent installations should be erected there. The only construction should be that necessary, and there should be a reduction in the rear areas. Everything should be based on the forward movement."

Officers who had attended both conferences of CinCPac and Commander, South Pacific, could not fail to have noted the sharp contrast between the harried, anxiety-ridden atmosphere of the September meeting and the confident, optimistic tone of the January meeting. The difference was partly the result of the vastly improved military outlook, but there was clear evidence also of much better administration, resulting mainly from Halsey's delegating authority to able men and backing them wholeheartedly.

The next morning the visitors departed, Nimitz and staff to Pearl Harbor,

McCain and Knox and their retinues via Pearl to Washington. Secretary Knox was much impressed by Halsey, feeling that he was perhaps not the best of administrators but every inch a leader, who attracted good men and won their confidence.

Secretary Knox returned to Washington with a couple of resolutions: to send Nimitz a decent flag plane with engines that wouldn't conk out and to provide Halsey with a sane and competent chief of staff. Miles Browning had been up to form, offending Knox and others repeatedly. Officers closely associated with Browning and recognizing his abilities learned to shrug off his temperamental vagaries, but Knox in a few hours of astonished observation had tagged him as a psychological basket case and, in his current post, a clear and imminent danger to the national security.

General Patch was now well launched on his westward offensive against an enemy who gave ground stubbornly, using cleverly sited artillery. More effective in slowing the drive was the problem of supplying front-line U.S. troops. As the main body of Patch's infantry advanced westward along Guadalcanal's north coast, a battalion was ferried around to a new beachhead west of Cape Esperance. The newly landed troops then advanced eastward to meet the approaching main body in order to nip off the enemy's communication with the coast and seal him up in the jungle for annihilation.

Meanwhile, Halsey's attention was focusing elsewhere. Allied aircraft and traffic analysts detected transports and destroyers assembling at Rabaul and in the upper Solomons. The Combined Fleet once more entered the waters north of Guadalcanal. Evidently the Japanese were about to make a fifth attempt at reinforcement, seizing the airfield, and recapturing the island. This time the South Pacific had power aplenty to turn them back. Halsey promptly dispatched to Guadalcanal a troop convoy supported by five task forces, including the repaired *Enterprise* and *Saratoga,* two escort carriers, and three battleships. No fleet action ensued, for the Combined Fleet had come down not to do battle but merely to create a diversion. Instead the Japanese struck from the air. At night, using parachute flares and floating lights, torpedo planes from the new Munda airfield attacked and succeeded in sinking the heavy cruiser *Chicago.*

While American attention was being diverted by the decoy force, a score of Japanese destroyers in three high-speed night runs down the Slot had carried away the twelve thousand half-starved survivors of their Guadalcanal garrison, all that remained alive of the thirty-five thousand Imperial Army troops who had occupied their end of the island in November. When the converging American land forces made contact on 9 February, they found that the quarry had slipped through their fingers. Thus on a note of mingled frustration and triumph for both sides, the Guadalcanal campaign came to an end.

Despite the enemy's escape, General Patch's report—"Total and complete defeat of Japanese forces on Guadalcanal effected today. . . . Tokyo Express no longer has terminus in Guadalcanal"—was received in Noumea, Pearl Harbor, and Washington with unalloyed rejoicing. As for Admiral Nimitz, in the hospital at Pearl recovering from his malaria, the good news did much to put him back on his feet.[9]

CHAPTER 13

CAESAR AND THE BULL

NEWSPAPERS AROUND THE WORLD commented on Admiral Halsey's prediction of an Allied victory before the end of 1943. In Washington the statement produced astonishment and some alarm. U.S. production chiefs were afraid that workmen on war projects, taking as gospel Halsey's word about an early end to hostilities, would quit their jobs. Draft authorities complained, and so did a good many other officials. Halsey was accused of everything from drunkenness to mental aberration.

In an interview in *The New York Times* in early 1945, with the war still raging, Captain Harold E. Stassen, then on Admiral Halsey's staff, explained the admiral's forecast:

> The admiral doesn't like alibis, but I'll take a chance and tell why he made that wrong prediction. . . . He made it during the darkest period of the Pacific War. We had very little navy afloat. Australia was very much concerned. The Japanese navy was still strong. It was a pretty gloomy situation. Halsey knew that if the Jap navy had attacked our force, it was doubtful if our fleet, even with its magnificent fighting spirit, could hold the line. So he made this bold assertive statement both to mislead the Japanese and to cheer up our force. It worked. The Japanese didn't attack for six months. Instead they tried to find out what in the world Admiral Halsey had that led him to make that statement.

Two years later, the war over, Halsey himself in somewhat more emphatic language undertook to explain his early published statements:

> God Almighty, I knew we wouldn't be in Tokyo that soon! I knew we wouldn't be there even by the end of 1944. I may be tactless, but I am not a damned fool! What the civilian bigwigs didn't consider is this: my forces were tired; their morale was low; they were beginning to think that they were abused and forgotten, that they had been fighting too much and too long. Moreover, the new myth of Japanese invincibility had not yet been entirely discredited. Prior to Pearl Harbor, the United States in general had rated Japan as no better than a class-C nation. After that one successful sneak attack, however, panicky eyes saw the monkeymen as supermen. I saw them as nothing of the sort, and I wanted my forces to know how I felt. I stand by the opinion that the Japs are bastards, and I stand by this one, too.[1]

One hesitates to pick out flaws in the testimony of such experienced officers, but Stassen and Halsey were talking about January 1943, and that was certainly not a time of low morale on Guadalcanal—or any other Allied territory. By late December 1942 all the U.S. island veterans, wasted by malaria and battered by incessant combat, had been relieved and were in more wholesome climes enjoying rest and recreation. Replacing them were men from the Americal and Second Marine divisions and from Joe Collins's hotshot Twenty-fifth Infantry Division—all spoiling for a fight. These men had been the target of aerial attacks to be sure, but nothing remotely like the heavy raids of the preceding months. Around the world the war was turning in favor of the Allies. British and American forces were closing in on the Germans and Italians in Tunisia. In Russia the Germans were facing imminent defeat at Stalingrad.

Meanwhile, the Japanese on Guadalcanal were dying. Since mid-November, they had received no reinforcements and precious little food or other supplies. By early December they were subsisting on grass roots and water. Foreseeing nothing but death, the men had worked out a mortality chart:

He who can rise to his feet	30 days left to live
He who can sit up	20 days left to live
He who must urinate while lying down	3 days left to live
He who cannot speak	2 days left to live
He who cannot blink his eyes	dead at dawn[2]

It is not surprising that Halsey, sending well-fed, newly arrived warriors against the stranded enemy, should have found one of his men equal to three, and eventually equal to twenty, dying Japanese. With respect to his forecast that the Allies would be in Tokyo in 1943, one is tempted to conclude that Halsey meant and believed what he said. Few officers were more careful about the image they projected. It seems unlikely that he would willingly have made a fool of himself in the international press.

Yet the truth may be, as Halsey's son and surviving members of the South Pacific staff insist, that the admiral began making such predictions during the dark days of October and November as a means of encouraging the embattled troops on Guadalcanal, a sort of coach's pep talk to hearten his apparently losing team, and that he continued to exude optimism through habit when better times arrived. According to this explanation, the newsmen who saw him regularly understood that such talk was for local consumption and did not report it. But when Halsey repeated it at general press conferences, the story reached the worldwide media with embarrassing repercussions.[3]

While Halsey in Auckland was proclaiming a 1943 ending for the war, or at least for the Pacific war, on the other side of the world in Casablanca, the Combined Chiefs of Staff (British and American) were meeting with President Roosevelt and Prime Minister Churchill to devise war plans for 1943 and 1944.

The United States had early agreed to join Britain in first defeating Germany, considered the most dangerous of the Axis powers because it was the nearest to England and the most likely to develop a decisive weapon. But Japanese aggression soon dashed British hopes that the United States would remain merely on the defensive in the Pacific theater until the Germans were defeated. Something had to be done to prevent Japan from consolidating its gains over a widening area.

The Americans, sometimes with help from Australia, blocked the Japanese advance in the Coral Sea and at Midway and hurled it back at Guadalcanal and New Guinea. So much they had achieved with only fifteen percent of Allied resources. The rest had gone to maintain operations against German and Italian forces in Europe, North Africa, and the Atlantic.

In Casablanca Admiral King and General Marshall argued that the Allied successes in the Pacific should be followed up promptly lest the Japanese regain the initiative they had lost. The strength deployed in the Pacific, they contended, should be raised to at least thirty percent of Allied resources, and the British chiefs of staff had no choice but to concur.[4]

The Combined Chiefs intended to make good their promise of reinforcements for the Pacific, but in the winter and spring of 1943 it seemed wiser to concentrate available military power in North Africa. In Tunisia British and American forces were closing the pincers on the enemy, and it was probable that they would capture enormous quantities of supplies and hundreds of thousands of Axis troops.

Though the concentration of Allied forces in Africa inevitably meant delaying the Allied shift to the offensive in the Pacific, Admiral King took comfort in the delay being temporary. Manpower for stepped-up Pacific operations was already available. Other requirements would soon be met. Under construction in the United States were weapons least needed in the European theater—carriers, battleships, dive-bombers, and torpedo planes. On the ways or nearing completion were twenty-two fleet carriers and eleven fast battleships. These, together with screening and amphibious vessels, would form a naval force of unprecedented power to lead a drive across the Pacific to the shores of Japan.

On 15 March King, anticipating the expansion of U.S. naval task forces to fleet strength, established a uniform numbering system, fleets in the Pacific being assigned odd numbers. The combatant ships of Halsey's South Pacific Force thus became the U.S. Third Fleet, and those assigned to the central Pacific, based at Pearl Harbor, became the U.S. Fifth Fleet. These, together with other American naval vessels operating in the Pacific Ocean areas, constituted the U.S. Pacific Fleet. Independent of the Pacific Fleet was MacArthur's small Naval Forces, Southwest Pacific, which became the U.S. Seventh Fleet. For operations, the fleets were divided into task forces, which in turn were divided into task groups and task units.

For the time being, Admiral Nimitz declined to dignify the few old battleships and supporting craft at Pearl Harbor with a fleet title, calling them instead Task Force 50. He and Admiral King, however, regarded this task force as the nucleus of the future Fifth Fleet, the main U.S. fleet, informally called the Big Blue Fleet, with which they intended to spearhead the drive directly across the Pacific.*

For senior U.S. naval officers who were privy to, or guessed accurately, what King and Nimitz had in mind, the future Fifth Fleet held tremendous interest. It was evidently destined to grow into a far-striking naval force that could become the mightiest in the history of the world. For a qualified officer, commanding such a force would be the supreme challenge. He would wield immense power, possibly be the chief victor over Japan, and thus earn for himself an unassailable place in history.

Since the principal punch of the new Fifth Fleet would presumably be provided by carriers, most naval aviators assumed that one of their own would be appointed to command it. Such was the attraction of the command, however, that half the flag officers in the navy, even some who had never set foot on a plane or carrier and others on permanent shore duty for health reasons, managed to dream up some reason why they were particularly eligible for the post. Admiral Nimitz did not have the power of appointment on such a high level, but it was believed, correctly, that his recommendation would be decisive. The navy awaited his decision.

The ever-discreet Nimitz has left us no record of his deliberations, but it is easy to make an educated guess why he early eliminated Bill Halsey from his list. Halsey was simply too valuable where he was. For the next few months his South Pacific Force would include more ships and more men than any other American command in the Pacific theater, and the south and adjoining southwest Pacific areas would be the major scene of operations against the Japanese.

In selecting an officer for the top seagoing command, Nimitz did not consult even Raymond Spruance, his chief of staff and current confidant. Spruance tells of words exchanged one morning in early April as he and Nimitz were walking from their living quarters to Pearl Harbor fleet headquarters.

"There are going to be some changes in high command of the fleet," said Nimitz casually. "I would like to let you go, but unfortunately for you, I need you more here."

*See footnote page 38, above.

"Well," replied Spruance, "the war is the important thing. I personally would like another crack at the Japs, but if you need me here, this is where I should be." And he stopped thinking of the matter.

The next morning, again on their way to headquarters, Nimitz said, "I have been thinking this over during the night. Spruance, you are lucky. I have decided I am going to let you go after all."

Spruance was pleased to be going to sea, but he counted on no more than a middle-level billet. He would have been amazed to know that Nimitz wrote King shortly afterward an "eyes only" letter recommending Spruance to command the future Fifth Fleet in the rank of vice admiral.

Spruance's promotion to vice admiral came through quickly. Before appointing him to the fleet command, however, King paused to consider the consequences. When at length he concurred in the appointment and announced his decision to Pearl Harbor, Spruance was stunned. So were Jack Towers and other senior naval airmen. To them it was unthinkable that the carrier-spearheaded Fifth Fleet should be commanded by a nonaviator. In their opinion, Spruance would bear watching.[5]

Halsey has left us no record of his reaction to the appointment. He was as aware as Nimitz that he could not be spared from his current post. Moreover, his area command outranked any fleet command, and as Commander, South Pacific, he faced early combat with the Japanese, whereas Spruance would have to postpone action for several months until a heavily augmented Task Force 50 was designated the Fifth Fleet.

Fighter that he was, Halsey must have found the possibility of commanding the future Big Blue Fleet in battle a tremendously attractive prospect. Generous of nature, however, he was doubtless glad that, if he could not have the command, it should go to his good friend Ray Spruance. Indeed, Halsey, when incapacitated by dermatitis the preceding May, had made the appointment possible by recommending Ray to head Halsey's own Task Force 16. Spruance's brilliant handling of that carrier force in the Battle of Midway was the evidence Nimitz needed to recommend him to head the future Fifth Fleet.

At his Noumea headquarters Halsey, in addition to war planning, had to concern himself with various extraneous problems. Most troublesome was the local population. In New Caledonia the dominant faction comprised the French settlers, who were served by both the Melanesian natives and Vietnamese and Indonesians imported as laborers and servants. The French themselves were divided politically among Vichyites and Gaullists and economically among true settlers, mostly families, and adventurers, chiefly men who lived in shacks and exploited the non-Europeans in an attempt to make a quick fortune in local agriculture and skip back home.

Into this mix had recently poured thousands of American servicemen, a situation that left the French families perplexed if not entirely hostile. Their solution in general was to isolate themselves as much as possible from the military newcomers. Even in stores the clerks would often turn their backs when American servicemen entered. This last gesture was understandable. After all, wartime shipping problems limited what could be brought in for sale to the locals, and the military had their own channels of supply.

Their exclusion from French society and places of entertainment meant that Americans coming in from long periods at sea had no place to relax. The Red Cross set up canteens that sold cigarettes and soft drinks, but men fresh from sea duty or combat wanted something more. When appeals to the local French authorities produced no results, Admiral Halsey took over the largest hotel on the island and set up clubs stocked with liquor for officers and men. Called informally the Club Pacifico, it helped boost morale.

That the French on New Caledonia did not totally avoid the Americans became evident when Admiral Halsey received an indignant letter from the commandant of the French garrison stating that a number of French girls were pregnant through association with men of the South Pacific forces. The commandant wanted to know what Halsey intended to do about the situation. Halsey dictated the following reply: "Fighting men are 'frolicking' men, and I'm not going to do a damned thing about it. If you Frenchmen can't keep your daughters out of trouble, don't count on the armed forces of the United States to do it for you."

Then there was the question of communication facilities. The growing importance of Noumea as rearward base for South Pacific operations resulted in the need for a greatly expanded radio station and a radio tower. A message sent to the governor asking permission to proceed with the work got nowhere, demonstrating anew the impotence of the local government. Halsey repeated the request by secret dispatch through the U.S. State Department to General De Gaulle in London. De Gaulle's reply was a flat negative—the expanded radio installation on New Caledonia would infringe on French sovereignty. Faced with an impasse, Halsey applied his usual solution. Ordering the Seabees to go ahead and build the radio facilities, he reported the action to nobody, confident that his seniors would approve but would rather not be told.

Another claim was more easily settled. The Americans who had fought and suffered and seen their comrades die in the struggle for Guadalcanal probably never gave a second thought to the fact that the island and the rest of the eastern Solomons belonged to Great Britain. But the British never forgot. All through the campaign they had an agent on Guadalcanal who kept a low profile and a large notebook.

After the Japanese had evacuated the island, Admiral Halsey received an official letter in an envelope bearing the printed inscription "On His Majesty's Service." It was from the British agent. He pointed out that in constructing Henderson Field the Americans had cut down thousands of coconut trees, an important source of income for the natives. On behalf of His Majesty's government he now requested from the United States a payment of two dollars per tree. He claimed to have a record of the exact number, but did not take into consideration that the trees had all been cut down by the Japanese, who had nearly completed the airfield when the Americans arrived. Halsey had his aide toss the agent's letter into the wastebasket.

Another impressive-looking letter arrived from Air Commodore Gottard, a British subject and high-ranking official in the Royal New Zealand Air Force who wanted to consult with Commander, South Pacific. Admiral Halsey, hoping to get some support from the New Zealand Air Force for Rear Admiral Marc Mitscher's Air Command, Solomons, invited the commodore to come to Noumea. Gottard arrived, not to offer military support but, so he said, to suggest how the South Pacific command could save time and money in the upkeep of its aircraft. He urged Halsey to recommend that the U.S. government construct bases in New Zealand, where Air Command, Solomons, could have its planes overhauled and repaired instead of sending them back to the United States. At the end of the war, all such construction would become the property of the Royal New Zealand Air Force. It was abundantly clear that Commodore Gottard's main object in offering his suggestion was long-range planning for his own air force at U.S. expense. It is said that the commodore left South Pacific headquarters more rapidly than he arrived.

Halsey, like Nimitz, believed in conferences to solve problems, but lacking Nimitz's gentlemanly patience, he sometimes used rough-and-ready means to reach solutions. There was, for example, a meeting to discuss how to set up a reserve fuel supply on New Caledonia for U.S. ships and planes. The South Pacific command had been depending on tankers from Hawaii and Australia. These were vulnerable to submarine attack and, moreover, were being escorted by destroyers, which were needed in the fleet. Halsey wanted ample quantities of reserve fuel to be stored in Noumea, close to the wharves and piers. He had brought his engineers and construction chiefs together to discuss how and when this project was to be carried out. Instead of giving him the answers he wanted, the officers commented on the problems they would encounter. When Halsey had heard them all out, he brought his fist down on his desk.

"You've told me all the reasons why the project is not feasible," he said. "This meeting is now adjourned and will reconvene in fifteen minutes. When you return I want to hear from you the action you propose to take in order to get the job done."

The men, thus challenged, found the answers. The project got under way and was completed sooner than anyone, except possibly Halsey, would have predicted. Some observers called it another of the Old Man's remarkable hunches. Others, in a position to observe Halsey closely, insisted that he did not base decisions on intuition but by quickly, possibly unconsciously, assessing all the factors and reaching a conclusion while the experts were still deliberating.[6]

The irritation such problems caused Halsey was nothing compared to his impatience over not getting on with the war. It was a feeling fully shared by General MacArthur and Admirals King and Nimitz. The longer the war in the Pacific remained on dead center and the longer Allied forces in that theater delayed shifting to the offensive, the more time the Japanese had to render impregnable such newly acquired strong points as Guam in the Marianas, Tarawa in the Gilberts, and Rabaul in the Bismarcks.

King had suggested a year earlier, and the Joint Chiefs had concurred, that as soon as the Japanese advance to the southeast had been halted, the Allies would advance to the northwest, beginning with a drive on Rabaul.

The town of Rabaul, near the tip of New Britain, main island of the Bismarck Archipelago, was blessed with a magnificent harbor that proved also to be its curse. The Japanese, observing Rabaul's fine harbor and its strategic location, commanding the Solomon Sea to the south and the Bismarck Sea to the west, early selected it as a primary target. Only seven weeks after Pearl Harbor they assaulted the position, wrested it from its small Australian garrison, and promptly began to develop it into a major base. By the end of 1942 the Japanese garrison there, numbering about ninety thousand men, had constructed five major airfields in the Rabaul area and fortified the surrounding mountains.

Rabaul had thus become a Japanese stronghold second in strength and importance only to Truk, 700 miles to the north. The latter, a ring of islands enclosed in a coral reef, was one of the world's finest anchorages. Held by Japan along with the rest of the Carolines under a League of Nations mandate since World War I, Truk had been illegally fortified, earning such names as the Japanese Pearl Harbor and the Gibraltar of the Pacific.

Japan counted on the bastions of Truk and Rabaul, supplemented by other strong points, to block any Allied advance into the western Pacific. Admiral Nimitz, who was planning a drive across the center, regarded Truk as a major barrier. General MacArthur, who planned to use New Guinea as his bridge for a return to the Philippines, considered the reconquest of Rabaul an essential preliminary.

New Guinea, next to Greenland the world's largest island, is shaped like a monstrous prehistoric bird, its head (the Vogelkop) facing west, its jaws agape as if about to gobble up the Moluccas, its tail pointing southeast, positioned to rise up and whack the Bismarcks. In the tail, known as Papua, MacArthur's American and Australian troops had fought to defend Port Moresby on the south coast and then crossed the Owen Stanley range to dislodge the Japanese from their footholds in Buna and other nearby positions on the north coast.

The fighting to reconquer Papua and Guadalcanal, 900 miles to the east, occurred simultaneously, and the two campaigns were completed at almost the same time. Each had been costly in terms of infantrymen: about three thousand American and Australian troops had been killed on Papua, about sixteen hundred American soldiers and marines on Guadalcanal. The disparity in numbers can be attributed to the fact that the Japanese on Papua and the Americans on Guadalcanal were on the defensive—digging out determined defenders from fortified positions is one of the most difficult and costly tasks of warfare.[7] Another reason for the difference was that the Japanese navy supported the army's efforts to seize Henderson Field on Guadalcanal. Allied naval efforts against the enemy fleet support, while ultimately successful, exacted a high price in ships and men. The loss of sailors added to the loss of marines and soldiers ashore made the conquest of Guadalcanal far more costly than that of Papua.

The simultaneous recapture of Papua and Guadalcanal, phase one of the reconquest of Rabaul, provided MacArthur and Halsey each a springboard for the rest of the campaign. Geographically, the campaign may be visualized as an inverted V with Rabaul at the apex. MacArthur's forces would advance along the left leg, via New Guinea and New Britain; Halsey's, along the right leg, via the Solomon Islands. Phase two, agreed upon by representatives of the Joint Chiefs, CinCPac, Commander in Chief, Southwest Pacific, and Commander, South Pacific, at a conference in Washington in March 1943, was to consist of the capture of a succession of positions suitable for bomber fields and ever closer to the ultimate target. As far as possible, assaults from the south and southwest Pacific would be launched concurrently in order to divide Japanese defenses. Phase three would be the joint recapture of Rabaul.

Execution of phase two presented a unique command problem. Admiral Halsey, as Commander, South Pacific, was subordinate to CinCPac-CinCPOA Admiral Nimitz, on whom he depended for all ships, planes, and men he needed for his expanding South Pacific Force. Yet when Halsey's force moved up the Solomons westward of Guadalcanal, it would enter MacArthur's Southwest Pacific Area. Who then would command what?

Old proposals and some new ones were made at various levels. Early revived was the sensible recommendation that the Pacific theater be placed under unified command, headed by either MacArthur or Nimitz. As before, the navy strictly opposed MacArthur, and the army as rigidly objected to Nimitz. The Pacific command would remain divided.

It was suggested that the dividing line between the south and southwest Pacific areas be altered to place the Solomons entirely within Halsey's South Pacific Area. The line had earlier been shifted at the navy's request to place Guadalcanal in the South Pacific Area. The army now opposed the sacrifice of more of MacArthur's Southwest Pacific Area to solve another command problem.

A plan submitted by MacArthur brought Halsey and him into close cooperation. Code-named Elkton, after the small Maryland town of quick marriages, it was in fact a specific design for control and step-by-step fulfillment of phase two of the campaign against Rabaul. After intensive discussion and modification of the plan, during which the code name was changed from Elkton to Cartwheel, the command and tasks for 1943 were set forth as follows:

A. Command
   1. Campaign to be conducted under overall command of MacArthur
   2. Operations in the Solomons to be carried out under the direct command of Halsey, operating under general directives from MacArthur
   3. Ships, planes, and ground forces of the Pacific Fleet to remain under control of Nimitz unless assigned by the Joint Chiefs to task forces engaged in specific operations
B. Tasks
   1. MacArthur: (a) establish airfields on Kiriwina and Woodlark islands; (b) seize Lae, Salamaua, Finchhafen, and Madang area; (c) occupy western New Britain
   2. Halsey: seize and occupy Solomon Islands, including southern Bougainville (see map, opposite page.)

To Halsey it was clear that if he was to move up the Solomons, he had to seize the Japanese airfield at Munda Point on New Georgia. Taking a preliminary step to that end, he followed his staff's advice and occupied the Russell Islands, sixty-five miles northwest of Henderson Field. Here he had a pair of airstrips constructed to extend the reach of his bombers and fighters a little farther up the Slot.[8]

Bull Halsey, or "the Bull," names by which he was now almost universally known in and out of the armed services, must have viewed with some misgivings the prospect of operating under MacArthur's "general directives." He is known to have shared his navy's lack of esteem for the general. To the admirals in Washington, who regarded the Pacific war as chiefly a naval show, MacArthur's persistent downplaying of sea power was a constant source of irritation. He assured the Australians that in spite of the U.S. Navy's all-out effort, the Japanese "have complete control of the sea lanes in the western Pacific and of the outer approaches to Australia." Such control, he said, "no longer depends solely or even perhaps primarily upon naval power, but upon air power operating from land bases held by ground troops. . . . A primary threat to Australia does not therefore require a great initial local concentration of naval striking power. It requires rather a sufficient concentration of land-based aviation."

The navy happily picked up the nickname Dugout Doug that some troops in the Philippines who had never seen MacArthur under fire had applied to him. During the bloody Papuan campaign, which the general fought chiefly

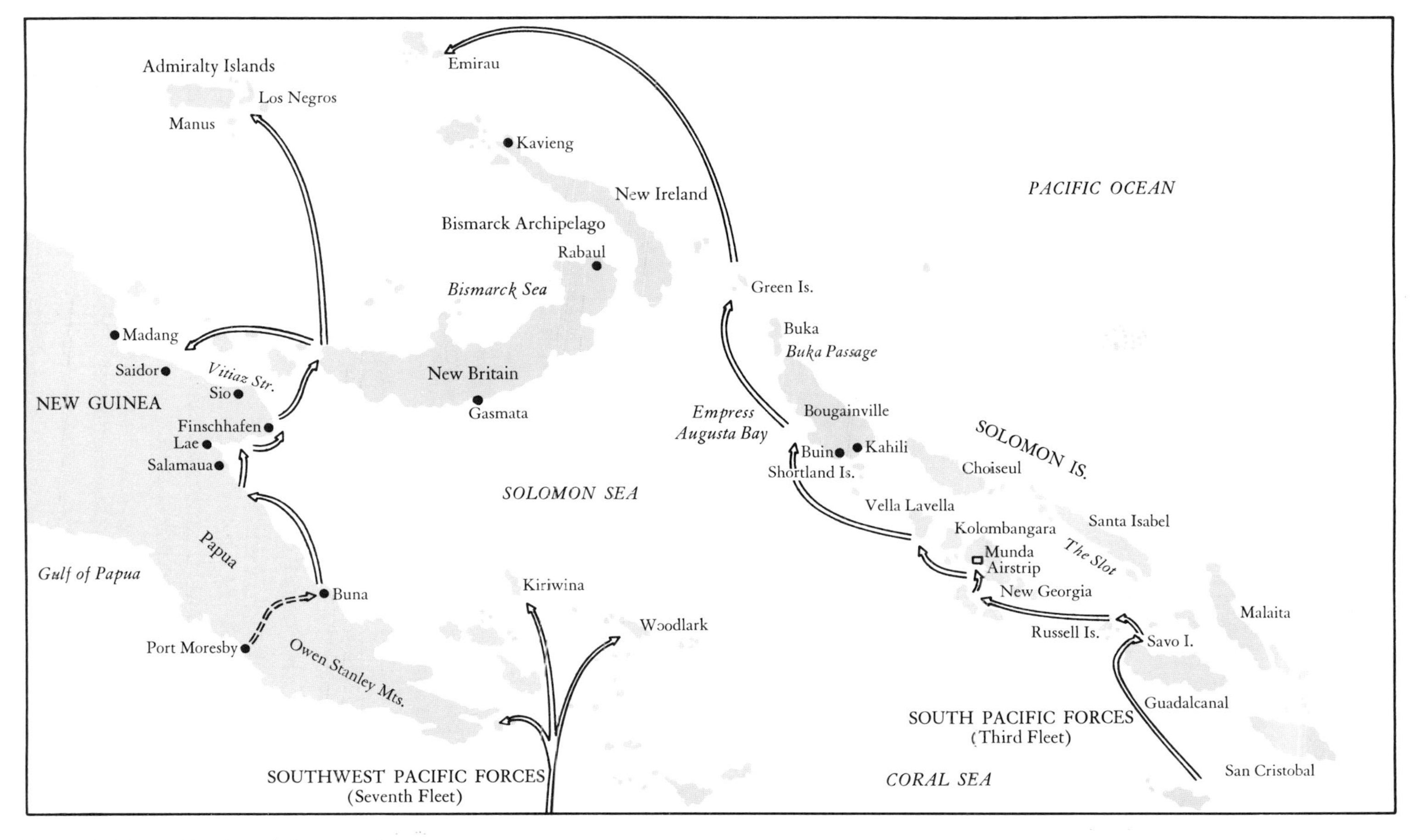

Rabaul Neutralized and Bypassed

from Brisbane, he seemed to have earned the name. The imputation of cowardice, however, was fully discredited in subsequent campaigns when MacArthur startled his subordinates by recklessly exposing his person to enemy fire. Nevertheless, no other nickname seems to have been so broadly applied to MacArthur during the war. It remained for talented wordsmith William Manchester to think up the striking title *American Caesar* for his biography of the general. In fact MacArthur had much in common with Julius Caesar—an imperious presence; unparalleled leadership abilities, both military and political; and a giant ego, shored up by ruthless self promotion. Caesar had his *Gallic War,* MacArthur his famous communiqués—in each the author was the lone hero and victor.

In late October 1942, when MacArthur moved from his comfortable hotel suite in Brisbane to the somewhat less comfortable governor's house at Port Moresby, still nearly a hundred miles from the fighting front, his communiqué announced, "The Supreme Commander has taken to the field." Instead, he sent Lieutenant General Robert L. Eichelberger to goad a faltering Allied army into capturing Buna, the toughest Japanese foothold in Papua.

"Go out there, Bob, and take Buna," said MacArthur, "or don't come back alive." When after several bloody battles Eichelberger succeeded in capturing the position, MacArthur coolly took the credit in his next communiqué. "I am convinced," wrote Eichelberger after the war, "that MacArthur's greatest interest was in the picture the world gained of him. That alone will explain how headlines went out of Port Moresby that MacArthur was leading charges at Buna."[9]

It seems strange that a man of MacArthur's intelligence should not have realized that his famous communiqués, which he either wrote or heavily edited, would ultimately sully his reputation. They were generally taken at face value by the current reading public, but many contemporary officers and journalists and all future historians, able to compare the general's publicity with the facts, would note the disparity between the two.

Admiral Halsey, in a position to compare at least some of the facts with the fiction in MacArthur's communiqués, early tagged the general a fraud. To scorn for the general he at length added resentment. In February 1943, when the Japanese, to cover their evacuation of Guadalcanal, staged diversionary raids by sea and air, the South Pacific command lacked adequate aircraft to meet the apparent crisis. In desperation Halsey asked MacArthur for the loan of a few heavy bombers. By radio dispatch the general refused the request, saying "my own operations envisage the maximum use of my air forces." He might, MacArthur said, be able to aid with support missions, provided Halsey gave him more information. "I am in complete ignorance of what you contemplate," the dispatch continued. "Before considering the dislocation of my plans and the diversion of my air force to your operations, it is necessary that I have some knowledge of your intentions. Moreover, effective support can only be given if sufficient information is available to me to permit of coordination."

Halsey was offended. In asking to know his intentions before agreeing to cooperate, MacArthur seemed to be questioning the admiral's competence. Halsey sent his deputy, Rear Admiral Theodore Wilkinson, to explain the situation to the general, now returned to Brisbane. To Nimitz Halsey sent a copy of the general's dispatch, which he called insulting. In a follow-up letter to Nimitz, Halsey said of MacArthur, "I refuse to get into controversy with him or any other self-advertising Son of a Bitch."[10]

In the months that followed, while Halsey was operating under MacArthur's strategic direction, the admiral's communications with the general were always polite but generally brief. On the other hand, Halsey exchanged with Nimitz a whole series of friendly letters, though for the South Pacific command's Solomons campaign CinCPac was little more than a supplier of troops, ships, and aircraft. Halsey would give Nimitz a full account of his plans and operations and add a little gossip on the side. Nimitz's replies, less informal but no less warm, carefully avoided giving orders but provided plenty of advice.

During the first months of 1943, when for lack of ships and planes neither Halsey nor MacArthur could begin the march on Rabaul, the Japanese went to work fortifying positions on both legs of the proposed Allied advance. The night-running Tokyo Express again went into high gear, pouring troops via the Slot into the central Solomons.

While awaiting the means to capture the troublesome airstrip at Munda, Halsey did what he could to weaken it. His planes made frequent bombing runs on Munda and a new auxiliary field at Vila on Kolombangara Island. They also laid mines on the approaches to both. South Pacific cruiser task groups commanded by Rear Admirals A. Stanton ("Tip") Merrill and Walden L. ("Pug") Ainsworth bombarded both fields at regular intervals. On the night of 5–6 March Merrill's group, while bombarding Vila, also managed to sink two Japanese destroyers.

Such setbacks scarcely slowed the revived Tokyo Express. Its reinforcement-resupply dashes were now much shorter than during the Guadalcanal campaign. The night runs down the Slot were less fraught with peril, being little exposed to air attack at dusk or dawn. Reinforcing the Japanese-held Lae-Salamaua area in New Guinea, however, remained risky, because it involved passage over open seas partly by daylight.

Early in March a convoy of eight transports escorted by eight destroyers met disaster while carrying seven thousand troops from Rabaul to Lae. Allied medium and light bombers out of Papua attacked it persistently almost at masthead level, using slow-fused bombs that permitted them to pull out of range of the explosions. This operation, the Battle of the Bismarck Sea, continued for three days, until all of the transports and four of the destroyers had been sunk and about twenty-five planes of the Japanese combat air patrol had been shot down by the Allied fighters. Some of the surviving troops made their way to New Guinea in boats and on rafts, but at least thirty-six hundred of them were lost. After additional Japanese vessels were sunk on this perilous route in the next few days, Imperial General Headquarters forbade sending convoys to New Guinea. Any further reinforcements or supplies would have to go by submarine or barge.

To blunt the forthcoming Allied advance, which they had long anticipated, the Japanese launched their most massive air attack of the war, first against the shipping in Ironbottom Sound and then against Allied positions in Papua. Using at least three hundred planes, they sank a destroyer, a corvette, a tanker, and two transports and destroyed twenty-five Allied planes, all at a cost of forty Japanese aircraft. The damage inflicted, while not negligible, was minute in proportion to the strength of the attack. Evidently the Japanese had expended their well-drilled first-line pilots. They were now sending into combat flyers less adequately trained. It was noted also that two-thirds of the attacking aircraft were carrier types. The Japanese were obviously weakening their fleet by using fleet planes to defend land objectives.[11]

The Allies did not know at the time that the massive air raid had been planned and directed by Japan's Admiral Isoroku Yamamoto, commander in chief of the Combined Fleet. Shortly afterward, the Pearl Harbor Combat Intelligence Unit broke a message announcing that Yamamoto was about to inspect the Japanese airfields of the upper Solomons, possibly in preparation for further raids. A remarkable fact about the announcement was that it gave the date, 18 April, and the hour and minute of the admiral's arrival by air at each base. Broadcasting such details by radio in however secure a code was at best ill advised, generally avoided by all armed forces. As it happened, the announcement of Yamamoto's schedule was in the same code—with a few minor changes—that the Americans had broken before the Battle of Midway.

The inspection tour would carry Yamamoto within 300 miles of Guadalcanal. Would it be possible for aviators from Henderson Field, counting on the Japanese commander in chief's known passion for punctuality, to intercept his plane? Nimitz put the question to Halsey, and Halsey passed it on to Mitscher. Mitscher replied that his flyers, using long-range army P-38 fighters, could do the job.

Yamamoto, planner of the attacks on Pearl Harbor, Midway, and elsewhere, was important quarry indeed. As Japanese fleet commander in chief, he was Nimitz's opposite number, and he had held his post longer than Nimitz had held his own. By 1943 Yamamoto had become a revered figure in Japan, second in prominence only to the emperor. He stood head and shoulders above any possible successor. His loss would stun the nation and demoralize the fighting navy. On 18 April he would be within reach of American aircraft. Halsey and Mitscher were struck by the coincidence. Exactly a year earlier, on 18 April 1942, they had conducted Doolittle's bombers into Japanese waters for the bombing of Tokyo.

Shooting down so prominent a figure as Yamamoto would have widespread political as well as military ramifications. It would be not only an act of war but also an assassination. For a final decision Nimitz passed the proposal to Washington, where it went all the way to the president. Back through the channels came an order: Get Yamamoto.[12]

Nothing would have pleased Bull Halsey more than to spend 18 April at his South Pacific headquarters and receive a prompt report on the assassination attempt, but he had made an appointment elsewhere, one he felt he could not cancel. Because he was supposed to synchronize his invasion of New Georgia with the southwest Pacific command's occupation of Kiriwina and Woodlark islands, and General MacArthur kept postponing the latter, Halsey concluded that a conference was in order and decided to beard Caesar, the "self-advertising Son of a Bitch," in his den. He wrote to MacArthur proposing a meeting and received a cordial invitation to come to Brisbane on 15 April.

MacArthur had not formed the unfavorable impression of the admiral that the latter had of the general. MacArthur had never met the character called Bull Halsey, but he knew him by reputation as a hard-fighting, outspoken warrior, ready to take necessary risks—qualities MacArthur admired in a man, provided he did not compete with the general for laurels.

On the fifteenth Halsey flew to Brisbane with members of his staff and arrived in mid-afternoon. General MacArthur, with some of his own staff, was at the wharf to meet them. As the South Pacific visitors emerged from their plane, the southwest Pacific group greeted them cordially. On Halsey's appearance, MacArthur stepped forward and seized his hand with every manifestation of friendship.

One small incident marred the genial atmosphere. The group was walking from the wharf up a small rise to where the cars were parked, MacArthur chatting with Halsey as they led the way. Something caught the eye of Julian Brown, now a brigadier general. He turned to Douglass Moulton, Halsey's flag secretary. "Say, Doug,—"

MacArthur spun on his heel and fixed Brown with a cold stare. It was widely known that even Mrs. MacArthur addressed her husband as General. When Brown indicated by an apologetic gesture that he was speaking to Commander Douglass Moulton, not General Douglas MacArthur, the latter turned back and resumed his conversation with Halsey.

Halsey's party was comfortably billeted at Brisbane's fine Lennons Hotel, which the military had taken over for the duration. The next morning Halsey joined MacArthur at the latter's headquarters, which occupied the nine-story AMP Insurance building. On entering the general's private office, Halsey noted that the room was simply furnished with a desk, a few chairs, and pictures of Washington and Lincoln on the wall.

MacArthur knew how to turn on the charm when he wished to make a favorable impression, and few persons could resist his fascinating personality. Halsey's bias against the general had begun to dissolve at their first meeting the day before. Now, in the presence of such charisma, his long-held prejudices entirely melted away.

"Five minutes after I reported, I felt as if we were lifelong friends," Halsey later wrote. "I have seldom seen a man who makes a quicker, stronger, more favorable impression. He was then about sixty-three years old, but he could have passed as fifty. His hair was jet black; his eyes were clear; his carriage was erect. If he had been wearing civilian clothes, I still would have known at once that he was a soldier."

MacArthur, while not overawed by Halsey, later wrote, "I liked him from the moment we met." The Bull lived up to Caesar's expections. MacArthur found Halsey "blunt, outspoken, dynamic" and noted that "the bugaboo of many sailors, the fear of losing ships, was completely alien to his conception of sea action."

The 15 April meeting established between the general and the admiral a lasting friendship. Not long after the Japanese surrender, Halsey wrote,

> The respect that I conceived for him that afternoon grew steadily during the war and continues to grow as I watch his masterly administration of surrendered Japan. I can recall no flaw in our relationship. We had arguments, but they always ended pleasantly. Not once did he, my superior officer, ever force his decisions upon me. On the few occasions when I disagreed with him, I told him so, and we discussed the issue until one of us changed his mind. My mental picture poses him against the background of these discussions; he is pacing his office, almost wearing a groove between his large, bare desk and the portrait of George Washington that faced it; his corncob pipe is in his hand (I rarely saw him smoke it); and he is making his points in a diction I have never heard surpassed.

In a series of amicable discussions, MacArthur accepted Halsey's plan to invade New Georgia on 15 May while the general simultaneously occupied Woodlark and Kiriwina islands.[13]

CHAPTER 14

CENTRAL SOLOMONS

GENERAL MACARTHUR lived with his wife and young son Arthur in a penthouse suite in Lennons Hotel. Members of the general's staff occupied quarters in the same building, and here too, as we have seen, Admiral Halsey and his party were housed during their April 1943 visit to Brisbane.

MacArthur neither entertained nor accepted invitations, preferring to spend evenings with his family, joined occasionally by a member of his staff. Halsey, apprised of the general's custom, expected to see no more of him following their daily conferences. The admiral dined a couple of evenings as guest of senior officers of the southwest Pacific command and then was glad to have an evening free to dine informally with his own staff members. The free time also provided him with an opportunity to contact his friend St. George Bryan's son Joseph, whom he knew to be on duty at southwest Pacific headquarters. The task of locating and inviting Joe he turned over to Commander Moulton.

Joseph Bryan III, like Halsey's son, was a Princeton graduate. Joe had been an associate editor of the *Saturday Evening Post* before setting up as a free-lance writer. Then the coming of war required his services for the U.S. armed forces. Commissioned in the naval reserve, he chose intelligence as his field, under the impression that intelligence had something to do with intellect.

From the Quonset Air Combat Intelligence School, Joe had been assigned not to carrier duty as he had requested, but to shore duty on the staff of Commander, Aircraft, Southwest Pacific, at Brisbane—the end of the line so far as Joe was concerned. Through some organizational overlap the command, despite its impressive title, had little to do. It consisted of fewer than a dozen officers, about the same number of enlisted men, and three planes. An idle mind being the devil's workshop, the underemployed officers turned to practical jokes for amusement. Lieutenant Bryan, the most junior and one of the youngest, was a favorite butt.

One April afternoon, which happened to be the afternoon preceding Halsey's free evening, the more senior officers of the command had the novel experience of being called into conference. Joe, left behind with other junior officers to mind the office, found little to do but read and conjure up new schemes for escaping his low position on an apathetic totem pole. A ringing telephone interrupted his daydreams.

"Bryan," Joe answered.

"Lieutenant Joseph Bryan?" an unfamiliar voice inquired.

"Yes."

"This is Commander Moulton, Admiral Halsey's flag secretary. I'm calling for the admiral. He wants to know if you will do him a favor."

Joe was unaware that Halsey and his father were friends or that Halsey was within a thousand miles of Brisbane. If this was a colleague up to another trick, he thought, Aircraft, Southwest Pacific, had reached new heights of absurdity. He wondered whom they had recruited to perpetrate this hoax. In a suave tone Joe replied, "I'll be glad to do the admiral a favor if the admiral will do me a favor first."

At the other end there was a startled pause. Then in an acid voice the speaker asked, "What is that, Lieutenant?"

Bryan made an unseemly suggestion about what the admiral could do.

Moulton was incredulous. "I *beg* your pardon?"

At that moment some kindly spirit intervened, whispering to Bryan, "This is no joke! Repeat: This is no joke!" And it occurred to Moulton that his announcement was subject to misinterpretation. After all, four-star admirals do not generally telephone lieutenants in foreign cities to ask favors. Bryan apologized for his misinterpretation, Moulton for his misleading announcement. The latter then explained that Admiral Halsey was inviting Bryan to dinner.

That evening Joe donned his best uniform and presented himself at Lennons, where he was directed to a private dining room. Here he was greeted warmly by Admiral Halsey. "Your father sends you his regards," said the admiral. "When I was in the hospital in Richmond last summer, he came to see me and mentioned that you were out here. I told him I'd try to look you up."

Halsey then introduced Bryan to the others as the son of a college fraternity brother and longtime friend. The South Pacific staff members received Joe as if he were one of themselves, and he and Moulton had a good laugh over the afternoon's misunderstanding. Joe decided that this was the sort of outfit he'd like to serve with. In the back of his mind he began figuring how he might use his new connection to shift from Brisbane to Noumea.

One thing Joe noticed and never forgot. Halsey both before and during dinner was clearly the leader, not because he maintained a commanding front but because he wore an air of calm authority so naturally that it in no way impaired the friendly and familiar manner he extended to all, regardless of rank.[1]

Joe didn't see Halsey again during the latter's visit. The admiral left Brisbane on the morning of 19 April for a goodwill tour of southeastern

Halsey in Noumea

Australia, which included a brief stop at Canberra and longer ones at Melbourne and Sydney.

His stay in the latter two cities brought back happy memories of calls at those ports thirty-five years earlier with the Great White Fleet, and older natives recalled the fleet's visit with pleasure. They assured him that the sailors who jumped ship had made good Australian citizens, and that some had risen to positions of eminence.

In both Sydney and Melbourne the press was waiting for him, but Halsey was wary. Of late, it seemed, reporters had been picking up something he said, perhaps offhand, and quoting it out of context to make him sound ridiculous. Bill, who formerly had been every newsman's best friend, had found he couldn't trust all journalists. Except to men he had learned to rely on, he now said as little as possible. Staff members traveling with Halsey urged him particularly to avoid making prophesies. Halsey agreed. Nobody was better aware than he that more than 100 days had passed since his Auckland prediction that the war with Japan would be over in less than 363 days.

During that period the only Allied advance in the Pacific theater had been the unopposed move from Guadalcanal to the adjacent unoccupied Russell Islands.

To the distress of his traveling staff, Halsey accepted a couple of invitations to speak. Nothing could induce him to prepare his speeches in advance, let alone write them down or have them written for him so that they could be scanned for statements that might prove embarrassing if quoted by the press. All of his speeches were ad-libbed. The Australians loved his bluff, outspoken style, and the press found nothing to quibble about after all.[2]

Halsey arrived in Noumea on 25 June to find the members of his staff who had stayed behind full of news. The plot to shoot down Admiral Yamamoto had apparently succeeded. The staff, on Halsey's orders, had not passed the information to him at Brisbane because the message, implying that the Americans were able to read Japanese codes, would be delivered via southwest Pacific communications and Halsey suspected the command of leaking secrets, chiefly through MacArthur's communiqués.

On the morning of the eighteenth, as planned, sixteen P-38s had taken off from Guadalcanal, four to attack and twelve to cover. Near the southeastern tip of Bougainville, right on schedule, the attackers encountered two bombers escorted by six Zero fighters. They shot down the bombers and three of the Zeros, losing only one P-38. The Americans believed, correctly, that Admiral Yamamoto was a passenger in one of the downed bombers. When the usually sobersided Admiral Turner displayed unwonted enthusiasm at the recitation of this achievement, Halsey remarked, "Hold on, Kelly! What's so good about it? I'd hoped to lead that bastard up Pennsylvania Avenue, with the rest of you kicking him where it would do the most good."

In fact, until 21 May Halsey was not certain that his aviators had actually got their man. On that date Admiral Yamamoto's ashes reached Japan in the superbattleship *Musashi,* and a newscaster on Radio Tokyo announced in a voice choking with emotion that Yamamoto "while directing general strategy on the front line in April of this year, engaged in combat with the enemy and met gallant death in a war plane."[3]

Halsey was impatiently marking time, his plans complete, his forces, except for a shortage of aircraft, ready for the assault on New Georgia. As noted, he had agreed with MacArthur to postpone the attack until 15 May, the earliest date on which the latter would be able to stage his concurrent occupation of Kiriwina and Woodlark islands. As it turned out, the southwest Pacific command could meet neither the new date nor a postponed date of 1 June. The demands of the Mediterranean campaign and the desperate antisubmarine Battle of the Atlantic withheld from MacArthur's newly organized Seventh Fleet the destroyers, transports, and amphibious craft it needed for landing operations. When at last they began arriving in the southwest Pacific in sufficient quantity, MacArthur designated the last day of June 1943 for the simultaneous assaults to begin.

Halsey, meanwhile, was anticipating the imminent arrival in the South Pacific of an additional air group. The new planes had reached the Fijis when South Pacific headquarters received an information copy of an order directing them to return to the United States. There the group was to be broken up and the pilots sent to the training command as instructors. The South Pacific had been counting heavily on those planes. The staff officer who brought the dispatch to Halsey remarked, "If they do that to us, we will have to go on the defensive."

The admiral turned contemptuous eyes on the speaker. "As long as I have one plane and one pilot," he growled, "I will stay on the offensive."

Halsey was less concerned than his subordinates about the shortage of aircraft. He believed that what he lacked in numbers his pilots more than made up for in skill. It was one of his so-called hunches, but the following week proved him right. The Japanese, alerted by search planes that naval forces were assembling in Ironbottom Sound, concluded that the Allies were about to launch their long-expected offensive and set out to crush it before it could get started. On 5 June eighty-one Zeros arrived over the Russells, intent on drawing Allied bombers into battle. They were met instead by American fighters, which shot down twenty-four of the Japanese planes while losing seven of their own. On the tenth U.S. fighters wiped out almost to the last plane an attack by two dozen dive-bombers and seventy Zeros at the cost of six American planes. Further Japanese air attacks on the twelfth and sixteenth resulted in similar losses, that on the sixteenth costing Japan 107 planes.

A major reason for the increasingly one-sided scores, it was learned after the war, was the previously mentioned heavy attrition of trained and experienced Japanese aviators. The Japanese had dispensed with armor and self-sealing fuel tanks, because the weight of such life-saving devices diminished the speed, range, and maneuverability of planes. Moreover, Japanese air groups were sent repeatedly into battle until they were wiped out, leaving no qualified flyers to train the next generation of aviators. After the spring of 1943 Japanese air power ceased to be a major factor, a situation that changed with the introduction of kamikaze suicide attacks in the fall of 1944.[4]

The transports, destroyers, and amphibious craft of Halsey's Third Fleet were designated the Third Amphibious Force, which in the forthcoming assault on New Georgia was to be commanded by Kelly Turner. Turner was at last out from under the shadow of the Savo Island defeat, an inquiry made at the order of the secretary of the navy having concluded that blame was too evenly distributed for any one officer to be censured.

Admiral Spruance, while serving with Turner on the staff of the Naval War College, had come to respect his professional competence. On being appointed to command the Fifth Fleet, he asked for Turner to head his Fifth Amphibious Force, "if I can steal him from Admiral Halsey." When the request had been approved by King, Nimitz, and Halsey, Turner was scheduled to transfer to the central Pacific on 15 July after the completion of the first stage of the New Georgia operation. Rear Admiral Theodore S. Wilkinson, Deputy Commander, South Pacific, would replace him as Commander, Third Amphibious Force.

In mid-June, in anticipation of the coming offensive, Admiral Nimitz visited the South Pacific to look over the men, ships, and planes he was providing. On the arrival of CinCPac and his party at Noumea, the first order of business was a review of Halsey's plan, approved by MacArthur, for carrying out phase two. It was to be staged in two parts: the first was the capture of the islands of New Georgia and Kolombangara and their airfields in the central Solomons, the second the capture of positions on and around the island of Bougainville in the upper Solomons.

The review completed, Nimitz, Halsey, and staff members set out from Noumea to inspect the forward area and invasion forces. At Halsey's suggestion he and Nimitz rode in separate planes—ostensibly to avoid the risk of losing two senior officers in a single crash. In fact, Halsey was thinking about himself and Nimitz's jinxed experiences in planes. To one of his staff members, who found the situation amusing, he retorted, "That's not superstition. It's common sense. Chester is bad joss in the air."

Arriving at Espíritu Santo, Nimitz and Halsey conferred with Admiral Fitch, Commander, Aircraft, South Pacific, and his staff. They visited the naval and air base at Segond Channel and the airfield at Pallikulo, where Fitch now had his headquarters. Nimitz and Halsey were gratified to learn that he intended to provide close air support to ground and surface operations rather than engaging in so-called strategic bombing with attacks on enemy airfields.

Fitch's planning officer, Commander George Van Deurs, explained that strategic bombing was in any event out of the question. Allied planes could not reach the fields in the Bougainville area with a bomb load, he said, but they could photograph them, and he produced some sample photos. These revealed that the enemy still had plenty of planes in the upper Solomons. Van Deurs pointed out that if the Japanese committed everything they had, including reserves, in one massive attack to oppose the upcoming New Georgia landings, they could swamp the Allied air defenses.

"Yeah," said Halsey, "they could come to us that way, but I've got a hunch they're not going to, so we're going ahead anyway." It was his conviction that, after their recent heavy losses in the air, the Japanese were not going to risk all their remaining planes in defense of the central Solomons.

At Guadalcanal Halsey and Nimitz observed with satisfaction that Henderson Field had been developed into a complete bomber base surrounded by three fighter strips. Five miles east of Henderson a new bomber base was nearing completion. Operating from these fields and from a pair of airstrips in the Russells, Admiral Mitscher's Air Command, Solomons, comprised some three hundred aircraft—bombers and fighters of the U.S. Army, Navy, and Marine Corps and of the Royal New Zealand Air Force.

The Halsey-Nimitz party next turned their attention to the ground forces earmarked for the coming operation. Since this was to be mainly an army show, General Millard Harmon, Commanding General, South Pacific, conferred at length with the principal officers responsible for the New Georgia land operations: Major General John H. Hester, commander of the Forty-third Infantry Division, which was to make the main landing with the task of capturing Munda Airfield, and Major General Oscar W. Griswold, Hester's immediate superior, commanding the Fourteenth Corps, which included the Forty-third Division.

The party next crossed to Tulagi, where Scrappy Kessing showed them through the motor-torpedo-boat base. In the Russell Islands they visited soldiers and marines and inspected the two airfields, informally known as Dagwood and Blondie after the comic-strip characters. On the way back to Noumea they stopped at Efate to look over the ships in Havannah Harbor. Here, and at Noumea and Espíritu, Nimitz was particularly gratified to note the improvement since his last visit in cargo handling and the resultant quick turnabout of ships. On 23 June Nimitz and Halsey were back at the latter's headquarters, satisfied that the forthcoming assault, code-named Operation Toenails, was ready to roll. Nimitz left for Pearl the following morning.[5]

The main South Pacific attack began on 30 June 1943, with a landing not on New Georgia but on lightly held Rendova Island, five miles to the south. Rendova was to serve as an unsinkable platform for the heavy artillery that would cover the troops crossing by boat to the mainland. Guns on the island would also support the subsequent drive on Munda. Fighters from Air Command, Solomons, chased away enemy aircraft whenever they appeared. Only one vessel of the amphibious force, Turner's flagship, the *McCawley*, was seriously damaged. Put out of action by a Japanese airborne torpedo, she was sunk the following night by an American torpedo boat that mistook her in the darkness for an enemy.

Some of Halsey's officers entertained the hope of emulating General Ulysses S. Grant's achievement exactly eighty years earlier when on the Fourth of July he presented the Union with the capitulation of beleaguered Vicksburg. But the forthcoming campaign against Munda would culminate in no Fourth of July triumph. Days passed with much of the Forty-third Division still on Rendova. The division's big guns sank into the mud and had to be hauled out and emplaced on the coral beaches of adjacent islets.

Army patrols, reconnoitering the shoreline, found the beaches nearest the

Munda airfield unsuitable for the assault. They could be approached from the sea only over a wide coral reef into the fire of massed artillery along the shore. Hester therefore sent his troops by landing craft to an unprotected, open stretch of beach four miles from their objective. Here the invasion force confronted the problem the Japanese had failed to solve on Guadalcanal—how to fight their way through jungle and wrest a well-defended airfield from brave and determined defenders.

The fact was that the Forty-third Division lacked combat training and conditioning for the sort of warfare they were now expected to wage. Based on World War I experience on the plains of Europe, their indoctrination was inadequate for jungle warfare. They had spent some time on Guadalcanal and the Russells, but there they seem mainly to have soaked up horror stories of Japanese atrocities and suicide tactics.

On 6 July the invaders reported themselves ready to penetrate the jungle. The 169th Regiment, leading the way, soon ran into enemy opposition, which brought it to a halt. At the approach of nightfall, the soldiers established a loose perimeter and went into bivouac. Some time later, in almost total darkness, word spread among the troops that they were being infiltrated by Japanese. Several of the Americans opened fire. Others tossed grenades. Panic spread. There followed several wild hours of gunfire, grenade bursts, and screaming. Dawn revealed no enemy dead within the perimeter, but there were numerous American casualties.

Whether Japanese infiltrators had indeed penetrated the regiment or the casualties were all self-inflicted, the men were jittery. The regimental commander sent 360 of them back to Guadalcanal as "war nerves" casualties. Here they were met by an indignant General Harmon, who ordered 300 of them back to the combat zone, along with a colonel to relieve the commanding officer who had sent them.

At some not clearly specified time, overall control of the forces on shore was to pass from Admiral Turner as Commander, Third Amphibious Force, to General Hester, who would remain commander of the Forty-third Division and become also commander of the New Georgia Occupation Force. In effect, the dual command could be meaningless, because in the drive on Munda the Forty-third Division and the occupation force would be identical unless reserves from other divisions were brought in.

It soon appeared that reserves would in fact have to be committed, because the Forty-third Division, despite its advantage of air and gunfire support, advanced on successive days by yards rather than miles. Harmon suggested that Griswold, not Hester, take over command of the occupation force. Turner opposed the change. Instead, he himself assumed increasingly active control of the land operations. Harmon, seeing little chance of reaching an agreement with Turner, flew off to Noumea to confer with Halsey, who ordered Griswold to proceed to New Georgia and report his findings. On 13 July General Griswold radioed Halsey and Harmon: "Things are going badly. Forty-third Division about to fold up. My opinion is that they will never take Munda. Enemy resistance to date not great." He recommended the immediate commitment of all reserves.

Halsey at once issued radio orders for Griswold to take command of the New Georgia Occupation Force, leaving Hester in nominal command of his Forty-third Division. He ordered Harmon to fly back to the Solomons and take whatever measures were necessary to get the offensive back on track. Harmon went first to Guadalcanal, where he busied himself with arrangements to move the reserve forces toward New Georgia.

Thus far everything had been done in accordance with regulations. It was fully within the authority of Halsey or his representative to replace or relieve Hester as commander of the New Georgia Occupation Force, a post to which Halsey had appointed him. Hester had correctly been left in command of the Forty-third Division, because he had been appointed to that duty by a higher authority.

When General Harmon followed the reserves to New Georgia and inspected the enlarged occupation force, he found the Forty-third Division failing to keep pace with the new arrivals. Hester himself appeared exhausted and had lost touch with his troops. Harmon promptly relieved him, sending in the assistant commander of the Twenty-fifth Division as his replacement.

Harmon relieved Hester more as an act of mercy than anything else, but in so doing he was acting illegally. He should have contacted Halsey, who in turn should have sought Nimitz's permission to relieve Hester as division commander—just as Nimitz the preceding October had checked with King before relieving Ghormley as area commander.

Admiral Halsey was in a quandary, determined to back Harmon, whom he had invested with full authority, yet anxious to avoid participating in an act of insubordination. In the end he did nothing, possibly hoping the irregularity would be overlooked or silently condoned.

Halsey had originally allotted six thousand men to make a swift capture of the airfield from its forty-five hundred defenders. The campaign, expected to last a few days, stretched to weeks while the Japanese guarding the field were reinforced until they numbered roughly eight thousand and Halsey committed all his available forces—thirty-two thousand soldiers and seventeen hundred marines. At last on 5 August the Americans reached the Munda field and blanketed its defenses with mortar and 37mm fire. The remnant of Japanese survivors, blasted out of their holes, "ran around in little circles like stunned chickens" until machine-gun fire mowed them down. Griswold reported by radio dispatch to Halsey: "Our ground forces have wrested Munda from the Japs and present it to you as the sole owner. Our Munda operation is the finest example in all my experience of a united all-service, all-American team."

To which Commander, South Pacific, replied, "Consider this a custody receipt for Munda and for a gratifying number of enemy dead. Such teamwork and unrelenting offensive spirit assures the success of future drives and the implacable extermination of the enemy wherever we can bring him to grips. Keep 'em dying."

Halsey, though he applauded the capture of the airfield, was disgusted at the amount of manpower and the length of time it had required. He recognized that it had been a tough job, tougher than anticipated, but with the Allied advantages of gunfire and air support the invaders should have moved much faster. Even after the fall of Munda, the army spent several more weeks dislodging and pursuing other island defenders, most of whom, when counterattack proved hopeless, slipped away by water to nearby Kolombangara. The delays bespoke poor leadership. "When I look back on Elkton," said Halsey after the war, "the smoke of charred reputations still makes me cough."[6]

Admiral Nimitz, who had been keeping track of events in the South Pacific, congratulated Halsey on the success of the New Georgia operations and on the splendid achievements of the air and surface forces under his direction. He had little reason to praise the soldiers, but he was sure, he said, that the army units participating in the campaign "learned many valuable lessons that will be profited by in future operations."

With respect to the irregular relief of the Forty-third Division commander, King would doubtless have given Halsey at least a sharp scolding. But that was not Chester Nimitz's way. He brought the matter up with just a touch of irony. "There is a rumor current here," he wrote, "that you found it necessary to relieve General Hester. Please let me know if this is true and, if so, the circumstances. I recognize, of course, that it may occasionally be necessary for you to relieve a flag or a general officer. If so, I desire, for obvious reasons, that you promptly inform me and let me know the reasons therefor."

Halsey recognized that he had been reprimanded, albeit gently. He hastened to assure Nimitz that the Hester case was no mere "yank-out"—that his relief as occupation force commander was incidental to the reorganization of the force and his relief as division commander was for reasons of health. He added:

> Hester had been in the rear occupied with corps matters and had lost immediate intimate touch with his division. It was also noted about this time that he looked very badly. . . . On Hester's arrival in the rear area (Guadalcanal), it was discovered that he was suffering from stomach ulcers. This had not been known at the time he went forward. He was travelling on his nerve. He has been sent to a hospital in New Zealand and will undoubtedly be sent to the States.

Thus Hester's ulcers, from which he soon recovered, preserved both his dignity and Halsey's reputation for conforming to regulations. Relief for physical disability was fully justified, and Hester was not disgraced.

Taking up other matters with Nimitz, Griswold, said Halsey, "had a very tough proposition thrown at him but got away with it nobly and things have been moving ever since he took over. He deserves much praise."[7]

Things were indeed moving, as Halsey said, but at the current rate of progress it would take the Americans ten years to reach Tokyo, not the admiral's prophesied 363 days. One matter Halsey had made up his mind about: there must be no more fighting through jungles to seize enemy airfields. In place of the costly Munda strategy, he would revert to the Guadalcanal scheme of building an airfield and presenting the enemy with the problem of fighting through the jungle to take it.

Halsey's staff offered a further solution. During the Munda campaign, the Japanese had been rapidly reinforcing Kolombangara, the major central Solomons island after New Georgia. Obviously they expected the Americans to land there and make a drive for the airfield at Vila. Why not, suggested the staffers, bypass Kolombangara and seize the island beyond it, lightly held Vella Lavella? Admiral Nimitz had recently set the example in the concurrent Aleutian campaign. Lacking sufficient force at the time to recapture the island of Kiska, he had sent his available fleet and army past Kiska to conquer the more distant, less heavily garrisoned Attu.

The Japanese were employing the defense-in-depth strategy of "fire and fall back," and so long as the Allies adhered to their island-hopping strategy, the enemy could delay them almost indefinitely. But the geography of the Pacific theater, with its many islands, presented a solution—that of bypassing enemy bases, intercepting their supplies, and leaving them to "wither on the vine."

There were of course dangers to bypassing—skipping over enemy bases that could block one's own line of supply and reinforcement, or occupying a position closer to enemy airfields than to one's own. The latter consideration prompted Halsey to turn down the recommendation of some his staff that they next invade the Treasury Islands south of Bougainville. He chose instead to accept the original staff suggestion and bypass only the big island of Kolombangara.

On 12 July Halsey sent a get-ready order to Admiral Wilkinson, whose duty it would be to execute the next assault, and to Admiral Fitch, who would direct air operations: "Bypass Vila area and allow to wither on the vine. Seize Vella Lavella and establish fighter field thereon. Such a plan would depend to a large extent on feasibility of establishing a fighter field on southwest coast of Vella Lavella for the purpose of giving close fighter aircraft support to the south Bougainville operation. When practicable, make aircraft reconnaissance on Vella Lavella to the above end."

Halsey and his commanders were capable of bypassing Kolombangara, but there was no bypassing General MacArthur. As they were expected to consult Nimitz before making major changes in personnel, it was their responsibility to get MacArthur's approval for any change in strategy. Because the general had already accepted the original island-hopping plan, Halsey needed his consent to the proposed bypass. Supposing it would be difficult to persuade MacArthur to abandon a project to which he had given his blessing, Halsey relied on no mere dispatch. Instead he sent as his emissary to Brisbane Vice Admiral Fitch, number two man in the South Pacific, second in seniority only to himself.

Fitch, believing he had a formidable selling job ahead, took along senior officers from surface ships, service forces, and submarines—a group able to answer any question that might come up. In Brisbane Fitch and his party were received in MacArthur's outer office and ushered into the presence of the general, who welcomed them most courteously. Hardly were they seated and hardly had Fitch made his introductory statement when MacArthur rose and began to talk, pacing back and forth and gesturing with his corncob pipe. It dawned on the navy group that the general's discourse had nothing to do with the question at hand. He was giving them a lecture on strategy, not of the Pacific war but of the ongoing conflict in Europe. At the end of fifteen minutes, MacArthur stopped, turned to the astonished naval officers with a smile, and said, "Thank you, gentlemen," in a tone that clearly indicated they were dismissed.

Fitch was baffled. Admiral Halsey had sent him to Brisbane to obtain a specific answer. He had been received and dismissed by MacArthur with nothing to report back to Noumea but a sovereign recipe for winning the war in Europe. He had made the mistake, he realized, of bringing along too many advisers. He had been warned that MacArthur, confronted by an audience, could not refrain from delivering a lecture.

Fitch telephoned MacArthur's office, only to be told that the general was busy. In desperation he called again and spoke to sundry colonels and generals, including the haughtiest of all, MacArthur's chief of staff, Major General Richard K. Sutherland. At length, the staff grudgingly vouchsafed him a brief interview.

Fitch returned to the sanctum, this time unaccompanied. He took a seat and stated his message as briefly as possible. MacArthur nodded. "Work it out with General Sutherland," he said. "I agree with anything you and Halsey want to do."[8]

Halsey, thus given a green light, scheduled the invasion of Vella Lavella for 15 August. On that date Admiral Wilkinson, commanding the Third Amphibious Force, began putting some six thousand men on the target island under cover of fighters operating from the captured strip at Munda. Despite persistent enemy air attacks, the assault forces suffered only a few casualties and slight material damage. Wilkinson avoided the high costs and delays of the Munda drive by invading the southern tip of the island, where there were no enemy forces, establishing a defense perimeter there, and setting his Seabees to work constructing a fighter airstrip.

When it became apparent that there was to be no attack against the American position, troops moved out of the perimeter in both directions along the coast to entrap or destroy the enemy garrison. In September New Zealanders relieved the Americans.

With Admiral King's March 1943 reorganization of the U.S. Fleet, Commander, South Pacific Force, acquired the alternate title of Commander, Third Fleet. As we have seen, Halsey entrusted the amphibious force to the command of Admiral Turner and his replacement, Admiral Wilkinson, but the rest of the Third Fleet, organized as Task Force 36, remained under his direct control. Task Force 36 comprised two battleship divisions, one carrier group with cruisers and destroyers, the two cruiser-destroyer groups under Rear Admirals Ainsworth and Merrill, several escort carriers, and eleven submarines.

During the central Solomons campaign, Halsey held his battleships and his two fleet carriers, the *Saratoga* and HMS *Victorious*, in ready reserve, to be sent into action only in the unlikely event that enemy battleships or carriers were again committed to battle. The function of Ainsworth's and Merrill's groups was bombardment of enemy positions and intercepting the supply and reinforcement missions of the Tokyo Express.

Ainsworth's group of three light cruisers and nine destroyers got off to a disappointing start on the night of 4 July, the date some of Halsey's officers were counting on for a victory on New Georgia. The Ainsworth group, after entering Kula Gulf and bombarding the Vila airfield, was sighted by an enemy destroyer division. The Japanese opened fire with torpedoes, one of which ripped open the hull of the U.S. destroyer *Strong*. After taking off most of the crew of the sinking vessel, the American group retired hastily to Ironbottom Sound.

Pug Ainsworth, deeply chagrined, thinking the *Strong* had been sunk by a submarine, had arrived off Guadalcanal when he received word from Halsey that a Tokyo Express was leaving port in the upper Solomons. Eager for battle, he promptly came about and with his three cruisers and five destroyers sped back to the Slot. After midnight on the sixth, his group tangled with two divisions of Japanese destroyers in the Battle of Kula Gulf. At dawn Pug radioed Halsey, "Think we got all of seven ships except one or two cripples still in Kula Gulf. *Helena* [cruiser] sunk probably by torpedoes. *Nicholas* and *Radford* [destroyers] standing by off Kula rescuing survivors. Will then rejoin."

Highly gratified, Halsey replied, "A grand night's record for an aggressive leader backed by indomitable officers and men! We will miss the *Helena,* but she took many times her weight in Jap meat. You paved many miles of the Tokyo road last night."

Through intelligence sources it became evident in the next few days that there had been ten Japanese destroyers in the battle. One had been sunk by U.S. gunfire. Another, stranded off the shore of Kolombangara, was destroyed the next day by American bombers. The rest returned to base.

A week later, again after midnight, Ainsworth with three cruisers and eight destroyers engaged a Japanese force consisting of a cruiser and five destroyers. In this action, the Battle of Kolombangara, Ainsworth's ships sank the enemy cruiser. The Japanese sank an American destroyer and so battered one of Ainsworth's cruisers, the *Leander* of the Royal New Zealand Navy, that she was out of action for most of the rest of the war.

This time Ainsworth avoided exaggerated claims, and Halsey withheld his congratulations until he knew the score. It was clear to all hands that the Allies did not yet rival the Japanese in night surface tactics. That the Americans were learning, however, was demonstrated on the night of 6–7 August in the Battle of Vella Gulf.

In that battle six U.S. destroyers in two columns, under Commander Frederick Moosbrugger, were hugging the coast of Kolombangara to avoid being seen or spotted by enemy radar detectors. Suddenly their own radar picked up four enemy destroyers approaching on an opposite course. Moosbrugger's first division raced past the enemy, launched torpedoes, and turned away. The other division took a course across the van of the enemy column to cap its T. Just as the torpedoes struck their targets, the two American divisions opened up with gunfire. Under this triple impact, three troop-carrying Japanese destroyers exploded, hurling eighteen hundred soldiers and sailors into the water and creating such a pyrotechnic display that PT boatmen thirty miles away in Kula Gulf thought a volcano on Kolombangara had blown its top.

Admiral Halsey, immensely relieved at this virtuoso performance by a force under his command, made sure the details were published widely as an example for all Allied tacticians. Admiral Nimitz wrote him from Pearl Harbor, "Especially do I want to offer congratulations on Moosbrugger's fine, clean-cut job with no losses to ourselves. It is a perfect example of economy of force."

The Allies, though they had bypassed Kolombangara, had not truly isolated it. The Japanese, instead of withering on the vine, prepared to do some reverse bypassing themselves. Their naval command in the upper Solomons waited until late September and the dark of the moon, then dispatched destroyers, submarines, and swift barges to evacuate the 12,400-man garrison. American destroyers sent out to intercept them succeeded in damaging a destroyer and sinking a submarine and about a third of the barges. Nevertheless, three quarters of the garrison escaped.

During the nighttime evacuation of Vella Lavella, which closely followed that of Kolombangara, a force of Japanese destroyers found themselves at such a numerical advantage that they disdained to turn tail and run away from the Americans. The resultant Battle of Vella Lavella brought little tactical credit to destroyermen on either side.

Warned by search planes of the approach of six Japanese destroyers escorting small craft, Captain Frank R. Walker took the destroyers *Selfridge, Chevalier*, and *O'Bannon* into the waters north of Vella Lavella to intercept them. In an exchange of torpedoes and gunfire, the Americans sank an enemy destroyer, Japanese torpedoes blew the bows off both the *Chevalier* and *Selfridge*, and in the confusion the *O'Bannon* rammed the *Chevalier*.

The timely arrival of three more Third Fleet destroyers obliged the enemy to retire, but while the Americans were looking after their crippled vessels and the sinking and helpless *Chevalier*, the enemy's small craft proceeded to Vella Lavella and carried out another evacuation.

Only about two hundred Japanese were left on the island, mostly unarmed, half-starved survivors of the Battle of Vella Gulf who had swum or drifted ashore from their sinking destroyers. These the New Zealanders quickly rounded up and captured.[9]

CHAPTER 15

SOUTH PACIFIC

In December 1942 the carrier *Saratoga*, after several months undergoing repair at Pearl Harbor, arrived in the South Pacific, where she joined the battered, scarcely seaworthy *Enterprise*. With cruiser-destroyer escorts they formed task forces commanded respectively by Rear Admirals DeWitt C. Ramsey and Frederick C. ("Ted") Sherman. These and a growing body of additional U.S. combatant vessels were stationed at Noumea, Espíritu, and Efate to back up the Guadalcanal line.

At the end of January 1943, as we have seen, the Combined Fleet briefly appeared north of the Solomons to divert attention from the evacuation of the remnant of starving Japanese troops from Guadalcanal. Halsey, supposing a renewed attack on Henderson Field was impending, rushed a troop convoy to the Guadalcanal area supported by all the naval strength he could assemble—the two carrier forces, plus a battleship force and two cruiser-destroyer forces. To Halsey's disgust, torpedo planes from Munda bored through all this defensive power in a night attack and sank the heavy cruiser *Chicago*.

Thereafter operations of the *Saratoga* and *Enterprise* forces were generally limited to the escort of troop convoys through sea areas within reach of enemy land-based aircraft. Whenever the Combined Fleet sortied from Truk, however, Halsey ordered the *Enterprise* out to sea from Espíritu Santo and the *Saratoga* out from Noumea. But there was no more sending them north of Guadalcanal. His loss of the *Hornet* at Santa Cruz had taught Halsey uncharacteristic caution in handling his limited carrier strength.

When it became increasingly evident that the *Enterprise* was in desperate need of overhaul, the United States borrowed from the Royal Navy the carrier *Victorious*, which proceeded via the Panama Canal to the Pacific, where she passed the *Enterprise* en route to Pearl Harbor and ultimately to the United States. On 17 May 1943 the British carrier arrived at Noumea and was absorbed into the *Saratoga* task force.

During the New Georgia campaign, the *Saratoga-Victorious* force, under Duke Ramsey, maneuvered south of the upper Solomons, ready to advance into action should an enemy carrier force intervene. Several times Halsey ordered Ramsey's carriers to sweep northward, but he stopped them before they came within range of attack by bombers from Rabaul.

Before the end of the campaign the *Victorious* was detached, having steamed more than 12,000 miles in twenty-eight days in company with the *Saratoga*. When she reached Pearl Harbor on her way home, her sailors saw why their services were no longer required in the Pacific. Riding at anchor were the recently built American carriers *Essex, Independence, Belleau Wood,* and *Princeton,* and the new *Yorktown* and *Lexington.*[1]

The frequent visits of the *Saratoga* at Noumea permitted Bill Halsey III, still an aviation supply officer, now a junior grade lieutenant, to see a good deal of his father. On shore leave he sometimes spent the night in the admiral's quarters. These visits gave him an opportunity to observe the routine the elder Halsey had evolved as Commander, South Pacific. It was early to bed and early to rise, but even when business or pleasure kept him up late, he arose at 0530, had a cup of strong black coffee, and smoked the first cigarette of his daily two packs.

The admiral breakfasted regularly at 0730, usually with some of his staff. What had occurred during the intervening two hours no one seemed to know, but his subordinates presumed he was a bathroom dawdler. At any rate, the elapsed time allowed him to indulge his devotion to neatness. When he arrived for the morning meal, he was always cleanshaven, his hair neatly combed, his nails freshly clipped. "When he eventually appears," Joe Bryan later observed, "he is immaculate enough to preside at an operating table instead of a breakfast table. He is never overdue on a haircut; his shoes are always polished, his buttons bright, his uniform crisp."

After breakfast Halsey walked to his office, arriving a few minutes after eight, and skimmed through the night's collection of dispatches. The daily morning conference, modeled roughly on those at Pearl Harbor, began at nine o'clock with a report from an intelligence officer and lasted anywhere from fifteen to forty-five minutes.

The admiral normally worked in his office till noon, then rode home for a light lunch. At 1330 he returned, usually for a series of meetings with individuals or small groups. To the distress of his staff, who could not go home before he did, Halsey often worked late. On leaving his office he always devoted at least an hour to swimming or walking. The evening mess awaited his return.

Following the meal, he went to a movie or read a newspaper or magazine. Though bedtime was normally 2200, he was always ready for a party and set a pace junior officers found hard to keep up with. He thought nothing of partying till three or four o'clock in the morning. Young Bill, after a merry New Year's Eve 1942 celebration with his father, protested when the admiral was up next morning as early as ever. "Most people," he said, "are going to bed at this time today, Dad, and here we are getting up!"

Both father and son were careful to see that Bill III neither sought nor was granted any special privileges. Some of young Bill's shipmates in the *Saratoga* did not even know that the admiral's son was on board. One, a lieutenant at the time, tells how he found out:

> Bill was hard-working and unassuming. And he certainly never traded on his father's reputation. In fact, I didn't know he was the admiral's son for quite some time after he came aboard. He acted like anything but a hotshot's kid. I only discovered his identity in a manner which was rather embarrassing to me. Bill sat near me at dinner and one night several of us, including Bill, were talking about a remark which the newspapers had credited to Admiral Halsey. My comment was, "I think the old son of a bitch is full of hot air."
>
> At first there was a deep silence; then Bill fairly howled with laughter, the others joining him. I said to the officer next to me, "What's so funny?" and he said, "The old son of a bitch is Bill's old man."
>
> I apologized, but Bill said it was perfectly okay. He was sure his father wouldn't have objected either.

A true story then going the rounds confirmed young Bill's conviction. Two South Pacific enlisted men were ambling down a passageway talking about Halsey. "I'd go to hell for that old son of a bitch," said one of them.

Just then he felt a stiff finger in his back. It was Halsey. "Young man," said the admiral in mock indignation, "I'm not so old."

Once, when the *Sara* was at Noumea, an aviation machinist's mate came on board and inquired his way to the aviation supply officer's duty station. The man, never dreaming he was dealing with the son of Commander, South Pacific, said he needed an ignition harness for Admiral Halsey's personal plane. Bill was dubious about letting one go. He had only five spares for the *Sara*'s ninety planes. However, he let the man have one. A couple of weeks later the same petty officer was back. He said the harness had broken and asked if he could have another one. Bill let him have it.

Two weeks after that, Bill got a call from an officer he didn't know and who didn't know Bill either. The stranger said, "I came out to get an ignition harness for Admiral Halsey's plane. I hear you have one."

Bill guessed the petty officer was afraid to come out again and ask for a third harness and had persuaded a commissioned officer, evidently one with enough rank to overawe a junior grade lieutenant, to pick it up. The officer had not bothered to come to Bill's station but had phoned from some point on the ship convenient to himself, expecting Bill to deliver the harness there. But the admiral's son had other ideas, figuring it was better to have three harnesses for ninety planes than for one plane to have three. "Yes," said Bill to the officer, "I have another three, but you can't have one."

A smoldering pause followed. When the officer spoke again, there was iron in his voice. "I guess maybe you don't understand," he said. "This harness is for Admiral Halsey's plane."

"Oh, I understand, all right," replied Bill cheerfully. "You can tell Admiral Halsey to shove it in his ear."

Bill heard a gasp, and the voice on the other end snapped, "What is your name, sir?"

"William Frederick Halsey," replied Bill and hung up. He never discovered what steps the officer took to discipline the insolent supply officer. Nothing was ever said to him about it, and he kept his three harnesses.

Bill was too much his father's son to be content with supplying and denying ignition harnesses below decks when combat was imminent. He pestered the ship's exec until the latter gave him additional duty as a gunnery officer in charge of six 20mm guns on the catwalk on the starboard side of the flight deck—one of the most exposed positions during battle.

Two days after the fall of Munda, on 7 August, the *Saratoga* put in to Havannah Harbor, Efate, and young Bill seized the opportunity to fly down to Noumea for some spare parts and to visit his father. After spending a night in the admiral's quarters, Bill started back early the next afternoon as a passenger in a return flight of three *Saratoga* torpedo planes.

That evening Admiral Halsey was stricken with the flu and ran a high fever. On the tenth, when his fever had subsided, Captain Raymond Thurber, his operations officer, came to him and said, "Admiral, I have some bad news. We have three torpedo planes missing for two days."

"Was my son on one of those planes?"

"Yes, sir." Thurber described the searches being made, then asked the admiral if he could suggest any further measures that might be taken.

"No," replied Halsey, "my son is the same as every other son in the combat zone. Look for him just as you'd look for anybody else."

Halsey went through two days of extreme anxiety and declining hope, which he felt he could not share with his associates. Finally at dusk on the twelfth a search plane reported sighting several rubber rafts on the beach of Eromanga, a small island between New Caledonia and Efate. The next day all ten missing men, including Bill, were picked up at the island and returned to their ship. They suffered from nothing more serious than flea bites, diarrhea, and sore feet.

Through a mixup at army headquarters in Noumea, the departure report of the three planes had failed to reach the *Saratoga*. The flight leader picked up the *Sara*'s radio beam and began to home in on it, neglecting his navigation. The operator on board the carrier, not knowing any planes were in the air, secured the beam and thus left the leader disoriented, not knowing his location. After dark the pilots spotted an island and made water landings near the beach.

When the final report of the incident reached Halsey's headquarters, his deputy added an endorsement properly condemning the flight leader for negligence.

"I'll be damned if I'll sign it," said Halsey when he had read the condemnation. Not wanting people thinking he was vindictive because his son was involved in the incident, he ordered the endorsement toned down.[2]

Before Halsey had got over the shock of his son's disappearance and while he was immersed in the final stages of the New Georgia campaign, word arrived that Eleanor Roosevelt was en route to tour the south and southwest Pacific and would arrive at Noumea on 25 August. On top of this distracting news came announcements from the Australian government and General MacArthur that they were sending sizable delegations to Noumea to give her an official welcome. South Pacific headquarters had no time for Mrs. Roosevelt and no quarters to accommodate the delegations.

Since early in the year, Halsey had been protesting to Nimitz about the arrival in the South Pacific of a stream of admirals, generals, politicians, and special correspondents who insisted that their duties included a visit to the combat zone. He complained as vehemently of do-gooders. These individuals, according to Halsey, convinced themselves and others that their presence near the front lines was indispensable to the morale of the fighting men. They took up badly needed space in planes and lodgings and interfered with the wartime duties of Halsey and his staff. The admiral had met and admired Mrs. Roosevelt, but by coming uninvited to the embattled South Pacific she made of herself, in his opinion, even more of a nuisance than most—for her he would have to put on a necktie and play the gracious host.

Admiral Halsey, as duty required, met Mrs. Roosevelt when her plane arrived. She stepped out wearing a Red Cross uniform. Halsey asked what her plans were.

"What do you think I should do?" she asked.

"Mrs. Roosevelt," replied the admiral, a shade grumpily, "I've been married for some thirty-odd years, and if those years have taught me one lesson, it is never to try to make up a woman's mind for her."

They decided that she would spend two days at Noumea, fly to Australia, and spend two more days at Noumea on her way home. That settled, Mrs. Roosevelt, to Halsey's consternation, handed him a letter from the president asking him to let his wife visit Guadalcanal if it was possible. Rather brusquely Halsey said, "Guadalcanal is no place for you, Ma'am."

"I'm perfectly willing to take my chances," she said. "I'll be entirely responsible for anything that happens to me."

"I'm not worried about the responsibility, and I'm not worried about the chances you'd take. I know you'd take them gladly. What worries me is the battle going on in New Georgia at this very minute. I need every fighter plane I can put my hands on. If you fly to Guadalcanal, I'll have to provide a fighter escort for you, and I haven't got one to spare."

Mrs. Roosevelt looked so downcast that Halsey couldn't resist adding,

"However, I'll postpone my final decision until you return." Despite his annoyance and the need to wear a tie, Halsey's good nature and ebullience took over at the reception and dinner he held for his guest that evening, but when he noted the number of marines stationed outside the Wicky-Wacky Lodge, where she was billeted, his grumpiness returned.

The next day Mrs. Roosevelt visited one army and two naval hospitals. These calls were not merely perfunctory. She went into every ward and stopped at every bed. She spoke to each patient, including those with horrible wounds, asking him his name, how he felt, if he needed anything, and if she could take a message home for him. She must have walked a dozen miles. The doctors assured Halsey that Mrs. Roosevelt's visit accomplished more good in less time than that of any civilian or civilian delegation during Halsey's entire tenure in the South Pacific.

When Mrs. Roosevelt returned from Australia, the New Georgia campaign was over, and Halsey, despite misgivings, arranged for her to stop at Guadalcanal on her way back to Pearl Harbor. When she departed from Noumea, he apologized for his original lack of hospitality. For what she had done for his men, he assured her, it was impossible to express his gratitude sufficiently.

While Mrs. Roosevelt earned her welcome, at least one other visitor quickly wore his welcome out. He was a young professor, admitted into the naval reserve for reasons not immediately apparent and holding the rank of lieutenant commander. The Office of Strategic Services (antecedent of the Central Intelligence Agency) sent him to Halsey. An authority on Tibet, he was presumed to be useful to the South Pacific campaign. The young man's credentials won him admission to Halsey's office, which he entered with an almost comically conspiratorial air. Impressed with his cloak-and-dagger role, he spoke so softly that Halsey had the dickens of a time finding out his business. It finally became clear that the visitor was promoting a one-man collapsible submarine. Halsey, dubious, asked him to describe it.

"I'd rather not. It's highly confidential," the man whispered. Halsey assured him that he could trust his discretion.

"The fact is," admitted the young professor, "we haven't got one yet, but I'll tell Washington to develop it."

"Get out of here!" snorted Halsey.

Another young officer requested an invitation to the South Pacific and was welcomed there. Ever since Halsey's visit to Brisbane, Joe Bryan had been dreaming up ways to ingratiate himself with the admiral and his staff, with a view to transferring from the torpid southwest Pacific to the active South Pacific command. At last he hit upon an idea.

Bryan sent a letter to the editor of the *Saturday Evening Post,* his old boss. "I have a very good contact with Admiral Halsey," Bryan wrote. "Could you use a firsthand profile of the admiral? If you want it, I suggest you cable me in these terms: URGENTLY REQUEST HALSEY PROFILE."

Halsey was figuring more and more prominently in the war news at that time, so Joe was not surprised to receive a cablegram from the editor of the *Saturday Evening Post* asking for the profile.

Joe wrote to Halsey's flag secretary, Doug Moulton. He quoted the cablegram and added, "I'm not doing anything. Why don't you get me over there and let me write the article? I can guarantee acceptance of it. Certainly it will be to the greater glory of Admiral Halsey and the United States Navy."

Moulton showed Bryan's letter to Admiral Halsey, who said, "Tell him to come on over." Because Lieutenant Bryan served an air command, Moulton sent the reply through the office of Vice Admiral Fitch, Commander, Aircraft, South Pacific. It arrived in Brisbane with Fitch's name on it: "Request services of Lieutenant J. Bryan III for temporary duty SoPac headquarters."

Faking surprise and distress, Joe took the dispatch to his top commanding officer, Rear Admiral Ralph Wood. "Good lord, Admiral," he said, "what am I going to do about this?"

Wood studied the message. "Well," he said, "you'd better go."

Joe packed in record time and was away for Noumea on the first available flight. At Noumea he was billeted in Halsey's quarters. The admiral granted him several long interviews. Then Joe latched on to officers who knew Halsey best or had been with him a long time—Bill Ashford, Doug Moulton, Bill Kitchell, Ray Thurber. At the end of two weeks he had copious notes on Halsey's personality, his wartime career, his daily routine.

Before returning to Brisbane to write his article, Joe sought an interview with Captain Thurber, with whom he had developed a warm friendship. "Please get me out of the Southwest Pacific," he pleaded. "I'm an air combat intelligence officer, and there's nothing over there to be intelligent about. I belong over here. I've been talking to the guys who run ACI here in your area. They're hard up for trained officers, and they can use me."

"Well," said Thurber, "I can't get you a definite assignment over here, but I think I can at least get you into this area, and we'll see what happens after that."

That was good enough for Joe, who hurried back to Brisbane where, with nothing much else to do, he completed a long article on Halsey in a short time. Hardly had he finished it when a dispatch arrived ordering his transfer.

Joe took the dispatch to Admiral Wood, again with outward manifestations of distress. Wood read the dispatch, then looked at Bryan narrowly. Evidently he suspected some monkey business. Still, the transfer was official. There was nothing he could do about it. "Well," said the admiral, "when rape is inevitable, relax and enjoy it."

Joe packed again, this time for good, said his farewells, and was off in a trice for Noumea, manuscript in hand. He handed it to Halsey, who read it from beginning to end. The admiral's only comment was, "This is very flattering."

Joe Bryan's article, "Four-Star Sea Dog," appeared along with pictures of Halsey in two installments in the *Saturday Evening Post* issues of 25 December 1943 and 1 January 1944. It was widely read and favorably received, the first in-depth treatment of the admiral and his achievements, known previously to the public mainly through newspaper stories.

Meanwhile, Joe was required to serve a token tour of duty on the battleship *Massachusetts,* after which he was attached to the air fighter command at Munda airfield.

Another welcome visitor at Noumea was Halsey's old sidekick Ray Spruance, now Vice Admiral Spruance, Commander, Fifth Fleet. He was accompanied by his chief of staff, Captain Charles J. ("Carl") Moore, sound planner, careful writer, and workaholic, whom Spruance had enlisted to take over paperwork and details, which he detested.

Spruance and Moore were making a tour of islands and commands to prepare themselves for the forthcoming central Pacific drive via the Gilberts, Marshalls, and Carolines, in accordance with the time-honored Orange Plan. The campaign was scheduled to begin in the autumn of 1943 with the main assault against Tarawa Atoll in the Gilbert Islands.

Halsey, as an area commander, had little useful advice for his visitor, a fleet commander. Moreover, the experience gained by South Pacific forces in the Munda campaign provided few lessons for the central Pacific. The landings in the Russells and on New Georgia had been over undefended beaches, and the Japanese overwhelmed in the Munda drive were able to escape to Kolombangara. Landings on the small islands of the central Pacific atolls would have to be made in the teeth of enemy defenses, and from such islands there could be no escape for the defenders. One thing both Halsey and MacArthur had learned was that the Japanese, when cornered, would fight to the last man. The new drive thus promised to be a bloody affair, but it would speed up the progress toward Tokyo, overshadowing Halsey's South Pacific and MacArthur's southwest Pacific campaigns.

Rear Admiral Randall Jacobs, chief of the Bureau of Naval Personnel, arrived at South Pacific headquarters wearing a new gray uniform with black braid, replacing the traditional colors all navies used, following the lead of Britain's Royal Navy. Admiral King's brainstorm, it was supposed to be less conspicuous in combat. Most U.S. naval officers heartily disliked the new uniforms. Halsey called them bus-driver suits. When this and similar comments reached King's ears, he issued a special all-navy bulletin "pointedly stating that grays had been authorized as an alternative uniform for the entire Navy, including *every theater* of the war."

At his next staff meeting Halsey, wearing his usual khakis, read the bulletin aloud. "Gentlemen," he added, "you have heard the edict. There will be no more derogatory remarks about that damned gray uniform." Then, after a pause, he continued, "Officers and chiefs in my command are wholly at liberty to wear the damn things—*if,* that is, they are so lacking in naval courtesy and have such limited intelligence as to prefer dressing differently from the commander of the force." Word got around, and no more gray uniforms were seen in the South Pacific.[3]

In the summer of 1943 (winter in the South Pacific) a number of key officers transferred into or out of Halsey's command. In mid-July Admiral Turner was scheduled to transfer to the central Pacific and be relieved as Commander, Third Amphibious Force, by Admiral Wilkinson. The assigned date, however, coincided with the period of confusion on New Georgia, General Griswold having just relieved General Hester in command of the occupation force there. Turner, who had characteristically involved himself in shore operations, believed that for the time being he was indispensable where he was. To Halsey he radioed, "In fairness to Wilkinson and me, recommend that I retain command of this operation until affairs are again going smoothly."

Halsey, who seems to have regarded Turner's participation at this time merely an added complication, replied without delay, "Your relief by Wilkinson will be effected on 15 July, as planned, in view of CinCPac's requirement for your services." Thus Admiral Turner departed from the South Pacific to become Commander, Fifth Amphibious Force, a post that was to win him fame as the war's outstanding expert in amphibious warfare.

Admiral Mitscher also was relieved in July, a move necessitated by his declining health. During his four months as Commander, Air Solomons, he had presided over the complex of aviators, aircraft, and airfields on Guadalcanal and the Russells with a sure hand. He was a pioneer of naval aviation and probably knew the subject better than any man alive. As a fighter he was reputed to be tough as nails, but he scarcely looked or seemed the part. For one thing, he rarely spoke above a whisper. Skinny, wrinkled, bald, he reminded one newsman of a village grocer. Halsey, however, recognizing his fighting spirit, had sought him for the Solomons post. As captain of the *Hornet*, it will be recalled, Mitscher had joined Halsey in carrying Doolittle's bombers into the waters off Japan and subsequently raced with him to the Coral Sea and back to Pearl Harbor.

"I knew we'd probably catch hell from the Japs in the air," said Halsey later, referring to Mitscher's assignment to Guadalcanal. "That's why I sent Pete Mitscher up there. Pete was a fighting fool, and I knew it."

Characteristically, Mitscher had given everything he had to the Solomons assignment, but unremitting nervous tension, together with heat and humidity, which he never stood well, soon sapped his strength, and a bout with malaria so undermined his health that his weight dropped to 115 pounds. Relieved by the army's Major General Nathan F. Twining, Mitscher left behind a proud record. His aviators, in destroying nearly five hundred Japanese planes and dropping more than 2,000 tons of bombs on the enemy, had ended the air threat to the Solomons.

Halsey requested that Mitscher be granted leave to restore his health. He then wanted him back in the South Pacific to command whatever carrier forces were assigned there. He was sure Pete would welcome the command, because, as Halsey knew, Mitscher's heart was with the carriers.

CinCPac and the Bureau of Personnel had other plans. The latter sent Mitscher to San Diego as Commander, Fleet Air, West Coast. The post was intended as a sinecure. Pearl Harbor passed informal instructions to San Diego to "keep him in the open and get him back in shape as soon as possible." During the next few months Pete Mitscher had his fill of fishing, his favorite sport. When he was sent back to the war zone the following year, it was not to head a South Pacific carrier group but to take command of the great Fast Carrier Task Force, which included all the fleet carriers of the U.S. Navy and had spearheaded the drive across the Pacific. No newsman called Pete a village grocer again. One conferred on him the title Admiral of the Ocean Air; others, to emphasize the contrast between his looks and his fighting spirit, called him the Ferocious Gnome.[4]

Bill Ashford, the South Pacific staff officer who had been with Halsey longest, was about to depart. He had joined the admiral as his aide in 1937 when the latter was commandant at Pensacola. He was still aide and flag lieutenant when Halsey became Commander, South Pacific. Since then Ashford had been air operations officer. Over the years there had developed between them a father-son relationship, but after New Georgia the admiral decided that Ashford had been on his staff long enough, perhaps too long, for the good of his career. He told the younger man that he was going to order him back to the United States for assignment and asked him to recommend a relief for himself. Ashford named Doug Moulton, a recommendation Halsey was pleased to accept. That posed the question of who should relieve Moulton as the admiral's flag secretary.

A couple of days later Ashford and Moulton were sitting in the staff duty office past working hours discussing prospects for Moulton's relief. A messenger came in and told them an officer was outside asking to see the staff duty officer.

"Send him in," said Ashford.

A lieutenant commander entered and presented his orders. Ashford, looking up, thought there was something familiar about the stranger's appearance. Then he glanced at the man's orders and did a double take. The officer was Harold Stassen. Ashford instantly recognized the name: Stassen had been the youngest governor of Minnesota and the keynote speaker of the 1940 Republican national convention. After reading the orders, Ashford handed them to Moulton with a raised eyebrow. Moulton read them and nodded knowingly. Ashford asked Lieutenant Commander Stassen if he had anywhere to stay for the night. When he said no, Ashford invited him to stay at Havoc Hall.

On offering his services for a third term as governor, Stassen, then an inactive officer in the naval reserve, had told the people of Minnesota that, if elected, he would resign after the legislative session to go on active duty. At the same time he recommended an able and experienced civil servant, a veteran of World War I, to be nominated and elected to the office of lieutenant governor.

In due course Stassen, elected to a third term, resigned the governorship as he had promised and went on active duty in the naval reserve with the rank of lieutenant commander. He considered the change his duty to his country and also perhaps a political necessity. In his middle thirties, with the nation at war, he needed a service record to attain the goal to which he aspired—the presidency of the United States.

Because Stassen's youthful achievements had won him national fame, his transfer from politics to military duty made headlines in the newspapers and was duly noted by the naval hierarchy. It gave Secretary Knox an idea. In his visit to Noumea the preceding January, the secretary had been impressed by Halsey's outstanding leadership but dismayed by his administration, which struck him as sloppy. Why not team this skilled young administrator, thrice elected state governor, with the seasoned leader? Knox contacted Stassen. Was he interested? Indeed he was! Operating in an active war zone would be the sort of challenge he had hoped for, and service with the most publicized admiral in the navy would keep him perpetually in the eye of the electorate.

The morning after Stassen's arrival, Ashford and Moulton paid a visit to Halsey's office while Stassen waited outside. Ashford told the admiral that he had located an officer who would make an excellent aide and flag secretary.

"Who is he?"

"Harold Stassen, the former governor of Minnesota."

Moulton began pointing out that experience as a state governor was superb indoctrination for a flag lieutenant. Halsey cut him short. "Show him in," he said and dismissed them with a gesture.

Halsey, who like most newspaper readers had a fair knowledge of Stassen's career and aspirations, seems to have been a little loath to serve as a vehicle for an ambitious politician, but at the same time he was intrigued and willing to take the ex-governor on as a calculated risk.

Seated at his desk, Halsey motioned Stassen to a chair facing him. After looking Stassen over, the admiral said, "Are you here to work?"

"Yes, Admiral."

"Good," said Halsey. "Go to it."

Stassen was perfectly aware that he had to sell himself to his new colleagues as well as to the admiral. At first he was startled by the freewheeling at South Pacific headquarters. But, accomplished politician that he was, he quickly accommodated himself to the staff's antics. Within a week the other officers had shed whatever awe or suspicion they had at first felt and were addressing the ex-governor as Stass. He made no secret of the fact that his ambitions included the national presidency, and his fellow staffers didn't hesitate to kid him about it.

"Of course," Doug Moulton told him, "we all expect White House sinecures when you're elected."

"I wouldn't have a chance to fix you up," replied Stassen. "If I'm elected, I'll have the shortest term in history. I'll be inaugurated one day, I'll announce my cabinet the next day, I'll give a SoPac party the third day, and on the fourth day I'll be impeached for it."[5]

Admirals King and Nimitz had long been dissatisfied with Halsey's chief of staff, attributing the admiral's occasional lapses in judgment at least in part to Miles Browning's influence. In the Battle of Santa Cruz, for example, Halsey had sent his two carrier forces to face the entire Japanese Combined Fleet, which sank the *Hornet* and a U.S. destroyer and damaged the *Enterprise* and *South Dakota*. Then there was the case of Captain Gilbert Hoover of the *Helena*. Following the November cruiser action, which cost Admirals Scott and Callaghan their lives, the *Helena*, the damaged *Juneau*, and a pair of destroyers were withdrawing from Ironbottom Sound when an enemy submarine fired a torpedo into the *Juneau*. She went down with all hands. Captain Hoover radioed a report of the sinking to a patrol plane and then continued on to Espíritu with the *Helena* and the two destroyers. For his failure to make further provisions to pick up survivors of the *Juneau*, Halsey relieved him of his command. Admiral Nimitz questioned the justice of this relief in view of Hoover's outstanding record—he had won three Navy Crosses—and the probability that, had he left a ship behind to pick up survivors, that ship also would have been sunk. Hoover had no way of knowing that his report to the patrol plane never reached headquarters.

Admiral Halsey's news conferences and prophesies of an early end to the war had raised further questions about his judgment, and Nimitz regarded his handling of General Hester's relief as at least questionable. However, such lapses faded into insignificance set next to his achievements—restoring morale in the South Pacific and turning prospective defeat there into victory. Nimitz and King believed that with a wiser counselor than Browning at his side, Halsey might be preserved from the painful and embarrassing errors that marred his otherwise sterling record.

Secretary Knox, shocked during his January visit by Browning's behavior, had been campaigning ever since to have him transferred. Halsey stoutly resisted the transfer, countering every move to relieve Browning with a recommendation to have him promoted to flag rank. Valuing his chief of staff's professional expertise, he was willing to put up with his eccentricities. Perhaps also he felt protective toward Browning because nobody else could stand him. At last King lured Browning away with a bait so attractive that Halsey would no longer stand in his way—nothing less than command of the new carrier *Hornet,* then nearing completion. Aviators resented Browning's being handed this choice assignment, but King insisted that "the idea was to get rid of him at once," whatever the price.

Predictably, Browning mishandled his new assignment. He berated the *Hornet*'s department heads savagely, usually without making clear what he was raving about. He kept his crew so on edge that a minor explosion on board incited a riot in which two men fell overboard and drowned. Browning's failure to muster and send out a boat led to a court of inquiry, which found him guilty of negligence, whereupon Admiral Mitscher, then commander of the Fast Carrier Task Force, requested his immediate relief. Browning spent the rest of the war exiled on the faculty of an army staff college.[6]

After Browning's departure from Noumea, Ray Thurber served as South Pacific chief of staff until 26 July 1943, when the new appointee, Robert B. ("Mick") Carney, arrived at Noumea. Admiral King had given Halsey a choice of three men, all competent, highly professional officers serving afloat in the South Pacific. Halsey selected Carney as "the least of the three evils."

Until the preceding September Carney had been chief of staff to Vice Admiral Arthur Bristol, stationed at Argentia, Newfoundland. In this billet his contributions to antisubmarine warfare won him the Distinguished Service Medal and the favorable attention of the Navy Department. He was given command of the new cruiser *Denver* with the understanding that it was temporary duty to prepare him for flag rank and a more important job. When, after less than a year in the *Denver,* hunting the Tokyo Express under Tip Merrill, Carney learned that the important job he had been promised was to be chief of staff at another island outpost, he felt distinctly let down.

But Carney took the appointment philosophically. For one thing, it was sweetened by promotion to rear admiral. Also, he liked Halsey, whom he had known socially before the war; and having served on the fringes of the South Pacific command, he was curious to observe operations at headquarters.

Admiral Halsey, despite his annoyance at losing Browning, received his new chief of staff cordially and saw that he was made comfortable. During the next few weeks, Carney was often surprised by what he observed. The day began with the boss in mysterious and extended seclusion. When he entered the dining room at breakfast time the staff officers invariably stood up. "Sit down, goddammit!" Halsey would shout. "How many times do I have to tell you?" He clearly meant what he said, but the men never failed to rise, usually grinning.

The way Halsey conducted his morning conferences would have pained General Robert of *Rules of Order* fame. He disregarded procedural details and brushed aside any business that could be handled out of council. But the necessary ground was usually covered. Later, in the series of interviews and small conferences that made up most of Halsey's work day, the admiral seemed mainly concerned with delegating administrative details and decisions to staff members or other officers under his command.

Before dinner Halsey always had a drink, sometimes a martini, more often his favorite, Scotch and water. He once remarked, "There are exceptions, of course, but as a general rule I never trust a fighting man who doesn't smoke or drink." When the occasion warranted, he might sound off with his favorite toast:

> I've drunk your health in company;
> I've drunk your health alone;
> I've drunk your health so many times
> I've damned near ruined my own.

On evenings when a party was in progress, Halsey could down an astonishing amount of Scotch. Carney never saw him get drunk, but at breakfast the next morning, he sometimes heard Halsey moan, "It seemed like a good idea last night." Then he would pitch in and do a full day's work with as much vigor as ever.

Halsey, Carney found, liked having his staff around him, talking and arguing. He encouraged them to express themselves, regardless of rank. Junior officers never hesitated to disagree sharply with him, his deputy, or his chief of staff. The staff members' familiarity in addressing the admiral stopped just short of calling him Bill. Sometimes, especially in the evening when the talk, enlivened by drink, approached the point of verbal backslapping, Halsey would shake his head or wag a finger. His men knew the signals and instantly toned down their discourse.

Arguments came to an end when Halsey made up his mind. "Okay, lads," he would say, "that's it. That's what we'll do." All hands knew the admiral expected them to carry out his decision just as though it had been their own.

When a major line of action was impending and time permitted, Halsey expected his staff to make a serious study of background and options before advising him. Sometimes he accepted their advice with little argument. At other times he chose to decide on the basis of one of his hunches. "It's convincing," he would say, "but I just have the feeling it's not right. We'll do it my way."

"In each of these instances," Carney said later, "his intuition was correct."

Even with plenty of advice, though, he occasionally made the wrong decision. A case in point was his relief of Captain Hoover of the *Helena*. He had made that decision on the recommendation of a court of inquiry consisting of three of his senior officers. Yet he felt uncomfortable about it, particularly when Admiral Nimitz questioned the justice of his action. One day he discussed the Hoover case with Carney and asked his opinion. Carney agreed with Nimitz, that the relief was unjust.

Halsey immediately dictated a letter to the Navy Department, stating that Captain Hoover's decision had been in the best interests of victory after all. He requested that the captain be restored to combat command, adding that he would be delighted to have Hoover serve under him. Halsey later made a public apology in his autobiography. "I have the comfort," he wrote, "of knowing that Hoover's official record is clean. I deeply regret the whole incident."

Carney found Halsey utterly uncomplicated. If he felt like saying something, he said it, but being of good will, he rarely hurt feelings. His humor was broad, lacking subtlety but never vulgar. His attitudes tended to extremes. His patriotism, for example, was absolute but he detested Japan and could see no good in anything Japanese. There was a touch of the theater in his makeup, his favorite role being that of Bull Halsey, a swashbuckler of the old tradition and, like most swashbucklers, part little boy who never grew up. On the other hand, he was completely honest, never offering alibis and despising those who did.

It was clear to Carney that Halsey's staff loved the guy and that the admiral returned their affection. He was intensely loyal to his officers and men, and they were loyal to him. Halsey praised in public and scolded in private. When his command had a success, he was promptly on the housetops acclaiming the achievements of his subordinates. When there was a setback, he took full responsibility.

Students of warfare have remarked that members of a military staff often grow to resemble their commanding officer in attitudes and personality—not surprising since these men, sometimes called the commander's family, spend months, even years, representing him, relaying and interpreting his orders, and anticipating his desires. For example, when Ray Spruance left Pearl Harbor to command the Fifth Fleet after thirteen months as Admiral Nimitz's chief of staff, another staff member remarked, "The admiral thinks it's all right to send Raymond out now. He's got him to the point where they think and talk just alike."

When the highly professional, slightly aloof Carney first joined the South Pacific staff, he regarded the Halsey carbon copies at headquarters with mild condescension, little suspecting that he too would in time fall captive to the Halsey charisma, that in little over a year he would be calling his strategy group "Halsey's Dirty Trick Department," and that he would regard liberty with Halsey "more damned fun than a circus."[7]

CHAPTER 16

BYPASSING RABAUL

JAPAN'S SHIPPING PROBLEM was complex. Having no industry in its resources areas and no resources in its industrial area, the country had to import all raw materials for manufacture and then distribute the products to consumers, which in war were the forces in the field. Aside from Manchuria, Japan's chief source of raw materials in 1943 was the East Indies and southeast Asia, its so-called Southern Resources Area, which the Japanese had conquered at the price of war with the United States, the Netherlands, and the British Commonwealth.

From the Southern Resources Area ships brought raw materials northward through the South China Sea and past Formosa (Taiwan) and the Ryukyus to Japan. Of all materials shipped to Japan on this route, the most vital was the oil from the wells of Borneo, Java, and Sumatra. Without this source of energy Japan could not long continue fighting. On the East Indies–to–Japan route, sometimes called Japan's oil line, the choke point was the Luzon-China-Formosa triangle. The Joint Chiefs of Staff directed both Nimitz's central Pacific and MacArthur's southwest Pacific drives toward this triangle, where bases could be set up on either Luzon or Formosa to block the flow of oil to Japan. The Joint Chiefs' planners estimated that one or the other of the Allied drives, or both, would reach Luzon or Formosa by the spring of 1945.

In 1943 the manufactured materials, including aircraft and munitions, flowed south from Japan through the Bonins, the Marianas, Truk, and Rabaul. Planes used the airfields at these bases, ships sailed under the protection of aircraft from the fields. The Joint Chiefs estimated that the most vulnerable point on this route was the Marianas, specifically the major islands of Saipan, Tinian, and Guam. U.S. submarines, ships, and aircraft operating from these positions could not only block the southward flow of Japanese products and thus starve Japan's forward bases but also protect American communications to the western Pacific. The Joint Chiefs assigned conquest of the major Marianas, to be achieved by mid-1944, to Nimitz's central Pacific drive.

In August 1943 the Joint Chiefs issued a directive for Allied operations in the Pacific theater through 1944. It ordered Halsey and MacArthur to continue their dual drive on Rabaul, after which MacArthur would advance the full length of the New Guinea north coast. "Rabaul," said the directive, "is to be neutralized rather than captured." Positions around Rabaul would be occupied and air bases set up from which it could be kept pounded down and isolated. Nimitz was ordered to sweep across the central Pacific and seize positions in the Gilberts, Marshalls, and Marianas, and in the Palau Islands in the western Carolines. Operations in 1945 would depend on successes achieved by the Allies in 1944.[1]

General MacArthur found little in the August directive that pleased him. He disliked leaving a powerful base such as Rabaul in his rear. Moreover, he had planned to make use of the excellent harbor there. On withdrawing from the Philippines, he had promised, "I shall return," and he proposed to do so by landing first on Mindanao, the southernmost of the islands. The directive did not mention the Philippines. It left MacArthur dangling at the western end of New Guinea. At the close of 1944 Admiral Nimitz's central Pacific forces arriving at the Palaus would be closer to Mindanao than the general's own southwest Pacific forces would be. MacArthur felt that the "Washington admirals" were plotting to halt his advance and turn the Pacific war into a completely navy-dominated operation. He grimly told Major General George Kenney, commanding his air force, that he would return to the Philippines even if he were "down to one canoe paddled by Douglas MacArthur and supported by one Taylor cub."[2]

Meanwhile, the immediate task of both MacArthur and Halsey was to seize bases for the neutralization of Rabaul. For the latter that meant, first, invading fiddle-shaped Bougainville, largest and most heavily fortified of the Solomon Islands. Here South Pacific forces were to seize enemy airfields or establish new fields from which short-range bombers could knock out enemy fields on Bougainville so that long-range bombers from Munda could get through to Rabaul, and from which fighters could support bombers from Munda and Papua in their attacks on Rabaul.

Halsey knew that invading Bougainville would be a formidable undertaking. On this and nearby islands were some sixty thousand Japanese, mostly in the south, at Kahili and Buin and on the offshore Shortland Islands. Others were in the north, at Buka and Bonis. The enemy occupiers manned several air bases supported from nearby Rabaul, which could be expected to meet any attack on Bougainville with a prompt counterattack by sea and air.

Early South Pacific strategy called for landings in the Shortlands and on the Bougainville mainland near Kahili, followed by an attack on Japanese airdromes. But after the bitter experience at Munda followed by the easy success at Vella Lavella, Halsey and his staff canceled the Shortlands-Kahili plan. They decided on another bypass, this time leapfrogging beyond enemy strongpoints in the south to seize a lightly defended Bougainville coastal area somewhere between the southern and northern enemy bases. Here the invaders would lay out their own airstrips and establish themselves behind a powerful perimeter before the Japanese at the bases could haul the necessary heavy equipment over primitive jungle trails to attack the Allied beachhead.

South Pacific reconnaissance parties, put ashore from submarines, searched the Bougainville coasts for suitable landing sites and at length recommended Kieta Harbor on the northeast coast and Cape Torokina at Empress Augusta Bay on the opposite coast. Neither position was heavily defended. The beach at Kieta was inside a cove; that at Cape Torokina was fairly open to the Solomon Sea, where there was often heavy surf. On the other hand, the soil at Torokina was more suitable for airfield construction. Prior to landing at either location, the Allies would have to safeguard their waterborne supplies by capturing enemy island bases lying athwart their lines of communication—Choiseul Island, if they chose to land at Kieta, or if they decided to take Torokina, the much smaller Treasury Islands.

The South Pacific staff debated the choice at length. Was it to be Kieta, Torokina, or elsewhere? As the discussion rambled on inconclusively, it occurred to Halsey that his officers were talking at least partly to postpone action. They evidently wanted to digest New Georgia and Vella Lavella and catch their breath before fully facing the formidable demands of a Bougainville invasion. Finally he lost patience. At a morning conference on 22 September he ended the debate by announcing, "It's Torokina. Now get on your horses!"

For so hazardous an operation Halsey had barely enough troops, some fourteen thousand men of the Third Marine Division for the assault, the Thirty-seventh Infantry Division for follow-up, and a brigade group of New Zealanders to seize the Treasuries. These together, about thirty-four thousand men in all, constituted the I Marine Amphibious Corps. Lieutenant General Vandegrift, commander of the corps, had been appointed commandant of the marine corps, and so on 15 September Major General Charles D. Barrett relieved him.

Because Kenney's bombers, operating out of Papua, would also be taking Rabaul under attack, Halsey felt Aircraft, Solomons, had enough planes for its mission, but he considered himself desperately short of combatant ships. Most new construction was being absorbed by the Mediterranean campaign and the U.S. Fifth Fleet, scheduled to invade Tarawa and Makin in the Gilberts on 20 November. For the Torokina assault, Admiral Wilkinson's Third Amphibious Force would carry the marines to the landing site in a dozen transports escorted by eleven destroyers. So many cruisers and destroyers had been sunk or damaged in the actions off the central Solomons that Halsey now had for surface support only Tip Merrill's Task Force 39, consisting of four new light cruisers and two destroyer divisions.

(*From left*) Admirals Nimitz, King, and Halsey at CinCPac headquarters, Pearl Harbor, 28 September 1943

After the departure from the South Pacific of the British carrier *Victorious,* Halsey had expected to receive some of the new U.S. carriers to join his venerable *Saratoga.* But Nimitz had retained all the new carriers at Pearl Harbor. They had come out with ill-trained crews and with aviators untried in battle. He was sending them on hit-run raids against Japanese-occupied islands to give them experience under fire before the Gilberts assault. Nimitz believed Halsey could make out with what he had. He was convinced the Japanese would not send their big ships to attack the South Pacific's small forces while a major fleet from Pearl Harbor was raiding their positions in the central Pacific.

After ordering the Torokina assault, Halsey flew to Pearl Harbor. There he must have used convincing arguments to persuade Nimitz and the CinCPac staff that he was in sore need of carriers and other combatant ships. When he headed back to the South Pacific he had been promised a loan of the light carrier *Princeton* and possibly an additional carrier group. A few cruisers and destroyers had also been offered, but these could not arrive until after the landing at Torokina, now scheduled for 1 November.

Pausing at Noumea on his return south, Halsey checked on the planning for the Bougainville campaign, found it satisfactory, and then with members of his staff flew to Brisbane to coordinate operations with the southwest Pacific. MacArthur was still fretting about the proposed central Pacific drive—its cost in casualties and what its demands in ships, planes, supplies, and men would do to his own drive across the southwest, an advance he was beginning to call his New Guinea–Mindanao Axis. In a letter to General Marshall he pointed to the Japanese disaster at Midway as an example of the hazards of attempting to capture enemy island bases.

MacArthur did not, however, protest Nimitz's forthcoming attacks on the Gilberts and the adjoining Marshalls. Since early in the Pacific war the Allies had worried lest the Japanese advance from the Gilberts via the Ellices and establish at Samoa a base for blocking communications from the United States to the southwest, which now would include supplies vital to his and Halsey's operational forces. And there could be no thought of taking the Gilberts and not the Marshalls, because enemy bombers based on the latter could make the Gilberts untenable.

The general also ceased protesting the bypassing of Rabaul. He acknowledged that it could be neutralized, and his projected capture of Manus in the Admiralty Islands 350 miles farther west would give him the use of Seeadler Harbor, as defensible as Rabaul's Blanche Bay and much more spacious. He insisted, however, that Halsey capture Kavieng at the western end of New Ireland, another Japanese Bismarcks base, second in strength only to Rabaul itself.

Back at Noumea, Halsey resumed his study and discussions of the plan being worked out for the assault on Bougainville. It was an intricate and ingenious scheme, guaranteed to perplex and delay the enemy if not confuse and paralyze him. Then on 20 October, just as Halsey was about to put his final okay on the plan, a setback occurred. General Barrett unaccountably fell out of the window of his quarters and died of a cerebral hemorrhage. There was only one remaining officer whom Halsey trusted to get his marines safely ashore on Bougainville. That was Vandegrift, then en route to Washington to head the marine corps. Priority messages sent out from Noumea overtook the

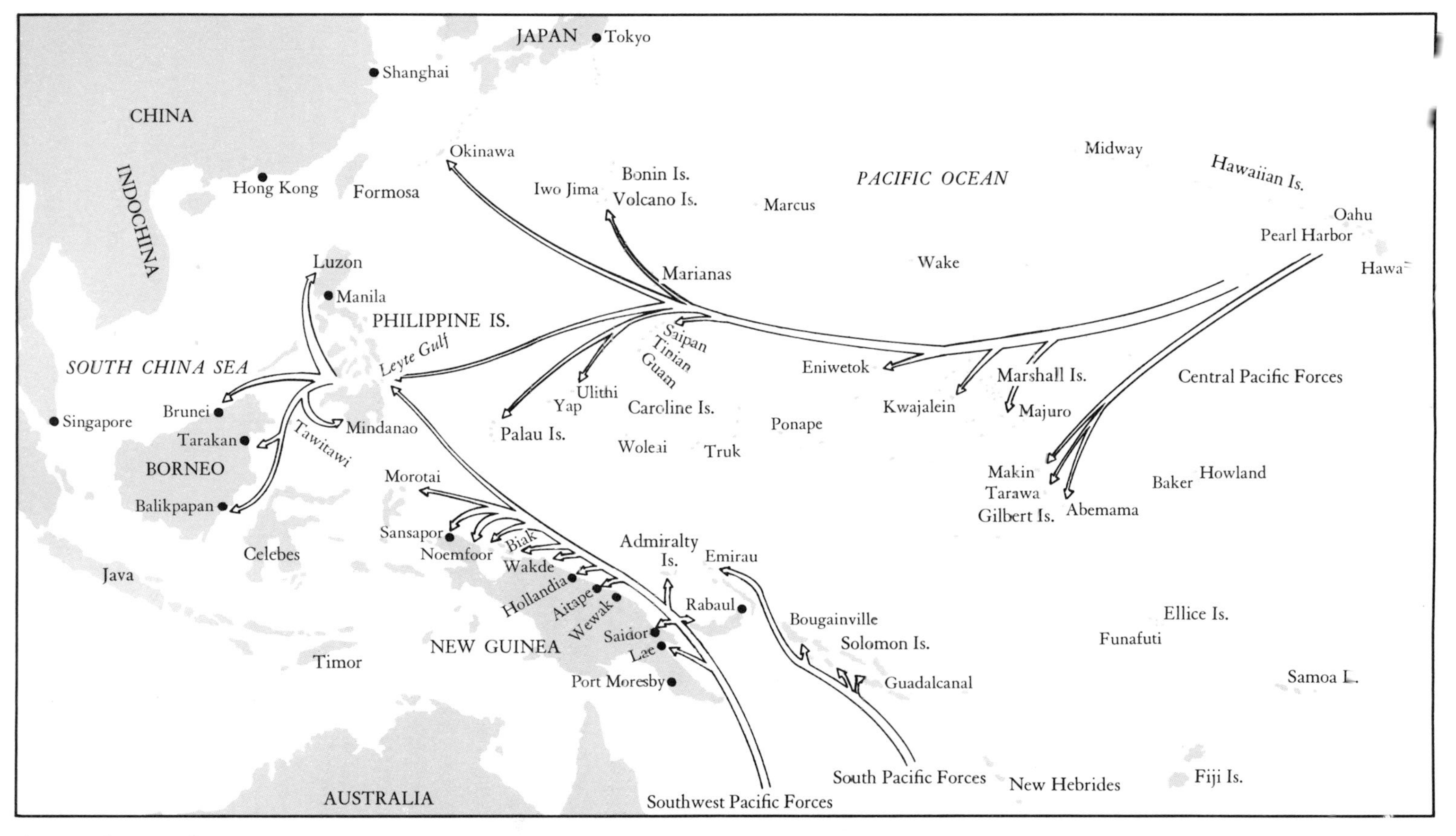

Across the Pacific

traveling general, pausing at Pearl Harbor. Could he come back to the South Pacific and resume his command of the I Corps for the assault? He could, but only for that and no more.

Halsey now faced the problem of finding a really good man to take over from Vandegrift. He discussed the possibilities with his new war plans officer, Brigadier General William R. Riley. Between them they could think of many men but none with enough experience to succeed Vandegrift in organizing and defending a perilous beachhead. After a fruitless discussion they decided to go to their rooms and think over the matter.

Alone in his room, Halsey reviewed in his mind his wartime experiences and the officers he had observed. One picture eventually obliterated the others. It was during the darkest days on Guadalcanal, when Halsey had just taken over as Commander, South Pacific. Pilots, worn out by too many missions, sleepless nights, and poor food, on returning from battles that were still raging, sometimes tumbled exhausted out of their cockpits and crawled sobbing under the wings of their planes. Brigadier General Roy Geiger, with seemingly iron nerves and tireless muscles, forced them back into their planes, slapping and kicking them if necessary. Rough measures, but necessary to save Henderson Field and the pilots themselves.

Halsey headed for Bill Riley's room. He met the general halfway.

Excitedly, Riley exclaimed, "I have the very man!"

Feigning casualness with a slight yawn, Halsey replied, "You mean Roy Geiger, of course."

"Right! How in hell did you know?" asked Riley, dumbfounded.

For his magnificent job on Guadalcanal, Geiger had been called to Washington as chief of marine aviation, but he was glad to come back to the South Pacific and combat duty. Archie Vandegrift would lead the troops ashore, and Geiger would relieve him at the end of the first week.[3]

The *Princeton,* on arriving in the South Pacific Area, was added to the *Saratoga* task group under Rear Admiral Frederick Sherman. Nimitz ordered all the carriers, including the *Saratoga,* and their escorts to be back in the central Pacific to support the Gilberts invasion on 20 November. The timing would be close indeed.

In mid-October bombers from Guadalcanal and New Georgia began working over the airfields on Bougainville. They struck at Rabaul too but left that base chiefly to General Kenney's New Guinea–based Fifth Air Force. Kenney's bombers achieved only indifferent success, however, because the intense antiaircraft fire and expert interception over Rabaul kept them too high to hit targets.

On 20 October, with the Torokina invasion imminent, Halsey and his whole operational staff headed for the Solomons. They paused at Efate and Espíritu Santo to inspect elements of the participating forces and talk with planners on subsidiary echelons. At Espiritu Halsey spent the night on board the flagship of Commodore Lawrence F. Reifsnider, commander of the transport group. The commodore was fretting over the unreliable old charts he was using to lead his heavy ships to the waters off Cape Torokina. South Pacific submarine reconnaissance had recently discovered uncharted shoals of less than four fathoms not far from his run-in point, and there were probably others still undetected.

"You won't have any trouble, Reif," said Halsey. "You're too good a sailorman." Reifsnider was not deceived and certainly not comforted by the admiral's feigned assurance.

On Guadalcanal, the officers from Noumea took temporary quarters at Koli Point, alongside "Camp Crocodile," where Admiral Wilkinson had his headquarters and trained his Third Amphibious Force. Here radio communication was adequate to keep Halsey and his South Pacific staff apprised of operations elsewhere. Here they would be able to interrogate returning flyers and sailors. And here, a thousand miles closer than Noumea to the combat area, they could perhaps with a little less sweat wait out the risky forthcoming attack.

Harold Stassen, wanting a still closer look at combat operations, requested permission to sail as an observer with Merrill's Task Force 39. Halsey granted his request. Intending to give Stassen duties more commensurate with his abilities, he concluded that sea duty under fire would season him.

By the last week in October, Aircraft, Solomons, in a series of massive raids, had pretty much bombed out the Japanese airfields on Bougainville. On the twenty-seventh, six thousand New Zealanders seized the Treasury Islands for a small-craft staging base and, more important, to prevent the enemy from using them as a base for attacking supplies en route to Torokina. That night 725 U.S. marines landed on Choiseul to draw Japanese attention away from the main Allied invasion area. A little after midnight on D-day, 1 November, Task Force 39 further diverted the enemy by bombarding the Buka and Bonis airfields northwest of Torokina. Then, while Merrill raced 200 miles to bombard the Shortlands southwest of Torokina at first light, Admiral Sherman's *Saratoga-Princeton* group sent in planes to continue the pounding of the Buka and Bonis fields.

While Japanese attention was thus drawn hither and yon, Wilkinson's amphibians made a dawn entry into Empress Augusta Bay. Despite determined resistance by about three hundred Japanese at the beachhead and an air attack from Rabaul, which fighters from Aircraft, Solomons, soon scattered, the Third Amphibious Force by nightfall had put ashore fourteen thousand troops and 6,000 tons of supplies. In early evening the transports pulled out, and four minelayers began laying a minefield off the beach.

Everybody expected the Japanese to attempt another cruiser night attack on the beachhead, as they had in the Savo Island battle. They did, but the results demonstrated how much the Americans had learned since that unhappy night in August 1942. This time U.S. army reconnaissance planes early spotted the cruiser-destroyer force coming down from Rabaul and accurately reported its composition, position, course, and speed.

The only force available to stop the oncoming enemy ships was Task Force 39. Though the crews were exhausted after having carried out two bombardments in the past sixteen hours, Admiral Halsey had no choice but to order them to Empress Augusta Bay. Merrill, mindful that his ships now constituted the principal Allied surface force in the whole South Pacific, did not plan a Nelsonian battle of annihilation. His goal was merely to repulse the attackers from the beachhead.

As Task Force 39 arrived off Torokina around 0230 on 2 November, American radar detected the enemy approaching in three columns. Merrill initiated the action known as the Battle of Empress Augusta Bay by detaching his two destroyer divisions, which raced along the enemy's flanks attacking with torpedoes. At the same time his cruisers, firing their guns, executed a series of 180° simultaneous turns, repeatedly crossing the enemy's T, each time a little closer, and thereby forcing the Japanese into confused retreat.

At dawn the Americans, somewhat scattered, broke off the chase and assembled for better defense against the inevitable air attack. They had sunk two enemy ships, a cruiser and a destroyer. None of their own ships were lost, but three were damaged. At 0800 a hundred carrier bombers and fighters from Rabaul arrived overhead. The Americans, with a combination of accurate antiaircraft fire and deft shiphandling, shot down seventeen of the planes and avoided all but two rather inconsequential bomb hits. The following afternoon Task Force 39, after a high-speed run down the Slot, entered Ironbottom Sound and received the routine signal from the base, "What do you require?" Back came a one-word reply, "Sleep."

On 4 November Solomons planes sighted a force of eight cruisers and four destroyers approaching Rabaul from Truk. Intelligence estimated that the new Japanese force would pause at Rabaul merely to refuel and then head for Torokina to redeem the failure of the first force. "This," said Halsey, "was the most desperate emergency that confronted me in my entire term as ComSoPac."

At Camp Crocodile Ray Thurber and Doug Moulton studied the operations chart. The new Japanese force was too strong for Merrill, and in any case he was too far away to reach Torokina ahead of the enemy. Sherman's *Saratoga-Princeton* group, however, by making a high-speed run northward, might be able to attack the new force while it was fueling.

It would be a perilous gamble. At that time carrier forces were definitely not supposed to attack powerful bases. The Japanese had done it on 7

December 1941, but they had achieved complete surprise against a base unready for war. Halsey's subsequent attacks among the mandates were against relatively primitive installations. But in the nearly two years the Japanese had been in possession of Rabaul, they had developed it into perhaps the most strongly fortified position in the Pacific. Moreover, it was backed by Kavieng and also by Truk, where the Combined Fleet was based.

With considerable trepidation Thurber and Moulton wrote a dispatch ordering Sherman to strike Rabaul, specifying as the priority among targets cruisers, then destroyers. They checked the order with Carney, who joined them as they took it to Halsey's Quonset hut for his approval.

"You're not going to send Merrill to Rabaul, are you?" asked the admiral as they handed him the paper.

"No, sir," replied Thurber. "This is Ted Sherman again."

Halsey had made his military reputation taking calculated risks. This time the risk he was being asked to take was almost unacceptable. The order he would be giving Sherman was comparable to the one he had given Scott and Callaghan the preceding November, directing them to take their cruisers against enemy battleships. He fully expected Sherman's carriers to be heavily damaged, possibly sunk. He tried not to remember that his son Bill was on board one of them. His duty and responsibility, however, were to protect the marines at Torokina.

Carney later recalled, "Every one of us knew what was going through the admiral's mind. It showed on his face, which suddenly looked 150 years old. He studied the dispatch for a few seconds, then handed it back. All he said was, 'Let 'er go!'" Subsequently Halsey ordered Aircraft, Solomons, to lend Sherman all the help it could.

In response to Halsey's order Sherman steamed northwest at high speed through the night. The following morning, as he maneuvered under a concealing cloud cover sixty miles southwest of Torokina, fighters from Vella Lavella arrived at his carriers and took over combat air patrol. Sherman was thus able to send all his planes, nearly a hundred, against the target. Striking from clear skies over Rabaul, his dive-bombers bored in through a steel curtain of antiaircraft fire, their objective the cruiser-destroyer force from Truk, which had anchored in Rabaul's Simpson Harbor just two hours before. At a cost of ten aircraft, the American dive-bombers and torpedo planes damaged six of the cruisers and two destroyers. There would be no surface attack on Torokina or its amphibious shipping. Halsey, receiving Sherman's report, was jubilant. "It is real music to me," he radioed back, "and opens the stops for a funeral dirge for Tojo's Rabaul."

Nimitz meanwhile had decided to lend Halsey the second carrier group, including the *Essex, Bunker Hill,* and *Independence,* under Rear Admiral Alfred E. Montgomery. On 11 November Halsey sent both Sherman and

Montgomery against Rabaul. Sherman attacked first from the waters north of Bougainville but was thwarted by foul weather. Montgomery had better luck. Striking from south of Bougainville under cover of fighters from Aircraft, Solomons, his carriers launched 185 planes, which thrust aside defending Zeros to hit shipping once more in Simpson Harbor. The cruiser-destroyer force that was the object of the 5 November attack had prudently departed, but there were other targets. The Americans sank a destroyer, torpedoed another, and played havoc among transports and cargo vessels.

This time Rabaul located the source of its attackers and struck back. In the afternoon 120 Japanese planes swooped down from the north and headed for Montgomery's carriers. Their raid cost them thirty-five aircraft and failed to damage a single ship. American losses in both attack and defense were limited to eleven planes. The opposition of carrier fighters, land-based combat patrol, and proximity-fused antiaircraft fire was too formidable for the hastily trained Japanese aviators who now replaced the veterans expended in the defense of the Solomons.

Their South Pacific assignment completed, Sherman's and Montgomery's carrier groups steamed away to participate with the Fifth Fleet in its assault on the Gilberts. They had settled the long-debated question whether carriers could be risked against powerful enemy bases. And they had already contributed more to the success of the Gilberts operation than the Americans then realized. Admiral Mineichi Koga, Yamamoto's successor in command of the Combined Fleet, had sent so many of his carrier planes to assist in the defense of Rabaul, and so many of these had been shot down, that his fleet was paralyzed for lack of air power. It was incapable of defending the Gilberts or even itself. Koga was obliged to send his carriers home to train new flyers and replace his losses.

With Sherman's and Montgomery's carriers gone, conduct of the Solomons campaign once more devolved upon local forces. Reconnaissance aircraft soon reported a worthwhile target: a Tokyo Express out of Rabaul taking soldiers to defend the Buka air base and evacuating the aviators. On the afternoon of 24 November Ray Thurber radioed Captain Arleigh Burke, then heading for Bougainville with a squadron of five destroyers: "Thirty-One-Knot Burke, get athwart the Buka-Rabaul evacuation line. . . . If enemy contacted, you know what to do."*

Burke, ardent for battle, knew very well what to do. Reaching the interception point a little before 0100, he made radar contact with the enemy. The resulting Battle of Cape St. George was in essence a duplication of

*This message, intercepted by various commands, conferred on Burke the nickname that soon became known around the world. Thurber, an old destroyer shipmate of Burke's, added the prefix as a gentle gibe at Burke's repeated reports that he was "making thirty-one knots" with a force previously reported as capable of no more than a thirty-knot sustained speed.

Moosbrugger's admirable Battle of Vella Gulf, followed by a chase. After his destroyers had sunk the two escorting destroyers with torpedoes, Burke pursued the three transport destroyers to within sixty miles of Rabaul, sinking one with gunfire.[4]

Halsey had arrived in Brisbane on 23 November for another of his periodic conferences with MacArthur. He and MacArthur discussed the ongoing Fifth Fleet invasion of the Gilberts, news of which was just coming in.* Apparently it was a success but at the price of heavy casualties. The general's reaction to the news seems to have been a mixture of distress at the losses and satisfaction that his warning about the cost of taking heavily manned enemy island bases had been vindicated.

In the midst of their discussion the general suddenly changed the subject. "I'll tell you something you may not know," he said. "They're going to give me a big piece of the fleet—put it absolutely at my disposal. And I'll tell you something else: the British are going to do the same." He paused to let the astonished admiral absorb this piece of information. Halsey knew, and he knew MacArthur knew, that Admiral King was adamantly opposed to having the general control any part of the Pacific Fleet. MacArthur continued, "I want my naval operations to be in [the]charge of an American. Whoever he is, he'll have to be senior enough to outrank the Britisher, or at least equal him." After another pause the general said, "How about *you,* Bill? If you come with me, I'll make you a greater man than Nelson ever dreamed of being."

Halsey replied that he was flattered but in no position to commit himself. He would, however, tell King and Nimitz about the general's offer.

MacArthur's statements are hard to explain. Perhaps the general believed or hoped that the heavy casualties suffered by Nimitz's forces in the Gilberts would lead to an early abandonment of the central Pacific drive, thereby freeing men, ships, and munitions for his own southwest Pacific advance, the only alternative. Perhaps if MacArthur had Halsey as his admiral, King might be less reluctant to let the Pacific Fleet operate solely in support of his New Guinea–Mindanao Axis.

During the next few days further details of the Gilberts losses became known in the south and southwest Pacific. Off lightly held Makin Atoll an enemy submarine had sunk the escort carrier *Liscome Bay,* causing the death of nearly 650 of her crew of about 900. It was at Tarawa Atoll, however, that the Americans suffered their heaviest casualties. Here they attacked the sole fortified island, two-mile-long Betio, occupied by about 3,000 Japanese combat effectives. The cornered enemy troops fought to virtually the last man. Of

*Initially the title *U.S. Fifth Fleet* was applied only to the *ships* of the Central Pacific Force. Early in 1944 the title was extended to include the amphibious troops and land-based planes, and the name *Central Pacific Force* was dropped. For simplicity, this account uses the title *Fifth Fleet* only in its extended meaning.

the 18,300 U.S. marines who stormed Betio, some 3,000 were casualties, and of these, more than 1,000 were killed or died of wounds.

The Fifth Fleet was scheduled to follow up the conquest of the Gilberts with an assault on the Marshalls at the end of January. It was hoped and expected that the new attack would result in far fewer casualties than the last one. Bombers from the Gilberts and the carriers would soften up the Marshalls, and lessons learned in assaulting the small, flat Gilbert islands should reduce casualties when the topographically similar islands of the new target were assaulted.

A far greater challenge was presented by the Marianas, next on schedule after the Marshalls. The Marianas targets—Saipan, Tinian, and Guam—were each much larger than any island in the Gilberts or Marshalls. They were beyond the reach of any Allied land-based planes but within range of Japanese land-based air support. If it had cost a thousand lives to take flat, two-mile-long Betio, what would it cost to conquer mountainous twenty-five-mile-long Guam?

General MacArthur, pointing to bloodletting at Tarawa and the probable cost of capturing the Marianas, urged the Joint Chiefs to direct Nimitz, after taking the Marshalls, to cancel further operations in the central Pacific. When they rejected this recommendation, the general, in defiance of regulations, tried to bypass the Joint Chiefs with a letter to Secretary of War Henry L. Stimson, to be shown to the president. "Give me central direction of the war in the Pacific," he urged, "and I will be in the Philippines in ten months. . . . Don't let the Navy's pride of position and ignorance continue this great tragedy to our country." The bearer of this plea, an army officer, quite properly showed the letter to General Marshall, who placed it in his files, where it remained.[5]

After Torokina the South Pacific Command had no further assault operations scheduled until mid-February 1944. The respite permitted Halsey to visit the United States and take a bit of rest and recreation to recover from the strains of the past year. His orders, probably engineered by Nimitz, sent him to Pearl Harbor, San Francisco, Los Angeles, and Washington for consultation, but Halsey understood that in the intervals he would be on leave, free to do as he pleased.

Putting South Pacific operations in Admiral Carney's hands, Halsey departed from Noumea the day after Christmas, accompanied by Bill Riley, Doug Moulton, and Bill Kitchell. The party paused four days in Pearl Harbor. Here Halsey and Nimitz, in a long conference, discussed the campaigns in the South Pacific. With Rabaul almost surrounded, Halsey had just about fought himself out of a job. He would soon have to move on to another.

Halsey mentioned MacArthur's recent offer to have him command naval forces in the southwest Pacific. Nimitz said that he and King had other plans.

They had discussed where next to employ Halsey and had tentatively decided to have him alternate command of the Big Blue Fleet with Spruance. For Bill Halsey this was an exciting prospect. Chester could not have given him a better Christmas present.

Nimitz next sought Halsey's advice. He needed a relief for the commander of his Fast Carrier Task Force, Rear Admiral Charles Pownall, who had been found lacking in aggressiveness. Admiral Towers, Commander, Air Forces, Pacific, had suggested Pete Mitscher for the command. What did Halsey think? Halsey, citing Mitscher's record as Commander, Aircraft, Solomons, heartily recommended him for the job.

With his party Halsey flew on to the States, arriving in San Francisco on the morning of New Year's Eve, 1943. They put up at the Fairmont Hotel, where the navy had taken over a large number of rooms and suites for the accommodation of naval personnel on business en route to and from the Pacific theater. Here, it will be recalled, Halsey had met with Jimmy Doolittle in the spring of 1942.

That afternoon, as Halsey and his officers were leaving the hotel, they encountered three young women in uniform—a sergeant followed by a corporal and a private. Puzzled, Halsey turned to one of his officers, who told him they were lady marines, something Bill had never seen before, mainly because Nimitz opposed admitting any servicewomen except nurses into the war zone.

"Halt!" said Halsey, and the women stopped in astonishment, the sergeant so suddenly that the revolving door barely missed clipping her nose.

"Left face!" Halsey ordered. The marines obeyed, their eyes wide with bewilderment.

As Bill explained later, "I told them that I had never seen a female marine before and I wanted a chance to look them over. They were good soldiers and appreciated my curiosity."

The next day, a rainy New Year, Admiral Halsey and General Riley went to the East-West football game. Getting to his seat, the admiral stumbled over a man who muttered something impolite. Halsey turned to apologize to the man and saw that he was a bluejacket. The sailor almost immediately recognized Halsey. "My God, Admiral," he said, "if I had known that was you I wouldn't have said anything. You can walk over me all you want."

The *Saratoga,* with Lieutenant Halsey on board, happened at that time to be at San Francisco. Young Bill, learning that his dad was in town, came ashore at the earliest opportunity and headed for the Fairmont. He had not seen his father since his adventure as a castaway in the New Hebrides. Admiral Halsey promptly gave him additional duty as his aide, and the two of them, with a navy car and driver, headed through drizzling rain for the airport. There they were to meet Mrs. Halsey, flying from the East Coast.

Fan's plane, grounded by bad weather at several points, did not get in until around 0300. On debarking, she joyfully threw herself into her husband's arms despite his wet raincoat. She turned to be introduced to Halsey's raincoated aide only to discover that it was her son. She had seen neither husband nor son in well over a year.

Admiral Halsey noticed an army officer getting off the plane and had Bill offer him a ride into San Francisco. The man was only too happy to accept. During the flight the officer had asked Mrs. Halsey if she was related to Admiral Halsey. She replied, "I believe my husband is a relation of his." On the way into town in the navy car, as they reached the first of the street lights, the officer glanced at Halsey and drew a sharp breath. His craggy features, seen in dozens of newspaper pictures, were recognizable anywhere. At this exposure of Mrs. Halsey's merry deception they all had a good laugh.

Now past middle age, Fan Halsey was still a beautiful woman. The extent of her recovery from the earlier days of alternate elation and deep depression was shown by her self-sufficiency in crossing the country alone. Her conversation was witty and informed and ever that of the cultured Virginia lady. Yet once in a while an erratic note marred her apparent composure. When Riley and Moulton dropped by the Halsey suite next morning to pay their respects, Fan suddenly interrupted her husband's discourse with a sharp "Shut up!" Her outburst was succeeded by an embarrassed silence. Then Bill Riley covered the situation handsomely by laughing and saying, "My God, I would have traveled thousands of miles to have heard somebody tell the boss that."

On 3 January Nimitz arrived from Pearl Harbor and King from Washington for another of their periodic CominCh-CinCPac conferences, and Halsey was invited to attend the meetings. A major task on the agenda was solving CinCPac's command problems, which included satisfying Undersecretary of the Navy James Forrestal's insistence that aviators be given more authority. The solution they reached was a game of musical chairs in which the dignity of all participants was enhanced. Mitscher would relieve Pownall in command of the fast carriers, Pownall would relieve Towers as Commander, Aircraft, Pacific, Towers would relieve Vice Admiral John H. Newton as deputy CinCPac, and Newton would go south as Halsey's deputy, to take over as Commander, South Pacific, on the latter's departure.

The discussion next turned to operations. Halsey proposed that he seize the Green Islands east of Rabaul and then take Emirau Island to the northwest, bypassing Kavieng, while MacArthur invaded the Admiralty Islands to the west. Thus the Allies would completely surround Rabaul and Kavieng, which could then be pounded down and neutralized by air attacks.

King, emphasizing that the key to the western Pacific was the Marianas, pointed out that capturing them would remove a barrier to Allied communications to the west, block the flow of supplies and reinforcements to Japan's southward bases, and provide airfields whence the new long-range B-29 bombers could blast Japanese cities.

From San Francisco Halsey and his party proceeded to Los Angeles, where the admiral had been ordered to attend a meeting of industrialists, evidently holders of major naval contracts. "As far as I could determine," said Halsey, "I was a monkey to be exhibited." But he was treated royally and, as always when thrown with people under circumstances of no great responsibility, he had a splendid time. The industrialists pronounced him a prince of a fellow.

Next Halsey reported to Washington for temporary duty. In conferences with King he again urged bypassing Kavieng in favor of Emirau. Secretary Knox, in recognition of Halsey's leadership and achievements in the South Pacific, awarded him a Gold Star in lieu of a second Distinguished Service Medal.

Now came the respite that Bill Halsey had been looking forward to—ten days' leave with Fan, daughter Margaret, son-in-law Lea Spruance, and his four grandchildren in Greenville, Delaware, where he had recovered from dermatitis in the summer of 1942. On 24 January he was obliged to bid his family farewell to attend a meeting called by Nimitz to discuss Pacific Ocean strategy.

Because Halsey's plane was grounded by bad weather at both Fort Worth and San Francisco, he did not arrive in Pearl Harbor until the twenty-ninth, the day after the meeting ended. Admiral Carney had represented him in his absence. MacArthur, also absent, had been represented by General Sutherland.

Sutherland, speaking for MacArthur, had accepted Halsey's plan to occupy the Green Islands and had scheduled their invasion for 15 February. MacArthur had rejected Halsey's Emirau proposal, however, and insisted on his storming of Kavieng—not on 1 May as originally scheduled but on 1 April, to coincide with the southwest Pacific's invasion of the Admiralties. Carney had already sent orders to Noumea to begin preparations for Kavieng.

More surprisingly, Sutherland, backed by General Kenney and Vice Admiral Kinkaid, newly appointed commander of MacArthur's small Seventh Fleet, had persuaded Nimitz and his staff to recommend canceling their scheduled invasion of the Marianas. Sutherland argued that taking the Marianas would be prohibitively costly, a conclusion the CinCPac staff, still in shock from the Gilberts losses, had already reached. Kenney contended that the B-29s would hamper Japan's war effort more effectively by operating from New Guinea bases against the East Indies oil wells than by raiding Japanese cities from the Marianas.

Nimitz, supported by the unanimous opinion of the assembled officers, said that he would recommend a single line of advance, along the New

Guinea–Mindanao axis. General Kenney wrote afterward, "The meeting finished with everyone feeling good and ready to work together and get the war over." Nimitz appointed his planning officer, Rear Admiral Forrest Sherman, to go to Washington and present the opinions of the conferees to the Joint Chiefs of Staff.

MacArthur was of course elated. To General Marshall he dispatched a message urging that all Pacific forces following the Marshalls operation be concentrated on his New Guinea–Mindanao axis, the shortest and most direct route to the Philippines. He wanted all the B-29s assigned to his Southwest Pacific Area and all naval forces placed under Admiral Halsey, whom he hoped to have as his naval commander. Believing that speed was essential, he sent General Sutherland to Washington to present his requests.

In Washington Admiral Sherman and General Sutherland ran into a stone wall named King. CominCh was opposed to bypassing the Marianas and assigning the B-29s, and in this opinion he was sturdily backed by General Arnold, air force commanding general.

Meanwhile, U.S. bombers from the Gilberts and Mitscher's aggressively handled fast carrier force had so softened up the Marshalls defenses that the American invasion, begun on the last day of January, was quickly concluded with relatively light losses. This conspicuous success swept away Nimitz's doubts and his dread of heavy casualties. He took another look at the map. The short, straight drive across the Pacific again began to look attractive to him, even though it would require conquest of the major Marianas.

Before Nimitz could communicate his revised opinion to Admiral King, he received from the latter a stern letter. After congratulating Nimitz for the happy outcome of the Marshalls invasion, King wrote, "I have read your conference notes with much interest, and I must add with indignant dismay. . . . I assume that even the Southwest Pacific advocates will admit that sometime or other this thorn [the Marianas] in the side of our communications to the western Pacific must be removed." In short, all recommendations were rejected. The major Marianas had to be taken.[6]

Back in the South Pacific, Halsey was keeping strictly out of the controversy and attending to his own assignments. On his orders, Wilkinson's Third Amphibious Force on 15 February 1944 put nearly six thousand New Zealand and American troops on the Green Islands. After the invaders had defeated the small Japanese garrison, Halsey's Seabees built a fighter strip on the main island, 115 miles due east of Rabaul.

The Fifth Fleet contributed to the isolation of Rabaul, first by conquering the Marshalls, a move so alarming to Admiral Koga that he hastily withdrew the bulk of his Combined Fleet from Truk to the Palau Islands. On 18 February Spruance led three of his Fifth Fleet carrier groups in a devastating attack that left Truk useless as a fleet or air base and as a backup for Rabaul.

At the same time another Fifth Fleet group invaded Eniwetok Atoll in the western Marshalls, and Spruance led his attack force a thousand miles farther west to raid the Marianas.

The speedup at the center persuaded MacArthur that he had better get moving if he hoped to win the race to the Philippines. According to his own schedule, he was to invade the Admiralty Islands on 1 April while Halsey's South Pacific forces simultaneously assaulted Kavieng. Instead, at the end of February he ordered a thousand-man American expeditionary force to invade the easternmost island, Los Negros, as a reconnaissance in force—which meant if it met heavy opposition it would pull out, and if not, it would occupy the island. Though outnumbered four-to-one by Japanese troops, the invaders were able, with the aid of ample air and naval support, to maintain their grip on the island while reinforcements were rushed in to take Los Negros and the much larger neighboring island of Manus.

The Joint Chiefs wanted the Admiralties' Seeadler Harbor developed as a major base for the use of Nimitz's Fifth Fleet as well as MacArthur's small Seventh Fleet. Since CinCPOA had the necessary Seabees and service troops for such a project, General Marshall had suggested to General MacArthur that he delegate the development of the Manus–Los Negros facilities to Admiral Halsey. Nimitz then sent a message to Admiral King, with a copy to MacArthur, in which he recommended that for this project Halsey remain under CinCPac command. That way the awkward arrangement whereby Halsey had been receiving orders from MacArthur and everything else from Nimitz would be avoided.

Nimitz should have known better. MacArthur exploded, regarding Nimitz's recommendation as a sinister attempt to encroach upon his authority. In a letter to General Marshall he declared that the proposal questioned his capacity to command and impugned his professional integrity, indeed his personal honor. He demanded an early opportunity to present his case to the secretary of the navy and the president.

At this point Captain Felix Johnson, Halsey's liaison officer on MacArthur's staff, had a brainstorm. He sent a dispatch to Halsey, urgently requesting him to come to Brisbane at once. Halsey flew over, accompanied by Mick Carney, Bill Riley, Doug Moulton, and his communication officer, Commander Leonard ("Ham") Dow. From the plane they went straight to MacArthur's office. The general was waiting for them, surrounded by his top staff officers, Captain Johnson, and his fleet commander, Admiral Kinkaid.

MacArthur was obviously fighting to control his temper. Ever the gentleman, however, he first greeted the new arrivals. Then he launched into his tirade. "Unlike myself," said Halsey later, "strong emotion did not make him profane. He did not need to be; profanity would have merely discolored his eloquence."

The general sounded off steadily for about a quarter of an hour, referring repeatedly and disparagingly to Admiral Nimitz, whose name MacArthur, when annoyed, tended to pronounce *neemitz.* He expounded two main topics: his refusal to submit to such interference with his authority, and his decision to restrict use of the Manus–Los Negros facilities to his Seventh Fleet until the question of jurisdiction was settled. Completing his diatribe, he pointed his pipestem at Halsey and demanded, "Am I not right, Bill?"

With one voice Halsey, Kinkaid, Carney, and Johnson replied, "No, sir!"

Smiling, MacArthur said, "Well, if so many fine gentlemen disagree with me, we'd better examine the proposition once more. Bill, what's your opinion?"

"General," replied Halsey, "I disagree with you entirely. Not only that, but I'm going one step further and tell you that by limiting use of the Manus naval base to the Seventh Fleet you'll be hampering the war effort." Halsey went on to say he didn't give a damn who commanded the construction at Manus. For all he cared Kenney or an Australian or an enlisted cavalryman could do the bossing, so long as the base was ready to service both fleets when the Americans and their allies moved toward the Philippines.

The argument, which began around 1700, lasted about an hour. At length MacArthur said, "Well. O.K. You can have it your way."

Halsey thought he had won the general over, but the next morning, as he and his party were preparing to head back to Noumea, Sutherland called Carney. "Sorry," he said. "The general's changed his mind." MacArthur wanted to see them again in his office at 1000.

When they arrived they found the same setup as before. Apparently MacArthur was mad all over again and once more determined to restrict work on the base. They repeated the arguments of the afternoon before, almost verbatim. At the end of an hour MacArthur again backed down. The work on full base facilities would proceed.

Halsey and his officers were about to say good-bye and fly back to Noumea when the general suddenly asked them to stick around and come back to his office at 1700. Says Halsey, "I'll be damned if we didn't run the course a third time!" On this occasion, however, MacArthur laid emphasis mainly on what he regarded as "Neemitz's" insult to his personal honor.

At last Halsey lost patience. "General," he said, "you're putting your personal honor before the welfare of the United States."

MacArthur's staff gasped. "I imagine," said Halsey, "they never expected to hear anyone address him in those terms this side of the Judgment Throne, if then."

"My God, Bull," said MacArthur, shocked. "You can't really mean that? We can't have anything like that." Turning to Sutherland, he continued, "Dick, there will be nothing like that."

It is doubtful whether anybody else could have addressed MacArthur as Halsey did without bringing down thunderbolts on his head. After this exchange the friendship between Caesar and the Bull remained as strong as ever.

Hardly had Halsey returned to Noumea and begun preparing for the coming assault on Kavieng when he received a dispatch from the Joint Chiefs canceling Kavieng and substituting Emirau, the latter to be occupied as soon as possible. Evidently he had done a better salesmanship job in San Francisco and Washington than he realized. He assigned the occupation to a regiment of the Third Marine Division on Guadalcanal. They shoved off on 18 March, made the 800-mile journey to Emirau through waters lately dominated by enemy air and sea power without encountering a ship, a plane, or even a submarine. As Halsey had suspected, there were no Japanese on Emirau. The sole casualty of the occupation was suffered by a Seabee who fell off a bulldozer and broke his leg.

Several weeks earlier the First Marine Division under MacArthur's command had landed at Cape Gloucester on New Britain, thus sealing off the only overland escape route for the hundred thousand Japanese isolated and encircled in the Rabaul area. In view of the unremitting pounding the base was now getting from bombers based at the surrounding Allied airfields, some uniformed wags recommended changing the name of the base from Rabaul to Rubble.

The only fighting still in progress in the South Pacific was at the new Allied air base that had expanded from the Torokina beachhead on Bougainville. By prodigious labor the Japanese had hauled through jungle trails the heavy equipment and ammunition needed to attack the Allied position. They struck first on 9 March and were repulsed. Thereafter they were repeatedly thrown back, their final attack fizzling out on the twenty-seventh, by which date twenty times as many Japanese as Allied troops had been killed. The enemy dead were buried with bulldozers, perhaps not deep enough. Halsey, who had arrived in time to observe the end of the fighting, was strolling behind the lines when he tripped over something and fell. He at first thought it was a root, but on closer inspection saw that it was a foot wearing a split-toed shoe. This was the only Jap, observed Halsey, who ever brought him to his knees.

Halsey supposed that the problems concerning the building of the Manus naval base had been settled during his recent visit to Brisbane, but not so. MacArthur insisted that the question of who was in command be submitted to the president. On 11 March Admirals Leahy, King, and Nimitz brought the matter up in a White House discussion on Pacific strategy. Somewhat impatiently, Mr. Roosevelt replied that he didn't know exactly where Manus was, and anyway the command problem was something the Joint Chiefs should handle. They did, leaving MacArthur in overall command. The general, as in the Solomons campaign, generally gave Halsey freedom to exercise his own judgment. Though he did not interfere, he considered his honor satisfied by the affirmation of his right to do so.

In early May Halsey was summoned to San Francisco for another conference with King and Nimitz, who told him that in June he would be relieved as Commander, South Pacific, but would retain his title of Commander, Third Fleet. In the latter capacity, they now confirmed, he would alternate command of the Big Blue Fleet with Spruance, replacing the latter for the first time after he had captured the major Marianas. Halsey's initial task on taking command of the fleet would be to seize positions in the Palau Islands.

Returning to the South Pacific, Halsey made a farewell tour of his old territory. In New Zealand the governor-general informed him that the king had appointed him an Honorary Knight Commander of the Order of the British Empire, an award that inspired his staff to address their boss as Sir Butch. After visiting various bases, where he found old battlefields replaced by baseball diamonds and enemy pillboxes supplanted by stores serving Cokes, Halsey returned to Noumea. Here General Harmon decorated him with the army's Distinguished Service Medal, and from General MacArthur he received a farewell message: "With deepest regret we see you and your splendid staff go. You leave behind you the unforgettable memory of a great sailor, a determined commander, and a loyal comrade. We look forward with eager anticipation to a renewal of our cooperative effort."

"On the morning of June 15," said Halsey, "I turned over my command to Vice Admiral John Henry Newton. . . . Next morning I took off for Pearl Harbor. Troops lined the way to the fleet landing. Their cheers and the bands and the flags stung my eyes. I never saw Noumea again."[7]

CHAPTER 17

THE BIG BLUE FLEET

GENERAL MACARTHUR, encouraged by the success of his early conquest of the Admiralties, next planned a tremendous 400-mile leap westward to Hollandia on the New Guinea north coast. Since Hollandia was almost beyond the range of his land-based planes, he requested the support of the Pacific Fleet for his landing. In a 12 March 1944 directive the Joint Chiefs of Staff approved his project and granted his request for Pacific Fleet support. The directive ordered the Southwest Pacific Force, again supported by the Pacific Fleet, to invade Mindanao on 15 November and establish air bases from which to reduce and contain Japanese forces in the Philippines "preparatory to a further advance to Formosa, either directly or via Luzon."

In late March Admiral Nimitz, complying with the Joint Chiefs' directive, set out to remove the Combined Fleet as a threat to MacArthur's forthcoming operation. He sent Task Force 58, his fast carrier force, into the western Pacific to lure the fleet out for a showdown battle. When the enemy refused to take up the gauntlet, the U.S. carriers advanced to smash the fleet at its new anchorage in the Palaus. But Japanese patrol planes spotted the approaching Americans, whereupon Admiral Koga, still unready for battle for lack of replacement aviators, promptly withdrew most of his ships. Task Force 58 planes struck the Palaus on the thirtieth and thirty-first, sinking a destroyer and sinking or heavily damaging thirty-five other vessels—mostly auxiliaries and freighters.

In mid-April Task Force 58 stood off New Guinea to provide direct support to the Hollandia assault, the southwest Pacific's largest amphibious operation up to that time, involving 113 ships and eighty-four thousand troops, but so thoroughly had Kenney's Fifth Air Force and Kinkaid's Seventh Fleet (including escort carriers lent by Nimitz) softened up the enemy defenses that support by the big carriers proved unnecessary. General MacArthur was now launched upon his westward drive to capture Japanese airstrips and convert them to his own use, advancing his fighter-escorted bomber line until at last it could cover his invasion of Mindanao.

In June, when Admiral Halsey and his staff reached Pearl Harbor, they found MacArthur's drive temporarily stalled on the Island of Biak off the New Guinea coast. His forces had to land there to secure an area of soil suitable for an airfield to be used by their heavy bombers. The general was experiencing the truth of his advice about the cost of assaulting a Japanese-held island from which there was no clear line of retreat. As usual in such an operation, the Japanese fought virtually to the last man. When Biak was secured after two months of hard fighting, American casualties amounted to 474 killed and 2,400 wounded.

Meanwhile, on 6 June, coinciding with the Anglo-American invasion of Normandy on the opposite side of the globe, the U.S. Fifth ("Big Blue") Fleet headed out of the Marshalls to assault the Marianas. Leading the way was Task Force 58 with Admiral Spruance in the *Indianapolis* and Vice Admiral Mitscher in the new carrier *Lexington*. Included were 15 fleet carriers, 7 battleships, 21 cruisers, 69 destroyers, 891 carrier aircraft, and 65 floatplanes. Following at a considerable distance was Vice Admiral Kelly Turner's Fifth Amphibious Force, comprising 535 ships carrying 127,000 troops. The simultaneous involvement of American fighting forces in Italy, China, France, and New Guinea and en route to the Marianas constituted the most titanic military effort put forth by any nation at any one time in history.

By the time Halsey arrived at Pearl Harbor on 17 June, the American landing force had secured its beachhead on Saipan and U.S. submarines had reported that the Japanese fleet had left its latest base, at Tawitawi, southwest of the Philippines, and was approaching the Marianas in two widely separated segments. Evidently a battle at sea was imminent. Admiral Halsey, due in a few weeks to take over command of Big Blue from Admiral Spruance, must have studied every piece of news from the Marianas with profound interest.

From intelligence sources, particularly submarines, the Americans knew quite a bit about the oncoming Japanese armada. It was the carrier-centered Mobile Fleet, comprising ninety percent of Japan's Combined Fleet. Its commander was Vice Admiral Jisaburo Ozawa, reputed to be one of the ablest officers in the Japanese navy. The Mobile Fleet was estimated to include nine carriers to oppose the fifteen of Task Force 58. Altogether Ozawa was believed to have between fifty and sixty ships and about four hundred planes. Mitscher had twice as many of each, and his aviators were far better trained than the Japanese. Persons aware of this disparity of force had reason to anticipate a devastating American victory.

On 19 June radio intercepts indicated to Pacific Fleet headquarters that a sea battle was in progress. At dusk Admiral Spruance reported to CinCPac, "Air attack on Task Force 58 commenced at 1045 coming in initially from westward and continuing for several hours. . . . Over 300 enemy planes are reported destroyed by our planes and AA fire. Own aircraft losses not yet reported. Only known damage to our ships: 1 bomb hit on *South Dakota*, which does not affect her fighting efficiency." The report was received at CinCPac headquarters with mingled relief and dismay—relief that Task Force

58 had suffered so little damage, dismay that the Japanese carriers had apparently received none at all.

Later that evening Spruance reported that with Task Force 58 he was heading westward to attack the Mobile Fleet itself, now apparently stripped of aircraft. A little before 1600 the following day, one of Mitscher's scout planes at last sighted the enemy ships fleeing toward Japan. Mitscher promptly launched a deckload strike. His planes found the Japanese with six carriers, six cruisers, and four battleships. The carriers did not have planes on deck and only a few aircraft were airborne. The Americans attacked at sunset and later reported sinking a *Hiyo*-class carrier, two destroyers, and two large oilers.

With Task Force 58 Spruance continued to pursue the fleeing enemy until the evening of the twenty-first, when, seeing no likelihood of overtaking it, he called off the chase. Officially the action of 19–21 June was named the Battle of the Philippine Sea, but to the American sailors who on the nineteenth had witnessed hundreds of Japanese planes falling into the sea, some like autumn leaves, others afire and streaking like comets, it would always be "the Marianas Turkey Shoot."

In the opinion of most American naval officers, the slaughter of enemy planes and aviators scarcely compensated for the fact that most of the Japanese carriers escaped destruction. They tended to blame Admiral Spruance. Mitscher, they learned, had in the early hours of 19 June strongly recommended heading westward "in order to commence treatment of the enemy at 0500," but Spruance had restrained him, wanting to remain near Saipan. The submarines had not observed the segments of the divided Mobile Fleet coming together. Spruance suspected that one of the segments might try to get between him and the island and attack the amphibious shipping at the beachhead.

Nonsense, said Spruance's critics. Scout planes would have detected and reported any such end run in time for Task Force 58 to head it off. Even if an enemy force had reached the beachhead area, it would have had to reckon with the combatant ships of the Fifth Amphibious Force, which included seven old battleships and seven escort carriers. If these could not defeat the intruder, they could at least so damage him that Task Force 58 would be able to overtake him and finish him off.

Spruance, said his detractors, should have heeded Mitscher's advice and without delay approached to within attack range of the enemy fleet. The approach would have to have been made under the cover of darkness. Otherwise the Japanese planes, greatly outranging the American aircraft because unencumbered with heavy body armor and self-sealing fuel tanks, could have found and attacked the American fleet while their own ships remained beyond the American reach.

Spruance himself expressed disappointment that he had not attacked the

Mobile Fleet on the nineteenth. "As a matter of tactics," he wrote, "I think that going after the Japanese and knocking their carriers out would have been much better and more satisfactory than waiting for them to attack us; but we were at the start of a very important and large amphibious operation and we could not afford to gamble and place it in jeopardy."

Both Nimitz and King stoutly defended Spruance's decision, and after the end of World War II, when Japanese records became available, many students of naval warfare agreed that Spruance on 19 June had placed Task Force 58 in the optimum position. But in 1944 most naval aviators, basing their opinion on the facts then available, insisted that Spruance had muffed the opportunity of the century. "This," they said, "is what comes of placing a non-aviator in command over carriers."

As for Halsey, he was too fond of Spruance, and in this instance possibly too discreet, to leave any record of what he thought of his friend's tactics. But from Halsey's subsequent actions at sea one may infer that he considered Spruance's insistence on remaining near Saipan a monumental blunder. There can be little doubt that, had he been in his friend's shoes on 19 June, Task Force 58 would have wasted no time racing after the Japanese carriers.

From the beginning of the central Pacific drive, Jack Towers, now deputy CinCPac, had been insisting that in amphibious operations carrier forces should not be tied to the beachheads. They should protect the landing forces not by close support but by striking at enemy fleets and bases that were the chief sources of counterattack. Tying the carriers to the beachheads, he said, made no use of their mobility, which was their sole advantage over airfields. Probably Halsey discussed the Battle of the Philippine Sea with Towers. Certainly he was in complete agreement with Towers's views concerning the use of carrier forces.[1]

During this period Halsey and his staff were spending most of their time preparing to assume command of the fleet and planning for their first operation, occupation of positions in the western Carolines. The targets assigned Halsey were the islands of Peleliu, Angaur, and Babelthuap in the Palau group; the island of Yap, some 280 miles northeast of the Palaus; and Ulithi Atoll, 120 miles farther in the same direction.

From the time Halsey learned he was to assault these islands, he had opposed all the operations except the occupation of Ulithi, which would provide a useful anchorage. Yap, his opponents argued, could serve as a staging point for aircraft, and capture of the Palaus would remove a possible threat to MacArthur's advance to Mindanao. Halsey believed, however, that Yap was not really needed and that U.S. carrier aircraft could readily neutralize the Palaus. These and Yap had been a long time in Japanese hands and most were reputed to be heavily manned and fortified. The advantages of capturing them, said Halsey, would not offset the cost. They should be bypassed. Nimitz consented only to bypassing Babelthuap, largest of the Palaus.

In the midst of preparations to assume the fleet command, Halsey was startled to receive an emergency telephone call from his daughter Margaret. Her mother had been plunged into a depression of such depth that Margaret believed only the presence of her husband could brighten her spirits. After checking with Nimitz, Halsey issued himself emergency leave orders, appointed Carney deputy in his absence, and flew to Delaware to do what he could to help Fanny weather the crisis.

Admiral Halsey's departure from Pearl Harbor very nearly coincided with Admiral King's arrival. With Admiral Nimitz King flew out to inspect the U.S.-occupied Marshalls and newly captured Saipan, where he conferred with Admiral Spruance and Spruance's senior commanders. On 20 July the travelers were back at Pearl, participating in a series of strategy conferences. Carney substituted for Halsey.

With respect to the western Carolines, King approved Nimitz's modifications, canceling Babelthuap and adding Yap and Ulithi. The conferees discussed tentative plans then under consideration for forthcoming operations:

September 15: Southwest Pacific forces occupy the island of Morotai, halfway between New Guinea and southern Mindanao; central Pacific forces occupy Peleliu and Angaur in the Palaus.
October 5: Central Pacific forces occupy Yap and Ulithi.
October 15: Southwest Pacific forces occupy the Talaud Islands, halfway between Morotai and southern Mindanao.
November 15: Southwest Pacific forces land in southern Mindanao.
December 20: Southwest Pacific forces land at Leyte, in the central Philippines.

On Mindanao and Leyte the invading Americans were to establish airfields to neutralize and contain Japanese forces in the rest of the Philippines. For the next move, King and Nimitz had espoused a plan to have southwest Pacific and central Pacific forces combine and land on Formosa on 1 March 1945. This would mean bypassing Luzon, the northernmost and principal Philippine island, but Formosa was closer to both China and Japan. The Americans had never given up hope of eventually breaking through Japanese defenses on the Asian coast and arming China's vast manpower, thus enabling it to oust the Japanese from the continent and spearhead an invasion of Japan from Chinese ports.

Earlier, when the King-Nimitz proposal had first come to MacArthur's attention, he was appalled. Any plan to bypass the many Filipinos of Luzon he considered morally wrong as well as strategically unsound. He sent a message to the Joint Chiefs: "I request that I be accorded the opportunity of personally proceeding to Washington to present fully my views."

President Roosevelt thought he had a better idea. Since he was planning to make an inspection tour of bases on the Pacific coast and in Hawaii after the forthcoming Democratic National Convention, he would meet General MacArthur and Admiral Nimitz at Pearl Harbor and arbitrate their differences. Contrary to his past practice when traveling overseas, this time he would be accompanied not by all the Joint Chiefs but only by Admiral William Leahy, who would be acting solely in his capacity as chief of staff to the president.

Both Admiral King and General MacArthur regarded the president's tour of inspection without the Joint Chiefs as a politically inspired grandstand play. Roosevelt had notified the chairman of the national Democratic party that he would accept the party's nomination for a fourth term. Following the nomination, a sure thing, the nominee would appear before the electorate in his capacity as commander in chief of the armed forces, an effect heightened by his meeting with MacArthur and Nimitz. So reluctant was MacArthur to participate in this political playacting that it took a direct order from General Marshall to force him to leave Brisbane for Pearl. At the same time King received a strong hint that he had better get out of the Pacific area before the president arrived.

Disgusted that politics should thus interfere with the conduct of war, King arrived at his final Pearl Harbor conference on 21 July in an ill humor. When Admiral Carney ventured to argue against King's preference for bypassing Luzon, King snapped, "Do you want to make a London out of Manila?"

"No, sir," replied Carney. "I want to make an England out of Luzon."

In fact, King was not entirely convinced that bypassing Luzon was good strategy. In his final instructions to Nimitz concerning the forthcoming presidential conference, he did not dictate which of the alternative strategies the latter was to espouse. He merely asked him to think over very carefully what he ought to recommend.

En route to the United States King's plane passed over the heavy cruiser *Baltimore* bearing President Roosevelt toward Pearl Harbor, where he arrived on 26 July. MacArthur's plane arrived from Brisbane the same day. Halsey, having done what he could to pull his wife out of the doldrums, returned to Pearl on the twenty-seventh.

That evening, in a conference with only the president, MacArthur, Nimitz, and Leahy present, the general pointed out that thousands of Filipino guerrillas were already harassing the Japanese occupation forces, that nearly the entire Filipino population could be counted on to join an American campaign of liberation, that to bypass and seal off these friendly people and the many American prisoners in the islands would expose them to frightful privations and to mistreatment at the hands of their Japanese captors, and that for the United States to renege on its promise to liberate the Filipinos at the earliest possible moment would be construed in the Orient as a second American abandonment of the Philippines. The president found these arguments convincing but did not impose his opinion on the Joint Chiefs. The final decision was to be made when the Combined Chiefs of Staff met with Roosevelt and Churchill at Quebec on 11 September.

Nevertheless, those in the know regarded the luncheon hosted by Nimitz the following day as a kind of victory celebration for MacArthur. All the flag officers on Oahu and in ships at Pearl Harbor were invited. Nimitz's flag lieutenant counted 146 stars on their collars. Admiral Halsey, among those present, was surprised by the alterations in Nimitz's quarters. Under the direction of Secret Service men, Seabees had temporarily removed palm trees and run a road around to the back, where the crippled president, sensitive about such matters, could be helped from his car to his wheelchair without being seen. The Seabees had also built a ramp to the back door, which they had widened to permit the wheelchair to pass through.[2]

Without delay Halsey again immersed himself in preparations for action. Like Spruance he elected to sail with the carrier force, spearhead of the fleet, rather than with the much larger amphibious force. For a flagship he requested one of the swift, new 45,000-ton *Iowa*-class battleships and was issued the *New Jersey*. He would have been more at home on a carrier, but carriers were vulnerable, and he could not risk having his flag functions disrupted by battle damage.

The *New Jersey,* with Halsey on board, sortied from Pearl Harbor on 24 August, escorted by three destroyers. Behind him, Halsey left a good many surprised and gratified officers and men. To each department that had helped his command prepare for action he had sent a letter of appreciation and thanks, and most department heads had ordered the letters posted for all to see.

The Marianas campaign had recently ended with Saipan, Tinian, and Guam in American hands, at a cost of more than five thousand American and nearly sixteen thousand Japanese lives. That exhausting and far-reaching operation completed, the time had come for a change of command. Until 26 August the U.S. Third Fleet consisted only of the *New Jersey* and her three destroyers. On that date Admiral Halsey relieved Admiral Spruance in command of the Big Blue Fleet, which thereupon changed its name from Fifth Fleet to Third Fleet; Vice Admiral Wilkinson relieved Vice Admiral Turner in command of the Fifth Amphibious Force, which became the Third Amphibious Force; and the carrier force, Task Force 58, became Task Force 38. Admiral Mitscher insisted on remaining on duty through the initial Philippines invasion, because there was nobody else he was yet ready to trust with the carriers in so crucial a mission, particularly one that might result in another battle at sea. Vice Admiral Slew McCain, who had been appointed Mitscher's relief, would temporarily command one of the carrier groups in a makee-learn capacity.

There were no change-of-command ceremonies, since neither Halsey nor Wilkinson was yet with their forces. On the twenty-sixth, in fact, the *New Jersey,* forging steadily westward, was 3,000 miles from Task Force 38, which was to the north bombing Iwo Jima, just 500 miles south of Tokyo. For the time being, the change of command was merely on paper.

Spruance and Turner and their staffs, and later Mitscher and his staff, were to take stateside leave, then return to Pearl Harbor to plan for operations to be conducted when they resumed their former commands under the old number designations. This double-echelon system, unique in the history of warfare, was counted on to speed up the war. It was feasible only because the Pacific theater enjoyed a surplus of skillful commanders. Use of the alternate titles of Fifth and Third Fleet confused the Japanese (and a good many Americans), who supposed that two Big Blue fleets were ranging the broad Pacific chewing up the remains of the expanded Japanese empire.

After pounding Iwo Jima, Mitscher brought Task Force 38 south to bomb Yap and the Palaus. He then shaped course westward for Mindanao, against which on 9 and 10 September he launched two heavy air strikes. On the eleventh the *New Jersey* at last joined up. Halsey, standing on board the battleship, must have been awed at the size of the carrier force. Stretching to the horizon, it comprised four circular groups, each considerably larger than his old Task Force 16.

Halsey told Mitscher to skip the usual courtesy call to the fleet flagship. He himself would do the visiting. He wanted to have a look at one of the new carriers and its planes. From the *New Jersey* he went by destroyer to Mitscher's flagship *Lexington,* a trip that required two ship-to-ship transfers. In the past he would have made the transfers in an undignified manner on a breeches buoy slung under a line. This time, however, he went over in style, riding in a fancy chair equipped with an ash tray and surry top.

Mitscher told Halsey that his attack on Mindanao had been a waste of time. Kenney's Fifth Air Force, striking out of western New Guinea bases, had already blasted the Mindanao installations. Only a few Japanese planes rose to meet the carrier aircraft.

Had Halsey intended to conform to the example of previous amphibious operations in the central Pacific, he would now have taken Task Force 38 to stand off the Palaus, which were scheduled to be assaulted in three days. But he was confident that Wilkinson's Third Amphibious Force, with old battleships, escort carriers, and many cruisers and destroyers, could give the landing forces all the close support they needed. With Task Force 38 he moved up the Philippine coast to lend distant support to the Palau operation by raiding enemy airfields and fending off any enemy fleet that approached to interfere.

As the Combined Chiefs, together with Roosevelt and Churchill, were convening in faraway Quebec, Halsey arrived off the central Philippines, where the mountains of Samar were visible from his flag bridge. On 12 and 13 September Task Force 38 flew twenty-four hundred sorties. About two hundred Japanese planes were shot down or destroyed on the ground, installations were flattened, a dozen freighters and a tanker were sunk—all at a cost of eight U.S. planes. Apparently the central Philippines were, in Halsey's words, "a hollow shell with weak defenses and skimpy facilities." Moreover, one of Halsey's downed aviators reported that the Filipinos who rescued him insisted there were no Japanese on Leyte. In this situation the old master of the calculated risk saw opportunity. Why not recommend scrapping the preliminaries and going right into Leyte, months ahead of schedule?

Halsey consulted with his staff. They restudied their combat reports and intelligence data and checked on the strength of forces available to Nimitz and MacArthur. Their conclusion: the proposed speedup could be carried out with a reasonable expectation of success.

Halsey sat alone in a corner of the bridge trying to make up his mind. "Such a recommendation," he said afterward, "in addition to being none of my business, would upset a great many applecarts, possibly all the way up to Mr. Roosevelt and Mr. Churchill." At last he sent for Mick Carney and Harold Stassen, the latter recently promoted from flag secretary to assistant chief of staff. "I'm going to stick my neck out," Halsey said. "Send an urgent dispatch to CinCPac."

Together they worded the message. As a result of Task Force 38's attacks in the central Philippines, it said, the Japanese had few serviceable planes remaining in the area, most of their oil storage had been destroyed, and there was "no shipping left to sink." The "enemy's non-aggressive attitude was unbelievable and fantastic," the message continued. On Leyte itself, it added, there were no Japanese; hence "the area is wide open." Halsey strongly recommended that the intermediary operations—against the Talauds, Mindanao, the Palaus, and Yap—be canceled and all the shipping and ground forces thus released be used to invade Leyte as soon as possible. Task Force 38 would be available to cover the landings until airfields could be established ashore.

Nimitz was not willing to cancel the Palau operation, but he did forward Halsey's recommendation by radio to the Joint Chiefs of Staff at Quebec, together with an offer to place at MacArthur's disposal the Third Amphibious Force and also the Twenty-fourth Army Corps, then loading at Pearl Harbor for Yap.

General Marshall referred Halsey's recommendation and Nimitz's offer by radio to General MacArthur, asking his opinion regarding the proposed changes. MacArthur was at sea, en route to Morotai and observing radio silence, so General Sutherland, at Hollandia, replied in his name. Sutherland, deciding that he too would stick his neck out, radioed back that the information about there being no Japanese on Leyte was false. But with the additional forces offered by Nimitz, he stated, the intermediate operations could be eliminated and an early attack made on Leyte.

When Sutherland's answer reached Quebec, the Joint Chiefs were being entertained at a formal dinner by Canadian officers. Staff members read the message, decided it was urgent, and rushed it to the banquet hall. Admirals Leahy and King and Generals Marshall and Arnold excused themselves, stepped outside, and conferred.

"Having the utmost confidence in General MacArthur, Admiral Nimitz, and Admiral Halsey," Marshall wrote afterward, "it was not a difficult decision to make. Within ninety minutes after the signal had been received in Quebec, General MacArthur and Admiral Nimitz had received their instructions to execute the Leyte operation on the target date 20 October, abandoning the three previously approved intermediary landings."

Morotai and Angaur proved to be lightly held and were occupied with few losses. Peleliu, on the contrary, was one of the most hotly contested islands of the Pacific war. It was defended by seven thousand elite troops, mostly holed up in natural and man-made caves. The veteran First Marine Division was busy until February of the next year digging them out, a slow and painful process that cost the Americans ten thousand casualties, including nearly two thousand deaths—a high price indeed for an island that proved of little value.

On the other hand, Ulithi Atoll, which the Americans occupied on 23 September without opposition, provided an invaluable anchorage and logistic base for the Third/Fifth Fleet. With an immense, deep lagoon, capable of accommodating seven hundred naval vessels, this atoll, "discovered" by Nimitz while pursuing his map-reading hobby, proved the hub of most naval operations in the final phase of the Pacific war.

Following his successful attack on the central Philippines, Halsey had signaled his carriers, "Because of the brilliant performance my group of stars has just given, I am booking you to appear before the best audience in the Asiatic theater."

The "audience" was Manila, Manila Bay, and the nearby cluster of airfields. While Mitscher was moving in on the new target area with Task Force 38, Halsey sped in the *New Jersey* to the vicinity of Peleliu to check on progress there and confer with Wilkinson and other senior officers. He was back with the carriers when they staged six raids on the Manila area on 21 and 22 September. The Task Force 38 aviators believed that they had destroyed or damaged 405 planes and sunk or damaged 103 ships. American losses were fifteen planes and twelve men. No American ship was touched.

After fueling, Task Force 38 moved in close to the Philippine coast. At dawn on the twenty-fourth it stood off San Bernardino Strait and launched a first strike against Coron Bay in the Calamian Islands, 350 miles away, on the far side of the Philippines. Here was a cluster of ships, including refugees from the strike on Manila Bay. In the course of the day, American planes sank or damaged several destroyer types and numerous tankers, cargo ships, and transports. At the conclusion of the attack, Carney prepared and sent to the task force in Halsey's name a lighthearted message of congratulation: "The recent exceptional performance yielded gratifying gate receipts, and although the capacity audience hissed very loudly, little was thrown at the players. As long as the audience has a spot to hiss in, we will stay on the road."[3]

The raid on Coron Bay practically ended the Third Fleet's support of the Palau operation. While one group of Task Force 38 remained off Peleliu and Angaur to cover, the other three withdrew to rearm and rest the crews, and the Third Amphibious Force, on loan to MacArthur, began moving piecemeal to Manus. The carrier group that included Halsey's flagship *New Jersey* headed for Saipan.

It was evidently en route that Halsey received Nimitz's operation plan for supporting the assault on Leyte. The plan directed all forces of the Pacific Ocean areas to "cover and support forces of the Southwest Pacific in order to assist in the seizure and occupation of objectives in the central Philippines." The Third Fleet (i.e., Task Force 38) was to "destroy enemy naval and air forces in or threatening the Philippines area."

The plan was in sentence outline form, each sentence preceded by a letter or a number—with a single exception. One unnumbered, unlettered sentence standing alone was apparently a late insertion. It read, "IN CASE OPPORTUNITY FOR DESTRUCTION OF MAJOR PORTION OF THE ENEMY FLEET OFFER OR CAN BE CREATED, SUCH DESTRUCTION BECOMES THE PRIMARY TASK." This was clearly an order for Halsey to advance and attack any major enemy fleet that presented itself rather than remain tethered to the beachhead as Spruance had been the preceding June by an operation plan that ordered him only to "capture, occupy, and defend Saipan, Tinian, and Guam."

After reading the op plan, Halsey wrote Nimitz a letter describing how he intended to deal with the enemy fleet if the opportunity offered:

> . . . I intend, if possible, to deny the enemy a chance to outrange me in an air duel and also to deny him an opportunity to employ an air shuttle (carrier-to-target-to-land) against me. If I am to prevent his gaining that advantage, I must have early information and I must move smartly.
>
> Inasmuch as the destruction of the enemy fleet is the principal task, every weapon must be brought into play and the general coordination of these weapons should be in the hands of the tactical commander responsible for the outcome of the battle. . . . My goal is the same as yours—to completely annihilate the Jap fleet if the opportunity offers. . . .[4]

From Saipan Halsey flew with members of his staff to Hollandia, where they spent Friday 29 September with MacArthur's staff working out a plan for cooperation between Task Force 38 and the southwest Pacific's Seventh Fleet in supporting the coming invasion. No overall commander had been assigned to be at the scene of action, a defect that this conference was intended to remedy. Halsey was responsible to Admiral Nimitz at Pearl Harbor, and Nimitz was responsible to the Joint Chiefs of Staff in Washington. Admiral Kinkaid, Commander, Seventh Fleet, was responsible to General MacArthur, who was responsible to the Joint Chiefs.

From Hollandia Halsey and his party flew to the Palaus and there witnessed the American flag being raised over conquered Angaur. In a jeep exploring Peleliu, where fighting was still going on, Halsey narrowly escaped being hit by mortar fire. However, this did not leave as lasting an impression on him as the newly available DDT, which had ridded the island of the flies, mosquitoes, and other insects that had made life miserable on Guadalcanal.

On Sunday, 1 October, Halsey and his party flew to newly occupied Ulithi Atoll. Riding at anchor in its immense lagoon was half of Task Force 38: Rear Admiral Gerald F. Bogan's Task Group 38.2, which included the *New Jersey*, and Rear Admiral Frederick Sherman's Task Group 38.3, with Admiral Mitscher's flagship *Lexington*. On 3 October a typhoon forced them to put to sea, but they returned the next day and finally departed on the sixth.

In the late afternoon of 7 October, some 375 miles west of Saipan, the two task groups rendezvoused with the rest of the task force: Vice Admiral McCain's Task Group 38.1 and Rear Admiral Ralph Davison's Task Group 38.4. Now that Nimitz had lent the Third Amphibious Force to MacArthur, the Third Fleet and Task Force 38 were identical. Halsey solved the obvious command problem by turning over to Mitscher, as Commander, Task Force 38, all air operations when the force worked as a unit, while he, as Commander, Third Fleet, assigned targets and controlled ship movements.

In preparation for the forthcoming invasion, all available U.S. air power was now committed to weakening the Japanese, particularly their air power, in and adjacent to the Philippines. From U.S. bases in western China, B-29s of the Twentieth Bomber Command and medium bombers of the Fourteenth Air Force operated against Formosa and the coast of China. General Kenney's Far Eastern Air Forces, based on New Guinea, Biak, and Morotai, hit the southern flank, striking repeatedly at Japanese airfields in Mindanao and the East Indies. The Third Fleet was assigned the northern flank, a great arc extending from the central Philippines through Formosa and the Ryukyu Islands to southern Japan.

To deceive the Japanese about Third Fleet objectives, on 9 October a U.S. cruiser-destroyer group attacked Marcus Island "with great fanfare," laying smoke screens, firing off pyrotechnics, and floating dummy radar targets. On

Admiral Halsey welcomes Vice Admiral Mitscher on board his flagship *New Jersey* for a conference just before the autumn 1944 strikes by the Pacific Fleet against Japanese defenses in the Philippines, Formosa, and the Ryukyus.

the tenth Task Force 38, having approached behind a weather front, struck the Ryukyus, concentrating on Okinawa, the largest of the islands. Not since the spring of 1942, when escorting Jimmy Doolittle's bombers, had Halsey been so close to Japan. This time, instead of skipping out fast, he spent the day, in the course of which his carrier planes flew 1,396 sorties, sinking a submarine tender, a dozen torpedo boats, two midget submarines, and four freighters and destroying about a hundred planes at the cost of twenty-one of their own. No American ships were damaged, either at Marcus or at the Ryukyus.

Before hitting Formosa, his main target, Halsey further isolated it by ordering two of his task groups to raid Aparri airfield in northern Luzon. This attack achieved little. Halsey had made a mistake, as he later confessed. He should have struck Formosa, his strongest target, first. The Ryukyu raid alerted the Japanese forces on the island, and the Aparri attack gave them a day of grace to bring in additional aircraft from Japan.

Early on 12 October Task Force 38 reached its dawn launching position fifty to ninety miles east of Formosa, with each of its four carrier groups assigned a sector of the island. They flew 1,378 sorties that day, the aircraft concentrating their efforts against enemy planes. The first wave met and shot down a third of the Japanese fighters. Only about sixty fighters contested the arrival of the second wave. None rose to intercept the third. The Americans must have destroyed about two hundred enemy aircraft that day, but at the heavy cost of forty-eight of their own planes.

On the second day, 13 October, the task force flew 974 sorties, which concentrated on airfields and hangars and other installations. At dusk came bad news. Halsey was informed that the heavy cruiser *Canberra* in McCain's task group had been hit by an aerial torpedo and was dead in the water. He glanced at the chart. The crippled cruiser was within range of several major enemy airfields and 1,300 miles from Ulithi, the nearest U.S. base. "We were squarely in the Jap dragon's jaws," said Halsey, "and the dragon knew it."

Under the circumstances, the prudent action would have been to abandon the damaged ship and sink her. Halsey decided on a bolder course—fighting his way out and towing her to Ulithi. He had a heavy cruiser take the *Canberra* in tow and scheduled an additional day of attacks on the enemy airfields. That day, 14 October, the Twentieth Bomber Command lent a hand by sending 109 B-29s from China to bomb the airfields around Takao. By the end of the three-day Formosa air battle, U.S. aircraft had destroyed nearly six hundred enemy planes, sunk some three dozen freighters and small craft, and inflicted fearful destruction on hangars, shops, barracks, ammunition dumps, and industrial plants.

In late afternoon of the fourteenth Bogan's task group came under attack by numerous Japanese torpedo planes. Most were shot down, but one slammed a torpedo into the light cruiser *Houston,* completely flooding her engineering spaces. Because she appeared to be breaking up, her captain ordered abandon ship, then changed his mind and called for a tow. McCain sent another heavy cruiser to take on that job. To assist with the towing of the two cripples, Halsey sent in three additional cruisers and eight destroyers, which promptly acquired the name CripDiv 1. For a cover unit, he detached three light carriers and four destroyers.

Both crippled ships were namesakes of former cruisers lost in the Pacific war. The original *Houston* had been sunk off Java. The earlier *Canberra,* an

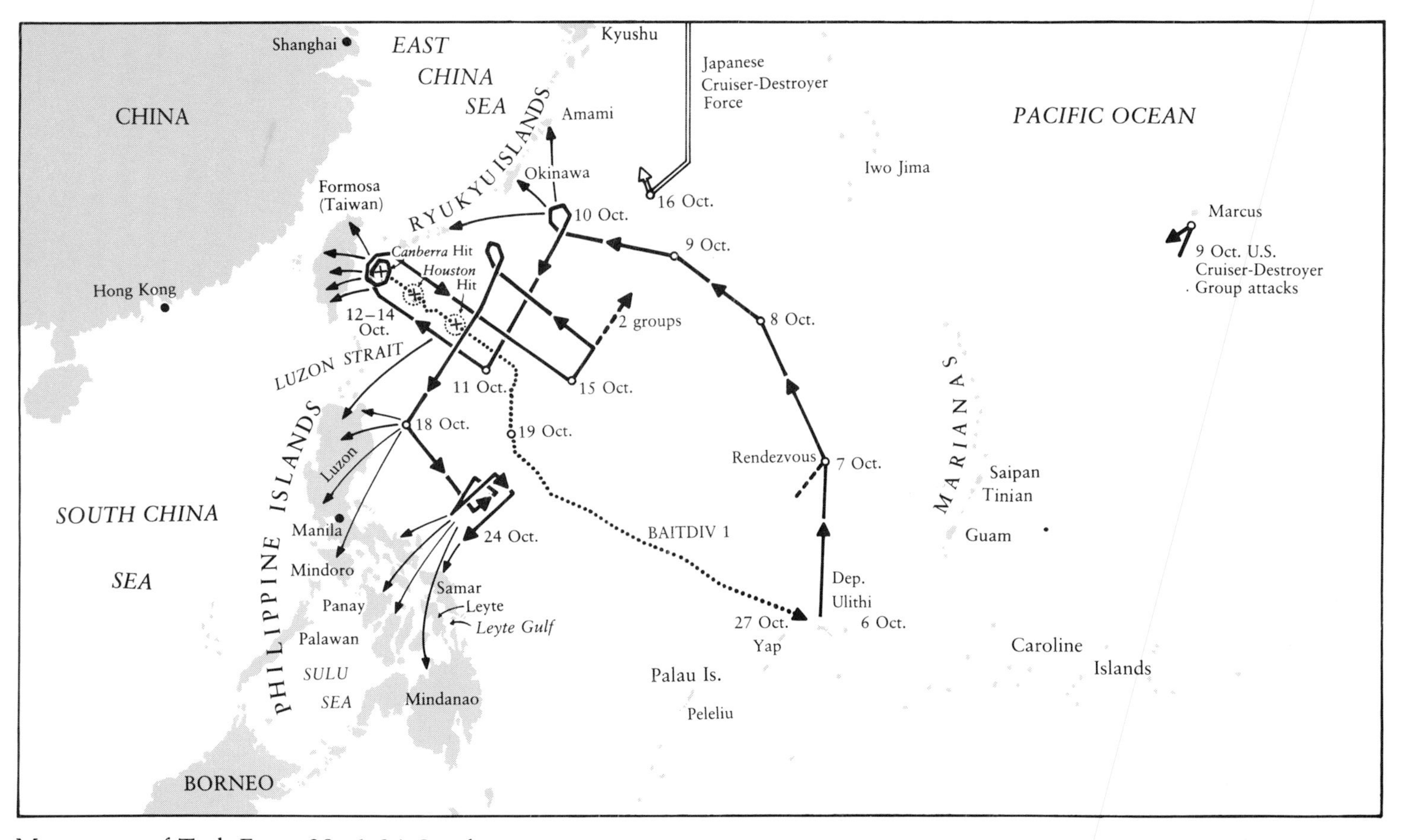

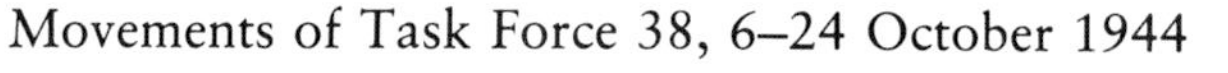
Movements of Task Force 38, 6–24 October 1944

Australian cruiser, had been lost in the Battle of Savo Island. The *Canberra* now under tow was the first American cruiser named after a foreign city.

With great fanfare Radio Tokyo began announcing that the intrepid Japanese aviators in a series of successful attacks had virtually annihilated the U.S. fleet. Most of the American ships that were not reported sunk were said to be on fire. A Japanese fleet, so the broadcast stated, was en route from the empire to destroy the American remnant. Subsequent broadcasts quoted an imperial proclamation and congratulatory messages from Hitler and Mussolini and announced that mass celebrations of the "glorious victory of Taiwan" were being held throughout Japan and at all armed forces headquarters in the Philippines.

Halsey had heard Radio Tokyo make false claims before, but nothing like this. Such hysterical jubilation persuaded him that this time even the Japanese high command believed the U.S. fleet had been crushed. After thinking the matter over, he arrived at a possible explanation for the extraordinary self-deception. He had noticed in preceding nights that some of his ships, when silhouetted against downed Japanese planes burning on the water, appeared themselves to be on fire. Probably the enemy pilots who escaped being shot down had observed the same phenomenon and reported the annihilation of the U.S. fleet in all honesty.

Meanwhile, Halsey kept glancing at the pin on his chart that represented the two damaged cruisers under tow. They could make less than four knots, and there were 1,300 miles to go. In an air attack neither they nor the ships towing them could maneuver out of danger.Trying to protect them endangered not only the additional ships Halsey had sent to join them but in fact jeopardized his whole fleet. After all, his overriding duty was covering MacArthur's landing, now only six days away. He was tempted to order the two cripples abandoned and sunk while the rest of his fleet sped out of reach of Japanese land-based planes.

Mick Carney and Captain Ralph Wilson, Ray Thurber's successor as operations officer, had a better idea. They pointed to the special order inserted in the operation plan: "In case opportunity for destruction of major portion of the enemy fleet offer or can be created, such destruction becomes the primary task." Here was the opportunity, handed to them by the enemy. The Japanese had announced that they were sending a force to destroy the remnant of the American fleet. Let CripDiv 1 represent that remnant to draw the Japanese on, while the rest of the fleet concealed itself, prepared to spring the trap.

Halsey, enthusiastically falling in with the plan, sent ships to reinforce CripDiv 1, which he renamed BaitDiv 1, and told its commander to keep the air busy with a series of mock distress messages. Said one of the captains in BaitDiv 1: "Now I know how a worm on a fishhook must feel."

On Halsey's orders two of his groups pulled off eastward, supposedly beyond observation by Japanese patrol planes, ready to pounce on any enemy naval force that advanced to take the bait. The other two groups moved south to carry out a scheduled strike on Luzon and the central Philippines. To Nimitz Halsey now sent a report: "The Third Fleet's sunken and damaged ships have been salvaged and are retiring at high speed toward the enemy."

On 15 October Halsey's ambush seemed on the verge of success. A submarine reported three heavy cruisers and a light cruiser heading south from Japanese home waters. Enemy aircraft attacked BaitDiv 1 several times during the day, suffering severe losses but achieving no damage. On the sixteenth sixty Japanese planes attacked the unhappy division, which shot down most of them. One of the enemy aircraft, however, succeeded in firing another torpedo into the *Houston*.

Air patrols from the two ambush groups to the east shot down every enemy plane that approached, but one that appeared suddenly out of a low cloud cover must have had time to broadcast a warning before it too was shot down. At any rate, the ships from Japan never found BaitDiv 1. Halsey assumed that they heard the warning and prudently retired.

The admiral said that watching the cripples limp across the ocean took years off his life, but he realized that the strain was far worse for the men on board. On the twenty-seventh the ships reached the safety of Ulithi, whence in due course they were dispatched via Manus and Pearl Harbor to East Coast yards for complete restoration. Meanwhile, after further strikes on Luzon's airfields, Task Force 38 took station east of Leyte to cover MacArthur's landing.

When Halsey's ambush failed, President Roosevelt, to the amusement and delight of the American public, released the admiral's dispatch about salvaging the Third Fleet's sunken vessels and retiring at high speed toward the enemy. To Halsey he sent a personal message which the admiral broadcast to all hands: "It is with pride that the country has followed your fleet's magnificent sweep into enemy waters. In addition to the gallant fighting of your flyers, we appreciate the endurance and superseamanship of your forces."[5]

CHAPTER 18

LEYTE GULF

On 17 October 1944, as the U.S. Third Fleet was approaching its covering position east of the Philippines, Admiral Halsey received news about the progress of the Leyte invasion. Rear Admiral Jesse Oldendorf, commander of the Seventh Fleet Bombardment and Fire Support Group, reported by radio that advance units of the fleet had put troops ashore on islands guarding the entrance to Leyte Gulf. The following day Oldendorf reported that his fire-support ships had entered the gulf and begun the bombardment of the Leyte beaches. On the twentieth General MacArthur announced that landings on Leyte, involving sixty thousand assault troops and 100,000 tons of supplies and equipment, had been made on schedule with extremely light losses.

Halsey had just about concluded that the Japanese fleet was not going to come out and fight. For days his own Third Fleet had been running wild in the western Pacific, destroying aircraft, sinking ships, and smashing installations almost on Japan's doorstep. The only visible reaction of the Japanese navy was to send out after BaitDiv 1 a cruiser-destroyer force that retreated at the first threat. A reasonable conclusion was that the Combined Fleet had again been paralyzed by loss of planes and aviators.

For Admiral Mitscher, normally ardent for battle, the Japanese navy's apparent unwillingness to fight was cause for relief. His men were tired, and he himself, always frail, was on the verge of exhaustion. He and his sailors and aviators had scarcely set foot on shore since the Fast Carrier Task Force departed Pearl Harbor in mid-January. Since then the force had supported the invasion of the Marshalls, the Marianas, and the Palaus; raided Truk, the Palaus, Iwo Jima, the Philippines, the Ryukyus, and Formosa; and fought the Battle of the Philippine Sea. "No other force in the world has been subjected to such a period of constant operation without rest or rehabilitation," said Mitscher. "The spirit of these ships is commendable," he added. "However, the reactions of their crews are slowed down. The result is that they are not completely effective against attack."

Halsey too was tired but, bellicose as ever, he was spoiling for a sea battle. His orders said that destruction of the enemy fleet was the primary task if the opportunity offered or could be created. He didn't know where the enemy carriers were, but he had reports from submarines and from search planes based on China and New Guinea that heavy surface units of the Combined Fleet had recently been observed in the Brunei-Singapore area. Halsey estimated that these would move into the South China Sea west of the Philippines, possibly basing themselves at Coron Bay to reinforce and supply their forces on Leyte. If the Japanese ships would not offer him an opportunity to destroy them by coming to him, he would create his opportunity by going to them. He broke radio silence to ask the Seventh Fleet commander, Admiral Kinkaid, whether the two openings in the Philippines, Surigao Strait, south of Leyte Gulf, and San Bernardino Strait, north of the gulf, were being swept of mines. He needed to know because, if and when the enemy ships arrived west of the Philippines, he intended to transit the straits and attack.

A copy of Halsey's message to Kinkaid was sent to CinCPac. Nimitz, startled, quickly reminded Halsey that he was still governed by that section of the op plan that required him to "cover and support forces of the Southwest Pacific." Moreover, said Nimitz, "movement of major units of the Third Fleet through Surigao and San Bernardino straits will not be initiated without orders from CinCPac."[1]

Forbidden to go looking for the Japanese fleet, which apparently was unwilling to come to him, Halsey planned to send his task groups in relays to Ulithi to reprovision, rearm, and rest their men. At the time the Third Fleet was organized as shown on page 288. At 2030 on 22 October Halsey initiated his rotation plan by ordering McCain's Task Group 38.1 to retire in Ulithi. Group 38.4 was scheduled to leave the following day. On the return of Groups 38.1 and 38.4 on 29 October, the remaining two groups would be ordered to Ulithi.

In the early hours of the twenty-third the submarine *Darter* began sending radio reports of enemy ships in Palawan Passage on the western side of the Philippines. Keeping the ships under surveillance, the submarine at dawn was able to observe and report at least eleven vessels, apparently battleships, cruisers, and destroyers, on course northeast. Halsey judged these to be the ships reported earlier in the Brunei-Singapore area and felt confirmed in his estimate that they were heading for Coron Bay, or possibly Manila Bay, to initiate a Leyte-bound Tokyo Express. He canceled his order for Task Group 38.4 to retire to Ulithi and directed it and Groups 38.2 and 38.3 to refuel and then to head closer to the Philippines.

Fanning out during the night, the three groups by dawn on 24 October had reached positions 125 miles apart—Sherman's Group 38.3 off Luzon, Bogan's Group 38.2, including Halsey's *New Jersey,* off San Bernardino Strait, and Davison's Group 38.4 off Leyte Gulf. McCain's Group 38.1, having received no change of orders from Halsey, plowed on toward Ulithi with five of the Third Fleet's sixteen carriers bearing 326 of the fleet's 595 planes.

THIRD FLEET
Admiral William F. Halsey in the *New Jersey*

Task Force 38
Vice Admiral Marc A. Mitscher in the *Lexington*

Task Group 38.1 Vice Admiral J. S. McCain	Task Group 38.2 Rear Admiral G. F. Bogan	Task Group 38.3 Rear Admiral F. C. Sherman	Task Group 38.4 Rear Admiral R. E. Davison
	Carriers		
Wasp (CV) *Hornet* (CV) *Hancock* (CV) *Monterey* (CVL) *Cowpens* (CVL)	*Intrepid* (CV) *Cabot* (CVL) *Independence* (CVL)	*Lexington* (CV) *Essex* (CV) *Princeton* (CVL) *Langley* (CVL)	*Enterprise* (CV) *Franklin* (CV) *San Jacinto* (CVL) *Belleau Wood* (CVL)
	Battleships		
	New Jersey *Iowa*	*Massachusetts* *South Dakota*	*Washington* *Alabama*
	Cruisers		
Chester (CA) *Pensacola* (CA) *Salt Lake City* (CA) *Boston* (CA) *San Diego* (CL) *Oakland* (CL)	*Biloxi* (CL) *Vincennes* (CL) *Miami* (CL)	*Santa Fe* (CL) *Birmingham* (CL) *Mobile* (CL) *Reno* (CL)	*Wichita* (CA) *New Orleans* (CA)
4 destroyers	16 destroyers	13 destroyers	15 destroyers

CV = carrier CVL = light carrier CA = heavy cruiser CL = light cruiser

Meanwhile, on the twenty-third the *Darter*, joined by the submarine *Dace*, had attacked the Japanese fleet in Palawan Passage. Torpedoes from the *Darter* sank one heavy cruiser and put a second out of action. Those from the *Dace* sank another heavy cruiser. Thus first blood had been drawn in the Battle for Leyte Gulf, which, measured by ship tonnage involved and area covered, was the greatest naval battle in history.

General MacArthur, when not ashore, was on board the light cruiser *Nashville* in Leyte Gulf. His fleet commander, Vice Admiral Kinkaid, was nearby in the amphibious command ship *Wasatch*. In the surrounding area was the enormously enlarged Seventh Fleet, composed mainly of the transports, cargo vessels, and amphibious craft of the Third and Seventh Amphibious forces; the cruisers, destroyers, and six old battleships of Oldendorf's Bombardment and Fire Support Group; and to the east, just outside Leyte Gulf, three carrier task units code-named Taffy 1, Taffy 2, and Taffy 3. These units, operating usually thirty to fifty miles apart on antisubmarine, antiaircraft, and ground support patrol, included altogether sixteen little escort carriers screened by destroyers and destroyer escorts.

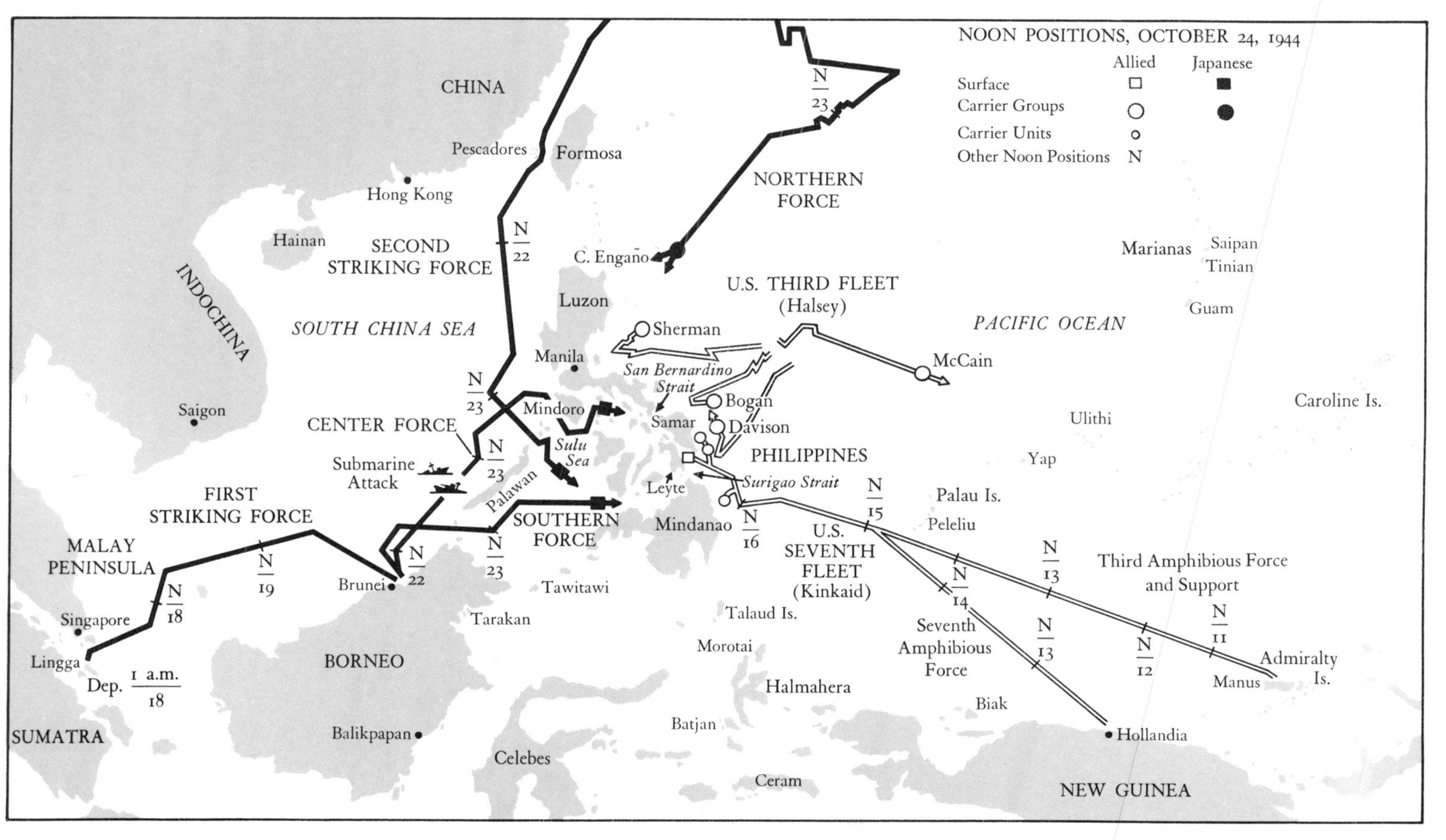

Approach of the Fleets to Leyte Gulf

Farther out, to the north and east, were Task Groups 38.2, 38.3, and 38.4 of the Third Fleet, which, as has been noted, had been reduced to Task Force 38, everything else having been lent to the Seventh Fleet. Halsey thought of himself as stripped for action, with orders to get the enemy fleet. He considered the beefed-up Seventh Fleet powerful enough for all defensive requirements. "The Third Fleet was offensive," he wrote later. "It prowled the ocean, striking at will with its new battleships and fast carriers."[2]

The forces involved in the Battle for Leyte Gulf did much reporting and communicating by radio, and the nearly static-free weather enabled CincPac's network of listening stations to pick up and relay most of the messages to ComInCh. Thus Nimitz at Pearl Harbor and King in Washington were able to follow the action closely.

Halsey, however, was sometimes poorly informed, because Kinkaid was forbidden to communicate with him directly. MacArthur, insistent on maintaining the independence of his command, forbade any uninterrupted channel of communication from the Seventh Fleet to the Third. If Kinkaid wanted to pass information to Halsey, he had to send it, usually in code, to the radio station at Manus to be retransmitted from there on the Fox schedule. This schedule, broadcast to the fleet, was copied in its entirety by operators on all U.S. naval ships, but the communicators were expected to decode only the messages that carried the call sign of their ship or force.

During the Battle for Leyte Gulf so many messages were graded urgent that nothing much else got through. The operators at Manus stacked the urgent messages and sent them out in the order they arrived or made a wild guess about which had priority. As a result it sometimes took hours for a dispatch to get from Kinkaid to Halsey, and often the messages arrived out of sequence. Kinkaid's staff, in an attempt to keep track of what was going on, defied orders and regulations by listening in on Halsey's frequencies and decoding everything, whether intended for them or not. The communication problem, compounded by messages obscurely worded, misinterpreted, and in one instance, accidentally corrupted, resulted in Halsey and Kinkaid basing several decisions on misinformation. Failure of the two fleet commanders to exchange clear and timely intelligence, aggravated by lack of a common superior close by, precluded effective coordination between their forces.[3]

At dawn on 24 October Halsey's three carrier groups off the Philippines launched scout planes to search the interisland waterways and the seas to the west for enemy ships, particularly the force the *Darter* and *Dace* had reported and attacked the preceding day. By now the ships could be in Coron or Manila Bay setting up the Tokyo Express Halsey and Kinkaid were expecting. A pilot from the carrier *Intrepid,* heading toward Coron Bay, which was included in his search sector, made a radar contact that prompted him to change course, gain altitude, and summon other nearby search planes. The pilots soon made out and reported no fewer than twenty-seven vessels—battleships, cruisers, and destroyers, a powerful armada the Americans were to call the Center Force—rounding the southern tip of Mindoro Island as if heading into the Sibuyan Sea.

For Halsey this information changed the picture drastically. The ships could only be heading for San Bernardino Strait and, ultimately, Leyte Gulf. The Japanese fleet was offering itself for battle after all. Halsey rebroadcast the contact report, summoned Sherman and Davison to close at best speed on Bogan's group off San Bernardino Strait, and gave all three groups their combat orders in one word: "Strike!" Halsey next directed McCain, then 600 miles east of the Philippines, en route to Ulithi, to reverse course, refuel, and be ready for whatever might develop.

The ships sighted off Mindoro were not the only oncoming Japanese vessels located that morning. Davison's search planes discovered a smaller force the Americans called the Southern Force eastbound in the Sulu Sea. The planes attacked this group, slightly damaging a battleship and a destroyer. To Halsey news of this second force implied a pincer movement, or double envelopment. Evidently the Southern Force was headed for Leyte Gulf also, via Surigao Strait. Davison, in closing on Bogan as ordered, would no longer be able to reach the Southern Force with his planes, but he would be in optimum position to join the attack on the larger Center Force in the Sibuyan Sea. That is how Halsey wanted it. He was convinced that the Seventh Fleet could easily prevent the ships in the Sulu Sea from entering the gulf.

In fact, Kinkaid was already making plans to repulse the Southern Force. To Oldendorf, commanding the Seventh Fleet's fire-support ships, he sent a message, listing Halsey, Nimitz, and King as information addressees: "Prepare for night engagement. Enemy force estimated 2 battleships, 4 heavy cruisers, 4 light cruisers, 10 destroyers reported under attack by our carrier planes in eastern Sulu Sea at 0910, 24 Oct. Enemy can arrive Leyte Gulf tonight."

Sherman's Task Group 38.3 was the only one of the Third Fleet groups discovered and attacked on the twenty-fourth by Japanese planes. Sherman could not comply with Halsey's order to close on Bogan because his ships were standing by his light carrier *Princeton,* which enemy aircraft based on Luzon had just set afire and left dead in the water. Damage to the *Princeton* was bad news indeed, but to Halsey it was no excuse for neglecting the attack mission he had assigned. To Mitscher, whose Task Force 38 flagship *Lexington* was in Sherman's group, he radioed, "Assume ComTaskGroup 38.3 is striking large enemy force near Mindoro. Advise results of strike earliest possible."

Between 0910 and 1350 on the twenty-fourth, the Third Fleet carriers launched five massive strikes against the Center Force as it plowed its way doggedly across the Sibuyan Sea. Though there were several Japanese airfields

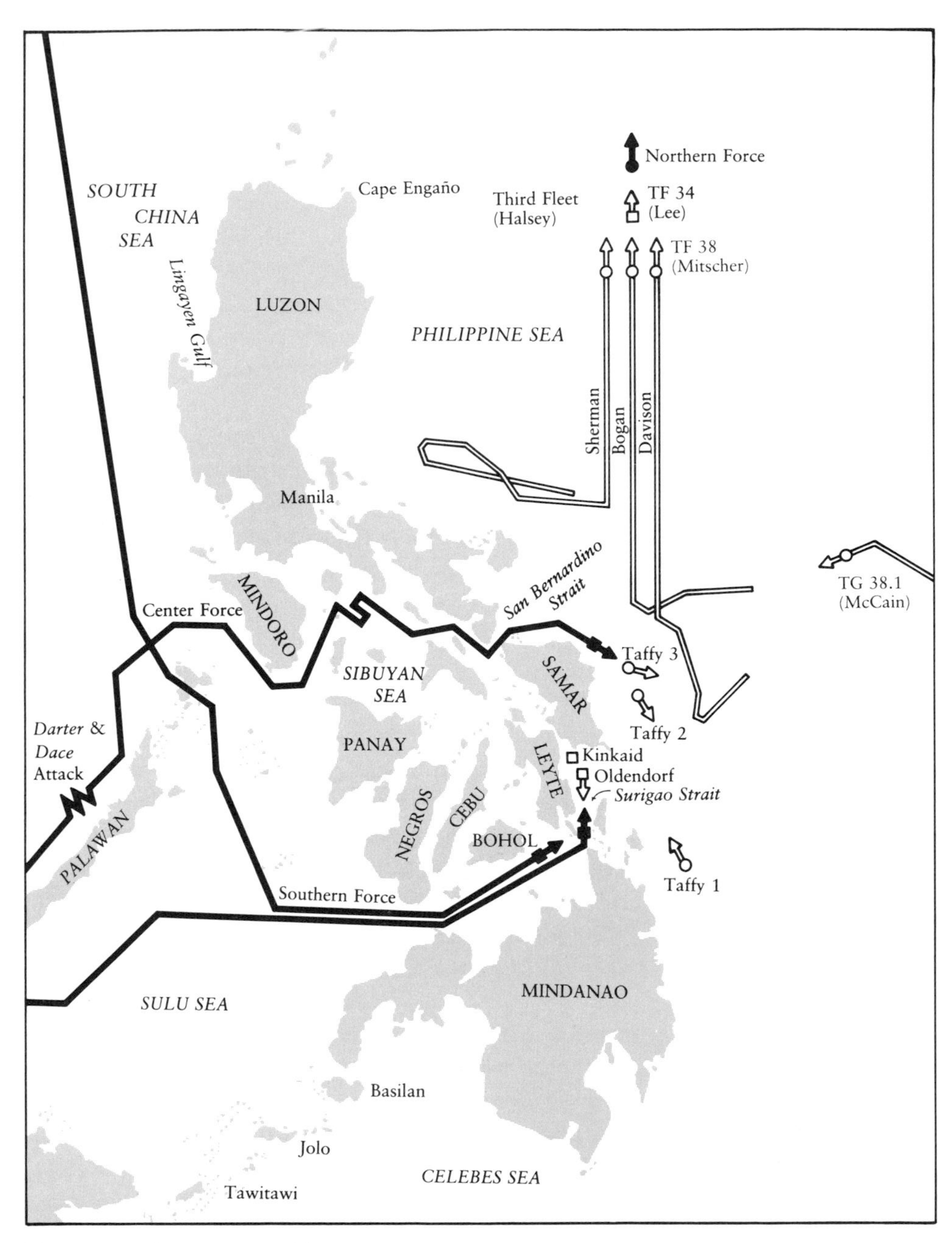

The Battle for Leyte Gulf, 23–25 October 1944

on Luzon and other nearby islands, the force received little air cover, and the few Japanese planes that the Americans saw they quickly shot down. The American planes aimed most of their bombs and torpedoes at the five enemy battleships, especially the two outsize vessels identified as the superbattleships *Yamato* and *Musashi,* the world's largest and most heavily armed combatant vessels. By early afternoon the Americans believed they had hit and seriously impaired the fighting ability of all the enemy battleships. One heavy cruiser was limping out of action and one of the superbattleships, identified as the *Musashi,* was listing, down by the head, and believed to be sinking. At about 1400 U.S. pilots reported that the whole enemy force had reversed course and was heading west, apparently in retirement. Though the enemy ships were heavily armed with antiaircraft guns, only eighteen of the hundreds of attacking American planes were destroyed in action.

At 1512 Admiral Halsey, thinking the Center Force might turn back east and transit San Bernardino Strait, sent a dispatch labeled "Battle Plan" to Vice Admiral Mitscher, Vice Admiral Willis A. Lee, his battle line commander, and his task group commanders. The addressees were to be prepared to form a new Task Force 34, consisting of the battleships *New Jersey, Iowa, Washington,* and *Alabama,* two heavy cruisers, three light cruisers, and two divisions of destroyers, all drawn from Task Groups 38.2 and 38.4. Lee, in the *Washington,* would be tactical commander of Task Force 34, which would engage the enemy at long ranges while the remainder of Task Groups 38.2 and 38.4 kept clear.

In his postwar autobiography Halsey wrote of the 1512 message, "This dispatch, which played a critical part in the next day's battle, I intended merely as warning to the ships concerned that *if a surface engagement offered,* I would detach them from TF 38, form them into TF 34, and send them ahead as a battle line. It was definitely *not* an executive dispatch, but a battle plan, and was so marked. To make certain that none of my subordinate commanders misconstrued it, I told them later by TBS, 'If the enemy sorties [through San Bernardino Strait], TF 34 will be formed *when directed by me.*'" This clarifying message was received only in Bogan's and Davison's nearby task groups, from which the ships for Task Force 34 would be drawn.

Probably nobody was more gratified by Halsey's plan than Kinkaid. His communicators, carrying out their illegal but widely practiced policy of eavesdropping across the radio spectrum, had intercepted the 1512 message. It was exactly in accord with Kinkaid's own plan. He expected Oldendorf's Seventh Fleet battleship force to block any attack on Leyte Gulf from the south and counted on Halsey to head off any enemy advance from Japan or San Bernardino Strait. Because of the divided command, they had made no agreement concerning their areas of responsibility. Kinkaid merely assumed that Halsey would order his battle plan executed—possibly by voice radio. King and

Nimitz, information addressees of the 1512 message, made the same assumption.[4]

Halsey and his staff were puzzled about the absence of Japanese carriers. From past experience the Americans expected enemy carrier forces to spearhead or at least support all-out drives such as the one that now appeared to be headed for the Leyte beachhead. But where were the carriers? Neither submarines nor search planes out of China and New Guinea had reported any in the Brunei-Singapore area. Evidently the carriers were now based in Japan and, if they were coming, would be approaching from the north.

Sherman, whose responsibility it had been to search to the north, had sent out no scout planes in the morning and early afternoon because he was busy warding off air attacks and covering the burning *Princeton*. As the afternoon wore on without the expected contact, Doug Moulton, now Halsey's aviation officer, repeatedly slammed his fist on the chart, saying, "Where in hell *are* those goddam Nip carriers?"

Finally, a little before 1700, Halsey and his staff received the news they had been impatiently expecting. Sherman had at last launched scouts, and these had sighted a force in two sections to the north. The more distant section, 180 miles east of Cape Engaño, the northern tip of Luzon, included at least three carriers, four to six cruisers, and half a dozen destroyers. The Americans promptly tagged these ships the Northern Force. Mitscher now recommended scuttling the *Princeton*, whose flames might serve after dark as a beacon for enemy planes. Halsey approved the scuttling and informed Nimitz and MacArthur that the enemy carrier force had been found.

When the enemy carriers were sighted Halsey and his staff immediately reviewed their charts. It had appeared all along that the Center and Southern forces were heading for a rendezvous in Leyte Gulf, evidently to attack the amphibious shipping there. Originally the staff estimated that these two forces would reach the gulf at dawn on 25 October. The Southern Force was on schedule, but the Center Force's reversal of course had spoiled its timing. Even if it turned back east, it could not reach Leyte Gulf before 1100 on the twenty-fifth. Thus Oldendorf's bombardment force, sent by Kinkaid to blast the small Southern Force in Surigao Strait, would have time to swing about and block the eastern entrance to the gulf against the entry of the more formidable Center Force. Though Oldendorf's old battleships were slow, in a static defense their fourteen- and sixteen-inch guns should be able to throw back an attacking enemy force that had been battered for several hours by Third Fleet carrier planes.

Halsey refrained from ordering an immediate strike against the Northern Force; if his attacking aircraft were launched at that hour of the day they would have to return to their carriers after dark, and few of the American pilots were trained to make night landings. Since Japanese planes could outrange American aircraft, Halsey's obvious move was to close the range under cover of darkness and attempt to get the jump on the enemy carriers with a dawn attack.

These circumstances presented Halsey with a choice of strategies:

1. *Guard San Bernardino Strait with all three available groups of Task Force 38.* This choice could place the Third Fleet between enemy airfields and enemy carriers, a situation naval commanders of World War II endeavored at all costs to avoid. Not only would the Third Fleet thus become a target for both land-based and carrier planes, it would permit the enemy carriers to stand out of range of the American carrier planes and shuttle-bomb the Americans—that is, have their planes hit the American ships, refuel and rearm at Luzon airfields, and hit the ships again on the return flight.

2. *Guard San Bernardino with Task Force 34 while attacking the Northern Force with part of Task Force 38.* At least one carrier group would have to remain near San Bernardino Strait to protect Task Force 34 from land-based enemy planes. McCain's Task Group 38.1, with more carriers and planes than any of the other groups, was probably still too far away to participate. The Americans would thus be obliged, with no more than two groups, at least one of which had been reduced in fire power after sending ships to form Task Force 34, to confront a force containing an undetermined number of carriers.

3. *Leave San Bernardino unguarded and attack the Northern Force with Task Groups 38.2, 38.3, and 38.4.* Halsey felt this was the strategy his orders obliged him to use. Certainly carriers, the ships with the longest reach and the hardest punch, constituted the "major portion of the enemy fleet" whose destruction had become "the primary task." He was convinced that by destroying enemy carriers he would be making the greatest contribution toward American victory.

Halsey was not particularly worried about the Center Force. Even if it transited San Bernardino Strait, to reach Leyte Gulf it would have to fend off air attacks by planes from the newly captured airfield at Tacloban, Leyte, and also from the three Seventh Fleet jeep carrier units, Taffies 1, 2, and 3. After that it would have to charge past the guns of Oldendorf's battleships and cruisers and the torpedoes of his destroyers. The Center Force would never reach the gulf, insisted Doug Moulton, who pointed out that U.S. pilots returning from the attacks that day in the Sibuyan Sea reported that the force had suffered such heavy damage to its guns and fire control that it was incapable of winning a decision.

Even if the Center Force did reach Leyte Gulf, Halsey reasoned, what could it do? Kinkaid, he assumed, had scout planes scrutinizing every move of the Center Force and thus would have ample time to have his defenses ready and his amphibious shipping out of reach. In the unlikely event that the Japanese broke through the defenses and entered the gulf, they could only hit and run. They could not consolidate their position, for obviously they were bringing no assault troops.

Halsey and his staff officers discussed the alternatives through the late afternoon and early evening. Their conclusions were based on two serious miscalculations. They overestimated the size and strength of the Northern Force and underestimated the fighting potential left in the Center Force. All of the officers present concurred in the final decision—to leave San Bernardino unguarded and attack the Northern Force with all available strength. "We will run north at top speed," said Halsey, "and put those carriers out for keeps."

"My decision to strike the Northern Force was a hard one to make," he afterward wrote, "but given the same circumstances and the same information as I had then, I would make it again."

Night was coming on. It was time to act. An earlier start northward might have been seen and reported by a Japanese scout plane, whereupon the Northern Force would have headed north to maintain a favorable range. A few minutes after 2000 Halsey strode into flag plot and, putting his finger on the Northern Force's last reported position, announced, "Here's where we're going." To Carney he said, "Mick, start them north." Having had no sleep for the past forty-eight hours, Halsey then retired to his emergency cabin to get some shut-eye before the coming battle.[5]

Carney now fired off a series of radio dispatches in Halsey's name, ordering Davison and Bogan to head due north at twenty-five knots; Sherman to join them as they sped past; McCain to head at high speed for the rest of Task Force 38; and the night fighters of the carrier *Independence* to search north to northwest. Kinkaid was sent the following dispatch, copies of which went to CominCh, CinCPac, and the Third Fleet: "Strike reports indicate enemy force Sibuyan Sea heavily damaged. Am proceeding north with three groups to attack enemy carrier force at dawn."

Kinkaid and other recipients of this message construed it to mean that three *carrier* groups were proceeding north and assumed that the Task Force 34 surface force had been formed and was left guarding San Bernardino Strait. "It was inconceivable," said Kinkaid later, "that Halsey would have scrapped a perfect battle plan." But it was also inconceivable to anyone acquainted with Halsey's character that he would send his carriers to fight a battle with an enemy carrier force of unknown size while he himself remained off a strait from which a heavily damaged enemy surface force might or might not emerge. What Kinkaid and others seem to have overlooked was that Halsey had included his flagship *New Jersey* in Task Force 34 and that his message said, "Am proceeding north," which meant Task Force 34 was not staying behind.

When it became apparent in the Third Fleet that Halsey was heading north with all his available ships, most of the officers seem to have heartily approved his decision. "The carrier forces to the north were our meat," said Admiral Sherman. "They were close enough so that they could not get away. The situation was entirely to my liking, and I felt that we had a chance to completely wipe out a major group of the enemy fleet, including the precious carriers, which he could ill afford to lose."

Captain Jimmy Thach, Mitscher's assistant chief of staff, was in entire agreement, then and later. "If I were Halsey and had the whole thing to do over again, even knowing what's been written in all the books," he said several years after World War II, "I'd still go after those carriers. I think he did exactly right. . . . There's a little calculated risk in everything, but in my opinion he certainly should have gone after those carriers."

Mitscher's chief of staff, Captain Arleigh Burke, Thach's immediate superior, felt otherwise. Carrier planes had participated in the air attack on Sherman's Task Group 38.3 earlier that day. Burke reasoned that these had come from the Japanese carriers, which must have been off Luzon north of Task Force 38 all day long. If so, why hadn't they coordinated with Luzon-based aircraft in a smashing attack on the Third Fleet to remove it from the path of the Center Force? Burke's conclusion was that the carriers had not done so because they could not. He had observed the terrible slaughter of enemy planes in the Marianas Turkey Shoot and had later seen Japanese carrier planes being shot down in great numbers in defense of Formosa. He now concluded that the Japanese carrier fleet no longer had enough trained flyers left to put up a decent fight. Their carriers must have been as helpless as they were when the United States invaded the Gilberts. If so, what were they now doing to the north? Why, they must be decoys. If they could not bomb the Third Fleet out of the Center Force's way, they could serve as bait to draw it away.

Burke went excitedly to Mitscher and asked him to pass this theory to Halsey. Mitscher demurred. "Well, I think you're right," he said, "but I don't know you're right." There was nothing worse, he insisted, than having a subordinate butt in and criticize a plan that was being executed. "I don't think we ought to bother Admiral Halsey," he concluded. "He's busy enough. He's got a lot of things on his mind."

Admiral Lee, who also had concluded that the Japanese carriers were decoys, was less reticent. Just before dark he conveyed his opinion to Halsey by flashing light. His message was acknowledged perfunctorily. Halsey and his staff had earlier discussed that possibility and rejected it as absurd. Priceless carriers, they concluded, would hardly be used as decoys for the benefit of less lethal, more expendable battleships.[6]

Meanwhile Mitscher had hatched a new plan. Why not proceed north at high speed, form and detach Task Force 34 after all and send it ahead to hit the Northern Force in a night battle, with Task Force 38 aircraft taking over at dawn to finish off whatever enemy ships remained afloat? The Third Fleet could then hasten back south, if not soon enough to bar the Center Force from entering Leyte Gulf, at least in time to smash it when it emerged. Mitscher's staff thought the plan excellent and urged him to offer it to Halsey. Mitscher refused lest it upset Halsey's operations. He told Burke, however, to work out the details and have the plan ready should an opportunity arise to use it. Then, bone-tired, he retired to his sea cabin.

The search planes from the *Independence* were now reporting that the Center Force was again headed east and that the navigation lights in San Bernardino Strait were illuminated for the first time since the recent U.S. invasion—news that was received with consternation by several senior officers. Admiral Bogan got on TBS to bring the reports to the attention of Admiral Halsey. Bogan planned to recommend that Task Force 34 be formed and sent back south with his own Task Group 38.2 in support, leaving Task Groups 38.3 and 38.4 to deal with the Northern Force. But the *New Jersey* communicators had heard the aircraft reports and had passed the information to Halsey. As soon as Bogan repeated the substance of the reports, the staff officer to whom he was speaking said, "Yes, yes, we have that information," in what seemed to Bogan "a rather impatient voice." Feeling brushed off, Bogan refrained from making his recommendation.

Burke wrote out a recommendation similar to Bogan's and showed it to Commander James Flatley, operations officer. The latter agreed that such action was imperative. They woke Mitscher, told him what the search planes had reported, and urged him to advise Halsey to detach Task Force 34 and head southward.

With a trace of annoyance in his voice, Mitscher asked, "Does Admiral Halsey have that report?"

"Yes," replied Flatley.

"If he wants my advice he'll ask for it," said the task force commander.

At about 2345, when Task Group 38.3, heading east, joined Task Groups 38.2 and 38.4, coming up from the south, Halsey ordered the three groups to slow down to sixteen knots on course north. The change of speed puzzled Burke. He telephoned Mitscher. "Do we have tactical command when we join?" he asked.

"Yes, we always do. We are the tactical commander," replied Mitscher. "Why do you ask?"

"Well, Admiral Halsey is giving tactical orders."

"Take it over," said Mitscher.

Burke, acting for Commander, Task Force 38, issued orders by voice radio for the three task groups to form a line of bearing approximately east-west, course north, at a speed of twenty-five knots. He hoped by thus racing ahead to implement Mitscher's plan for a night battle and dawn air strike. A Third Fleet staff officer countermanded Burke's order and told the fleet to decrease speed to sixteen knots. Halsey had given the order for slower speed because he was anxious to avoid passing the Northern Force in the dark. If the enemy turned south and got past the fleet on the right, he could shuttle-bomb it, using Luzon airfields. If southbound he passed the fleet on the left, between the Third Fleet and Luzon, he could race to join the Center Force in an attack on Leyte Gulf.

Burke, unaware of Halsey's reasons for slowing down, was anxious to put Mitscher's plan into effect. Taking a chance that the Third Fleet staff officer, in countermanding the speedup, was acting on his own and not on orders from Halsey, Burke in a series of orders by TBS inched the task force forward until it was again making twenty-five knots.[7]

A little before 0100, Halsey, awakening, entered the *New Jersey*'s flag bridge and, noticing the increase in speed, brought the fleet back down to sixteen knots, apparently not realizing that Burke was the villain who had disregarded his orders. Now more fearful than ever of overrunning the enemy fleet, he ordered a night air search launched from the *Independence*. Burke, still acting for Mitscher, heard the order and respectfully recommended that it be canceled, pointing out that the Japanese might detect the search planes by radar and change course.

"Have you any information that we don't have?" Halsey asked.

Burke replied that he had no such information.

"Launch the search," Halsey ordered.[8]

Five radar-equipped Hellcat night fighters promptly took off and sped to the north. One of these made radar contact with the enemy at 0205 and again at 0235. The Northern Force was still in two sections, now evidently headed for a rendezvous. To the dismay of Halsey and the satisfaction of Burke and Mitscher, the search plane reported the enemy fleet at considerably less than a hundred miles ahead. Evidently the Mitscher plan of a night battle followed by a dawn air attack was inevitable. Mitscher had Burke get on TBS to recommend that Task Force 34 be formed and sent ahead.* Halsey approved the recommendation. He didn't want his carriers involved in a night battle.[9]

Mitscher lost no time ordering Lee to form an enlarged Task Force 34, to include not four but all six battleships of Task Force 38. Halsey, disregarding

*Halsey and Mitscher rarely spoke on TBS. They generally relied on a staff officer to transmit their verbal orders or announcements.

the requirements of radio silence, sent a message to King, Nimitz, MacArthur, and Kinkaid announcing his renewed contact with the Northern Force and concluding with the words, "Own force in three groups concentrated," a statement that should have notified all recipients that Task Force 34, which was to have included Halsey's *New Jersey,* was not off San Bernardino Strait.

Officers on watch in Task Force 38 observed on their radarscopes the intricate ship movements of Lee's operation—some with great satisfaction, expecting the ships extracted from Task Force 38 to dash back south and cover San Bernardino Strait. Instead, to their astonishment, Task Force 34 moved out ahead of the carrier groups and continued north.

Mitscher ordered all the carriers to arm first deckloads without delay. Hours then passed with no contact between the new Task Force 34 and the Northern Force. At first light Mitscher sent out search planes. Without waiting for these to regain contact with the enemy, he at once launched combat air patrol and a 180-plane first strike. He hoped thus to get the jump on the enemy, supposedly nearby, and avoid having his own carriers come under attack with planes on board. Having now planned and launched the air attack, Mitscher in utter exhaustion returned to his cabin, leaving the execution to Burke.[10]

Halsey, out ahead in the *New Jersey* with Task Force 34, watched with satisfaction as Mitscher's planes passed overhead. There followed a long, nerve-wracking delay. The night search plane's report had been in error. The enemy force was much farther north than stated. Finally, at 0710, one of the search planes launched at dawn made new contact with the enemy fleet. It reported the fleet's position and apparent composition: one large and three light carriers; a pair of hybrid battleships, the *Ise* and *Hyuga,* with flight decks aft; several cruisers; and a few destroyers—about seventeen combatant vessels in all. Against these Halsey was taking sixty-four warships, including five large and six light carriers. So much the better, he believed. The Northern Force would be the more quickly disposed of, permitting the Third Fleet to hasten back to Leyte Gulf in the unlikely event that it was needed there.

Halsey and his staff had a long, impatient wait for news of the first strike. Meanwhile, the admiral's attention was increasingly diverted from the impending battle with the Northern Force. At 0412 Admiral Kinkaid had informed him by radio that Seventh Fleet surface forces were engaging enemy surface forces in Surigao Strait. To reassure himself, Kinkaid asked Halsey if Task Force 34 was guarding San Bernardino Strait. This message, sent by the *Wasatch*'s powerful transmitter, could have been received directly by the *New Jersey* had the latter been assigned the appropriate frequency. But in compliance with the southwest Pacific communication plan, it was sent to Manus, 1,500 miles away, to be relayed as part of the crowded Fox schedule. As a result Halsey did not receive Kinkaid's communication until 0648.

The dispatch was handed to Halsey on a long paper ribbon, which meant that it had been sent in cipher. The communicators, under a standing order not to take time transferring "hot" messages to a dispatch form, had merely torn the strip from the ciphering machine and rushed it to flag country by pneumatic tube.

In reply to Kinkaid's question whether Task Force 34 was guarding the strait, Halsey radioed back, "Negative. Task Force 34 is with carrier groups now engaging enemy carrier force." The reply dumbfounded Kinkaid.

At 0802 Halsey received a message sent by Kinkaid at 0623: "Enemy surface vessels Surigao Strait retiring, pursued by our light forces," followed shortly by Kinkaid's announcement that his forces were "closing to polish off four Nip cripples." Evidently the Seventh Fleet had won a resounding victory over the enemy Southern Force. Halsey confidently predicted an even more resounding victory for his own Third Fleet. He expected the combination of Mitscher's planes and Lee's guns to make a clean sweep of the Northern Force.

Toward 0830, however, Halsey was handed a message that checked his euphoria. It was a plain-language dispatch from Rear Admiral Ziggy Sprague, commander of Taffy 3, northernmost of the three escort carrier units off Leyte Gulf. Sprague reported that enemy battleships and cruisers were firing on his unit from fifteen miles astern. The attacking ships were evidently part of the Center Force, which must have come through San Bernardino Strait during the night.

Halsey was surprised but not greatly alarmed. "I figured," he wrote afterward, "that the sixteen little carriers had enough planes to protect themselves until Oldendorf could bring up his heavy ships." What puzzled him most was how Kinkaid and Sprague, with search planes at their disposal, could have permitted Taffy 3 to be taken so unaware.

In fact, Kinkaid had ordered searches by both seaplanes and carrier planes. Of five Black Cat Catalinas assigned to reconnaissance, only three were able to take off, and the one that flew over San Bernardino Strait did so before the Center Force had arrived. The jeep carrier assigned to search was slow getting planes respotted on her dark and rain-whipped flight deck. After dawn, when her scout planes were at last ready to take off, the ships of the Center Force were coming over the horizon and opening fire.

Just after 0800 Halsey was handed another surprising message from Kinkaid: "Fast battleships are needed immediately at Leyte Gulf." This struck Halsey as absurd. It was not his job, he believed, to provide direct protection to the Seventh Fleet. He felt he was being distracted while speeding to attack a force that menaced both the Third and the Seventh fleets—in fact the whole Allied Pacific strategy. However, he directed McCain, fueling to the east, to proceed with Task Group 38.1 at "best possible speed" and strike the enemy force northeast of Leyte Gulf. Then Halsey notified Kinkaid of the order.

At 0850, right after he had sent his messages to McCain and Kinkaid, Halsey was handed the long-awaited flash report of Task Force 38's first strike against the Northern Force: "One carrier sunk after tremendous explosion. Two carriers, one light cruiser hit badly. Other carrier untouched." The U.S. pilots reported heavy antiaircraft fire from the Japanese ships but almost no enemy planes in the air. Halsey assumed that the Americans had taken the Japanese by surprise before they could get planes launched. A second strike from Task Force 38 was on its way northward.

The enemy force was reported on course nearly due north, making no better than seventeen knots. Halsey ordered Lee to increase speed to twenty-five knots. He now assigned to Task Force 34 the function of completing the work of Mitscher's planes by sinking cripples, stragglers, and any other Japanese vessels it could overtake. If the Northern Force maintained course and speed, it would be under gunfire by Task Force 34 before noon. Halsey eagerly anticipated what thus far he had missed in his varied career—an old-fashioned fire-away-Flanagan surface battle.

The admiral considered the pending battle very much his responsibility. As for the Seventh Fleet, he was making the considerable sacrifice of sending his most powerful task group, McCain's 38.1, to aid Kinkaid. He devoutly hoped he had heard the last cry for help from that quarter.

It was not to be. At 0900 came another desperate plea from Kinkaid, in plain English: "Enemy force attacking our CVEs [escort carriers] composed of 4 battleships, 8 cruisers, and X other ships. Request Lee proceed top speed cover Leyte. Request immediate strike by fast carriers." Such persistent distractions, about which Halsey could do nothing further, infuriated him and tied his stomach in knots. It was unlike Kinkaid, ordinarily calm and self-controlled under pressure, to be screaming for help.

At 0922 Halsey was handed still another message from Kinkaid. The new dispatch merely stated that Taffy 3 was under attack by vessels that must have come through San Bernardino Strait during the night. It requested an immediate air strike and support from heavy ships, and concluded, "My OBBs [old battleships] low in ammunition."

This last statement shocked Halsey. If Oldendorf's battleships lacked the means to defend Leyte Gulf, the situation there was far more serious than Halsey had suspected. Why hadn't Kinkaid told him before? He glanced at the date-time group on the new dispatch. It had been filed at 0725, nearly two hours earlier, before several of the messages he had received since. Halsey never learned what caused the delay, but we may be sure the trouble was at Manus, where the relay operators were either having trouble fitting messages into the Fox schedule or overwhelmed by the sheer volume of dispatches from various transmitters in and out of the war zone.

That Oldendorf's old battleships might now be short of ammunition could have been anticipated. Too slow to operate with the carriers, the OBBs had until the Leyte operation been used solely for shore bombardment. Hence they carried mostly high-capacity bombardment ammunition, with only a small proportion of armor-piercing projectiles for use against armored vessels. Oldendorf's battlewagons had evidently used up most of the latter repulsing the Southern Force.

Summoning his last shreds of patience, Halsey spelled out to Kinkaid the situation of his Third Fleet: "Am now engaging enemy carrier force. Task Group 38.1 with 5 carriers and 4 CAs [heavy cruisers] has been ordered to assist you immediately. My position with other 3 carrier task groups lat. 17-18 N long. 126-11 E." Nearly 400 miles from Leyte Gulf, Halsey's northbound carriers and battleships could not possibly get back in time to intervene in the ongoing Seventh Fleet action.

Shortly after 1000, two dispatches arrived in flag country almost simultaneously. The first was another shocker from Kinkaid: "My situation is critical. Fast battleships and support by air strikes may be able to keep enemy from destroying CVEs and entering Leyte."

The other dispatch, from Admiral Nimitz, with copies to CominCh and Commander, Seventh Fleet, read, "WHERE IS RPT WHERE IS TASK FORCE THIRTY-FOUR RR THE WORLD WONDERS." Halsey was stunned. His commander in chief and good friend Chester Nimitz appeared to be taunting him with heavy-handed sarcasm while calling on King and Kinkaid to witness his humiliation. The admiral plucked off his cap, hurled it to the deck, and broke into sobs. Carney rushed over, grabbed him by the shoulders, and shouted, "Stop it! What the hell's the matter with you? Pull yourself together!"

Halsey, speechless, handed the dispatch to his chief of staff and turned away. A check with the *New Jersey*'s communicators identified the final words of the dispatch as padding. Padding was nonsense phrasing placed by encipherers at the beginning and end of radio messages to bury the often stereotyped opening and closing words, which enemy cryptanalysts might easily decipher. The communicators at the receiving end were expected to remove all padding before passing the messages on. In this case they had removed it from the opening, but the end read so much like a part of the message that they left it, trusting Halsey would be told in flag country that the double consonant preceding the closing phrase marked it as padding. He was not so informed, at least not until he had read the dispatch and received the shock of his life.

Even without the final phrase the message sounded peremptory enough to demand action. Not until weeks later did Halsey learn that the message Nimitz had authorized was a mere question: "Where is Task Force 34?" The staff officer who dictated it added Admirals King and Kinkaid as information addressees. In dictating, he employed so emphatic a tone that the yeoman who wrote up the message interpreted the officer's intention by inserting "RPT [repeat] where is." The ensign who prepared the dispatch for transmission added the padding—the nonsense phrase "Turkey trots to water" at the beginning, and the misleading phrase "the world wonders" at the end. In all the ships and stations that received and recorded the message, only the *New Jersey*'s communicators failed to delete both padding phrases.

Thinking he had no choice, a little before 1100 Halsey ordered Task Force 34 to change from course 000 to course 180—from due north to due south. Mitscher's second strike was now pounding the Northern Force, leaving cripples to be finished off by the battleship guns. Until he reversed course, Halsey believed himself on the threshold of a spectacular victory. "I turned my back on the opportunity I had dreamed of since my days as a cadet," he afterward moaned. "For me, one of the biggest battles of the war was off, and what has been called 'the Battle of Bull's Run' was on."

Halsey detached Bogan's Task Group 38.2 from Task Force 38 to provide air cover for his battleships and released four cruisers and ten destroyers from Task Force 34 to give additional surface support to the two groups remaining under Mitscher, who pressed on northward in pursuit of the Northern Force. Halsey reported to CinCPac, "Task Force 34 with me engaging enemy carrier force. Am now proceeding with Task Group 38.2 and all fast battleships to reinforce Kinkaid. No damage own force. . . . Task Group 38.1 already ordered assist Kinkaid immediately." To Kinkaid he signaled, "I am proceeding toward Leyte with Task Group 38.2 and 6 fast BBs . . . but do not expect to arrive before 0800 tomorrow."[11]

During the early afternoon Halsey received another series of dispatches from Kinkaid: "Situation looks better. Enemy forces retiring"; "Enemy forces returning to attack CVEs"; "Situation Leyte Gulf again very serious"; "Enemy apparently attempting to force entrance Leyte Gulf." A puzzling final message gave the impression that the Center Force was retiring toward San Bernardino Strait. To intercept it, Halsey detached his two fastest battleships, the *New Jersey* and *Iowa,* together with three light cruisers and eight destroyers, and sped ahead. The race was futile. When Halsey reached the vicinity of San Bernardino Strait a little after midnight, the only ship of the Center Force that had not passed back through the strait was a destroyer that had lingered to pick up Japanese survivors of the battle with Taffy 3. The American cruisers and destroyers darted ahead and sank the vessel with gunfire and torpedoes, while Halsey, on board the distant *New Jersey,* observed with satisfaction "the first and only surface action I saw during my entire career." His battleships had steamed 300 miles north and then 300 miles back south between the two main enemy forces without quite making contact with either.[12]

Afterward, when U.S. naval officers reviewed the Battle for Leyte Gulf, they gave each of the four main actions a name. The series of air attacks made on the Center Force as it plowed its way eastward on 24 October toward San Bernardino Strait they called the Battle of the Sibuyan Sea. In this action Halsey's carrier planes put a heavy cruiser out of action, damaged several other ships, and sank the superbattleship *Musashi.*

The Southern Force was actually two enemy groups that never came together. The first group, consisting of two battleships, one heavy cruiser, and four destroyers, was nearly annihilated in the Battle of Surigao Strait, fought before dawn on 25 October. Oldendorf had set a trap for the group by lining the sides of the strait with his destroyers and PT boats and placing his battleships and cruisers on T-capping courses across the northern end. The second Japanese group, seeing what happened to the first, prudently withdrew.

The action fought a few hours later between the Center Force and Taffy 3 was named the Battle off Samar. The Center Force opened fire on the six jeep carriers of the unit, sinking the *Gambier Bay* and heavily damaging two others. The unit's destroyers and destroyer escorts made smoke and in an act of extraordinary courage charged against the huge Center Force and attacked it with torpedoes. Three of these little vessels were sunk by gunfire, but their suicidal charge threw the enemy into confusion. Planes from the Taffies and from Leyte struck at the Center Force, sinking three of its cruisers and inducing the remainder of the force to retire. On the afternoon of 25 October aircraft from McCain's Task Group 38.1 attacked the Center Force but did little damage. Striking from extreme range, they were hampered by wing tanks and thus obliged to carry bombs instead of the heavier, more lethal torpedoes. That same afternoon Japanese pilots, flying land-based planes, crashed into five carriers of Taffy 3 and nearby Taffy 1, heavily damaging all and sinking one. These suicide attacks marked the beginning of a development that would bring great destruction to American ships.

Task Force 38's attack on the Northern Force was called the Battle off Cape Engaño. In this operation U.S. carrier planes sank the big carrier *Zuikaku,* last of the Pearl Harbor raiders, three light carriers, and two destroyers. They also damaged a cruiser, which as she limped homeward was sunk by an American submarine. Of the Northern Force's thirteen surface vessels ten, including the converted battleships *Ise* and *Hyuga,* returned to Japan. Had Task Force 34 continued northward, it might have sunk most if not all of these ships.

Because the Northern Force carriers attempted no counterattack and appeared almost bare of planes, a number of officers in addition to Lee and Burke concluded that the force was as impotent as the Combined Fleet had been two years earlier and was being used merely to lure Halsey away from Leyte so that the Southern and Center forces could close in on American shipping in the gulf. After the war the Japanese confirmed this conclusion. Their carriers had lost most of their planes in the Battle of the Philippine Sea. Any Japanese fleet aviators who had attained proficiency after that had been sacrificed to protect the Formosan bases from Halsey's carrier attacks. The four carriers of the Northern Force carried only 116 planes, approximately half their normal complement. At 1145 on the twenty-fourth the carriers launched a seventy-six-plane strike against Sherman's Task Group 38.3. Three of the ill-trained, inexperienced pilots got lost and returned to their flight decks. The rest, having achieved nothing in their attack, flew to friendly fields on Luzon, where they remained.

As long as he lived, Admiral Halsey rejected all evidence and every assertion that the Northern Force had been bait. The notion that he had been lured away to the north did not sit well with him. His only mistake, he continued to insist, was turning back south in the late morning of 25 October, but he believed he had no choice after receiving Admiral Nimitz's dispatch inquiring the whereabouts of Task Force 34.

During his afternoon and evening run south on 25 October, Halsey found time to look over the many dispatches reporting recent operations at sea. On the basis of these he concluded that the Americans had been victorious, and at 2126 he radioed Nimitz, "It can be announced with assurance that the Japanese navy has been beaten, routed, and broken by the Third and Seventh fleets." Nimitz passed the message to the Navy Department. King told him not to release it because Halsey had not had sufficient time or opportunity to evaluate the situation completely. Secretary Forrestal concurred with King but nevertheless informed President Roosevelt.

The navy's hand was forced by MacArthur, who on his own released a victory communiqué to the Reuters news agency. Harry Hopkins, special assistant to the president, called Forrestal and suggested that Halsey's message be given to the press. Forrestal was hesitant to release good news without being absolutely certain of the facts, but Hopkins thought it was worth taking a chance. Consequently, at 1800 (Washington time) on 25 October the president called in White House reporters and read them a paraphrase of Halsey's victory message to Nimitz.

When all the facts became known, they more than justified Halsey's optimistic report. Not only had the Japanese been thwarted in their scheme to sink American shipping in Leyte Gulf, but they had lost 306,000 tons of their own combatant ships—three battleships, four carriers, ten cruisers, and nine destroyers. The Americans, at a cost of 37,000 tons of warships—one light carrier, two escort carriers, two destroyers, and one destroyer escort—had terminated Japan's capacity to wage another fleet battle.

An hour after sending his victory dispatch to Nimitz, Halsey sent a top-secret message to Nimitz and King explaining his conduct in the battle:

> Searches by my carrier planes revealed the presence of the Northern carrier force on the afternoon of 24 October, which completed the picture of all enemy naval forces. As it seemed childish to me to guard statically San Bernardino Strait, I concentrated Task Force 38 during the night and steamed north to attack the Northern Force at dawn. I believed that the Center Force had been so heavily damaged in the Sibuyan Sea that it could no longer be considered a serious menace to the Seventh Fleet.

This dispatch, said Nimitz in a letter to King, indicated that Halsey was feeling defensive. And well he might, since his leaving the strait unguarded cost Taffy 3 an escort carrier, two destroyers, and a destroyer escort and permitted the bulk of the Center Force to escape. Yet, considering the information he had in the afternoon of 24 October, the destructive power he believed the Northern Force with its carriers wielded, his negative reaction to Spruance's remaining off the Saipan beachhead the preceding June, the permissive orders under which he was operating, and above all his record of taking calculated risks that won victories, it is scarcely conceivable that Halsey would have acted otherwise.

Certainly the admiral had not diminished himself in the eyes of his friend MacArthur. Overhearing criticism of Halsey while at dinner with his staff, the general pounded on the table for attention. "That's enough," he said. "Leave the Bull alone. He's still a fighting admiral in my book." To Halsey himself he sent a message of thanks, concluding, "Everyone here has a feeling of complete confidence and inspiration when you go into action in our support."

Reporting in person to Admiral King the following January, Halsey said, "I made a mistake in that battle."

King held up his hand. "You don't have to tell me any more," he said. "You've got a green light on everything you did."

"I still think it was a mistake to turn south when the Japs were right under my guns."

"No. It wasn't a mistake. You couldn't have done otherwise."

Rarely in history have two successive battles presented problems as similar as those of the Philippine Sea and Leyte Gulf, and rarely have two commanders responded so differently to similar battle situations. Long afterward Halsey somberly suggested that it might have been better had he commanded in the Philippine Sea and Spruance at Leyte Gulf.[13]

CHAPTER 19

THE PHILIPPINES

On orders from Halsey, Bogan's Task Group 38.2 and McCain's Task Group 38.1 rendezvoused north of Samar at 0500 on 26 October and an hour later launched over the Sibuyan Sea the first of three strikes against the fleeing Japanese Center Force. Because of the distance the enemy force had covered during the night, the attacking planes had to be armed with bombs rather than torpedoes, but they succeeded in sinking a light cruiser and further damaging a straggling heavy cruiser that had lost her bow in the Battle off Samar the day before. Meanwhile, Task Groups 38.3 and 38.4, having sunk the four carriers of the Japanese Northern Force, were fueling to the northeast, under the temporary command of Mitscher.

That morning Halsey had received a request from Kinkaid to provide combat air patrol over Leyte Gulf. With planes of two of his groups over the Sibuyan Sea and the other two groups fueling in the distance, he could not immediately comply, but he ordered Mitscher's groups to move in toward the gulf when they had finished fueling and be "prepared to make strikes or furnish fighter cover over Leyte Area."

Halsey was nettled by Kinkaid's request. Having played a major role in destroying Japanese air power before the American invasion of Leyte and in repulsing the enemy fleet afterward, he felt that he had fully complied with his orders and knew no reason why the army air force should not now take over air support of the Leyte operation. His impatience showed in a dispatch sent to MacArthur that evening: "After seventeen days of battle, my fast carriers are unable to provide extended support for Leyte, but two groups are available 27 October. The pilots are exhausted, and the carriers are low in provisions, bombs, and torpedoes. When will land-based air take over at Leyte?"

As it turned out, Halsey continued to provide the requested support, always hoping in vain that the next day or so army air would take over and release his ships. He and Nimitz had plans for Task Force 38 that did not include cruising off the Philippines. It was Halsey's intention to allow his ships and crews a brief stay at Ulithi for rest and replenishment and then lead them northward to join the Marianas-based B-29s in an attack on Tokyo, the first bombing of the Japanese capital since the Doolittle Raid of April 1942. The big land-based bombers had postponed raids on Japan because fighter planes lacked sufficient range to support them in the long flight to the target and back. Halsey's flyers would provide the fighter support and also participate in the bombing.

But the Third Fleet was desperately needed in Philippine waters, especially after Kinkaid sent away the battered escort carriers of the three Taffies. Fifth Air Force planes could not take over support of the Leyte operation, mainly because the one usable airport, at Tacloban, could not handle enough planes at one time to assure continuous offense and defense. Torrential rains brought by the monsoons delayed the building of additional airfields. Army engineers saw steel matting and truckloads of gravel sink before their eyes in soupy mud. Meanwhile, the Japanese were bringing in fresh planes from Formosa and Japan, and these were operating from the all-weather airfields of Luzon.

On 27 October, in response to Kinkaid's request, Task Group 38.3 provided fighter cover over the gulf and sent fighter sweeps over the central Philippines. Planes from the *Essex* attacked an enemy convoy with bombs and rockets, sinking two destroyers. The following day, Task Groups 38.2 and 38.4 took over close support of U.S. ground forces on Leyte and also attacked enemy airfields and shipping, while the remaining two groups shaped course toward Ulithi for quick replenishment.

On the twenty-ninth enemy aircraft from Luzon attacked the two groups of Task Force 38 remaining in Philippine waters. Combat air patrol and antiaircraft fire shot down most of the planes, but one plane dived into Bogan's flagship, the carrier *Intrepid*. Striking a glancing blow at the ship's gun gallery, the plane caused only minor material damage, but it killed ten men and wounded six others.

Halsey, watching from the bridge of the nearby *New Jersey*, was witnessing his first kamikaze in action. It will be recalled that in February 1942, when Halsey's task force was withdrawing from its raid on the Marshalls, a Japanese plane had dived into his flagship *Enterprise* and skidded across the flight deck, spraying gasoline from its ruptured fuel tanks. But that plane was on fire and doomed; the pilot was about to lose his life anyway. The *Intrepid*'s attacker, on the contrary, had come in flying an undamaged aircraft. All hands recognized it as one of the newly organized Kamikaze ("divine wind") Special Attack Corps, about which naval intelligence had warned them. The corps, taking its name from the typhoons that in 1274 and 1281 saved Japan by scattering Kublai Khan's invasion fleets, was made up of aircraft pilots who, unable to hit ships with torpedoes or bombs, made up in guts what they lacked in skill by hurling themselves and their planes into their targets.

Halsey and his officers regarded the attack on the *Intrepid* as an isolated event, a kind of token terror. The idea of combat by deliberate suicide was utterly alien to American psychology. The U.S. fighting man, however brave, seldom undertook a mission that did not promise him at least an outside chance of survival. As Halsey said afterward, "We could not believe that even the Japanese, for all their hara-kiri traditions, could muster enough recruits to make such a corps really effective."

The Americans were violently disabused of that notion the following day. Four Zeros managed to evade the combat air patrol guarding Davison's group, and at a straight, unbroken 45° angle the leader glided right through the flight deck of Davison's flagship, the big, new *Franklin.* A bright burst of flame aft of the carrier was followed by a column of black smoke. The second plane dived through the flight deck of the *Belleau Wood,* setting off explosions that hurled huge chunks of burning debris in all directions. One of the remaining Zeros headed for the *San Jacinto* but was hit just in time by antiaircraft fire and splashed short of her bow. The fourth aimed for the venerable *Enterprise* and, in almost a repeat of the 1942 attack, skidded across her flight deck and exploded in the sea. Both the *Franklin* and *Belleau Wood,* heavily damaged, retired under escort to Ulithi. Between them they had lost forty-five planes and had 148 men killed and 70 injured.[1]

While Task Group 38.3 was en route to Ulithi, Mitscher spent most of the time resting in his sea cabin, and Burke gave orders that he was not to be disturbed. The admiral was now ready to relinquish command of Task Force 38. On his arrival at Ulithi on 30 October, Slew McCain relieved him as task force commander, and Rear Admiral Alfred E. Montgomery relieved McCain in command of Task Group 38.1.

Halsey had hoped at least to be able to rotate his task groups to Ulithi for rest and replenishment, a plan that had been interrupted by the Battle for Leyte Gulf. It was interrupted again by events beginning on 1 November. That day Japanese aircraft attacking the ships in the gulf sank one destroyer and damaged five others.

In the evening Halsey received an information copy of a message from Kinkaid to MacArthur describing the enemy attack and urging the general to request further help from Task Force 38, since army air was apparently still incapable of providing adequate fighter cover. Halsey, recognizing Kinkaid's message as an indirect appeal to himself, wearily set out to relieve the emergency. He could not stomach the thought of cruising off the gulf merely to provide fighter cover to the ships within. His style called for crushing enemy air power at its source—in this case, the feeder fields on Luzon. After checking with MacArthur and Nimitz, he proceeded to undertake that task.

Because the *Franklin* and *Belleau Wood* would have to withdraw to major shipyards to have their heavy damages repaired, Halsey temporarily disbanded Task Group 38.4 and distributed its ships among the other three groups. With these he headed back toward the Philippines. They refueled on the third, and that night while they moved, zigzagging, toward their assigned positions, a submarine torpedoed the light cruiser *Reno,* producing violent internal explosions. Admiral Sherman called a tug from Ulithi to take her in tow and left behind four destroyers to form an antisubmarine screen and escort her back to the anchorage.

At dawn on 5 November Task Force 38 reached its selected operational area eighty miles east of central Luzon and launched a fighter sweep, then successive deckloads of fighter-escorted bombers. The bombers, attacking airfields and shipping from northern Luzon to Mindoro, generally caught the enemy napping. A little after noon, however, he struck back. Four Zeros evaded the combat air patrol and made suicide dives on the Task Group 38.3 carriers. One of the planes was shot down and two others barely missed the *Ticonderoga* and McCain's flagship, the *Lexington*. The fourth slammed into the *Lexington*'s island, wrecking her secondary control, killing 50 men and injuring 132 more, many very seriously.

On 6 November Task Force 38 struck again at enemy airfields and shipping. After two days the U.S. aviators claimed to have destroyed 439 aircraft, mostly on the ground, while in the bays and seas U.S. dive- and torpedo bombers sank a cruiser and sank or damaged numerous smaller craft. The wholesale destruction of enemy aircraft resulted in a sharp decrease in attacks on shipping at the Leyte beachhead.

In consenting to have Halsey carry out the two-day raid, Nimitz asked General MacArthur "to release the forces of the Third Fleet as soon as the situation permitted." CinCPac was under increasing pressure from the independent Twenty-first Bomber Command to provide seaborne fighter support for its projected B-29 raids on Japan. Nimitz sent his deputy chief of staff, Rear Admiral Sherman, to MacArthur's headquarters at Tacloban to discuss the possibility of releasing Task Force 38, if only for the three or four weeks needed to bomb Japan effectively. The upshot of the discussion was that, because the Japanese were obviously determined to hold Leyte at any cost, continued support by the fast carriers was essential. Halsey is reported to have "accepted this decision, a bitter disappointment to him, with good grace."

The B-29s began their bombing of Japan without fighter support, lack of which obliged them to make fuel-consuming climbs to 28,000 feet, an altitude from which precision bombing was impossible. The situation was not remedied until the following February, when the long-projected capture of Iwo Jima gave the United States a fighter base halfway between the Marianas and Tokyo.

At Leyte Gulf Japanese night raiders were particularly trying for U.S. sailors bringing in supplies. The enemy planes did not often hit anything, but antiaircraft fire and repeated red alerts kept the Americans awake. More worrisome to MacArthur were the expresses rushing enemy troops and supplies into Leyte from all over the Philippines and landing them on the west coast, usually at Ormoc Bay. U.S. army aviators, untrained for overwater operations, were of little help in plugging the enemy inflow. Under the circumstances, Halsey took the liberty of offering MacArthur some advice. In the Solomons there was a marine air group specially trained to blast enemy vessels. When Halsey left the South Pacific, these came under the direct command of General Kenney, MacArthur's air officer, but he had made little use of them. Halsey suggested bringing the marine aviators to Leyte as soon as an airfield could be made ready for them.

Meanwhile, the expresses continued to bring in reinforcements. On or about 9 November an American search plane reported a particularly large convoy departing from Manila Bay, evidently bound for Leyte. It consisted of four destroyers, a minesweeper, a subchaser, and five or six transports estimated to be carrying ten thousand men. A worried MacArthur requested help from Task Force 38, then approaching a fueling rendezvous far out in the Pacific. Halsey ordered the force to cancel fueling and proceed at high speed to Philippine waters. At dawn on 11 November the carriers, then 200 miles off San Bernardino Strait, launched search planes, which found the big convoy approaching Ormoc Bay. The first attack wave of 347 planes sent out by the carriers sank all the transports. The second wave sank the four destroyers and sixteen of twenty-five or thirty intercepting enemy aircraft. Total American losses were nine planes. All the Japanese troops being convoyed to Leyte drowned except a few strong swimmers who reached distant shores. Two weeks elapsed before the Japanese could assemble enough vessels for another troop convoy.

To decrease further the number of enemy vessels, Task Force 38, after fueling, returned to the Philippines and on 13–14 November launched a series of strikes against Japanese shipping. The carrier aircraft sank a light cruiser, four destroyers, and seven transports and destroyed an estimated eighty-four planes in the air and on the ground—at a cost of twenty-five American aircraft, most of which succumbed to antiaircraft fire from Japanese ships.

When Task Force 38 returned to the Philippines on the nineteenth, its flyers found few ships, but they destroyed more than a hundred aircraft on the ground, losing thirteen of their own. Enemy aircraft followed the American planes back to their carriers and made a series of raids, none of them successful. Because there was not much left to attack in and around Luzon, Halsey canceled strikes scheduled for the twentieth, and Task Force 38 withdrew to refuel and give the Japanese time to bring in more targets.[2]

Halsey had by now developed a fairly regular personal seagoing routine. At 0500 he was usually seated on his high steel chair on the flag bridge to watch the first planes take off. On days when his carriers were launching a series of strikes, he was likely to remain on the bridge all day, making occasional visits to the adjacent flag plot to look over the big chart. This was overlaid with paper on which the watch officers traced American ship movements in blue pencil and marked reported sightings of Japanese ships in orange. On these days he took his meals off a tray, and at sea he always slept in his sea cabin just off the bridge.

On quiet days outside the combat zone he would descend the ladder to his office and living quarters directly under flag plot and take his time to bathe, shave, and dress for the day. Flag mess, just outside his office, was dominated by a large oval table that served both for conferences and meals. Here at breakfast, lunch, and dinner Halsey was the genial host to some twenty staff officers—his official family. He frowned on any discussion of fleet problems at meals unless they were especially urgent.

After breakfast the admiral returned to his office and tackled the day's paperwork. In the afternoon, in quiet zones, he enjoyed a game of deck tennis, which he didn't want interrupted. Once a rain squall stopped his game. As soon as the rain ceased, an order was passed by bull horn: "Dry down all weather decks!" Without waiting for a work party, Halsey grabbed a swab and invited his fellow players to do likewise and turn to.

After dinner came the regular evening movie, which Halsey rarely missed. Once, after a long series of second-rate films, he sent a letter of complaint to Nimitz. Following the movie, the admiral sat in on the nightly conclave of his Dirty Trick Department—Mick Carney, Ham Dow, Doug Moulton, Harold Stassen, and Johnny Lawrence—and listened with admiration as the conspirators devised new schemes to harass and bewilder the gullible enemy.

The Dirty Tricksters, while concocting their plans, often remained in session until 0100, but Halsey generally left a little before midnight. He went out on flag bridge for a last look at the formation and visited flag plot for a last look at the charts and dispatches. In his sea cabin, before turning in, he had his tenth and final cup of coffee of the day and his fortieth and last cigarette. He always tried to get five hours of sleep but seldom succeeded.[3]

The next strikes of Task Force 38 were scheduled for 25–26 November. They were to be executed by Bogan's and Sherman's groups, which, after a high-speed approach, reached the launching point at dawn on the twenty-fifth and sent the first of several projected strikes winging over Luzon. Off Luzon beaches the American planes sank two cruisers, three beaching craft, and two freighters.

A surprising aspect of the 25 November raid was the number of Japanese planes already airborne when the Americans arrived. Of the fifty-five enemy aircraft destroyed, only twenty-nine were on the ground; the rest were shot down. It seemed as if Japanese air forces had been expecting the Americans that day and were resolved not to be caught napping again.

More surprising was the magnitude and destructiveness of the Japanese counterattack. In early afternoon, when the two American task groups, about thirty-five miles apart, were launching their third strike of the day, their radar screens suddenly filled with bogies. Zeros were approaching in such numbers that the combat air patrol could not repulse them all. Bogan's group, with Halsey in the *New Jersey,* took the first blows. One of the Zeros dived at the *Hancock.* The carrier's antiaircraft guns shot it down directly overhead, but a piece of its wing fell onto her flight deck, knocking out a 20mm gun.

Halsey having Thanksgiving dinner with the crew of the *New Jersey*, November 1944

Two bomb-laden kamikazes dived into the luckless *Intrepid.* One crashed through her flight deck before its bomb exploded, blasting a huge hole in the deck and starting raging fires. The other dived into the deck at a shallow angle. The plane disintegrated into flaming scraps that scattered in all directions and started more fires, while its bomb streaked through to the hangar deck, where it exploded. One kamikaze rammed into the flight deck of the light carrier *Cabot;* another narrowly missed her and exploded alongside. The combination of a hit and near miss left the *Cabot* with thirty-six men killed, sixteen seriously injured, and gaping holes in her deck and hull. Over in Sherman's group, two kamikazes dived on the *Essex.* She shot one down, but the other slammed into her flight deck. Though the crash killed fifteen of her crew, the ship was not severely damaged.

The *Intrepid,* rocked by internal explosions, continued to blaze, while oily black smoke, hiding everything but her bow, trailed alongside and astern and billowed thousands of feet into the air. Because of her damaged flight deck and arresting gear, she could not land her seventy-five planes then in the air, nor was there room for them in the other carriers. The pilots solved their problem by landing on the *Essex, Hancock,* and *Ticonderoga* long enough to refuel and then flying to the Tacloban airfield on Leyte.

By mid-afternoon the *Intrepid* had extinguished her fires. Throughout her ordeal she had maintained her speed and station in the formation, but sixty-nine of her men were killed or missing, thirty-five others seriously injured, and seventeen of her planes destroyed. Her extensive damages could be repaired at no base closer than Pearl Harbor. Since 29 October the suicide planes had cost the Third Fleet 328 men, some ninety planes, and the services of three carriers that would have to be sent to distant shipyards for major repairs.

Damage to Task Force 38 carriers obliged Halsey to cancel a scheduled 26 November strike on Japanese shipping. Nimitz now backed Halsey in a proposal to refrain from further casual strikes. "Only strikes in great force for valuable stakes or at vital times," Halsey argued, "would justify exposure of the fast carriers to suicidal attacks—at least until . . . defensive techniques were perfected."

Hardly had Task Force 38 withdrawn from active support of the Leyte operation when the kamikazes began inflicting serious damage on ships in the gulf. On 27 November they damaged a battleship and two cruisers; on the twenty-ninth, a battleship and two destroyers. MacArthur now lost no time following Halsey's advice about summoning the marine aviators from the Solomons. They arrived at Tacloban on 3 December flying eighty-five Corsairs and twelve navy B-25s. On the same date a squadron of marine corps night-fighting Hellcats arrived from Peleliu. MacArthur had obtained the latter through a deal with Nimitz. Concerned over the poor success of his army air force Black Widow night fighters on Leyte, he had turned them over to CinCPac in exchange for a dozen Hellcats. The marines and the army-flown Hellcats went into action without delay, whereupon the air situation over Leyte took a turn for the better.

MacArthur's next major move was an invasion of Mindoro, scheduled for 5 December. Because the army air force had by no means gained control of the air over the central Philippines, support from the fast carriers was essential. Halsey, all too aware that his sailors and aviators desperately needed a rest period to unwind, reluctantly asked MacArthur to postpone the operation. On 1 December, having received no reply, he sortied from Ulithi, en route to support the Mindoro operation. Several hours later word came from the general rescheduling the invasion for the fifteenth, news that was received by all hands with heartfelt cheers. Halsey immediately ordered the task force to reverse course and head back to the atoll.

Halsey was grateful to MacArthur for responding to his request. He did not know that Admiral Kinkaid, backed by Generals Sutherland and Kenney, had been trying since mid-November to induce MacArthur to delay the landing, and that all three had just arrived at MacArthur's headquarters to argue postponement once more. When Halsey's request arrived, followed by a strong endorsement from Nimitz, the stubborn general at last gave in.[4]

Ulithi Atoll, a meandering string of coral reefs enclosing a lagoon fifteen miles across at its widest, was broken by half a dozen channels and dotted with a score of small islands. The largest of the islands, measuring about a mile across, served as an air base with a 1,200-yard-long airstrip. The adjoining island was the seat of the advanced fleet base. Of most interest at this time to the officers and men of Task Force 38 was tiny, helmet-shaped Mogmog, northernmost of the atoll's islands. This was the atoll's recreation center. No Riviera or Waikiki, Mogmog was nevertheless joyfully embraced by men who had been too long at sea and faced death too often. The atoll commander, Halsey's friend Commodore Scrappy Kessing, who had previously dispensed hospitality as commander at Tulagi, had done what he could to provide entertainment in an unlikely setting. Mogmog boasted a swimming beach, basketball courts, horseshoe pitches, baseball diamonds, even a football field. Soft drinks were available, and enlisted men were allowed two bottles of beer a day, usually paid for by ships' welfare funds. For officers there was a bar where Scotch or bourbon was available at twenty cents a shot.[5]

During the ten-day pause at Ulithi, conversations, particularly among officers from several different ships of Task Force 38, were likely to center at times on the two fleet commanders under whom most of them had served in recent months. Spruance and Halsey each had his loyal adherents. The former had taken his staff with him when he turned over the Big Blue Fleet to Halsey, and they were known to regard their boss with admiration. Of those who had had limited contact with Spruance, some shared his staff's partiality, others regarded him as cold and austere. It seemed that affection for Spruance tended to increase in proportion to one's intimacy with him. The gregarious Halsey was generally liked, and the officers who served him most closely tended to be fiercely loyal. On the other hand, some individuals found Halsey's humor a bit on the crude side and some of his remarks uncouth, particularly those expressing his opinion of the Japanese.

Officers were more sharply divided with respect to the two admirals' command styles. Many preferred Spruance's detailed advance planning and his close adherence, so far as combat conditions permitted, to his announced program. Spruance apparently foresaw everything, and his adherents took satisfaction in watching his minutely thought-out operations run their course. Other officers preferred Halsey's imaginative improvisations. His admirers pointed out that if they, and perhaps Halsey himself, never knew what he was going to do next, his operations must completely bewilder the enemy. Spruance's partisans were likely to brand Halsey's command procedures sloppy and reckless. Admirers of Halsey called Spruance's style overcautious and inflexible and pointed out that, in their respective battles with the Japanese sea forces, Spruance had sunk only one out of nine enemy carriers, while Halsey had sunk four out of four.[6]

At Ulithi Halsey was deliberately casual. During the ten days granted him and his crews for rest and relaxation, he did not expect anyone to be much concerned with protocol. His temporary waiving of the usual military courtesies, however, raised some eyebrows among certain distinguished visitors. These comprised the Special Joint Chiefs of Staff Committee on the Reorganization of National Defense, a group of senior army and navy officers touring fleets, bases, and major army posts to sample attitudes about a proposed postwar unification of the U.S. armed forces. The senior member was retired Admiral J. O. Richardson, who in 1940 had been CinCUS. Halsey had served under him as Commander, Aircraft, Battle Force.

The committee, which had just visited General MacArthur at Leyte, was finding that for the most part the army favored unification while the navy opposed it.

From Leyte the group had flown to Ulithi to call on Commander, Third Fleet. The army officers, anxious to behave properly when they boarded Halsey's flagship, enlisted the services of the committee's junior naval officer, Rear Admiral Malcolm F. Schoeffel, to give them some instructions. Schoeffel held rehearsals in the corridor of their plane, showing the army officers how one went on board and saluted the quarterdeck and exchanged salutes with the officer of the deck. He told them that under wartime conditions there might not be gun salutes but there would be side boys and probably a marine guard.

Their plane landed at Ulithi's airstrip, and the committee embarked in a boat and headed for the *New Jersey,* riding at anchor in the lagoon. "As we approached," recalls one of the group, "we could see Halsey up there on the forward quarterdeck ahead, pacing back and forth. He could see us coming, and he leaned over the side, raised his arms, and shouted, 'Hey, Joe!' Richardson leaned out of our boat and shouted back, 'Hey, Bill!' That was all the protocol there was."*

What Halsey lacked in protocol he more than made up for in hospitality. Having the visitors on board, especially his boss of prewar days, delighted him. He had all his flag officers assembled to greet and confer with them. Messengers had been sent out to commandeer delicacies afloat and ashore, and thus Halsey was able that evening to serve a dinner to remember. "Good God!" murmured one of the army officers to another, "why didn't we join the Navy?"[7]

During Task Force 38's stay at Ulithi, Slew McCain, sometimes with members of his staff, visited the *New Jersey* several times to confer with Halsey. Skinny and wrinkled like Mitscher, whom he slightly resembled, Slew sported on his head something even more nonregulation than Mitscher's famous baseball cap. McCain's headgear consisted of a green drab fatigue cap, on which his wife had sewn an old "scrambled eggs" visor. The crown was threadbare, the visor encrusted with verdigris. Halsey found the combination revolting. McCain's cap, he said, "was the most disreputable one I ever saw on an officer." But Slew, superstitious like most sailors, would not part with his hat when in the combat zone. He never wore it elsewhere. He moved in a series of jerks, reacted to provocations with strings of muttered oaths, and smoked cigarettes that he rolled himself, rather too loosely, so that he scattered tobacco wherever he went. Once Halsey had a steward's mate follow him about with a brush and dustpan.

"What the hell's *this* for?" demanded Slew.

"So you won't dirty up my clean ship," replied Halsey, "that's what!"

During their brief holiday, Halsey, McCain, and their staffs sought a solution to the problem of kamikazes. First, however, they tried to determine why the Japanese had been expecting them and were prepared to counterattack on 25 November, the first time Task Force 38 had failed to attain tactical and strategic surprise. Strongly suspected was General MacArthur's headquarters, notorious for leaking information. Or perhaps the Japanese had been alerted by the sudden inactivity of Kenney's planes, a precaution taken to prevent U.S. Army and Navy planes from attacking each other by mistake.

The reason, when it was figured out, came as a surprise. Task Force 38 had been advancing into Philippine waters to attack at regular intervals and had

*Admiral Richardson's first name was James, but his friends generally called him by his initials, J. O., which they often shortened to Joe.

Vice Admiral McCain in conference with Admiral Halsey on board the *New Jersey* in December 1944.

launched from virtually the same ocean area each time. Moreover, similar patterns of radio traffic had preceded the attacks.

To test the radio traffic theory, Third Fleet communicators broadcast a series of dummy messages duplicating the pattern previously transmitted before strikes. Kenney's scout planes reported that Japanese merchant shipping promptly scurried to safety on the far side of the China Sea. Halsey called this test his Picnic Strike, because it was "launched" on the day he and his staff picnicked at a beach named Kessing's Last Resort, in honor of the illustrious Scrappy. Following the test, Halsey decreed that as far as possible patterns in operations and radio traffic were to be avoided. Ironically, his sharpest critic had complained, "Halsey never does things the same way twice."[8]

On 11 December Admiral Halsey again departed Ulithi with Task Force 38 to pave the way for and support MacArthur's Mindoro invasion by paralyzing Japanese air power on Luzon. At the same time General Kenney's Southwest Pacific Air Forces would try to maintain control of the air over

Mindoro and its approaches. Halsey planned to strike Luzon on 14, 15, and 16 December, refuel on the seventeenth, and strike again on 19, 20, and 21 December.

The Seventh Fleet invasion convoy, during its approach to Mindoro via Surigao Strait and the Mindanao and Sulu seas, became the target of numerous kamikazes, one of which hit the convoy flagship *Nashville,* killing 133 men, injuring 190, and obliging the cruiser to return to Leyte. Another suicide plane severely damaged a destroyer, which also had to turn back. However, with tactical cover by planes from Leyte and from escort carriers accompanying the convoy, and with strategic support from Halsey's fast carriers, the Americans invaded Mindoro on 15 December without opposition. Only after the assault troops had landed did the kamikazes succeed in making a D-day strike, which cost the expeditionary force two tank landing ships.

A remarkable fact is that every one of the aircraft that attacked Mindoro and the invasion convoy between 14 and 16 December was from the central Philippines. None of the enemy planes came from Luzon. The Third Fleet was keeping them there. This it achieved by means of the Big Blue Blanket (BBB), a tactical measure not tried before for lack of planes. The BBB was an umbrella of carrier-based fighters that flew over Luzon airfields around the clock to prevent planes from taking off. While maintaining the umbrella, the Third Fleet planes destroyed nearly two hundred enemy aircraft, most of which were on the ground.

The BBB was just one of several innovations Admiral McCain had introduced into Task Force 38 to meet the threat of the kamikazes. He had also halved the number of dive-bombers and doubled the number of fighters per carrier, and modified the Hellcat and Corsair fighters to carry 2,000 pounds of bombs each, making them dual-purpose planes. These measures actually increased the striking power of the carrier.

As a further countermeasure McCain had reduced the number of task groups from four to three, thereby concentrating his antiaircraft fire and combat air patrol. During strikes, he stationed radar picket destroyers sixty miles from the task force on the flanks of the target-bearing line to give early warning of approaching enemy planes. The pickets had their own combat air patrol, and U.S. aircraft returning from a strike were required to make a turn around a specified picket so the destroyer's air patrol could weed out any kamikazes that had joined the returning planes to locate the carriers. Aircraft approaching the task force from a direction other than that of the designated picket destroyer were assumed to be enemy and treated accordingly.[9]

On 17 December Task Force 38 withdrew eastward to refuel, but worsening weather obliged Halsey to discontinue fueling in early afternoon. He scheduled a new rendezvous with the fueling group for 0600 the following morning, 200 miles to the northwest, a location recommended by the Third

Fleet staff aerologist because a tropical disturbance 500 miles to the east and estimated to be moving north-northwest was expected soon to collide with a cold front and bounce off to the northeast.

An hour later Halsey received a weather warning from a seaplane tender at Ulithi. At 0500 that morning one of her scouts had sighted a storm center less than 200 miles southeast of the *New Jersey*'s 1400 position. Halsey wondered at the delay in reporting. Much later he learned that the scout pilot had made his report only after returning to base, and that it had been encrypted by means of the slow, tedious cipher required for weather reports rather than by the swift electric ciphering machine.

If, as estimated, the storm center was moving northwest at twelve to fifteen knots, it was now much closer to Task Force 38 than when it was sighted by the scout plane. By 0600 on the eighteenth it would probably be passing close aboard the new fueling rendezvous. Halsey set up still another rendezvous to the southwest, but because the oilers of the fueling group would be unable to cover the distance in the heavy seas, he soon had to cancel that in favor of a position closer by. Halsey's commitment to support MacArthur on Mindoro meant that he must refuel not later than the morning of the eighteenth and remain close enough to Luzon to be able to strike Luzon airfields on the nineteenth, as scheduled. The storm warnings betokened an element of risk, but this he accepted.

In fact, the risk was far greater than Halsey or anyone else suspected. What the scout plane from Ulithi had seen but not recognized was a typhoon making up. During the evening of the seventeenth Task Force 38 and the fueling group plowed steadily westward through mounting seas. At midnight, hoping to find smoother water, Halsey ordered a course change from due west to due south. He thus took his carriers and their escorts directly into the path of the oncoming typhoon.

By dawn on the eighteenth Halsey knew that fueling would be even more difficult than on the day before, but he had to attempt it, not only to carry out his commitment but for the safety of his smaller vessels, particularly the destroyers, which after three days of high-speed operations had nearly exhausted their fuel. As their tanks emptied, they rode higher in the water and became increasingly unseaworthy. To offset this effect, destroyers encountering rough weather usually filled their empty tanks with seawater. But pumping out the water could take up to six hours. Hence the destroyer skippers, with fueling pending, were reluctant to take this precaution.

At 0700 the task force began fueling, but in the prevailing conditions the task was impossible. A little after 0800 Halsey canceled the fueling directive and regretfully notified MacArthur that he would be unable to support the Mindoro operation. Shortly afterward he started receiving reports of mishaps from his smaller vessels. Men were going overboard. There was loss of steering control. On the light carriers and escort carriers with the fueling group, planes were being swept from their flight decks and, worse, aircraft were breaking loose in their hangar decks, slamming against bulkheads, and catching on fire.

After 1000 the barometer fell rapidly, the first clear evidence that there was a typhoon approaching. Shortly afterward the aerologists observed the wind moving counterclockwise and the sea making up fast. The wind velocity increased sharply to seventy-three knots, piling up mountainous waves. Describing the peak of the storm, Halsey wrote in his autobiography:

> No one who has not been through a typhoon can conceive its fury. The 70-foot seas smash you from all sides. The rain and the scud are blinding; they drive you flat-out, until you can't tell the ocean from the air. At broad noon I couldn't see the bow of my ship, 350 feet from the bridge. The *New Jersey* once was hit by a 5-inch shell without my feeling the impact; the *Missouri,* her sister, had a *kamikaze* crash on her main deck and repaired the only damage with a paintbrush; yet this typhoon tossed our enormous ship as if she were a canoe. Our chairs, tables, and all loose gear had to be double-lashed; we ourselves were buffeted from one bulkhead to another; we could not hear our own voices above the uproar.

What it was like on a destroyer one-twentieth the *New Jersey*'s size Halsey could only imagine. Later he learned that some destroyers were heeled over on their beam ends with their stacks almost horizontal, pinned in that position by the gale while seawater poured into their ventilators and intakes, shorting circuits, killing power, steering, lights, and communications, and leaving them helplessly adrift.

During the afternoon the winds abated and by dusk ships that were still operational began looking for survivors, a task that lasted three more days. Halsey called it the most exhaustive search in the navy's history. Men were picked up on rafts and in the water. From these Halsey compiled his casualty list. Three ships had capsized and sunk, all destroyers that had not ballasted their empty tanks with seawater. Of their combined complement of 831 only 74 were rescued. Other men killed or missing brought the number lost to nearly eight hundred. Seven ships were heavily damaged; 186 planes had collided, burned, been jettisoned, or been blown overboard. Task Force 38 was as badly battered as if it had fought a major battle.[10]

Because of the delay in fueling and the rescue operations, Task Force 38 could not carry out the strikes on Luzon scheduled for 19–20 December. On the twenty-first the strikes still could not be executed because the typhoon was then passing over Luzon. So the Third Fleet returned to Ulithi, where the crews were allowed some much-needed rest and a service squadron began repairing the storm-damaged ships.

Nimitz, who had been promoted to fleet admiral just ten days before, flew to Ulithi and arrived on Christmas Day. He had already appointed a court of inquiry, but he wanted to find out for himself why the carrier force had been caught by the typhoon. As he was piped aboard, a five-star flag was broken at the main. He had thoughtfully brought along a decorated Christmas tree for the *New Jersey*'s wardroom and was a little piqued to notice that the ship's officers were much prouder of a tree the crew had fashioned out of nuts, bolts, and metal scraps.

While Task Force 38's disaster was being investigated by the court of inquiry, Nimitz flew to Leyte, where organized Japanese resistance had just ended. At MacArthur's Tacloban headquarters he conferred with the general concerning Task Force 38 support for the forthcoming invasion of Luzon. On 28 December Nimitz, en route to Pearl Harbor, stopped again at Ulithi to pass on to Halsey the agreements he had reached with MacArthur.

Halsey requested permission to take Task Force 38 into the South China Sea to attack the Japanese carrier-battleships *Ise* and *Hyuga,* refugees from the Battle for Leyte Gulf, which had been sighted in this area and posed a threat to any supply line to the Luzon beachhead in Lingayen Gulf. Nimitz consented but stipulated that Halsey was not to make his foray west of the Philippines until his fast carriers had finished supporting the Lingayen landings.

Halsey brought to Nimitz's attention the misleading padding at the end of the message CinCPac had sent to him during the Battle for Leyte Gulf. Nimitz, shocked, promised to find out who was at fault and take appropriate action. Halsey wrote in his autobiography, "Chester blew up when I told him about it; he tracked down the little squirt and chewed him to bits." The facts are somewhat different. On his return to Pearl Harbor, Nimitz had the matter looked into. When he learned that the author of the offending padding was an ensign, he said to his head communicator, "If that ensign can't keep his thoughts out of operational dispatches, you'd better transfer him to a less sensitive spot." The ensign was transferred.

The court of inquiry, presided over by Vice Admiral John Hoover, put most of the blame on Admiral Halsey. Nimitz, in his endorsement for the court of inquiry's record, moderated the verdict by stating his opinion that Halsey's mistakes "were errors of judgment committed under stress of war operations and stemming from a commendable desire to meet military requirements." King softened this by adding after the word "judgment" the phrase "resulting from insufficient information" and changing "commendable desire" to "firm determination."

Though the modified endorsement practically nullified the court's verdict, Halsey never deigned to mention the court, its verdict, or the endorsement. He makes no reference to it in his otherwise generally candid autobiography. Nimitz, after reviewing the testimony of witnesses before the court and pondering what he had learned in discussions at Ulithi, wrote a fleet letter of advice for dealing with severe storms. A major theme of the letter was summed up in the concluding sentences: "The time for taking all measures for a ship's safety is while still able to do so. Nothing is more dangerous than for a seaman to be grudging in taking precautions lest they turn out to have been unnecessary. Safety at sea for a thousand years has depended on exactly the opposite philosophy."[11]

During the Third Fleet's stay at Ulithi, communicators were careful to keep radio traffic at a routine level, since any sudden increase might alert the Japanese to an impending naval operation. All important radio messages from the fleet were flown by special plane to Guam and transmitted from there.[12]

On 30 December the Third Fleet, still stripped down to Task Force 38, left Ulithi to pave the way for and support the Seventh Fleet landings at Lingayan Gulf, scheduled for 9 January. Halsey and McCain planned to alternate strikes on Luzon with attacks on Formosa and the Ryukyus, the latter to block the flow of aircraft from Japan to the Philippines. They opened the campaign on 3 January with raids on Formosa and Okinawa. The weather was so foul that it was impossible to blanket the airfields, and few Japanese planes took off to resist the attackers. That afternoon and the next, visibility was so poor that all strikes and searches had to be recalled. Nevertheless, the Americans destroyed about a hundred enemy planes on the ground at a cost of only twenty-two of their own.

After fueling on 5 January Task Force 38 attacked airfields in northern Luzon, while the army air force struck at those in southern Luzon and the central Philippines. Again foul weather did not permit effective blanketing. The Third Fleet carriers lost seventeen of their aircraft that day and destroyed thirty-two of the enemy's.

Because of continuing bad weather, neither the Third Fleet, nor the army air force, nor accompanying escort carriers could provide adequate support for Vice Admiral Oldendorf's bombardment group spearheading the Seventh Fleet invasion force that was heading for Lingayan Gulf via the Mindanao, Sulu, and South China seas. On 4 January, after a bomber dived into the deck of one of the escort carriers and set off raging fires and explosions, she had to be abandoned and sunk. On the fifth suicide planes crashed into five of Oldendorf's vessels and damaged four others with near misses. On the sixth, when the bombardment group entered the gulf, the kamikazes sank one of the American ships and damaged eleven others, killing hundreds of men, including a rear admiral and a lieutenant general.

On 7 January the skies cleared, enabling Task Force 38 at last to spread its BBB effectively over Luzon airfields. Halsey, hoping to take full advantage of the change in weather, sent his pilots a personal message insisting on "extra effort in support of our comrades of the Southwest Pacific in their Luzon

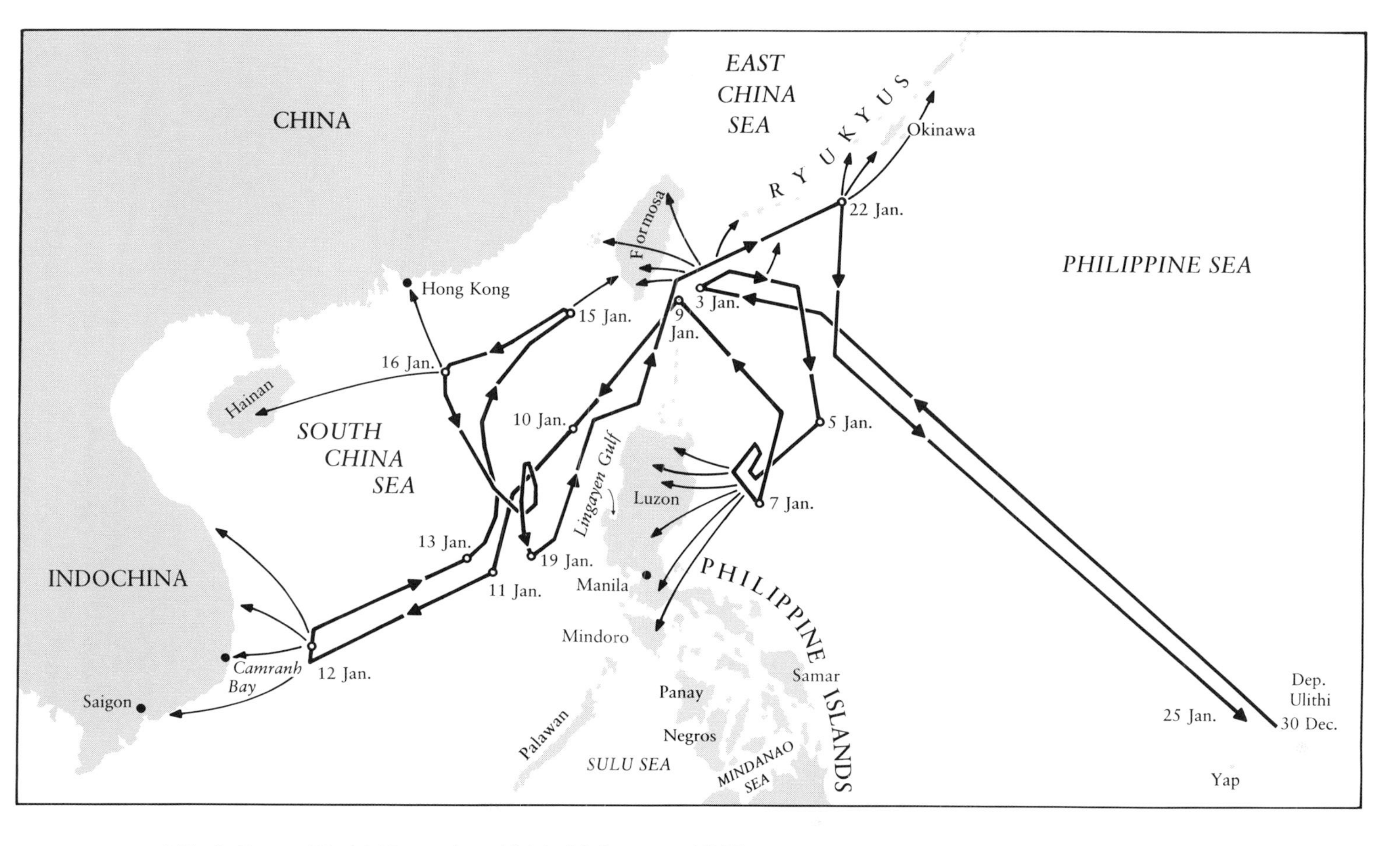

Movements of Task Force 38, 30 December 1944–25 January 1945

attack." Only a few enemy planes appeared over Lingayan Gulf that day, and most of these were shot down. Thereafter the Japanese made only sporadic air attacks against the American invaders.

Task Force 38 fueled again on the eighth and on the ninth attacked Formosa and the Ryukyus once more in support of the concurrent landings on Luzon. The weather again closed in, but it made little difference. The Japanese had decided to send no additional aircraft to the Philippines.

That night Halsey boldly led the Third Fleet through Luzon Strait, north of Luzon, into the South China Sea. His basic mission, as stated, was to

Halsey with staff members, on a barge, en route to inspect kamikaze damage inflicted on the carrier *Ticonderoga*, 21 January 1945

safeguard the Mindoro-Lingayan supply line, and the surest way to do that was to destroy enemy combatant ships that might attack it. At that time American naval intelligence concluded that about half the Combined Fleet was in the South China Sea with the *Ise* and *Hyuga,* probably based in Camranh Bay. Nimitz had given Commander, Third Fleet, the green light to attack "if major Japanese fleet units were sighted." Thus Halsey hoped at last to command a battle between fleets at sea, an experience that had eluded him throughout the war.

On 12 January 1944 Halsey stood off Camranh Bay with the Third Fleet, excitedly anticipating action. McCain's carrier aircraft flew nearly fifteen hundred sorties over the Indochina coast without finding any signs of the enemy fleet, which had prudently departed for the Singapore area some time before. But the carrier planes still found plenty of targets to attack. They raided the coast of Indochina, southern Formosa, and the Hong Kong area, sinking forty-four ships and destroying large numbers of enemy aircraft. As the task force slipped out through Luzon Strait on the twenty-first, its planes again struck Formosa. This time kamikazes struck back, damaging two carriers and a destroyer.

On 25 January Task Force 38 steamed back into Ulithi Lagoon, having completed its mission of supporting MacArthur's Southwest Pacific Forces in their invasion of the Philippine Islands. Admiral Spruance and his staff were waiting to resume their command of the Big Blue Fleet, which would again be called the Fifth Fleet.

Always appreciative, Halsey never left a command or ended a campaign without words of thanks or commendation for his subordinates. Few of his officers or men forgot the substance of his farewell message when he took his leave of them at Ulithi: "I am so proud of you that no words can express my feelings. This has been a hard operation. At times you have been driven almost beyond endurance but only because the stakes were high, the enemy was as weary as you were, and the lives of many Americans could be spared in later offensives if we did our work well now. We have driven the enemy off the sea and back to his inner defenses. Superlatively well done!"[13]

CHAPTER 20

OKINAWA

ON THE MORNING of 27 January 1945, as Admiral Halsey was about to leave the *New Jersey* for a flight to Pearl Harbor, he was handed a dispatch from General MacArthur: "Your departure from this theater leaves a gap that can be fouled only by your return." At first startled, the admiral then assumed that "fouled" was a garble; the general had in fact written "filled."

At Pearl Halsey and his staff spent a couple of weeks completing reports and winding up other Third Fleet business. One afternoon the admiral took off from these chores and hosted a party for friends, using a residence the navy had rented for the convenience of senior officers between tours of sea duty. Helping serve was Filipino Chief Steward Benedicto Tulao, who had long been in Halsey's service. Halsey and Carney were sipping old-fashioneds when the radio announced that U.S. Army troops had entered Manila. Halsey at once called Tulao and, giving him a great bear hug, told him the good news. When the young man's eyes filled up, Carney said, "Tulao, bring me an old-fashioned, please."

Tulao prepared the cocktail and brought it. "Now," said Carney, "I want you to join us in a toast to your wonderful people."

Tulao turned his eyes appealingly to Halsey, then said to Carney, "The admiral knows I don't drink, sir."

"This time you do," replied Carney. "It's an order."

Everyone in the room, including Tulao, drank to the health of the Philippine nation.

Nearly all the Third Fleet staff had leave coming, and most of them took it stateside. Halsey and Carney, after visits with their families, accepted an invitation to hunt quail and wild turkey on John Hay Whitney's 4,000-acre estate near Titusville, Georgia. Halsey, in boots and flannel shirt, looked the part of a veteran hunter, but he shot only a few birds. "I'm learning this kind of hunting for the first time," he explained. From long experience however, Carney had become an excellent wing shot. "On the rare occasions when he missed," Halsey recalled, "he always had an unimpeachable ballistic explanation of why the shot had been impossible in the first place."

Halsey returned to Wilmington to be with his family, but, always restless, he took several trips to inspect schools and installations where replacement personnel were being trained for the fleet. He spent March in Washington on temporary duty. Summoned to the White House, he sent for Fan, who would pin on him the Gold Star that President Roosevelt was awarding him in lieu of a third Distinguished Service Medal. The accompanying citation concluded, "Under his forceful and inspiring leadership, the recovery of the Philippines was painstakingly prepared for, covered and effectively supported during operations which evidenced his daring tactics and the devotion to duty of his gallant command."

After the ceremony and lunch, the president took Bill to his upstairs office for an hour's conversation, mostly about prospects for the war. It was the last meeting of the two old friends. Roosevelt had a little over a month left to live.

At the president's request, Halsey temporarily detached Harold Stassen and sent him to San Francisco to take part in drafting and signing the United Nations Charter. Some high officials expressed fear that the Japanese might stage a carrier raid against San Francisco while the UN was in session there. Halsey and King knew that the Japanese had hardly any carrier air groups left and no carriers to put them on, but something had to be done, and King had Nimitz appoint Halsey Commander, Mid-Pacific Striking Force, "charged with interception and destruction of enemy raiding forces." The force, comprising two big carriers and all surface units available in the Hawaiian and U.S. West Coast ports, never even assembled. The army placed some antiaircraft guns around San Francisco, and that was as far as the defense project got.

While Halsey was on duty in Washington, the public relations section of the Navy Department induced him to be interviewed by newsmen. One of the questions they asked him was, "Is the mikado's palace a military objective?"

"No," Halsey replied. "If by chance the B-29s or somebody came over there in an undercast, they might hit it by mistake, but it would have been a mistake." Never one to let well enough alone, he added, "I'd hate to have them kill Hirohito's white horse, because I want to ride it."

The public relations people considered Halsey's quip unfortunate. Specialists on Japan were aware of the deep reverence the Japanese people had for their emperor. A time might come, as indeed it did, when he, and only he, could make the bellicose Japanese stop fighting. Perhaps the quip would go unnoticed.

Quite to the contrary. The comment made headlines, and soon, said Halsey, "I found myself connected with it [the White Horse] as inseparably as if I were a centaur." The Reno chamber of commerce sent him a fine saddle. The Lions Club of Montrose, California, sent him another, together with a bridle, blanket, and lariat, and offered to ship him a mustang should he be denied a ramble on the imperial steed. The Military Order of the World Wars sent him a toy horse, and a Texas sheriff sent him a pair of spurs. The equestrian gifts followed him to sea, until his cabin began to look like a tack

Admiral Halsey presents the Legion of Merit to Commander Harold E. Stassen, USNR.

room—strange surroundings for a man not known to have been near a horse since his wild ride in 1914 at Veracruz.

On 7 April Halsey and most of his staff returned to Pearl Harbor to plan further operations for the Third Fleet, which as the Fifth Fleet under Spruance had captured Iwo Jima and assaulted Okinawa.

The Joint Chiefs had anticipated no serious difficulty in capturing Iwo Jima, a triangular heap of lava and ashes in the Japanese Volcano Islands. They estimated that the three marine divisions assigned to the operation could take it in five days or less. Nevertheless, bombers from the Marianas pounded Iwo for seventy-four consecutive days, and U.S. gunnery ships gave it three days of heavy bombardment. Task Force 58, with Spruance and Mitscher on board, blasted airfields around Tokyo, destroying hundreds of aircraft that might have been used against the American forces at Iwo.

Iwo Jima was no pushover. The preceding year, when the Americans captured Saipan, the Japanese had promptly identified Iwo as a future U.S.

target, because of its location halfway between Japan and the Southern Marianas and its relatively flat surface, suitable for airfields. Onto this small island they poured more than twenty-three thousand defenders, who set up hundreds of pillboxes and blockhouses and gouged out gun positions and interconnected tunnels in the lava until they had made Iwo into the most formidably defended eight square miles in the Pacific. Instead of the estimated five days, the American conquest required nearly a month of vicious fighting and mutual slaughter. All the Japanese garrison except 216 prisoners of war were at length killed or sealed up in caves. Casualties among the assault forces exceeded losses among the defenders: nineteen thousand Americans were wounded and nearly seven thousand were killed or died of wounds.

The conquest of Iwo Jima proved worth the cost. The island was used mainly as a haven for planes damaged or short of fuel, and by the end of the war, some twenty-four hundred B-29s, with crews numbering about twenty-seven thousand, made emergency landings there. However, the low-level precision bombing, rendered practical when fighters based on Iwo accompanied the big bombers, produced meager results. Far more effective were incendiary night bombings of Japanese cities by unaccompanied B-29s. The first of the fire raids, against Tokyo on the night of 9–10 March 1945, destroyed 250,000 houses and burned 83,793 persons to death, more destruction than either of the atomic bombs inflicted.

The next target for American invasion was sixty-mile-long Okinawa, suitable for airfields that could tighten the blockade of Japan and intensify the bombing of its cities. The island could also be used as a base for staging an invasion of Kyushu, southernmost of the Japanese home islands. Under Admiral Spruance, Commander, Fifth Fleet, Admiral Mitscher commanded the carrier force; Admiral Turner, the amphibious force; and army Lieutenant General Simon Bolivar Buckner, the Tenth Army, which comprised three marine corps divisions and four army divisions, with a fifth army division in reserve—a total of 183,000 combatant and 115,000 service troops to oppose the 77,000 defenders. On 1 April 1945 the Tenth Army began going ashore on west coast beaches.

Off to the east steamed Task Force 58, providing air cover to the American troops and their incoming supplies. Performing a similar function to the southwest, between Okinawa and Formosa, was a British fleet of four carriers, two battleships, five cruisers, and fifteen destroyers. Commanded by Vice Admiral Sir Bernard Rawlings and serving in the U.S. Fifth Fleet, it was designated Task Force 57.

Japanese bombers and suicide planes lost no time attacking the American ships off Okinawa, at first as single aircraft and then in a series of mass raids. The fleet flagship *Indianapolis* was so badly damaged by one kamikaze that Spruance sent her to Mare Island for major repairs and shifted his flag to the battleship *New Mexico.* To participate in the suicide operations, the superbattleship *Yamato,* a cruiser, and eight destroyers sortied from Japan's Inland Sea for a one-way passage to Okinawa, planning to sink as many American ships as possible before being destroyed. But Task Force 58 planes pounced on the Japanese attack force southwest of Kyushu, quickly sending down the *Yamato,* the cruiser, and a destroyer and mauling three other destroyers, which the surviving vessels sank before returning to base.

While the Okinawa campaign was in progress, the United States was planning future invasions. These included the assault against Kyushu, scheduled for 1 November 1945, to be followed by an invasion of the main Japanese home island of Honshu, set for 1 March 1946. An alternative plan called for a series of operations, including two landings on the coast of China, intended to further isolate and weaken Japan before the home islands were invaded.

The first task given Halsey and his staff was to prepare for this alternative plan of gradual encirclement and strangulation. They carried out their assignment, but with little enthusiasm. The admiral believed that such time-consuming peripheral operations would not make invasion of the home islands any less costly and that they would prolong the agony for war-weary Americans.

Toward the end of April Halsey made a brief trip to Guam, where Nimitz had established advanced headquarters nearer the scene of action. Halsey's team was supposed to relieve Spruance's at the conclusion of the Okinawa operation. Nimitz now informed him that he would have to take over from Spruance in about thirty days, whether or not Okinawa had been conquered. CinCPac estimated that under the constant threat of mass kamikaze attacks, the senior commanders, who never left the scene of action, would then have reached the limit of their endurance.

Halsey, anxious to get back into action, was delighted. He was less pleased to learn that he could not have back his old flagship *New Jersey.* She was being overhauled, so Halsey would hoist his flag in her sister ship, the *Missouri.* Since Nimitz expected Halsey to employ the Third Fleet as a raiding force, as he had in the Philippine campaign, the ground and amphibious forces would again be detached from his command.

After a quick trip to Okinawa to confer with Spruance, Halsey returned to Pearl Harbor. He was there when Germany surrendered. His reaction to that event was not so much jubilation as eagerness—to get the men and supplies released from the European theater and step up the drive to defeat Japan.

News from Okinawa, meanwhile, was increasingly grim. In mid-April the main body of the invading U.S. Tenth Army, driving south against growing opposition, had reached the enemy's chief defense citadel, a warren of hills, caves, and pillboxes like a king-sized Iwo Jima but dug into solid rock rather than soft lava. For six weeks the Americans, receiving and inflicting heavy casualties, had scarcely moved forward.

The campaign was proving the most costly in the U.S. Navy's history. By mid-May in Okinawan waters enemy aircraft had damaged 133 ships and sunk 26, killing nearly two thousand sailors. The ships most often hit, because they were usually the first sighted by oncoming suicide planes, were destroyers stationed at sea to give early warning. But two battleships and six fleet carriers were among the vessels seriously damaged. Admiral Mitscher had lost a large part of his staff, some killed, some severely injured, and had been obliged to change flagships twice in four days as crashing kamikazes put the carriers *Bunker Hill* and *Enterprise* successively out of action.

At Guam on 18 May Admiral Halsey hoisted his flag in the *Missouri.* To Captain Stuart S. ("Sunshine") Murray, her captain, he said as he came on board, "This is a significant day. I served in the *Missouri* forty years ago, and here I am back again."[1]

Halsey was due to arrive at Okinawa on 25 May, but because another mass kamikaze attack against ships in the area was expected that day, Spruance recommended that his arrival be delayed. So Nimitz ordered the *Missouri,* then en route, to take temporary refuge with Rear Admiral Donald B. Beary's logistic support group, Service Squadron 6.

Under a combat air patrol provided by accompanying escort carriers, Service Squadron 6 operated within a rectangular ocean area 600 to 700 miles southeast of Okinawa, prepared to replenish ships of the Big Blue Fleet with fuel, ammunition, and provisions. Halsey welcomed the opportunity to observe this huge floating supply base and to meet its commander, with whom he would have many dealings in the next few months. On 24 May Beary and members of his staff came on board the *Missouri* to explain the services his squadron was equipped to render. The next day the *Missouri* set out for her destination, arriving at her anchorage off the west coast of Okinawa a little after dawn on the twenty-sixth.

With his chief of staff and flag lieutenant, Admiral Spruance paid an early courtesy visit to the *Missouri,* and later that morning Halsey and part of his staff boarded the *New Mexico* for a conference. Spruance, who had just survived four months of some of the toughest fighting of the war, including seven weeks of massive kamikaze raids, looked remarkably fit and composed, but some of his officers appeared on the verge of exhaustion. Spruance would much have preferred to remain with the Okinawa operation until the island was secured, but for the sake of his haggard officers he was prepared to leave without protest.

At the conference it was agreed that Halsey would relieve Spruance at midnight on 27 May and that McCain would relieve Mitscher the next day.

Admiral Halsey and Admiral Spruance on board the *New Mexico*, 27 May 1945

Vice Admiral Harry Hill had already relieved Kelly Turner in command of the amphibious force.

Halsey now learned firsthand something of the terrible cost to the navy of the Okinawa campaign—sailors killed by the hundreds and wounded by the thousands, scores of ships sunk or put out of action. Many of the wounded were hideously burned by the gasoline fires that usually accompanied kamikaze strikes. Most of the sunk and damaged ships were victims of the Japanese suicide planes. The radar picket ships continued to suffer the heaviest losses.

Halsey wondered why it was necessary to expose seaborne pickets to such slaughter. Why hadn't the army relieved them by establishing radar early-warning stations on the shores? The army was establishing such stations, he was told, but not fast enough, despite written complaints from Spruance.

It will be recalled that Halsey had little patience with the strategy of using carriers to support troops on shore. Why hadn't the carrier task force simply blanketed the airfields on Kyushu as it had blanketed those on Luzon? He was informed that carrier task groups had approached Kyushu four times and sent in planes to bomb the airfields, but because they were numerous, widely scattered, and well protected by antiaircraft batteries, it had proved impossible to blanket them.

The British carrier force, Task Force 57, had done a commendable job of attacking airfields in the southwestern Ryukyus and, for a while, on Formosa. But this task force had recently withdrawn to Sydney for upkeep. A U.S. escort carrier group had taken its place to destroy planes in the lower Ryukyus, and the southwest Pacific air force based in the Philippines had assumed the task of neutralizing Formosa.

When Halsey, always suspicious of southwest Pacific air, asked how well it was carrying out the assignment, Spruance replied bitterly, "They've destroyed a great many sugar mills, railroad trains, and other equipment."

Halsey exploded. "Sugar mills can't damage our fleet!" he thundered. "Why the hell don't they destroy their *planes?*"

For lack of airfields, U.S. ground forces on Okinawa could not deploy enough aircraft to protect themselves, and the stubborn Japanese defense prevented them from capturing enough level ground to build more airfields. Until this impasse was solved, the carrier force had to stand by and do the protecting. Admiral Nimitz, increasingly aware of the problem, had prodded General Buckner. During a visit to Okinawa at the end of April, he told the general, "I'm losing a ship and a half a day. So if this line isn't moving within five days, we'll get someone here to move it so we can all get out from under these stupid air attacks." Shortly after that the press launched such a bitter attack on Buckner's tactics that, to head off a potential interservice wrangle, Secretary of the Navy Forrestal and Admirals Turner, Mitscher, and Nimitz issued statements supporting the general, after which he was unassailable. Relieving an officer thus praised could prove awkward.

On the afternoon of the twenty-sixth, Halsey went ashore to confer with Buckner. One of the matters the admiral took up was the business of the army building more early-warning radar stations. This was the first time Buckner had been informed that the delay was causing the navy losses and that Spruance had complained. He promised to correct the situation immediately. "I will always maintain," said Halsey, recalling this incident, "that if you want something done quickly, a five-minute conversation is infinitely better than a five-thousand-word report in triplicate."

At noon on the twenty-seventh the *Missouri* left her anchorage at Okinawa and went to join the carrier force. As she steamed down Okinawa's west coast, Halsey ordered her gunners to fire a few salvos at Japanese positions. "I just wanted to leave my calling card," he said. At midnight, while soundly asleep, he again became commander of the Big Blue Fleet, which resumed its former title of Third Fleet.

The next morning, as Spruance headed for Guam in the *New Mexico*, the *Missouri* joined the big carriers. Mitscher came on board for a conference, at the end of which Halsey detached him and directed McCain to take command of the carrier force, again designated Task Force 38. Because Nimitz was taking Hill's amphibious force and Buckner's Tenth Army under his direct control, Third Fleet and Task Force 38 were identical once more.

Halsey was shocked at Pete Mitscher's appearance. Always thin, he now looked like a walking skeleton. He weighed less than a hundred pounds and was too weak to mount a ship's ladder without assistance. Pete returned to the carrier that had been his flagship, and as he was departing, Halsey sent him a farewell dispatch expressing the sentiment of the whole Third Fleet: "It is with the very deepest regret that we watch a great fighting man shove off. I and my staff and the fleet send all luck to you and your magnificent staff."

Halsey, recalling how MacArthur had solved the problem of too few airfields on Leyte by bringing forward a highly effective marine air group based on the Solomons, recommended that a similar group currently based on the Philippines be brought forward to Okinawa. Pending its arrival, the carrier task force continued to support operations ashore.[2]

Task Force 38 was now operating in three groups: 38.1, commanded by Rear Admiral J. J. Clark; 38.3, by Rear Admiral F. C. Sherman; and 38.4, by Rear Admiral A. W. Radford. In accordance with an established rotation plan, Halsey sent Sherman's group to Leyte for a rest period. On 2 June he ordered Radford northward to strike Kyushu airfields. Halsey and McCain remained with Clark's group in a supporting position off Okinawa, but no enemy aircraft penetrated the heavy rainstorms that brought ground operations on the island to a virtual standstill. On Radford's return in the afternoon of 3 June, Halsey sent Task Group 38.1 some 140 miles to the southeast to rendezvous with a fueling group from Admiral Beary's Service Squadron 6.

Meanwhile, ships and search planes were reporting a tropical storm, possibly a typhoon, boiling up from the south. The Third Fleet flag aerologist, after studying the reports and consulting his charts, concluded that Okinawa was not in the path of the storm and advised Halsey to stay where he was.

"You are probably right," said the admiral, "but I can't take a chance. If I should be forced to go westward, I would be in shallow waters with no room to maneuver in and be in range of Japanese aircraft from China. If possible, I should like to be south of the typhoon."

The weather man studied his charts again, and on his advice Halsey in the

Missouri and McCain in his flagship *Shangri-La* headed southeast with Radford's Task Group 38.4. Halsey ordered the amphibious command ship *Ancon,* en route from Okinawa to Subic Bay and presumably close to the center of the storm, to change course from south to east-southeast and report weather conditions.

In the evening of 4 June Radford's Task Group 38.4 joined Clark's group and Beary's fueling group, and all three headed east-southeast on a 110° course. At about the same time the *Ancon* reported having sighted the storm on her radar, and it was indeed a typhoon. Unfortunately the *Ancon*'s report did not reach Halsey until 0100 the next morning, 5 June. It had been encrypted in the laborious weather code and thus had had to wait before the decoders tackled it. Had Halsey received the report promptly, he could have ordered the *Ancon* to track the typhoon, reporting its course and speed. But the *Ancon*'s captain, finding that he was within fifty miles of a typhoon, had prudently reversed course to put as much distance as possible between his ship and the storm.

Halsey at once called a conference of aerological team and staff. The *Ancon*'s report located the typhoon farther south than the original reports had placed it. Halsey would not have had time to get south of it after all. A comparison of reports indicated that the typhoon was heading rapidly northeast, almost directly toward the Third Fleet. In the hours since the *Ancon*'s report it should have traveled almost to the Third Fleet's doorstep. The problem now was how to get out of its way. Halsey asked his weatherman if their present course, 110°, would achieve that end. The aerologist thought not, and on his advice Halsey at 0134 ordered a change of course to 300°, almost a complete reversal from southeast to northwest. This unexpected turnabout surprised some members of his staff and dismayed Clark and Beary. Halsey then surrendered the tactical command to McCain. Carney, who seems to have had doubts about the wisdom of the course change, observed prophetically, "Some day we are going to maneuver blindly right into a typhoon."

Halsey explained his change of course as a move to get his fleet into the so-called safe semicircle of the approaching typhoon. Within range of a typhoon there is no truly safe area, but in one semicircle of the whirling, circular storm the winds and gusts are more moderate than in the other. For a typhoon on a northerly course in the northern hemisphere that moderate area is in the west semicircle. Halsey believed that he was now moving at right angles to the extended track of the oncoming typhoon, and that he could cross in front and ahead of it and be in the safer semicircle when it arrived.

It is possible also that Halsey had his military responsibility in mind. In the December typhoon he had headed west, towards Luzon, so as to be able to support General MacArthur's operation. Now by heading west he would be in a position, when the storm abated, to support General Buckner's operation on Okinawa.

When the barometer began to fall and the weather worsened, Beary signaled McCain, "Believe this course is running us back into the storm." Thus prompted, McCain at 0314 changed course to due north. The three groups were now strung out in column, Radford's, including Halsey's and McCain's flagships, leading, with Clark's group fifteen miles to the south and Beary's fueling group eighteen miles south of Clark's.

After about twenty minutes on course north, Beary signaled McCain, "My CVEs riding very heavily on this course, am coming to previous course." Course 300°, which Beary now resumed, took his group right into the center of the typhoon, as he had predicted it would.

Meanwhile, Clark and his Task Group 38.1 staff had sighted the typhoon on radar and, plotting its motion, realized that its north-northeast course would intersect with the task group's course 000°. At 0401 Clark signaled McCain, "My radar shows center storm bearing 245 moving 030," but received no reply. At 0420 Clark signaled, "I can get clear of the center of the storm quickly by steering 120°. Please advise."

McCain replied, "We have nothing on our scope to indicate storm center."

"We very definitely have," Clark signaled back. "We have had one for one and a half hours."

McCain asked Halsey's advice, and the latter replied, "Posit," which meant maintain relative position with respect to the guide. Halsey didn't want his fleet scattered. If and when they emerged and found weather fit for air operations, he wanted to be able to put up a concentrated combat air patrol to fend off kamikaze attacks.

At 0435 McCain asked Clark the current position and bearing of the eye and was told that it now bore 240° thirty miles away. At 0440 McCain signaled, "We intend holding present course [000°]. Use your own judgment." Had McCain released Clark when he first made the request, course 120° would have carried Task Group 38.1 clear, but he had spent twenty minutes consulting Halsey and his own aerologist, and now it was too late. So small and tight was the typhoon that Clark found his group being sucked into whirling winds and towering waves, while Radford's Task Group 38.4, just fifteen miles to the north, was moving through comparatively calm seas. Presently Radford's group passed in front of the oncoming typhoon and into the safe semicircle, while Clark's group, caught in the typhoon's coils, was desperately trying to find a course it could hold. At last Clark ordered his ships to stop their engines and heave to.

Meanwhile, Beary's fueling group was passing through the eye of the typhoon, after experiencing waves seventy-five feet high and gusts of wind up to 127 knots. When at length it emerged from the storm Beary found that his group had not been battered as severely as he had feared. Of his forty-eight ships, only four—two escort carriers, a tanker, and a destroyer escort—were seriously crippled.

Clark's task group passed through the eye an hour and a half after Beary's. Nearly all of his thirty-three ships suffered some damage, but none were sunk. Most severely battered was the cruiser *Pittsburgh,* which had 104 feet of her bow section wrenched off—fortunately after the men had withdrawn from the forward berth compartments and the watertight bulkheads behind the rupture had been shored up with heavy timbers. The frame of another cruiser was twisted, and the bow of a third had been buckled upward by the mountainous seas. All four of Clark's carriers were damaged. The forward flight decks of the *Hornet* and *Bennington* had collapsed. The *San Jacinto*'s hull was buckled, and the starboard forward catwalk of the *Belleau Wood* had been carried away. The *Pittsburgh*'s bow section remained afloat and drifted out of sight but was finally rounded up by a fleet tug, which reported, "Have sighted the suburb of *Pittsburgh* and taken it in tow."

In Clark's task group and Beary's fueling group together, six men were killed or swept overboard and four were seriously injured. Their aircraft losses amounted to seventy-six—some planes were swept overboard, others were jettisoned or damaged beyond repair.[3]

Before he received a report of these damages and losses, Halsey thought that "it possibly was not a typhoon after all." After being apprised of the facts, he knew that he was in for another court of inquiry and decided to take the offensive in advance. He fired off an angry message to Admiral Nimitz in Guam, reporting that the early-warning messages had been garbled, that their estimates of storm conditions had been at variance, and that coding regulations had critically delayed the *Ancon*'s message. He strongly recommended the establishment of regular weather reconnaissance squadrons and advocated a change in regulations to permit vital typhoon warnings to be sent as urgent messages in plain English.

On 6 June Clark's and Radford's task groups were once more off Okinawa providing combat air patrol and direct support. On the eighth Radford's Group 38.4 again attacked airfields in southern Kyushu. It was becoming apparent, however, that the presence of the Third Fleet in Okinawan waters was no longer vital. The American offensive on shore was now well under way. The marine air group from the Philippines had arrived. Additional airfields were under construction, and additional radar stations were being installed on Okinawa and adjacent islands. Recent kamikaze raids had employed fewer than a hundred planes. Obviously the Japanese had written off Okinawa and were hoarding planes and suicide pilots for use against an anticipated American attempt to invade Japan.

By 10 June the decline in kamikaze attacks, coupled with the buildup of air power on Okinawa and the successes of the B-29s operating against Kyushu out of China and the Marianas, at last permitted Task Force 38 to be released from Okinawan waters. The fast carrier force arrived at Leyte Gulf on the thirteenth after ninety-two days at sea.

Hardly had Task Groups 38.1 and 38.4 and Service Squadron 6 dropped anchor in the gulf when Admirals Halsey, McCain, Clark, and Beary were handed orders to appear before a court of inquiry scheduled to convene on 15 June on board the *New Mexico*, in nearby San Pedro Bay. Again presiding was Vice Admiral John H. Hoover, whose harshness of temperament had earned him the ironic nickname Genial John.

The court, after sitting for eight days, reported its opinion that the main cause of the damage to the Third Fleet was Halsey's change of course from 110° to 300° at 0134 on 5 June, and a secondary cause was McCain's twenty-minute delay in granting Clark permission to change from course 000° to 120°. According to the court, serious consideration should be given to assigning Halsey and McCain to other duties. The opinion would have to travel up the chain of command to the secretary of the navy, collecting endorsements en route, before it could be acted on or its contents revealed to the admirals under scrutiny.

When the opinion reached the Navy Department, Secretary Forrestal was ready to retire Halsey. Fleet Admiral King, for his part, agreed with the court that Halsey and McCain had botched their operation, that with the weather information available to them they should have avoided the typhoon. On the other hand there were good reasons, in his opinion, why Halsey should not be relieved. In view of his earlier contributions to victory, it would be harsh treatment. He was a popular hero. His relief would depress American morale, boost the enemy's, and dim the luster of the navy's hour of victory. Forrestal saw the point and, like King, decided to let Halsey alone.

McCain, however, was vulnerable. Nimitz had long doubted his competence, but Halsey had supported him, and King, who had assigned him to the task force command, had protected him. McCain's blunder now forfeited King's protection. He had to go.

One of Halsey's first acts on arriving at Leyte Gulf was to give all the fleet's Filipino stewards whose homes had been freed leave to visit their families. Once the court was adjourned, he gave himself a vacation and flew to Manila, his first visit since 1908 with the Great White Fleet. He took with him Chief Steward Tulao and his brother Maximiliano for seven days' leave in the city. Halsey's pilot toured Manila Bay, which the admiral was gratified to see littered with wrecked enemy ships. The next morning Commodore William A. Sullivan, who was restoring the port facilities, conducted him on a surface tour. Sullivan informed Halsey that close to six hundred Japanese craft of all sizes had been sunk in the bay, a good many of them between September and January, when Third Fleet aircraft were operating in the area.

Halsey had lunch with General MacArthur. It was their first meeting in almost exactly a year. Both were in high spirits. The Philippine campaign was nearly over, and a final victory over Japan appeared in the offing. The general and Mrs. MacArthur had been delighted to find that their house in Manila, instead of being demolished as they had feared, was only slightly damaged—no doubt because the Japanese ambassador to the Philippines had used it as his residence during the occupation.

The battle for Okinawa was winding down. On 21 June the island was declared secured. The next day the Japanese general and his chief of staff acknowledged defeat by ceremoniously committing suicide. Mopping-up operations continued until the end of the month. By then practically all the defending forces except eleven thousand prisoners of war had been killed. The American dead numbered almost thirteen thousand, including thirty-four hundred marines and forty-nine hundred sailors. By air attack alone fifteen U.S. vessels had been sunk and more than two hundred had been damaged, some beyond repair.

These sacrifices had brought the Americans to the brink of victory. Japanese leaders, shocked by the loss of Okinawa, their last outpost, were almost convinced that Japan must soon surrender. U.S. air and sea forces reinforced that growing conviction. Bombers from Okinawa and the Marianas were beginning to appear over Japan in waves of five hundred, burning out vast areas in its major cities. Submarines and mine-bearing planes were drawing the blockade of the home islands ever tighter.[4]

CHAPTER 21

VICTORY

ON 1 JULY 1945 the U.S. Third Fleet sortied from Leyte Gulf to join in the battering of Japan. Its specific assignment was to attack the home islands, destroying the remnants of Japan's navy, merchant marine, and air power and crippling its factories and communications. Planes were to strike inland while big guns bombarded coastal targets. Preparations for the campaign were rigorous. B-29s reconnoitered and photographed the fleet's objectives. Other land-based planes flew barrier patrols ahead of the fleet to screen its approach from enemy scouts. Submarines probed the assigned bombardment areas for mines. A line of submarines preceded the U.S. ships to detect and destroy enemy pickets and serve as lifeguards for the fleet's pilots.

The initial target was Tokyo. Halsey was at last about to carry out the raid formerly denied him by the requirements of the Philippine campaign. Riding a weather front, the Third Fleet arrived at the launching point in the early hours of 10 July. At dawn its strike was over Tokyo. In daylong raids, which destroyed at least a hundred planes on the ground, the American pilots met no airborne opposition and encountered little antiaircraft fire. Two snoopers approaching the carrier force were shot down. Halsey, who had predicted that Japan would cave in by October, now believed the collapse would come earlier.

Task Force 38 withdrew eastward to be fueled by a group from Admiral Beary's Service Squadron 6, then headed to attack northern Honshu and Hokkaido, areas thus far unscathed because they were beyond B-29 range. On 14 July McCain's carriers launched aircraft from only eighty miles off shore. Again there was no air opposition. The attacking pilots destroyed only twenty-five planes, but they wrought heavy destruction on the ships at Muroran and Hakodate. They sank a destroyer, two destroyer escorts, eight naval auxiliaries, thirteen freighters, and seven car ferries—vital links between Honshu and Hokkaido. That day a battleship group detached from Task Force 38 moved to within sight of the coast and spent two hours bombing the ironworks at Kamaishi without provoking an enemy response.

On the fifteenth the carrier planes concentrated on the car ferries, sinking twelve. They also destroyed ten steel freighters and some seventy sailing colliers. Meanwhile, another detached bombardment group steamed boldly into the landlocked waters between Hokkaido and Honshu and bombarded a steel company and an ironworks at Muroran. Halsey, on board the *Missouri* with this group, kept one eye on the target and the other on the sky. During the three-hour approach, the hour's bombardment, and the three-hour retirement, the group was in plain view from both shores. Halsey says these were the longest hours of his life. He felt confirmed in his theory that the Japanese were hoarding their aircraft to hurl against an anticipated American invasion.

That same day Vice Admiral McCain was shocked to receive from the Navy Department notification that on 14 August, when the Third Fleet was due at Eniwetok, he would be relieved of command of Task Force 38 by Vice Admiral John H. Towers and, after leave, would proceed to Washington to serve as deputy head of the Veterans Administration under General Omar Bradley. McCain knew this meant the end of his naval career. He rightly guessed it was a direct outcome of the board of inquiry's opinion concerning his actions in the June typhoon.

Task Force 38 steamed out to sea for another fueling rendezvous. It was joined by Vice Admiral Rawlings's British carrier force, fresh from its period of upkeep at Sydney. Now designated Task Force 37, it became a part of the Third Fleet, which thus was no longer identical with Task Force 38. Rawlings's 29 men-of-war were added to Halsey's 105, making the Third Fleet the most powerful striking force in history.

The enlarged Third Fleet now headed again for Tokyo. While en route the gunnery ships bombarded major industrial plants at Hitachi, about eighty miles northeast of the enemy capital. The strikes on 18 July were directed mainly at the Yokosuka Naval Base in Tokyo Bay. Here they sank a destroyer, a submarine, two escort vessels, and a PT boat. The principal target, however, was the battleship *Nagato,* which the bombers heavily damaged but could not sink. Heavy antiaircraft fire at the base cost the Americans and British together fourteen planes and eighteen men.

The Third Fleet now retired for a three-day refueling and replenishment rendezvous with Service Squadron 6, which provided 6,369 tons of ammunition, 379,157 barrels of fuel oil, 1,635 tons of stores and provisions, 99 replacement aircraft, and 412 replacements of officers and men. This is believed to have been the largest logistics operation ever carried out on the high seas.

One of the officers transferred from Service Squadron 6 came with a message. Rear Admiral William R. Purnell, as an emissary from CinCPac, brought Halsey information that the Twentieth Army Air Force was going to drop an atomic bomb on Hiroshima. This was the first time Halsey heard of the bomb. Now he understood why CinCPac had earlier forbidden him to attack certain cities, including Hiroshima and Nagasaki. Purnell brought

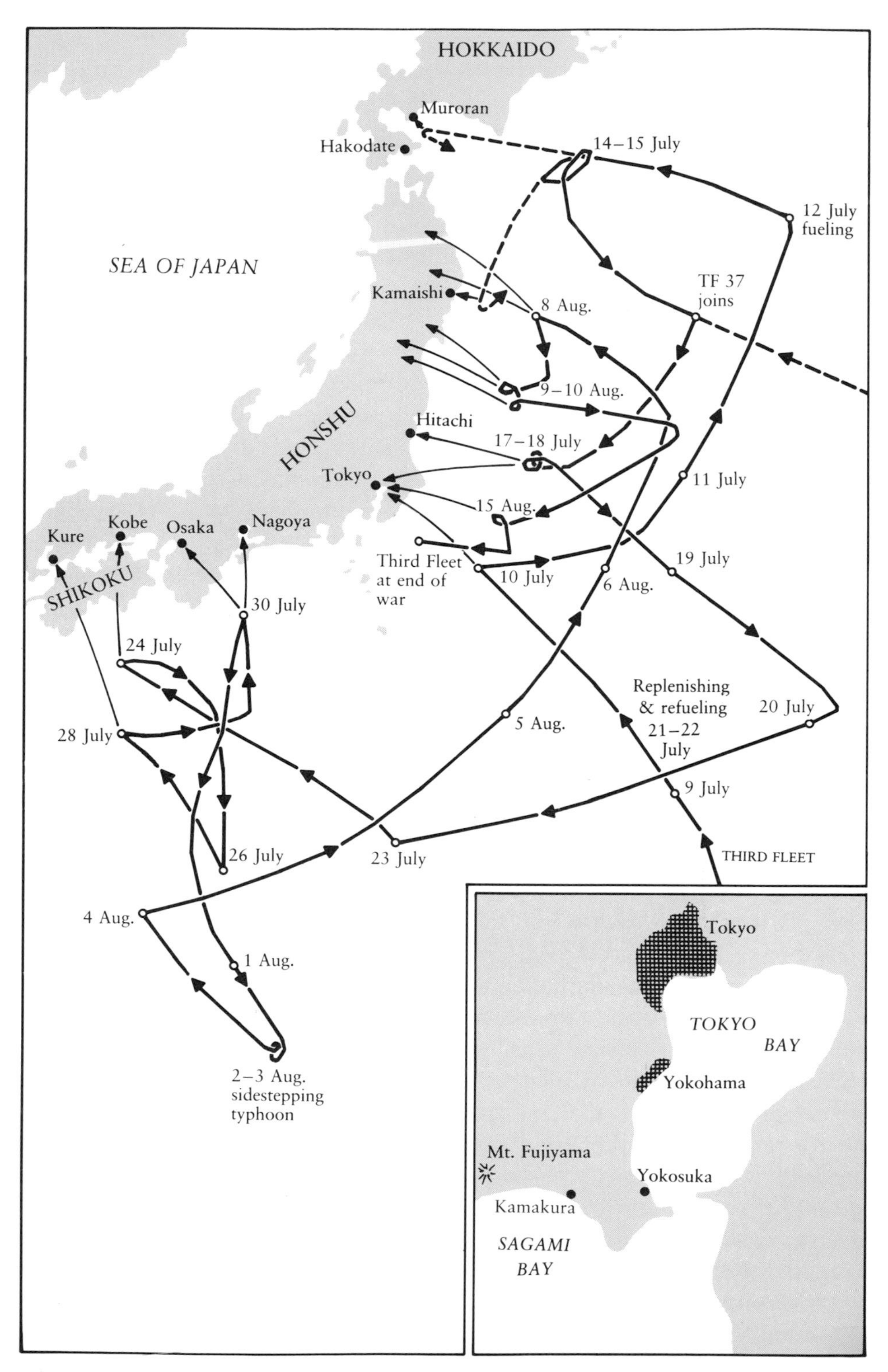

Movements of the U.S. Third Fleet, 1 July–15 August 1945

further instructions that after 1 August Halsey was to keep his planes at least fifty miles from each of the cities listed.

CinCPac ordered Halsey to destroy what was left of the Japanese fleet. The American public demanded nothing less in retaliation for the sneak attack on Pearl Harbor. Besides, if Japan retained any serviceable warships at all, she might be able to interfere with seaborne supplies from the United States to Russia, which was about to declare war on Japan. Lastly, if the Japanese were left any part of their fleet, they might try to use it as a post-surrender bargaining makeweight, as the Germans had used their fleet at the end of World War I.

Mick Carney had another thought. He reminded Halsey that Task Force 37 had been sent to the Pacific mainly to shore up British prestige. Prime Minister Churchill, hoping that a victory in that part of the world would offset in Oriental minds the memory of the crushing British defeats in 1941–42, had insisted on having ships of the Royal Navy in on the final defeat of Japan. U.S. naval leaders neither needed nor wanted them. Their presence merely intensified the logistics problems posed by the swelling flow of American warships coming to the Pacific from shipyards and the European theater. Now, in the hour of victory, Carney pointed out, the British must not be permitted to claim even a small part of the credit for destroying the Japanese fleet, credit that the U.S. Navy had justly earned in nearly four years of bitter and costly fighting.

"I hated to admit a political factor into a military equation," Halsey recalled. "My respect for Bert Rawlings and his fine men made me hate it doubly, but Mick forced me to recognize that statesmen's objectives sometimes differ widely from combat objectives, and that an exclusively American attack was therefore in American interests."

Halsey reserved the big naval base of Kure and the important port of Kobe as American targets. To the British he assigned Osaka, a major port but one offering only minor warships for destruction. The British, old hands at mingling politics and warfare, knew they were being shunted and resented it, but they carried out their attack in the best traditions of the Royal Navy.

The American attacks on Kure and Kobe on 24 and 28 July were among the heaviest of the war. The carrier planes sank the battleship *Haruna,* the hybrid battleships *Ise* and *Hyuga,* and four cruisers and heavily damaged a cruiser, five destroyers, and the carriers *Amagi, Katsuragi,* and *Ryuho.* The only major warship left in the Japanese navy that was in any sense operable was the bomb-resistant *Nagato* at Yokosuka.

After raiding various targets in central Honshu, the Third Fleet headed south at the end of July to sidestep a typhoon. Pearl Harbor was at last providing adequate warnings of potentially disastrous weather conditions. On 4 August, after fueling and replenishing, Halsey received orders to head north again and destroy a concentration of bombers reported in northern

Honshu. The Russians thought the aircraft menaced the Vladivostok area; MacArthur thought they were intended for Okinawa, which he had taken under his command. In fact they were scheduled to convey two thousand suicide troops to crash-land on the major B-29 bases in the Marianas.

The northbound Third Fleet was passing opposite Tokyo on 6 August, the day a B-29 from the Marianas dropped the first atomic bomb on Hiroshima. As the carrier forces approached their launching area on the eighth, Russia declared war on Japan and the Red Army marched into Manchuria. On the ninth, while Third Fleet aircraft launched strikes against northern Honshu and a detached battleship force was again bombarding Kamaishi, a second airborne atomic bomb devastated Nagasaki.

Third Fleet carrier planes broke up the planned crash mission to the Marianas by destroying or heavily damaging nearly four hundred enemy aircraft. During the attack on Kamaishi, the *Iowa,* by previous arrangement, transmitted the sounds of the bombardment to the United States for simultaneous broadcast by public radio. The following day, 10 August, the Third Fleet hurled more strikes against northern Honshu, pounding two newly discovered airfields where bombers were assembling for the Marianas crash mission.

That evening, while the crew on board the *Missouri* was watching a movie, word passed around that a radio flash from San Francisco had reported a rumor that the Japanese were willing to surrender. A little later a communications watch officer brought Carney the transcript of a radio intercept. Carney glanced at it, stopped the movie, and read it aloud: "Through the Swiss government, Japan stated that she is willing to accept Allied surrender ultimatum issued at Potsdam, provided they can keep their emperor."

Halsey growled, "Have we got enough fuel to turn around and hit the bastards once more before they quit?"

The admiral, like several senior commanders in the Pacific theater, had for weeks believed the Japanese to be so near the end of their resources that they would soon have no choice but to surrender. If so, preparations for the invasion of Japan were a waste of time and the dropping of the atomic bombs was unnecessary. Not only were the bombs unnecessary; they were, in Halsey's opinion, misleading. Many people would believe that it was the bombs that ended the war, and not the strenuous efforts made by the armed forces, especially the U.S. Navy. Halsey liked to quote a postwar statement of Admiral Soemu Toyoda, chief of the Japanese Naval General Staff: "I do not think it would be accurate to look upon use of the atomic bomb and the entry and participation of Soviet Russia as direct causes of the termination of the war, but I think that those two factors did enable us to bring the war to a termination without creating too great chaos in Japan."

Halsey canceled plans for the Third Fleet to retire to Eniwetok. He had the logistics pipeline kept full in order to meet any turn of events that would require the fleet's continuing presence in Japanese waters. He ordered the organization of a landing party of marines and bluejackets to serve as occupation troops.

As the only military unit in place and with sufficient strength to begin an occupation, the Third Fleet began receiving a flood of instructions but no orders to curtail its attacks. Accordingly, Halsey planned to strike Tokyo again on 12 August, but because of uncertain weather he ordered McCain to hold his planes for twenty-four hours.

Late that night Carney brought to Halsey's cabin an intercept from the Army News Service: "The American secretary of state, speaking for the Allied Powers, has accepted the surrender of Japan, provided that the supreme allied commander rule Japan through the authority of the emperor."

If Japan had actually surrendered, Halsey was reluctant to attack it and still more reluctant to risk his flyers' lives needlessly. Still, the thing was not yet official, and the Japanese might conceivably rebel at the provision subordinating their sacred emperor. He discussed the problem with his staff. The majority believed the surrender genuine except for a technicality and counseled a cease-fire. Halsey agreed and signaled McCain to call off the attack.

Carney, not one of the majority, followed Halsey to his room, still arguing. He pointed out that they had never trusted the Japanese before, and with good reason. Why begin trusting them at this critical time? Halsey's armistice was premature, he argued, and might easily prove to be one-sided. Halsey, persuaded, signaled Slew to proceed with the attack.

From CinCPac, who had been cut in on these signals, came a dispatch ordering Halsey to cancel the strike. Halsey did so but directed McCain to maintain a strong, defensive combat air patrol. Presently another signal came from Nimitz canceling his previous order. Halsey, wondering what in the world the diplomats were up to, signaled McCain, "Follow original schedule of strikes."

Within an hour the first strike was airborne, bound for Tokyo. Third Fleet flyers claimed to have destroyed more than four hundred planes that day. Nineteen of them were shot down by the combat air patrol. The fleet refueled on 14 August, and at dawn the next morning McCain began launching what turned out to be the final air attack against the Japanese capital. The first strike this day was over Tokyo, and a second was nearing the coast when Halsey was handed a top-secret, high-priority dispatch from CinCPac: "Suspend air attack operations."

On 7 December 1941 Admiral Halsey was at breakfast on board the *Enterprise* when Doug Moulton informed him that the Japanese had started the war. On 15 August 1945, while Halsey was at breakfast on the *Missouri*, it was Moulton who brought him word that the Japanese had ended the war. He dashed in, waving a dispatch. "Admiral," he shouted, "here she is!" It was President Truman's official announcement.

The first thing that crossed Halsey's mind, he tells us, was the joyous, solemn word *victory!* "God be thanked," he breathed, "I'll never have to order another man out to die!" To the men around him he said, "I am grateful for the honor of being in command of the Third Fleet this day." Then he began pounding the shoulders of his staff and yelling exuberantly.

After CinCPac broadcast his cease-fire order, coupled with a warning to beware of Japanese treachery, Halsey had battle flags hoisted on the *Missouri*, his four-star flag broken at the main, and the whistle and siren sounded for one minute. The rest of the fleet followed his example. The admiral ordered a flag hoist run up conveying the message "Well done!" to all hands. He took the precaution, however, of maintaining a combat air patrol lest some kamikaze make a last-minute attack for the honor of his ancestors. To the pilots in the air he signaled, "Investigate and shoot down all snoopers—not vindictively, but in a friendly sort of way."[1]

At 1300 Admiral Halsey broadcast a message to the fleet, saying in part,

> Men, . . . the war is ended. You, in conjunction with your brothers in arms, of all services and all branches of all services have contributed inestimably to this final result. You have brought an implacable, treacherous, and barbaric foe to his knees in abject surrender. This is the first time in recorded history of the misbegotten Japanese race that they as a nation have been forced to submit to this humiliation. . . .
>
> Your names are writ in golden letters on the pages of history—your fame is and shall be immortal. . . . Whether in the early days, when fighting with a very frayed shoestring, or at the finish, when fighting with the mightiest combined fleet the world has ever seen, the results have been the same—victory has crowned your efforts. The forces of righteousness and decency have triumphed. Victory is not the end—rather, it is but the beginning. We must establish a peace—a firm, a just, and an enduring peace.

Admiral Nimitz had sent a regiment of marines from Guam to join two Third Fleet marine regiments and four naval landing battalions of bluejackets, one British. These were intended for the immediate occupation of the Tokyo Bay area, so that the Allies' will could be enforced pending the arrival of regular occupation forces. General of the Army MacArthur, appointed supreme commander of the Allied powers in the Pacific, turned down this plan. The naval force, he said, was not strong enough for the proposed assignment. At any rate, it would be better to wait awhile, giving Japanese hotheads enough time to face defeat and realize that further resistance was useless. Moreover, it was only just, the general insisted, that representatives of all the armed services, land, sea, and air, arrive simultaneously to occupy the conquered territory. He scheduled the occupation for 26 August, but a severe

On board the *Missouri*, 22 August 1945, Halsey toasts the end of World War II. *Left to right*: Rear Admiral R. B. Carney; Captain J. P. L. Reid, RN; Vice Admiral Sir Bernard Rawlings, RN; Admiral Halsey; Vice Admiral J. S. McCain; and Rear Admiral Wilder D. Baker.

typhoon passing over the intended flight path of his airborne troops from the Philippines prompted him to postpone it until the twenty-eighth. The surrender ceremony was to follow on 2 September.

At Manila, meanwhile, General MacArthur's staff, with Rear Admiral Forrest Sherman representing Admiral Nimitz, set to work planning the occupation and surrender. They summoned Japanese government officials to Manila to receive instructions for Japanese reception of the occupation forces and participation in the surrender ceremony.

To honor President Truman's native state, the *Missouri* was designated the scene of the ceremony. Admiral Halsey was delighted. He asked the Naval Academy Museum to lend him the American flag Commodore Matthew Calbraith Perry had flown when he entered Tokyo Bay in 1853. Halsey wanted to display it on the surrender deck. The selection of their ship sent Captain Murray and his crew into a flurry of activity. Sailors set to work scouring the dull wartime finish from the brasswork and holystoning through the gray battle paint of the decks to expose the white teak beneath.

Day by day additional vessels of various types were joining the Third Fleet to assist in the occupation. Some of the ships brought correspondents and photographers, officers invited to attend the surrender ceremony, and representatives of the Allied powers to sign the surrender document.

One of the new arrivals was Jack Towers, who as Deputy CinCPac–CinCPOA had been senior naval officer at Pearl Harbor since Nimitz's move to Guam. Though he was not now scheduled to take command of Task Force 38 until 1 September, he immediately boarded the *Shangri-La* and, by virtue of his ten months' seniority as vice admiral, replaced McCain's flag with his own.

That day or the next, Admiral Carney, receiving a message that McCain wanted to see him on board the *Shangri-La*, asked Halsey what he should do about this somewhat irregular summons. Halsey told him to go ahead. On board the carrier, Carney found McCain sick in his bunk. McCain said now that the fighting was over he wanted to go home. "Go back and tell Bill that," he continued. "I've had it. I fought all the way from the South Pacific up to here. It's all over now, and I want to go home."

Carney said his long, hard campaign against the enemy was all the more reason he should stay and witness the surrender.

"I don't give a damn about seeing the surrender," said McCain. "I want to get the hell out of here!"

When Carney conveyed McCain's request to Halsey, the latter said, "Of course, I'm not going to let him go home. The old SOB is entitled to witness the surrender, and that's what he's going to do. He was commanding this task force when the war ended, and I'm making sure that history gets it straight." Halsey paused a moment in thought, then added, "I'll tell you what I'll do. The minute the thing is over, I'll put him on a plane and start him home."

Reluctant to keep the growing force at sea in typhoon weather, Halsey secured orders for the Japanese navy to send out a destroyer and guide his fleet through the minefields to an anchorage in Sagami Bay, gateway to Tokyo Bay. On the morning of 27 August Halsey and Carney were watching from the *Missouri*'s flag bridge when the destroyer appeared—dirty, rusty, with, as stipulated, her guns depressed, breeches open, torpedo tubes empty, and only enough crew topside to handle a small boat.

"You wanted the Jap navy, Admiral," said Carney, pointing to the woebegone vessel. "Well, there it is."

The Japanese ship brought officers authorized to arrange the surrender of the Yokosuka Naval Base. Carney treated them with the "cold, impersonal formality" that he had instructed all the Third Fleet staff to maintain in dealings with the erstwhile enemy. When one of the Japanese officers lit a cigarette in his presence, Carney immediately made him extinguish it. When another requested the return of the side arms of which he had been relieved, saying that they were an essential part of his uniform, Carney informed him that the Americans were now prescribing his uniform, and it did not include side arms.

Deeply suspicious of the Japanese, Halsey left all but one of his carriers in the open sea. To the battleships and cruisers he assigned targets before they stood in, and their guns were loaded and trained. By late afternoon the ships were at anchor in the bay, their crews viewing the breathtaking panorama of the Japanese coast, from Fujiyama in the distance, bathed in sunlight, to nearby Kamakura, the Japanese riviera, site of the emperor's summer palace.

The peacefulness of the scene by no means lulled the fleet into letting down its guard. After sunset the ships were darkened as usual, and picket boats and destroyers patrolled the perimeter of the anchorage. One of the pickets, hearing a shout in English from the beach, investigated and took on board two British officers, escapees from a POW camp near Tokyo. To Commodore Rodger W. Simpson, appointed by Halsey to head rescue operations, they described the inhumane treatment they and their fellow prisoners had been receiving. Their horrifying account of men subjected to beatings, starvation, and solitary confinement was corroborated the following day by a Swiss doctor who had been visiting the camps as a representative of the International Red Cross. MacArthur had sent instructions to the fleet not to begin recovering POWs until the army was ready to participate, but when Halsey heard the prisoners' story, he ordered Simpson to take to Tokyo a rescue group—the hospital ship *Benevolence* and two transports, escorted by a light cruiser and a destroyer—and stand by for further orders.

On Tuesday the twenty-eighth elements of an airborne U.S. Army division landed at Atsugi airfield, twenty miles northwest of Yokosuka, and Third Fleet minesweepers began searches inside Tokyo Bay for mines planted by the Japanese or dropped from B-29s. These vessels were followed by an advance force of ten ships headed by the light cruiser *San Diego*. Carrier planes roared overhead.

On the twenty-ninth the *Missouri, South Dakota,* and *Duke of York,* the flagship of Admiral Sir Bruce Fraser, commander in chief of the British Pacific Fleet, entered Tokyo Bay, accompanied by two cruisers and several destroyers. Early that afternoon a Coronado seaplane arrived in the bay with Nimitz and a few of his staff and taxied to the *South Dakota*, which was to serve as the admiral's flagship. Meanwhile the *Missouri*, partly as a symbolic gesture, had anchored near where Perry, intent on opening Japan to world intercourse, had dropped anchor ninety-two years before.

Nimitz was hardly settled on board his temporary flagship when Halsey contacted him to explain the urgency of the prisoner-rescue operation.

"Go ahead," said Nimitz. "General MacArthur will understand."

Simpson lost no time going ashore with his rescue detail, which included Harold Stassen. Over the past few days aircraft had searched diligently and located most of the POW camps in eastern Honshu. Now planes from the fleet guided the detail up rivers in ships' boats to reach them. At one notorious camp, Omori 8, the commandant demanded to see written orders.

"I have no authority to release these men," he said.

Replied Stassen, "You have no authority, period!"

When one released bluejacket learned who had sent the rescue party, his haggard face lit up. "I knew it!" he shouted. "I told these Jap bastards that Admiral Halsey would be here after us!"

On 29 August, the first day of the rescue mission, POWs began reaching the *Benevolence* at 1910. By midnight 794 men had come on board.

Admiral Nimitz, arriving in Tokyo Bay on 29 August 1945 to participate in the surrender ceremony, is welcomed on board the *South Dakota* by Admiral Halsey.

H-hour for the Third Fleet landing forces was 1000 on the thirtieth. U.S. marines occupied Yokosuka Air Base, U.S. bluejackets occupied Yokosuka Naval Base, and British bluejackets took over Azuma peninsula. Like the soldiers over at Atsugi, the occupation forces at Yokosuka met no resistance or any signs of violence. Most of the Japanese acted as if they did not even see the Americans and British in their midst.

A special naval detail had been assigned to take over the battleship *Nagato,* battered but still afloat at the naval base. When he boarded the ship, the American commanding officer ordered the captain to haul down his colors. The captain directed one of the Japanese enlisted men to carry out the order, but the American intervened. "No," he said. "Haul them down yourself."

At 1030 Vice Admiral Michitare Totsuka officially turned over the Yokosuka facilities to Admiral Carney, who was acting as Halsey's representative. Headquarters of the Third Fleet and of the landing force were established there, and Halsey's flag was raised over the base. Admiral Nimitz promptly sent a signal ordering it hauled down. He later sharply reminded Halsey of the impropriety of breaking his flag ashore in the presence of a senior officer. "All the same," wrote Halsey gleefully, "it is the first United States admiral's flag to fly over Imperial Japanese territory."

A little after 1400 that afternoon General MacArthur arrived by plane at Atsugi airfield and in an automobile furnished by the Japanese headed for headquarters at Yokohama. At about the same time, Admirals Nimitz and Halsey went ashore to inspect the Yokosuka Naval Base. In a limousine of doubtful vintage, also provided by the Japanese, they toured the shipyard and inspected the dry dock, the officers' club, and the hospital, passing through cheering lanes of U.S. sailors and marines. The two admirals were gratified to see that the bomb damage to the base was so slight that facilities could be quickly restored for American use during the occupation. On the other hand, it was obvious that the Japanese had made little effort to comply with orders specifying that "on delivery to the Allies, all facilities will be cleared of debris, scrupulously clean, and in full operating condition." In fact, the base was filthy, and much of the equipment was in poor shape or inoperable. Nimitz told newsmen there was no evidence that the Japanese had made any effort to clean the place or put the machinery in working order. "Most of Admiral Halsey's remarks," said the *New York Times,* "were unprintable." The disgust of the two admirals reached a climax when their limousine ran out of gas and left them stranded. Meanwhile, because his Japanese car kept breaking down, it took two hours to drive General MacArthur the fifteen miles from Atsugi to Yokohama.

That same afternoon Admirals Halsey and Carney, Captain Murray, and General Sutherland, MacArthur's chief of staff, joined Admiral Nimitz in the

South Dakota for a conference on the surrender ceremony. Sutherland outlined the procedure, and Nimitz told Murray to execute the plan and spare no pains to make sure that everything went according to schedule. Nimitz said he would send Halsey a complete list of visitors to the *Missouri,* including the names of photographers, correspondents, participants, and witnesses. Leaving the others to continue the discussion, Murray hustled back to his ship. From that point on, practically every officer and man in the *Missouri* who could be spared from other duties was pressed into service preparing for the ceremony. Carney and Murray superintended the operation, while Bill Kitchell, Halsey's flag lieutenant, acted as general coordinator.

As soon as Murray received Nimitz's list, he and his assistants, using off-duty sailors as stand-ins, began marking the areas on deck where each participant in the ceremony was to stand or sit. Besides the Allied signatories and a few official observers, the only persons on the starboard veranda deck, where the surrender document was to be signed, would be flag officers who had led the fight against Japan and, briefly, the Japanese surrender party.

MacArthur wanted the surrender party to arrive on the veranda deck at precisely 0900, not a second earlier or later. To attain such precision, the Americans would have to find out exactly how long it would take the Japanese to get there from their boat, which could be delayed. They would have to mount the accommodation ladder leading up the side of the vessel to the quarterdeck and a second ladder leading from the quarterdeck to the veranda deck. The situation was complicated by the fact that the delegation would be led by Foreign Minister Mamoru Shigemitsu, who had a wooden leg, having lost his own long before to a would-be assassin's bomb.

To play the role of Shigemitsu, Murray had young sailors strap a swab handle to one leg so they couldn't bend it and go from boat to veranda deck, crossing the quarterdeck between ladders. The sailors were pretty good, said Murray; the slowest in about twenty runs took only ninety seconds. Allowing for the foreign minister's age, the captain doubled that time and added a minute, scheduling Shigemitsu for a four-minute trip.

Then a series of unexpected factors threw the planning askew. The secretary of the navy was sending out some visitors for the ceremony, and he wanted them to have a good view. Captain Murray had assigned all the best places, but somebody pointed out that the top of the no. 2 turret was available. From there the visitors could look down on the proceedings. Assuming that the secretary's guests would be older men and might fall off if they stood, Murray had chairs placed for them a safe distance from the edge.

Next General MacArthur let it be known that he would like to have his flag displayed on the *Missouri* during the ceremony. Breaking a general's flag on a naval vessel was unheard of. According to regulations and by tradition, the flag of the senior *naval* officer on board, in this case Admiral Nimitz, should be broken at the main. Neither MacArthur's nor Nimitz's flag could be shifted to the fore peak because neither was senior to the other. Admiral Nimitz said he had no objection to sharing honors with the general, provided the flags were at exactly the same height. Murray turned the problem over to his technicians, who after some head scratching welded to the top of the mainmast a transverse bar with pulleys at each end. Admiral Halsey's four-star flag would remain hoisted until the first of the five-star flags was broken.

Admiral Fraser offered to send Halsey a table to hold the surrender document at the signing and a pair of chairs, one for the Japanese signatories, the other for the Allied signatories. All hands thought it would be good if the British were able to contribute something to the surrender ceremony. Halsey accepted with thanks. Presently there arrived from the *Duke of York,* along with a pair of upholstered chairs, a handsome mahogany table, about forty inches square, along with a note stating that it was of historic interest, having been in the Battle of Jutland.[2]

On 1 September Commander Horace Bird, the *Missouri*'s gunnery officer, assembled three hundred sailors on deck to represent the dignitaries, correspondents, and photographers who would participate in the ceremony. They would rehearse the whole thing, and the next day it would be the duty of each man, with a few exceptions, to escort the man he had represented to the spot where he was to stand or sit.

The rehearsal was proceeding smoothly when the band began the "Admiral's March," announcing the arrival of Admiral Nimitz. Nimitz did not arrive. His stand-in, a hefty chief boatswain's mate nicknamed Two-Gut, was found transfixed at the foot of the accommodation ladder, scratching his head and muttering in awe, "I'll be damned! Me an admiral!"

The next day, the day of the surrender ceremony, every precaution was taken to protect the *Missouri* while there were so many senior officials on board. Marine guards were stationed throughout the ship with instructions to keep a wary eye on the few Japanese newsmen and photographers invited. All the ship's antiaircraft guns were manned except those on the starboard side, where the visitors were standing. Small boats circled the vessel to watch for suicidal swimmers with explosives, and high overhead a strong combat air patrol was maintained. Some distance away several hundred airborne B-29s and carrier planes orbited. These, however, were not for protection. At a signal originating with Halsey, then transmitted by radio, they would carry out their assigned role in the proceedings.

Shortly after 0700 correspondents and photographers of all nationalities arrived by destroyer and were conducted to their assigned places. The choice location for photographers was a temporary wooden platform constructed outboard from the veranda deck, opposite the surrender table. Another platform for photographers had been built on the quarterdeck forward of the veranda deck.

A little after 0800 high-ranking officers and officials began coming on board the *Missouri* from various craft. Admiral Halsey, playing the genial host, greeted each one, calling the officers, mostly old friends, by their first names or nicknames. He almost choked up when he spied General Jonathan Wainwright, now more gaunt than ever. "Skinny!" he cried and grasped his hand. Wainwright had been flown in for the ceremony from a POW camp in Manchuria, where he had been incarcerated after surrendering the Philippines in 1942.

The *Missouri*'s officers and sailors escorted the new arrivals to their places. Representatives of the United Nations, both signatories and observers, took station abaft the mahogany table facing forward. To the right of these, next to the number two turret, stood row upon row of U.S. flag and general officers in khaki uniforms with open-necked shirts. Behind and above, in every toehold of the masts and superstructure, the *Missouri*'s sailors were perched, many with Kodaks, all in white uniforms.

Admiral Nimitz and his party came from the *South Dakota* by barge. His blue flag was broken at the starboard end of the bar on the mainmast, he was piped aboard, and the band played the "Admiral's March." Halsey saluted him and extended his hand in welcome.

A long wait ensued. Finally, at 0840, General MacArthur arrived with staff officers in the destroyer *Buchanan*. When his red flag had been broken at the port end of the bar and honors had been duly rendered, he walked up to Nimitz, Halsey, and Carney, who were awaiting him. "Chester! Bill! Mick!" he exclaimed, happily shaking their hands. "It's grand having so many of my sidekicks from the shoestring SoPac days meeting here at the end of the road!"

Arriving with MacArthur and his staff was an army colonel who had flown out from Washington with the surrender documents, one bound in leather for the Allies, the other in canvas for the Japanese. When Captain Murray saw the documents, he was dumbfounded. They were several times the size he had imagined, and they had to be laid side by side for signing. The beautiful mahogany table couldn't hold them.

Calling four sailors, Murray headed for the wardroom, where they grabbed a table. It was bolted to the deck—something the captain in his excitement had forgotten. They dashed to the crew's mess compartment, where the messcooks were folding tables and hanging them on the overhead before watching the ceremony. When Murray and his sailors grabbed a table, the cooks reacted with loud protests. "You'll get it back," said the captain as he and his sailors made off with it. But the messcooks never did. The table wound up at the Naval Academy Museum, together with a facsimile of the Allied copy of the surrender document and one of the two pens Admiral Nimitz used in signing.

While passing again through the wardroom, Captain Murray snatched a coffee-stained green baize cloth off one of the tables. He told the sailors to get rid of the mahogany table, set up the mess table in its place, and spread the green cloth over it.

Meanwhile, MacArthur, Nimitz, and Halsey had been conversing on the quarterdeck. Eventually they turned to go to the flag cabin and await the Japanese surrender party. Since they were to cross the veranda deck on their way, Commander Bird dashed ahead of them to make sure the officers there were in position. Reaching the top of the ladder, he was appalled at the sight before him. In the long wait for MacArthur, the officers on the veranda deck, happy to be together and exhilarated by the occasion, had drifted from their assigned spaces and were sounding off enthusiastically. "Gentlemen," Bird shouted, "General MacArthur and Admiral Nimitz are approaching!"

His words drowned out by the lively chatter, he filled his lungs and bellowed, "Attention, all hands!" Instantly the generals and admirals fell silent, took their assigned places, and snapped to attention. Escorted by Bill Kitchell, MacArthur and Nimitz, followed by Halsey, crossed in front of the ranks of generals and admirals and mounted another ladder to Halsey's cabin. Bird went back down to the quarterdeck to join Captain Murray, who was now at the head of the accommodation ladder.

The Japanese surrender delegation had left the destroyer that brought them and were in a boat coming over to the *Missouri*. In addition to the signatories, Foreign Minister Shigemitsu and General Yoshijiro Umezu, there were three more army officers, three naval officers, and three officials from the Foreign Office. One of the civilians wore white, in mourning; the other civilians were in formal morning dress and top hats.

When the coxswain, as instructed, brought the boat alongside the ladder platform at precisely 0856, Shigemitsu, carrying a cane, struggled for nearly a minute getting out. Then, obviously in pain, he began a slow and halting climb up the steps. Bird reached down to give him a helping hand, which Shigemitsu at first shook off and then briefly accepted. Bird next led the way across the quarterdeck and up the second ladder to the veranda deck.

Bill Kitchell had gone to notify MacArthur, Nimitz, and Halsey of the arrival of the Japanese. At precisely 0900 MacArthur stepped outside the flag cabin. When he looked down and saw Shigemitsu's top hat just reaching the level of the veranda deck, he went back inside to allow a couple of minutes for the Japanese to take their places and receive their initial instructions. He then descended with the two admirals. Nimitz joined the Allied signatories, Halsey took his place in the front line of the officers under the turret, and MacArthur stepped up to a microphone behind the cloth-covered mess table, on which the two copies of the surrender document now lay.

"We are gathered here," the general began, "representatives of the major warring powers, to conclude a solemn agreement whereby peace may be restored." He concluded his remarks with these words: "It is my earnest hope—indeed the hope of all mankind—that from this solemn occasion a better world shall emerge out of the blood and carnage of the past, a world founded upon faith and understanding, a world dedicated to the dignity of man and the fulfillment of his most cherished wish for freedom, tolerance, and justice." Then, pointing to the chair at the opposite side of the table, MacArthur said, "I now invite the representatives of the Emperor of Japan and the Japanese Government and the Japanese Imperial Headquarters to sign the instrument of surrender at the places indicated."

Foreign Minister Shigemitsu limped to the table, accompanied by his secretary. He took off his gloves and silk hat. Then, sitting down heavily, he dropped his cane and accidentally banged his wooden leg against one of the tie rods that held the table legs in place. Captain Murray, on the quarterdeck, heard the noise and shuddered, expecting the table to collapse. It did not.

Shigemitsu seemed in a daze. He picked up his cane, which he handed to his secretary. He fumbled with his hat and gloves and felt in his inside pocket for a pen. The secretary handed him one from a holder on the table. Shigemitsu then seemed confused about where he was to put his name. Halsey, thinking he was stalling, wanted to slap his face and snarl, "Sign, damn you! Sign!"

"Sutherland," MacArthur said to his chief of staff, "Show him where to sign." Sutherland pointed, and Shigemitsu affixed his signature in behalf of the Emperor of Japan and the Japanese government.

General Umezu then stepped forward stiffly and, not deigning to sit down, scrawled his name on the two documents in behalf of the Japanese General Headquarters.

General MacArthur beckoned Lieutenant Generals Jonathan Wainwright and Sir Arthur Percival to stand behind his chair as he signed the acceptance of the surrender on behalf of all the Allied powers. Percival, who had surrendered Singapore in 1942, had like Wainwright been flown from a POW camp in Manchuria. Next Admiral Nimitz, with Admiral Halsey and Rear Admiral Forrest Sherman behind his chair, signed for the United States. While Nimitz was signing the two documents, MacArthur put an arm around Halsey's shoulders and whispered, "Start 'em now!"

"Aye, aye, sir!" Halsey replied and waved a prearranged signal to an officer watching for it, and the latter relayed the signal to main radio, which ordered the bombers orbiting in the distance to head for Tokyo Bay.

The Japanese surrender, 2 September 1945. Admiral Halsey stands between General of the Army Douglas MacArthur (*left*) and Rear Admiral Forrest Sherman as Fleet Admiral Nimitz signs the instrument of surrender for the United States.

Nimitz was followed at the surrender table by the signatories for China, the United Kingdom, the Soviet Union, Australia, Canada, France, the Netherlands, and New Zealand. When all had signed, MacArthur again addressed the assemblage: "Let us pray that peace be now restored to the world and that God will preserve it always. These proceedings are now closed." At that moment the sun came from behind the clouds and the carrier planes and B-29s that Halsey had summoned swept over Tokyo Bay and the British and American ships.[3]

As the Japanese were turning to depart, one of their Foreign Office aides came forward to pick up the Japanese copy of the surrender document. He glanced at it and hurried off, calling out to the Japanese delegates, who stopped. There was an excited conversation among them.

MacArthur said to Nimitz's flag lieutenant, who was standing by, "Go over and find out what's going on."

The aide pointed to a blank space in the column of acceptance signatures. The Canadian representative had skipped his space and written his name where the French representative should have signed. The rest had followed, all one line too low, and the last one, the New Zealand representative, had perforce signed in the margin at the foot of the column, which made him, as he afterward put it, "an humble footnote to the document."

"Change the thing," MacArthur said to Sutherland.

With a fountain pen, Sutherland marked out the names of the countries above the misplaced signatures and wrote them below the signatures. The Japanese then somberly took the corrected document and left. As they approached the gangway, they were given the customary honors betokening the fact that they were no longer enemies.

As the gathering of Allied observers was breaking up, Halsey was surprised to see an aviation rating among the generals and admirals. Carney reminded him that a number of newly rescued POWs had been invited. Most POWs were emaciated, but the young man Halsey noticed was exceptionally husky. Carney asked him how he managed to keep in such good shape in prison camp. "Sir," said the lad, grinning, "they had me working in the railroad yards that all their food passes through. Those bastards were lucky to get anything to eat at all!"

Halsey invited to his cabin all the foreign representatives, along with some of his senior officers and friends. He apologized for the U.S. Navy regulation forbidding alcohol on board; certainly champagne was in order on such an occasion as this. His guests, filled with a sense of accomplishment, were happy to accept coffee and doughnuts. Halsey spoke to each of the representatives, chatting to the Russian and Chinese generals through interpreters. He was particularly amused when the Chinese general remarked that he was glad to see Halsey alive; the Japanese had often reported the admiral killed.

When the party broke up Slew McCain remained behind. "Thank God you made me stay, Bill," he said. "You had better sense than I did."

McCain headed for the States that evening. He reached his home in Coronado and died of a heart attack the next day. Carney, discussing McCain's health with his chief of staff, came to the conclusion that the attack was not Slew's first, that he had had a heart attack at sea and kept quiet about it. "He knew his number was up," concluded Carney, "but he wouldn't lie down and die until he got home."

The day following the surrender ceremony Admiral Nimitz returned to Guam. On 5 September Admiral Halsey shifted his flag to the *South Dakota*.

President Truman had ordered the *Missouri* to New York so that he could make his Navy Day speech from her bridge. Halsey was to stay at Tokyo until 20 September, when Admiral Spruance would relieve him of command of all naval forces remaining in Japan. These would be designated the Fifth Fleet. Ships heading for West Coast ports would constitute the Third Fleet and come under the command of Halsey.

General MacArthur invited Admiral Halsey to join him for the official occupation of the Japanese capital on 8 September. When the day arrived they drove, with MacArthur's staff, from the general's headquarters at Yokohama to the undamaged American embassy in Tokyo. Here an honor guard of the Twenty-first Cavalry Division was drawn up. Halsey and the staff took position in front of the line of troops, and MacArthur stood alone in front of the other members of his party. The band played "General's Colors" and, after four ruffles from the drums and four flourishes from the trumpets, "The Star Spangled Banner." Then, in a sonorous voice, MacArthur said, "Have our country's flag unfurled, and in Tokyo's sun let it wave in its full glory as a symbol of hope for the oppressed and as a harbinger of victory for the right." To the sound of bugles, while officers saluted and an honor guard presented arms, the Stars and Stripes rose slowly on the flagpole. General MacArthur was now proconsul of Japan.

Pointing to the slightly damaged U.S. chancellery nearby, MacArthur said, "Your flyers did that, didn't they, Bill?"

"No, sir," replied Halsey, "not my boys." He gave credit for the trivial damage to the B-29s from the Marianas.

Later they drove past what had been Imperial General Headquarters, now reduced to rubble. "But my boys did *that,*" said Halsey.

There was a good deal of work for the Third Fleet: demilitarizing installations, rescuing and evacuating Allied prisoners, arranging the return and discharge of men with sufficient service points. Halsey left these chores to his staff, who were capable of handling them without superintendence. He appointed Scrappy Kessing commandant of the Yokosuka Naval Base. One of Kessing's first tasks was to clean up the officers' club and enlisted men's recreation building for the use of the occupation forces. Both were incredibly filthy.

Though at Nimitz's insistence Halsey had ordered the forces not to loot, he indulged in a little looting himself. A music box and two vases at the officers' club having caught his eye, he had them carried to his cabin to take home as souvenirs. Of three battered but serviceable automobiles found hidden in a cave, Halsey appropriated one for his own local transportation and subsequently arranged through Kessing to have it shipped to the United States for his use there.

If this conduct was unbecoming to an officer, it did not seem so to Halsey.

Once, during the Solomons campaign, his officers found Japanese money at a captured enemy headquarters and offered some to Halsey "to spend when he got to Tokyo."

"I don't need it," Halsey replied. "When I get to Japan, I don't intend to pay for a damn thing."

Fondness for his men made him particularly sensitive to accounts of Japanese brutality—mutilation of the wounded and mistreatment of captives. He was deeply shocked to learn of the Bataan death march. Every day he heard more horror stories from ex-POWs reaching the Tokyo area. Apparently some Japanese doctors even went so far as to practice vivisection on sick and wounded Americans. At length Halsey concluded that the Japanese were a subhuman species unworthy of respect or consideration.

When MacArthur put out an order forbidding confiscation of Japanese officers' swords, Halsey was indignant. The next time he saw the general he protested, saying he considered the order unwise for two reasons. First, the sword, a symbol of militarism, would keep its spirit alive. He gave the example of Germany, where he had served as an attaché shortly after World War I. In many homes there he had seen a bust of Napoleon with a sword hung above it. Such displays, he was convinced, helped preserve in Germany the spirit of militarism that exploded into World War II.

"That's true," said MacArthur, "but I was thinking of Appomattox, when Grant allowed Lee's troops to keep their side arms."

"That brings me to my second point," Halsey replied. "Grant was dealing with an honorable foe. We are not."

The general pondered a few moments, pacing his office. "You're right!" he exclaimed. "You're right! I'll revoke the order." He did.

During the occupation Halsey had a surprising experience. He was invited to luncheon as a guest of Major General William C. Chase, commander of the First Cavalry Division. General Chase met him wearing his tin hat and conveyed him out to his camp in a car escorted by MPs and four tanks. On arrival, Chase asked Halsey to inspect his troops—"as magnificent a body of men," said Halsey, "as ever I've seen."

The inspection over, the general sprang his trap. At a gesture from him a white horse was led out. "Not *the* white horse," Halsey says, "but a reasonable facsimile [of the emperor's]." His sportsmanship thus challenged, he warily mounted the animal, to great applause. As past experience proved, Halsey was no horseman, and he was relieved to find that this was no fiery steed. It had only two speeds: very slow and stop. At the first stop Bill dismounted, to the relief of both himself and the horse.

On 17 September Ray Spruance arrived in Tokyo Bay in his flagship, Halsey's old one, the *New Jersey,* and boarded the *Mississippi* to confer with Halsey. The next evening the two friends and their staffs were entertained by

Vice Admiral Rawlings on board his flagship, HMS *King George V*, which the Americans were calling the Cagey Five. Like all Royal Navy ships, she was well stocked with liquor. "It was quite a celebration," Spruance wrote his wife, "and, as Bill was having a thoroughly good time and feeling no pain whatever, it was 1:30 A.M. before we got back to our ships."

Somehow Halsey managed to squeeze in a farewell call on MacArthur. As they parted, the general said, "When you leave the Pacific, Bill, it becomes just another damned ocean!" These words Halsey always treasured.

On the evening of the nineteenth, his final night in Japan, the Third Fleet officers gave Halsey a send-off in the newly renovated officers' club at the Yokosuka Naval Base. Of this gathering Spruance wrote, "I left early, but I judge that the party lasted well into the night, with Bill the life of the party and again feeling no pain." At midnight, as Spruance was sound asleep in his bunk and Halsey was feeling no pain, Commander, Fifth Fleet automatically relieved Commander, Third Fleet. At 0630 the following morning Halsey departed by air for Pearl Harbor.

At Pearl Halsey formed Task Force 30, consisting of homeward-bound ships, and sortied with them on the morning of 9 October. After parading past Diamond Head, the task groups separated and proceeded independently to their assigned West Coast ports. The group including Halsey's flagship *South Dakota* headed for San Francisco, which it reached on the fifteenth.

Bill Halsey had come home.[4]

CHAPTER 22

LAST YEARS

OUTSIDE THE GOLDEN GATE the *South Dakota* slowed down to receive the pilot from his tug. The tug also brought out to the battleship Governor Earle Warren of California, Mayor Roger Lapham of San Francisco, Admiral Royal E. Ingersoll, commander of the Western Sea Frontier, and other dignitaries. On reaching the quarterdeck, Ingersoll threw his arms around his old friend Halsey.

At noon on 15 October 1945 the *South Dakota* passed under the Golden Gate bridge, her band playing "There'll Be a Hot Time in the Old Town Tonight." Inside San Francisco Bay the flagship took station, and the rest of the task group, thirteen ships, including three battleships and a cruiser, passed before her in review. While whistles screeched and sirens howled and planes roared overhead, thousands of would-be spectators lined the shores and crowded the bridges. Unfortunately, the morning fog had not yet lifted, so the sailors could not see the cheering crowds or read the welcoming signs posted everywhere.

The next morning Halsey was surprised when Chester Nimitz arrived on board the *South Dakota* for a friendly call. Nimitz had just completed a round of welcoming parades and ceremonies in San Francisco, Washington, New York, and his native state of Texas and was on his way back to Pearl Harbor. He had been in the San Francisco area a couple of days but had been careful to remain incognito, not wanting to divert attention from Bill's welcome.

At noon that day officers and men of the fleet, with Admiral Halsey at their head, began marching up Market Street to City Hall, whence the welcoming speeches and Halsey's reply were broadcast by radio to the nation. The following day Halsey flew in his personal Douglas R5D to Los Angeles for more welcoming receptions and ceremonies. Then he visited Indianapolis, St. Louis, and Boston for more of the same.

In each city Halsey urged the nation to keep the navy strong, as a deterrent. "I'm barnstorming," he told newsmen, "barnstorming in the interest of the children and grandchildren of all of us. . . . I'm too damned old to fight another war, and I don't want them to have to fight one." In what seemed to him a logical extension of that plea, he decried the ongoing movement to merge the armed forces under a single department. In his Navy Day speech in Indianapolis he said that he was "a hundred percent for unified command" of forces in the field but just as much against merging departments at home. "Now that it [the war] is over," he said, "I pray that we shall not gamble away all we've gained by any hasty, ill-considered decision."

In Boston Fan joined her husband in his triumphant tour. The citizens there gave Halsey the usual hero's welcome with a parade, speeches, and ceremonies. The next morning, 7 November, Bill and Fan flew to Elizabeth, New Jersey, which was prepared to stage another "Halsey Day," one that would eclipse the extravaganza of November 1942. From the Newark airport the admiral and his wife drove directly to Pingry School, Bill's boyhood alma mater. Awaiting him in the gymnasium were some of his old classmates together with the current generation of Pingry boys. When the latter had exhausted themselves cheering, Admiral Halsey made a little speech.

"I haven't much to say to you," he began, "except that I envy you. I would give anything I have today to change places with you—to be starting out instead of ending up."

As the Halsey motorcade moved from Pingry School to Scott Park, scene of the official ceremony, church bells tolled, fire sirens wailed, and the crowds lining the streets—many thousands from Elizabeth and surrounding towns—roared their welcome and nearly smothered Bill and Fan with confetti and paper ribbons.

Awaiting the admiral in the park were more cheering thousands and the official welcoming party consisting of the mayor, New Jersey's governor, and both of the state's U.S. senators. After the dignitaries had paid their tributes and the mayor had presented the Halseys with a silver tea service, gift of the city, the admiral replied in his usual modest style. He accepted the silver and the great ovation "as the representative of the finest fighting men in the world, whom I have been privileged to command. I cannot say enough for them."

At the end of the day Bill and Fan were entertained at a reception, held appropriately in the admiral's birthplace, the former home of the redoubtable James Drew Brewster, Bill's stern, word-conscious grandfather.

Next Halsey made a private visit to Wilmington, where, in addition to his daughter Margaret and her husband, the admiral's mother and sister Deborah had established residence. He ended his tour on 9 November in Philadelphia with the usual parade and ceremony.[1]

Before leaving Japan, Halsey had sent a formal request to Nimitz and King: "Due to the capitulation of Japan and the cessation of hostilities throughout the world, the Navy will soon return to peacetime functions. It is my belief that the younger officers should be given higher commands with wider responsibilities. Therefore, upon completion of my duty as Commander Third Fleet . . . it is requested that I be placed on the retired list of the United States Navy."

To newsmen at Pearl Harbor Halsey gave another reason for his request. Though he was more than a year below the retirement age of sixty-four, he considered his job was finished, and he was tired. "I'm an old man," he said. "Let the young fellows take over. . . . I've applied for retirement, but they haven't told me yet what they plan to do about it."

At the end of his tour Halsey received his answer from the Navy Department: request granted. In his endorsement Nimitz said, "It will be difficult—if not impossible—to overestimate the value of Admiral Halsey's splendid services to our country." King added, "Well done!"

On 22 November, at Long Beach, California, some fifty officers headed by Rear Admiral Robert B. Carney stood behind Admiral Halsey on the bow of the *South Dakota* as ships of the Third Fleet passed in review, roaring seventeen-gun salutes. Halsey turned command of the fleet over to his successor, Rear Admiral Howard F. Kingman. "In hauling down my flag," said Halsey, "I am terminating a seagoing career of slightly over forty-five years. This is far from a pleasure, but I deem it necessary for men of my age to step aside so that younger men can take over the greatest navy in the world."

Admiral Carney personally piped Halsey over the side. To newsmen Halsey remarked that, for him, leaving the fleet was like cutting off his right arm. As it turned out, however, he was not actually terminating his naval career, for a week later President Truman nominated him for promotion to fleet admiral.

In December 1944 the U.S. Senate had approved a House bill authorizing the appointment of four fleet admirals and four generals of the army—five-star ranks that presumably would enable senior Amerian officers to stand on an equal footing with senior British officers. The president at once appointed Marshall, MacArthur, Eisenhower, and Arnold generals of the army, and Leahy, King, and Nimitz fleet admirals. Many persons were surprised that Halsey did not get the fourth appointment to the new naval rank, but King was reluctant to see Halsey promoted if Spruance was not. Instead of expressing a choice, he sent Secretary Forrestal a memorandum naming Spruance, Halsey, and four other senior admirals as candidates for the fifth star. Forrestal, equally unwilling to express a preference, left the appointment undecided for several months. He then passed the buck to Truman, who selected Halsey.

In April 1946 the Senate approved a House-Senate committee recommendation to keep the eight five-star U.S. officers, now including Halsey, on active duty for life. Each was to be provided with an office and an aide and to receive fixed pay and allowances of $15,750 a year. In the Navy Department on 13 May the judge advocate general swore in Halsey and Nimitz as permanent five-star admirals.

Fleet Admirals Nimitz and Halsey being sworn in as permanent fleet admirals of the navy, 13 May 1946, by Rear Admiral Oswald S. Colcloug, judge advocate general, representing the secretary of the navy

"My only fear," Halsey wrote to a friend, "is that the extra stripe is going to interfere with my drinking arm."[2]

Meanwhile, Joe Bryan had again entered Halsey's circle. Bryan had spent the latter part of the war in carriers, but that duty did not keep him from his free-lance writing. With Philip Reed he wrote *Mission Beyond Darkness,* published in 1945, a vivid account of the twilight attack of Mitscher's aviators on the Japanese fleet in the Battle of the Philippine Sea.

At war's end Bryan's literary agent suggested that he collaborate with Admiral Halsey in writing the latter's autobiography. Bryan being willing, the agent asked the *Saturday Evening Post* editors if they would like to have it. The editors, recalling the success of Bryan's two-part profile of Halsey, jumped at the opportunity. The agent contacted Halsey, who agreed to the enterprise. Agent and lawyers then entered into negotiations, the upshot of which was that the *Saturday Evening Post* paid sixty thousand dollars for the magazine rights, and McGraw-Hill advanced twenty thousand for book rights—princely sums of which Halsey was to receive sixty percent.

Retired heavyweight boxing champion Gene Tunney, a friend of Halsey's and Bryan's, offered the use of his comfortable home in Hobe Sound, Florida, as a workshop. Joe Bryan reported to Hobe Sound with his wife, who would keep house. Admiral Halsey arrived with two yeomen. The admiral's son and daughter each came for a short visit.

The work began in early February 1946. Joe would ask Halsey questions. One of the yeomen would take the questions and answers down in shorthand and afterward type up a rough draft from his notes. Joe would then go over the draft with Halsey, correcting or expanding as needed. Frequently the admiral would interrupt, reminded of something that Bryan might find interesting.

When the need arose for further details or a fact check, Bryan would send the drafts to some member of Halsey's former staff—Mick Carney, Ray Thurber, Ralph Wilson, Julian Brown, Bill Kitchell, Ham Dow, Bill Ashford, Doug Moulton, Harold Stassen, or Herb Carroll. Louis Bolander, the Naval Academy librarian, provided details pertinent to Halsey's early days at the Academy. From these sources, but chiefly from Halsey's dictated recollections, Bryan, with the help of the yeomen, assembled and arranged a succession of typescripts, concluding with a formidable document of around seven hundred pages. Before the end of March this phase of the work was finished. The workshop broke up, and Bryan retired with his seven hundred pages to the solitude of his family's country home to write the book.

When a chapter was completed, Bryan would send it to Halsey for approval and corrections. At last the work was done and the typescript submitted. To Joe's dismay, the *Saturday Evening Post* editors, considering the narrative too long for their purpose, cut the text heavily, particularly the part covering Halsey's childhood.

Joe forwarded the galleys, when they came, to Halsey's former staff members and other persons who had contributed to the manuscript. When these sent in words of praise for Halsey, Bryan inserted their remarks in the text, in smaller type, to offset the admiral's natural modesty in describing his own accomplishments.

Part one of "Admiral Halsey Tells His Story" appeared in the 14 June 1947 issue of the *Post,* with successive installments in the next eight issues. Not long after the final installment was printed, McGraw-Hill published the autobiography under the title *Admiral Halsey's Story.*[3]

Bryan was wise to retain a good deal of the original dictated narrative, sometimes at the expense of unity and in defiance of chronology. The result catches Halsey's personality strikingly; the reader almost seems to hear the admiral talking. In the biography, as in life, Halsey had abundant praise for most of his colleagues and associates but did not hesitate to criticize individuals or actions of which he disapproved.

In the summer of 1946, while Bryan was still wrestling with his text, Halsey at the request of President Truman made a goodwill tour of parts of

Latin America, in the course of which he was awarded the Order of Liberator (Venezuela), the Order of Ayacucho (Peru), the National Order of the Southern Cross (Brazil), and the Grand Cross of the Legion of Merit (Chile). The nature and success of the mission may be judged from the following letters:

The White House

Sept. 3, 1946

My dear Admiral Halsey,

I am enclosing you a letter from Claude G. Bowers, our Ambassador in Chile.

I am very happy over the outcome of your visit to South America.

Sincerely yours,
Harry Truman

Santiago, August 13, 1946

Dear Mr. President:

I think you should know directly from here that the visit of Admiral Halsey to Chile was of immeasurable value to the United States and to our people here. His robust personality, his simplicity and modesty, his perfect tact in brief addresses, made a deep impression on everyone. The navy men here have been enthusiastic in their praise and they appear to feel that a compliment was paid them by his coming. When that fighting face of his broke into an infectious smile he won the hearts of all. I have never seen a better reaction to the visit of a citizen of our country. His visit will be of value to our Naval Mission which has been unfortunate because of our seeming inability to furnish it with the material necessary for its complete success.

I am sure you will be glad to know that like Caesar he came, and saw and conquered—an old habit of his.

In the meantime, Halsey had been receiving offers to serve in executive positions in industry. These had proved tempting, offering salaries to supplement the stipend he was receiving from the government, which postwar inflation was making increasingly inadequate. Admiral Nimitz, by economizing and entertaining simply, even when he was chief of naval operations, got by on his navy pay as long as he lived. But Admiral Halsey had the burden of constant and expensive medical care for Fan.

In early December 1946 Halsey, at his own request, was relieved of active participation in the navy but remained on full pay. Though this news raised some eyebrows, naval officers generally understood that the continuing monthly stipend was in fact a pension—pay not for what he was expected to do but a reward for what he had already accomplished.

Before the end of the month, the president of the Carlisle Tire and Rubber Company of Pennsylvania announced that Admiral Halsey had been elected a member of its board of directors. Since his duty as director required only that he attend the quarterly meetings, for each of which he was paid three hundred dollars and expenses, he was able in February 1947 to accept the chairmanship of a University of Virginia development fund drive.

Halsey, who had had a warm feeling for the university since his year there as a medical student, undertook his new duties with enthusiasm, writing letters, chairing meetings, and making public appearances. At this time he and Fan lived at the Farmington Country Club in Charlottesville.

Admiral Halsey's mother, now a feisty old lady of eighty-seven, had been bedridden since breaking her hip the preceding summer. Halsey made several trips to Wilmington to visit her. He was last at her bedside on 23 May 1947 in Delaware Hospital. She died two days later and was buried beside her husband in Arlington National Cemetery.

Not long afterward Admiral and Mrs. Halsey moved from the club into a comfortable residence that had park-like surroundings and a view of the Blue Ridge Mountains. Fan employed her considerable talents decorating the interior and seeing to the garden outside. "We've moved in," Halsey wrote a friend, "and are actually keeping house and thoroughly enjoying it. It is the first time I have had a home of my own for nearly fifteen years, and you can imagine what a joy it is."

Halsey was settled in Charlottesville and engaged in his fund-raising activities when his autobiography began appearing in the *Saturday Evening Post*. One of the earliest reactions came in the form of a letter from Admiral Kimmel, Halsey's old commander in chief. Kimmel, bitter at having been made the scapegoat for the Pearl Harbor disaster, was gratified by Halsey's spirited defense of him, particularly in the conclusion, which for emphasis Halsey had put in italics: *"In all my experience, I have never known a Commander in Chief of any United States Fleet who worked harder, and under more adverse circumstances, to increase its efficiency and to prepare it for war; further, I know of no officer who might have been in command at that time who could have done more than Kimmel did."*

"Thanks for your kind words about me in your articles," Kimmel wrote. "I'm sure they will give the public a better understanding of my actions. I am sincerely grateful and appreciate what you have done."

On the other hand, Halsey's opening installment brought him a blast from a national temperance society in the form of a six-column spread in its newsletter. The society was particularly shocked at his statement, "There are exceptions, of course, but as a general rule, I never trust a fighting man who doesn't drink or smoke." It called the report that he had ordered a hundred gallons of bourbon brought on board the *Enterprise* to soothe the nerves of returning pilots "an astonishing breach of Navy discipline." The article conceded that there was no evidence of Halsey's ever having been drunk in public and allowed that he may not have imbibed anything stronger than hot coffee during the Battle for Leyte Gulf. "But we do know," it added insinuatingly, "that this was the man who was tricked into doing what the Japanese wanted him to do."

In subsequent installments of his autobiography Halsey violated military custom by publicly criticizing a fellow officer who was still living, General George Kenney. Kinkaid, Halsey wrote, "wasn't satisfied with the cover that Kenney was providing," and "what balked us was . . . Kenney's inability to give Leyte effective air support. I had to stand by and attend to his knitting for him."

Halsey's seventh installment, published on 26 July, caused ripples throughout the navy. This piece covered the Battle for Leyte Gulf, and Halsey, aware that his tactics in that battle were being criticized, had seized the opportunity to vindicate himself. At the beginning of his narrative and again at the end, he blamed the less-than-complete victory on the divided command, which left the Third and Seventh fleets without a common superior at the scene of action. He diverted attention from his failure to prevent the Center Force from attacking Sprague's task unit by stating, "I wondered how Kinkaid had let 'Ziggy' Sprague get caught like this." Commenting on Kinkaid's demand for fast battleships at Leyte Gulf, Halsey wrote, "That surprised me. It was not my job to protect the Seventh Fleet. My job was offensive, to strike with the Third Fleet." As for the fruitless run back south that had stripped Mitscher of the power to protect his force at night from Japanese battleships, Halsey put the blame mainly on the corrupted language of Nimitz's dispatch.

Lastly, with respect to Kinkaid, Halsey endeavored to have his cake and eat it too. "I have attempted to describe the Battle for Leyte Gulf in terms of my thoughts and feelings at the time," he wrote, "but on rereading my account, I find that this results in an implication grossly unfair to Tom Kinkaid. True, during the action, his dispatches puzzled me. Later, with the gaps in my information filled, I not only appreciate his problems, but frankly admit that had I been in his shoes, I might have acted precisely as he did."

Admiral King, in a letter to Halsey dated 30 July 1947, had a few words to say about this installment:

> Since reading the 7th installment of your "Story" in the Saturday Evening Post of July 26th, I have debated in my own mind whether to write to you about it. . . .
>
> The comment chiefly has to do with two points—your remarks about Kinkaid [and] your statement that things would have been different if the command set-up had been different.
>
> Your "strictures" on Kinkaid are severe even though you have a "note" in which you say that you would have done as he did in the circumstances. In fact, an inference readily to be drawn from your remarks about the command

> set-up is that if you had had the control of the 7th Fleet, its readiness to oppose the Japanese Central Force would have been adequate, or more nearly so. . . .
>
> Personally, I must say that I did not like the tenor of the installment, neither as to Kinkaid . . . nor as to the command set-up. . . .
>
> You would do well to review—and rewrite—the matter contained in the 7th installment. . . .

Halsey replied on 12 August, "I have given your letter and my article much thought and study, and have asked for and received counsel. I regret that your point of view and mine do not coincide."

Others besides King took exception to Halsey's seventh installment. Probably the most regrettable outcome was that it turned his old friend Kinkaid into an implacable enemy.[4]

After 1948 Halsey became increasingly dissatisfied with life in Charlottesville and with his post at the University of Virginia. For one thing, the university's goal for the development fund was set at eighteen million dollars, an unrealistic figure. When it was evident that the drive under his chairmanship was not going to bring in anywhere near that amount, Halsey was frustrated by an unaccustomed sense of failure. Fan, plagued by ill health, made few friends. With Bill frequently away from home on business, she was lonely. Moreover, in Charlottesville, despite the presence of the university hospital, she was unable to get the medical attention she needed.

Halsey's basic problem was sheer boredom. He had accepted the chairmanship eagerly, but for an officer who had commanded the world's largest fleet, collecting dollars for a university fund at last proved less than exhilarating. For a military leader who had reversed the course of the war in the South Pacific and pounded the Japanese empire from Mindanao to Hokkaido, the serenity of Charlottesville was soporific. The letdown following a major war is a phenomenon that many commanders of large military forces have had to face. Admiral Nimitz, confronted with it, at length came to terms with the problem, but it killed Admiral King.[5]

After the war many clubs and societies, most based in New York, offered Admiral Halsey honorary memberships in recognition of his military achievements. In his trips to the big city on business for the university or for Carlisle Tire and Rubber, Halsey took advantage of these connections for some stimulating company.

One of the most memorable occasions, before Halsey joined either the university or the rubber company, was the evening he was guest of honor, "fall guy" in circus parlance, of the New York Circus Saints and Sinners society. As fall guy he was subjected to a program of good-natured ribbing about his career. Another memorable evening with the Saints and Sinners was at the Waldorf-Astoria on 24 June 1948, when the fall guy was Governor William

Tuck of Virginia. Participating in the ribbing, besides Admiral Halsey, were Dwight Eisenhower, Lowell Thomas, Babe Ruth, Jack Dempsey, Gene Tunney, Fiorello La Guardia, Irving Berlin, Lauritz Melchior, Winthrop Rockefeller, Eddie Rickenbacker, and a score of U.S. senators, state governors, and members of the president's cabinet.

Among the club men Halsey met and admired in his New York rounds was Colonel Sosthenes Behn, cofounder and chairman of the board of the International Telephone and Telegraph Corporation. Unlike in many ways, Behn being a connoisseur of the arts, the two men nonetheless formed a close and enduring friendship.

In late 1949, learning that the Virginia development fund drive was drawing to a close, Behn offered Halsey chairmanship of the board of the All-American Cable and Radio Corporation, an affiliate of ITT. Halsey immediately accepted. Subsequently he became a director of ITT itself and president of the International Telecommunications Laboratories, another ITT affiliate.

Despite his high-sounding titles, Halsey was in no sense an executive of these enterprises. His services were limited to public relations. Bill, who at the Naval Academy had been "everybody's friend," was a natural goodwill ambassador. His services for ITT could not be performed at occasional meetings. A convivial table companion, he was in much demand for the lunches and dinners at which company representatives made some of their most useful contacts. It turned out that he was getting higher pay than at any time in his life for doing what he enormously enjoyed.

It quickly became clear that Halsey could not operate from his base in Charlottesville or even from the Wilmington residence of his sister, which he considered his second home. He resigned from both the University of Virginia fund committee and from the tire and rubber company, now known as the Carlisle Corporation, and prepared to settle in New York.

There was a major flaw in this arrangement. Fan refused to live in New York. She believed that her tender health could not stand the hurly-burly of the big city, particularly with Bill away much of the time at lunches and dinners or on trips for his companies. After thrashing the matter out, Bill and Fan reached a painful conclusion. She would move to the West Coast, where her son and many of her navy friends lived. Bill would reside in New York, where he would make enough money to provide her with the best of care.

In New York Halsey first took residence at the Ambassador Hotel, 51st Street and Park Avenue, and later moved into an apartment at 530 Park Avenue, the building in which his former aide Bill Kitchell resided. Halsey had two offices, one at 67 Broad Street, the ITT building, the other at 90 Church Street, the navy building. His health was declining, and in an exception to a statute making the five-star rank permanent, Halsey was put on the retired list for physical disability, an arrangement that eased his tax burden. But he retained his navy pay, aide, yeoman, and office and never ceased to conduct a certain amount of navy correspondence.

In April 1951, when General MacArthur, in defiance of orders to the contrary, continued to issue statements criticizing State and Defense department plans for the Korean War, President Truman relieved him of all his Far East commands. Admiral Halsey predictably took the general's side in the dispute, and New York prepared to give the general a hero's welcome with a traditional ticker-tape parade. Halsey was to ride in the parade showing support for his old friend, but en route to Idlewild Airport to meet the general's plane he collapsed with pneumonia. He was taken to Roosevelt Hospital while Bill Kitchell pinch-hit for him in the parade.

The following summer, fully recovered, Halsey sailed for Europe on ITT business, specifically to convey greetings and encouragement from the home office to various ITT officers abroad. Combining pleasure with business, he brought his sister Deborah and his daughter Margaret, both divorced, on a seven-week tour that took them to London, Paris, Zurich, Milan, Florence, and Naples.

In 1952 Colonel Behn and Admiral Halsey attended a world telecommunication conference in Buenos Aires. While they were there, the Argentine government decorated Halsey with its Order of Naval Merit in recognition of his war record.

In the spring of 1954 Admiral Halsey flew to Australia as a guest of the government to participate in Coral Sea Week, a commemoration of the battle that saved Port Moresby and was widely believed to have preserved Australia from invasion by the Japanese. As soon as the New Zealanders heard of the visit, they invited the admiral to visit their country, which had been part of his area of command as Commander, South Pacific. The old admiral received great acclaim in Brisbane, Sydney, Canberra, Melbourne, Adelaide, and Perth in Australia and Wellington, Auckland, and Christchurch in New Zealand.[6]

Operation Remember, held in May 1957 at the Naval Academy, gave Halsey a great deal of pleasure. This was a gathering of the top U.S. naval commanders of World War II. Because Leahy was in poor health and King had died the year before, Nimitz was expected to be the senior officer present. He made the trip from his home in California to the East Coast, where, stricken with a severe case of laryngitis, he was obliged to remain at the home of his daughter and son-in-law. Thus Halsey, the senior officer present, reviewed the midshipmen's parade in honor of the visitors.

Just before the march past, Halsey was standing on the parade ground beside the academy superintendent, Rear Admiral William R. Smedberg, facing the midshipman brigade commander and his staff. The band sounded off and played ruffles and flourishes. That was the cue for the gun salute to Halsey, but nothing happened.

"I'm a little deaf," Halsey muttered, "but I don't hear any guns."

"I don't hear any guns either," muttered Smedberg out of the side of his mouth, "and I'm *not* deaf!"

During this period the salute guns were stationed on Stribling Walk, out of sight of the parade ground. To back up the cue from the band, an officer on the field gave the order to fire by telephone line. This time of all times, in the presence of the aging war leaders, the gunners failed to hear the band, and the telephone line went dead.

After an embarrassing silence, the brigade commander said, "Sir, the brigade of midshipmen."

Admiral Halsey arrives at the New York Naval Shipyard to attend the launching of the carrier USS *Independence* (CV 62), 6 June 1958. (Courtesy of S. N. Pyne)

"Pass in review," said Halsey.

Before the next parade, and forever after, the guns were positioned alongside the parade ground, a hundred yards from the band.

Admiral Halsey, in addition to his public relations duties with ITT and its affiliates, accepted the chairmanship of a drive to preserve his old flagship, the carrier *Enterprise.* From his office at 67 Broad Street he conducted a vigorous campaign to raise the necessary million dollars. In mid-1957 he went to Washington to urge approval of a bill calling for the carrier to be turned into a national naval shrine and museum. To the press he remarked that he was "getting along in years but trying to live to save the *Enterprise.*"

Bill was in his middle seventies, long past the usual retirement age. His efforts on behalf of the Big E may have contributed to the mild stroke he suffered at the end of July. At any rate, on his doctor's orders he retired from active participation in the drive, remaining honorary chairman until December 1957, when he withdrew entirely from the project. To his sorrow, in August 1958 the famous old carrier left her mooring off New York City and moved down the East River to the Naval Industrial Reserve Shipyard at Kearny, New Jersey, to be cut up and sold for scrap. But her name would be perpetuated in the new *Enterprise,* the first nuclear-propelled carrier, which was under construction at the Newport News Shipyard. The new *Enterprise* would displace more than three times the tonnage of Halsey's flagship.[7]

From time to time Admiral Halsey flew to the West Coast to visit his son, living at La Jolla, and Fan, who had retired to a nursing home to get the continuous care she needed. On one occasion the admiral and his son went to Camp Pendleton, the huge marine corps base between Los Angeles and San Diego. Here Cagney-Montgomery Productions was shooting a movie, *Admiral Halsey's Story,* later renamed *The Gallant Hours.* By terms of the contract between Cagney-Montgomery and Halsey, the admiral would receive ten percent of the profits. When the admiral's son saw James Cagney in makeup for the leading role, he was startled at the actor's resemblance to his father as he had appeared during World War II. In fact, Cagney looked more like the wartime admiral than the aging Halsey did, now walking with a cane and wearing thick glasses to compensate for cataract operations on both eyes.[8]

Few things annoyed Admiral Halsey in the postwar years more than repeated criticism of his strategy in the Battle for Leyte Gulf. At first, even among officers and others conversant with the details, opinion was divided as to whether Halsey had made a mistake in abandoning San Bernardino Strait and heading north to attack the Japanese Northern Force. A few officers speculated that the Northern Force might have been a decoy sent to draw the Third Fleet away from the strait, but this view was not widely held.

In 1946, however, the U.S. Strategic Bombing Survey published the two-volume *Interrogations of Japanese Officials,* containing a statement by Vice

Admiral Jisaburo Ozawa, commander of the Northern Force, who said he had indeed been sent as bait and had considered his assignment a suicide mission. This was not an unrealistic expectation. The whole Northern Force would probably have been destroyed had Halsey not taken his six battleships on their fruitless run back south in response to Admiral Nimitz's botched message.

Publication of *Interrogations* had little immediate effect on public thinking because it was not widely distributed. The volumes came to the attention mainly of naval historians and other specialists. Eventually, however, the public was brought into the controversy by a series of books and articles published in 1947. Early that year two small volumes appeared: James A. Field's *The Japanese at Leyte Gulf* and C. Vann Woodward's *The Battle for Leyte Gulf*. Field, writing from the Japanese point of view, as set forth chiefly in the *Interrogations,* was strictly objective with respect to American operations. Woodward, telling the story from both the Japanese and American points of view, was rather sympathetic toward Halsey and his strategy. Both books, however, repeated and emphasized Ozawa's testimony, supported by other interrogations, that the Northern Force was sent on a supposed suicide mission to lure the U.S. Third Fleet north. The fact that Halsey took the bait did not necessrily mean that he had made a mistake, but in the minds of many persons his run to the north was a blunder simply because he did what the Japanese wanted him to do.[9]

This was in effect the view espoused by Bernard Brodie in the summer 1947 issue of *The Virginia Quarterly Review*. Brodie's article, "The Battle for Leyte Gulf," in part a review of the Field and Woodward books, called Halsey's handling of his forces

> anything but "well done." Despite the sympathy which at least Mr. Woodward displays towards Halsey, the facts which he presents make the tally of errors against the American admiral more extensive and more astonishing than before. . . . His accomplishments prior to the Battle for Leyte Gulf were spectacular. But his judgments were not equal to his boldness, and boldness alone does not make a Nelson. . . . It is the skill of the commander that matters. And the United States Navy will have learned the greatest lesson of the Battle for Leyte Gulf if it concludes that in the supreme commander it is brains that matters most.

This imputation of stupidity on Halsey's part naturally outraged the admiral, and he complained bitterly to his friends about it. Wisely, though, he avoided issuing a statement, which could only bring the article to wider attention.

Almost immediately after the article's appearance, the Halsey series began appearing in the *Saturday Evening Post*. Because the admiral insisted his only mistake was turning back south with his battleships, a move made unwillingly in response to what he took to be an order from Nimitz, the series was widely regarded as a reply to Brodie—though in fact the autobiography had been submitted to the publisher even before the Field and Woodward books were published. Thus inadvertently Halsey set off a controversy, at first limited mainly to wardrooms, clubs, and history symposia.

The 14 November 1947 issue of *Life* magazine went public with a feature article by Gilbert Cant:

> Bull's Run
> Was Halsey Right at Leyte Gulf?
> *The greatest naval battle in history is being refought between supporters of Admiral ("Bull") Halsey and Admiral Tom Kinkaid. MacArthur's return to the Philippines and the whole course of the Pacific war were at stake. Did a Japanese blunder save an American Army and Fleet from a Halsey mistake?*

Cant asked a question and provided an answer, of sorts:

> The four-day, four-ring battle left one great question unanswered: was Admiral William F. ("Bull") Halsey right in dashing off to destroy the Japanese aircraft carriers instead of the battleships—or did he leave a fellow American admiral in the lurch? . . . No one can deny the brilliance of Halsey's leadership. But in the matter of Bull's run his judgment seems so questionable that even one of his most loyal former subordinates, after vigorously defending him, admitted, "Still, it's a damned shame it turned out the way it did, with all those battleships getting away."

In January 1951 Halsey learned that Professor Samuel Eliot Morison of Harvard University, the country's most prolific naval historian, winner of many literary and history prizes, had recently lectured on the Battle for Leyte Gulf before the Naval Historical Foundation in Washington, and that in the course of his lecture he had called the Third Fleet run to the north "Halsey's blunder."

Admiral Halsey, suppressing his wrath, penned Morison a dignified if not particularly coherent letter, saying in part,

> I realize that long after the event it is very difficult if not impossible to place oneself in the position of a Fleet Commander at the time of the specific occurrence. Information which has subsequently become available [the lack of air strength in the Northern Force] tend [*sic*] to intrude upon any determination based only on the facts and on the information which were [*sic*] available to the Commander at the time of his decision. To correctly evaluate any decisions made at a prior time it is necessary to consider only the information available to the person who made the decision at the time such a decision was made. . . . I still feel that my only real error was in not continuing my advance to the North and completely annihilating the Northern Force, and this I would have done had it not been for the dispatches from Kinkaid and Nimitz.

It was apparently about this time that Halsey, in view of his declining health and strength, began assembling and editing his voluminous papers. The editing, carried out with the assistance of his naval aide, consisted mainly of removing personal papers such as letters Halsey sent to and received from his family. The remainder, some twenty-two thousand items, he left to the Naval Historical Division, Washington, D.C., which subsequently turned them over to the Library of Congress.

In 1958 Professor Morison had Little, Brown and Company, his publisher, send Admiral Halsey a copy of his new book, *Leyte, June 1944–January 1945*, volume twelve of his monumental *United States Naval Operations in World War II*.

Morison may have thought to please the admiral with his gift, but it produced the opposite reaction. In his account of the Battle for Leyte Gulf, which occupies the latter half of the volume, the historian failed to explain Halsey's decisions strictly on the basis of the facts known to the admiral at the time—a procedure recommended in Halsey's 1951 letter. Instead, Morison repeatedly interrupted his narrative with reminders that the Third Fleet was speeding north after an enemy force far weaker than itself on the surface and in the air—a force sent down specifically on a supposed suicide mission to lure Halsey away from San Bernardino Strait and thus allow the Japanese Center Force a free passage to Leyte Gulf. Halsey and his staff were made to look like a parcel of prime dunces. This effect Morison heightened by a statement that the fleet had been informed by naval intelligence that the Japanese were planning to use carriers as a decoy. Halsey was so startled that he sent letters to his former staff members asking if they had seen the intelligence report. None could recall having seen anything of the sort. Investigation finally turned up the item Morison had based his statement on. The document was so vague and subject to misinterpretation that no one had considered it worth sending up the line to the admiral.

Halsey, incensed, wrote to his former staff members asking them to find ammunition to use against Morison, items that would enable the admiral "to poke fun at him as a very poor historian and cite some instances to prove our point. In other words, make a laughingstock of him." Mick Carney, however, was able to pacify Halsey. "My initial thought," Carney wrote,

> is that any reply you make should be completely devoid of sarcasm or any effort to discredit Morison's general reputation as a historian. My natural reaction is always the same as yours: to fight. However, despite the fact that Morison is stuffy, and has an exaggerated opinion of Morison's importance, he *has* done excellent work at times, his flair for writing readable history is widely acclaimed, and on the basis of the volume of his research and output he is firmly established in public opinion as a professional and competent historian. No blast of yours, however justifiable, will destroy that structure; it would far more likely boomerang.

"Once again," replied Halsey, "I shall probably keep my mouth shut about this matter. . . . Again, I thank you for your always good advice when I get mad—which I do frequently."

Hardly had Halsey's anger over Morison's account subsided when he had more trouble from professors. In the late spring of 1959 a Naval Academy professor wrote asking Halsey to inspect several chapters he had written for a textbook, *Sea Power: A Naval History,* which he and his colleagues were preparing for the use of midshipmen. Permission was granted, and in due course two chapters arrived covering Halsey's operations in the South Pacific. The admiral read them carefully, in fact took them with him for a second reading on what proved to be his last visit to his son and wife on the West Coast. Finding nothing seriously wrong with the material, Halsey returned it to the professor with a few minor comments.

In July another chapter arrived from Annapolis, this one including a narrative of the Battle for Leyte Gulf. Halsey proceeded to scrutinize the new version. He perused the first few pages with general satisfaction. Then he came to two sentences that gave him a jolt. Of the Third Fleet's run to the north the author wrote, "Halsey had made the wrong decision. In the light of what we now know, there can be no question about that."

On reading this, the admiral burst out, "I consider this statement one of the best examples of Monday-morning quarterbacking I have ever read." Then, restraining his choler, he added, "The author has leaned over backwards in trying to be fair to me, so I dislike very much picking him up on this statement."

But the sentences rankled Halsey, and presently he returned to them. This time he let both the Academy professor and Morison have it, with both barrels:

> Referring again to the author's statement, "Halsey had made the wrong decision . . . etc." This, to my mind, is a very wrong statement to make. It places the author in the class of another so-called Naval Historian, Samuel Eliot Morison, who does not hesitate to drop objectivity, but categorically makes statements about strategical decisions of commanders afloat, saying some decisions were all wrong, and he, in his high understanding and knowledge of the rather difficult subject of strategy, pontificates on what the decision should have been and spreads it for all to see. . . . It comes to mind that the U.S. Government wasted much money on the education of many Naval officers throughout the years, when they were not needed as Samuel Eliot Morison could have stepped in and done their jobs better than the Americans trained as naval officers did—and think what their education cost!*

Admiral Halsey need not have worried. The offending sentences never saw

*Morison, shown this passage, wrote to the Academy professor, "I am gratified to be in Bill Halsey's doghouse along with you."

print. The general editor of the textbook, also author of the submitted chapters, had sought and obtained the counsel of Admiral Nimitz, who served as associate editor of the 1960 edition of *Sea Power*. It was on Nimitz's advice that the editor sent chapters covering their operations to major American commanders. Admiral Nimitz was reading the Leyte Gulf chapter at the same time Admiral Halsey was reading it. He urged that the offensive passage be eliminated and proposed a guiding principle: "Give all the facts, as accurately, objectively, and fairly as you can, but don't draw the conclusions. Let the reader do that. Let the facts speak for themselves."[10]

In August 1959, as in several preceding summers, Halsey vacationed at the country club on Fisher's Island, administratively an extension of Long Island but lying in fact in Block Island Sound, five miles south of Mystic, Connecticut. On the fifteenth, as usual, he relaxed, waded along the beach, and sunbathed. The next morning, when he failed to appear for breakfast, the club manager investigated and found him alone in his room, dead from a heart attack. The body was flown by helicopter to New York.

For the funeral Halsey's son sought the advice of Mick Carney. The admiral's old friend said that for a man of Halsey's fame and achievements the public would expect nothing less, and the admiral deserved nothing less, than a state funeral with full military honors. Bill consented with misgivings, thinking his father might have preferred something simpler. He and his mother flew east to be present.

At Floyd Bennett Field in Brooklyn the admiral's flag-draped white casket was loaded on a plane while a navy band played "Eternal Father." Accompanying the casket to Washington were Halsey's son and daughter, his former and most recent aides, Commanders William Kitchell and William Neville, and Halsey's old friend Rear Admiral Walden Ainsworth, designated escort commander for the trip.

The body lay in state in the National Cathedral's Bethlehem Chapel until the funeral service on Thursday, 20 August, following which the casket was placed on a caisson and drawn by horses through crowd-lined streets to Arlington Cemetery. As the caisson passed through the memorial gate, guns began firing at intervals. Next came a nineteen-gun salute. At the end of a winding drive, enlisted pallbearers, accompanied by an honor guard of senior generals and admirals, bore the casket up a steep hill to the burial site, next to the admiral's parents' graves, while jet fighters thundered overhead.

In the presence of dignitaries and friends of the deceased, with the family seated under a canopy and Admiral Nimitz, representing President Eisenhower, standing at the head of the casket, Chaplain D. J. Zimmerman read prayers and committed the body to the grave. Another nineteen-gun salute followed, then three rifle volleys, and taps.[11]

Thus passed one of the most courageous, colorful, and beloved heroes of his time.

SOURCES

PUBLISHED BOOKS

Adams, Henry H. *1942: The Year That Doomed the Axis*. New York: David McKay Co., 1967.

———. *Years of Expectation: Guadalcanal to Normandy*. New York: David McKay Co., 1973.

———. *Years to Victory*. New York: David McKay Co., 1973.

Adamson, Hans Christian, and George Francis Kosko. *Halsey's Typhoons*. New York: Crown Publishers, 1967.

Alden, Carroll Storrs, and Allan Westcott. *The United States Navy: A History*. Chicago: J. B. Lippincott Co., 1943.

Bailey, Thomas A. *A Diplomatic History of the American People*. New York: F. S. Crofts & Co., 1942.

Baldwin, Hanson W. *Sea Fights and Shipwrecks: True Tales of the Seven Seas*. New York: Hanover House, 1955.

Belote, James H. and William M. *Titans of the Seas: The Development and Operations of Japanese and American Carrier Task Forces During World War II*. New York: Harper & Row, 1975.

Blair, Clay, Jr. *Silent Victory: The U.S. Submarine War Against Japan*. Philadelphia and New York: J. B. Lippincott Co., 1975.

Buell, Thomas B. *Master of Sea Power: A Biography of Fleet Admiral Ernest J. King*. Boston: Little, Brown and Co., 1980.

———. *The Quiet Warrior: A Biography of Admiral Raymond A. Spruance*. Boston: Little, Brown and Co., 1974.

Burns, Eugene. *Then There Was One: The USS* Enterprise *and the First Year of the War*. New York: Harcourt, Brace, 1944.

Cant, Gilbert. *America's Navy in World War II*. New York: The John Day Co., 1944.

Casey, Robert J. *Torpedo Junction: With the Pacific Fleet from Pearl Harbor to Midway*. Indianapolis: The Bobbs-Merrill Co., 1942.

Clark, J. J., and Clark G. Reynolds. *Carrier Admiral*. New York: David McKay Co., 1967.

Costello, John. *The Pacific War*. New York: Rawson, Wade Publishers, 1981.

Craig, William. *The Fall of Japan*. New York: The Dial Press, 1967.

Craven, Wesley F., and James S. Cate, eds. *The Army Air Forces in World War II*. Vol. 4. Chicago: University of Chicago Press, 1950.

Davis, Burke. *Get Yamamoto*. New York: Random House, 1969.

Dyer, George Carroll. *The Amphibians Came to Conquer: The Story of Admiral Richmond Kelly Turner.* 2 vols. Washington, D.C.: U.S. Government Printing Office, 1971.

Falk, Stanley L. *Decision at Leyte.* New York: W. W. Norton & Co., 1966.

Field, James A., Jr. *The Japanese at Leyte Gulf: The Sho Operation.* Princeton, N.J.: Princeton University Press, 1947.

Forrestel, E. P. *Admiral Raymond A. Spruance, USN: A Study in Command.* Washington, D.C.: U.S. Government Printing Office, 1966.

Frank, Benis M. *Halsey.* New York: Ballantine Books, 1947.

Fuchida, Mitsuo, and Masatake Okumiya. *Midway: The Battle That Doomed Japan.* Annapolis, Md.: U.S. Naval Institute, 1955.

Geffen, William. *Command and Commanders in Modern Warfare.* Colorado Springs: U.S. Air Force Academy, 1969.

Glines, Carroll. *Doolittle's Tokyo Raiders.* Princeton, N.J.: D. Van Nostrand Co., 1964.

Griffith, Samuel B., II. *The Battle for Guadalcanal.* Philadelphia: J. B. Lippincott Co., 1963.

Halsey, Jacob Lafayette, and Edmund Drake Halsey. *Thomas Halsey of Hertfordshire, England, and Southampton, Long Island, with His American Descendants to the Eighth and Ninth Generations.* Morristown, N.J., 1895. Library of Congress. Microfilm.

Halsey, William F., and J. Bryan III. *Admiral Halsey's Story.* New York: McGraw-Hill Book Co., 1947.

Hart, Robert A. *The Great White Fleet: Its Voyage Around the World, 1907–1909.* Boston: Little, Brown and Co., 1965.

Heinl, R. D. *The Defense of Wake.* Washington, D.C.: U.S. Marine Corps Headquarters, n.d.

The History of the Lives and Bloody Exploits of the Most Noted Pirates. Hartford: Silus Andrus & Son, 1847.

Holmes, W. J. *Double-Edged Secrets: U.S. Naval Intelligence Operations in the Pacific During World War II.* Annapolis, Md.: Naval Institute Press, 1979.

Hough, Frank O., Verle E. Ludwig, and Henry I. Shaw, Jr. *History of U.S. Marine Corps Operations in World War II.* Vol. 1. Washington, D.C.: Historical Branch, U.S. Marine Corps Headquarters, n.d.

Hoyt, Edwin P. *The Battle of Leyte Gulf: Death Knell of the Japanese Fleet.* New York: Weybright and Talley, 1972.

———. *How They Won the War in the Pacific: Nimitz and His Admirals.* New York: Weybright and Talley, 1970.

Isely, Jeter A., and Philip A. Crowl. *The U.S. Marines and Amphibious War: Its Theory and Practice in the Pacific.* Princeton, N.J.: Princeton University Press, 1951.

James, D. Clayton. *The Years of MacArthur.* Vol. 2, 1941–45. Boston: Houghton Mifflin Co., 1975.

Jordan, Ralph B. *Born to Fight: The Life of Admiral Halsey.* Philadelphia: David McKay Co., 1946.

Kahn, David. *The Codebreakers: The Story of Secret Writing*. London: Weidenfeld and Nicolson, 1967.

King, Ernest J., and Walter Muir Whitehill. *Fleet Admiral King: A Naval Record*. New York: W. W. Norton & Co., 1952.

Knox, Dudley W. *A History of the United States Navy*. New York: G. P. Putnam's Sons, 1932.

Lewin, Ronald. *The American Magic: Codes, Ciphers and the Defeat of Japan*. New York: Farrar, Straus and Giroux, 1982.

Lockwood, Charles A., and Hans Christian Adamson. *Battles of the Philippine Sea*. New York: Harper & Row, 1967.

Lord, Walter. *Incredible Victory*. New York: Harper & Row, 1967.

Lundstrom, John B. *The First South Pacific Campaign: Pacific Fleet Strategy, December 1941–June 1942*. Annapolis, Md.: Naval Institute Press, 1976.

MacArthur, Douglas. *Reminiscences*. New York: McGraw-Hill Book Co., 1964.

Manchester, William. *American Caesar: Douglas MacArthur, 1880–1964*. Boston: Little, Brown and Co., 1978.

Matloff, Maurice. *Strategic Planning for Coalition Warfare, 1943–1944*. Washington, D.C.: Office of the Chief of Military History, Department of the Army, 1959.

———, and Edward M. Snell. *Strategic Planning for Coalition Warfare, 1941–1942*. Washington, D.C.: Office of the Chief of Military History, Department of the Army, 1953.

Merillat, Herbert Christian. *Guadalcanal Remembered*. New York: Dodd, Mead, 1982.

Merrill, James M. *A Sailor's Admiral: A Biography of William F. Halsey*. New York: Thomas Y. Crowell Co., 1976.

Miller, Thomas G., Jr. *The Cactus Air Force*. New York: Harper & Row, 1969.

Mitchell, Donald W. *History of the Modern American Navy: From 1883 Through Pearl Harbor*. New York: Alfred A. Knopf, 1946.

Morison, Elting E. *Admiral Sims and the Modern American Navy*. Boston: Houghton Mifflin Co., 1942.

Morison, Samuel Eliot. *History of United States Naval Operations in World War II*. Boston: Little, Brown and Co., 1947–62. Vol. 3, *The Rising Sun in the Pacific, 1931–April 1942* (1948). Vol. 4, *Coral Sea, Midway, Submarine Actions, May 1942–August 1942* (1949). Vol. 5, *The Struggle for Guadalcanal, August 1942–February 1943* (1949). Vol. 6, *Breaking the Bismarcks Barrier, July 22, 1942–May 1, 1944* (1950). Vol. 7, *Aleutians, Gilberts and Marshalls, June 1942–April 1944* (1951). Vol. 12, *Leyte, June 1944–January 1945* (1958). Vol. 13, *The Liberation of the Philippines, 1944–1945* (1959). Vol. 14, *Victory in the Pacific, 1945* (1960).

———. *The Two-Ocean War: A Short History of the United States Navy in the Second World War*. Boston: Little, Brown and Co., 1963.

Morton, Louis. *Strategy and Command: The First Two Years*. Washington, D.C.: Office of the Chief of Military History, Department of the Army, 1962.

Pogue, Forrest. *George C. Marshall: Ordeal and Hope, 1939–1942*. New York: The Viking Press, 1966.

———. *George C. Marshall: Organizer of Victory, 1943–1945.* New York: The Viking Press, 1973.

Potter, E. B. *Nimitz.* Annapolis, Md.: Naval Institute Press, 1976.

———, and others. *Sea Power: A Naval History.* Englewood Cliffs, N.J.: Prentice-Hall, Inc., 1960.

———, and others. *Sea Power: A Naval History.* Annapolis, Md.: Naval Institute Press, 1981. Revision of the 1960 edition.

———, and others. *The United States and World Sea Power.* Englewood Cliffs, N.J.: Prentice-Hall, Inc, 1955.

Prange, Gordon W. *At Dawn We Slept: The Untold Story of Pearl Harbor.* New York: McGraw-Hill Book Co., 1981.

Pratt, Fletcher. *The Navy: A History.* Garden City, N.Y.: Garden City Publishing Co., 1941.

Reynolds, Clark G. *The Fast Carriers: The Forging of an Air Navy.* McGraw-Hill Book Co., 1968.

Richardson, James O., and George C. Dyer. *On the Treadmill to Pearl Harbor: The Memoirs of Admiral James O. Richardson, USN (Retired).* Washington, D.C.: Naval History Division, Department of the Navy, 1973.

Sherman, Frederick C. *Combat Command: The American Aircraft Carriers in the Pacific War.* New York: E. P. Dutton & Co., 1950.

Spector, Ronald H. *Eagle Against the Sun: The American War with Japan.* New York: The Free Press, 1985.

Stafford, Edward P. *The Big E: The Story of the USS* Enterprise. New York: Random House, 1962.

Stewart, Adrian. *The Battle of Leyte Gulf.* New York: Charles Scribner's Sons, 1979.

Stillwell, Paul, ed. *Air Raid: Pearl Harbor! Recollections of a Day of Infamy.* Annapolis, Md.: Naval Institute Press, 1981.

Sweetman, Jack. *The U.S. Naval Academy.* Annapolis, Md.: Naval Institute Press, 1979.

Taylor, Theodore. *The Magnificent Mitscher.* New York: W. W. Norton & Co., 1954.

Toland, John. *But Not in Shame: The Six Months After Pearl Harbor.* New York: Random House, 1961.

———. *The Rising Sun: The Decline and Fall of the Japanese Empire, 1936–1945.* New York: Random House, 1970.

Vandegrift, A. A., and Robert B. Asprey. *Once a Marine: The Memoirs of General A. A. Vandegrift, United States Marine Corps.* New York: W. W. Norton & Co., 1964.

Westcott, Allan, ed. *American Sea Power Since 1775.* Chicago: J. B. Lippincott Co., 1952.

Wilson, Eugene E. *Slipstream.* New York: McGraw-Hill Book Co., 1950.

Woodward, C. Vann. *The Battle for Leyte Gulf.* New York: The Macmillan Co., 1947.

Y'Blood, William T. *Red Sun Setting: The Battle of the Philippine Sea.* Annapolis, Md.: Naval Institute Press, 1981.

NEWSPAPER AND MAGAZINE ARTICLES

New York Times, as dated in notes.
Shipmate, as dated in notes.
Time, as dated in notes.
Bryan, J., III. "Four-Star Sea Dog." *Saturday Evening Post. In two parts.* 25 Dec 1943, pp. 28–34. 1 Jan 1944, pp. 26, 50–52.
Potter, E. B. "The Command Personality: Some American Naval Leaders in World War II." *United States Naval Institute Proceedings* (Jan 1969): pp. 18–26.

U.S. GOVERNMENT PUBLICATIONS

The Battle for Leyte Gulf, October 1944: Strategical and Tactical Analysis. Newport, R.I.: U.S. Naval War College, 1957–58.
CinCPac Command Summary, or Gray Book. In operational archives branch of Naval Historical Center, Navy Yard, Washington, D.C. A diary of the Pacific war as seen from CinCPac headquarters, organized by dates.
Combat Narratives. Washington, D.C.: Office of Naval Intelligence, 1943. Accounts of battles and other combat operations issued to U.S. naval officers during World War II. Often incorrect regarding Japanese participation but containing useful details.
Interrogations of Japanese Officials. 2 vols. Naval Analysis Division, United States Strategic Bombing Survey. Interrogations of Japanese officers and other officials by U.S. naval officers in Tokyo during October and December 1945.
Pearl Harbor Attack: Hearings Before the Joint Committee, 79th Congress. 40 parts. Washington, D.C.: U.S. Government Printing Office, 1946.
"The Role of Radio Intelligence in the American-Japanese Naval War, August 1941–December 1942." In the National Archives and Naval Historical Center. Encrypted Japanese radio dispatches, broken and translated by the U.S. Navy's combat intelligence units. Included are the intercepted messages that enabled the navy to meet the enemy on favorable terms in the battles of the Coral Sea and Midway.
U.S. Naval Academy Notice, 31 August 1942: Seating Allocation for Address by Vice Admiral Halsey. In the U.S. Naval Academy archives.

U.S. NAVAL DOCUMENTS (Naval Historical Center)

USS *Enterprise* (CV 6) action report, 23 April 1942.
USS *Hornet* (CV 8) action report, 28 April 1942.
USS *Enterprise* (CV 6) war diary, 1942.
USS *Saratoga* (CV 3) war diaries, 1942 and 1943.
CinCPOA operation plan 8-44, 27 Sep 1944, for Pacific Fleet support of Southwest Pacific Force invasion of Leyte in October 1944.

U.S. NAVAL COMMUNICATIONS (Naval Historical Center)

CinCPac classified radio message file.
Commander, South Pacific, classified radio message file.

Commander, Task Force 77 (Admiral Kinkaid), classified radio message file.
Commander, Third Fleet, classified radio message file.

MacARTHUR'S DISPATCHES

Classified radio dispatches in Records of General Headquarters No. 4, United States Army Forces, Pacific, in the archives at the MacArthur Memorial in Norfolk, Virginia.

HALSEY'S MEMOIR

This is the story of Halsey's life as dictated by him. It served as the main source for *Admiral Halsey's Story,* which was put into its final form by Joseph Bryan III. It served also as the main source for this book.

When I interviewed Mr. Bryan at his home in Richmond, he told me that he had given the transcript to the Virginia Historical Society. I went there, saw the usefulness of the source, and asked the society to have it copied for me, which they did. On the completion of this book, I gave my copy to the Naval Historical Center.

Though Admiral Halsey dictated the memoir, he also read and approved or amended the chapters of *Admiral Halsey's Story* before they were published. Where quotations in the two sources differ, I have preferred the published version unless the testimony of another person supported the memoir version.

The memoir contains a good deal that is not in the published autobiography, because Bryan made selective use of the former and because the editors of the *Saturday Evening Post* cut the autobiography heavily to make it conform to space limitations.

THE HALSEY PAPERS

These roughly twenty-two thousand items are housed in the manuscript division of the Library of Congress (James Madison building). Included are Halsey's orders, together with itineraries, schedules of his other travels, announcements, telegrams, and letters. Halsey's replies to the communications are copies; everything else is an original. Of the letters, the official wartime correspondence is most useful to the biographer. The other correspondence relates mainly to business and honors or expresses congratulations or thanks. There is also a good deal of fan mail and some crank mail. Personal papers, such as letters to and from family and close friends, have been withdrawn from the collection.

LETTERS NOT IN THE HALSEY PAPERS

Ashford, Rear Admiral William H., Jr., USN (Ret.), to author, 22 September 1982, 27 March 1984.
Beardall, Rear Admiral John R., USN, superintendent, U.S. Naval Academy, to Vice Admiral W. F. Halsey, Jr., USN, 31 July, 11 and 21 August 1942. U.S. Naval Academy archives.
Bogan, Vice Admiral Gerald F., USN (Ret.), to Clark G. Reynolds, 11 May 1964.
Bryan, J., III, to author, 15 December 1982; 31 May, 30 August 1984.
Burke, Admiral Arleigh A., USN (Ret.), to author, 29 October, 31 May, 22 November 1984.

Carney, Admiral Robert B., USN (Ret.), to author, 31 October, 17 November, 3 December 1984.
Farrington, Captain Robert F., USN, to Clark G. Reynolds, 19 March 1961.
Halsey, Vice Admiral William F., Jr., USN, to Rear Admiral John R. Beardall, USN, 6 and 19 August 1942. U.S. Naval Academy archives.
Kinkaid, Admiral Thomas C., USN (Ret.), to author, 15 August 1959, 20 February 1960.
Layton, Rear Admiral Edwin T., USN (Ret.), to author, 12 July 1983.
Moulton, Rear Admiral H. Douglass, USNR (Ret.), to author, 27 December 1982; 29 May 1983; 28 May, 26 June 1984.
Schoeffel, Rear Admiral Malcolm F., USN (Ret.), to author, 3 September 1984.
Smedberg, Vice Admiral William R., USN (Ret.), to author, 22 February 1985.
Stassen, Harold, to Reverend Glen H. Stassen, 16 June 1964; to Clark G. Reynolds, 12 August, 13 October 1964; to author, 3 July 1984.
Tobin, John R., Jr., administrator of Johnston-Willis Hospital, to author, 24 January 1973.
Wilson, Vice Admiral Ralph E., USN (Ret.), to Clark G. Reynolds, 15 August 1967.

INTERVIEWS

1. Oral Histories

Most of the oral histories below are part of the U.S. Naval Institute collection. The interviews, conducted (often in series) by John T. Mason, Jr., and his assistants, are bound in volumes and available for research at the U.S. Naval Institute in Annapolis, the U.S. Naval Academy's Nimitz Library in Annapolis, and the Naval Historical Center in Washington, D.C. The exception is the William W. Ashford oral history, conducted by East Carolina University and available only at the East Carolina manuscript collection in Greenville, North Carolina.

Ashford, Rear Admiral William H., Jr., USN (Ret.). Interviewed by Donald R. Lennon, 1978–79, in Raleigh, N. C.
Bogan, Vice Admiral Gerald F., USN (Ret.). Vol. 1. Interviewed by Commander Etta-Belle Kitchen, USN, 25 October 1969, in La Jolla, California.
Burke, Admiral Arleigh A., USN (Ret.). Vol. 1. Interviewed by John T. Mason, 1978–79, in Bethesda, Md.
Colwell, Vice Admiral John Barr, USN (Ret.). Interviewed by Mason, 1973–74, in Washington, D.C.
Doolittle, Lieutenant General James Harold, USA (Ret.). Interviewed by Captain Paul B. Ryan, USN (Ret.), 1983, in Monterey, California.
Dyer, George C., USN (Ret.). Interviewed by Mason, 1969–71, in Annapolis, Md.
Faulk, Captain Roland W., CHC USN (Ret.). Interviewed by Mason, November 1974, in San Diego.
Hooper, Vice Admiral Edwin B., USN (Ret.). Interviewed by Mason, 1970–78, in Washington, D.C.
Jackson, Vice Admiral Andrew McBurney, Jr., USN (Ret.). Interviewed by Mason, 1971–72, in Annapolis, Md.

Jurika, Captain Stephen, Jr., USN (Ret.). Vol. 1. Interviewed by Ryan, 1975–76, at Univ. of Santa Clara, California.

Lee, Vice Admiral Fitzhugh, USN (Ret.). Interviewed by Kitchen, 1970, in Coronado, California.

McCollum, Rear Admiral Arthur H., USN (Ret.). Vol. 2. Interviewed by Mason, 1971, in McLean, Va.

Mack, Vice Admiral William Paden, USN (Ret.). Vol. 1. Interviewed by Mason, 1979, in Annapolis, Md.

Minter, Charles S., Jr., USN (Ret.). Vol. 1. Interviewed by Mason, 1979, in Annapolis, Md.

Moorer, Admiral Thomas H., USN (Ret.). Vol. 1. Interviewed by Mason, 1975, in Washington, D.C.

Murray, Admiral Stuart S., USN (Ret.). Vols. 1 and 2. Interviewed by Kitchen, 1970–71, in Montecito, Ca.

Pirie, Vice Admiral Robert B., USN (Ret.). Interviewed by Mason, 1973–74, in Washington, D.C.

Royar, Vice Admiral Murrey L., SC USN (Ret.). Interviewed by Mason, 1972–73, in McLean, Va.

Russell, Admiral James S., USN (Ret.). Interviewed by Mason, November 1974, in Takoma, Wa.

Schoeffel, Rear Admiral Malcolm F., USN (Ret.). Interviewed by Mason, 1979, in Naples, Fl.

Smedberg, Vice Admiral William R., III, USN (Ret.). Vol. 1. Interviewed by Mason, 1975–77, in Annapolis, Md., and Crystal River, Fl.

Smith, Vice Admiral J. Victor, USN (Ret.). Interviewed by Mason, 1976, in Annapolis, Md.

Smoot, Vice Admiral Roland N., USN (Ret.). Interviewed by Kitchen, 1970–71, in Laguna Hills, Ca.

Stroop, Vice Admiral Paul D., USN (Ret.). Interviewed by Kitchen, 1969–70, in San Diego, Ca.

Tarbuck, Rear Admiral Raymond D., USN (Ret.). Interviewed by Kitchen, 1970–71, in Coronado, Ca.

Thach, Admiral John Smith, USN (Ret.). Vols. 1 and 2. Interviewed by Kitchen, 1970–71, in Coronado, California.

Van Deurs, Rear Admiral George, USN (Ret.). Vol. 2. Interviewed by Kitchen, 1969, in Belvedere, Ca.

Wheeler, Rear Admiral Charles J., USN (Ret.). Interviewed by Kitchen, 1969, in Menlo Park, Ca.

Worthington, Rear Admiral Joseph M., USN (Ret.). Interviewed by Mason, 1972, on Gibson Island, Md.

2. Other interviews and personal communications

Ashford, Rear Admiral William H., Jr., USN (Ret.). Interviewed by author, 25 Feb 1983, in Raleigh, N.C. Available at U.S. Naval Institute.

Bryan, J., III. Interviewed by author, 10 Nov 1982, in Richmond, Va. Available at U.S. Naval Institute.

Burke, Admiral Arleigh A., USN (Ret.). Telephone conversation with author, 26 Oct 1984.

Carney, Admiral Robert B., USN (Ret.). Interviewed by Benis M. Frank, 17 May 1973, in Washington, D.C. Available at Naval Historical Center and at U.S. Marine Corps Headquarters, Washington, D.C. Interviewed by author, 3 Aug 1984, in Washington, D.C.

Driver, Louise. Telephone conversation with author, 3 Dec 1984.

Dyer, Vice Admiral George C., USN (Ret.). Interviewed by author, 23 May 1968, in Annapolis, Md. Available at U.S. Naval Institute.

Halsey, William F., III. Interviewed by author, 7–9 Jan 1985, in La Jolla, Ca.

Layton, Rear Admiral Edwin T., USN (Ret.). Interviewed by author, 7 May 1979, in Carmel, Ca.

Smedberg, Vice Admiral William R., III. Telephone conversation with Grace Potter, 25 Feb 1985.

MISCELLANEOUS

Lamar, H. Arthur, "Anecdotes." A collection of wartime experiences of Admiral Nimitz, as recalled by his personal aide. Typed copy at the Naval Historical Center.

U.S. Naval Academy chapel records.

NOTES

Where facts in successive pages of this book are drawn from the same group of sources, only one note is provided below, showing the sources of all material going back to the preceding note. References are shortened, usually to the last name of the author (or one of the authors). Where necessary a short title has been added.

CHAPTER 1. PEARL HARBOR AND WAKE

1. Prange, 370; Halsey, *Story,* 72–73.
2. Prange, 400–401.
3. Halsey, memoir, 306.
4. *Pearl Harbor Attack,* part 26, 323; Prange, 401, 406.
5. Halsey, *Story,* 74.
6. Ashford interview, 39.
7. Halsey, memoir, 307.
8. Stafford, 6.
9. Burns, 7–8.
10. Halsey, *Story,* 76; Halsey, memoir, 304; Toland, *Shame,* 10.
11. Burns, 9–10; Halsey, *Story,* 76.
12. Stillwell, 263, 269.
13. Prange, 410.
14. Burns, 11; Halsey, *Story,* 77; Stafford, 14.
15. Prange, 513, 517.
16. Stafford, 16.
17. Prange, 564–66, 569; Halsey, *Story,* 79.
18. Halsey, *Story,* 79; Stafford, 19; Burns, 14.
19. Stafford, 20; Ashford interview.
20. Halsey, *Story,* 80; Halsey, memoir, 317.
21. Stafford, 23.
22. Halsey, *Story,* 81; Halsey, memoir, 318–19.
23. Burns, 17; Stafford, 21.
24. Halsey, *Story,* 81; Stafford, 23–24.
25. Halsey, memoir, 320; Prange, 516.
26. Halsey, *Story,* 81–82; Halsey, memoir, 321.
27. Stafford, 24–25.
28. Stafford, 26–28; Spector, 103; Halsey, memoir, 322–24; Halsey, *Story,* 82–83.
29. Prange, 589–90.

30. Buell, *Master,* 153.
31. Spector, 105–6; Hough, 130–31, 143; Heinl, 37–39; Burns, 20–21; Stafford, 30; Halsey, *Story,* 83–84; Halsey, memoir, 324–26.

CHAPTER 2. ORIGINS OF A WARRIOR

1. Hoyt, *How They Won,* 23–24; Holmes, 40.
2. Halsey, *Story,* 2; *The History of the Lives and Bloody Exploits,* 96–104.
3. Halsey, memoir, 1, 11–13; Halsey, *Story,* 3; J. L. Halsey, *Thomas Halsey,* 139, 263, 347, 376, 436.
4. Halsey, *Story,* 2–7; Jordan, 13. I use Jordan with caution. His book is undocumented and contains obvious errors, but he interviewed Admiral Halsey's wife and mother and possibly the admiral himself.
5. Halsey, *Story,* 3–4.
6. Halsey, memoir, 7–8, 12–16; Halsey, *Story,* 4–5; J. Bryan III, letter to author, 15 Dec 1982; Jordan 31–32.
7. Sweetman, 135, 142, 143; Halsey, *Story,* 5.
8. Halsey, memoir, 18–37; Halsey, *Story,* 5–8.

CHAPTER 3. COUNTERATTACK

1. Potter, *Nimitz,* 8–10, 14, 16, 18–21.
2. W. F. Halsey III interview; Halsey Papers: Halsey to Calhoun, 10 Jan 1942.
3. Prange, 591, 594–97.
4. *Pearl Harbor Attack,* part 23, 2 Jan 1942, 605, 613–14.
5. Halsey, memoir, 326, 328.
6. Potter, *Nimitz,* 33.
7. Told to author by Admiral Nimitz.
8. Halsey, memoir, 326–28.
9. Stafford, 30; Ashford oral history, 49.
10. Costello, 196; Stafford, 31.
11. Halsey, memoir, 329–32; Halsey, *Story,* 85–89; Stafford, 31–34; Blair, 115–16; Ashford oral history, 51; Burns, 24–25.
12. Potter, *Nimitz,* 37.
13. Halsey, memoir, 334; Halsey, *Story,* 90.
14. Stafford, 37–41; Halsey, *Story,* 90.
15. Stafford, 38, 43.
16. Buell, *Quiet Warrior,* 102–6.
17. Merrill, 25; Stafford, 44–46; Casey, 154; Burns, 30–32; Halsey, memoir, 337–39.
18. Halsey, *Story,* 94.
19. In the Battle of Midway (June 1942), Gaido occupied the rear seat of one of the dive-bombers that sank the Japanese carriers. Shot down, he and his pilot were picked up from an inflated life raft by a Japanese destroyer. After interrogating the Americans for several days, the Japanese attached weights to their legs and threw them overboard. (Robert E. Barde, "Midway: Tarnished Victory," *Military Affairs,* December 1983, p. 191. Mentioned also in Clark G. Reynolds, *The Carrier War,* Alexandria, Va.: Time–Life Books, 1982, p. 99.)

20. Halsey, *Story,* 95; Halsey, memoir, 340–41.
21. Stafford, 47–48; Halsey, *Story,* 95–96; Halsey, memoir, 340–43.

CHAPTER 4. TARGET: TOKYO

1. Potter, *Nimitz,* 39–40; Casey, 167.
2. Buell, *Quiet Warrior,* 29, 42, 107, 436.
3. Halsey, *Story,* 97; Halsey, memoir, 343; Buell, *Quiet Warrior,* 109.
4. Stafford, 58–59. Stafford erroneously places this episode after Halsey's Wake Island raid.
5. Cant, 173.
6. Potter, *Nimitz,* 37–42.
7. Halsey, *Story,* 98–199; Halsey, memoir, 344–49; Buell, *Quiet Warrior,* 110–15.
8. Fuchida, 53–54; Morison, *Rising Sun,* 268.
9. Glines, 13–14, 55, 61; Morison, *Rising Sun,* 389–90; Halsey, *Story,* 101.
10. Halsey, memoir, 350. The text follows Halsey's version, dictated in 1946. Doolittle, recalling the incident years later, said that the discussion occurred at a table in a restaurant, and several books have accepted this account. I have preferred Halsey's version because it was recorded earlier, Halsey's memoir reveals an excellent memory, and I simply do not believe officers would discuss top-secret operations in a public restaurant.
11. Glines, 69–70, 76–77; *Hornet* action report, 28 April 1942.
12. Halsey, memoir, 351; Halsey, *Story,* 102.
13. Halsey, memoir, 351–52; Com 12 Naval District dispatch 071044.
14. Glines, 90.
15. Stafford, 60.
16. *Enterprise* action report, 23 April 1942; *Hornet* action report, 28 April 1942.
17. Stafford, 40, 76.
18. Halsey, memoir, 352.
19. Toland, *Rising Sun,* 305.
20. Glines, 96–111, 318; Toland, *Rising Sun,* 306–8; Doolittle oral history, 29–31; Jurika oral history, 469–72; Holmes, 68; *Hornet* action report, 28 April 1942.

CHAPTER 5. BATTLES MISSED

1. Glines. 112–15; Halsey, *Story,* 103; Ashford oral history, 59.
2. Casey, 309–11; Stafford, 66; Halsey, *Story,* 104; Glines, 380–81. Shangri-La was a mysterious, imaginary Tibetan city in James Hilton's 1933 novel *Lost Horizon.* The name was subsequently given to *Essex*-class carrier CV 38.
3. Ashford oral history, 60–61; Buell, *Quiet Warrior,* 125–26.
4. Casey, 320.
5. Lundstrom, 78–87; Potter, *Nimitz,* 66–69; Lewin, 91–94; "Role of Radio Intelligence."
6. James, 98–109, 120–23; Pogue, *Ordeal,* 248–51; Adams, *Axis,* 96–98, 136; Buell, *Master,* 190–92.
7. Casey, 325; Halsey, memoir, 358; Lundstrom, 88–89.
8. Holmes, 70–71; Lewin, 93–94.

9. James, 159; Potter, *Nimitz,* 70; Spector, 158–63; Stafford, 68; Casey, 329; Worthington oral history, 170.
10. Casey, 331, 337.
11. Lundstrom, 144–57; Casey, 348–59; Halsey, memoir, 360–61; Halsey, *Story,* 105. Lundstrom assumes from Halsey's operations that he was acting on secret orders from Nimitz. In reply to my inquiry on this point, Edwin Layton, Nimitz's wartime intelligence officer, stated in a letter of 12 July 1983, "Nimitz *did* send an 'eyes only' message to Halsey directing that he be seen and reported by the Japs!"

    Halsey's account of his operations in the period from 10 to 16 May 1942 as dictated in his memoir is more convincing than the version in his published *Admiral Halsey's Story,* which says, "I wanted to make sure that they weren't re-forming to break through between the New Hebrides and the Fijis" (p. 105). Break through from where to attack what? Halsey's disgusted exclamation on receiving ComInCh's order is softened in *Admiral Halsey's Story* to, "I was mad as the devil!" It is fascinating to compare Halsey's account of what he was doing between 10 and 16 May with Lundstrom's theoretical reconstruction and with the shrewd guesses of Robert Casey, a civilian newsman on board one of the cruisers. Casey was privy to no classified information, but knew how to use his eyes and ears.
12. Lewin, 303; Lundstrom, 159; "Role of Radio Intelligence"; Morton, 280–81; Holmes, 90–91.
13. Lundstrom, 156–62.
14. Halsey, memoir, 363; Ashford oral history, 11; Lord, 30.
15. Buell, *Quiet Warrior,* 120–22; Ashford interview; Lord, 31.
16. Holmes, 91–94; Lord, 33; Lewin, 96–109; "Role of Radio Intelligence."
17. Halsey, memoir, 364; Buell, *Quiet Warrior,* 122; Potter, *Nimitz,* 89, 93, 99, 105–6; Spector, 169–77.
18. Ashford interview; Ashford oral history, 63–64; John H. Tobin, Jr., letter to author.

CHAPTER 6. JUNIOR OFFICER

1. Halsey, *Story,* 8–9; Halsey, memoir; 38–47; Hart, 53.
2. Halsey, *Story,* 10; Halsey, memoir, 49–53.
3. Halsey, *Story,* 15–16; Halsey, memoir, 55–56.
4. Halsey, *Story,* 10; Halsey, memoir, 54–55; Driver interview.
5. Halsey, memoir, 57; *Halsey's Story* places Halsey's proposal and acceptance *after* the world cruise (p. 16). The memoir, however, makes it abundantly clear that the proposal took place before the cruise.
6. Halsey, memoir, 63; Hart, 28, 29, 48, 49, 54, 57, 58, 60; Potter, *Sea Power* (1981), 192, 194, 195; Pratt, 448.
7. Halsey, memoir, 64–67.
8. Halsey, memoir, 64, 67–69, 73–74; Hart, 165–69.
9. Halsey, memoir, 78, 79, 83; Hart, 187, 192, 193, 197; Halsey, *Story,* 11–12.
10. Halsey, memoir, 85, 86; Hart, 206, 215, 216, 218, 219, 226, 227, 230, 231; Halsey, *Story,* 12–13. In 1905 Passed Midshipman Chester W. Nimitz used one

of the invitations sent to his ship, then in Tokyo Bay, to attend the Japanese emperor's garden party honoring his senior officers, recent victors over Russia. Here Nimitz met Admiral Togo and was deeply impressed by him. Again in Tokyo Bay in 1934, when Togo died, Nimitz attended his funeral. At the end of World War II Nimitz placed a marine guard on board the *Mikasa,* Togo's flagship, to prevent looting. Subsequently, when the *Mikasa* fell into neglect, Nimitz wrote an article, published in Japan, to remind the Japanese of the part Togo's victory had played in their naval heritage and donated his renumeration for the article toward the flagship's restoration, which soon followed. When a Japanese edition of the Pacific war portion of the book *Sea Power* was published, Nimitz wrote a special foreword to it and contributed his remuneration for that toward the restoration of the Togo Shrine, damaged in the firebombing of Tokyo. The restored shrine, a Shinto temple, contains mementos of Horatio Nelson and Nimitz as well as of Togo ("the three great admirals"), including a small bronze statue of Togo shaking hands with Passed Midshipman Nimitz in the emperor's garden.

11. Halsey, memoir, 87, 89–91; Halsey, *Story,* 12; Hart, 229, 243, 247–48, 256, 260.
12. Halsey, memoir, 89, 91, 92; Halsey, *Story,* 13; Hart, 261, 262, 265, 272, 282–84.
13. Halsey, memoir, 93–95; Halsey, *Story,* 14, 16; Hart, 290–95, 299.

CHAPTER 7. DESTROYERMAN

1. Halsey, memoir, 95–96; Halsey, *Story,* 15.
2. Halsey, memoir, 97, 100, 101; Jordan, 75. The exchange between Bill and Fanny on page 98 certainly sounds stilted, but it is apparently part of the family tradition.
3. Halsey, memoir, 102, 104.
4. Halsey, memoir, 105, 106; Halsey, *Story,* 16–17.
5. Halsey, memoir, 106, 110, 112, 113; Halsey, *Story,* 17.
6. Halsey, memoir, 118–24; Halsey, *Story,* 17–19.
7. Halsey, memoir, 124–135; Halsey, *Story,* 19–21; Morison, *Sims,* 288–312; Bailey, 604–7.
8. Halsey, memoir, 139–40; Halsey, *Story,* 22–23.
9. Halsey, memoir, 143–47; 149, 152–54, 157–58; Halsey, *Story,* 24–26; Jordan, 77–78; Morison, *Sims,* 337–66, 368, 373n; Potter, *Sea Power* (1981), 226–27.
10. Halsey, memoir, 158–80; Halsey, *Story,* 27–37; Morison, *Sims,* 382–83; Knox, 401; Mitchell, 219, 239; Wheeler oral history, 250–54. When Commander Joseph Taussig, commanding the first U.S. destroyer division to reach Queenstown, reported to Admiral Bayly after a tempestuous crossing, the admiral asked, "When will you be ready to go to sea?" Much has been made of Taussig's prompt reply, "We are ready now, sir," but chances are British destroyermen had told him this was the answer to give. Even Bayly did not take it seriously. He allowed four days. Taussig used to make light of the incident by insisting that what he had understood Bayly to say was, "When will you be ready to go to eat?"

CHAPTER 8. AVIATOR

1. Halsey, memoir, 183–225; Halsey, *Story,* 37–47; Buell, *Quiet Warrior,* 40–42; Alden, 378.
2. Halsey, memoir, 227–33; Halsey, *Story,* 47–49; Jordan, 96–98.
3. Halsey, memoir, 233, 235, 237–38; Halsey, *Story,* 49.
4. Buell, *Quiet Warrior,* 48; Jordan. 99; Halsey, memoir, 238–44, 247; Halsey, *Story,* 49–52.
5. Halsey, *Story,* 53–54; Halsey, memoir, 247–48, 252–53; Jordan, 105–6; chapel records, U.S. Naval Academy.
6. Halsey, memoir, 253–55; Halsey, *Story,* 54–55; Forrestel, 11–12; Buell, *Master,* 44–45, 79, 94–97; Potter, *Nimitz,* 136–42; King, 207–11, 240–43; Morison, *Sims,* 505–9, 522–28; Frank, 15.
7. Halsey, *Story,* 56–60; Halsey, memoir, 256–70; Lee oral history, 16–17.

CHAPTER 9. CARRIER COMMANDER

1. Halsey, memoir, 271–83; Halsey, *Story,* 60–64; Potter, *Sea Power* (1960), 636–39; Wilson, 135–48.
2. Bogan oral history, 48; Ashford oral history, 34–35; Ashford interview; Halsey, *Story,* 65; Halsey, memoir, 283–86.
3. Halsey, *Story,* 65–66; Halsey, memoir, 286–88; Moorer oral history, 74–77; Bogan oral history, 50–51; King, 289–92; Richardson, 2–7.
4. Halsey, *Story,* 66–72; Morison, *Rising Sun,* 38, 45–86; Halsey, memoir, 288–305; King, 293–94, 305–6; Buell, *Master,* 124–25; Dyer interview; Layton interview; Buell, *Quiet Warrior,* 89–91; Thach oral history, 159–60; Van Duers oral history, 361.

CHAPTER 10. COMMANDER, SOUTH PACIFIC

1. Halsey, memoir, 364, and insert no. 6; Halsey, *Story,* 108; Ashford interview; Ashford oral history, 64–67; Tobin, letter to author; W. F. Halsey III interview; Halsey to Beardall, 6 and 19 Aug 1942; Beardall to Halsey, 21 Aug 1942; U.S. Naval Academy notice, 31 Aug 1942.
2. Halsey, memoir, 365; King, 388; Spector, 185–98; Morton, 296–304.
3. Halsey, *Story,* 109; Reynolds, 41; W. F. Halsey III interview; war diaries, *Saratoga* and *Enterprise.* Both Halsey's memoir and *Admiral Halsey's Story* have the date for the ceremony on board the *Saratoga* wrong.
4. Adams, *Axis,* 341–44; Potter, *Sea Power* (1960), 698–99; Stafford, 147, 149; Griffith, 127–30.
5. Hoyt, *How They Won,* 153–58; Griffith, 140–42.
6. Spector, 200–201; *Combat Narratives,* "Solomon Islands Campaign," parts 4 and 5, 18–30.
7. Buell, *Warrior,* 156; Halsey Papers: CinCPac orders to Halsey, 10 Oct 1942; Belote, 134; Ashford oral history, 70; Halsey, *Story,* 108–9; *Enterprise* war diary.
8. Spector, 208–9; Halsey, *Story,* 109; Halsey, memoir, 367; Buell, *Warrior,* 157; Potter, *Nimitz,* 196–98; Forrestel, 63; Griffith, 163.

9. Halsey, *Story,* 109, 111–12, 116–17, 119; Halsey, memoir, 367–68; CinCPac Command Summary; Griffith, 141, 164; Hough, 341.
10. Ashford oral history, 72–73.
11. Ashford interview; Ashford oral history, 73; Morison, *Struggle for Guadalcanal,* 188–224; *Combat Narratives,* "Battle of Santa Cruz Islands," 30–31.

CHAPTER 11. THE CRISIS

1. Morison, *Struggle for Guadalcanal,* 226.
2. Vandegrift, 174, 179; Halsey, memoir, 383–85; Halsey, *Story,* 123; Van Deurs oral history, 467; Halsey Papers: Commander, South Pacific, orders to Halsey, 7 Nov 1942. An area commander issued himself travel orders for purposes of record keeping.
3. Stafford, 184–85; Halsey, memoir, 385–86; Halsey, *Story,* 124–26; Potter, *Sea Power* (1960), 702.
4. Adams, *Axis,* 360–64; Halsey, memoir, 386–89; Halsey, *Story,* 126–27; Potter, *Sea Power* (1960), 702–4; Vandegrift, 198.
5. Morison, *Struggle for Guadalcanal,* 259–62; Halsey, *Story,* 128; Halsey, memoir, 389.
6. Merillat, 234; Vandegrift, 198; Halsey, *Story,* 129; Halsey, memoir, 390.
7. Potter, *Sea Power* (1960), 704; Morison, *Struggle for Guadalcanal,* 263–69; Halsey, 129–30; Merillat, 235.
8. Morison, *Struggle for Guadalcanal,* 270–82; Vandegrift, 199; Merillat, 236; Halsey, *Story,* 130–31.
9. Vandegrift, 199–200; Merillat, 237.
10. Halsey, *Story,* 131–32; Halsey, memoir, 393–97.
11. Halsey, memoir, 399; Halsey, *Story,* 132; *Time,* 30 Nov 1942, "World Battlefronts," 28.
12. Halsey, memoir, 398–99; *Time,* 30 Nov 1942, "World Battlefronts," 28; Halsey, *Story,* 132.

CHAPTER 12. GUADALCANAL RECAPTURED

1. Halsey, *Story,* 136; Potter, "The Command Personality"; Geffen, 225–39.
2. Halsey, *Story,* 136–37; Morton, 208–12; Morison, *Coral Sea,* 253; Halsey Papers: Halsey to Secretary of the Navy Knox, n.d., filed but never sent.
3. Halsey, *Story,* 138–39.
4. Potter, *Sea Power* (1960), 705–6; Adams, *Axis,* 371–72.
5. Morison, *Struggle for Guadalcanal,* 310–12; Smedberg oral history, 224–37.
6. Potter, *Sea Power* (1960), 707; Morison, *Struggle for Guadalcanal,* 334–35; Halsey, *Story,* 140.
7. Halsey, *Story,* 141–45; Halsey Papers: Halsey to Nimitz, 20 Dec 1942.
8. Halsey, *Story,* 145–47; Stroop oral history, 176; Van Deurs oral history, 506.
9. Hoyt, *How They Won,* 200–202; Halsey, *Story,* 147–48; Potter, *Sea Power* (1960), 707; Costello, 389–90; Morison, *Struggle for Guadalcanal,* 333–44.

CHAPTER 13. CAESAR AND THE BULL

1. Halsey, *Story,* 142–45.
2. Toland, *Rising Sun,* 418–21.
3. W. F. Halsey III interview.
4. Morton, 379–85; James, 304–5.
5. Buell, *Quiet Warrior,* 164–65; Potter, *Nimitz,* 97, 211, 237–39, 243, 248–49.
6. Ashford oral history, 79–84; Van Deurs oral history, 404.
7. Morton, 218, 288–89; James, 260–74; Potter, *Sea Power* (1960), 707–8, 754.
8. Morton, 388–99; Halsey, *Story,* 153; James, 306–10; Morison, *Bismarcks Barrier,* 95–100.
9. James, 54–55, 74, 153, 244, 247, 281, 296, 384; Ashford oral history, 94.
10. Morton, 288; MacArthur dispatch to Halsey, 9 Feb 1943 (090915); Halsey Papers: Halsey to Nimitz, 13 Feb 1943.
11. Morison, *Bismarcks Barrier,* 54–65, 107–10, 117–20; Potter, *Sea Power* (1960), 715–17.
12. Toland, *Rising Sun,* 441; Kahn, 596–601; Davis, 116–88; Halsey, *Story,* 155–56; Taylor, 149–52.,
13. James, 315–16; Halsey, *Story,* 154–55; Moulton, letter to author, 28 May 1984.

CHAPTER 14. CENTRAL SOLOMONS

1. Bryan interview; Bryan, letters to author, 3 and 31 May 1984.
2. Bryan, "Sea Dog," Dec, p. 37; Van Deurs oral history, 464; Halsey Papers: Commander, South Pacific, orders to W. F. Halsey, 14 April 1943, with itinerary attached; Hart, 195.
3. Kahn, 596–601; Davis, 116–88; Halsey, *Story,* 155–56; Taylor, 149–52. Davis says the shooting down of Yamamoto was plotted and executed before Halsey left for Australia. Halsey and Bryan say that both the plotting and the execution took place after Halsey returned from Australia. Neither is correct. The Halsey Papers contain a "Dear Chester" letter to Nimitz dated 26 May 1943. Halsey in guarded language discusses a possible leak, which might reveal to the Japanese that the Americans were reading their naval operational code. He writes, "I shall attempt to give you my present knowledge about the 'leak' in regard to the mid-April operation. The operation was organized and alerted before my departure for Australia. The actual successful completion of the operation took place during my stay in Australia and I was informed on my return that we had accomplished our desires."
4. Morison, *Bismarcks Barrier,* 139–40; Potter, *Sea Power* (1960), 717; Taylor, 157–58.
5. Ashford interview; Van Deurs oral history, 411; Halsey, *Story,* xii; Buell, *Quiet Warrior,* 167–68; Potter, *Nimitz,* 243.
6. Hough, 79–118; Morison, *Bismarcks Barrier,* 144, 146–59; Halsey, *Story,* 159–61; Dyer, 586; Morton, 509–11.
7. Halsey Papers: Nimitz to Halsey, 8 Aug 1943, and Halsey to Nimitz, 19 Aug 1943.

8. Halsey, *Story,* 170–71; Halsey radio dispatch 110421 (July 1943) to Wilkinson and Fitch; Hoyt, *How They Won,* 260–61.
9. Potter, *Sea Power* (1960), 719–22; Spector, 240; radio dispatches: Ainsworth to Halsey and Fitch, 051710, and Halsey to Ainsworth, 052000. Reynolds, 35; Halsey Papers: Nimitz to Halsey, 8 Aug 1943.

CHAPTER 15. SOUTH PACIFIC

1. Reynolds, 34–35; Belote, 159, 165–68.
2. Bryan, "Sea Dog," Dec, p. 37; Halsey, *Story,* xii–xiii, 165; Jordan, 106–7; Potter, *Nimitz,* 218; Halsey, memoir, inserts nos. 7–10, 25–26; Ashford oral history, 96.
3. Halsey, *Story,* 139–40, 166–68, 170; Bryan interview; Bryan, letter to author, 31 May 1984; Ashford oral history, 97; Buell, *Quiet Warrior,* 176; Halsey Papers: Nimitz to Halsey, 8 Aug 1943; R. B. Carney, *Shipmate*, March 1983, 8.
4. Dyer, 587; Taylor, 145, 157, 160–63.
5. Ashford oral history, 109–10; Moulton, letter to author, 28 May 1984; Stassen, letter to author, 3 July 1984; Ashford oral history, 97; Halsey, *Story,* 184–85.
6. Halsey, *Story,* 133–34; Halsey, memoir, 394–96; Reynolds, 147; Clark, 157–58; Buell, *Master,* 478–79.
7. Halsey, *Story,* xiii, 134; Carney interviews, 17 May 1973 and 30 July 1984; Bryan, "Sea Dog," Dec, pp. 37–38.

CHAPTER 16. BYPASSING RABAUL

1. Morton, 644–53; Potter, *Sea Power* (1960), 809.
2. James, 330–34; Craven, 615.
3. James, 319, 340; Isely, 175–76; Morison, *Bismarcks Barrier,* 279–91; Halsey Papers: Admiral Robert B. Carney to Rear Admiral John B. Heffernan, 1 Mar 1951, and Halsey to Heffernan, 2 Apr 1951.
4. Halsey, *Story,* 176–86; Adams, *Expectation,* 245–58; Potter, *Sea Power* (1960), 722–28. In writing *Nimitz* I concluded that Halsey and Bryan must have been mistaken in their dating of MacArthur's statement about expecting a large part of the U.S. and British fleets to be put under his command. MacArthur would have no reason for anticipating anything of the sort until immediately after the January strategy meeting at Pearl Harbor. That is where I put the general's statement in *Nimitz.* In working on the Halsey materials for this book, however, I concluded that Halsey and Bryan were correct and MacArthur and Potter were wrong. I asked Admiral Carney why MacArthur would have made such a statement at that time. He replied, "Wishful thinking."
5. James, 348; Pogue, *Organizer of Victory,* 440–41; Halsey, *Story,* 186; Potter, *Sea Power* (1960), 741–48, and (1981), 319–23.
6. Halsey, *Story,* 186–88; Potter, *Nimitz,* 267, 282–83; Halsey, memoir, 446–50; Potter, *Sea Power* (1981), 323–25.
7. Halsey, *Story,* 188–93; Halsey, memoir, 450–52; Potter, *Sea Power* (1960), 730–31, 745–55; Carney interview, 17 May 1973; Pogue, *Organizer of Victory,*

441. In presenting the three-part argument between MacArthur and Halsey and their staffs, I leaned a little toward Carney's recollection of the episode, but where logic seemed to require I drew from Halsey and Bryan and from the memoir. MacArthur's farewell dispatch ("Personal to Admiral Halsey from MacArthur"), dated 10 June 1944, is in Records of General Headquarters No. 4, U.S. Army Forces Pacific. Halsey's reply (120440 June 1944, "For General MacArthur") is in the same records: "I am deeply grateful for your message and proud that my team earned your approval. I envy and admire your newest lashing blows against the enemy, and I sincerely share your hope that we may again join forces."

CHAPTER 17. THE BIG BLUE FLEET

1. Morison, *Aleutians,* 9, 27–41, 133, 171–73, 313–14; Potter, *Sea Power* (1960), 760–61, (1981), 325; Potter, *Nimitz,* 259, 289, 292, 294, 296–303; Y'Blood, 204–206. The differences between the views of Spruance and Towers parallel those between the navy and air force at the Sicily invasion; the former demanded tactical air support at the landing area, the latter insisted on fighting the enemy aircraft on or over their own airfields, never permitting them to reach the beachhead.
2. Halsey, *Story,* 194; Halsey, memoir, 460–61, 468; Pogue, *Organizer of Victory,* 451–52; James, 526–32; Buell, *Master,* 466–69; Halsey Papers: Commander, Third Fleet, orders to Admiral W. F. Halsey, with itinerary from Pearl Harbor to Wilmington, Delaware, and return; Lamar, "Anecdotes."
3. Halsey, *Story,* 197–203; Halsey, memoir, 462–65, 481–85; James, 537–39. As executive officer of the Pearl Harbor Registered Publication [codes and ciphers] Issuing Office, I personally posted our copy of Halsey's letter of thanks and appreciation.
4. Halsey, memoir, 468, 485; Lockwood, 135–39; CinCPOA Operation Plan 8-44, 27 Sep 1944; Halsey to Nimitz, 28 Sep 1944, in Hoyt, *How They Won,* 424–25. Admiral Schoeffel, who in September 1944 was assistant chief of staff to Admiral King, says in his oral history (p. 267) that the sentence "In case opportunity, etc." was put into CinCPOA Op Plan 8–44 by order of King, but in a letter to me dated 8 Sep 1984, he seemed less sure of that fact. It would be interesting to know who actually wrote it. The sentence is either ungrammatical or makes use of the old-fashioned subjunctive, neither of which was characteristic of King or Nimitz.
5. Halsey, memoir, 485–501; Halsey, *Story,* 203–9; Morison, *Leyte,* 86–109.

CHAPTER 18. LEYTE GULF

1. War College, *Leyte Gulf,* vol. 3, 341, 345, 563, 566; Woodward, 43; Halsey, memoir, 501–2.
2. War College, *Leyte Gulf,* vol. 3, 768–69, 772; Halsey, *Story,* 210–11; Woodward, 44–45; Potter, *Sea Power* (1960), 780.
3. Van Deurs oral history, 487.
4. Adams, *Victory,* 184–85; Stewart, 47–65; Woodward, 47–64, 74; Halsey, *Story,* 214; radio dispatches: CTF 77 (Kinkaid) 240315, Commander, Third Fleet (Halsey), 240252, 240400, 240612, 240829.

5. Halsey, memoir, 505–9; Halsey, *Story*, 216–17; Woodward, 70–81; Reynolds, 268; Merrill, 158.
6. Halsey, memoir, 509–12; Kinkaid, letter to author, 15 Aug 1959; Halsey, *Story*, 217; Woodward, 134–35; Thach oral history, 387–88; Morison, *Leyte*, 195; Bogan oral history, 84–85; Burke oral history, vol. 1, 398.
7. Taylor, 260; Bogan oral history, 84–85; Burke oral history, vol. 1, 399–401; Halsey, *Story*, 217.
8. Taylor, 262–68.
9. Woodward, 136; Morison, *Leyte*, 322.
10. Woodward, 136; Bogan oral history, 85; Royar oral history, 180–81; Morison, *Leyte*, 322–24; Commander, Third Fleet, radio dispatch 241800.
11. Halsey, *Story*, 218–21; Hoyt, *Leyte Gulf*, 206–7; Morison, *Leyte*, 245, 289–90; Potter, *Nimitz*, 339–40; Halsey, memoir, 513–14; radio dispatches: CTF 77 241912, 242123, 242203, 242225, 242227, 242239, 242329; Commander, Third Fleet, 242204, 242348, 242355, 242334, 250027, 250215, 250217; CTU 77.4.3 242207; CinCPac 250044. The ensign who enciphered the CinCPac 250044 dispatch, in adding the end padding, may have been echoing the line "All the world wonder'd" from Tennyson's poem celebrating the magnificent, futile charge of the Light Brigade in the Battle of Balaklava, fought on 25 October 1854. When Nimitz sent the message "Where is task Force 34?" he was not merely asking for information. By 1414 Pearl Harbor time (0944 in the Philippines), when the message was sent, it was clear that Task Force 34 was nowhere near San Bernardino Strait. Nimitz figured the force could only be with Halsey attacking the Northern Force. Strongly opposed to interfering with a commander at the scene of action, Nimitz told me he intended the message as a nudge, to make Halsey reconsider whether he was making the wisest use of his battleships in the prevailing conditions. As for Halsey's weeping on reading the corrupted version of the message, I have followed his dictated memoir, which says that he "burst out crying" (p. 514). I assume the version in *Admiral Halsey's Story*, "shouted something I am ashamed to remember" (p. 220), is the product of editing to give the story a more macho tone.
12. Halsey, *Story*, 222–25; Potter, *Sea Power* (1960), 794; radio dispatches: CTF 77 250146, 250231, 250403.
13. Field, 63; James, 565; Halsey, *Story*, 226; Potter, *Nimitz*, 341–45; Morison, *Leyte*, 191–92; radio dispatches: Commander, Third Fleet, 251226, 251317; Halsey, letter to author, 29 June 1959; Carney, letter to author, 31 July 1959.

CHAPTER 19. THE PHILIPPINES

1. Halsey, *Story*, 228–29; Halsey, memoir, 521–27; Stafford, 412–14; Adams, *Victory*, 279–80.
2. Morison, *Leyte*, 344–56.
3. Halsey, *Story*, 234–35; Merrill, 178–79; Adamson, *Typhoons*, 24, 33–34; Halsey, memoir, insert no. 33.
4. Halsey, *Story*, 231–32, 34; Morison, *Leyte*, 351, 357–60, 366–68, and *Philippines*, 7–9, 55.
5. Adams, *Victory*, 294; Morison, *Philippines*, 49–50.

6. Conversations with officers during and since World War II.
7. Schoeffel oral history, 253–54.
8. Halsey, *Story,* 284–85; Morison, *Philippines,* 357.
9. Morison, *Philippines,* 22, 55–59; Potter, *Sea Power* (1960), 816.
10. Adamson, *Typhoons,* 28–148; Halsey, *Story,* 237–40; Halsey, memoir, 535–45; Morison, *Philippines,* 59–84; Potter, *Sea Power* (1960), 816.
11. Halsey, *Story,* 241–42; Potter, *Nimitz,* 350–51; Merrill, 201; Morison, *Philippines,* 84.
12. Halsey, memoir, 546.
13. Morison, *Philippines,* 88–89, 106–7, 157–83; Potter, *Nimitz,* 351–52; Potter, *Sea Power* (1960), 817–21.

CHAPTER 20. OKINAWA

1. Halsey, *Story,* 247–51, 289–90; Halsey, memoir, 558–61; Merrill, 209; Stassen, letter to author, 3 July 1984; Potter, *Sea Power* (1960), 824–32, (1981), 348–50; Spector, 494–505, 532–40; Reynolds, 320.
2. Murray oral history, 355, 362–66; Buell, *Quiet Warrior,* 361–63; Morison, *Victory,* 158, 160, 169, 266, 272; Potter, *Sea Power* (1960), 832; Halsey, *Story,* 251–53; Forrestel, 215; Potter, *Nimitz,* 375–76; Halsey, memoir, 561–64; Westcott, 575; Adamson, *Typhoons,* 170.
3. Adamson, *Typhoons,* 170–90; Clark, 232–37; Reynolds, 347–49; Merrill, 216–23.
4. Merrill, 223; Halsey, *Story,* 254–55; Buell, *Master,* 492–93; Halsey, memoir, 570–71; Potter, *Sea Power* (1960), 832–33.

CHAPTER 21. VICTORY

1. Halsey, *Story,* 257–73; Merrill, 230–36; Reynolds, 361; Westcott, 577; Carney interview, 17 May 1973; Morison, *Victory,* 309–16, 330–35.
2. Halsey, *Story,* 274–80; Merrill, 237–42; Murray oral history, 425–63; James, 785–86; Potter, *Nimitz,* 390–94; Carney interview, 17 May 1973.
3. Toland, *Rising Sun,* 866–70; Murray oral history, 445–63; Halsey, *Story,* 281–83; Manchester, 448–54; Halsey, memoir, 607–12; Potter, *Nimitz,* 394–96.
4. Carney, letter to author, 17 Nov 1984; Halsey, *Story,* 283–91; Potter, *Nimitz,* 396; Toland, *Rising Sun,* 871; Carney interview, 17 May 1973; Wheeler oral history, 336; Faulk oral history, 157; Halsey, memoir, 614–28.

CHAPTER 22. LAST YEARS

In the notes for this chapter referring to material in the Halsey Papers that is widely scattered, I have simply given Halsey Papers as the source, confident that the excellent cataloguing of this collection in the Library of Congress will enable researchers to locate the items. Numbers in parentheses following dates of *New York Times* articles indicate page and column (for example, 15:3).

1. Halsey, *Story,* 291; Merrill, 246–47; *New York Times,* 16 Oct (1:2), 17 Oct (5:4), 28 Oct (32:8), and 30 Oct (3:5) 1945, and 6 Nov (6:3), 8 Nov (21:1), and 10 Nov (5:2) 1945.

2. Halsey, *Story,* 292; Merrill, 245, 248; Potter, *Nimitz,* 349; Buell, *Master,* 386–88; *New York Times,* 15 Nov (3:6), 23 Nov (3:1), and 29 Nov (2:3) 1945, and 16 March (1:2), 3 April (21:5), and 14 May (11:5) 1946.
3. Bryan interview; Bryan, letter to author, 13 Dec 1958. Bryan gave the uncut manuscript of *Admiral Halsey's Story* to the Naval Academy library, which lost it. The old Mahan Hall library had no provision for protecting rare books or documents. Everything, regardless of value, was placed on the open shelves. Midshipmen sometimes left the library without checking out books. Some of the midshipmen, through neglect, never got around to returning items thus informally borrowed. At the end of each academic year, the cleaning people gathered up baskets of library books from the dormitory rooms and returned them to the library. It was probably at this stage that the Bryan manuscript got tossed out as trash.

   During a photo session for *Saturday Evening Post* installments, Halsey good-naturedly consented to Bryan having a picture taken wearing the former's blouse with the fleet admiral's stripes. Afterward Joe had great fun sending copies of the picture to friends with the note, "Promotion is now on the merit system. Fleet Admiral J. Bryan, III, USNR"—with the *R* in red. In a letter to Halsey he reported that he had sent a copy to Roger Kent, his senior in the Solomons, with the inscription, "To Lt. Comdr. Kent, whose dogged refusal to be dislodged from the Waikiki Line was an inspiration to my men in Okinawa." Joe added, "Kent lives in San Francisco, but I could hear his screams of rage all the way across the Continent" (Bryan interview; Halsey Papers: Bryan to Halsey, 14 Aug 1947).
4. W. F. Halsey III interview; Merrill, 250–51; Potter, *Nimitz* 416; *New York Times,* 7 Dec (9:6) and 27 Dec (28:3) 1946, 15 Feb (17:8) and 29 Sep (1:2) 1947; Halsey Papers: letters and other items concerning the death and burial of Admiral Halsey's mother, schedule of the admiral's goodwill tour of Central and South America, and letters of Bowers toTruman (13 Aug 1946), Truman to Halsey (3 Sep 1946), King to Halsey (30 July 1947), Halsey to King (12 Aug 1947), and Kimmel to Halsey (12 Aug 1947).
5. Halsey Papers; W. F. Halsey III interview; Potter, *Nimitz,* 436, 455; Buell, *Master,* 508–9.
6. Halsey Papers; W. F. Halsey III interview; Merrill, 252–54; *New York Times,* 15 May 1954 (3:7).
7. Halsey Papers; *New York Times,* 30 July (11:1) and 31 July (9:2) 1957; Merrill, 254; Smedberg interview.
8. Halsey Papers; W. F. Halsey III interview; Merrill, 254.
9. *Interrogations of Japanese Officials,* vol. 1, 220–21; Field, 24, 35, 35n, 36, 38; Woodward, 132, 134, 135.
10. Halsey Papers; Merrill, 172–76; W. F. Halsey III interview; Morison, *Leyte,* 160, 160n, 167, 193–97, 289–93, 317–18, 321–22, 329–31; Halsey Papers: Carney, letter to Halsey, 14 Nov 1958; Potter, *Sea Power* (1960), chapters 37, 38, and 41 (in the manuscript sent to Admiral Halsey these chapters were numbered respectively 34, 35, and 39); Halsey Papers: Halsey to author, 29 June 1959 (added in handwriting at the end: "I have a copy of chaps 34 & 35 with me. I may be able to

do something with [them] while at my son's home at La Jolla. This has been written & signed in the air. We have just left Tucson, Arizona and are en route to Mitscher's field at Miramar in La Jolla."); Halsey, letter to author, 27 July 1959 (with enclosure, three pages of comment on chapter 39 of *Sea Power,* "The Battle for Leyte Gulf"); Potter, *Nimitz,* 465. Hanson W. Baldwin, while writing his book *Sea Fights and Shipwrecks* (1955), sent the manuscript of his chapter on the Battle for Leyte Gulf to Admirals Halsey and Kinkaid, inviting each to write a commentary, which he would publish in his book at the end of the chapter. Each complied and neither saw the other's commentary until it was in print. Much of Kinkaid's commentary consists of criticism of Halsey's strategy in the battle. Most of Halsey's consists of defense or explanation of his strategy.

11. W. F. Halsey III interview; Merrill, 254–55; *New York Times,* 17 Aug (1:2), 18 Aug (30:5), and 21 Aug (21:1) 1959. The Naval Academy professor mentioned in the text was myself. I sent the Battle for Leyte Gulf chapter to Admiral Kinkaid as well, who in a letter to me dated 15 August 1959 expressed great bitterness over *Admiral Halsey's Story.* "When the Saturday Evening Post first published a chapter of Halsey's book," Kinkaid wrote, "after careful thought, I decided that I would not engage in a public controversy with him, despite pressure that was put on me by those who had been with me at Leyte and other personal friends. That this decision was fitting was confirmed to me when one of my highly respected and admired wartime commanders said to me, 'You remember what our mutual friend, Senator Swanson, used to say—never get into a controversy with a skunk.'" In a postscript, obviously written a few days later, Kinkaid added, "The radio has just announced that Halsey died this morning at Fishers Island. All of these comments were written before this announcement. I have no time to change them, nor do I desire to do so."

ACKNOWLEDGMENTS

THIS BOOK OWES A GREAT DEAL to my former colleagues and coauthors Henry H. Adams and J. Roger Fredland and to my wife Grace, all of whom read the manuscript and made numerous suggestions for improvement in style and organization. After William F. Halsey III, son of the subject of this biography, had read the manuscript, I spent three days going over it with him at his home in La Jolla, California, seeking greater accuracy. Admiral Robert B. Carney, USN (Ret.), Admiral Arleigh Burke, USN (Ret.), the late Rear Admiral Edwin T. Layton, USN (Ret.), and Joseph Bryan III read portions of the manuscript and gave helpful advice. It must not be inferred, however, that this book is in any sense an authorized biography. I alone am responsible for its contents.

I owe a special debt to Joseph Bryan for directing me to the document referred to in the notes and sources as Halsey's memoir. This book is based largely on that valuable record. Virginius C. Hall, Jr., associate director of the Virginia Historical Society, had a copy made for me.

The oral histories of the U.S. Naval Institute proved another major source for this book. I worked with these volumes chiefly at the U.S. Naval Academy's Nimitz Library with the assistance of Alice Creighton, head of the special collections section. The single most useful oral history for this book, however, was East Carolina University's transcript of the reminiscences of William Ashford, Halsey's aide from 1937 to 1943. I researched this volume with the help of Donald R. Lennon, director of the East Carolina manuscript collection.

Dean C. Allard, director of the operational archives at the Naval Historical Center, and his assistants were helpful in solving research problems. Jane H. Price, assistant archivist of the U.S. Naval Academy, unearthed for me several facts about Halsey's activities in Annapolis. Edward J. Boone, Jr., archivist at the MacArthur Memorial in Norfolk, sent me copies of messages passed between Halsey and MacArthur. The archivists at the Library of Congress manuscript division, where I spent a good deal of time, were unfailingly helpful.

My wife assisted me in research and conducting interviews. My former colleague Edwin M. Hall devoted many hours to scanning the galleys for misprints and other slips. Constance Buchanan of the Naval Institute Press skillfully edited my text.

INDEX

William F. Halsey, Jr., is abbreviated WFH. Ships, unless otherwise noted, are U.S. Page numbers in italics show the location of pictures.